BEST PLACES®

SEATTLE

BEST PLACES®
SEATTLE

Edited by
GISELLE SMITH

EDITION 8

SASQUATCH BOOKS
SEATTLE

Printed in the United States
Distributed in Canada by Raincoast Books Ltd.

Eighth edition.
02 01 00   5 4 3

ISSN: 1095-9734
ISBN: 1-57061-155-6

Series editor: Kate Rogers
Cover and interior design: Nancy Gellos
Cover photograph: Rick Dahms
Fold-out and interior maps: GreenEye Design

Cover note: The Public Market Center logo is a trademark of the Pike Place
Market Preservation and Development Authority.

BEST PLACES®. Reach for it first.

SPECIAL SALES
BEST PLACES® guidebooks are available at special discounts on bulk purchases
for corporate, club, or organization sales promotions, premiums, and gifts.
Special editions, including personalized covers, excerpts of existing guides,
and corporate imprints, can be created in large quantities for specific needs.
For more information, contact your local bookseller or Special Sales,
BEST PLACES® Guidebooks, 615 Second Avenue, Suite 260, Seattle, Washington
98104, 800/775-0817.

SASQUATCH BOOKS
615 Second Avenue
Seattle, WA 98104
206/467-4300
books@SasquatchBooks.com
www.SasquatchBooks.com

CONTENTS

Introduction

Seattle is changing. The city best known 20 years ago for Boeing and a decade ago as the birthplace of grunge music has also gone from being the home of Microsoft to being the home of Starbucks. Currently, cutting-edge internet companies (amazon.com, drugstore.com, etc.) and high-tech do-gooders (the so-called "Microsoft millionaires" who retired to do philanthropic work or to start their own companies) are redefining Seattle yet again.

So, it only makes sense that the city's most popular guidebook, *Seattle Best Places*, change, too.

The editors at BEST PLACES° elected to completely revamp the eighth edition. Part of this decision came from on-going reader suggestions about what restaurants, hotels, and other places deserve to be mentioned in the book—or don't. But there was also a recognition that the city is growing and prospering at an ever-increasing rate. *Seattle Best Places* has always been an insider's guide written by and for locals, and now it's time to expand our audience and let all the visitors and newcomers in on our secrets.

Although the book still contains all the information BEST PLACES° readers have come to trust over the years—star-rated restaurant reviews, a complete shopping guide, a handy city map—it also has several new features, including the Lay of the City and Planning a Trip chapters, which orient you to the city and help you get started. You'll find a handful of informative "boxes" that tell the stories behind local businesses and offer insider tips, and helpful icons that quickly lead you to places for romance or family fun. In addition to outlining the city's many neighborhoods in the Exploring chapter, we also now spotlight the Top 25 Attractions—are your favorites represented here?

Special thanks go to the many writers and reviewers who contributed their expertise, words, and time to this project: Molly Dee Anderson, Rachel Bard, Ellen L. Boyer, Fred Brack, Tori Breithaupt, Jo Brown, Providence Cicero, Charles R. Cross, Caroline Cummins, Roger Downey, Sheila Farr, Jim Goldsmith, Kelly A. Harvill, Sarah E. Henderson, Sarah Hilbert, Tom Keogh, Philippa Kiraly, Nancy Leson, Eric Lucas, Chris Maag, Shannon O'Leary, J. Kingston Pierce, Courtney Reimer, Kristine Richardson, Byron Ricks, Charles Smyth, and Barbara Spear. Thanks, too, to series editor Kate Rogers, copyeditor Alice Smith, proofreader Sherri Schultz, and assistant editor Meghan Heffernan.

Whether this is your first copy of *Seattle Best Places* or your eighth, we hope you'll find this guide as useful as we intend it to be. Here is Seattle—to explore, experience, and enjoy.

—*Giselle Smith, Editor*

About Best Places® Guidebooks

People trust us. BEST PLACES® guidebooks, which have been published continuously since 1975, represent one of the most respected regional travel series in the country. Each guide is written completely independently: no advertisers, no sponsors, no favors. Our reviewers know their territory, work incognito, and seek out the very best a city or region has to offer. Because we accept no free meals, accommodations, or other complimentary services, we are able to provide tough, candid reports about places that have rested too long on their laurels, and to delight in new places that deserve recognition. We describe the true strengths, foibles, and unique characteristics of each establishment listed.

Seattle Best Places is written by and for locals, and is therefore coveted by travelers. It's written for people who live here and who enjoy exploring the city's bounty and its out-of-the-way places of high character and individualism. It is these very characteristics that make *Seattle Best Places* ideal for tourists, too. The best places in and around the city are the ones that denizens favor: independently owned establishments of good value, touched with local history, run by lively individuals, and graced with natural beauty. With this latest edition of *Seattle Best Places*, travelers will find the information they need: where to go and when, what to order, which rooms to request (and which to avoid), where the best music, art, nightlife, and shopping is, and how to find the city's hidden secrets.

We're so sure you'll be satisfied with our guide, we guarantee it.

NOTE: *Readers are advised that places listed in previous editions may have closed or changed management, or may no longer be recommended by this series. The reviews in this edition are based on information available at press time and are subject to change. The editors welcome information conveyed by users of this book. A report form is provided at the end of the book, and feedback is also welcome via email: books@ SasquatchBooks.com.*

How to Use This Book

This book is divided into twelve chapters covering a wide range of establishments, destinations, and activities in and around Seattle. All evaluations are based on numerous reports from local and traveling inspectors. BEST PLACES reporters do not identify themselves when they review an establishment, and they accept no free meals, accommodations, or any other services. Final judgments are made by the editors. Every place featured in this book is recommended.

STAR RATINGS *(for Top 200 Restaurants and Lodgings only)* Restaurants and lodgings are rated on a scale of one to four stars (with half stars in between), based on uniqueness, loyalty of local clientele, performance measured against the establishment's goals, excellence of cooking, cleanliness, value, and professionalism of service. Reviews are listed alphabetically, and every place is recommended.

★★★★   The very best in the city

★★★   Distinguished; many outstanding features

★★   Excellent; some wonderful qualities

★   A good place

[unrated]   New or undergoing major changes

(For more on how we rate places, see the BEST PLACES Star Ratings box on page xii.)

PRICE RANGE *(for Top 200 Restaurants and Lodgings only)* Prices for lodgings are based on peak season rates for one night's lodging for two people (i.e., double occupancy). Peak season is typically Memorial Day to Labor Day; off-season rates vary but can sometimes be significantly less. Prices for restaurants are based primarily on dinner for two, including dessert, tax, and tip. When prices range between two categories (for example, moderate to expensive), the lower one is given. Call ahead to verify, as all prices are subject to change.

$$$ Expensive (more than $80 for dinner for two; more than $125 for one night's lodgings for two)

$$ Moderate (between expensive and inexpensive)

$ Inexpensive (less than $30 for dinner for two; $85 or less for one night's lodgings for two)

ADDRESSES All listings are in Seattle unless otherwise specified. If an establishment has two Seattle-area addresses, we list both at the top of the review; if there are three, we list the original, downtown, or recommended branch, followed by the words "other branches"; the other two addresses are in the review text. If there are more than three branches, we list only the main address.

CHECKS AND CREDIT CARDS Most establishments that accept checks also require a major credit card for identification. Note that some places accept only local checks. Credit cards are abbreviated in this book as follows: American Express (AE); Diners Club (DC); Discover (DIS); Japanese credit card (JCB); MasterCard (MC); Visa (V).

EMAIL AND WEB SITE ADDRESSES With the understanding that more people are using email and the internet to access information and to plan trips, BEST PLACES° has included email and Web site addresses for establishments, where available. Please note that the World Wide Web is a fluid and evolving medium, and that Web pages are often "under construction" or, as with all time-sensitive information, may no longer be valid.

MAP INDICATORS The letter-and-number codes appearing at the end of most listings refer to coordinates on the fold-out map included in the front of the book. Single letters (for example, F7) refer to the downtown Seattle map; double letters (FF7) refer to the Greater Seattle map on the flip side. If an establishment does not have a map code listed, its location falls beyond the boundaries of these maps (for example, Bainbridge Island locations).

HELPFUL ICONS Watch for these quick-reference symbols throughout the book:

 FAMILY FUN Family-oriented places that are great for kids—fun, easy, not too expensive, and accustomed to dealing with young ones.

 GOOD VALUE While not necessarily cheap, these places offer you the best value for your dollars—a good deal within the context of the city.

 ROMANTIC These spots offer candlelight, atmosphere, intimacy, or other romantic qualities—kisses and proposals are encouraged!

 UNIQUELY SEATTLE These are places that are unique and special to the Emerald City, such as a restaurant owned by a beloved local chef or a tourist attraction recognized around the globe. (Hint: If you want to hit several of these special spots at once, turn to the Top 25 Attractions in the Exploring chapter. They're all uniquely Seattle!)

&. Appears after listings for establishments that have wheelchair-accessible facilities.

INDEXES In addition to a general index at the back of the book, there are five specialized indexes: restaurants are indexed by star-rating, features, and location at the beginning of the Restaurants chapter, and nightspots are indexed by features and location at the beginning of the Nightlife chapter.

READER REPORTS At the end of the book is a report form. We receive hundreds of reports from readers suggesting new places or agreeing or disagreeing with our assessments. They greatly help in our evaluations, and we encourage you to respond.

MONEY-BACK GUARANTEE Please see page 482.

BEST PLACES® STAR RATINGS

Any travel guide that rates establishments is inherently subjective—and BEST PLACES® is no exception. We rely on our professional experience, yes, but also on a gut feeling. And, occasionally, we even give in to a soft spot for a favorite neighborhood hangout. Our star-rating system is not simply a AAA-checklist; it's judgmental, critical, sometimes fickle, and highly personal. And unlike most other travel guides, we pay our own way and accept no freebies: no free meals or accommodations, no advertisers, no sponsors, no favors.

For each new edition, we send local food and travel experts out to review restaurants and lodgings anonymously, and then to rate them on a scale of one to four, based on uniqueness, loyalty of local clientele, performance measured against the establishment's goals, excellence of cooking, cleanliness, value, and professionalism of service. That doesn't mean a one-star establishment isn't worth dining or sleeping at—far from it. When we say that *all* the places listed in our books are recommended, we mean it. That one-star pizza joint may be just the ticket for the end of a whirlwind day of shopping with the kids. But if you're planning something more special, the star ratings can help you choose an eatery or hotel that will wow your new clients or be a stunning, romantic place to celebrate an anniversary or impress a first date.

We award four-star ratings sparingly, reserving them for what we consider truly the best. And once an establishment has earned our highest rating, everyone's expectations seem to rise. Readers often write us letters specifically to point out the faults in four-star establishments. With changes in chefs, management, styles, and trends, it's always easier to get knocked off the pedestal than to ascend it. Three-star establishments, on the other hand, seem to generate healthy praise. They exhibit outstanding qualities, and we get lots of love letters about them. The difference between two and three stars can sometimes be a very fine line. Two-star establishments are doing a good, solid job and gaining attention, while one-star places are often dependable spots that have been around forever.

The restaurants and lodgings described in *Seattle Best Places* have earned their stars from hard work and good service (and good food). They're proud to be included in this book—look for our BEST PLACES® sticker in their windows. And we're proud to honor them in this, the eighth edition of *Seattle Best Places*.

PLANNING A TRIP

PLANNING A TRIP

How to Get Here

BY PLANE

SEATTLE-TACOMA INTERNATIONAL AIRPORT (206/431-4444; map:O06), better known as simply **SEA-TAC**, is located 13 miles south of Seattle, barely a half-hour freeway ride from downtown. Successful expansion, multimillion-dollar renovations to concourses in the main terminal, and a new, easily accessible parking facility have helped turn Sea-Tac into one of the most convenient major airports in the country. It now serves more than 23 million passengers a year. A high-speed computer-controlled subway system links the main terminal to two adjoining satellite terminals; allow an extra 10 minutes to reach gates in those terminals.

TRAVELERS AID, on the ticketing level, offers assistance weekdays from 9:30am to 9:30pm, and weekends from 10am to 6pm. Besides providing free information on getting around town, the organization will escort children, the elderly or infirm, and disabled travelers within the airport. Sea-Tac's Operation Welcome sends bilingual staff to meet incoming international flights and help foreign passengers with customs and immigration procedures. The airport nursery, on the ticketing level of the main terminal near the Northwest Gift Shop, has space for changing and feeding children (complete with chairs, couches, and cribs), and infant changing tables are located in women's and men's restrooms throughout the airport. For exhaustive information on airport services and operating conditions, call the airport information line (206/431-4444) from a touchtone phone: you can listen to any of a list of recorded messages on everything from parking to paging to lost and found.

The Sea-Tac **PARKING** complex, which holds 8,000 vehicles, is a short walk from the main terminal through enclosed walkways. Express, short-term metered parking (up to two hours) costs $2 for 40 minutes. Long-term parking costs $16 per day, with no limit on the number of days. Valet parking is available for $21 per day. Major credit cards are accepted. The pedestrian plaza on the third floor of the parking garage offers load-and-unload facilities, and you can even grab an espresso-to-go from carts stationed there.

For less expensive long-term parking, try the numerous commercial parking lots in the vicinity of the airport. The following operate 24 hours a day and offer free shuttle service for their parking and car-rental patrons: Budget Car and Truck Rental (17808 International Blvd; 206/244-4008), Thrifty Airport Parking (18836 International Blvd; 206/242-7275), Park Shuttle and Fly (17600 International Blvd; 206/433-6767), and Doug Fox Airport Parking (2626 S 170th St; 206/248-2956).

TOP OF THE LIST

"Try as we might, we couldn't keep Seattle off the top," *Fortune* magazine reported in November 1996 when it named Seattle first on its **Best Cities** list.

That seems to be the quandary of a lot of magazine editors. Either the facts (for example, low crime and high employment) or their readers' choice keep landing Seattle at or near the apex of those "best of" lists. It's getting to be a little embarrassing.

It all started in 1989 with the stunning selection of Seattle as *Money* magazine's **Most Livable City**. Until then, much of the nation thought the city was a suburb of Alaska. (The magazine repeated the compliment in 1998, picking Seattle as the **Best Place to Live in America**.)

Other kinds of acclaim soon followed. Medically speaking, Seattle is in peak form. The TV show *60 Minutes* decreed in 1974 that the city was "the "safest place to have a heart attack." *U.S. News & World Report* selected the University of Washington as **Best Research Medical School** in 1994, and in its 1998 ranking of best grad schools rated the UW as tops in primary care, family care, and nursing. *Parade* magazine picked Seattle as the second **Safest City** (out of 75 U.S. cities) in 1994. Seattle was one of the few American cities to make the grade in *Condé Nast Traveler* magazine's internationally competitive Best Cities list in 1997; Seattle corporations Alaska Airlines and Microsoft made the top 10 of *Fortune* magazine's **America's Most Admired Companies** in 1997; *American Health for Women* magazine picked Seattle the number one **City for Women** in 1998; and, of course, for several years running, Microsoft CEO Bill Gates has topped *Fortune* magazine's **World's Richest** list. And in the ultimate pop-culture plaudit, Seattle Mariner shortstop Alex Rodriguez was numbered among *People* magazine's "50 **Most Beautiful People** in the World" in 1998—the only athlete to be so honored in the issue.

It's enough to make a city blush.

— *Shannon O'Leary*

Airport Transportation

Stop by the airport information desk, near the baggage claim, for information about ground transportation services. One of the easiest and least expensive ways of getting to Sea-Tac Airport from downtown (or vice versa) is on the **GRAY LINE AIRPORT EXPRESS** (206/626-6088). Going to the airport, the shuttle stops at 20- to 30-minute intervals at downtown hotels, including the Madison Renaissance, Crowne Plaza, Four Seasons Olympic, Hilton, Sheraton, Roosevelt, Paramount, Warwick, and Westin, from about 5am until about 11pm. Going to the hotels, it runs from about 5am to midnight at the same intervals, from the north and south ends of the airport baggage area. Additional runs are added in the summer months. The ride is about 30 to 45 minutes between the Madison Renaissance and Sea-Tac. Cost is $13 round trip ($7.50 one way), or $9.50 round trip ($5.50 one way) for children ages 2 to 12.

SHUTTLEEXPRESS (206/622-1424 or 800/487-RIDE) provides convenient door-to-door van service to and from the airport, serving the entire greater Seattle area, from Everett to Tacoma. The cost ranges from $18 (from within the city) to $26 (from outlying suburbs) one way. Groups traveling from a single pickup point pay reduced rates. You may share the ride with other passengers, so expect to stop elsewhere en route. To ensure availability, make reservations two to three days ahead for trips to the airport. The shuttle from Sea-Tac operates 24 hours a day and requires no advance notice; the service desk is located at the south end of the baggage claim area.

TAXIS to the airport from downtown Seattle (or vice versa) run about $30.

METRO TRANSIT (206/553-3000; transit.metrokc.gov) offers the cheapest rides to the airport ($1.25 one way, $1.75 during rush hour), via two routes: the #174 (can take up to an hour from downtown) and the #194 Express (a 30-minute ride). Both run every half hour, seven days a week. The #194 uses the downtown transit tunnel, except on weekends, when it travels through downtown along Third Avenue. The #174 travels through downtown along Second Avenue. Both buses stop on the baggage level of the airport.

By Charter or Private Airplane

Most airplane and helicopter charter companies are based at Boeing Field/King County International Airport (206/296-7380; map:KK6). Others are located north of the city at Snohomish County Airport (Paine Field, 425/353-2110). Services include flying lessons and aircraft rentals. Call the Seattle Automated Flight Service Station (206/767-2726) from a touchtone phone for up-to-date weather reports and flight-related information.

By Seaplane

See Air Tours in the Exploring chapter.

BY BUS

GREYHOUND BUS LINES (811 Stewart St; 800/231-2222; map:I4) has the greatest number of scheduled bus routes connecting Seattle to other cities and is usually the least expensive way to get to Seattle. The station is within walking distance of the downtown retail core.

If you're traveling up the West Coast to get to Seattle, another option (especially for the young and/or adventurous) is the **GREEN TORTOISE** (800/867-8647). The line offers two runs a week between Seattle and San Francisco with stops along the way in Washington, Oregon, and California in buses equipped with benches in front, a small dinette area in the middle, and a cushioned platform in back for passengers to lounge on. The station is located near Pike Place Market at the Green Tortoise Hostel (1525 2nd Ave; 206/340-1222; map:K7).

BY TRAIN

The wide seats and beautiful scenery make **AMTRAK** (800/872-7245) the most comfortable and scenic mode of transportation to Seattle. Especially beautiful is the Portland-to-Seattle route, much of which runs along Puget Sound. Trains leave Seattle headed south to Portland, San Francisco, Los Angeles, and San Diego; headed north to Vancouver, British Columbia; and headed east to Chicago. The train pulls up to King Street Station (3rd Ave S and S Jackson St; map:P8) at the edge of the International District. Call for passenger information and reservations. For baggage offices, package express, and lost and found, call 206/382-4128.

BY CAR

Interstate 90 is Seattle's primary connection to all points east, crossing the Cascades at Snoqualmie Pass before dropping down to the plains of Eastern Washington and curving its way towards Spokane, 280 miles east. The primary north-south artery is Interstate 5, which runs south from Seattle through Tacoma and the state capital of Olympia, to Portland, Oregon (185 miles south of Seattle), and on through California. To the north via I-5 lies Vancouver, British Columbia, just 143 miles away. To go to and from the Olympic Peninsula, take a scenic ferry ride across Puget Sound (see "Ferry Rides" box in the Day Trips chapter). More or less parallel to I-5 is the old north-south route, Highway 99, which becomes Aurora Avenue for a stretch through the city. Just south of downtown, I-5 meets I-90; from downtown, I-90 crosses a floating bridge over Lake Washington to the eastern suburbs. The other link to the Eastside suburbs is Highway 520, which leaves I-5 just north of downtown, crosses another floating bridge, and passes near the Bellevue and Kirkland town centers before ending in Redmond. Both east-west highways connect with I-405, which runs north-south through the suburbs east of Lake Washington.

A cautionary note: Seattle's traffic seems to get worse by the day. Try to plan your arrival and departure times to avoid rush hours, generally 7–9:30am and 4:30–7pm. For information about renting a car in Seattle, see Getting Around in the Lay of the City chapter.

When to Visit

When you decide to visit Seattle is a matter of personal preference, but if weather is a factor in your decision, you'll want to know what to expect.

Remember that the table below shows averages, though; what you'll experience is unpredictable. For other considerations, check the Calendar of Events at the end of this chapter. Keep in mind that although the season from November through February may have more rain and be a little cooler, hotel rates, airfares, and admission fees are often lower at that time as well.

WEATHER

The toughest job in Seattle is being a weather forecaster—everyone thinks you're a liar, an idiot, or both. Between the mountains, the warm offshore currents, and the cold fronts sweeping down from the north, predicting weather here is an exercise in equivocation. Predictions are even more difficult because a torrential downpour in West Seattle might occur at the same time as blinding sunshine in Wallingford. If you're trying to avoid the rain altogether, July and August are the warmest and driest months. Things get wet in the winter, averaging around five inches of rain a month from November through January, but temperatures are mild enough that snow and ice are infrequent. On those rare days when they do appear, though, watch out: the town grinds to a halt and the streets become one big roller derby.

Average temperature and precipitation by month

Month	Daily Maximum Temp. degrees F	Daily Minimum Temp. degrees F	Monthly Precipitation in inches
JANUARY	45	35	5.38
FEBRUARY	49.5	37.5	3.99
MARCH	52.7	38.5	3.54
APRIL	57	41.2	2.53
MAY	63.9	46.3	1.7
JUNE	69.9	51.9	1.5
JULY	75.2	55.2	0.76
AUGUST	75.2	55.7	1.14
SEPTEMBER	69.3	51.9	1.88
OCTOBER	59.7	45.8	3.23
NOVEMBER	50.5	40.1	5.83
DECEMBER	45.1	35.8	5.9

Source: U.S. National Oceanic and Atmospheric Administration

TIME

Seattle is on Pacific Standard Time (PST), which is three hours behind New York, two hours behind Chicago, one hour behind Denver, one hour ahead of Anchorage, and two hours ahead of Honolulu. Daylight Saving Time begins in early April and ends in late October. Because Seattle is located so far north (between the 47th and 48th latitudes), residents enjoy long daylight hours in summer, with sunrises before 6am and sunsets as late as 9:45pm.

WHAT TO BRING

Given the highly variable nature of Seattle's weather, it's best to be ready for anything, especially if you're visiting between May and October. Bring layers that you can add or remove, from short-sleeved shirts to long-sleeved ones, with a sweater or a light jacket just in case, as even summer evenings can be cool. From June through September, be sure to bring shorts and sunglasses. In the winter months, it's easy: dress for rain. No matter when you visit, pack a rain jacket. If you plan to take walking tours of the city, wear wool socks and be sure to bring an extra pair.

When choosing what to wear, remember that Seattle pioneered the art of dressing casual. Suits and ties are seen only on those unfortunate souls who work in the downtown business district; otherwise jeans, khakis, and T-shirts are ubiquitous.

With a few exceptions, even the most expensive restaurants allow patrons to wear jeans, and only a select few require a jacket.

General Costs

Booming. No other word describes Seattle's economy, thanks to the continued success of Seattle's landmark companies and upstart industries. Seattle used to be known (not quite correctly) as a one-company town. The company, of course, was Boeing. Today, with a raft of new orders for its commercial jetliners, combined with renewed global interest in its defense and aerospace products, Boeing remains the largest employer and greatest revenue generator in the state—despite its occasional layoffs. Other longtime local titans, such as Weyerhaeuser and Nordstrom, are also thriving. Their success is joined by a group of relatively young industries, especially high-technology ones. Microsoft, now the world's largest software manufacturer for personal computers, continues to grow exponentially, both in profits and in the size of its Redmond campus. Many of Microsoft's young retirees are investing their considerable money and talent in a growing wave of startups, adding to the more than 1,500 computer-related firms already in the area. The state's leadership in biotechnology, focused primarily in the Seattle area, is promising to spur further economic growth. In 1997, biotech contributed $500 million to the state economy; by 2003, that figure is expected to mushroom to $3 billion annually.

Seattle's economic growth is made possible by a diverse, well-educated work force. Two-thirds of King County residents have attended college (one-third of residents graduated), and 33 percent are in professional or managerial occupations. In 1998, the unemployment rate in King County was just 2.8 percent, compared to 4.2 percent in Washington State and 4.6 percent nationally. Low unemployment means high buying power; retail sales grew 9 percent in a two-year period during the 1990s. The strong economy also pushes prices higher, making the average price of Seattle's goods and services 15 percent higher than the national average. Housing costs in Seattle are 125 percent, and health care costs 143 percent, of the national average.

Average costs for lodging and food

Double room:

INEXPENSIVE	**$59–$80**
MODERATE	**$80–$150**
EXPENSIVE	**$150 AND UP**

Lunch for one:

INEXPENSIVE	**$8–$12**
MODERATE	**$12–$18**
EXPENSIVE	**$19 AND UP**

Beverages in a restaurant:

GLASS OF WINE	**$5–$7**
PINT OF BEER	**$3.50**
COCA-COLA	**$0.75**
DOUBLE TALL LATTE	**$2.50**

Other common items:

MOVIE TICKET	**$7**
ROLL OF FILM	**$5.50**
TAXI PER MILE	**$1.80**
RAIN JACKET FROM REI	**$29–$549**
SEATTLE SOUVENIR T-SHIRT	**$12–$15**

Tips for Special Travelers

FAMILIES WITH CHILDREN

In an emergency, call 911, 24 hours a day. For questions about your child's health, growth, or development, call the Children's Hospital Resource Line (206/526-2500). If you think your child has ingested a toxic substance, call the Washington Poison Center (206/526-2121 or 800/732-6985). A local publication, *Seattle's Child*, serves as a resource for parents and is available free at many coffee shops, newsstands, and newspaper boxes. It's produced by Northwest Parent Publishing (206/441-0191).

The majority of downtown hotels cater almost exclusively to business travelers. This means that family-oriented amenities such as swimming pools, game rooms, and inexpensive restaurants are more readily found at hotels outside the downtown area. Many hotels allow kids to stay free when traveling with their parents, so ask when you make reservations. Most major restaurants have children's menus.

 Watch for this icon throughout the book; it indicates places and activities that are great for families.

SENIORS

Senior Services of Seattle/King County (1601 2nd Ave, Suite 800; 206/448-3110) runs a referral service for seniors, offering information about health and welfare resources and transportation and mobility services. It also publishes a newsletter called ACCESS that lists upcoming events for seniors including fairs, opportunities for flu shots, and some happenings at neighborhood senior centers. For public transit, senior bus passes are $3 for people 65 and older. They are good for life, and reduce the fare to 25 cents on all buses. Senior passes can be purchased in person either at the downtown Metro office (201 S Jackson St; 206/553-3060; map:P7) or in the transit tunnel station underneath Westlake Center (map:J6).

PEOPLE WITH DISABILITIES

For information about using public transportation, call the Metro handicapped information line (206/553-3095). For faster or more personalized transportation, Pierce-King Cabulance (253/838-3522) operates a wheelchair-accessible taxi service, as does Cabulance TLC (206/233-9259). For tour companies and other private companies offering mobility services, call the Seattle/King County Convention and Visitors Bureau (206/461-5840). The Easter Seals Society (206/281-5700) offers a handbook detailing all the places in Seattle that are wheelchair accessible. The Deaf/Blind Service Center (206/323-9178) offers volunteers who help deaf or blind Washington State residents take walks, go grocery shopping, or go to the bank. The service is sometimes available to visitors for $10 an hour, with advance notice.

WOMEN

Seattle is known as a relatively safe city, but as in most cities, women travelers should take extra precautions at night, especially in downtown and the Pioneer Square neighborhood. For health and reproductive services, call Planned Parenthood (2211 E Madison; 206/328-7700; map:HH6). Particularly rich in resources for women is Bailey/Coy Books (414 Broadway E; 206/323-8842; map:HH6), a community bookstore on Capitol Hill.

READ ALL ABOUT IT

Seattleites are bookworms. They spend double the national average on books every year and are avid borrowers from the public library system. Their page-turning proclivities ensure that you don't have to go far in this town to find a store selling new or used titles or both. Although they don't often write about the city, many well-known authors live and work in the area: Tom Robbins, Charles Johnson, Jonathan Raban, Rebecca Brown, Jon Krakauer, Brenda Peterson, and Pete Dexter, to name just a few. True-crime masters John Saul and Ann Rule, as well as science-fiction novelists Vonda McIntyre and Greg Bear, also live here. But it's crime novelists—from J. A. Jance to G. M. Ford to K. K. Beck—or visiting writers who seem to best capture the city.

Here's a short list of diverse works that will help you learn more about Seattle and the Puget Sound region:

Nonfiction

The Forging of a Black Community, by Quintard Taylor (University of Washington Press, 1994). Taylor examines the often-troubled evolution of Seattle's Central District from the year 1870 through the civil-rights struggles of the 1960s.

Rains All the Time: A Connoisseur's History of Weather in the Pacific Northwest, by David Laskin (Sasquatch Books, 1997). Laskin recounts the history of this region's relationship with its "liquid sunshine."

Walt Crowley's *National Trust Guide Seattle* (John Wiley & Sons, 1998) gives a wonderful overview of the city's architecture and history that both locals and visitors can enjoy. *Seattle City Walks,* by Laura Karlinsey (Sasquatch Books, 1999), provides easy-to-use walking tours of various city neighborhoods, with historical and cultural details, directions to lovely viewpoints, and profiles of Seattle personalities.

Skid Road, by Murray Morgan (Comstock, 1978). A lively, irreverent look back at some of the events and eccentrics most responsible for creating the Seattle we know today. This is the essential guide to the first 100 years of the city's history.

One of our most beloved regional books, *The Egg and I,* by Betty MacDonald (J. R. Lippincott Co., 1945), is a delightfully whimsical memoir of life on a Washington chicken ranch.

In *The Natural History of Puget Sound Country* (University of Washington Press, 1991), Arthur R. Kruckeberg offers insights into the region's development.

Northwest history is recorded by the people who lived it in *A Voyage of Discovery to the North Pacific Ocean and Round the World* (C. G. and J. Robinson, 1798), by explorer George Vancouver, and books by early pioneers and visitors: *Pioneer Days on Puget Sound* (The Alice Harriman Co., 1908), by Arthur A. Denny; *West Coast Journeys, 1865–1879: The Travelogue of a Remarkable Woman* (Sasquatch Books, 1995), by Caroline C. Leighton; and *The Canoe and the Saddle* (J. W. Lovell, 1862), by Theodore Winthrop.

Writer Sallie Tisdale (*Stepping Westward: The Long Search for Home in the Pacific Northwest;* Henry Holt, 1991) and *New York Times* correspondent Timothy Egan (*The Good Rain: Across Time and Terrain in the Pacific Northwest;* Alfred A. Knopf, 1990) offer contemporary perspectives on the region. Northwest poet Richard Hugo's work reflects the Seattle area he called home in *Making Certain It Goes On: Collected Poems of Richard Hugo* (W. W. Norton, 1984).

Fiction

Catfish Café, by Earl Emerson (Ballantine Books, 1998). Seattle private eye Thomas Black is hired by a former partner to rescue his daughter, a former crackhead and an eyewitness to the recent killing of a straitlaced white schoolteacher.

Indian Killer, by Sherman Alexie (Warner Books, 1998). Native American novelist and screenwriter Alexie tells the story of an Indian serial killer in Seattle who is raising racial tensions by murdering whites in revenge for his people's treatment.

Slant, by Greg Bear (Tor Books, 1997). Seattle in the year 2050 is one of the principal settings for this innovative tale of nanotechnology and national madness.

Slow Burn, by G. M. Ford (Avon Books, 1998). Seattle private eye Leo Waterman, together with his motley cronies, tracks down both the killer of an influential food critic as well as the whereabouts of a Black Angus bull destined for barbecue fame.

Snow Falling on Cedars, by David Guterson (Vintage Contemporaries, 1995). This history-based novel about the murder trial of a Japanese-American fisherman working on Puget Sound won considerable local and national acclaim.

Lastly, Oregonian Ken Kesey captures the Northwest timber history in *Sometimes a Great Notion* (Viking Press, 1964), a regional classic.

— J. Kingston Pierce

PET OWNERS

Travelers with pets will find themselves welcome in the most surprising places—including downtown Seattle's four-star Four Seasons Olympic Hotel. Refer to guidebooks such as *The Seattle Dog Lover's Companion* by Steve Giordano for other places your dog or cat is welcome to share your room.

If Seattle has one militant, vocal political force, it's dog owners. When the City Council discussed whether to allow pets to roam free in designated areas within some city parks, those were the best-attended and most passionate council meetings in many years. The hard-fought right to unfetter your critter comes with certain responsibilities, though; owners must make sure their dogs don't jump on other owners, and they must pick up their dogs' waste. Here are Seattle's off-leash areas:

GOLDEN GARDENS PARK, 8498 Seaview Place NW, in Ballard. The area is in the eastern portion of the park.

I-90 BLUE DOG POND PARK, on Martin Luther King Jr. Way at Massachusetts Street. The area is in the northwest corner of the park.

MAGNUSON PARK, 6500 Sandpoint Way, in View Ridge. The area runs along the park's eastern and northern boundaries, with some water access to Lake Washington.

VOLUNTEER PARK, 1400 E Prospect Street, on Capitol Hill. The area is located behind the Seattle Asian Art Museum.

WESTCREST PARK, 8806 8th Avenue SW, in West Seattle. The area runs along the southern border of the reservoir.

WOODLAND PARK, N 50th Street and Aurora Avenue N, in Wallingford. The area is in the park's northeastern portion, west of the tennis courts.

OUTSIDE SEATTLE, area off-leash parks include Mercer Island's Luther Burbank Park as well as Marymoor Park in Redmond.

GAYS AND LESBIANS

Seattle is well known for being a gay-friendly city. Its large gay community is mainly centered around the Capitol Hill neighborhood, with a variety of gay-focused bars, dance clubs, bookstores, and bed-and-breakfast inns. The *Seattle Gay News* (206/324-4297) is the community newspaper, available at many shops and bars around Capitol Hill. There are two guides to the businesses and services of the community: the *GSBA Guide & Directory*, available at stores in the area or by contacting the Greater Seattle Business Association (2150 N 107th, Suite 205; 206/363-9188; map:DD7); and the *Pink Pages* (1122 E Pike St, Suite 1226; 206/328-5850; map:GG6), also available in stores or from the business office. Two community bookstores, Beyond the Closet (518 E Pike St; 206/322-4609; map:K2) and Bailey/Coy Books (414 Broadway E; 206/323-8842; map:HH6), offer community bulletin boards and have staffs who are knowledgeable about local resources and events. The Lesbian Resource Center (2214 S Jackson St; 206/322-3953; map:HH7) provides business referrals, therapy services, and housing and job information. For information on the city's many gay clubs and bars, see the Nightlife chapter.

FOREIGN VISITORS

Seattle hosts a number of foreign exchange brokers and foreign banks. Thomas Cook (400 Pine St; 206/467-1600; map:I6; 10630 NE 8th St, Bellevue; 425/462-8225; map:HH3; and various Sea-Tac Airport locations) is a foreign exchange broker. Foreign banks with branches in Seattle include Bank of Tokyo (1201 3rd Ave, Suite 1100, 206/382-6000; map:L7), Hong Kong Bank of Canada (700 5th Ave, Suite 4100,

206/233-0888; map: N7), and Sumitomo Bank (1201 3rd Ave, Suite 5320; 206/625-1010; map:L7).

A multitude of services are available for the foreign visitor who does not speak English as a first language. The American Cultural Exchange (200 W Mercer St, Suite 504; 206/217-9644; map:GG8) offers language classes and arranges for summertime exchanges and visits by foreigners to American homes. The ACE's Translation Center (206/281-8200) provides interpreters and written translations. Yohana International (425/771-8465) and The Language Connection (425/277-9045) provide document translation as well as interpreters in dozens of languages, including those of Asia, Africa, and Europe. The Milmanco Corporation (651 Strander Blvd, Suite 100; 206/575-3808) can help those involved in international business and in need of technical written translations (from and into foreign languages); rates vary. The Red Cross Language Bank (206/323-2345) provides on-call interpretive assistance at no charge.

For general visa information, contact U.S. Immigration at Sea-Tac Airport (206/553-0466). Seattle's importance as a port city has brought it many foreign consulates.

AUSTRIA	1111 3RD AVE, SUITE 2626	206/633-3606
BELGIUM	3214 W MCGRAW ST, SUITE 301	call for appt; 206/285-4486
BOLIVIA	5200 SOUTHCENTER BLVD, SUITE 25	206/244-6696
CANADA	PLAZA 600, SUITE 412	206/443-1777
ESTONIA	500 UNION ST, SUITE 930	206/467-1444
FINLAND	11045 SE 28TH PL, BELLEVUE	425/451-3983
FRANCE	P.O. BOX 1249, SEATTLE	call for appt; 206/256-6184
GERMANY	600 UNIVERSITY ST, SUITE 2500	206/682-4312
GREAT BRITAIN	900 4TH AVE, SUITE 3001	206/622-9255
GUATEMALA	2001 6TH AVE, SUITE 3300	206/728-5920
HUNGARY	4416 134TH PL SE, BELLEVUE	425/643-0563
ICELAND	5610 20TH AVE NW	206/783-4100
JAPAN	601 UNION ST, SUITE 500	206/682-9107
MEXICO	2132 3RD AVE	206/448-3526
NETHERLANDS	4609 140TH AVE NE, BELLEVUE (not open to the public)	call for appt; 425/861-4437
NEW ZEALAND		call for appt; 206/525-0271
NORWAY	1402 3RD AVE, SUITE 806	206/623-3957
PERU	3717 NE 157TH ST, SUITE 100	206/714-9037
RUSSIA	2001 6TH AVE, SUITE 2323	206/728-1910
SOUTH KOREA	2033 6TH AVE, SUITE 1125	206/441-1011
SWEDEN	1215 4TH AVE, SUITE 1019	206/622-5640
TAIWAN	2001 6TH AVE, SUITE 2410	206/441-4586

WEB INFORMATION

With so many high-tech companies in Seattle, it's little wonder the city is the subject of a wide range of Web sites operated by private as well as government organizations, nonprofit and for-profit ventures. One catchall site is www.pan.ci.seattle.wa.us, which is useful for both residents and visitors, offering information on history, tours, employment, and even a Spanish-language guide. The site forks off into home pages for entities such as the city parks department. Other helpful sites include:

WWW.SEATTLE.NET
WWW.WASHINGTON.EDU (University of Washington)
WWW.SEATTLETIMES.COM (Seattle Times)
WWW.SEATTLE-PI.COM (Seattle Post-Intelligencer)
WWW.SEESEATTLE.ORG (Seattle/King County Convention and Visitors Bureau)
See listings within other chapters for specific site addresses, where available.

Calendar of Events

FEBRUARY

Chinese New Year INTERNATIONAL DISTRICT; 206/623-5124 Held in either February or March (depending on the lunar calendar), this International District celebration greets the Chinese and Vietnamese New Year with a fanfare of festivals, displays, and a lively parade complete with lion dancers. *www.wingluke.com*

Fat Tuesday PIONEER SQUARE; 206/622-2563 Seattle's weeklong Mardi Gras celebration brings a colorful parade and the beat of Cajun, jazz, and R & B to the streets and clubs of Pioneer Square. Nightclubs levy a joint cover charge, and proceeds from several events benefit Northwest Harvest, a local food bank. Held the week before Lent.

Northwest Flower and Garden Show WASHINGTON STATE CONVENTION & TRADE CENTER, 9TH AVE AND PIKE ST; 800/229-6311 For five days in mid-February, this enormous horticultural happening occupies almost 5 acres at the Convention Center. Landscapers, nurseries, and noncommercial gardeners outdo themselves with more than 300 demonstration gardens and booths. Shuttle-bus service is available from Northgate. General admission is $12.50 (evenings $10.50). *www.gardenshow.com*

MARCH

International Chocolate Festival NORTHWEST ROOMS, SEATTLE CENTER; 206/684-8582 Indulge in chocolate cuisine prepared by more than 25 vendors. Demonstrations and workshops are also held. Usually the first weekend of March.

Imagination Celebration/Arts Festival for Kids CENTER HOUSE, SEATTLE CENTER; 206/684-7200 Free activities and workshops in the visual and performing arts are features of this weekend-long, fun-filled, child-centric event. Kids and their parents can participate in hands-on learning activities, including arts, crafts, and music. Call for dates and schedule. *www.seattlecenter.com*

St. Patrick's Day Parade FROM CITY HALL, 600 4TH AVE, TO WESTLAKE CENTER, 1601 5TH AVE; 206/329-7224 Faith 'n' begorra, this downtown parade features bagpipes, singing, dancing, and the laying of a green stripe down the center of Fourth Avenue. *www.irishclub.org*

Whirligig CENTER HOUSE, SEATTLE CENTER; 206/684-7200 From late March through early April, this indoor winter carnival fetes the coming of spring with rides, music, and games just for kids. The entertainment is free; rides cost 25 cents to 50 cents apiece. *www.seattlecenter.com*

Kulturefest LANGSTON HUGHES CULTURAL ARTS CENTER, 104 17TH AVE S; 206/684-4757 The Pacific Northwest is home to numerous cultures, and this fair celebrates that diversity, focusing on the artistry of clogging, square dancing, blues, folk, and gospel music. Usually held the last Saturday of March.

APRIL

Skagit Valley Tulip Festival MOUNT VERNON, 60 MILES NORTH OF SEATTLE VIA I-5; 360/428-5959 When the 1,500 acres of tulip fields burst into brilliant color in early April, Mount Vernon seizes the moment and entertains visitors with a street fair and parades. Makes a nice—and flat—bicycle trip.

MAY

Opening Day of Boating Season ALONG THE MONTLAKE CUT BETWEEN LAKE WASHINGTON AND LAKE UNION; 206/325-1000 (SEATTLE YACHT CLUB) Boat owners from all over the Northwest come to participate in this festive ceremonial regatta, which officially kicks off the nautical summer on the first Saturday in May. Arrive early to watch the world-class University of Washington rowing teams race other nationally ranked teams through the Montlake Cut. Parade registration for watercraft is free. *www.seattleyachtclub.org*

International Children's Festival SEATTLE CENTER; 206/684-7338 Professional children's performers come from all over the world for this popular event. Crafts, storytelling, puppet shows, and musical and theater performances (some free) entertain kids and their parents for six days in early May. *www.seattlecenter.com*

Seattle International Film Festival VARIOUS THEATERS AROUND TOWN; 206/324-9996 Founded in 1976 by Darryl Macdonald and Dan Ireland, the 3½-week Seattle International Film Festival brings films for every taste—art house to slapstick—to Seattle theaters every May and June. Fans of the obscure will appreciate SIFF's archival treasures and independent films. Series tickets (full and partial) go on sale in January. *www.seattlefilm.com*

University District Street Fair UNIVERSITY WAY NE; 206/527-2567 On the third—and usually the hottest—weekend in May, this juried festival features more than 400 artists' booths in a 10-block area. Street mimes and clowns hold court in the crowd, which is as kaleidoscopic as the selection of crafts.

Northwest Folklife Festival SEATTLE CENTER; 206/684-7300 The largest folk fest in the nation happens Memorial Day weekend, and brings ethnic groups and their folk-art traditions (dance, music, crafts, and food) to stages all around Seattle Center. A must. *www.nwfolklife.org*

Pike Place Market Festival PIKE PLACE MARKET, FIRST AVE AND PIKE ST; 206/682-7453 The Pike Place Market Merchant Association sponsors a free celebration of the Market on Memorial Day weekend: food, drink, and crafts aplenty, as well as clowns, some of the city's finest jazz musicians, and an entire Kids' Alley chock-full of activities. *www.pikeplace market.org*

JUNE

Northwest Microbrewery Festival THE HERBFARM, 32804 ISSAQUAH–FALL CITY RD, FALL CITY; 425/784-2222 Nearly 50 microbrewers convene at The Herbfarm for this outdoor fun fest held on Father's Day. Live music, food, beer tasting, and forums highlight the event. A $12.50 admission fee ($10 in advance) buys six taste tickets, a beer glass, and the chance to wander around the herb gardens. *www.theherbfarm.com*

Gay Pride Week BROADWAY AND OTHER CAPITOL HILL LOCATIONS; 206/323-1229 (FREEDOM DAY COMMITTEE) A week of sporting events, dances, forums, and a pride festival, culminating on the last Sunday of June with the all-in-good-fun parade down Broadway (attracting over 60,000 revelers and gawkers) and a rally at Volunteer Park. *www.gay seattle.com*

Fremont Fair N 34TH ST, ALONG THE FREMONT SHIP CANAL; 206/632-1500 Fremont celebrates the beginning of summer with a solstice parade, music, crafts booths, food, and dance. This event gets bigger, better, and crazier every year.

Summer Nights on the Pier PIER 62/63 ON ALASKAN WAY; 206/622-5123 Two former working piers transformed into a 3,000-seat concert ground have become a perfect place to spend a summer evening—listening to the sounds of acts such as the Indigo Girls, Ben Harper, Ringo Starr, or Robert Cray against a backdrop of sailboats and the setting sun. The concert series extends through the summer. *summernights.org*

JULY

AT&T Family Fourth at Lake Union GAS WORKS PARK; 206/281-8111 A day full of outdoor activities at Gas Works Park is capped by a multi-level show of fireworks, exploding to a score played by the Seattle Symphony. *www.onereel.org*

Fourth of Jul-Ivar's MYRTLE EDWARDS PARK; 206/587-6500 Enjoy a fun-filled day with live entertainment, culminating in a spectacular array of fireworks over Puget Sound. Ivar's Elliott Bay show is best viewed from Myrtle Edwards Park. A lucky few who think to make reservations for a late dinner at the Space Needle can view both dueling fireworks shows. The pyrotechnics start just after dark. *www.keepclam.com*

Lake Union Wooden Boat Festival CENTER FOR WOODEN BOATS, 1010 VALLEY ST (SOUTH END OF LAKE UNION); 206/382-2628 For three days, around the Fourth, the Center for Wooden Boats lures the nautically minded with rowing, sailing, and team boat-building competitions, plus workshops, food, and crafts. Spectators can board various wooden boats (including the *Wawona*, a schooner built in 1897). Water taxis shuttle people from events to demonstrations during the day. Donations of $5 per person are suggested. *www.cwb.org*

Marymoor Heritage Festival MARYMOOR PARK, REDMOND; 425/296-2964 The rich ethnic heritage of the Puget Sound area comes to life over the Fourth of July, with food, crafts, and music in the pastoral setting of Marymoor Park. There's plenty to fascinate kids; admission is free, though parking on the grounds sets you back $5.

Bite of Seattle SEATTLE CENTER; 206/232-2982 A chomp-fest that brings cheap nibbles from more than 60 restaurants to Seattle Center in mid-July. All tastes are under $5. Admission is free. *biteofseattle.com*

Caribbean Festival—A Taste of Soul MYRTLE EDWARDS PARK; 206/329-8818 Be transported to the islands during one of Seattle's most temperate months. Let yourself be tempted by luscious Caribbean and African foods while calypso, soca, gospel, and reggae music soothe your soul. There's a limbo contest if you're feeling flexible; otherwise, you can just pretend the winds off the Sound are the gentle breezes of Montego Bay. Mid-July.

Chinatown International District Summer Festival HING HAY PARK, INTERNATIONAL DISTRICT; 206/382-1197 The International District's mid-July extravaganza celebrates the richness and diversity of Asian culture with dancing, instrumental and martial arts performances, food booths, and arts and crafts. A children's corner features puppetry, storytelling, and magic shows; craft demonstrations (classical ikebana, a Japanese tea ceremony, basket weaving, calligraphy, and Hawaiian lei-making) take place in the cultural corner.

King County Fair KING COUNTY FAIRGROUNDS, ENUMCLAW; TAKE I-5 SOUTH TO AUBURN EXIT, HWY 104; 360/825-7777 The oldest county fair in the state is also its best, featuring live music with country headline acts, a rodeo, 4-H and FFA exhibits, a loggers' show (remember axe-throwing contests?), crafts, and food. Begins the third Wednesday in July. *www.metrokc.gov/park/*

Seafair VARIOUS LOCATIONS THROUGHOUT TOWN, INCLUDING THE LAKE WASHINGTON SHORE AND DOWNTOWN SEATTLE; 206/728-0123 Seattle's frenzied summer fete has been around since 1950 and—to the chagrin of many locals—isn't likely to go away. The hoopla begins on the third weekend of July with the milk carton–boat races at Green Lake and ends on the first Sunday in August, when the hydroplanes tear up the waters of Lake Washington. Bright spots include a couple of triathlons and some excellent ethnic festivals (Bon Odori, late July; Chinatown International District Summer Festival, mid-July; Hispanic Seafair Festival, late July; and Black Mardi Gras, mid-July). The Torchlight Parade (the Friday before the hydroplane races) is a full-scale march through the downtown area and a kids' delight. Practically all Seafair events are free. *www.seafair.com*

Nordstrom Anniversary Sale 5TH AVE AND PINE ST (AND BRANCHES); 206/628-1690 A bonafide Northwest event—folks actually line up for this annual sale at Seattle's favorite store. Prices on upcoming fall apparel are excellent. Happens for two weeks in late July. *www.nordstrom.com*

Pacific Northwest Arts and Crafts Fair BELLEVUE SQUARE, NE 8TH ST AND BELLEVUE WAY NE, BELLEVUE; 425/454-4900 The Northwest's largest arts-and-crafts fair covers Bellevue Square with an excellent juried selection of West Coast arts and crafts and a juried exhibition in the Bellevue Art Museum, the last weekend in July. *www.bellevueart.org*

SEPTEMBER

Bumbershoot SEATTLE CENTER; 206/281-8111 The longest multi-arts festival north of San Francisco is a splendid, eclectic celebration. Select craftspeople, writers, poets, and performing artists entertain the hordes on stages throughout Seattle Center over Labor Day weekend. Music is the main draw, with past performers ranging from Bonnie Raitt and Bela Fleck to Sonic Youth, Beck, and even George Clinton. A $14 daily pass ($10 if you buy in advance) is all you need to stay thoroughly entertained. *www.onereel.org*

Northwest AIDS Walk STARTS AND FINISHES AT SEATTLE CENTER; 206/323-WALK (JULY–SEPT) OR 206/329-6923 Begun in 1986, this annual event just keeps growing—in number of participants, and in the amount of money raised. In recent years, more than 15,000 walkers have raised more than $1.3 million annually for AIDS care and education agencies statewide. *www.nwaids.org*

Puyallup Fair (Western Washington State Fair) PUYALLUP, 35 MILES SOUTH OF SEATTLE VIA I-5; 253/841-5045 Everybody "does the Puyallup." This 17-day extravaganza begins in early September, and it's the rural county fair you remember from your childhood—only bigger. Rodeo, music, barnyard animals, carnival rides, exhibits, and vast amounts of food (including legendary scones).

Salmon Homecoming VARIOUS LOCATIONS AROUND TOWN, INCLUDING THE SEATTLE AQUARIUM (1483 ALASKAN WAY), PIER 62/63, AND WATERFRONT PARK; 206/386-4300 A celebration of Native American heritage, and an examination of how salmon and Seattleites affect each other, Salmon Homecoming takes place the second weekend of September, with pow-wows, Coastal Indian cultural dances and storytelling, and lectures and forums. *www.seattleaquarium.org* or *aquarium.programs@ci.seattle.wa.us*

Greek Festival ST. DEMETRIOS CHURCH, 2100 BOYER AVE E; 206/325-4347 For three days in late September (or early October, depending on Husky football games), enjoy traditional Greek food and festivities galore at this noble Byzantine church. Church tours, folk-dancing performances, music, arts and crafts, and wonderful baklava make this a favorite neighborhood and Grecophile event.

OCTOBER

Issaquah Salmon Days ISSAQUAH, 15 MILES EAST OF SEATTLE ON I-90; 425/392-7024 Issaquah celebrates the return of the salmon the first weekend of October with a parade, food, crafts, music, dancing, displays, shows, and 5K and 10K runs. A kids' fair keeps the tykes entertained with pony rides and face painting, and the hydro races at Lake Sammamish are fun for kids of all ages. At the state hatchery you can get excellent views of chinook and coho thrashing up the fish ladder; it's even more affecting to see them struggling up Issaquah Creek from any number of vantage points in town. *www.frontstreet.org*

OUR HUMOR'S ALL WET

After a brief visit to Seattle some years back, comedian Bill Cosby worked up a skit about the rarity of good weather here. When the sun manages to claw out from behind gray clouds, he said, natives bound from their homes and run about frantically yelling, "What have we DONE? What have we DONE?"

Maybe he overstated things. Just a tad. Yes, the city's favorite event is a Labor Day festival called Bumbershoot, after the British term for umbrella. Yes, a lot of visitors would take issue with the old TV theme song from *Here Come the Brides* that claimed, "The bluest skies you've ever seen are in Seattle." But this place doesn't really deserve its reputation as the wetness capital of the United States. The rain that drenches Seattle every year is typically less than what falls on Miami, New York, Boston, or Atlanta.

Yet Seattle's drippy rep hasn't been all bad. It has kept weather wimps away and even inspired a wealth of dry humor.

"What comes after two straight days of rain in Seattle?" runs one popular riddle. The answer? "Monday." "The most popular movie in Seattle? *The Sound of Mucus*." "It's so wet in the Northwest you can watch people walk their fish." To the query "Whaddya do around here in the summer?" Northwesterners are said to reply cheerfully, "Well, if it falls on a weekend, we go on a picnic."

The rain joke is the local equivalent of the Chicago wind joke, the Michigan black-fly joke, and the Texas brag. It's a corny spill of overstatement that unites a diverse people because they all understand the exaggeration. Humor also helps fend off dampened spirits. Nobody wants to listen to somebody else whine over the rain. Too depressing. But if they tell you they were knocked unconscious by a huge raindrop and that it took six buckets of sand in the face to bring them around, that makes it all right.

More surreptitious motives may be behind this brand of humor, of course. Residents who want to keep Seattle all to themselves use the rain—and the rain joke—as their first line of attack.

— *J. Kingston Pierce*

Northwest Bookfest WASHINGTON STATE CONVENTION AND TRADE CENTER; 206/378-1883 Seattle's first book festival debuted in 1995 with a wide range of programs, including author appearances and signings, bookseller and publisher exhibits, multimedia demonstrations, children's activities, panel discussions, writing workshops, and more. Now it's held annually in late fall. *nwbookfest@speakeasy.org; www.speakeasy.org/nwbookfest*

Earshot Jazz Festival VARIOUS LOCATIONS THROUGHOUT SEATTLE; 206/547-9787 Each October, Seattle celebrates this innovative music form with swing bands, Afro-Caribbean rhythm groups, bebop quartets, brass trios, and many more quality musicians. Tickets are $8 to $18, with some free concerts. If there's a certain vocalist you've been wanting to check out, this is a great way to do it, and to support jazz in the Emerald City. Held October through early November. *www.earshot.org*

NOVEMBER

KING 5 Winterfest SEATTLE CENTER; 206/684-7200 Each holiday season, Seattle Center comes alive with a dizzying array of festive lights and props, sponsored by the local NBC-affiliate TV station. Winter activities include the ever-popular ice-skating rink, sure to bring out the kid in all of us. Held the last weekend of November through the first week of January. *www.seattlecenter.com*

DECEMBER

A Christmas Carol A CONTEMPORARY THEATRE (ACT), 700 UNION ST; 206/292-7676 Based on an original adaptation written for ACT, this festive production has become a holiday tradition for many families, and sells out every year. Runs Thanksgiving through several days after Christmas.

Christmas Ship VISITS BEACHES CITYWIDE; 206/623-1445 One of Seattle's cherished Christmas traditions comes to life every December, as area musical groups climb aboard a lit-up boat to serenade folks gathered on various shores. Call for a schedule. *argosy@argosycruises.com; www. argosycruises.com*

Community Hanukkah Celebration STROUM JEWISH COMMUNITY CENTER, 3801 MERCER WAY, MERCER ISLAND; 206/232-7115 The largest community Hanukkah celebration around offers arts and crafts, holiday wares, children's games, food, and music. Everyone is welcome to take part when members of the area's Jewish community gather for the Festival of Lights—complete with the traditional symbolic candlelighting ceremony.

Fruits of the Harvest: Kwanzaa CHILDREN'S MUSEUM, CENTER HOUSE, SEATTLE CENTER; 206/441-1768 To teach youngsters about the African-American festival Kwanzaa, the Children's Museum holds a seven-night candlelighting celebration to introduce Kwanzaa's seven principles: unity, self-determination, responsibility, cooperative economics, purpose, creativity, and faith. Children are invited to make candles and mkeka hats. Held the last week of December. *www.thechildrensmuseum.org*

The Nutcracker PACIFIC NORTHWEST BALLET, OPERA HOUSE, SEATTLE CENTER, 351 MERCER ST; 206/441-2424 Pacific Northwest Ballet's annual production is a Northwest tradition, notable for the spectacular set designs of Maurice Sendak. A good introduction to the ballet for children. Early December through the end of the month; tickets go on sale in mid-October. *www.pnb.org*

Seattle Men's Chorus Holiday Concert BENAROYA HALL, 200 UNIVERSITY ST; 206/323-2992 A premier vocal group, Seattle Men's Chorus serenades sold-out audiences year after year with a soulful holiday concert. Tickets for two make a great gift if you can get them. Concerts are presented the second week of December. *info@seattlemenschorus.org; www. seattlemenschorus.org*

Seattle Symphony's *Messiah* BENAROYA HALL, 200 UNIVERSITY ST; 206/215-4747 With an internationally acclaimed orchestra led by a world-class conductor, this production of Handel's 18th-century classic performed by the Seattle Symphony Chorale will certainly grab you with its sheer 20th-century volume and excitement. Mid-December. *www.seattle symphony.org*

Westlake Center 1601 5TH AVE; 206/467-1600 The heart of downtown gets dressed up and decked out for the season with two miles' worth of holiday lights. A carousel, the Great Figgy Pudding Street Corner Caroling Competition, the Jingle Bell Run/Walk, and a great big Christmas tree add to the fun. Downtown Seattle, through the month of December.

LAY OF THE CITY

LAY OF THE CITY

Orientation

Seattle is a city defined by water. Contrary to popular myth, however, it's not what falls from the sky that is most important when you're getting to know this city. Situated on a narrow isthmus of land between **PUGET SOUND** and **LAKE WASHINGTON**, and bisected by **LAKE UNION** and the Lake Washington Ship Canal, Seattle has a unique character that is largely defined by the wet stuff surrounding it. The city's distinct neighborhoods developed in relative isolation, cut off from one another by the many canals and lakes and by the forested slopes that tumble down to the water's edge.

Water is also a critical element of Seattle's awe-inspiring natural beauty, attracting droves of tourists and residents to this growing metropolitan area of nearly three million people. Across Puget Sound to the west loom the Olympic Mountains. Mount Rainier plays hide-and-seek 40 miles south of downtown. The Cascades stretch in a jagged line just 50 miles to the east. And on clear days, Glacier Peak can be glimpsed 50 miles north.

Within the boundaries of these imposing geographic landmarks lies a rapidly growing urban area. The major city landmarks of Seattle are tightly contained in a small, bustling area centered around downtown. At its heart stands the famous **PIKE PLACE MARKET** (Pike St and 1st Ave; map:J8), an authentic smorgasbord of food, flowers, and art that has served local residents and visitors for more than 90 years. Taking the steps down the steep hill behind the Market leads you to the Seattle waterfront, brimming with shops, restaurants, and the always-busy **FERRY DOCKS** (map:M9). Directly east of the Market is an ever-growing shopping district anchored by **WESTLAKE CENTER** (Pine St and 4th Ave; map:I6) and fanning out in all directions. Seattle's major office and financial district lies south of the shopping area.

At the southern end of downtown lies historic **PIONEER SQUARE** (along 1st and 2nd Aves, between Cherry and King Sts; map:N8), the first area of Seattle to be rebuilt after the great fire of 1889 and a longtime home of Seattle's artistic community. The **KINGDOME** (Occidental Ave S and S King St; map:Q9), slated for demolition in January 2000 to make way for a new football stadium in 2001, squats immensely just south of Pioneer Square.

Traveling north from Pike Place Market through the trendy, swiftly gentrifying **BELLTOWN** neighborhood (north of Virginia St and south of Denny Way, between Western and 5th Aves; map:G7), one comes upon the sprawling **SEATTLE CENTER** complex (north of Denny Way and Broad St, between 1st Ave N and 5th Ave N; map:B6). It's home to the

Pacific Science Center and a wide variety of festivals and fairs, as well as Seattle's best-known landmark, the **SPACE NEEDLE** (Broad St and 5th Ave N). A few blocks east of downtown, **CAPITOL HILL** rises steeply from I-5 into a neighborhood of funky shops, coffee shops, and nightspots.

Visitor Information

Ever since the Klondike gold rush, Seattleites have been known to lend a helping hand to travelers. If people on the street can't point you in the direction of gold, or whatever else you seek, try the administrative office of the **SEATTLE/KING COUNTY CONVENTION AND VISITORS BUREAU** (520 Pike St; 206/461-5800; map:J4; www.seeseattle.org). It's open from 8:30am to 5pm Monday though Friday, as is the main visitors bureau, on the first floor of the Washington State Convention & Trade Center (8th Ave and Pike St; 206/461-5840; map:J4). An additional information booth stands in Pioneer Square, on the corner of Occidental and Main (map:O8), from Memorial Day to Labor Day, and another is located at the foot of the Space Needle (map:C6). Free maps of Seattle can be picked up at any of these locations or requested over the phone.

The **WESTLAKE INFORMATION CENTER** (206/467-1600), on the third floor of Westlake Center at Fourth and Pine (map:I6), offers a wealth of information, from where to eat cheaply to how to pronounce the word *geoduck* ("goo-ey duck"). **PIKE PLACE MARKET** operates an information booth (206/682-7453, ext. 226) near its main entrance at First and Pike (map:J8) to help visitors navigate the maze of shops and restaurants. The **SEA-TAC AIRPORT VISITORS INFORMATION CENTER** (206/433-5288) is located on the airport's baggage-claim level, and offers trip-planning assistance along with a plethora of splashy travel brochures (map:OO6).

For more information about Seattle, or anything else you could possibly think of, call the research wizards at the **SEATTLE PUBLIC LIBRARY QUICK INFORMATION LINE** (206/386-INFO). The *Seattle Survival Guide* by Theresa Morrow is a thorough, reliable resource for newcomers and longtime residents alike.

Getting Around

BY BUS

It is exceptionally easy to get around downtown Seattle without a car. **METRO TRANSIT** (201 S Jackson St; 206/553-3000; transit.metrokc.gov; map:P7) operates more than 200 bus routes in Seattle and surrounding King County. Many of the coaches are wheelchair-accessible, and all are

HOW TO PASS FOR A LOCAL

Every city has its own set of idiosyncrasies. Visitors who want to mesh more naturally with the locals might benefit from these insights into Seattle's native style.

Umbrellas: Despite the city's rep, it doesn't rain buckets here daily (Miami has more rain annually). A sure way to spot a newcomer is to see an unfurled umbrella during a light shower.

Shades: Residents have to combat glare more than raindrops. As a result, sunglasses are de rigueur nearly year-round.

Attire: It varies widely by neighborhood. For example, while the Capitol Hill crowd favors black ensembles, body piercings, and Doc Martens, Green Lakers sport spandex, bare midriffs, and Nikes. The main thing is, Seattleites are flexible when it comes to degrees of formality. A night at the opera here can mean evening gowns or Gap wear.

Coolness: This isn't a climate reference but an attitudinal one. Frankly, natives aren't an effusive lot—just ask any touring actor waiting for a standing ovation. Rumor has it that it takes two years to make a real friend here (unless, of course, the new friend is another lonely newcomer). It's not that we're unfriendly—we're just politely reserved.

Vocabulary: "Yeah" is as common a part of Seattle speech as "Oh my gawd!" is to

equipped with bike racks (mounted on the front of the bus) for bike-and-bus commuters. Bus stops have small yellow signs designating route numbers, and many have schedules posted. The fare is $1 in the city ($1.25 during peak commuter hours—6–9am and 3–6pm), $1.25 if you cross the city line ($1.75 peak). Exact fare is required. Seniors, youths, and handicapped riders are eligible for discount cards. All-day passes ($2) are available from drivers on the weekends and holidays only. Printed schedules and monthly passes are available at Metro headquarters and the Westlake Center bus tunnel station. You can also buy passes at many Bartell Drug Stores, at the Federal Building branch of the NW Federal Credit Union (915 2nd Ave; 206/682-7622; map:M7), and by phone (206/624-PASS). Bus schedules are also available at a number of downtown office buildings as well as the downtown Seattle Public Library (1001 4th Ave; 206/386-4683; map:M6).

One of Metro's most valued services is the **RIDE FREE AREA** in downtown's commercial core. In the area bordered by the waterfront, I-5, Jackson Street to the south, and Battery Street to the north, you can ride free on any Metro bus until 7pm. Avoid above-ground traffic snags by catching a bus in Metro's sleek, L-shaped transit tunnel within the Ride Free Area; it has five underground stations, from near the Washington State Convention & Trade Center, at Ninth and Pine, to the International District at Fifth and Jackson. The tunnel will be part of a future light-rail

a suburban teenager. Not to be confused with the intimidating interrogative "Oh *yeah?!*" favored by East Coasters, Seattle's "Yeah" is simply a laid-back form of assent or agreement. (In the more heavily Scandinavian sections of the city, "Ya sure, you betcha" can be used as a synonym.)

Jaywalking: That crowd on the corner isn't making a drug deal, they're simply waiting for the crosswalk sign to change. Natives are notorious sticklers for obeying these signs—and so are the police. Newcomers blithely crossing against lights may find themselves ticketed, at about $38 a pop.

Bicyclists: Some days they seem to outnumber cars. Observing the traditional politeness of the city, locals resist the urge to bump off cyclists who unconcernedly hold up traffic.

Travel espresso cups: They're everywhere. Isn't that why car cup holders were invented? Besides, a swig of caffeine takes drivers' minds off dawdling cyclists.

Cellular phones: How do you tell a California transplant from a native Seattleite? The native tries to hide that fact that he or she even *owns* a cell phone—making a call in public requires the secrecy of an FBI operative.

— *Shannon O'Leary*

system set for completion around 2006; till then, frustrated commuters will continue to grind their teeth at the length of time it takes Metro to travel the short distance through downtown on surface streets during rush hour.

Metro also operates the **WATERFRONT STREETCAR**. The vintage 1927 Australian mahogany-and-white-ash trolleys run from Myrtle Edwards Park along Alaskan Way on the waterfront to Main Street, then jog east through Pioneer Square to Fifth and Jackson. They depart at 20-minute to half-hour intervals from 7am (weekdays) or around 10:30am (weekends) until 6pm, with extended hours in summer. The ride takes 20 minutes from one end to the other and costs $1 (exact change only), $1.25 during Metro peak hours. Metro monthly passes and discount permits are good on the streetcar.

The **MONORAIL**, which connects Seattle Center to the downtown retail district, was a space-age innovation of the 1962 World's Fair. The 90-second, 1.2-mile ride—presently the only stretch of rapid transit in town—is a great thrill for kids. A smart way to avoid the parking hassle at Seattle Center is to leave your car downtown and hop on the Monorail at Westlake Center (3rd floor, Pine St and 4th Ave; map:I6); the station is on a platform outside, just east of the top of the escalator. Adults pay $1 one way, and children ages 5 to 12 pay 75 cents. Trains leave every 15 minutes from 9am to 11pm.

For trips from as far out as Darrington, **COMMUNITY TRANSIT** (425/778-2185 or 800/562-1375; www.riderlink.gen.wa.us) runs buses on a regular schedule. Fare is $2 per adult to Seattle from any point outside the city; fare within Snohomish County is $1.

GRAY LINE OF SEATTLE (4500 W Marginal Way SW; 206/624-5077) has the largest fleet of charter buses and the most competitive prices for sightseeing tours of the city. The company also offers organized tours to destinations such as Mount Rainier and Vancouver. (For other bus information, see Motor Tours under Organized Tours in the Exploring chapter.)

BY CAR

Despite ongoing efforts to make mass transit accessible to more people, sometimes it takes a car to get around Seattle. Most large **RENTAL CAR COMPANIES** have offices at Sea-Tac Airport, in downtown Seattle, and in downtown Bellevue. Some larger ones, such as Enterprise (for out-of-town reservations call 800/325-8007) and Budget (800/527-0700), have locations in other suburbs and in various Seattle neighborhoods. Hertz (800/654-3131) is the preferred rental car company of **AAA WASHINGTON** (330 6th Ave N; 206/448-5353; emergency road service 425/462-2001 or 800/AAA-HELP). The Washington State Department of Public Affairs (206/440-4697) will send out free state maps. Visitor Information Centers, operated by the Seattle/King County Convention and Visitors Bureau, offer free **ROAD MAPS** of Seattle (see Visitor Information in this chapter).

Centrally located **PARKING** lots charge around $15 a day; lots on the fringes of downtown—the International District, Belltown, and Alaskan Way on the waterfront, for instance—are usually less expensive. In downtown, most of the meters have a maximum of 30 minutes, and many are off limits to all but delivery trucks. Most parking tickets cost $20 to $23; parking illegally in a space reserved for the disabled costs $250. Large facilities such as the Kingdome, Seattle Center, and Husky Stadium generally have their own parking areas. Meters cost 60 cents to $2 an hour throughout town. In an attempt to draw shoppers to the city's retail core, the Pacific Place garage (6th Ave and Pine St; map:I5) opened with reduced parking rates in 1998, with a promise not to exceed $7 for 4 hours during the day. Evenings are just $2 for up to 4 hours after 5pm, and Sundays are $4 for up to 4 hours.

For **LOST CARS**, begin by calling the Seattle Police Department's Auto Records Department (206/684-5444) to find out whether your car is listed as towed and impounded. If there's no record, it may have been stolen; call 206/625-5011, or in an emergency call 911.

BY TAXI

There are about 2,300 cabs operating in Seattle, but taking a taxi is fairly uncommon. A cab from the airport to downtown costs about $30. The standard drop is $1.80, with the meter running at $1.80 per mile or 50 cents per minute. Most cabs are directed by dispatchers, which makes it difficult to hail one anywhere but at the airport or near one of the major downtown hotels. Call ahead and one will meet you at most downtown locations within 5 to 10 minutes. Local companies include Farwest Taxi (206/622-1717); Graytop (206/282-8222); Yellow Cab (206/622-6500); and Stita (206/246-9999).

BY BICYCLE

Seattle is a relatively bicycle-friendly city. **BIKE LANES** on arterial streets throughout the city are fairly safe routes for cyclists, and bike trails offer a reprieve from huffing and puffing up Seattle's steep slopes. For both commuting and recreation, the **BURKE-GILMAN TRAIL** is the bicycling backbone of Seattle. Extending 16.5 miles from Kenmore at the north end of Lake Washington through the University of Washington campus to Ballard, and connecting to downtown Seattle via either the Ballard Bridge and 15th Avenue, or the Fremont Bridge and Dexter Avenue, the Burke-Gilman Trail follows a former railroad line and is essentially flat. The trail connects in Kenmore with the Sammamish River Trail, which takes riders around the north end of the lake and through Woodinville to Redmond's Marymoor Park. The Elliott Bay Trail is a scenic 2.5-mile spur running northwest from downtown along the waterfront through Myrtle Edwards and Elliott Bay Parks. The recently rebuilt Alki Trail stretches along Alki Beach in West Seattle and will soon connect with the 11-mile Duwamish Trail, which roughly follows the Duwamish River south to Kent. Recreational riders especially enjoy the bike trail in Seward Park, which circles the wooded peninsula jutting into Lake Washington. For a **MAP OF BIKE ROUTES** in Seattle, call the City of Seattle Bicycle and Pedestrian program (206/684-7583). Maps include in-depth insets on difficult-to-navigate areas, but they become scarce during summer, so call ahead if you can. For bike maps of Bellevue, call the City of Bellevue Transportation Department (425/452-2894).

If in your travels you come upon a hill or body of water that looms too large, hop on a bus or ferry. All Metro buses come equipped with bike racks on the front, and using them is free. The only restriction is that you can't load or unload bicycles in the downtown Ride Free Area between 6am and 7pm, except at the Convention Place and International District bus tunnel stations. For more information, call Metro's Bike and Ride program (206/553-3000). Taking a bike on most ferry routes costs about 50 cents on top of the regular passenger fare. For more ferry information, see the next section.

To **RENT A BIKE**, try Gregg's Greenlake Cycle (7007 Woodlawn Ave NE; 206/523-1822; map:FF7) near popular Green Lake, or Al Young Bike and Ski (3615 NE 45th St; 206/524-2642; map:FF6), across the street from the busy Burke-Gilman Trail. Downtown, check out Blazing Saddles (1230 Western Ave; 206/341-9994; map:K8) or Ti Cycles (824 Post Ave; 206/624-9697; map:L8).

BIKE RACKS are conveniently located outside the downtown Seattle Public Library (1000 4th Ave; map:L6), Key Tower (700 5th Ave; map:N6) on the Cherry Street side, and City Centre (1420 5th Ave; map:J5). In addition, racks can usually be found within a block of most bus stops in commercial areas.

BY FERRY

In the Puget Sound area, ferries are commuter vehicles, tourist magnets, and shortcut alternatives to driving around large bodies of water. You can take a ferry from the downtown terminal at Pier 52 on the waterfront (map:M9) across the Sound to semiresidental/rural Bainbridge or Vashon Island (many people who live on the islands or the Kitsap Peninsula catch daily ferries into the city), or hop one from Anacortes, north of town, to the San Juan Islands or even Vancouver Island, British Columbia. Travelers headed for the Olympic Peninsula use them as a scenic way to cut across the Sound; some passengers just go for the ride; and people have even gotten married on them. For complete schedule and route information, call **WASHINGTON STATE FERRIES** (206/464-6400, 800/84-FERRY, or 888/808-7977; www.wsdot.wa.gov/ferries/). Schedules vary from summer to winter (with much longer lines in summer); cash only. For more information on ferry routes, see the "Ferry Rides" box in the Day Trips chapter.

Essentials

PUBLIC REST ROOMS

Public rest rooms are located at the base of the ramp in the Main Arcade of Pike Place Market (Pike St and Western Ave; map:J8), at Freeway Park (6th Ave and Seneca St; map:L5), and on the Main Street side of the Pioneer Square fire station (corner of 2nd Ave S and S Main St; map:O8). Public buildings are another option (e.g., Seattle Public Library, King County Courthouse, the Federal Building). Many larger parks, such as Volunteer Park and Gas Works Park, also have public facilities (although most are open only until dusk).

MAJOR BANKS

Money-changing facilities are available at almost every major downtown bank. All of Seattle's larger banks also provide the full range of services, and you can locate neighborhood branches by contacting their downtown headquarters: Washington Mutual (national headquarters located in the neoclassical Washington Mutual Tower, 1201 3rd Ave; 206/461-6475; map:L7), Seafirst (Columbia Seafirst Center, 701 5th Ave; 206/358-3000; map:N6), Wells Fargo (999 3rd Ave; 206/292-3435; map:M7), US Bank (1420 5th Ave; 206/344-3795; map:K6), and Key-Bank (1329 4th Ave; 206/447-5768; map:L6).

POLICE AND SAFETY

In emergency situations, dial 911. In nonemergency situations, call the Seattle Police Department at 206/625-5011. Seattle is known as a relatively safe city. There are fewer violent crimes here than in many large cities, although pickpockets are a problem in crowded areas such as Capitol Hill and Pike Place Market. As in any large city, be particularly aware of your surroundings when walking around downtown at night. (A fun bit of trivia: Seattle was the first city in the nation to have bicycle cops.)

HOSPITALS AND MEDICAL/DENTAL SERVICES

Seattle has so many hospitals located near the heart of the city that the First Hill neighborhood is known to locals as Pill Hill. One of the best facilities is Harborview Medical Center (325 9th Ave; 206/731-3000 info or 206/731-3074 emergency; map:P4). Owned by King County and managed by the University of Washington, Harborview is a full-service hospital and home to the leading trauma center in a four-state region. Other hospitals include Swedish Medical Center (747 Broadway; 206/386-6000 info or 206/386-2573 emergency; map:N2) and the University of Washington Medical Center (1959 NE Pacific St; 206/548-3300 info or 206/548-4000 emergency; map:FF6).

Doctors Referral and Appointment Service (206/622-9933 or 800/622-9933) can put you in touch with a doctor 24 hours a day. The Seattle/King County Dental Society offers a Dentist Referral Service (206/443-7607) that refers callers to a dentist or a low-cost dental clinic. Healthsouth Medical Clinics (drop-in health clinics) have numerous locations around Puget Sound, including one downtown at Denny Way and Fairview Avenue N (1151 Denny Way; 206/682-7418; map:G3).

POST OFFICE

Downtown Seattle's main U.S. Post Office (301 Union St; 800/275-8777; map:K6), is open weekdays 8am–5:30pm. Hours at neighborhood branches vary, and some are open on Saturdays, so call ahead.

GROCERY STORES

If you can't find what you need in the recesses of Pike Place Market, the closest major grocery stores to downtown are the Capitol Hill QFC (523 Broadway E; 206/322-8200; map:L1), at the corner of Broadway and

PLACES OF WORSHIP

Houses of reverence vary widely in Seattle, from classical grandeur to eclectic jumble to tumbledown storefront. Here are a few noted for their architecture, community importance, and welcoming attitudes.

In Islam, the oldest set of doctrines are those of the Sunnis. North Seattle contains a small, attractive home for local adherents in the form of the **Sheikh Abdul Kader Idriss Mosque** (1420 NE Northgate Way; 206/363-3013; map:DD6). The compact dome and minaret-evocative tower, topped with a crescent, routinely slow down traffic.

Synagogues in Seattle serve Reform, Conservative, Orthodox, and Sephardic communities. Freestanding fluted columns lend a Hellenistic air to **Temple de Hirsch Sinai** (1511 E Pike St; 206/323-8486; map:HH6), an airy, modern Reform complex on the fringe of Capitol Hill. An extensive library includes over 500 films with Jewish themes.

The twin towers of **St. James Cathedral** (804 9th Ave; 206/622-3559; map:N4) announce an elegant and solidly impressive Roman Catholic church. At New Year's, festive light-filled streamers sway lightly over the circular dais marking the meeting of the nave and the transept. Concerts of sacred music (from Hildegard von Bingen to Mozart) are suitably awesome. The cathedral choir sings Sundays at 10am, the women's choir Sundays at 5:30pm.

Standing taller than all the rest, **St. Mark's Episcopal Cathedral** (1245 10th Ave E; 206/323-0300; map:GG6) looks out over Lake Union from the north end of Capitol Hill. Designed along traditional Gothic lines in the late 1920s, the cathedral was never finished due to the Depression; after a yearlong closure for renovation, the interior is now filled with pastel light streaming from a new rose window. A popular compline mass is held Sundays at 9:30pm (www.scn.org/arts/compline).

Tiny between the looming tower blocks of downtown, but spacious under its central dome, the **First United Methodist Church** (811 5th Ave; 206/622-7278; gbgm-umc.org/churches/FirstWA001; map:M6) is a calm oasis on a frenetic corner.

Pike, and three stores on the western edge of Seattle Center: Larry's Market (100 Mercer St; 206/213-0778; map:A7), QFC (100 Republican; 206/285-5491; map:A7), and Safeway (516 1st Ave W; 206/282-7388; map:A9).

PHARMACIES

Bartell Drug Stores is the biggest local chain in the area, and most locations have prescription departments. Downtown stores are at 1404 Third Avenue (206/624-1366; map:K6) and at Fifth Avenue and Olive Way (206/622-0581; map:I6). The branch on Lower Queen Anne (600 1st Ave N; 206/284-1354; map:A7) is open 24 hours a day. Other 24-hour

Early music concerts and readings by visiting authors such as Isabel Allende are often packed.

In the land of sleek downtown hotels, the white stucco curves of **Plymouth Congregational Church** (1217 6th Ave; 206/622-4865; www.halcyon.com/plymouth; map:L5) are both intriguingly intricate and refreshingly simple. Black-and-white abstract crosses dance in starry columns down the sides of the building, inviting passersby in to lunchtime jazz services (September–June).

The lofty central dome of the **St. Demetrios Greek Orthodox Church** (2100 Boyer Ave E; 206/325-4347; map:GG6) is a friendly home to Eastern Christianity. It stages an enjoyable bazaar in the fall.

First Covenant Church (400 E Pike St; 206/322-7411; map:K1), with its gold-tipped dome surmounting a heavy classical front, is a roomy space smack in the middle of Funkytown. The cheeky live-comedy show *Late Nite Catechism*, performed here to great success throughout 1998, indicates the neighborhood tone.

First Presbyterian Church (1013 8th Ave; 206/624-0644; www.firstpres.org; map:L4) is a streamlined sculptural complex dating from the 1960s; the modern architecture hides the fact that, at 130 years, this is one of Seattle's oldest congregations. Tune in to the radio broadcasts at 10am Sundays on KGNW 820 AM.

Look for the Buddhist festival held every July at **Seattle Buddhist Church** (1427 S Main St; 206/329-0800; map:R4). A long brick building with upturned roof corners, the temple sits across from a park displaying the temple bell (under a canopy) and a statue memorializing the founder of Jodo Shinsu Buddhism.

Red, white, and blue upside-down triangles along the edge of the roof make **Mount Zion Baptist Church** (1634 19th Ave; 206/322-6500; map:HH6) easy to spot. Led for 40 years by renowned African-American activist the Reverend Samuel McKinney (who retired in 1998), the church draws congregants from five counties.

— *Caroline Cummins*

pharmacies are located in Walgreen Drug Stores in Ballard (5409 15th Ave NW; 206/781-0056; map:EE8) and Kirkland (12405 NE 85th; 425/822-9202; map:EE3).

DRY CLEANERS AND LAUNDROMATS

Several dry cleaners operate throughout the city, and many hotels have in-house services. A couple to consider: Downtown Cleaners and Tailoring (920 3rd Ave; 206/622-1433; map:M7), open Monday–Saturday; and Fashion Care Cleaners (1822 Terry Ave; 206/382-9265; map:I3), which has an express service.

Downtown, the slightly seedy but well-lit St. Regis laundromat (116 Stewart St; 206/448-6366; map:I8) is open every day, 7am–10pm. And in funky Belltown is the unusual Sit & Spin (2219 4th Ave; 206/441-9484; map:G6), where you can listen to live music, eat dinner, play board games, or admire the art on the walls while you do your wash. It's open 9am–midnight Sunday through Thursday, and 9am–2am Friday and Saturday (see Nightlife chapter).

LEGAL SERVICES

Lawyer Referral Services (206/623-2551) puts clients in touch with lawyers who are members of the King County Bar Association. The call to the service is free; lawyers charge varying rates for consultations, with a pro bono program for low-income clients. Columbia Legal Services (206/464-5911) is a federally funded program that provides free consultation for clients with very low incomes. Northwest Women's Law Center (206/621-7691) provides basic legal information and attorney referrals, as well as advice on self-help methods.

BUSINESS, COPY, AND MESSENGER SERVICES

Business Service Center (1001 4th Ave, 32nd floor; 206/624-9188; map:M6) rents office and conference space for periods of 3 to 12 months. Open weekdays only, the reception services include answering the phone and providing coffee. Olympic Suites (411 University St, Suite 1200; 206/467-9378; map:K6) is geared toward business executives and occupies the 12th floor of the Four Seasons Olympic Hotel (it's available to hotel guests only). Two word processors, two phones, and a fax machine, plus hourly conference room rentals, are available Monday though Friday.

If you're not staying at the Four Seasons, another option is Globe Secretariat (2001 6th Ave, Suite 306; 206/448-9441; map:H5). Services available include word processing, typing, tape transcription, résumés, 24-hour dictation, copying, and faxing. Or try CEO Professional Services (1600 Dexter Ave N, Suite E; 206/285-3062; map:GG7), a company offering business services such as word processing, typing, transcription, dictation, and faxing, as well as desktop publishing and scanning.

Kinko's (1833 Broadway and branches; 206/329-7445; map:GG6), with its myriad locations all over town, is open 24 hours every day and offers copying, in-house IBM and Macintosh computer rentals, desktop publishing facilities, Internet access (on rental computers), and résumé and fax services, among many other business necessities. Kinko's even offers a customer service hotline: 206/634-1350. Superior Reprographics (1927 5th Ave and branches; 206/443-6900; map:I5) is a complete graphics and copy center with black-and-white and color copying, and diazo (blueprint) printing. Open weekdays, Superior will deliver jobs within city limits.

Elliott Bay Messenger (206/340-9525) is considered the best and fastest bicycle courier service downtown. Packages weighing over 20 pounds have a $10 surcharge. Downtown rush deliveries within a half hour, standard delivery within an hour, and more economical rates available for less rapid service. Elliott Bay is open weekdays only and does car deliveries to the entire Puget Sound area. Fleetfoot Messenger Service (206/728-7700) has quick-service radio-dispatched bicyclists delivering up to 20 pounds downtown Monday though Friday. Vehicle delivery of packages up to 250 pounds—or whatever fits—statewide. And then there's always Federal Express (800/463-3339) and United Parcel Service (UPS) (800/742-5877).

PHOTOGRAPHY EQUIPMENT AND SERVICES

Seattle's professional photographers swear by Cameratechs (5254 University Way; 206/526-5533; map:FF6). The shop services all makes and models, usually within 24 hours, and is open Monday through Saturday. For developing, the pros take their film to Ivey-Seright (424 8th Ave N; 206/623-8113; map:D3). Another good option downtown is Ken's Cameras (1327 2nd Ave; 206/223-5553; map:K7), where you can have almost any brand of camera repaired or have your film developed in as little as one hour; it's also open Monday through Saturday.

COMPUTER REPAIRS AND RENTALS

PC Fixx (601 Union St and branches; 206/624-2700; map:K5) is the best name in town for PC repair. And if you need your computer fixed right now, and right now happens to be 2am Saturday, PC Fixx is the only shop in town. The 24-hour mobile repair service costs anywhere from $125/hour on weekdays to $250/hour on weekends from midnight to 8am. The shop fixes laptops and desktops with an average two-day turnaround (in-shop repairs during regular hours are about $65 per hour), and also services business networks. Store hours are 8am–6pm Monday–Friday and 10am–2pm Saturday.

According to those in the know, Westwind (510 NE 65th St; 206/522-3530; map:EE7) is "head and shoulders above the rest" for Macintosh repair. The shop does laptops and desktops, has a priority service for $80, and is open 9am–6pm Monday–Friday.

Bit-by-Bit Computers (2715 152nd Ave NE, Bldg 6, Redmond; 425/881-5353; map:GG1) rents Macs and IBM-compatibles by the day, week, or month, and delivers anywhere in the state. Laptop models are also available. A complete system, with printer, runs about $200 to $700 a week. Bit-by-Bit is open weekdays and offers free on-site repair; no in-house rentals. Known for accommodating service.

Business Computer Systems Rentals (BCSR) (12015 115th Ave NE, Suite 130, Kirkland; 425/823-1188; map:DD3) rents IBM, Compaq,

Macintosh, Toshiba, and Zenith by the day, week, or month. One- to two-year leasing available. No in-house rentals, but they'll deliver to you and make on-site repairs. Prices begin at $160 per week and climb from there.

PETS AND STRAY ANIMALS

If you spot a stray animal or lose your pet in Seattle, call Seattle Animal Control (206/386-4254). They hold animals for three days before putting them up for adoption, so make sure Rover has a legible license. For veterinary services, the Elliott Bay Animal Hospital (2042 15th Ave W; 206/285-7387; map:FF8) is highly recommended by local vets. If your pet needs immediate attention after hours, contact the Emerald City Emergency Clinic (206/634-9000).

SPAS AND SALONS

Downtown Seattle has numerous spas and salons where you can get everything from a hydromassage to a haircut. Some of the finest in the city include Robert Leonard (2033 6th Ave, Suite 151; 206/441-9900; map:H5), Jaroslava (1413 4th Ave; 206/623-3336; map:K6), Ummelina (1525 4th Ave; 206/624-1370; map:K6), Gene Juarez (607 Pine St and branches; 206/326-6000; map:F9), and the 5th floor at the flagship Nordstrom (500 Pine St; 206/628-1450; map:J5). Outside downtown, in the residential area of Ballard you'll find Habitude (5350 Ballard Ave NW; 206/782-2898; map:FF8), and in Kirkland look for Spa Csaba (1250 Carillon Point; 425/803-9000; map:EE3).

Local Resources

NEWSPAPERS

Seattle's two daily papers have merged their business functions under a joint operating agreement but retain entirely separate editorial operations. The evening paper, the **SEATTLE TIMES** (1120 John St; 206/464-2000; map:F2), maintains its editorial and administrative offices downtown but has moved its production facilities to a Bothell location, where tours are offered Tuesday through Thursday (425/489-7000; reservations required). The waterside offices of the early-morning **SEATTLE POST-INTELLIGENCER** (101 Elliott Ave W; 206/448-8000; map:B9) are home to one of the city's most eye-catching landmarks: a rotating neon-enhanced world globe high atop the building. The free **SEATTLE WEEKLY** (1008 Western Ave, Suite 300; 206/623-0500; map:M8) provides coverage of politics, the arts, and civic issues. Another free alternative weekly, **THE STRANGER** (1202 E Pike St; 206/323-7101; map:GG7), offers irreverent editorial comment and concise day-by-day music and dance-scene listings. Both are available beginning on Thursday of every week. On the Eastside, the **EASTSIDE JOURNAL** (1705 132nd

Ave NE, Bellevue; 425/455-2222; map:GG2) provides a local voice and a hedge against the hegemony of the *Seattle Times*. Want more local flavor? Most neighborhoods have their own weekly newspapers, usually available at grocery stores.

NAMING NAMES

Most people know that Seattle was named in honor of Chief Sealth, the peace-loving leader of two local Indian tribes (the Suquamish and the Duwamish) at the time when the first white settlers landed at Alki Point in 1851. But the sources of names for other landmarks, streets, and sights are less well remembered.

Denny Way. This busy street near Seattle Center recalls David Denny, one of the town's pioneers, who arrived here in 1851 with 25 cents in his pockets and eventually made a fortune with his investments—before losing it all during the Panic of 1893.

Elliott Bay. Today's harbor was christened by Lieutenant Charles Wilkes, who commanded an 1841 exploration of Pacific Northwest waterways. The bay was supposedly named after one of three Elliotts in his party. But whether it was the Reverend J. L. Elliott, Midshipman Samuel Elliott, or 1st Class Boy George Elliott is open for debate.

King County. The area containing Seattle was originally dubbed King County in honor of William Rufus DeVane King, Franklin Pierce's vice president. But it was renamed in 1986 to honor the slain civil rights leader Martin Luther King Jr.

Mercer Island. There's some doubt as to which of two pioneering Mercer brothers gave his name to this lump of land in Lake Washington. The probable honoree was Thomas Mercer, who arrived here in 1852 with a team of horses to become Seattle's first teamster and later its first judge. But it could also have been Asa Mercer, first president of the Territorial University (now the University of Washington) and the man who brought the famous "Mercer Maidens," a cargo of potential brides from the East Coast, to this virgin territory in the 1860s—an entrepreneurial feat immortalized in the 1960s TV show *Here Come the Brides*.

Puget Sound. Our "inland sea" was named after Peter Puget, a second lieutenant under British Captain George Vancouver, who commanded an exploration of the Sound in 1792.

Starbucks Coffee. Our best-known latte purveyor takes its moniker from Mr. Starbuck, a java junkie in Herman Melville's *Moby Dick*.

Yesler Way. In the early 1850s, Henry Yesler built the town's first steam sawmill on Elliott Bay. The Pioneer Square street that bears his name was originally a path down which logs were skidded from surrounding hills for processing.

— J. Kingston Pierce

PUBLIC LIBRARIES

Squeezed into a drab building whose architecture betrays its construction in the *Brady Bunch* era, the downtown branch of the **SEATTLE PUBLIC LIBRARY** was the subject of a long, contentious debate over the site of its future home. In 1998, a $196 million bond measure passed with an unprecedented 72 percent approval, allowing the library to upgrade facilities, technology, and books throughout the system. A new $156 million building is scheduled to open on the site of the old structure in 2003. Despite its current cramped quarters, however, the downtown Seattle Central Library (1000 4th Ave; 206/386-4636; www.spl.lib.wa.us; map:M6) continues to be a valuable resource. The librarians are friendly and extremely helpful, and the library has 10 computer terminals where the public can reserve time to surf the Internet, plus 15 terminals in the community learning center. The main branch also hosts the Quick Information Line (206/386-INFO), for answers to almost any question you can think of. In addition to lending books, video and audio recordings, and even artwork, the Seattle Public Library system offers lectures, films, and many other events in 24 branch libraries around the city. Call the individual branches for specific events.

For mobile library service, call 206/684-4713. The **KING COUNTY PUBLIC LIBRARY** system has 40 branches countywide, as well as a traveling library service, a video library, and an answer line (425/462-9600 or 800/462-9600).

MAJOR DOWNTOWN BOOKSTORES

Seattle's population is legendarily literary (see "Read All About It" box in the Planning a Trip chapter), so it's not suprising that the city is filled with bookstores. The Elliott Bay Book Company (101 S Main St; 206/624-6600; map:O9) is the best locally owned bookstore in town. The downtown branch of the University Book Store (1225 4th Ave; 206/545-9230; map:K6) features a vast selection of technical and computer titles. Large chains with downtown branches include Borders Books & Music (1501 4th Ave; 206/622-4599; map:J6) across from Westlake Center, and Barnes & Noble at Pacific Place (7th Ave and Pine St; 206/264-0156; map:I5). For more bookstores, see the Shopping chapter.

RADIO AND TV

Amid the usual horde of stations offered by the usual huge, nationwide radio conglomerates lie some gems. Small, upstart 90.3 KCMU offers younger, generally more cutting-edge music and no commercials. For a quick introduction to the issues and politics of Seattle, nothing beats the University of Washington's National Public Radio affiliate, 94.9 KUOW, and its daily *Weekday* program, running every morning from 9 to 11am. Here's a quick guide to the local radio dial.

Radio Stations

TALK RADIO	570	KVI AM
NEWS/TALK	710	KIRO AM
SPORTS	950	KJR AM
MORNING TALK	1000	KOMO AM
CNN-STYLE NEWS	1090	KIRO AM
NATIONAL PUBLIC RADIO & JAZZ	88.5	KPLU FM
AVANT-GARDE	90.3	KCMU FM
BELLEVUE COMMUNITY COLLEGE, JAZZ, FOLK	91.3	KBCS FM
TOP 40, R&B	93.3	KUBE FM
COUNTRY	94.1	KMPS FM
NATIONAL PUBLIC RADIO	94.9	KUOW FM
OLDIES	97.3	KBSG FM
CLASSICAL	98.1	KING FM
CLASSIC ROCK	102.5	KZOK FM
ADULT CONTEMPORARY	103.7	KMTT FM
ALTERNATIVE	107.7	KNDD FM

TV Stations

ABC	4	KOMO
NBC	5	KING
CBS	7	KIRO
PBS	9	KCTS
UPN	11	KSTW
FOX	13	KCPQ
WARNER/INDEPENDENT	22	KTZZ

INTERNET ACCESS

Many major hotels now offer the option of Internet access for their guests with double phone lines in rooms or sometimes even computers and business centers (see the Lodgings chapter).

It can get crowded at times, but the downtown SEATTLE PUBLIC LIBRARY (see above) has more than 20 computers available to the public with free Internet access. Hours are 9am–9pm Monday–Thursday, 9am–6pm Friday–Saturday, and 1–5pm Sunday.

Some copy centers also offer Internet access. Kinko's (206/292-9255), with 18 locations in the region open 24 hours a day, offers PC and Macintosh computers for use at $12 an hour. Seattle is also home to a few cybercafes where, for a fee, you can log on and surf—or just check your email. At the Capitol Hill Internet Café (219 Broadway E; 206/860-6858; map:HH6), using the PCs will cost you $6 an hour; hours are 10am–midnight daily. Habitat Espresso (202 Broadway E; 206/329-3087; map:HH6), also on Capitol Hill, is a not-for-profit cafe with email access for $6 an hour and similar hours. The Speakeasy Cafe

(206/728-9770), a virtual cafe, has computer terminals in more than a dozen satellite cafes around the city. Unfortunately, the Speakeasy closed its own non-virtual Belltown cafe in 1999. Call for alternate locations.

UNIVERSITIES

The University of Washington (Visitor Information Center: 4014 University Way NE; 206/543-2100; map:FF6) is the largest of the Washington State public universities and has the second-largest university bookstore in the country (4326 University Way NE, 206/634-3400). Seattle Pacific University (3307 3rd Ave W; 206/281-2000; map:FF8) is a private college associated with the Free Methodist Church. Seattle University (Broadway and Madison; 206/296-6000; map:N1) is a private Jesuit school. Seattle Community Colleges (206/587-4100) operate three separate campuses in the city.

Important Telephone Numbers

AAA WASHINGTON	206/448-5353
AAA EMERGENCY ROAD SERVICE (24 HOURS)	800/AAA-HELP
AIDS HOTLINE	206/296-4999
ALCOHOLICS ANONYMOUS	206/587-2838
AMBULANCE	911
AMTRAK	800/872-7245
ANIMAL CONTROL	206/386-4254
AUTO IMPOUND	206/684-5444
BETTER BUSINESS BUREAU	206/448-8888
BIRTH AND DEATH RECORDS	206/296-4769
BLOOD BANK	206/292-6500
CHAMBER OF COMMERCE	206/389-7200
CHILD PROTECTIVE SERVICES CRISIS HOTLINE	206/721-4306
CITY OF SEATTLE INFORMATION	206/386-1234
CITY PARKS INFORMATION AND SCHEDULING OFFICE	206/684-4075
COAST GUARD	206/286-5450
COAST GUARD 24-HOUR EMERGENCY	800/286-5400
COMMUNITY INFORMATION LINE	206/461-3200
CUSTOMS (U.S.)	206/553-4676
DIRECTORY INFORMATION (60 CENTS PER CALL)	206/555-1212
DOMESTIC VIOLENCE HOTLINE	800/562-6025
DWI (DRUNK DRIVERS) HOTLINE	800/223-7865
FBI	206/622-0460
FIRE	911
GREYHOUND BUS LINES SEATTLE TERMINAL	206/628-5526
IMMIGRATION AND NATURALIZATION SERVICE	206/553-5956
LOST PETS	206/386-7387

MARRIAGE LICENSES	206/296-3933
METRO TRANSIT RIDER INFORMATION LINE	206/553-3000
MISSING PERSONS	206/684-5582
NORTHWEST SKI REPORT	206/634-0071
PASSPORTS	206/553-7941
PLANNED PARENTHOOD	206/328-7700
POISON CENTER	206/526-2121
POST OFFICE INFORMATION	206/285-1650
RAPE RELIEF	206/632-7273
RED CROSS	206/323-2345
SEATTLE/KING CTY CONVENTION & VISITORS BUREAU	206/461-5840
SEATTLE/KING CTY DEPARTMENT OF PUBLIC HEALTH	206/296-4600
SENIOR INFORMATION CENTER	206/448-3110
SEXUAL ASSAULT CLINIC	206/223-3047
STATE PATROL	206/455-7700
SUICIDE PREVENTION	206/461-3222
TICKETMASTER	206/628-0888
TRAVELERS AID SOCIETY	206/461-3888
WASHINGTON STATE FERRIES	206/464-6400
WEATHER	206/526-6087
ZIP CODE INFORMATION	206/285-1650

TOP 200 RESTAURANTS

Restaurants by Star Rating

★

Armadillo Barbecue
Bahn Thai
Bakeman's Restaurant
Bistro Lautrec
Boat Street Café
Burk's Cafe
Cafe Da Vinci's
Copacabana
Coyote Creek Pizza
Cucina! Cucina!
Dixie's BBQ
Emmett Watson's
   Oyster Bar
Filiberto's Italian
   Restaurant
Huong Binh
Ivar's Indian Salmon
   House
Luna Park Cafe
Mae's Phinney Ridge
   Cafe
Maggie Bluffs
Pagliacci Pizza
Philadelphia Fevre
   Steak & Hoagie
   Shop
Pho Bac
Pon Proem
Ruby's on Bainbridge
Siam on Lake Union
Sisters European
   Snacks
Still Life in Fremont
   Coffeehouse
Streamliner Diner
13 Coins Restaurant
Three Girls Bakery
Trattoria Mitchelli
Triangle Lounge
Wildfire Ranch BBQ
Zula

★☆

André's Eurasian
   Bistro
Ayutthaya
Bizzarro Italian Cafe
Buca di Beppo
Chandler's Crabhouse
   and Fresh Fish
   Market

The Chile Pepper
Ciao Bella Ristorante
El Puerco Lloron
Fremont Noodle
   House
Gravity Bar
Jitterbug Cafe
Luau Polynesian
   Lounge
Moghul Palace
Nicolino
Panos Kleftiko
Piecora's
Queen City Grill
Roy's
Saigon Bistro
Salvatore Ristorante
   Italiano
Si Señor
Siam on Broadway
Six Degrees
The Slip
Taqueria Guaymas
Thai Ginger
Two Bells Tavern
Union Square Grill
Waters, A Lakeside
   Bistro

★★

Afrikando
Anthony's Beach Cafe
Anthony's HomePort
Assaggio Ristorante
Bell Street Diner
Big Time, The
   Uncommon Pizzeria
Bistro Pleasant Beach
Bistro Provençal
Black Pearl
Blowfish Asian Cafe
BluWater Bistro
Burrito Loco
Chinook's at Salmon
   Bay
Ciao Italia
Coastal Kitchen
Daniel's Broiler
Desert Fire, A
   Southwestern Grill
El Camino

Firenze Ristorante
   Italiano
Fireside Room
5 Spot Cafe
Golden Goat Italian
   Café
Golkonda
Hi-Spot Cafe
icon Grill
Il Bacio
Italianissimo
Izumi
JaK's Grill
Kabul
Kaizuka Teppanyaki
   and Sushi Bar
Macrina Bakery & Café
Madison Park Cafe
Maltby Cafe
Maple Leaf Grill
Maximilien in the
   Market
McCormick &
   Schmick's
Mediterranean Kitchen
Ming Place Chinese
   Seafood Restaurant
Nikko
Noble Court
Palisade
Pecos Pit BBQ
Phoenecia at Alki
The Pink Door
Plenty Fine Foods
Pontevecchio
Provinces Asian
   Restaurant & Bar
Raga
Red Mill Burgers
Ristorante Buongusto
Ristorante Machiavelli
Ristorante Paradiso
Salute of Bellevue
Sanmi Sushi
Santa Fe Cafe
Sea Garden
Sea Garden of
   Bellevue
Serafina
Shamiana
Shuckers

Spazzo Mediterranean
  Grill
Swingside Cafe
Tandoor
Thai Restaurant
Thai Thai
Tosoni's
22 Fountain Court
Yakima Grill
Yanni's Greek Cuisine
Yarrow Bay Beach
  Café
Zeek's Pizza

★★☆

Adriatica
Al Boccalino
Andaluca
Avenue One
Axis
Bandoleone
Brie & Bordeaux
Cactus
Cafe Flora
Cafe Nola
Carmelita
Chutneys
Cutters Bayhouse
Dulces Latin Bistro
El Greco
Fullers
I Love Sushi
Il Gambero
Isabella Ristorante

Kingfish Café
Lead Gallery and Wine
  Bar
Lush Life
Marco's Supperclub
Metropolitan Grill
Mona's
Place Pigalle
Ray's Boathouse
Roy St. Bistro
Salish Lodge
Seattle Catch Seafood
  Bistro
Shallots Asian Bistro
Shanghai Café
Shanghai Garden
Shea's Lounge
Snappy Dragon
Union Bay Cafe

★★★

Anthony's Pier 66
Cafe Campagne
Cafe Juanita
Cafe Lago
Canlis
Cassis
Chez Shea
El Gaucho
Etta's Seafood
Flying Fish
The Hunt Club
Il Bistro
Il Terrazzo Carmine

Kaspar's
La Medusa
Le Gourmand
Matt's in the Market
Nishino
The Painted Table
Palace Kitchen
Ponti Seafood Grill
Sazerac
Shiro's
Sostanza Trattoria
Szmania's
Third Floor Fish Café
Tulio
Wild Ginger Asian
  Restaurant and
  Satay Bar
Yarrow Bay Grill

★★★☆

Dahlia Lounge
Georgian Room
Rover's

★★★★

Campagne
Lampreia

Restaurants by Neighborhood

BAINBRIDGE ISLAND
Bistro Pleasant Beach
Cafe Nola
Ruby's on Bainbridge
Streamliner Diner

BALLARD/SHILSHOLE
Anthony's HomePort
Burk's Cafe
Le Gourmand
Ray's Boathouse

BELLEVUE
André's Eurasian
  Bistro
Coyote Creek Pizza
Daniel's Broiler

Dixie's BBQ
Firenze Ristorante
  Italiano
Golkonda
I Love Sushi
Mediterranean Kitchen
Ming Place Chinese
  Seafood Restaurant
Moghul Palace
Noble Court
Raga
Salute of Bellevue
Sea Garden of
  Bellevue
Shanghai Café
Spazzo Mediterranean
  Grill

Thai Ginger
Tosoni's
22 Fountain Court

BELLTOWN
Afrikando
Axis
El Gaucho
Flying Fish
Il Gambero
Lampreia
Lush Life
Macrina Bakery & Café
Marco's Supperclub
Queen City Grill
Shallots Asian Bistro
Shiro's

Two Bells Tavern
Zeek's Pizza

BURIEN
Filiberto's Italian
    Restaurant
Thai Thai

CAPITOL HILL
Ayutthaya
Bistro Lautrec
Cassis
Chutneys
Coastal Kitchen
El Greco
Gravity Bar
Kingfish Café
Pagliacci Pizza
Piecora's
Ristorante Machiavelli
Siam on Broadway
Zula

COLUMBIA CITY
La Medusa

CROWN HILL
Burrito Loco

DES MOINES
Anthony's HomePort

DOWNTOWN
Andaluca
Assaggio Ristorante
Avenue One
Blowfish Asian Cafe
Dahlia Lounge
Desert Fire,
    A Southwestern Grill
Fullers
Georgian Room
icon Grill
Isabella Ristorante
Lead Gallery and
    Wine Bar
McCormick and
    Schmick's
Metropolitan Grill
Nikko
The Painted Table
Palace Kitchen
Roy's
Sazerac
Shuckers
Tulio
Union Square Grill
Yakima Grill

EASTLAKE
Bandoleone
Serafina

EDMONDS
Anthony's Beach Cafe
Anthony's HomePort
Ciao Italia
Provinces Asian
    Restaurant & Bar

FIRST HILL
Fireside Room
The Hunt Club

**FISHERMAN'S
    TERMINAL**
Chinook's at Salmon Bay

FREMONT
El Camino
Fremont Noodle House
Pontevecchio
Ponti Seafood Grill
Seattle Catch Seafood
    Bistro
Still Life in Fremont
    Coffeehouse
Swingside Cafe
Triangle Lounge

GREEN LAKE
Brie & Bordeaux
Luau Polynesian Lounge
Mona's
Six Degrees

**GREENWOOD/PHINNEY
    RIDGE**
Burrito Loco
Carmelita
Mae's Phinney
    Ridge Cafe
Red Mill Burgers
Santa Fe Cafe
Yanni's Greek Cuisine
Zeek's Pizza

**INTERNATIONAL
    DISTRICT**
Huong Binh
Kaizuka Teppanyaki and
    Sushi Bar
Pho Bac
Saigon Bistro
Sea Garden
Shanghai Garden

ISSAQUAH
Cucina! Cucina!
JaK's Grill
Nicolino
Shanghai Garden
Wildfire Ranch BBQ

KIRKLAND
Anthony's HomePort
Bistro Provençal
Cafe Da Vinci's
Cafe Juanita
Coyote Creek Pizza
Cucina! Cucina!
Izumi
Ristorante Paradiso
Shamiana
The Slip
Third Floor Fish Café
Waters, A Lakeside
    Bistro
Yarrow Bay Beach Café
Yarrow Bay Grill

LAKE UNION
Adriatica
BluWater Bistro
Boat Street Café
Buca di Beppo
Chandler's Crabhouse &
    Fresh Fish Market
Cucina! Cucina!
I Love Sushi
Ivar's Indian Salmon
    House
Siam on Lake Union
13 Coins Restaurant

LESCHI/MADRONA
Daniel's Broiler
Dulces Latin Bistro
Hi-Spot Cafe
Plenty Fine Foods

LYNNWOOD
Buca di Beppo
Taqueria Guaymas

**MADISON PARK
    /MADISON VALLEY**
Cactus
Cafe Flora
Madison Park Cafe
Nishino
Philadelphia Fevre Steak
    & Hoagie Shop
Rover's
Sostanza Trattoria

MAGNOLIA/INTERBAY
Maggie Bluffs
Palisade
Red Mill Burgers
Sanmi Sushi
Szmania's

MALTBY
Maltby Cafe

MERCER ISLAND
Pon Proem

MONTLAKE
Cafe Lago

MUKILTEO
Ivar's Mukilteo Landing

PIKE PLACE MARKET
Cafe Campagne
Campagne
Chez Shea
Copacabana
Cutters Bayhouse
El Puerco Lloron
Emmett Watson's
  Oyster Bar
Etta's Seafood
Il Bistro
Matt's in the Market
Maximilien in the Market
The Pink Door
Place Pigalle
Shea's Lounge
Sisters European Snacks
Three Girls Bakery
Wild Ginger Asian
  Restaurant and
  Satay Bar

PIONEER SQUARE
Al Boccalino
Bakeman's Restaurant
Il Terrazzo Carmine
Pecos Pit BBQ
Trattoria Mitchelli

**QUEEN ANNE/
  SEATTLE CENTER**
Bahn Thai
Canlis
Chutneys
5 Spot Cafe
Kaspar's
Mediterranean Kitchen
Pagliacci Pizza
Panos Kleftiko

Ristorante Buongusto
Roy St. Bistro
Zeek's Pizza

RAVENNA/WEDGWOOD
Black Pearl
Ciao Bella Ristorante

REDMOND
Big Time, The
  Uncommon Pizzeria
Desert Fire,
  A Southwestern Grill
Il Bacio
Si Señor
Thai Ginger

ROOSEVELT/MAPLE LEAF
Maple Leaf Grill
Salvatore Ristorante
  Italiano
Santa Fe Cafe
Shamshiri
Snappy Dragon

**SANDPOINT/
  LAURELHURST**
Union Bay Cafe

UNIVERSITY DISTRICT
Boat Street Café
Pagliacci Pizza
Tandoor

WALLINGFORD
Bizzarro Italian Cafe
The Chile Pepper
Chutneys
Jitterbug Cafe
Kabul

WATERFRONT
Anthony's Pier 66
Bell Street Diner
Ivar's Acres of Clams
  and Fish Bar

WEST SEATTLE
Luna Park Cafe
Phoenecia at Alki
Taqueria Guaymas

WHITE CENTER
Taqueria Guaymas

WOODINVILLE
Armadillo Barbecue
Golden Goat Italian Café
Italianissimo

47

Restaurants by Food and Other Features

AFGHAN
Kabul

ALL-NIGHT
13 Coins Restaurant

BAKERY
Macrina Bakery & Café
Three Girls Bakery

BARBECUE
Armadillo Barbecue
Dixie's BBQ
Pecos Pit BBQ
Wildfire Ranch BBQ

BREAKFAST
Andaluca
Blowfish Asian Cafe
Cafe Campagne
Cafe Nola
Chinook's at Salmon Bay
Coastal Kitchen
5 Spot Cafe
Georgian Room
Gravity Bar
Hi-Spot Cafe
The Hunt Club
Ivar's Mukilteo Landing
Jitterbug Cafe
Luna Park Cafe
Mae's Phinney
   Ridge Cafe
Maggie Bluffs
Maltby Cafe
Maximilien in the Market
The Painted Table
Roy's
Saigon Bistro
Salish Lodge
Sazerac
Sisters European Snacks
The Slip
Still Life in Fremont
   Coffeehouse
13 Coins Restaurant
Three Girls Bakery
Trattoria Mitchelli
Tulio
Waters, A Lakeside
   Bistro
Yakima Grill

BREAKFAST ALL DAY
Coastal Kitchen
Mae's Phinney
   Ridge Cafe
13 Coins Restaurant

BRUNCH
Anthony's HomePort
Bandoleone
Bistro Pleasant Beach
Bizzarro Italian Cafe
Boat Street Café
Brie & Bordeaux
Cafe Campagne
Cafe Flora
Chandler's Crabhouse
   and Fresh Fish Market
Cutters Bayhouse
El Greco
Etta's Seafood
Georgian Room
The Hunt Club
Ivar's Indian
   Salmon House
Kingfish Café
Macrina Bakery & Café
Palisade
Ponti Seafood Grill
Ruby's on Bainbridge
Salish Lodge
Seattle Catch
   Seafood Bistro
Swingside Cafe
Yarrow Bay Grill

BURGERS
Maggie Bluffs
Maple Leaf Grill
Red Mill Burgers
The Slip
Two Bells Tavern

CAJUN/CREOLE
Burk's Cafe

CHINESE
Black Pearl
Ming Place Chinese
   Seafood Restaurant
Noble Court
Sea Garden
Sea Garden of Bellevue
Shallots Asian Bistro·

Shanghai Café
Shanghai Garden
Snappy Dragon

COFFEEHOUSE
Still Life in Fremont
   Coffeehouse

CONTINENTAL
Boat Street Café
Canlis
Georgian Room
Roy St. Bistro
Salish Lodge
Szmania's
Tosoni's
22 Fountain Court

DELIVERY
Black Pearl
Pagliacci Pizza
Piecora's
Snappy Dragon
Zeek's Pizza

**DESSERTS
   (EXCEPTIONAL)**
Adriatica
Dahlia Lounge
Etta's Seafood
Il Bacio
Kaspar's
Palace Kitchen
Tulio

DINER
5 Spot Cafe
Hi-Spot Cafe
Jitterbug Cafe
Luna Park Cafe
Mae's Phinney
   Ridge Cafe
Streamliner Diner

DINING ALONE
Blowfish Asian Cafe
Cafe Campagne
Carmelita
Fullers
I Love Sushi
Kaspar's Wine Bar
La Medusa
Luna Park Cafe

Marco's Supperclub
Matt's in the Market
Nikko
Nishino
Pagliacci Pizza
Palace Kitchen
Place Pigalle
Sazerac
Shiro's
Szmania's
Yakima Grill

ETHIOPIAN/EAST AFRICAN
Zula

FAMILY 👫
Anthony's Beach Cafe
Anthony's HomePort
Anthony's Pier 66
Bell Street Diner
Buca di Beppo
Burrito Loco
Cucina! Cucina!
Ivar's Acres of Clams
    and Fish Bar
Ivar's Indian Salmon
    House
Ivar's Mukilteo Landing
La Medusa
Mae's Phinney Ridge
    Cafe
Maggie Bluffs
Ray's Boathouse
Shuckers
Si Señor

FIREPLACE
Avenue One
Bistro Provençal
BluWater Bistro
Cafe Juanita
Canlis
Desert Fire, A
    Southwestern Grill
Dulces Latin Bistro
Filiberto's Italian
    Restaurant
The Hunt Club
Ponti Seafood Grill
Ristorante Buongusto
Rover's
Sostanza Trattoria
22 Fountain Court

FISH 'N' CHIPS
(see also Seafood)
Anthony's Beach Cafe
Chinook's at Salmon Bay
Emmett Watson's
    Oyster Bar
Ivar's Acres of Clams
    and Fish Bar
Ivar's Indian Salmon
    House
Ivar's Mukilteo Landing

FRENCH
Avenue One
Bistro Provençal
Brie & Bordeaux
Cafe Campagne
Cafe Nola
Campagne
Cassis
Le Gourmand
Madison Park Cafe
Maximilien in the Market
Place Pigalle
Rover's

GERMAN
Szmania's

GOURMET TAKE-OUT
Brie & Bordeaux
Cafe Campagne

GREEK
Panos Kleftiko
Yanni's Greek Cuisine

GRILL
Desert Fire, A
    Southwestern Grill
El Gaucho
icon Grill
JaK's Grill
Maple Leaf Grill
McCormick and
    Schmick's
Metropolitan Grill
Palisade
Ponti Seafood Grill
Queen City Grill
Six Degrees
Triangle Lounge
22 Fountain Court
Union Square Grill
Yarrow Bay Grill

Waters, A Lakeside
    Bistro

HEALTH-CONSCIOUS
Afrikando
Cafe Flora
Cafe Nola
Carmelita
Gravity Bar
Plenty Fine Food
Still Life in Fremont
    Coffeehouse

INDIAN
Chutneys
Golkonda
Moghul Palace
Raga
Shamiana
Tandoor

INVENTIVE ETHNIC
Andaluca
André's Eurasian Bistro
Axis
Bistro Lautrec
BluWater Bistro
Cafe Flora
Cafe Nola
Coastal Kitchen
Cutters Bayhouse
Dahlia Lounge
Etta's Seafood
Fullers
Hi-Spot Cafe
Jitterbug Cafe
Kingfish Café
Luau Polynesian Lounge
Lush Life
Maple Leaf Grill
Marco's Supperclub
Matt's in the Market
Mona's
Ponti Seafood Grill
Roy's
Ruby's on Bainbridge
Sazerac
Shea's Lounge
Sostanza
Swingside Cafe
Szmania's
Triangle Lounge
Union Bay Cafe
Waters, A Lakeside
    Bistro
Yarrow Bay Beach Café

Yarrow Bay Grill

ITALIAN
Al Boccalino
Assaggio Ristorante
Bizzarro Italian Cafe
Buca di Beppo
Cafe Da Vinci's
Cafe Juanita
Cafe Lago
Ciao Bella Ristorante
Ciao Italia
Cucina! Cucina!
Filiberto's Italian
  Restaurant
Firenze Ristorante
  Italiano
Golden Goat Italian Café
Il Bacio
Il Bistro
Il Gambero
Il Terrazzo Carmine
Isabella Ristorante
Italianissimo
La Medusa
Lush Life
Nicolino
The Pink Door
Place Pigalle
Pontevecchio
Ristorante Buongusto
Ristorante Machiavelli
Ristorante Paradiso
Salute of Bellevue
Salvatore Ristorante
  Italiano
Serafina
Sostanza Trattoria
Swingside Cafe
Trattoria Mitchelli
Tulio
Union Bay Cafe

JAPANESE
I Love Sushi
Izumi
Kaizuka Teppanyaki and
  Sushi Bar
Nikko
Nishino
Sanmi Sushi
Shiro's

KITSCHY
Armadillo Barbecue
Bizzarro Italian Cafe
Buca di Beppo

5 Spot Cafe
icon Grill
Luna Park Cafe
Mae's Phinney
  Ridge Cafe
The Pink Door

LATE-NIGHT
Bandoleone
Campagne
Cucina! Cucina!
El Gaucho
5 Spot Cafe
Flying Fish
Mona's
Queen City Grill
Sea Garden
Spazzo
13 Coins Restaurant
Trattoria Mitchelli
Two Bells Tavern
Union Square Grill

LATIN
Bandoleone
Dulces Latin Bistro
Yakima Grill

MEDITERRANEAN
Adriatica
Andaluca
Bistro Pleasant Beach
El Greco
Mediterranean Kitchen
Mona's
Phoenecia at Alki
Shea's Lounge
Spazzo Mediterranean
  Grill

MEXICAN
Burrito Loco
Cactus
The Chile Pepper
El Camino
El Puerco Lloron
Sante Fe Cafe
Si Señor
Taqueria Guaymas

NORTHWEST
Chez Shea
Dahlia Lounge
Etta's Seafood
Fireside Room
Fullers
Georgian Room

The Hunt Club
Ivar's Indian Salmon
  House
Kaspar's
Lampreia
Le Gourmand
The Painted Table
Palace Kitchen
Place Pigalle
Queen City Grill
Rover's
Szmania's
22 Fountain Court
Union Bay Cafe

OUTDOOR DINING
Anthony's Beach Cafe
Anthony's HomePort
Anthony's Pier 66
Assaggio Ristorante
Bistro Pleasant Beach
Cactus
Cafe Da Vinci's
Cafe Flora
Cafe Nola
Campagne
Carmelita
Chandler's Crabhouse
  and Fresh Fish Market
Chinook's at Salmon Bay
Copacobana
Cucina! Cucina!
El Camino
El Puerco Lloron
Emmett Watson's
  Oyster Bar
Filiberto's Italian
  Restaurant
Fremont Noodle House
Hi-Spot Cafe
The Hunt Club
Il Terrazzo Carmine
Ivar's Acres of Clams
  and Fish Bar
Ivar's Indian Salmon
  House
Ivar's Mukilteo Landing
Madison Park Cafe
Maggie Bluffs
Marco's Supperclub
Palisade
The Pink Door
Place Pigalle
Ponti Seafood Grill
Ray's Boathouse
Rover's

Serafina
Shuckers
Sostanza
Still Life in Fremont
  Coffeehouse
Streamliner Diner
Triangle Lounge
22 Fountain Court
Union Bay Cafe
Waters, A Lakeside
  Bistro
Wildfire Ranch BBQ
Yarrow Bay Beach Café
Yarrow Bay Grill

OYSTER BAR
Chandler's Crabhouse
  and Fresh Fish Market
Chinook's at Salmon Bay
Emmett Watson's
  Oyster Bar
McCormick and
  Schmick's
Shuckers

PAN-ASIAN
André's Eurasian Bistro
Blowfish Asian Cafe
Palisade
Provinces Asian
  Restaurant & Bar
Roy's
Shallots Asian Bistro
Wild Ginger Asian
  Restaurant and
  Satay Bar

PERSIAN
Shamshiri

PIZZA
Assaggio Ristorante
Big Time, The
  Uncommon Pizzeria
Cafe Da Vinci's
Cafe Lago
Ciao Italia
Coyote Creek Pizza
Cucina! Cucina!
Filiberto's Italian
  Restaurant
Isabella Ristorante
Pagliacci Pizza
Piecora's
Salvatore
Zeek's Pizza

PRIVATE ROOMS
Anthony's HomePort
Bistro Provençal
Cafe Juanita
El Gaucho
Firenze Ristorante
  Italiano
Flying Fish
Georgian Room
Kaizuka Teppanyaki and
  Sushi Bar
Kaspar's
McCormick and
  Schmick's
Metropolitan Grill
Nikko
Nishino
Palace Kitchen
Ponti Seafood Grill
Ray's Boathouse
Sea Garden
Szmania's
Third Floor Fish Cafe
Tulio
Wild Ginger Asian
  Restaurant and
  Satay Bar
Yarrow Bay Grill

ROMANTIC 🗲
Adriatica
Al Boccalino
Andaluca
Bandoleone
Bistro Lautrec
Brie & Bordeaux
Cafe Juanita
Campagne
Chez Shea
Dahlia Lounge
Dulces Latin Bistro
Fireside Room
Georgian Room
Golkonda
The Hunt Club
Il Bistro
Il Gambero
Il Terrazzo Carmine
Lampreia
Lead Gallery and
  Wine Bar
Lush Life
Mona's
The Painted Table
Place Pigalle
Ponti Seafood Grill

Ray's Boathouse
Ristorante Buongusto
Ristorante Paradiso
Salish Lodge
Serafina
Sostanza Trattoria
The Third Floor
  Fish Café
Tosoni's
22 Fountain Court
Yarrow Bay Grill

SEAFOOD
Anthony's Beach Cafe
Anthony's HomePort
Anthony's Pier 66
Bell Street Diner
Chandler's Crabhouse &
  Fresh Fish Market
Chinook's at Salmon Bay
Cutters Bayhouse
Emmett Watson's
  Oyster Bar
El Gaucho
Etta's Seafood
Flying Fish
I Love Sushi
Ivar's Acres of Clams
  and Fish Bar
Ivar's Indian Salmon
  House
Ivar's Mukilteo Landing
Kaizuka Teppanyaki and
  Sushi Bar
McCormick and
  Schmick's
Ming Place Chinese
  Seafood Restaurant
Nikko
Nishino
Palisade
Ponti Seafood Grill
Queen City Grill
Ray's Boathouse
Roy's
Sanmi Sushi
Sea Garden
Sea Garden of Bellevue
Seattle Catch Seafood
  Bistro
Shiro's
Shuckers
Third Floor Fish Café
Yarrow Bay Beach Café
Yarrow Bay Grill

SOUP/SALAD/SANDWICH

Bakeman's Restaurant
Boat Street Café
Hi-Spot Cafe
Luna Park Cafe
Macrina Bakery & Café
Maltby Cafe
Philadelphia Fevre Steak & Hoagie Shop
Sisters European Snacks
Still Life in Fremont Coffeehouse
Streamliner Diner
Three Girls Bakery
Two Bells Tavern

SOUTH AMERICAN

Copacabana
Si Señor

SOUTHWESTERN

Cactus
Desert Fire, A Southwestern Grill
Santa Fe Cafe

SOUTHERN

Kingfish Café
Sazerac

STEAK

Canlis
Daniel's Broiler
El Gaucho
The Hunt Club
JaK's Grill
Metropolitan Grill
22 Fountain Court
Union Square Grill

SUSHI

I Love Sushi
Kaizuka Teppanyaki and Sushi Bar
Nikko
Nishino
Sanmi Sushi
Shiro's

TAKEOUT (MOSTLY)

Dixie's BBQ
Pagliacci Pizza
Plenty Fine Foods
Red Mill Burgers
Taqueria Guaymas
Three Girls Bakery

TAPAS

Bandoleone
Cactus
Mediterranean Grill
Mona's
Spazzo

TAVERN

Maple Leaf Grill
Six Degrees
Triangle Lounge
Two Bells Tavern

THAI

Ayutthaya
Bahn Thai
Fremont Noodle House
Pon Proem
Siam on Broadway
Siam on Lake Union
Thai Ginger
Thai Thai

UNIQUELY SEATTLE

Cafe Juanita
Canlis
Chez Shea
Chinook's at Salmon Bay
Dahlia Lounge
Emmett Watson's Oyster Bar
Etta's Seafood
Fireside Room
Flying Fish
The Hunt Club
Ivar's Indian Salmon House
Macrina Bakery & Café
Matt's in the Market
The Pink Door
Place Pigalle
Ponti Seafood Grill
Shea's Lounge
Still Life in Fremont Coffeehouse
Streamliner Diner
Third Floor Fish Café
13 Coins Restaurant
Two Bells Tavern

VALUE, GOOD

André's Eurasian Bistro
Bakeman's Restaurant
Bistro Provençal
Buca di Beppo
Chinook's at Salmon Bay

Chutneys
Coastal Kitchen
Golden Goat Italian Café
Golkonda
Hi-Spot Cafe
Huong Binh
Il Gambero
Kaizuka Teppanyaki and Sushi Bar
Kingfish Café
Ming Place Chinese Seafood Restaurant
Pho Bac
Shallots Asian Bistro
Si Señor
The Slip
Union Bay Cafe

VEGETARIAN

Cafe Flora
Carmelita
Gravity Bar

VIETNAMESE

Huong Binh
Pho Bac
Saigon Bistro

VIEW

Adriatica
Anthony's Beach Cafe
Anthony's HomePort
Avenue One
BluWater Bistro
Cafe Da Vinci's
Canlis
Chandler's Crabhouse & Fresh Fish Market
Chez Shea
Chinook's at Salmon Bay
Copacabana
Cucina! Cucina!
Cutters Bayhouse
Daniel's Broiler
I Love Sushi (Seattle)
Ivar's Acres of Clams and Fish Bar
Ivar's Indian Salmon House
Ivar's Mukilteo Landing
Matt's in the Market
Maximilien in the Market
Palisade
The Pink Door
Place Pigalle
Ponti Seafood Grill
Ray's Boathouse

I Love Sushi (Seattle)
Ivar's Acres of Clams
    and Fish Bar
Ivar's Indian Salmon
    House
Ivar's Mukilteo Landing
Matt's in the Market
Maximilien in the Market
Palisade
The Pink Door
Place Pigalle
Ponti Seafood Grill
Ray's Boathouse
Salish Lodge
Sanmi Sushi
Shea's Lounge
Third Floor Fish Café
Waters, A Lakeside
    Bistro
Yarrow Bay Beach Café
Yarrow Bay Grill

WEST AFRICAN
Afrikando

WINE BAR
Boat Street Café
Brie & Bordeaux
Kaspar's
Lead Gallery and
    Wine Bar

RESTAURANTS

Adriatica / ★★☆

1107 DEXTER AVE N; 206/285-5000

Climbing the two challenging flights of stairs leading to Adriatica may be the culinary equivalent of reaching the summit of Mount Rainier: always worth the effort. In 1980, Jim Malevitsis opened this handsome trilevel restaurant high above Lake Union, where he continues to preside over the comfortably cloistered warren of small dining rooms. The menu hasn't changed dramatically over the years, but the once-stunning view is now obstructed by an office complex. Lately, the kitchen has experienced some missteps, but chef Jay Knickerbocker continues to turn out former longtime chef Nancy Flume's time-tested renderings of herb-kissed grilled meats and other Mediterranean-inspired fare. Start with one of the Greek appetizers; the calamari fritti is renowned for the garlic quotient of its *skorthallia*. Pastas include smoked trout farfalle. Only a fool would skip dessert here, and the proof is literally in the pudding of an airy chocolate espresso soufflé and a feathery puff pastry layered with lemon custard. *$$$; AE, DC, MC, V; checks OK; dinner every day; full bar; reservations recommended (weekends only); map:B2*

Afrikando / ★★

2904 1ST AVE; 206/374-9714

Men in Senegal don't cook, which is why chef/co-owner Jacques Sarr opened his first restaurant far, far away from home—in Washington State's hippest neighborhood, Belltown. Seattle's port of entry into West African cooking, Afrikando is decked out in Senegalese prints, imported masks, and African music (Sarr has been known to sing and dance in the kitchen). Fervent regulars come for a taste of Senegal's national dish, *thiebu djen*, a stewed white fish (usually halibut) stuffed with hot peppers and parsley and served over red rice. And everyone loves the *mafe*, a stunningly simple combination of jasmine rice, sweet potato, carrots, and yam doused with an oniony, garlicky, peppery peanut sauce. Order the airy fritters as an appetizer, and, if you like fire with the heat, ask for Jacques's "special sauce from hell." No alcohol is served, but there's a selection of homemade juice—ginger, tamarind, and hibiscus—that shouldn't be missed. For dessert, try a bowl of *thiakry*, a thick pudding of couscous, fruit, sour cream, yogurt, and vanilla sauce. It's a rich, creamy mouthful that's gloriously delicious. This is a vegetarian-friendly establishment. *$; MC, V; local checks only; lunch Mon–Sat, dinner every day; no alcohol; reservations accepted (large parties only); map:G8* &

Al Boccalino / ★★☆

I YESLER WAY; 206/622-7688

Intoxicating drifts of herbs and garlic wafting from the antipasti table greet you when you enter the old brick building just off Pioneer Square. Its chic, mottled-mustard-and-raw-brick walls are accented with dark wood and stained glass; a skewed shape to the two rooms creates the desired atmosphere of intimacy and intrigue. Carlos Tager, former maître d' and longtime friend of founder Kenny Raider, bought the restaurant in 1996 and has changed it little. The menu traverses Italy from north to south, and seafood is prominent on the daily fresh sheet. The simplest preparations work best, like the pan-seared halibut draped in a fresh red pepper puree. Pasta sauces are beautifully balanced. The formidable bistecca alla Fiorentina is a perfectly delicious, perfectly enormous aged porterhouse simply broiled with olive oil and fresh ground pepper. The still solidly Italian wine list lacks the depth and breadth it once had, but the servers are among the most polished in town. This is a great place for a quiet lunch, a dinner for two, or a party for 20, but when the house is full the noise level rises accordingly. *$$$; AE, DC, MC, V; checks OK; lunch Mon–Fri, dinner every day; beer and wine; reservations recommended; map:N8* &

Andaluca / ★★☆

407 OLIVE WAY (MAYFLOWER PARK HOTEL); 206/382-6999

Soulful, sexy, small, and sophisticated, Andaluca is a feast for the senses. Romance is in the air, even when the room is filled with business folk, as it often is at lunch. Glowing rosewood booths, fresh flowers, and textured walls in deep jewel tones that match the fancy glass bread plates create an intimate setting for the lusty dishes put before you. The menu marries Northwest ingredients and Mediterranean influences: expect a bit of Spain, a touch of Italy, a soupçon of France, a hint of Greece, and traces of the Levant. Every dish is as dramatic on the palate as it is on the plate: a soaring tower of crab, avocado, and palm hearts; zarzuela, a cumin-scented shellfish stew; fideua Andaluca, a paella-like platter of sausage, chicken, and shellfish on a bed of vermicelli; Cabrales-crusted beef tenderloin in marsala glaze; or rack of lamb in a pungent chorizo-Rioja sauce. Linger at the bar over a Gilded Manhattan sprinkled with gold dust, or nibble a few "small plates and sharables," perfect partners for one of the many sherries available by the glass. For dessert, the opulent pineapple napoleon will conquer utterly. *$$$; AE, DC, DIS, MC, V; checks OK; breakfast every day, lunch Mon–Sat, dinner every day; full bar; reservations recommended; map:I6* &

André's Eurasian Bistro / ★☆

14125 NE 20TH ST, BELLEVUE; 425/747-6551

More than a decade ago, before the fusion concept began its first half-life, André Nguyen—raised Vietnamese, educated French—ran his little (*very* little) Bellevue strip-mall eatery featuring Asian and European cuisines on menu pages side by side, but gradually the two interbred. After a 1996 fire caused by a van plowing through an adjacent computer store, he and host/spouse Noel rebuilt and expanded, creating smart, contemporary new digs. It's a comfortable cafe, not a shoot-the-moon, VISA-maxing kind of place. Flavors range from Phnom Penh beef or pork with a ginger-soy-chile sauce to Bombay prawns in curry coconut sauce to gingery Eurasian pork to chicken Parisienne with a white wine–lemon sauce. Our favorite is the Asian crab ravioli: fresh pasta clinging to fresh crabmeat, flavored with a pink ginger-butter sauce. *$$; AE, DC, MC, V; no checks; lunch Mon–Fri, dinner Tues–Sat; beer and wine; reservations recommended; map:GG2* &

Anthony's HomePort / ★★
Anthony's Beach Cafe / ★★

135 LAKE ST S, KIRKLAND (AND BRANCHES); 425/822-0225
465 ADMIRAL WAY, EDMONDS; 425/771-4400

In a city where most seafood restaurants come in multiples and are based more on marketing concepts than on culinary ideas, Anthony's stands out. The original HomePort restaurant on Kirkland's waterfront continues to clone itself on other nearby shores (Everett, 425/252-3333; Des Moines, 206/824-1947; Edmonds, 425/771-4400; Seattle (Shilshole Bay), 206/783-0780; Tacoma, 253/752-9700; Olympia, 360/357-9700), banking heavily on the excellent quality of its seafood. Well-deserved raves go to culinary director Kelly Degala for overseeing the fishified menu: robust cioppino filled with local mussels and Discovery Bay clams; buttery, crab-packed Dungeness crab cakes with a ginger-plum sauce; a fine rendition of fish 'n' chips; a simple piece of grilled halibut or salmon. Sunday brunch, available at all HomePorts except Olympia, is ordered from a menu—what a refreshing surprise at a waterside restaurant—and Sunday nights draw family crowds for all-you-can-eat crab feeds. Lunches are served at the Everett, Des Moines, Olympia, and Shilshole HomePorts only. The views, of course—over whatever body of water happens to be outside your particular branch's window—are peerless.

The popular Edmonds extension, Anthony's Beach Cafe, sells summer year-round: cheeriness, generous drinks, and all-you-can-eat fish 'n' chips on Monday. Tuesday sees the ante upped with all-you-can-eat prawns. Salads, steamed shellfish, pastas, and great fish tacos round out the inexpensive menus both here and at Anthony's Oyster Bar & Grill (downstairs from the Des Moines HomePort). Both are open for lunch and dinner. *$$/$; AE, DC, DIS, MC, V; checks OK; dinner every day, brunch Sun; full bar; reservations recommended; www.anthonys-restaurants.com; map:EE3* &

Anthony's Pier 66 / ★★★
Bell Street Diner / ★★

2201 ALASKAN WAY (AT PIER 66); 206/448-6688

Ever since this upscale/midscale, upstairs/downstairs, sprawling restaurant complex opened downtown, seafood with a view hasn't been the same. Upstairs at Anthony's Pier 66 you might drink a bracing ginger-infused martini at the bar while you hold out for a snug booth in the graceful arc of the handsome koa wood–accented dining room. Thrill to such appetizers as the "Poke Trio"—a Hawaiian-style starter that elevates ahi to new heights—or the "Potlatch"—a feast of local shellfish, known to cause a swoon—and then make your way through a menu heavy with more seafood (don't miss the crab cakes). Presentation points are well earned here, and service deserves a nod, as it does downstairs at the decidedly more casual Bell Street Diner. Fans of its sister restaurant, Chinook's at Salmon Bay (see review), will appreciate the menu and the industrial-style decor that has been cloned here to great effect. Sit at the open kitchen (where stools flank a gleaming stainless-steel counter), in the bar (with seating both indoors and out), or in the bustling dining room, and order the justly popular mahi-mahi tacos or the excellent tempura-fried seafood. For quick-stop cheap eats, there's Anthony's Fish Bar, an adjoining walk-up window on the promenade. *$$$/$$; AE, DC, DIS, MC, V; local checks only; dinner every day (Anthony's Pier 66); lunch, dinner every day (Bell Street Diner); full bar; reservations required (Pier 66), reservations recommended (Bell Street Diner); www.anthonys-restaurants.com; map:H9* &

Armadillo Barbecue / ★

13109 NE 175TH ST, WOODINVILLE; 425/481-1417

Sensible parents alert! Get take-out, or leave impressionable youth at home—otherwise, prim Auntie Rose might hear tell of a "killer hot sauce" concocted by "a group of perverts in Texas bent on destroyin' armadillos," many of which now reside in Woodinville—stuffed (the armadillos, not the perverts). This is the home of the "Snake Plate," described as "three bucks worth o' stuff" for only $4, a place where a waiter might pass by wielding a giant spray bottle of disinfectant, explaining, "You just can't use enough of this." The droll, wacko humor might amuse or appall, but the barbecue is first-rate. The chewy/smoky beef and pork ribs are irresistible though messy, and the fall-apart chicken comes with a citrusy, molasses-y sauce, which brave (or foolish) souls can replace with the aforementioned killer hot sauce. Food writers and hip newspapers have been known to hire Armadillo's catering services. *$; AE, DIS, MC, V; checks OK; lunch, dinner every day; beer and wine; reservations not accepted (but required for parties of 5 or more); map:BB1* &

Assaggio Ristorante / ★★

2010 4TH AVE (CLAREMONT HOTEL); 206/441-1399

There's an air of festivity at Assaggio, and we're not sure whether it's because the high-ceilinged two-room trattoria is always packed with customers (making for an agreeable din), or because owner Mauro Golmarvi handshakes, hugs, and/or kisses everyone who enters. (He seems to know half the people walking through the door.) Whatever it is, Assaggio brings Roman ambience to this downtown hotel space, especially when the weather's warm and the sidewalk seats are filled. Chef Don Curtiss brings untraditional ideas (baby bok choy with the lamb shank) to what had been a traditional menu, though many classics remain. Fusilli with currants and pine nuts in a saffron-tinted cream sauce proves he's on the right track. To wind up, choose the tiramisu. The other desserts are not made in-house. *$$; AE, DC, DIS, MC, V; checks OK; lunch Mon–Fri, dinner Mon–Sat; beer and wine; reservations recommended; map:H7* &

Avenue One / ★★☆

1921 1ST AVE; 206/441-6139

A million-dollar makeover transformed the former, funkier Cafe Sophie into a handsome interpretation of a 1930s-era Parisian bistro that strikes a pose midway between casual and casually elegant. A stylish crowd sips the cocktail of the moment along the curvy, copper-topped bar, often until the late-night hours. In the peach-tinted dining room under the buttery glow of vintage fixtures, enjoy a French-inspired menu that has more hits than misses. We were disappointed with the lackluster bouillabaisse but delighted by the tender duck confit bedded on tiny green lentils. Onion soup did not impress, but a thickly musseled billi-bi did. You might start with a well-composed salad, such as endive and frisée with sautéed sweetbreads and crisp pancetta, then find happiness in braised lamb shank, blanquette of veal, or beef fillet in black olive demiglace. Goat cheese tart topped with plumped dried fruits makes a fine, not-too-sweet finish. The lengthy wine list is a hodgepodge, with very little of France represented. A fireplace lures diners desiring intimacy to the small back room, which has a Sound view. *$$$; AE, DC, MC, V; no checks; dinner every day; full bar; reservations recommended; map:I8* &

Axis / ★★☆

2214 1ST AVE; 206/441-9600

The sleek, soaring, multilevel space occupied by Axis is filled with light and color—and noise, when the place gets packed, as it often does. The bar became an instant hang for Belltownies and wannabes who are looking for action and big, bold cocktails. Executive chef Alvin Binuya, also of Ponti Seafood Grill (see review), developed the vast global menu that's geared for sharing. It has something for everyone—from macaroni and cheese to knockwurst to grilled ahi. We can't resist the crisp duck in an Asian-inspired reduction of soy, ginger, scallions, and brown sugar; the seared sea bass in roasted tomato sauce; the garlicky, oven-roasted mussels with tomato and basil; or the beef tenderloin rubbed with chile pepper. Mama Binuya does the desserts—a killer banana cream pie among them. *$$; AE, DC, MC, V; no checks; dinner every day; full bar; reservations accepted; map:G8* &

Ayutthaya / ★☆

727 E PIKE ST; 206/324-8833

Soothing pastel colors and clean, smooth lines create a calming antidote to the fiery Thai food, which is prepared carefully and authentically here on Capitol Hill. It's good to make reservations; there's little waiting room. The seafood is excellent—a sizzling platter of shrimp spiked with basil, chiles, and garlic is a show in itself. Local businesspeople crowd the place at lunch for one of the best deals in town, so arrive early. Service is patient, and the only thing smoking here is the food. *$; AE, DC, JCB, MC, V; no checks; lunch Mon–Fri, dinner every day; beer and wine; reservations accepted; map:L1* &

Bahn Thai ★

409 ROY ST; 206/283-0444

The cozy, romantic aura created by soft candlelight and the proximity to Seattle Center make Bahn Thai a great date spot before a night at the opera or the theater. Don't worry about making it to your show on time; service is speedy (although, since the dining room closes between lunch and dinner, a call ahead is advised and reservations are recommended on show nights). The choice of one- to four-star spice rating makes Bahn Thai's cuisine accessible to every palate and has earned the establishment a reputation as a place to bring novice Thai eaters. A variety of curries and vegetarian options pepper the extensive menu, and the chef, kindly, is open to substitutions. Raves go to the noteworthy *tom kah gai* soup, yellow curry, peanut sauce with spinach, and sautéed scallops with *prik pao*. We also love the coconut ice cream as a sweet last dish. *$; AE, DIS, MC, V; no checks; lunch Mon–Fri, dinner every day; beer and wine; reservations recommended; map:A5*

Bakeman's Restaurant / ★

122 CHERRY ST; 206/622-3375
Bakeman's is headquarters for the working-class sandwich, now an institution among Seattle's office workers. No sprouts, just shredded iceberg lettuce; no gherkins or cornichons, just crunchy dills; handmade meat loaf instead of pâté; and real turkey sandwiches made from honest-to-God real, juicy, baked turkey with big hunks of skin sometimes still attached. As you move down the counter, be ready with your choices: white or wheat bread; light or dark meat, or mixed; mayo or no mayo; cranberry, double cranberry, or hold the cranberry. If the waiting line is snaking around the room, don't let it scare you off; things move with amazing speed here. You want stats to prove it? Bakeman's employees make over 500 sandwiches per day—3,000 per week—and move through 240 pounds of turkey daily (that's 30 eight-pounders). Go ahead and order a cup of chili or a bowl of soup to accompany your sandwich (the turkey noodle will remind you of Grandma's), and be sure to say yes when jivemeister Jason tries to fast-talk you into a piece of carrot cake. *$; no credit cards; checks OK; lunch Mon–Fri; no alcohol; reservations accepted; map:N1*

WHO'S ON FIRST?

Not Virazon anymore. The chef and owner at this lovely French bistro succumbed to professional differences and closed the doors. Say adieux to 3½-star-rated **Relais**, as well. At press time, owner/chef Eric Eisenberg abruptly shifted gears at this former Bothel temple of French haute cuisine, and is now serving up casual American fare at the renamed **Hillside Bar & Grill.**

In the past few years, Seattle has come into its own as a city of fine dining and innovative new restaurants. Competition is fierce as restaurants open and close faster than you can shake a martini. And by far the chic-est new place to enjoy one of those is at Jeremiah Tower's **Stars Bar & Dining,** which sets a new standard in town for glamorous sipping and supping. Stars is the pinnacle of downtown's posh, new Pacific Place mall, where four other restaurants stand ready to vanquish your hunger and thirst. All are California or Texas imports but for one, **Cafe Starbucks**, a stretch-limo version of the ubiquitous coffeehouse serving all-American meals. **Il Fornaio** has staked out a virtual Italian empire with a bakery, risotteria, and sandwich cafe for quick bites, as well as a dining room so elegant Catherine di Medici would feel at home. For something more energetic and contemporary, sample the around-the-world menu and ales at **Gordon Biersch Brewery Restaurant**. Next door is a branch of **Desert Fire**, a tranquil oasis of better-than-average Southwestern food (see review).

Bandoleone / ★★☆

2241 EASTLAKE AVE E; 206/329-7559

A place of many moods, Bandoleone can be lively, romantic, or just plain mellow—sometimes all in one evening. The equally peripatetic menu at this cozy neighborhood joint lined with Caribbean primitive paintings pursues Latin cuisine from Mexico to the tip of Chile, from the Caribbean to Spain and Portugal. Seafood and meat are handled with equal skill. Though the menu changes with the seasons and/or the whim of the chef, you might start with the chorizo-stuffed empanadas or the nubbins of rock shrimp sautéed in butter with lime and chipotle pepper and served with fluffy corn pancakes. Entrees that linger in our memory include grilled ahi basking in a spicy red pepper sauce in company with sweet papaya and black bean salsa and a silky corn and roasted garlic flan, and *cordero asada*, skewered chunks of lamb imbued with the flavors of black plums and chile negro. Half of the small storefront space is given over to the bar, where cigars are as popular after 10pm as the limited late-night tapas menu. There's a cozy deck out back. Local bands playing jazz, blues, and salsa draw a youngish crowd. *$$; MC, V; checks OK; dinner every day, brunch Sun; full bar; reservations recommended; bandoleone@earthlink.net; www.earthlink.net/~bandoleone; map:GG7* &

Big Time, The Uncommon Pizzeria / ★★

7824 LEARY WAY, REDMOND; 425/885-6425

In the face of Big Competition, Big Time maintains its hold on the top spot in byte-land. Even if the pizzas—built on a rich, flavorful crust from hand-tossed dough, with toppings representing styles from Greece to

That flashy new Mediterranean venture behind the iron gates on Third Avenue at Lenora Street is **Brasa**, recently launched by **Campagne** (see review) alums, chef Tamara Murphy and general manager Bryan Hill. Acclaimed chef Laura Dewell, who closed the beloved **Pirosmani** in December 1997, resurfaced at **Credenzia** on lower Queen Anne, while chef Kerry Sear, formerly of the Four Seasons Olympic Hotel's **Georgian Room** (see review) flies solo in Belltown, creating his version of Northwest cuisine at **Cascadia**, which will open some time in 1999. Other pre-millennium changes? Bicoastal restaurateur Drew Nieporent will make his Seattle debut with **Earth & Ocean** in the luxurious new W Hotel downtown, and one of the city's favorite restaurants, **Wild Ginger** (see review), will leave its popular Western Avenue locale for larger digs uptown, near Benaroya Hall.

Beyond that, our crystal ball gets a little cloudy. . . .

—*Providence Cicero*

Mexico to Thailand—were not as good as they are, we would go for the eight wines offered by the glass. There are plenty of beers on tap as well. Our fave pies remain the Pesto Plus (with fontina, sun-dried tomatoes, mushrooms, artichoke hearts, and pesto) and the Greek (feta, kalamata olives, Roma tomatoes, green peppers, and oregano). Best is Big Time's attention to unusually savory toppings: blue cheese, Montrachet, and portobello mushrooms. The calzone oozes mozzarella, encased in a deliciously chewy, handmade crust. A few pan-tossed pastas and green salads round out the menu. *$; AE, DC, DIS, MC, V; local checks only; lunch, dinner every day; full bar; reservations accepted (large parties only); map:EE2* &

Bistro Lautrec / ★

315 E PINE ST; 206/748-0627

Formerly Cafe Sabika, this tiny Capitol Hill spot was redecorated and renamed by its new owners, who retained its ambience as a cozy, romantic bistro. Seeking inspiration globally, co-owner/chef Rob Zahel goes overboard at times by piling on influences and flavors—grilled ahi, for example, is drizzled with sesame-ginger oil and sided by bitter greens, pasta, and red pepper–tomato coulis. Stick to simple preparations such as the crab cakes in herb-chardonnay sauce or one of the pastas, reach across the table to touch hands, and bliss out. *$$; AE, DC, DIS, MC, V; no checks; dinner Tues–Sat; beer and wine; reservations recommended; map:J1*

Bistro Pleasant Beach / ★★

241 WINSLOW WAY W, BAINBRIDGE ISLAND; 206/842-4347

Hussein and Laura Ramadan closed their white-linen place in an old Tudor mansion on Bainbridge Island's southwest corner, built a smart new place on the edge of downtown Winslow, dumped the white linen, and became the island's chic-est spot the moment they opened. Though the bistro seats as many as 160 when the weather's fair (60 on the main floor, 40 on the mezzanine level, and another 60 on the broad patio), when dinnertime rolls around it fills to the gills. Then it's kiss-kiss, wave-wave, and everyone settles down to Mediterranean-inflected, local-ingredient food: baked Brie with walnuts, five-onion bisque, wood oven–fired pizza, curried lamb stew, grilled Atlantic salmon from Bainbridge's fish farm. *$$; AE, MC, V; local checks only; lunch Tues–Fri, dinner Tues–Sun, brunch Sat–Sun; beer and wine; reservations recommended* &

Bistro Provençal / ★★

212 CENTRAL WAY, KIRKLAND; 425/827-3300

For more than 25 years, Philippe Gayte has been purveying perfectly sauced French fare in the heart of downtown Kirkland. And believe us, that is a lot of sauce. One of our favorite meals involves three medallions of meat—veal, lamb, and pork—with three different sauces—marsala, béarnaise, and berry, respectively. In recent years Gayte has emphasized a less formal, more easily accessed menu, featuring a range of à la carte dishes plus a terrific value in a $25 prix-fixe menu—soup or pâté, appetizer, salad, entree, and dessert. The cozy, country-inn atmo remains, as does the creaky old dessert tray, which could have served napoleons to Napoleon. Service is likely to be erratic, lacking some attention to detail; Gayte always manages to have one or more French-accented waiters on board with condescending attitude intact. (After we had coughed up an $18 cork fee, our man studiously avoided refilling our glasses.) But the food has been, is, and probably always will be well worth that minor inconvenience. Two rustic rooms share a two-sided fireplace. *$$; AE, DC, MC, V; local checks only; dinner every day; full bar; reservations recommended; map:EE3* &

Bizzarro Italian Cafe / ★★☆

1307 N 46TH ST; 206/545-7327
Nestled in a former garage in Wallingford, Bizzarro demonstrates clearly that it deserves its name. When it's good, it's very, very good; but don't be surprised if you encounter a good meal and terrible service, or vice versa. Frequently redecorated, the cafe might resemble anything from an upside-down garden—complete with picnic and plastic ants—to a resurrected dinosaur park. The food, too, is varied and imaginative, with ingredients ranging from the sublime to the ridiculous. This is clearly a neighborhood favorite, with servers greeting regulars by name and placing their standard orders without prompting. Appetizers might include an appealingly simple warm goat cheese with roasted garlic. Bread is nothing special. Among the pastas, an outstanding choice is the mix-and-match, where diners choose a pasta shape and marry it with their favorite sauce. Full dinners are a bargain, with soup or salad included. On any given evening, though, salads may be less than fresh, and soups overseasoned. The menu changes seasonally, so watch for the return of the consistently good roast chicken. There's a limited selection of wines by the glass and by the bottle. *$; AE, DIS, MC, V; checks OK; dinner every day, brunch Sat–Sun; beer and wine; reservations not accepted; map:FF7*

Black Pearl / ★★

7347 35TH AVE NE; 206/526-5115
Starting out as Panda's, then becoming Pandasia and then Black Pearl (after the owners split and the Pandasia name stayed with a Magnolia spot), this Wedgwood place is still busy, busy, busy. Its little white 4x4s whiz around the neighborhood delivering house-made, hand-cut noodles and dozens of other fresh-from-the-wok, inexpensive, familiar Chinese dishes. Evidence that take-out and delivery dominate is found behind the

counter. Five or six serious-looking cooks silently toil, even though only 6 booths and 10 counter stools occupy the clean, lavender-tinted place. You can't go wrong with the thick, chewy noodles or the tea-smoked chicken, duck, or sea bass. Nearly every first-timer orders Lovers' Eggplant (crisply battered outside, meltingly soft inside) or General Tso's chicken, both swathed in thick, sweet, orange-flavored sauce. Lunch combos rank among the city's best bargains. *$; AE, MC, V; checks OK; lunch, dinner Mon–Sat, dinner only Sun; beer and wine; reservations recommended; map:EE6* &

Blowfish Asian Cafe / ★★

722 PINE ST (PARAMOUNT HOTEL); 206/467-7777

Not your typical hotel restaurant, Blowfish is the first restaurant venture for the Kikuchi family of Japan, and it's proved such a successful concept that another is planned for Bellevue. The whimsical contemporary Asian decor mixes posters of Japanese baseball stars, pachinko machines, brightly colored origami mobiles, and sleek black tables. Two exhibition kitchens—a wok station and a robata grill—add to the fun. The pan-Asian menu offers pleasant grazing. We liked skewered salmon with asparagus, the elegant seafood stir-fry, and especially the Chinese sausage paired with shrimp in a vegetable-laced fried rice. Iceberg lettuce finds its perfect calling as a wrap for minced chicken, shiitakes, and pine nuts in a pungent ginger-and-garlic-spiked oyster sauce. Breakfast is a traditional American affair: oatmeal, flapjacks, bacon, eggs, and hash browns. Jump-start your day with a sassy Wasabe Mary, or smooth out the day's wrinkles in the evening with a gleaming Silvertini from the enticing cocktail list. *$$; AE, DC, DIS, MC, V; checks OK; breakfast, lunch, dinner every day; full bar; reservations recommended; blowfish@nwlink.com; map:J5* &

BluWater Bistro / ★★

1001 FAIRVIEW AVE N; 206/447-0769

Among the restaurant Goliaths that line the south end of Lake Union sits the unassuming BluWater Bistro, the kind of place where everybody is likely to know your name after only a couple of visits. Chef Peter Levine takes a classy approach to the American bistro menu: smoky chipotle pepper in the aioli that accompanies excellent fried calamari; pineapple and jicama relish under the tepee of skewered Jamaican jerk chicken; ancho chile and honey brushed over the grilled salmon. Whatever the pasta special is—order it. Salads are equally fresh, light, and appealing. Steaks are he-man-size and cooked to perfection. Only sandwiches and service occasionally disappoint. Nearby office workers fill the generous marina-side patio at lunch or sit fireside when the weather is foul. The 20-something owners attract an equally youngish bar crowd for the latest last call on the lake. They're probably knocking back single-malt scotches or small-batch bourbons; we favor the smooth, blue Bada Margarita. *$$; AE, DC, DIS, MC, V; checks OK; lunch, dinner every day; full bar; reservations not accepted (but required for large parties); www.wolfenet.com/~bluwater; map:D1* &

Boat Street Café / ★

909 NE BOAT ST; 206/632-4602

The Boat Street Café is a gem in the middle of nowhere, on one of the most difficult-to-find little streets in Seattle. That doesn't mean that no one knows where it is, though: You'll recognize it by the long line outside, especially for weekend brunch. What looks like a fisherman's shack from the outside is utterly airy and light-filled inside. The unfinished ceilings, glowing walls, and open kitchen make this the ideal space for low-toned conversations, newspaper reading, and leisurely cups of tea—in short, the perfect place for a quiet, civilized weekend brunch, a lovers' lunch, or an intimate dinner. On the weekend, break into a coddled egg, using a bit of crusty bread to sop it all up. At lunch, try one of the sandwiches, made from a Le Fournil baguette, or an artfully dressed salad--all favorites with the university folks nearby. Dinner is pricier, but you get more bang for the buck as well: candlelight, a good wine list (the back room is now a wine bar serving 30 different bottles), and a rotating selection of dishes that reflects the offerings of the season. Start with an appetizer of fresh sliced pears, carmelized walnuts and gorgonzola cheese; entrees include pastas as well as vegetarian and meat dishes. *$; no credit cards; checks OK; lunch Tues–Sun, dinner Wed–Sat, brunch Sat–Sun; beer and wine; reservations recommended; map:FF7* &

Brie & Bordeaux / ★★☆

2227 N 56TH ST; 206/633-3538

When Green Lake's neighborhood wine-and-cheese shop stepped across the street and added a kitchen and a charming bistro, it quickly proved that bigger (in this case, at least) is definitely better. Owners Alison and Mary Leber have assembled a polished staff both on the retail side, where a vast international array of cheeses, olives, wines, pâtés, and cured meats are available to go, and in the bistro, where chef Scott Samuels displays increasing finesse with each new seasonal menu. Start or end your dinner with hand-picked cheeses from the shop. If it's summer, revel in the freshness of sweet corn soup or the lushness of seared foie gras with grilled peaches and nectarine chutney. Fish of the day might be pan-seared halibut or sea bass, or king salmon and rock shrimp mousse steamed in savoy cabbage. Madeira and mushroom jus moistens grilled rabbit. Honey and lavender demiglace bathes rack of lamb. No room for dessert? The sweet Brie ice cream will change your mind. At lunch and brunch the fare is no less inventive. Choices include lamb burger topped with Gorgonzola dolce, chive-potato pancakes with grilled chicken and apple sausages, and an omelet of grilled portobello, braised leek, and smoked Gouda. *$$; AE, MC, V; local checks only; dinner Tues–Sat, brunch Sat–Sun; beer and wine; reservations accepted for dinner only; brbordeaux@aol.com; map:FF7* &

Buca di Beppo / ★★

701 9TH AVE N; 206/244-2288

4301 200TH ST SW, LYNNWOOD; 425/744-7272

Count on good fun, good food, and good value at this restaurant-cum–ethnic theme park. But come prepared to wait for it, particularly on weekend evenings; you won't be seated until everyone in your party shows. Buca di Beppo is big, boisterous, and decorated with tongue-in-cheek Italian kitsch. But Italians don't joke about food, and the soul of Buca di Beppo is a celebration of that most sacred of Italian rituals—family dinner. The enormous family-size platters require at least a party of four to do them justice, but the more the merrier is the rule when it comes to indulging in the dozen or so pastas, half a dozen pizzas, and such entrees as a sassy and superb chicken cacciatore. For dessert, save room for a slice of cheesecake the size of New Jersey. *$$; AE, DC, MC, V; checks OK; dinner every day; full bar; reservations not accepted; map:C3* &

Burk's Cafe / ★

5411 BALLARD AVE NW; 206/782-0091

"Indolent" and "tropical" are not words one usually associates with Ballard, but at Burk's, an exception must be made. This brightly painted wood-frame building looks as though it belongs on a lazy wharf in Biloxi. The illusion is fostered inside, where ceiling fans whirl and tile floors make for a pleasant racket when the room is full. What Burk's lacks is the down-and-dirty attitude that makes for a real deep-fried Southern experience; only in Seattle would a Cajun joint ban smoking, even at the bar. It all feels just a little too clean, despite the good-natured attempts of the waitstaff to juice the place up a bit. But the food is fiery and down-home, starting with the crock of pickled okra that graces each table. The appetizers are all dependable, including a wonderful squid with chile butter. For dinner, there's both filé and okra gumbo, homemade sausage (too dry on one visit), crawfish in season, and an excellent specials list that sometimes includes various blackened fish, pork in barbecue sauce, and fresh catfish (no bargain and not so nice to look at). All the dinners come, classically, with red beans and rice. Though the pecan pie is the best in town, other desserts—such as bread pudding with whiskey sauce served chilled and gelatinous—can disappoint. *$$; MC, V; local checks only; lunch, dinner Tues–Sat; beer and wine; reservations not accepted; map:EE8*

Burrito Loco / ★★
9211 HOLMAN RD NW; 206/783-0719

A storefront attached to a gas station seems an unlikely place to find a good meal, but Burrito Loco confounds expectations with fresh ingredients, clean-flavored sauces, and lard-free beans. The big signature burrito exemplifies this care and quality. Even better are two chicken dishes: chicken enchiladas, swathed in dark mole, and chicken in *pipian*, a sauce of crushed sesame, sunflower, and pumpkin seeds originating in the owners' hometown of Cuatula, Jalisco. Burrito Loco also serves tortas— Jalisco-style sandwiches of soft white Mexican rolls filled with fish, fowl, pork, or beef. Ceviche refreshes, especially in warm weather, and makes for either a great appetizer or a light meal. Don't miss the agua frescas: lemonade, melon, honeydew, or horchata (sweetened rice milk scented by cinnamon). *$; DIS, MC, V; checks OK; lunch, dinner every day; beer and wine; reservations not accepted; map:DD8* ㅊ

Cactus / ★★★
4220 E MADISON ST; 206/324-4140

On many evenings, the crowd at Cactus spills out onto the sidewalk— on weekends, prepare to wait an hour or more for a table. Armed with a restaurant-supplied beeper, you can stroll the charming neighborhood of Madison Park knowing the wait will be worth the while. It may be that the sun-drenched cuisines of Mexico and the Southwest are a great antidote to yet another gray Seattle day, but more likely Cactus owes its popularity to the consistent quality and originality of its food. Brightly painted tables and hanging peppers (some illuminated) enhance the festive atmosphere. So what if the decor borders on kitsch—the kitchen turns out the real thing. Start with tapas and you may not need to go any further: a few make a very satisfying light meal, especially calamari flavored with roasted garlic, tomato, raisins, and pine nuts; mussels in creamy fennel and vodka broth; or chile-spiked garlic shrimp in a sherry-laced sauce. The familiar Mexican reliables—fajitas, enchiladas, and tacos—are well done, but other options can be more interesting: chicken marinated in chili, cinnamon, and chocolate, glazed with honey and more cinnamon; or grilled pork steak adobo infused with orange and chipotle peppers under a layer of fruit mojo. Most entrees come with a basket of incomparable Navajo Indian fry bread. The beverage list features fruit drinks, margaritas, beer, and mineral water, but the wine list is limited. Three-milk Cuban flan is the must dessert. *$$; DC, DIS, MC, V; checks OK; lunch Mon–Sat, dinner every day; full bar; reservations not accepted; map:GG6* ㅊ

Cafe Da Vinci's / ★

89 KIRKLAND AVE, KIRKLAND; 425/889-9000
It seems like Da Vinci's always has been and always will be the buzz of Kirkland on a weekend night. Even when the weather is dicey and the staff can't open the glass wall looking out on Lake Street, 20-somethings get drawn into the dark, loud bar, where sporting events blare from big TVs. It's the kind of place where love, or at least lust, blooms as willingly as summer impatiens. It's also a place that needs a strong arm hanging around, just in case things take a turn. A glow-in-the-dark paint job remains, even though the "Flying Pizza" moniker has flown. But there's another side to DaVinci's as well: the other side of the building, actually, where a dining room looks out on the lake and a large streetside patio area offers some of the best seats in town on a fine day. What a pleasant surprise to find not only decent pizza but some pleasing pasta preparations as well, especially the cannelloni. *$$; AE, DC, DIS, MC, V; checks OK; lunch, dinner every day; full bar; reservations accepted; www.davincis.com; map:EE3* ⅙ *(bar only)*

Cafe Flora / ★★☆

2901 E MADISON ST; 206/325-9100
Cafe Flora's original meatless, smokeless, boozeless ethic was rooted in a larger vision: multiculturalism, responsible global stewardship, and a fervid righteousness about health. Political and social agendas aside, this very attractive, modern place has become a mecca for vegetarians and even their nonveggie friends. Concessions have been made for the regulars who longed to sip something more potent than rosemary-laced lemonade; you may now enjoy a glass of merlot with your portobello Wellington (mushroom-pecan pâté and grilled portobellos wrapped in pastry) or drink a beer with your Oaxaca tacos (a pair of corn tortillas stuffed with spicy mashed potatoes and cheeses, set off by a flavorful black bean stew and sautéed greens). Soups are always silky and luscious, salads sport interesting (and often organic) ingredients, and diners who don't do dairy will always discover something cleverly prepared to suit their dietary needs. Never hesitate when the dessert tray makes the rounds. *$$; MC, V; checks OK; lunch Tues–Fri, dinner Tues–Sun, brunch Sat–Sun; beer and wine; reservations recommended; map:HH6* ⅙

Cafe Juanita / ★★★

9702 NE 120TH PL, KIRKLAND; 425/823-1505

As Cafe Juanita celebrates its 20th birthday, little has changed in the last two decades—at least visually. It is still a converted white-brick house with hardwood floors, a small collection of Italian etchings, and a high shelf along one wall with empty wine bottles elbow to elbow, just waiting for a good earthquake. There are a couple of recent changes: a private room downstairs and a patio just outside it, with a lawn sloping down to a small creek. The only menu, as ever, is written in chalk on one of three boards. And many of the items on it—*spiedini misti, pollo pistacchi, agnello verdure*—also remain virtually constant. If anything, the list of items that rotate in and out has grown shorter. This is because owner Peter Dow has one of the most loyal followings in the area, and they want their *pollo pistacchi* forever available. So much practice ensures impressive consistency. Start with a fresh pasta, move on to a meat or seafood course, share a family-style plate of greens, and save room for creations from the dessert cart. Try one of Dow's own Cavatappi wines, or choose from a good list featuring Italian and Northwest selections. Know that when you return, you will tread familiar ground. *$$; AE, MC, V; local checks only; dinner every day; full bar; reservations recommended; map:DD4* ঙ

Cafe Lago / ★★★

2305 24TH AVE E; 206/329-8005
Owners Jordi Viladas and Carla Leonardi (he's the chef, she's the pastry chef) fuel the fires at this rustic Montlake cafe reminiscent of trattorias that dot the hills of Tuscany. A flaming brick oven, butcher paper–topped tables nestled together, and prettily stenciled walls entice a loyal neighborhood clientele. The menu, which changes regularly, includes a strong selection of antipasti, a quartet of pastas, and a half-dozen pizzas. When compared to other not-so-fancy Italian restaurants, the offerings may seem somewhat expensive, but rest assured, your money's well spent here. Start with the astounding antipasti sampler, which might include thick slices of fresh mozzarella, salty Asiago cheese, herby goat cheese nudging up against roasted red peppers, grilled and marinated eggplant, a head of roasted garlic, a selection of cured meats, and crostini swabbed with olive paste. Fruitwood imparts a smoky flavor to the fabulous thin-crust pizzas, and the handmade pastas give new meaning to the word ethereal. The lasagne con melanzane—"unlike any lasagne you have ever had," according to the menu—lives up to the billing. The sheets of pasta come rolled thin as a wonton, layered with eggplant, béchamel, and ricotta, with a bright red tomato sauce. Simply extraordinary. The wine list runs the gamut in prices, with some rather fine Italian bottlings. The high ceilings make for a noisy room, but, hey, that's Italian. *$$; DC, MC, V; checks OK; dinner Tues–Sun; beer and wine; reservations accepted (large parties only); map:GG6* ঙ

Cafe Nola / ★★☆

101 WINSLOW WAY, BAINBRIDGE ISLAND; 206/842-3822
Imagine holding a bowl of café au lait in both hands and having a heart-to-heart with a friend. Thanks to sisters Melinda Lucas and Mary Bugarin, you don't have to take the Concorde to France for the experience. Improbably, they turned their backs on successful California

careers and migrated to Bainbridge Island, where they established this elegant French provincial cafe complete with lavender-lined patio for good-weather idling. Melinda (a former pastry chef at L.A.'s illustrious Spago) bakes the scrumptious pastries, beautiful desserts, and exceptional breads. Mary (a former San Francisco caterer) prepares the extraordinary soups, salads, sandwiches, pastas, and pizzas. Breakfast features the freshest eggs imaginable, along with perfect fruits for topping granola and oatmeal. Heavenly Hots (tender sour-cream pancakes) with huckleberry compote mark Sundays as special. Cafe Nola keeps many small island farmers busy growing organic produce—and gathering organic eggs—to satisfy the cafe's exacting standards. Monthly wine dinners give the sisters opportunities to prepare the likes of seared wild salmon ravioli, served open-faced with white-corn sauce, grilled pea vines, and roasted pepper–infused oil. *$–$$; MC, V; checks OK; breakfast, lunch Tues–Sun; beer and wine; reservations not accepted (except for wine dinners and large parties)* &

Campagne / ★★★★
Cafe Campagne / ★★★

86 PINE ST; 206/728-2800; 1600 POST ALLEY; 206/728-2233 (BOTH IN PIKE PLACE MARKET)

Linen tablecloths, tiny vases of flowers, and wall space dedicated to wine bottles help set the mood for country French in a very urban setting at Campagne. Located in a courtyard off Pike Place Market, the restaurant takes its cue from the cuisine of southern France. Owner Peter Lewis (one of the city's most gracious hosts) and some of Seattle's finest servers will ensure that you dine with gusto. Campagne offers a deliciously rich cassoulet; other nightly specials reflect the day's catch, the season's offerings, and the soothing inspirations of chef James Drohman. There are many successes here—an inspired, carefully wrought wine list not the least

among them. A wonderful late-night menu is available in the exceptionally romantic (but often smoky) bar. Dining at a courtyard table while sipping a Framboise Sauvage is the next best thing to a trip to France.

Lewis's Cafe Campagne, which opened in 1994 just below its stylish sibling, often proves too small to accommodate those who throng to this casual bistro-cum-charcuterie. Wherever you sit (at a cherrywood table or the elegant counter), be sure to utter the most important words spoken here: garlic mashed potatoes. At lunch or dinner, the herby rotisserie chicken or classic steak frites will put you over the edge. *$$$/$$; AE, DC, MC, V; no checks; breakfast, lunch, dinner Mon–Sat, brunch Sun (Cafe Campagne), dinner every day (Campagne); full bar; reservations recommended; map:I7* &

Canlis / ★★★

2576 AURORA AVE N; 206/283-3313

Everyone has an opinion about Canlis. Some say it's Seattle's finest cele-
bratory restaurant; others say it's an anachronism. We say you gotta love
a place this dedicated to making the customer feel like visiting royalty.
Owners Chris and Alice Canlis, intent on enticing the "next generation"
of Canlis-goers, recently sank $1.5 million into a structural remodel of
the nearly 50-year-old restaurant, updated the menu to take better
advantage of the Northwest's bounty, and traded in their waitresses'
cumbersome traditional kimonos for swaying pantsuits, while continuing to offer luxe dining in luxe surroundings at luxe prices. There
remains a timeless quality about the place—from the twinkling lights
around Lake Union below, to the well-heeled, well-aged patrons sipping
martinis, to the sound of "Happy Birthday" being played for the
umpteenth time at the splendid piano bar. Yes, you can still order Peter
Canlis Shrimp Capri and the famous Canlis Salad (an overdressed
knockoff of a caesar), but the menu also boasts an exceptional sashimi
appetizer and crisp, moist Dungeness crab cakes. The wine list makes the
phone book look like Cliff Notes, and though you can spend $1,000 on
a single bottle, there are options in the $30 range worth savoring. *$$$;
AE, DC, DIS, MC, V; checks OK; dinner Mon–Sat; full bar; reservations
required; canlis@canlis.com; www.canlis.com; map:GG7* &

Carmelita / ★★☆

7314 GREENWOOD AVE N; 206/706-7703

In their first restaurant venture, owners and interior designers Kathryn
Newmann and Michael Hughes transformed a dilapidated retail space
into a theatrically lit, art-filled haven of color and texture. This is a place
to be alone with a pot of tea and a newspaper in the charming lounge,
dine intimately with a friend, or celebrate with the whole family. Neigh-
bors from Greenwood and Phinney Ridge embraced Carmelita warmly
from the beginning, and though the opening chef has since departed, the
sophisticated, seasonal vegetarian menu remains enticing. Start with the
daily changing bruschetta sprinkled with luscious aged balsamic vinegar.
Entrees we favor include a dramatically plated caponata-stuffed, mari-
nated tofu coated with cornmeal and pan-fried, and a leek-wrapped por-
tobello stuffed with asparagus, roasted peppers, and caramelized onion.
The wine list is short, with nothing over $30; teas, tisanes, juices, and a
refreshing tamarind-ginger lemonade round out the beverage options. In
summer, there's also a charming, plant-filled deck. *$$; DC, MC, V; local
checks only; dinner Tues–Sun; beer and wine; reservations accepted;
map:EE8* &

Cassis / ★★★

2359 10TH AVE E; 206/329-0580
Small, sexy Cassis looks, outside and in, as if it had anchored the north end of Capitol Hill since the '20s. A neighborhood-size bistro that draws from beyond the neighborhood, it serves up true French bistro fare, such as freshly cut and fried pommes frites alongside a sturdy grilled rib-eye awash in marchands de vin; or a pan-roasted half capon, seasoned under the skin; or sautéed calf's liver. From appetizers (think mussels marinière or house-smoked fish or capon breast) to dessert (beautifully burnished tarte Tatin or bread pudding), the food consistently excels. The tiny bar area crowds up quickly; the tiny dining room, brown-walled and dimly lit by period sconces, can't hold all who want in; tiny linen-topped tables quickly crowd with plates and glasses. (Smoking is allowed in the bar and on the deck after 9pm.) The only thing big here is heart and French soul. *$$; MC, V; no checks; dinner every day; full bar; reservations recommended; map:GG6*

Chandler's Crabhouse and Fresh Fish Market / ★☆

901 FAIRVIEW AVE N; 206/223-2722
Chandler's is quintessential Seattle, due in part to the view of Lake Union with its boats and seaplanes coming and going, the lights of Queen Anne Hill in the distance, and the representative cross-section of Seattle types at the bar and in the dining room. The menu offers a gastronomic geography lesson on Puget Sound with a variety of local oysters, Dungeness crab, clams, and mussels, not to mention the wide selection of fresh fish, all cooked with tender attention. Crab cakes are moist and delicious, with the true crab flavor coming through, and the menu boasts a healthy salmon component. Chandler's recipes often bow to a cross-cultural mix of ingredients: cherry-smoked Alaskan halibut with apricot ginger glaze, or a wonderful Grays Harbor sturgeon with lemongrass, asparagus, and jasmine rice. Service is attentive, and there's an extensive wine list, heavy on Northwest labels. Even the desserts have a local tang with fruits in season. *$$$; AE, DC, MC, V; local checks only; lunch Mon–Fri, dinner every day, brunch Sat–Sun; full bar; reservations recommended (weekends only); map:D1* &

Chez Shea / ★★★
Shea's Lounge / ★★☆

94 PIKE ST, THIRD FLOOR (PIKE PLACE MARKET); 206/467-9990

Chez Shea is one of Seattle's gems. You might walk through Pike Place Market a hundred times and not know that Sandy Shea's tiny, romantic hideaway is perched just above in the Corner Market Building, looking out over Puget Sound. Dinner at Chez Shea is a prix-fixe affair, with four courses reflecting the bounty of the season and ingredients fresh from the market stalls below. A winter meal might begin with an asparagus soufflé with yellow-pear-tomato vinaigrette, followed by gingered soup. The main-course choices might include sautéed halibut moistened by lemon-sorrel butter; grilled portobello and roasted vegetables layered with goat cheese, baked and served with sherried red onion sauce; beef fillet sided by caramelized Walla Walla sweets and bathed in a blue cheese–spiked demiglace; and pepper-crusted duck complemented by rhubarb purée and mango salsa. Service is always sure and gracious. Next door is Shea's Lounge, a deep, narrow, sexy bistro that's wed to Chez Shea by a common door. The menu offers about a dozen Mediterranean-accented dishes, including superb pizzas and a vivid salad or two. The perfect place to meet a friend for a little something before or after. *$$$/$$; AE, MC, V; no checks; dinner Tues–Sun; full bar; reservations recommended (Chez Shea only); map:J8*

The Chile Pepper / ★★☆

1427 N 45TH ST; 206/545-1790
It's an odd eating experience: food that's sometimes fiery, sometimes subtly distinctive, but always wonderfully complex, served in a dining room that's as dull as any we've seen in Seattle. Maybe the ploy is to throw the brilliance of the food into high relief. The Gonzalez family purveys the regional cuisine of the upland Mexican state of Guanajuato, where the sauces are rich marriages of flavor, not unlike a good curry. An outstanding mole poblano sauce served on chicken is neither the sweet chocolate Oaxacan mole nor the bland, pale nut sauce other eateries seem to buy by the tub. It's as dark as chocolate, redolent of cinnamon, clove, laurel, sesame, almonds, peanuts, tart tomatillos, black pepper, and several kinds of chiles. Chiles rellenos is the most popular dish here, lightly battered and laden with cheese. Ceviche is served in a tall glass, topped with guacamole; the slight fire of the guac plays nicely against the citrus and cilantro flavor of the fish. *$; no credit cards; checks OK; lunch, dinner Mon–Sat; beer, wine, and margaritas; reservations not accepted; map:FF7* &

Chinook's at Salmon Bay / ★★

1900 W NICKERSON ST; 206/283-4665
It's big, busy, and formulaic, but the Anthony's HomePort folks seem to be using the right bait here at their showplace in the heart of Fishermen's Terminal. The industrial-strength design—very high ceilings, steel countertops, visible beams and ventilation ducts—matched with an appealing collection of action-packed fishing photos, fits well with the bustle around the working marina. The seemingly never-ending menu ranges from broiled, steamed, fried, and sandwiched seafood to stir-fries and big, juicy burgers. We suggest you nab a few things off the regular menu (tempura onion rings and a half-dozen oysters) and pay close attention

to the daily special sheet (say, Copper River salmon char-grilled with sun-dried tomato–basil butter. For dessert, try a big piece of blackberry cobbler—if you haven't already overdosed on the warm focaccia brought to you in baskets by friendly servers. *$$; AE, DC, MC, V; checks OK; breakfast Sat–Sun, lunch, dinner every day; full bar; reservations not accepted; map:FF8* &

Chutneys / ★★⯪

519 IST AVE N; 206/284-6799

Chutneys opened in 1995 with at least one certain advantage: the owners include Bill Khanna, formerly of the Eastside's popular Raga and New York's Bombay Palace. Clearly, Khanna and his partners have left no consideration neglected. The casually elegant Queen Anne dining room is a tranquil oasis, presided over by dozens of carved bas-relief gods and goddesses who appear to be smiling. And who could blame them? If you're not yet familiar with the zesty flavors of the Asian subcontinent, this is an excellent place to begin. Gracious servers are happy to explain dishes and make recommendations. Before you can scan the menu, a basket of pappadams appears with two of the restaurant's namesake chutneys. Among the excellent starters are the onion *bhaji*—a variation on onion rings—and remarkably light vegetable pakoras. Entrees can be ordered at varying degrees of heat, to be chased with a cocktail, an Indian beer, or a mug of milky, cardamom-infused tea. Though Indian food can be fiery, here even the curry vindaloo—synonymous in some restaurants with tongue-searing heat—is spicy without going overboard. The many delicious main-dish options include chicken tikka masala (which combines the appeal of the tandoor with a creamy tomato yogurt sauce) and a mixed tandoori grill (with succulent lamb chops, chicken, fish, and prawns). Individual portions of perfectly cooked basmati rice are served in shiny copper pots, and there are many appealing vegetarian choices. Don't overlook the breads, especially the garlic naan. For dessert, indulge in a slice of mango cheesecake. At $5.95, the lunchtime buffet is a considerable bargain. Sister restaurants are Capitol Hill's Chutneys Grill on the Hill (605 15th Ave E; 206/726-1000) and Chutneys Bistro (Wallingford Center, 1815 N 45th St; 206/634-1000). *$$; AE, DC, DIS, MC, V; checks OK; lunch, dinner every day; full bar; reservations recommended; map:GG8* &

Ciao Bella Ristorante / ★⯪

5133 25TH AVE NE; 206/524-6989

In a romantically dark dining room or on a well-lighted porch that on summer evenings calls to mind his native Umbria, Gino Borriello serves enormous portions of unpretentious food. The seafood appetizers are all good, especially the prawns in a slightly creamy tomato sauce (with plenty left over for sopping up with bread). There's a sort of first-things-first approach to dinner here: minimal effort is exerted on salads so that utmost attention can be paid to entrees. The specials list shines: from *trinette mare e moti* (a plentiful collection of clams, mussels, prawns, mushrooms, and peas over pasta) to tender veal in a sauce of artichoke hearts, mushrooms, and cream. Pastas can be uneven; a simple penne with mozzarella, basil, and tomato, which should be light and fresh, can be gummy and leaden. Ciao Bella is neither groundbreaking nor flawless, just simple and charming, as a neighborhood Italian place should be. *$$; AE, MC, V; local checks only; dinner every day; beer and wine; reservations recommended; map:FF6*

Ciao Italia / ★★

546 5TH AVE S, EDMONDS; 425/771-7950

Every neighborhood needs a homey Italian restaurant to call its own, and Ciao Italia has been Edmonds's favorite for nearly a decade. Looking for fancy? Fuggetaboutit. Even the requisite red-checkered, hanging-grape Italo-kitsch is absent—unless you count that "O Sole Mio" on the sound system. Owners Patrick and Claire Girardi are enchanting young hosts who bring a casual tableside charm to their unpretentious, candlelit dining room. In the kitchen, chef Bruno Girardi prepares meat-and-pasta standards in a better-than-standard fashion. Don't miss his simple, elegant pizza Margherita with its perfect, yeasty-chewy crust. Nor should you forgo anything made with his spirited tomato sauce (which helps makes the spaghetti puttanesca—that savory dish with an unsavory name—a perpetual favorite here). Entrees include a complimentary salad, but that shouldn't dissuade you from sharing a delectable bowlful of *cozze saltate* (mussels treated to a garlicky wine bath). *$$; MC, V; local checks only; dinner every day; beer and wine; reservations accepted (parties of four or more); pgirardi@isomedia.com*

Coastal Kitchen / ★★

429 15TH AVE E; 206/322-1145

Neighborhood restaurant kingpins Peter Levy and Jeremy Hardy (of Wallingford's Jitterbug and Queen Anne's 5 Spot fame; see reviews) oversee their third joint, on the eastern reaches of Capitol Hill. This is the food of the coast—any coast, tweaked with a Jersey diner/mom-for-the-millennium sensibility. The regular menu sports some serious winners, like a tender half roast chicken and a grilled pork chop dinner plate with juicy, spicy chops nudging up against mashed potatoes and gravy so good you'll be begging for seconds. There's fresh fish, simply grilled, and the All Day Long Breakfast, with maple-smoked bacon, hash browns, toast, and eggs. The menu features getaways to far-flung coastal locales—which change every quarter—and this is where the cooks get rowdy and imaginative. We've scarfed Gulf Coast fried green tomatoes with aioli and crowder peas; epazote- and lime-laced Michoacán seafood stew; and Thai-style spring rolls with a spicy-sweet dipping sauce. Exotic cocktails like the Blue Moon Martini (it's very, very blue) make imbibing more fun than usual. Be forewarned: the menu is written in such fractured Huck Finnified vernacular (y'all know they're duckin' and dippin' and tryin' to be interestin') that it may get on your nerves as much as the clattery din. *$$; MC, V; local checks only; breakfast, lunch, dinner every day; full bar; reservations accepted (large parties only); map:HH6* &

Copacabana / ★

1520½ PIKE PL (PIKE PLACE MARKET); 206/622-6359

Seattle's only Bolivian restaurant doesn't provide the authenticity of Ramon Paleaz's original Pike Place Market dive—the one with the counter that tilted so much that servers had to jam forks beneath the plates to keep them level. But why object, when the second-floor balcony offers the best seat in the Market for viewing the kaleidoscope below? Don Ramon's family still runs the place, and the original recipes are still used for spicy shrimp soup, meat and vegetable pies called *salteñas*, a piquant corn pie topped with cheeses called *humita*, and halibut in a saffron-tomato sauce. Like the Spanish, Bolivians seem to cook everything to death, and everything here is a tad pricier than you'd expect. Visit on a warm day, when lingering over a chilly beer and eating light is on your mind, sit on the balcony, and contemplate the Market's astounding drawing power. *$; AE, DC, MC, V; no checks; lunch, dinner Mon–Sat in summer; lunch every day, dinner Sat only in winter; beer and wine; reservations accepted before noon only; map:J8*

Coyote Creek Pizza / ★

228 CENTRAL WAY NE, KIRKLAND; 425/822-2226
15600 NE 8TH ST, BELLEVUE; 425/746-7460

Sodden Northwesterners find allure in desert images. Coyote Creek takes advantage of this, with a pair of comfortable, attractive restaurants (one in trendy downtown Kirkland, the other a calzone toss from the big screen at Crossroads Cinema) decorated in a sort of pleasing, spare, Southwest and Native-art style. In addition to knowing the value of image, the owners also know the value of a delightfully crisp crust that never sogs or sags—or gets depressed under the weight of an anything-goes, "Hey-I-got-an-idea!" topping combo. Funny thing: some of these preposterous admixtures even work. We love the North by Northwest, a combo of Granny Smith apples, roasted hazelnuts, Gorgonzola, mushrooms, and onions, which jams like a jazz quintet. Any of the salads makes a fresh preface, including one with mandarin oranges, feta, and barbecued chicken, called the Coyote in the Coop. Though it's possible to indulge more conventional cravings with such mundane stuff as pepperoni or sausage or just plain cheese, why not walk on the wild side? *$; DC, MC, V; local checks only; lunch, dinner every day; beer and wine; reservations not accepted; map:EE3; map:HH1* &

Cucina! Cucina! / ★

901 FAIRVIEW AVE N (AND BRANCHES); 206/447-2782

Cucina! Cucina! translates as "Kitchen! Kitchen!"—but "Empire! Empire!" would be more appropriate. The most ambitous of Roman emperors would have admired the Schwartz Brothers for developing a concept that first conquered Puget Sound and then swept outward in waves (including phalanxes of small, swarming, pasta/pizza-as-fast-food Cucina Presto!s). Oregon, California, and Arizona have all felt their incursions. At Lake Union one of the original bastions still stands, bright and loud, hung with bicycles and shimmering with possibilities, only some of which have anything to do with food. But if food is your object of desire, check out the menu with its multitudinous antipasti, zuppe, insalate, pizze, paste, and griglie. The wood-fired yellow-tile oven kicks out excellent pizzas, from simple quattro formaggios to combos that might make Wolfgang Puck raise an eyebrow. Pastas succeed often, on the basis of fresh noodles and well-tested formulas. A few meat and fish entrees also testify to the virtues of Practice! Practice! Cost-cutting measures in the past year have reduced the quality of ingredients—the longtime favorite chopped salad recently disappointed—but we hope the brothers will return to the formula that worked so well for the first several years. Don't overlook the "not spumoni" at meal's end, a generous slab of rich, fruity ice cream. *$$; AE, DC, DIS, MC, V; checks OK; lunch, dinner every day; full bar; reservations recommended (required for large parties); map:D1* &

Cutters Bayhouse / ★★★

2001 WESTERN AVE; 206/448-4884

Given its location, Cutters is inevitably heavy with tourists, but now Seattleites are rediscovering it. A million-dollar remodel and a new menu of global cuisine, both unveiled in 1998, have reinvigorated this glitzy fish house overlooking Elliott Bay on the north edge of Pike Place Market. Overall, the spirited cooking of executive chef Brad Komen makes a better impression than does the many-patterned, flashy red decor (complete with tartan carpet). Asian influences have the upper hand on the eclectic menu: mussels in Thai curry sauce, whole wok-seared Dungeness crab in a jolting garlic-and-chile-laced black bean sauce, and sake-and-soy-glazed soba noodles under succulent house-smoked prawns all delight. The daily fresh sheet highlights the bounty of Northwest waters, much of it reaping the aromatic benefits of the applewood grill. Though seafood is the focus, meat is deftly prepared as well, amply demonstrated by pan-seared beef tenderloin astride a blue cheese risotto cake in veal demi-glace enriched with portobello mushroom and cognac. The extensive wine list contains many Northwest gems available by the glass. A long list of specialty cocktails and microbrews contribute to the popularity of the bar. *$$$; AE, DC, MC, V; checks OK; lunch, dinner every day, brunch Sun; full bar; reservations recommended; map:J8* &

Dahlia Lounge / ★★★⯪

2001 4TH AVE; 206/682-4142

The Dahlia Lounge is, for many locals and out-of-towners, synonymous with the Seattle food scene. Many of us learned about Northwest foods from kitchen maverick Tom Douglas, and grew accustomed to his clever juxtaposition of cultures within a meal—indeed, often within a plate. With his star ever rising, Douglas opened the fabulous Etta's Seafood, followed by his most recent project, the chic Palace Kitchen (see reviews). He now shuttles among the trio of very different restaurants, yet even in his absence, the food at the Dahlia—under chef John Sunstrom—is executed with an artist's eye and an epicure's palate. The restaurant's scenic appeal lies in the interplay between the stylish two-level dining landscape of vermilion and gold and brocade, with papier-mâché fish lamps between the booths, and the intriguing presentations on your plate. Pan-seared calamari, in a broth fragrant with chiles, Chinese black beans, and Thai basil, comes paired with coconut rice cakes. A Persian play on ravioli marries Middle Eastern flavorings—yogurt, mint, and cumin—with such Asian ingredients as cilantro and ginger. And you'll not find a better version of the salty-sweet Japanese specialty kasu cod than that served here. As for desserts, we're inclined to say they're the best in town—and we'd consider bestowing our first fifth star on the perfect coconut cream pie. *$$; AE, DC, DIS, MC, V; local checks only; lunch Mon–Fri, dinner every day; full bar; reservations recommended; www.tomdouglas.com; map:H7* ⅙

Daniel's Broiler / ★★

10500 NE 8TH ST (SEAFIRST BUILDING), BELLEVUE; 425/462-4662
200 LAKE WASHINGTON BLVD; 206/329-4192

Noisy steak-house chains might hold more appeal for family-oriented Eastsiders (and their pocketbooks), but we say forget the rest and go for the best. Daniel's corn-fed USDA prime steaks, offered in appropriately masculine surroundings, with a panoramic view from the 21st floor of the Seafirst Building, put other grillmeisters to shame. Perhaps your server will suggest cutting into your filet mignon or well-marbled rib-eye (a bargain at lunch) to see if it's seared to your liking (laughing, knowing it will be). The day's fresh catch is among the worthy options for those who don't do red meat. Expect straightforward steak-house fare with all the trimmings: potatoes mashed, baked, or shoestringed beyond compare. To start, there are prawn cocktails, oysters on the half shell, or a velvety cup of clam chowder. The wine list is praiseworthy. So is Daniel's Seattle twin restaurant, perched across Lake Washington at Leschi Marina. *$$$; AE, DC, DIS, MC, V; checks OK; lunch Mon–Fri, dinner every day; full bar; reservations recommended; map:HH3; map:HH6* ⅙

Desert Fire, A Southwestern Grill / ★★

600 PINE ST (PACIFIC PLACE); 206/405-3400

7211 166TH AVE NE (REDMOND TOWN CENTER), REDMOND; 425/895-1500

The word "desert" is enough to fire the imagination of a chilled, water-logged Northwesterner. Throw in "fire" and you've got a hot concept, the first Northwest incursions of a Texas-based chain that tries to do for Southwestern cuisine what Cucina! Cucina! does for Italian. They picked a pair of hot spots for locations: the Redmond Town Center shopping mall and tony Pacific Place in the heart of Seattle. Sandstone, tile, and wood create a pleasing, rustic appeal, with both places hubbed by circular gas fireplaces and marked outside by flaming sconces (at Pacific Place on an outside deck). On Fiestaware plates, chiles provide the heat—mostly mild—in some outstanding dishes. Skip the appetizers, except for the poblano chicken chowder, and focus on entrees such as a jalapeño-and garlic-marinated roast chicken, or chile-rubbed tuna or shrimp, or succulent corn-husk salmon. *$$; AE, DC, MC, V; checks OK; lunch, dinner every day; full bar; reservations recommended; map:EE1* &

Dixie's BBQ / ★

11522 NORTHUP WAY, BELLEVUE; 425/828-2460

The bad news is you can no longer get your brakes repaired here, as you could in the early days, when Porter of Porter's Automotive Repair wheeled in a smoker like a steam locomotive and started selling the ribs that had long made his family so popular at church picnics. The good news is that you can get a brake job most anywhere, but there's only one Dixie's BBQ. It's near the junction of Highway 520 and I-405. Appreciative hordes line up out the door and across the parking lot as early as 11:30am on weekdays. Dixie's has achieved its legendary status not on its good looks but on its good food. About its only advertising efforts are the bumper stickers and T-shirts that brag, "I met The Man at Dixie's BBQ." The Man, by the way, is not Porter but his secret hot barbecue sauce. Rumor has it that state health inspectors once tried to have the stuff banned under the terms of the Geneva Convention. The beef brisket sandwich really doesn't need it, and neither do the well-smoked ribs and chicken. Sides, such as red beans and rice, corn bread, potato salad, and baked beans, hold up their end of the plate, as does the family's lemon cake. *$; no credit cards; checks OK; lunch, early dinner Mon–Sat; no alcohol; reservations not accepted; map:GG1* &

Dulces Latin Bistro / ★★★

1430 34TH AVE; 206/322-5453

 Owner/chef Julie Guerrero cooks most nights in the semi-open kitchen in one corner of this handsome Madrona bistro, while her partner, Carlos Kainz, acts as host. Their long, low-ceilinged, rust-toned dining room, with its soft, jazzy Latin guitar pulsing in the background, is the perfect place to relax on a rain-soaked night, but its candlelit and comfortable atmosphere warms patrons in any weather. Though the owners' heritage—and dishes such as chiles rellenos, prawns a la diabla, and saffron-scented paella—lend the menu its Latin coloring, Guerrero paints with a far broader palette. You might sample New England clam chowder one night, black bean soup the next. Homemade ravioli may arrive stuffed with chorizo and sauced with tomatillos—or enfolding smoked duck, ricotta, and mascarpone. The ruffled phyllo cup lined with roasted garlic custard and topped with cilantro and tomato-studded crab is a triumph. Meat lovers will delight in rack of Ellensburg lamb finished with pomegranate demiglace or wild boar steeped in tamarind. Desserts are homey and delicious. The handsome, fireplace-warmed cigar lounge is also a dining room. *$$; AE, DIS, MC, V; checks OK; dinner Tues–Sun; full bar; reservations recommended; map:GG7* &

El Camino / ★★

607 N 35TH ST; 206/632-7303
The mood is just right at this relaxed Fremont cantina where the regional Mexican cuisine never veers into Tex-Mex schlock. The seriously social bar scene, stoked by superb fresh-juice margaritas, often goes into the wee small hours. In the dining room, hardwood floors, wrought iron, ceramic tiles, a sequin-bedecked icon or two, and the inevitable ceiling fan add to the authentic south-of-the-border ambience. Standouts on the lengthy menu include a killer chile relleno, quesadillas de camarones (stuffed with cheese, rock shrimp, and cilantro paste), grilled pork in pasilla chile sauce, and crackling crisp duck in green mole sauce. Finish with the mile-high chocolate torte and forks all around. *$$; AE, MC, V; no checks; dinner every day; full bar; reservations recommended; bigfood@amazon.com; map:FF8* &

El Gaucho / ★★★

2505 IST AVE; 206/728-1337
Paul Mackay, who managed Seattle's original El Gaucho (known for its mink-lined booths, flaming shish kebabs, cafe diablo, and other tableside hanky-panky), resurrected the gone-but-not-forgotten steak house in a new venue: Belltown. The current version—a big, dark, dramatic, windowless space—brings a kitschy chic to the memory of the hallowed haunt where Sinatra would have felt at home. The bar crowd sips martinis as jazz standards emanate from a baby grand; those so inclined head into the two cigar lounges to puff a stogie. Patrons seated at comfy banquettes in the theater-in-the-round-style dining room share chateaubriand-for-two or custom-aged steaks and big, honking baked potatoes with all the trimmings. They watch in awe as swords of lamb

tenderloin are vodka-flamed before their eyes. Seafood lovers don't get short shrift here, either: they can dredge garlic bread in buttery Wicked Shrimp or spoon saffron-scented broth from an artful bouillabaisse. Bananas Foster proves both decadent and sublime. When El Gaucho's offshoot, a supper club called the Pampas Club, closed, it was rechristened the Pampas Room, a hole was cut in El Gaucho's floor, and now the two connect via a stairway. The Pampas Room is open for dancing and drinking on Fridays and Saturdays (the space is available for private parties on other occasions) and offers El Gaucho appetizers on its menu. *$$$; AE, DC, MC, V; checks OK; dinner every day; full bar; reservations recommended; www.elgaucho.com; map:F8* &

El Greco / ★★☆

219 BROADWAY E; 206/328-4604

Warm colors, linen napkins, and fresh flowers make this Mediterranean-inflected bistro a calm oasis amid the crowded bustle on see-and-be-seen Broadway. Hummus and baba ghanouj are to be expected, but such fabulous dishes as creamy, fennel-spiked arborio rice topped with five perfectly cooked prawns and scented with ouzo (we've had risotto half as good at twice the price) and a wild mushroom ragout (an earthy concoction of mushrooms and vegetables served with crisp, smoked-mozzarella potato cakes) are a welcome surprise. Expect everything to be fresh, appetizing, prepared precisely, and served in portions that won't bust a gut. Come for a latte served in a big cup and hope for the warm apple-and-rhubarb crisp served à la mode with fabulous house-made ice creams. *$; MC, V; checks OK; lunch, dinner Tues–Sat, brunch Sat–Sun; beer and wine; reservations accepted (recommended on weekends); map:HH6* &

El Puerco Lloron / ★☆

1501 WESTERN AVE; 206/624-0541

This place transports you back to that cafe in Tijuana, the one with the screaming hot pink and aquamarine walls and the bent, scarred "Cerveza Superior" tables. Remember the wailing jukebox and the cut-tin lamps and the woman quietly making corn tortillas by the door? They're all here. Belly up to the cafeteria line, place your order (dishes run a paltry $5 to $6), and fight for a table—in warm weather those outdoors are as hard to get as parking spots. Try the taquitos plate, three excellent corn-masa tortillas rolled around a meat filling and served with rice, beans, and a scallion. The chiles rellenos, so often bungled by American chefs, are fresh and bright with flavor. At the end of the counter, pick up a cool Mexican beer. *$; AE, MC, V; no checks; lunch, early dinner every day; beer and wine; reservations accepted (large parties only); map:J8*

Emmett Watson's Oyster Bar / ★

1916 PIKE PL (PIKE PLACE MARKET); 206/448-7721

Occupying a cheery back-alley cranny in the Soames-Dunn Building, the namesake restaurant of Seattle's most curmudgeonly journalist embodies some of the casual irreverence of this town. The tiny flowered courtyard is nice when warm noontime sunlight drifts down to the tables; when the weather is wet, take refuge inside at one of the booths. Part of the draw is the oysters. Regulars drop in just to slip down one or a half-dozen on the half shell or fried up hot and sandwiched on a French roll. Others love the salmon soup, a clean, clam-based broth with big chunks of the pink fish. Still others come for the chowder and a Guinness (one of many bottled brews and drafts available) or for the fish 'n' chips—true cod dipped in a spicy breading and fried in canola oil. *$; no credit cards; checks OK; lunch, dinner every day; beer and wine; reservations not accepted; map:J8* &

Etta's Seafood / ★★★

2020 WESTERN AVE; 206/443-6000

The second of Tom Douglas's restaurant triumvirate, Etta's is a buoyant, hip seafood house that occupies the husk of the late Cafe Sport, where Douglas first made his mark in the '80s. The colorful, casual space features one small, conversation-friendly dining room and another larger and much noisier noshery complete with a bar and counter seating. The menu is a freewheeling affair within a seafood framework. Starter courses such as fire-grilled tamales with Jack cheese and ancho chiles are offered alongside a two-bite morsel of foie gras paired with a single seared scallop in a buttery brown pepper jus. Entrees range from fish 'n' chips to whole tilapia, deep-fried and sauced with black soy and garlic. Prepare to be wowed by whole Dungeness crab or Maine lobster, either simply steamed or wok-seared in a kick-ass chile-and-black-bean sauce. Etta's spice-rubbed pit-roasted salmon ranks as one of Seattle's signature salmon preparations. Side dishes—from red Bliss mashers to garlic-sautéed ruby chard—are equally compelling. Lush desserts won't disappoint. Start weekend brunch with a scorching Bloody Mary, and then cool your jets with a smoked salmon and goat cheese omelet or fan the flames with corned beef hash and habanero ketchup. *$$$; AE, DC, MC, V; checks OK; lunch, dinner every day, brunch Sat–Sun; full bar; reservations recommended; www.tomdouglas.com; map:I8* &

Filiberto's Italian Restaurant / ★

14401 DES MOINES MEMORIAL DR, BURIEN; 206/248-1944

Since 1975, Filiberto's has been serving to Seattle's sprawling southern reaches the sort of fare Americans once assumed was the height of Italian cuisine. That we know better now hasn't diminished Filiberto's appeal to the regulars who've made this their favorite dining room. The look is cheery, if a bit worn around the edges. Out back, next to an umbrella-shaded patio, a brick-dust bocce court, covered and lighted for night play, draws the old-timers. The lengthy menu includes nearly every familiar Italian pasta, veal, chicken, and seafood dish from the '60s and '70s. What's best—pizzas and calzones—comes slightly, and nicely, charred from the wood-fired pizza oven. One wall contains a large, well-priced, help-yourself selection of Italian wines. *$$; AE, MC, V; checks OK; lunch, dinner Tues–Sat; full bar; reservations recommended Fri–Sat; map:NN7* &

Firenze Ristorante Italiano / ★★

15600 NE 8TH ST, BELLEVUE; 425/957-1077

Owner Salvatore Lembo squeezes considerable Mediterranean atmosphere out of this small mall restaurant just a skip and a jump from Crossroads Cinema: terra-cotta floor, sun-yellow stucco walls, one antique sideboard, one old chandelier, and many wine bottles. Sinatra knocks out a tune to the crash of dishes dumped in a serving station just outside the kitchen. Expect traditional Italian offerings among the pasta, veal, and chicken dishes. Spaghetti carbonara is dreamily creamy, generously spiced, and loaded with pancetta. A tender chicken breast rests in a lake of Gorgonzola sauce. Skip the veal marsala and move on to a veal piccata, sauced with sun-dried tomatoes, capers, and lemon—simple, elegant, sublime. Nightly specials can include osso buco, risotto, and the occasional salmon. There's a room for private parties, including cigar aficionados, who will find a selection here. Servers know their stuff and don't try to force dessert on you, though you wouldn't mind being forced to eat the dainty little tiramisu. *$$; AE, DC, MC, V; local checks only; lunch Mon–Fri, dinner every day; full bar; reservations recommended; map:HH1* &

5 Spot Cafe/ ★★

1502 QUEEN ANNE AVE N; 206/285-SPOT

Most mornings there's a line under the big neon coffee cup outside this Queen Anne landmark. It's a Big Fun kind of place at the top of the Counterbalance and, in fact, it counterbalances an architecturally pretty cafe with a kitschy menu and calm, pleasant service. That menu brags, "We're all over the map." No kidding. Expect such standard regional American fare as Southern-style tasso ham, red beans, and rice; Northwest salmon cakes; and New England roast chicken supper. A Food Festival Series mixes in a different region (say, Florida or Texas) on a rotational basis, while a late-night menu sports $5 items. We give a "hubba hubba" to the moist coconut-pineapple coffee cake and the updated red-flannel hash at breakfast, which may be the best you'll ever eat. A great pair of dinner pork chops comes with rib-sticking mashed potatoes and gravy, though we know folks who can make a meal out of an order of french fries and a Lucky Lager in the bar (aka the Counterbalance Room). Burgers are not the forte here, and vegetarians have some good choices. Don't pass up the bread pudding or the chocolate cake. *$; MC, V; local checks only; breakfast, lunch, dinner every day; full bar; reservations accepted (recommended for brunch; required for large groups); map:GG8* &

Flying Fish / ★★★

2234 1ST AVE; 206/728-8595

In terms of national recognition, this Belltown landmark since 1995 ranks, in the superhot Seattle dining scene, perhaps second only to Wild Ginger. Accordingly, every summer you'll see groups of tourists getting their picture snapped by practiced server/camerapersons as they mug together around the trademark whole fried rockfish—a gnarly-looking critter they then pick apart with their fingers and wrap in rice paper along with a pineapple-anchovy sauce. Sound like a party? It is. We're talking about conviviality vivified by platters (large, small, and in-between) meant to be shared, especially those where you order by the pound— crab, lobster, seafood antipasti, mussels in chile-lime dipping sauce—or oysters by the dozen. Owner/chef Christine Keff deftly combines flavors and influences as disparate as Catalonian and Thai and everything in between. In addition to the usual Northwest sea critters, she brings in interesting oddities—barracuda one week, opah or escolar the next. If you don't like fish, choose another destination, or settle for one of perhaps two other choices. Flying Fish is obviously no meat market, though the bar scene attracts a glamorous crowd, drawn to a great-looking room: industry meets gallery, with a balcony, and with front windows that roll up to provide access to streetside tables. A late-night menu keeps the party rolling. The private dining room seats 36 for dinner or accommodates as many as 70 people for a reception. *$$$; AE, DIS, MC, V; local checks only; dinner every day; full bar; reservations recommended; map:G8* &

Fremont Noodle House / ★★☆

3411 FREMONT AVE N; 206/547-1550

Finally, a Thai restaurant where the atmosphere can compete with the food for your sensory pleasure. You can't help but be drawn in off Fremont's main drag to inspect this wood-filled temple of Thai good taste, where rice-paper lampshades hang from the ceiling, a curio cabinet displays Thai photos, and mirrors make the oft-crowded room appear much larger than it is. A short menu offers fragrant noodle-based soups and sautés and simple rice dishes spiked with various meats, seafoods, and vegetables. Among the half-dozen appetizers is *mieng kahm*, a most sensually appealing starter. Arranged on a large wooden platter are tiny individual bowls of colorful, freshly chopped condiments—toasted coconut, ginger, Thai chile, peanuts, red onion, and lime—meant to be folded into the accompanying *bai cha plu* (dark green leaves), then dipped into a sweet sauce to assuage the heat. At $7.95, it's the most expensive dish on the menu. Service is swift and exceptionally polite. *$; AE, DIS, MC, V; checks OK; lunch, dinner Tues–Sun; beer and wine; reservations recommended (weekends and large parties only); map:FF8*

Fullers / ★★☆

1400 6TH AVE (SHERATON SEATTLE HOTEL AND TOWERS); 206/447-5544
Rumors of Fullers's demise following the departure of celebrated chef Monique Barbeau in August 1998 were exaggerated. The high-backed banquettes and soothing water music of a George Tsutakawa–designed fountain remain. Barbeau's replacement and former sous chef, Tom Black, introduced his first menu as this book went to press and while some of his improbable combinations work, others don't. Start off on the right foot with fat, golden Dungeness crab cakes and roasted potatoes intriguingly drizzled with horseradish aioli and cinnamon-scented carrot oil. Avoid the sautéed scallops, which stumble in a white wine sauce overpowered by beet glace, and their plate-mate, crispy chèvre spaetzle, which is neither crispy nor cheesy. The spaetzle shows to better advantage in a dish of tender, Madeira-sauced rabbit that includes the whole leg, sliced loin, and marvelously savory sausage. There's mostly salmon in the tomatoey bouillabaisse garnished with a rollicking rouille. King of the sea here, though, is Chilean sea bass paired with an earthy mushroom ragout, frizzled leek and risotto doused with a carrot reduction. The room's understated elegance still serves as a backdrop for the stunning display of contemporary Northwest glass and artwork, but the kitchen artistry that once put this restaurant at the leading edge of contemporary Northwest cuisine is absent. Seamless service and fancy coffee fixings remain unchanged. For dessert, the pineapple tarte Tatin with (no kidding) rosemary ice cream was way too delicious to share, but at these prices we want wow from beginning to end. *$$$; AE, DC, MC, V; checks OK; dinner Mon–Sat; full bar; reservations recommended; www.sheraton.com; map:K5* &

Georgian Room / ★★★☆

411 UNIVERSITY ST (FOUR SEASONS OLYMPIC HOTEL); 206/621-7889
A grand space for those grand occasions (or for times when a little pampering is what's needed), the Georgian Room boasts high ceilings, ornate chandeliers, gleaming silver, and touches of gilt which will transport you to a time and place that—happily—still exists. As you sink back into your plush banquette-built-for-two, the tuxedoed maître d' pours your martini from an elegant shaker; a smiling, impeccably uniformed, and well-trained professional waitstaff tends to your every need; and a pianist tickles the ivories in the center of the room. This kind of cosseting doesn't come cheap, but the inventive, seasonally changing menu—replete with

luxury ingredients from truffles to foie gras—may make you forget the high tariff. Each dish is an objet d'art, beginning with the colorful vegetable cocktail—tiny baby vegetables splashed with tomato butter in a large martini glass. The intense earthy flavors of black and white truffles, mushrooms, and goat cheese infuse almost-translucent sheets of fresh pasta, while crab cakes crowned with Alaskan spot prawns in a pungent crab broth fairly sing of the sea. Other inspired couplings include crisp-skinned rock cod and caramelized ramps in a rich red wine sauce; nubbins of duck cracklings and foie gras in a salad of dandelion and fennel; and rosy-centered veal tenderloin slices ringed around a beehive of rich and delicious yellow Finn mashed potatoes. Longtime executive chef Kerry Sear departed to open his own restaurant in 1999; taking the helm is Gavin Stephenson, most recently of the Ritz-Carlton, Chicago, who is expected to continue the tradition here of superb fine dining. Private parties can arrange for seclusion in the Georgette Petite room. Afterward, step into the Georgian Terrace for a very civilized cognac and a cigar. *$$$; AE, DC, MC, V; no checks; dinner Mon–Sat; full bar; reservations recommended; www.fshr.com; map:K6* &

Golden Goat Italian Café / ★★
14471 WOODINVILLE-REDMOND RD, WOODINVILLE; 425/483-6791

The Golden Goat fits in the category of great little neighborhood cafe—with no neighborhood thereabouts. But no matter, since people in Woodinville are used to driving all over creation to get anywhere anyway. From around the entire Eastside, as well as from Seattle, those in the know recognize this restaurant as having just about the deepest list of Italian wines in the region, which helped earn owner/chef Jeff Boswell a *Wine Spectator* Award of Excellence. The Goat is a little place, seating about three dozen, with a small menu derived from and inspired by the regions of Tuscany, Emilia-Romagna, and Piedmont. The wine list is user-friendly, and Boswell is more than happy to hop out of the kitchen and discuss your options. Or your lamb chop, nestled in a red wine–porcini sauce, snugged up to silky eggplant and Parmigiano-dusted squash. *$$; AE, DC, DIS, MC, V; checks OK; dinner Tues–Sat; beer and wine; reservations recommended; goldengoat@aol.com; map:CC1* &

Golkonda / ★★
15600 NE 8TH ST, BELLEVUE; 425/649-0355

Yes, it's an Indian restaurant. But naan? None. Fuchsia-colored chicken? Nope, no tandoori specials either. Instead, Lakshma and Usha Reddy (who also own Bite of India in the Crossroads Mall food court) serve up the cuisine of their native Southern India: *dosas,* for instance, which are sourdough lentil and rice crepes wrapped around a number of fillings. This is the original "wrap," a meal in hand. *Dum-ka-murga,* a garlic-and-ginger game hen marinated overnight in a yogurt sauce, is an incredibly messy, delectable feast. Spice mixes tend to be a little simpler here than at other Indian restaurants, with heavy emphasis on black cumin, cinnamon, cardamom, and cloves. A bowl of *rasam*—thin, spicy, tomato-tamarind soup—and a plate of crisp, wafery pappadams start each dinner. A bowl of *pala payasam*, a sort of tapioca pudding bursting with cardamom, should end it. Surroundings are pleasantly appointed, with linen-set tables. *$$; AE, DC, DIS, MC, V; checks OK; lunch, dinner Mon–Sat; beer and wine; reservations recommended; map:HH1* &

Gravity Bar / ★★☆
415 BROADWAY E; 206/325-7186
Meet George Jetson. His boy Elroy. Daughter Judy. Jane, his wife. Need we say more about Seattle's slickest vegetarian restaurant and juice bar, with its conical tables of galvanized metal and green frosted glass lit from within for the ultimate Jetsons effect? Chic patrons down shots of wheat-grass juice, becoming rejuvenated before your very eyes, but most others shy away from the dark green sludge and opt instead for a banana-pineapple or carrot-spinach-beet blend. Entrees are luscious, healthful, and beautifully presented: mounds of brown rice and steamed vegetables with a glistening lemon-tahini sauce; chapatis rolled with hummus and fresh vegetables; miso soup with buckwheat noodles; tempeh burgers with barbecue sauce on herb and onion buns; sun-dried tomatoes, avocados, black beans, and provolone on thick fingers of whole wheat. The freshest of fresh juices can get expensive, but indulge. You'll feel like a million bucks later. *$$; MC, V; local checks only; breakfast, lunch, dinner every day; no alcohol; reservations not accepted; map:HH6*

Hi-Spot Cafe / ★★
1410 34TH AVE; 206/325-7905
Joanne Sugura and Michael Walker's old multilevel Victorian, with its outdoor deck for warm-weather dining, is ever inviting. The bakery is out of sight, while a sleek espresso bar and a few cafe tables fill the front room. Breakfast is still breakfast: baked eggs, great cinnamon buns, and long lines. Lunch includes the requisite soups, salads, and groovy '90s sandwiches. But dinner (where chef Sugura gets to strut her stuff with a menu that changes monthly) is the real reason to head here. You'll find appetizers such as a Gorgonzola cheesecake with roasted red pepper sauce, or brandade de morue—a classic rendering of the warm, spreadable mash of potato and salt cod. Spicy Caribbean seafood stew gets its bright coloring from fiery-hot harissa mellowed with coconut milk. A mixed grill comes with an innovative version of dolmades: Swiss chard leaves stuffed with rice and garbanzo beans over a peppery tzatziki. Well-conceived salads and a quartet of pastas are always ready for the less adventuresome. Entrees won't set you back much more than $15 and wine list prices hover in the low end, making it worthwhile to stray from

your own neighborhood to this Madrona neighborhood destination. *$$; DIS, MC, V; no checks; breakfast every day, lunch Mon–Fri, dinner Tues–Sat; beer and wine; reservations accepted (recommended on weekends); map:GG5* &

Hilbo's Alligator Soul / ★

7104 WOODLAWN AVE NE; 206/985-2303

No, the curtains didn't become scorched by brushing against the food at this storefront near Green Lake. They're part of the burning-Atlanta decor, though the fare is largely New Orleans Creole, with touches of Cajun and low-country South. It's all hot, sweet, and salty: panéed (fried) rabbit, crab gumbo, smoked duck crawfish in a fried-eggplant boat; Creole shrimp; stuffed pork tenderloin. It's standing room only on Sunday evenings as patrons with butter-smeared fingers suck on crawfish while pounding down corn-on-the-cob, andouille sausage, and boiled potatoes. Nice touch: the background jazz recalls the music of New Orleans before it came upriver and lost its innocent rawness. *$$; DIS, MC, V; checks OK; dinner Tues–Sun, brunch Sun; beer and wine; reservations recommended; map:EE7* &

The Hunt Club / ★★★
Fireside Room / ★★

900 MADISON ST (SORRENTO HOTEL); 206/343-6156

With new chef Brian Scheehser firmly in control and a subtle but unmistakable lightening of the burnished mahogany, weathered-brick, men's-clubby room, the Hunt Club is fully prepared for a new century. Scheehser produces a short, Mediterranean-accented menu while employing superb Northwest ingredients. We especially like his way with meats: trimming and cutting them beautifully and then marinating them in olive oil and herbs. His prime-grade New York steak is wondrous, arguably the best in town. Look for pink, tender, flavorful duck, too. And the lamb chops—but we get ahead of ourselves. Start with terrific house-cured salmon. Don't miss the frothy mussel bisque (or one of the other fabulous soups). Fish receive respectful medium-rare treatment. Desserts rise nearly to the same standard. The wine list runs deep and broad. Only service falls short of world-class. Savvy patrons take dessert, coffee, and cognac in the octagonal, mahogany-lined Fireside Room off the lobby, where piano music and card and board games frequently draw crowds. Scheehser serves light meals there, too. In summer, half the hotel's circular, fountain-centered driveway (lined by underground-heated palm trees) becomes a civilized but traffic-noisy alfresco cafe. This kitchen has been a launching pad for chefs' careers, but we fervently hope Scheehser stays around. *$$$/$; AE, DIS, MC, V; checks OK; breakfast, lunch, tea, dinner every day, brunch Sat–Sun; full bar; reservations recommended; map:L4* &

Huong Binh / ★

1207 S JACKSON ST; 206/720-4907

While other less successful eateries come and go, this tidy Vietnamese restaurant in one of the many strip malls marking the ever-expanding Vietnamese commercial area near the International District continues to hold its own. We've had feasts here, huge brimming tablefuls, for less than $20. One such: *banh beo* (steamed rice cake topped with brilliant orange ground shrimp), *cha hue* (a steamed pork roll), *bahn hoi chao tom* (grilled shrimp on sugar cane—hint to novices: you eat the shrimp, then suck the cane), and a couple of dishes starring pork and shrimp skewers with rice. Pork is particularly nicely done: tender, pounded thin, and marinated in garlic and lemongrass. Best of all, these grilled dishes come in traditional Vietnamese fashion with an accompanying fragrant garden of herbs, to allow you to dress your food to your liking. *$; no credit cards; checks OK; lunch, early dinner every day; no alcohol; reservations not accepted; map:HH6*

I Love Sushi / ★★☆

1001 FAIRVIEW AVE N; 206/625-9604
11818 NE 8TH ST, BELLEVUE; 425/454-5706

Chef Tadashi Sato has created a pair of premier Japanese restaurants, one on either side of Lake Washington. Both feature bustling, bright, high-energy sushi bars with exquisitely fresh fish—and a friendly, helpful staff to keep things running smoothly. At the sushi bar, Sato and his minions attract many Japanese customers who know a good thing when they eat one. The sushi combinations are a veritable bargain (particularly at lunch), while such traditional Japanese specialties as sea urchin, abalone, and fermented bean paste may raise the stakes somewhat. The hot dishes, including flame-broiled fish cheeks, the ubiquitous tempura, and *chawan mushi*—a steamed custard egg soup that's the ultimate in Japanese comfort food—are excellent. *$$; AE, MC, V; no checks; lunch Mon–Fri, dinner every day (Seattle); lunch Mon–Sat, dinner every day (Bellevue); full bar; reservations accepted (weeknights only); www.ilovesushi.com; map:GG7; map:HH3* &

icon Grill / ★★

1933 5TH AVE; 206/441-6330

The overwrought decor (done in every imaginable shade of pink) includes a plaid carpet, potted orchids, a 10-foot iron-and-glass fountain, art glass dripping from the chandeliers and atop the tables, and literally hundreds of gewgaws, many of which light up, like a '50s-era toaster studded with Christmas bulbs. Still, the booths are cozy, the lights are soft, and the American menu is pleasantly straightforward. Opening chef and co-owner Philip Kephart sticks to comfort food, deftly reworking standards such as macaroni and cheese (its velvet texture actually comes from Velveeta); meat loaf glazed with molasses and wrapped in bacon; potato skins loaded with gratinéed crabmeat; and Smithfield ham and Gruyère in a crisp wonton wrapper. Desserts range from a seven-layer chocolate cake (served with an ice-cold bottle of milk) to lemon cheese-cake on a gingersnap crust to three scoops of fruit sorbet afloat in water-melon consommé. At press time, Nick Musser has been promoted to executive chef. *$$$; AE, MC, V; checks OK; lunch Mon–Fri (Mon–Sat in summer only), dinner every day; full bar; reservations recommended; map:I6* &

Il Bacio / ★★

16564 CLEVELAND ST, REDMOND; 425/869-8815

In three neat, simple rooms that never impart the illusion you're any-where but a Redmond strip mall, master chef Rino Baglio works his art. He's a man of impeccable credentials: helped prepare the wedding feast for Chuck and Di, cooked for Princess Caroline of Monaco and for the Pope, won numerous awards. A northern Italian, he largely forsakes tomato sauce, a southern specialty, for his own brand of home cooking. Venison-stuffed ravioli comes in a rich cream sauce, topped by shaved black truffles. White truffle oil accents a buttery white-wine sauce hosting three islands of veal scaloppine. Though the excellent pasticceria that established his and spouse/host Patsy's original foothold here is now gone, it's still foolish not to leave room for beautifully baked desserts. *$$; AE, DC, DIS, JCB, MC, V; local checks only; lunch Mon–Fri, dinner every day; beer and wine; reservations recommended; map:EE1*

Il Bistro / ★★★

93-A PIKE ST (PIKE PLACE MARKET); 206/682-3049

For a quarter-century, Il Bistro has been a cherished refuge down a narrow cobblestone street in Pike Place Market. It's an intimate grotto, like a room from the set of *Casablanca:* low-ceilinged, rounded arches, whitewashed walls. A step-down bar draws a lively crowd of regulars—and smokers—who dispatch clouds and conversation to engulf the nearest dining-room tables. Though chefs come and go, Il Bistro still serves Seattle's best rack of lamb, six ribs of surpassing texture and flavor. The menu three-steps through the classic Italian dinner journey: appe-tizer, pasta, and main course. Sign up for the full trip, and the knowl-edgeable staff will offer a half-portion of the pasta—or gnocchi or polenta. The fare also follows Italian culinary tradition by celebrating straightforward flavors of first-rate ingredients. Escarole is sautéed in fruity olive oil and paired with olives and pecorino Romano. And simple roast chicken comes with an American touch: superb mashed potatoes. With some 500 choices, the wine list can be daunting. Here servers can be invaluable. Dessert? The Marquis, a deadly piece of chocolate, is divine. Afterward, a broad selection of boutique grappas beckons behind the bar. Play it for me, Sam. *$$$; AE, DC, MC, V; no checks; dinner every day; full bar; reservations recommended; map:J8*

Il Gambero / ★★☆

2132 1ST AVE; 206/448-8597

Romance and garlic—there's lots of both at this warm and inviting Belltown trattoria owned by chef Gaspare Trani and his wife Dianne, proprietors also of Gaspare's in Maple Leaf. Il Gambero means "the shrimp" in Italian, and here they make a good impression, whether brushed with olive oil and grilled on a rosemary skewer or sautéed and served over linguine. Clams, mussels, and squid also benefit from a quick sauté with lemon, garlic, and white wine. Pastas are good, particularly fettuccine in a tomato-mushroom broth. Funghi fanciers will also love the veal smothered in shiitakes. After dinner, as candlelight flickers on the warm brick walls, hold hands over the last of your wine (from a value-oriented, mostly Italian list) and then share the rich, ice cream–filled truffle called *tartufo*. *$$; AE, MC, V; checks OK; lunch Mon–Fri, dinner Mon–Sat; beer and wine; reservations recommended; map:H7* &

Il Terrazzo Carmine / ★★★

411 1ST AVE S; 206/467-7797

Be prepared to spend an entire evening at Il Terrazzo, for dining at Carmine Smeraldo's restaurant is an event. Graze through the glistening array of antipasti and watch for Seattle's rich and famous, who are likely to be dining to the strains of classical guitar beside you in this comfortably airy restaurant or outside on the small terrace. For a lusty starter try *calamari in padella*, tender squid in a heady tomato-garlic sauté. Deciding among the pastas is a feat, but it's the sauces on the stunning array of meat entrees here that get the greatest applause. Sweetbreads with prosciutto and peas are lightly smothered in a wonderful wine sauce. The fork-tender veal has an equally good reduction sauce, just slightly zingy from capers. Robust nebbiolo grapes lend a richness to the barolo sauce that cloaks the tender fillet of beef. A mighty veal chop is as carefully cooked as a delicate fillet of fish. The extensive wine list is international in scope but retains a sharp focus on premier Italian producers. Prices here are high, but there are tables in the bar where you might share the antipasti and a couple of glasses of wine, and call it dinner. Either way, you'll want to keep dessert simple—perhaps a silky flan, or house-made biscotti with a glass of vin santo for dipping. *$$$; AE, DC, DIS, MC, V; checks OK; lunch Mon–Fri, dinner Mon–Sat; full bar; reservations recommended; map:O8* &

Isabella Ristorante / ★★½

1909 3RD AVE; 206/441-8281
Gino Borriello gambled and lost when he opened this lovely eatery on the fringe of the hot downtown dining area already inundated with Italian restaurants. He retreated to Ciao Bella Ristorante, his place near University Village (see review), and Kamyar Khoshdel took up the risk of keeping this place alive. So far, Khoshdel's proved up to the task. With its slick decor (towering carmine walls, cobalt columns, and uncluttered spaces), Isabella is chic but not intimidating. That goes for the food too. For instance: a smashing, mint-tinged panzanella salad, exceptional crab cakes, succulent grilled meats and braised lamb shank, toothsome risotto, and chewy thin-crust pizzas baked in a wood-fired oven. *$$; AE, MC, V; checks OK; lunch Mon–Fri, dinner every day; full bar; reservations recommended; map:I7* &

Italianissimo / ★★

17650 140TH AVE NE, WOODINVILLE; 425/485-6888
Good under the direction of founder/legend Luciano Bardinelli, Italianissimo is even better thanks to current owner Kent Betts, who ensures the quality of cooking by doing most of it himself. It is he who stuffs the fresh-rolled ravioli with spinach and ricotta and rolls out paper-thin pasta layers for lasagne. He also buys his veal by the leg and then dresses it himself to ensure lean, braised shanks and the tenderest of scaloppine. Add a stable, skilled staff and an airy, pleasant dining room, and you get fine Italian dining even in a Woodinville strip mall. *$$; AE, DC, MC, V; checks OK; lunch, dinner Mon–Sat; full bar; reservations recommended; map:AA1* &

Ivar's Indian Salmon House / ★

401 NE NORTHLAKE WAY; 206/632-0767
Ivar Haglund was a legend in this town—entrepreneurial dynamo, master of the corny pun ("Keep clam"), prolific fish fryer. He passed away (God rest his sole), but his gastronomic populism lives on in the form of three waterside restaurants, two take-out fish bars, and fast-food outposts all over the city (not recommended here). Best loved is North-lake's Indian Salmon House, a replica of a Coastal Indian longhouse where salmon and black cod are properly grilled over a smoky alder fire and served with corn bread. Consistent it's not, but Seattleites often take guests here anyway. Ivar's Acres of Clams and Fish Bar on the Elliott Bay waterfront (Pier 54; 206/624-6852; map:L9) draws hordes of tourists. It's got fireboats next door and seagulls swooping for midair french-fry snacks, and kids love the place. Both the Salmon House and Acres of Clams have take-out adjuncts with outdoor seating—wonderful for cod 'n' chips or excellent clam nectar, enjoyed in quintessentially Seattle set-

tings. Well-regarded chef Barbara Figueroa is attempting to sun-dry-tomato Ivar's food into contemporary 21st-century chic, with mixed success. Stick with the simplest preparations. And, at Ivar's Mukilteo Landing (710 Front St, Mukilteo; 425/347-3648; map:FF7), try the rotisserie meats. *$$; AE, MC, V; checks OK; lunch, dinner every day (Acres of Clams); lunch Mon–Sat, dinner every day, brunch Sun (Salmon House); lunch, dinner every day, breakfast Sat–Sun (Mukilteo); full bar; reservations recommended (Acres of Clams and Salmon House), reservations accepted (Mukilteo); map:L9; map:FF7 &*

Izumi / ★★

12539 116TH AVE NE, KIRKLAND; 425/821-1959

Tucked into taco-and-burger land in a Kirkland shopping center, Izumi is a favorite among the local Japanese community. Part the dark blue half-curtain inside the front door, and suburbia is left behind: you're in the competent care of servers in traditional sea green kimonos. Things move briskly at lunch, when Japanese families sometimes mingle with the business crowd. Unagi (broiled freshwater eel) and mirugai (geoduck) sushi are outstanding; roe enthusiasts can sample the eggs of four different sea creatures. Tonkatsu—pork cutlet in a light, crisp breading—is juicy, tender, and generously portioned. Those who prefer to venture cautiously into Japanese cuisine will find the tempura crust exceedingly light and the teriyaki excellent (and not overly sweet). Makunouchi can be had at lunch, or in two sizes at dinner—the larger Izumi Special is a feast of sushi, sashimi, tempura, teriyaki, and cooked vegetables presented in a lacquer box. Wash everything down with a big Asahi beer. *$$; AE, DC, MC, V; checks OK; lunch Tues–Fri, dinner Tues–Sun; beer and wine; reservations not accepted; map:DD3 &*

JaK's Grill / ★★

14 FRONT ST N, ISSAQUAH; 425/837-8834

Started in West Seattle in 1996, JaK's (the annoying typography stands for owners Jeff Page and Ken Hughes) looked eastward and saw Issaquah spreading faster than Irish potato blight. New money, good steaks—what a fit! And good they are: aged prime quality, most of them, grilled near perfection and slathered with herb butter. Such a success it was that within a year JaK's moved down the street to the current larger spot, still centrally located in the older section of downtown Issaquah (the original West Seattle branch is now closed). JaK's doesn't mess around: with nary an appetizer to be had, you get right to the heart of the matter—a big salad, then steak (and there's a line outside the door to be served). Trucked-in desserts don't merit lingering for, though the bar is a pleasant spot for an after-dinner sip or two. *$$; AE, MC, V; checks OK; dinner Tues–Sun; full bar; reservations not accepted; map:II8 &*

Jitterbug Cafe/ ★★☆

2114 N 45TH ST; 206/547-6313

A sliver of a place, Jitterbug is a diner with ambition: white linen napkins, terra-cotta-colored walls, a cast-iron chandelier in the bar, and servers dressed in white shirts and ties. Like its siblings, the Coastal Kitchen and the 5 Spot Cafe, Jitterbug supplements its regular offerings every few months with a loosely interpreted ethnic menu. Local artists produce works on each theme (all are for sale), and mock language lessons complete with droll English translations are piped into the restrooms. Fending off boredom seems to be the intent, and it works. Breakfast fare also stimulates: gingerbread waffles, or an omelet of Serrano ham, white beans, pecorino Romano, tomato, and asparagus—eating is fun! Entertaining, too, like the films at the Guild 45th theater across the street, which get endlessly rehashed in the Jitterbug's cozy booths as the movie house's neon paints the night. *$; MC, V; checks OK; breakfast, lunch every day, dinner Mon–Sat; full bar; reservations recommended; map:FF7* &

Kabul / ★★

2301 N 45TH ST; 206/545-9000

In Afghanistan the king's cooks marinated and grilled the finest meats, infusing dishes with mint, cilantro, and dill, and applying the cooling touch of yogurt and the zing of scallions. Recipes were guarded jealously and passed down through the generations. Sultan Malikyar and his family emigrated from Kabul, Afghanistan, to Seattle in the late '70s. Malikyar still cooks from his father's kabob recipe; his *chaka* (garlic-yogurt sauce) and rice come from his mother's side. This is fragrant, elegant food: crisp *bolani* (scallion-potato turnovers with *chaka* for dipping); *jan-i amma* (a sort of Afghan version of tzatziki); *ashak* (delicate scallion dumplings topped with beef sauce—or a vegetarian tomato sauce—and more *chaka*); kabobs served on lovely heaps of basmati rice. Service is unfailingly friendly, and the room—with its simple decor, glass-topped tables, and colorful accents—is almost as soothing as *firni*, the cardamom-and-rosewater-flavored custard served as dessert. *$; AE, DC, DIS, MC, V; local checks only; dinner every day; beer and wine; reservations accepted; map:FF7*

Kaizuka Teppanyaki and Sushi Bar / ★★

1306 S KING ST; 206/860-1556

Kaizuka holds much appeal for neighbors in from Mount Baker and Madrona—folks who consider this homey Japanese joint their best-kept secret. Tucked into the space long occupied by the original Nikko restaurant, this quiet, mom-and-pop-run sushi and teppanyaki house is perched on the far eastern fringe of the International District. Beautifully and simply decorated, it boasts six teppanyaki tables, four tatami rooms, and a separate, comfortingly small sushi bar. Smiling Jeff Kaizuka entertains at the cooktop tables, wielding his knives and flash-searing beef, chicken, and seafood. As for the sushi, generous cuts of maguro, hamachi, and saba are folded over lightly seasoned rice, and they're decidedly less expensive than those purveyed elsewhere. Running between rooms, Lisa Kaizuka works the floor, tending tables as well as the door, making sure everyone feels at home. *$$; AE, DC, JCB, MC, V; no checks; lunch Tues–Fri, dinner Mon–Sat; beer and wine; reservations recommended; map:II6*

The Kaleenka / ★★

1933 1ST AVE; 206/728-1278
You'll rarely find food more comforting than that served in this richly decorated Russian cafe whose menu borrows from many regions of the former Soviet Union. Eastern European accents drift from talk at nearby tables as you sit down to a pot of black currant tea served in a graceful Uzbek teapot. Try a filling plate of *varniky* (Ukrainian dumplings stuffed with farmer cheese or spicy potato) or some fragrant *samsa* (pastries filled with cumin-spiced lamb, served with a sour cream–based dill sauce). The garlicky *pilmeny* (ravioli-like beef dumplings) float in a huge bowl of beef consommé topped with a dollop of sour cream. Lunch is a bargain. *$$; AE, DIS, MC, V; checks OK; lunch, dinner Mon–Sat; beer and wine; reservations accepted (recommended on weekends); map:I8*

Kaspar's / ★★★

19 W HARRISON ST; 206/298-0123
It's not just the pre-theater/opera/ballet crowd that loves Kaspar's—though if necessary, the staff always gets them seated, sated, and out the door in time for opening curtain. Lodged in a cool, multi-tiered building just west of Seattle Center, Swiss-born Kaspar Donier imaginatively couples classic international cooking styles with fresh Northwest ingredients. The room exudes relaxation in shades of brown and green, with the lower level a kind of solarium, shaded by wood lattice. Well-trained servers make you feel immediately welcome and always well cared for. Some just stop by for a bite and duck into the cozy wine bar, with an outstanding wine-by-the-glass program drawn from a broad list of mostly West Coast labels. In the dining room, Donier has been serving his signature dish for years: pink-fleshed Muscovy roasted duck breast, paired with crispy duck confit and served with licorice sauce and pumpkin spaetzle. Though seafood gets the royal treatment, don't overlook the classical influence on meats, such as a scrumptious merlot-braised lamb shank. Side dishes never disappoint, and neither does dessert. *$$$; AE, MC, V; no checks; dinner Tues–Sat; full bar; reservations recommended; info@kaspars.com; www.kaspars.com; map:A8* &

Kingfish Café / ★★☆

602 19TH AVE E; 206/320-8757

In 1996 the Coaston sisters opened their dream restaurant, a stylish, casual, contemporary space with blown-up sepia-tinted photos from the family album on the walls—including one of distant cousin Langston Hughes. Buoyed by long lines of people waiting for a taste of chef Tracey McRae's sassy Southern soul food (and, OK, maybe for a glimpse of silent partner Supersonic Gary Payton), they expanded into the space next door less than a year later. People still wait, but it's worth it for the likes of Big Daddy's Pickapeppa Skirt Steak, topped with a cool peach; velvety pumpkin soup; crab and catfish cakes with green-tomato tartar sauce; seafood curry with coconut grits; and buttermilk fried chicken. Lunch is even more of a bargain—try the pulled pork sandwich with peach-and-watermelon barbecue sauce. At Sunday brunch those crab and catfish cakes are topped with a poached egg and hollandaise. *$$; no credit cards; checks OK; lunch Mon, Wed–Fri, dinner Mon, Wed–Sat, brunch Sun; beer and wine; reservations not accepted; map:HH7* &

La Medusa / ★★★

4857 RAINIER AVE S; 206/723-2192

Columbia City may seem an unlikely place to go for fine food, but plenty of Seattleites are making the 15-minute drive from downtown to sample Sherri Serino and Lisa Becklund's scintillating Sicilian soul food. It's not uncommon to find customers queuing up on the sidewalk for a seat inside the cheery yellow space filled with bare wood tables and chairs varnished to a golden glow. (Becklund brings out focaccia if the wait drags on.) The exemplary waitstaff knows when to leave two lovers alone to enjoy their wine (good, inexpensive, mostly Italian choices by the glass or bottle) along with a marvelous thin-crust pizza, perhaps topped with caramelized onion, cured black olives, and mozzarella. They also know just when to bring a restless toddler a lump of pizza dough to play with. And they have the patience to explain to elderly first-timers exactly what *pasta con le sarde* is: spaghetti doused in garlicky tomato sauce thickened with sardines, capers, pine nuts, olives, fennel, and golden raisins. Dreamy risotto, savory braised greens, salt-cod fritters as light as angels' wings—these are just some of the dishes that will lure you back to La Medusa again and again. *$$; MC, V; no checks; dinner Tues–Sat; beer and wine; reservations not accepted; map:KK6* &

Lampreia / ★★★★

2400 1ST AVE; 206/443-3301

Lampreia is where you go when you want to taste food the way God intended it to taste. West Seattle native Scott Carsberg, having earned culinary renown in Europe, returned to his hometown and eventually established this elegantly simple restaurant in what was then the wasteland of Belltown. Here he demonstrates the gastronomic virtue of simplicity. One or two asparagus spears might bridge three perfect divers' scallops (freshly hand-harvested), while a dollop of truffle oil infuses mashed potatoes with an ethereal quality. Slices of smoked duck need only a balsamic reduction to thrill a focused palate. From appetizers, one moves to an "intermezzo" course, priced and sized between appetizers and main courses. Intermezzos might include sections of Dungeness crab simply braised in lobster stock, fanning out from a hillock of mashed potatoes rendered pink by lobster roe. Meat and fish entrees echo the minimalist theme, such as an oven-roasted veal chop finding all the adornment it needs in a cheese sauce. Servers then bring a selection of handcrafted local cheeses, along with a wealth of tempting descriptive detail. These make a fine end to a meal or an even better prelude to a delicate lemon tart paired with strawberry sauce. Carsberg's elegantly simple, sophisticated restaurant—jazz in the air, artwork on the walls, wood-framed windows hung with cafe curtains—is often likened to the urbane fine-food haunts of New York and San Francisco. *$$$; AE, MC, V; no checks; dinner Tues–Sat; full bar; reservations recommended; map:F8* &

Le Gourmand / ★★★

425 NW MARKET ST; 206/784-3463

An unprepossessing storefront on the edge of Ballard doesn't seem like much of a destination, and the city's foodies always seem to be buzzing about some more fashionable place. But Bruce Naftaly, one of the founding fathers of Northwest regional cooking, quietly puts out some of the most delectable plates of Northwest bounty in the city, with admirable consistency, in a room as serene as a garden. Seasonal produce and fish arrive daily from Naftaly's carefully chosen list of local suppliers, all to be generously embellished with his forte—sauces—and garnished with edible blossoms from his backyard garden. A pair of capable servers attend a diminutive dining room—its trompe l'oeil wall complete with trees and flowers, its ceiling painted like a clear spring day—and deftly answer questions about the small seasonal menu and the French/Northwest wine list. Dinner here is composed of appetizer, entree (which determines the price of the meal), and salad. Every dish is carefully considered as to season, taste, and presentation—the entree arrives on its own plate, center stage, with vegetables on a separate dish. Depending on the time of year, you might begin with an earthy nettle soup or a delicate leek-and-onion tart crowned with juniper berries. A meal might include impossibly tender veal medallions in a sublime chanterelle sauce or a noble rack of lamb followed by a salad of wild greens feathered with calendulas, nasturtiums, and rose petals. *$$$; AE, MC, V; checks OK; dinner Wed–Sat; beer and wine; reservations recommended; map:FF8*

Lead Gallery and Wine Bar / ★★☆

1022 1ST AVE; 206/623-6240
Unique on the West Coast (and perhaps anywhere), this place seamlessly blends contemporary art gallery into chic wine bar into sparkling-food cafe. Leopard-print triangular bar stools, a slate bar, pale plastic bucket seats, bone-white vinyl table coverings, a dark epoxied floor, and metal-racked wines shining with gathered light in the shadowed space might be ultra-cool, but redemption comes in the form of plush antique couches on an Oriental rug up front. Improbably, it all adds up to the "social gathering place" owner Marsha Sleeth envisioned when she moved her Lead Gallery a couple of blocks south in early 1998. Blond-and-beautiful chef Drew McPartlin conjures remarkably good soups, salads, sandwiches, appetizers and "small plates" using just a small oven. His seafood stew, reflecting what's fresh in Pike Place Market, ranks among the city's best. Add plenty of by-the-glass wines, great breads, good cheeses, and casual, friendly service, and what you get is even better than what you see. *$$; AE, DC, DIS, MC, V; checks OK; lunch, dinner Mon–Sat; beer and wine; reservations not accepted (but recommended for large groups); map:L7* &

Luau Polynesian Lounge / ★☆

2253 N 56TH ST; 206/633-5828
Inventive chef Gavin McMillan (he and proprietors Thomas and Jessica Price are alumni of various Tom Douglas establishments) experiments with tropical flavors and seasonings as exuberantly as a kid with a giant box of Crayolas. This leads to dishes as complex and compelling as a steaming pot of clams and mussels in hot and sour miso broth flavored with lemongrass and kaffir lime, and to curiosities like wasabe gnocchi sauced with sweet onion confit, tomato, and ginger. Generally speaking, South Pacific trappings are kept to a minimum, but there is a flaming pupu platter. Pair this with any of Thomas's umbrella-bedecked cocktails and you're on your way to a fun time. *$$; MC, V; checks OK; dinner every day; full bar; reservations accepted; map:FF7* &

Luna Park Cafe / ★

2918 SW AVALON WAY; 206/935-7250
West Seattle's Luna Park Cafe, with its anachronistic hodgepodge of memorabilia, provides the perfect clubhouse for those souls who love to feel cast adrift on the waters of time. The food is, for the most part, as retro as the atmo. Burgers, turkey dinners, and meat loaf are all served with a straight face: no sage stuffing, no imaginative spices, just good old-fashioned cookery. (The authenticity stops at the salads, which are 1990s tossed rather than 1950s iceberg.) More concessions are made to the health-conscious in the form of spinach salads and the delicious veggie burger. Servings are enormous; when they say jumbo hot fudge sundae,

they mean it. There's a solipsistic satisfaction to be found here, whatever you order: sitting in a booth, flipping through the tableside jukebox, you can forget about the world on the other side of the Viaduct. *$; MC, V; checks OK; breakfast, lunch, dinner every day; beer and wine; reservations accepted (large parties only); map:JJ9* &

Lush Life / ★★⯪

2331 2ND AVE; 206/441-9842
The husband-and-wife team of Marco Rulff and Donna Moodie, who helped launch the restaurant invasion of Belltown with Marco's Supperclub (see review), are behind this sensuous restaurant inspired by the lyrics of the Billy Strayhorn jazz classic "Lush Life." The mood is as mellow as the single-malt Scotch you might nurse at the secluded, intimate bar. The shadowy, candlelit dining room is made for lovers. The menu leans toward Italy, with a winning antipasti platter; an elegant, thin-crusted yellow potato, roasted garlic, and pecorino pizza; and linguine in a blissful melange of prosciutto, peas, and Gorgonzola. Bacon-wrapped grilled beef tenderloin topped with Gorgonzola in a nebbiolo wine reduction is surely among the lushest of Lush Life's *piatti principali;* it makes the rosemary-scented, double-cut pork chop in juniper marinade seem almost restrained. Chocolate-sambuca cake will make a suitably soulful finish to your meal. *$$; AE, MC, V; checks OK; dinner every day; full bar; reservations recommended; map:F8* &

Macrina Bakery & Café / ★★

2408 1ST AVE; 206/448-4032
Leslie Mackie has gained national acclaim as a bread baker, first as originator of the rustic bread program at Grand Central Bakery and later with her own ovens at Macrina. Today, she and her small army of bakers can hardly keep up with the demand for her gutsy, exceptional breads, which you'll find on the tables at the city's finest restaurants.

Mornings, Belltown regulars show up for buttery pastries, bowls of fresh fruit and house-made granola, and creamy lattes, enjoyed in the sunny Euro-chic cafe setting. Others hasten out the door with a loaf of potato bread, warm from the oven. Lunch brings simple, artful soups, salads, and panini, and a classy meze trio of daily-changing Mediterranean-inspired noshes. *$; MC, V; local checks only; breakfast, lunch Mon–Fri, brunch Sat–Sun; beer and wine; reservations not accepted; map:F8* &

Madison Park Cafe / ★★

1807 42ND AVE E; 206/324-2626
What began 20-plus years ago as a neighborhood coffee shop, a happy partnership between Karen Binder and Peggy Stamm, matured and ripened into a comfortable neighborhood cafe, home of sublime break-

fasts and excellent lunches. In a clapboard house just off Madison Park's main drag, lovingly crafted weekend brunches still draw in a neighborhood crowd. But dinner is now the main event, five nights a week. Specialties include oysters with Pernod cream sauce, rack of lamb with celeriac-flavored mashed potatoes, steak au poivre, and cassoulet. Moderate prices at dinner carry over to the small, mostly French wine list. Winter draws diners fireside for French-accented bistro fare prepared by chef Michael Richman. Best of all worlds is summer and a table in the sun-dappled brick courtyard. Catering is more than a sideline. *$; MC, V; checks OK; dinner Tues–Sat, brunch Sat–Sun; full bar; reservations accepted (dinner only); map:GG6*

Mae's Phinney Ridge Cafe / ★

6412 PHINNEY AVE N; 206/782-1222

On weekend mornings, the line outside Mae's is a microcosm of North Seattle—couples in athletic clothes; others in Birkenstocks, looking as if they had just crawled out of bed; families with young children; youths with varicolored hair, tattoos, and body piercings. These patrons line up because Mae's offers one of the most dependable breakfasts in the neighborhood. The wait may look long, but it rarely is because there are four sprawling dining areas. Of particular interest to bovine fans is the Moo Room, where everything is Holsteins and milk shakes. Although Mae's offers lunch, breakfast is the specialty and is served all day. No one leaves hungry, thanks to the Paul Bunyan–size portions of breakfast potatoes (or grits) and toast served with nearly every breakfast variation. Pastry lovers should opt for the coffee cake (the cinnamon rolls tend to be oversized and underflavored). Spud fans should order the Spud Feast, a mountain of potatoes topped with onions, green peppers, cheese, sour cream, and salsa. In addition to omelets, pancakes, and the breakfast regulars, there's a selection of egg scrambles, made with everything from veggies to seafood. Service is casual and friendly, though you may need to flag down your server for a coffee refill. An espresso bar offers access from a walk-up window. *$; AE, MC, V; checks OK; breakfast, lunch every day; no alcohol; reservations accepted (large parties only); map:FF8*

Maltby Cafe / ★★

8809 MALTBY RD, MALTBY; 425/483-3123

Upstairs, the 1937 WPA project Maltby School gymnasium remains as it was. Downstairs, in what used to be the school cafeteria, the Maltby Cafe remains what it is, year after year: home of outstanding country breakfasts and equally satisfying lunches. Logger-size portions abound for those who can find the place their first time out or for repeaters whose wheels know the way to the Big Fill-Up: a Saturday morning repast can do you for the weekend. Unhurried, bountiful breakfasts feature delicious omelets—the Maltby is a huge affair, stuffed with more than a cup of assorted veggies and even chunks of prime rib. Freshly roasted turkey is heaped high on sandwiches built on homemade bread. If you have to wait for a table (which is usually the case on weekends), order one of the legendary, giant cinnamon rolls, then savor it on the steps outside, or wander to the nearby crafts gallery, Back Alley Art. At lunch, enjoy great sandwiches and soups (try a Reuben, made with their own corned beef). *$; MC, V; local checks only; breakfast, lunch every day; beer and wine; reservations accepted (large parties only)* &

Maple Leaf Grill / ★★

8929 ROOSEVELT WAY NE; 206/523-8449
Don't let the pub atmosphere fool you. And whatever you do, don't insult the culinary artistry of chef Pauline Wickery by calling her food "pub grub." One look down the plate-filled bar or into the big wooden booths proves that "grub" doesn't come close to describing the food served here. The flannel-and-denim-clad regulars are as likely to be forking into red-pepper fettuccine with chipotle-spiked cream sauce or grilled skewers of escolar (a mild, sweet white fish) with chile-garlic sauce as munching a burger with fries. And they are as likely to be hoisting a glass of red (by-the-glass selections are extensive as the hot-sauce choices) or even a kir royale as they are a brew. With blues on the sound system and convivial customers gratefully digging in or tacking their names to the waiting list while trading gibes with frontman David Albert, you get the feeling that you're at a housewarming in the home of an exceptionally good cook. *$$; MC, V; checks OK; lunch Mon–Fri, dinner every day; beer and wine; reservations recommended; map:DD6* &

Marco's Supperclub / ★★☆

2510 1ST AVE; 206/441-7801
Expat Chicagoans Marco Rulff and Donna Moodie opened their first bistro in Belltown well before the neighborhood became the hippest food corridor in Seattle. From the day the doors opened, the husband-and-wife team have had more than luck going for them. Their formula for success includes years of tableside experience, an adventurous and capable chef, and a strong staff of friendly yet sophisticated servers. Their sexy, noisy, and busy restaurant has welcomed hordes of savvy diners who come for the warm, funky atmosphere and the trip-around-the-world menu. Forgo the pastas, but certainly order the fried sage appetizer, the subtly spiced Jamaican jerk chicken served up with sautéed greens and mashed sweet potatoes, or seasonal specials such as pork tenderloin marinated in juniper berries and herbs, or cumin-and-coriander-spiked Moroccan lamb. A bar running the length of the room is a great perch for those dining alone. In summer a colorful, plant-filled deck out back practically doubles the seating capacity. *$$; AE, MC, V; local checks only; dinner every day; full bar; reservations recommended; map:F8* &

Matt's in the Market / ★★★

94 PIKE ST, THIRD FLOOR (PIKE PLACE MARKET); 206/467-7909

Barely two dozen seats occupy this seafood bar and restaurant that might be one of Seattle's best-kept secrets. Nine of them are at the mosaic-tiled counter, behind which chef Erik Cannella nimbly jockeys sauté pans between two portable gas burners and one small oven, gentling each dish to its moment of perfection. Owner Matt Janke does just about everything else, acting as host, waiter, busperson, dishwasher, and sommelier with friendly aplomb. The interplay of flavors in the best dishes ranges from subtle to explosive; salmon and scallop pâté is so light it's almost a mousse, while sturgeon in a jacket of coriander and mustard seed more than holds its own under fiery lime pickle sauce. Daily specials augment the short menu that changes every couple of months, but everything is fresh because the cooks shop the Market twice a day. For lunch, nearby office workers climb the stairs for a perfect oyster po' boy, a dense and satisfying filé gumbo, or perhaps steamed mussels and clams in an ouzo-infused liquor that also includes butter, garlic, bitter greens, and new potatoes. After dark a vintage floor lamp and a row of bare-bulbed fixtures throw diffused light on small candlelit tables draped in twilight blue damask under white cloths. No one will rush you if you choose to linger over a silky chocolate pot de crème while enjoying live jazz (every Wednesday night), or savor one last glass of wine (from a wonderfully quirky and reasonably priced list) while watching the sun sink into Elliott Bay. And no one will take your reservation, either—but they will hold tables for 15 minutes if you call ahead. *$$; MC, V; no checks; lunch Mon–Sat, dinner Tues–Sat; beer and wine; reservations not accepted; map:J8*

Maximilien in the Market / ★★

81-A PIKE ST (PIKE PLACE MARKET); 206/682-7270

After nearly a quarter-century, this undeniably French cafe has undergone a needed revitalization. François and Julia Kissel graced the Seattle restaurant scene at various venues for three decades. By selling this, their last place, to two former employees—both French—they presented the city with one final gift. Chef Eric Franey and frontman Axel Mace put together a new menu, added dramatic silk-flower arrangements, and placed linen and fresh flowers on tables at night, but didn't alter the dark green walls or remove the collection of natural wood-framed mirrors. Many patrons bring a book or newspaper, now and then gazing pensively at the windows framing views of Elliott Bay. A French person would feel right at home with the fare: escargots, mussels, foie gras, onion soup, duck with orange sauce, rack of lamb, sole Normandy. Friday and Saturday breakfasts and Sunday brunch draw crowds for the likes of smoked-salmon Benedict and sage-flavored sausage. The menu says country omelet, but the kitchen will prepare the soft, small-curd, tender

French classic on request. That's characteristic of the accommodating owners. No Gallic shrugs from them. *$$; AE, DIS, MC, V; no checks; lunch, dinner Tues–Sat, breakfast Sat, brunch Sun; full bar; reservations accepted; map:J8* &

McCormick & Schmick's / ★★

1103 1ST AVE; 206/623-5500

No, you're not in New York or San Francisco. It just feels that way in this big seafood restaurant that bows to chophouse tradition with dark wood paneling, booths, glittery bar, and waiters with black bow ties. You'd think they'd been grilling lamb chops and salmon steaks since the turn of the century. Don't smirk—they do it well, if not with perfect consistency. Just remember to keep it simple: order seafood (if it swims or clings to rocks, it's probably on the astounding fresh sheet), and stay away from the pasta. Start with fresh oysters; then hope there's steelhead in season. The straightforward work at the grill includes meat, game, and poultry. Suits sit at the lengthy counter, reading the *Wall Street Journal* while knocking back single-malt Scotch and waiting for double-cut pork chops. At lunch M & S is too busy for its own good—service adopts a hurry-up attitude, and you have to sit in the hall until your whole party assembles—but dinners are more relaxed. A private room holds up to 24 guests. The bar holds a crowd. *$$; AE, DC, DIS, JCB, MC, V; no checks; lunch Mon–Fri (Mon–Sat in summer), dinner every day; full bar; reservations recommended; www.mccormickandschmicks.com; map:L7*

Mediterranean Kitchen / ★★

366 ROY ST; 206/285-6713

103 BELLEVUE WAY NE, BELLEVUE; 425/462-9422

You can practically whiff the garlic from one end of 520 to the other, thanks to these twin versions of the same restaurant. The Middle Eastern fare is powered by the founder's belief in the healthful as well as gustatory properties of this edible bulb. Son Bassam Aboul Hosn has taken the idea and run with it, setting up shop on the Eastside, just down Bellevue Way from the Square. He carries on the tradition of his father, Kamal Aboul Hosn, which stretches back to his grandfather in old Lebanon: chicken wings marinated in red-wine vinegar, charbroiled, and slathered with enough roasted garlic to render downtown Bellevue a vampire-free zone. Kamal, who has worked similar magic on Lower Queen Anne since 1980, recently moved to newer, larger digs nearer Seattle Center. Large digs seem appropriate given the gargantuan portions of terrific eastern Mediterranean fare. Vegetarians love both these places, while only the undead disagree. *$; AE, DC, MC, V; no checks; lunch Mon–Fri (Seattle), Mon–Sat (Bellevue), dinner every day; beer and wine; reservations accepted (recommended on weekends); map:A5; map:HH3* &

Metropolitan Grill / ★★☆

820 2ND AVE; 206/624-3287
The steakhouse Seattle loves to love, the Met Grill is a handsome, money-colored haunt in the heart of the financial district that does a booming business among stockbrokers and Asian tourists. The bovine is divine here at Suit Central—prime-grade, corn-fed, and dry-aged—so you'd do well to stick to the steaks. Pastas and appetizers are less well executed, but a list of large, appealing salads, sandwiches, and a daily fish special present good alternatives to beef for the lunch crowd. Waiters are of the no-nonsense school, which suits the table-hopping power brokers just fine. Not surprisingly, big reds dominate the lengthy, pricey wine list. Financiers count on the Met's 30-person private room as a dependable dinner venue. *$$$; AE, DC, MC, V; local checks only; lunch Mon–Fri, dinner every day; full bar; reservations recommended; map:M7* &

Ming Place Chinese Seafood Restaurant / ★★

13200 NORTHUP WAY, BELLEVUE; 425/643-3888
What with Noble Court and Sea Garden in the same general neighborhood, Ming Place gets overlooked. Yet, though it hasn't quite the same scope as its competitors, it does offer tempting bargains: a Peking duck for nine bucks one night, a Dungeness crab for ten another. There's a catch, natch—this one a requirement to purchase two other entrees as well. That's not a hardship, however, given the long and varied menu, frequently including preparations of live prawns, abalone, geoduck, and lobster, plus a plethora of other Hong Kong–style specialties. Service and language problems abound—but bargain hunting is rarely easy. For easy, try the daily dim sum lunch. *$$; JCB, MC, V; local checks only; lunch, dinner every day; beer and wine; reservations recommended (weekends only); map:GG2* &

Moghul Palace / ★☆

10303 NE 10TH ST, BELLEVUE; 425/451-1909
You've gotta like a place that makes its own mango ice cream, all fruity and chunked up with pistachios and almonds. It's a fine way to top off a beautifully spiced meal that comes rich in saffron, exotic as Marco Polo, and warming to the core with clove, cumin, and coriander. Owner Shah Kahn's prettily decorated restaurant just a block north of Bellevue Square offers a solid lunch-buffet special. But the place is best in evening, when you can indulge in a heartwarming curry or one of the tantalizing tandoori specialties, such as a marinated salmon fillet. Everything is better with a chunk of onion-cilantro naan in one hand. *$$; AE, DC, DIS, MC, V; local checks only; lunch Mon–Sat, dinner every day; full bar; reservations recommended; map:HH3* &

Mona's / ★★☆

6421 LATONA AVE NE; 206/526-1188

Tito Class and Annette Serrano had the *Mona Lisa* in mind when they named their restaurant, though the ghost of Frida Kahlo seems to have inspired the decor. Mona's has been such a successful addition to the burgeoning Green Lake restaurant scene that in 1997 the couple annexed the storefront next door, allowing room for a cozy lounge where a well-constructed cocktail may be enjoyed at the imposing bar built by Class himself. In the glowing, candlelit dining room, Serrano's original artwork adorns the stippled green walls. The small menu, which ranges from Spain to Greece to Tunisia to Italy, changes frequently, but you will usually find among the appetizers a superb duck confit and steamed mussels or clams. Salads are pungent with innovative dressings, while entrees—from a hefty paella to a simple, pan-seared salmon to pork chops marinated in pomegranate juice—are delicious and modestly priced. A late-night tapas menu is available in the lounge. *$$; AE, MC, V; checks OK; dinner Tues–Sat; full bar; reservations recommended; map:EE7* &

Mondo Burrito / ★

2121 1ST AVE; 206/728-9697

Mondo Burrito wraps its way around the world. These giant burritos, fresh and flavorful, range from a traditional chile-packed Mexican job to Thai (peanut-coconut rice, bean sprouts, cilantro, carrots, green onions, and Indonesian sweet-and-hot sauce); Hawaiian (rice, romaine, pineapple–green pepper salad, toasted coconut, and tropical barbecue sauce); and Cajun (red beans, rice, smoky cheddar, and sweet corn in a spicy sauce). A couple of salads, high-voltage chili, and very good soup of the day round out the menu. Most people grab and go, but it's pleasant to linger in the tropical red and green storefront dining room hung with the work of local artists. *$; MC, V; checks OK; lunch, dinner every day; beer and wine; reservations not accepted; map:H8* &

Nicolino / ★★☆

317 NW GILMAN BLVD, ISSAQUAH; 425/391-8077

At Issaquah's Gilman Village, you'll find several places to head once you've shopped till you're ready to drop. Or just drop by Nicolino, and forget shopping altogether. On warm days, the sunny brick courtyard is the place to be. Other times, head for the cheerful little dining room, pleasantly cluttered with wine bottles, art prints, murals, a mandolin, maps—it might be quicker to list what *isn't* on the walls. Music is in the air—Italian crooners, percussion courtesy of kitchen help pounding chicken breasts. Hearty slices of peasant bread are meant to be soaked with herb-infused olive oil, or dredged in tomato sauce as bright as a mandolin note, zestily spiced. Pastas are the thing here, washed down with a fruity chianti. New ownership—Jessica Robertiello and Derek

Schaubroeck, longtime workers here—promises an infusion of enthusiasm. *$$; DIS, MC, V; checks OK; lunch, dinner every day; beer and wine; reservations not accepted* &

Nikko / ★★

1900 5TH AVE (WESTIN HOTEL); 206/322-4641

When Nikko moved several years ago from its inconspicuous International District location to the Westin, a flashy, highly decorated, $1.5 million remodel awaited it. Nikko's current incarnation offers one of the most attractive Japanese dining rooms in the city. The enormous sushi bar is a great place to enjoy impeccable raw fish, including the astounding Nikko Roll (seven different pieces of fish rolled with avocado and rice). Perennial non-sushi favorites include black cod marinated in sake lees and then broiled to flaky perfection, or crisp soft-shell crab. One of the most satisfying rainy-day dishes here is the often-maligned sukiyaki, a soulful one-pot meal. And you can always enjoy a plate of grilled this-and-that from the robata bar. *$$$; AE, DC, JCB, MC, V; no checks; dinner Mon–Sat; full bar; reservations recommended; www.nikkorestaurant.com; map:I6* &

Nishino / ★★★

3130 E MADISON ST; 206/322-5800

Kyoto-born Tatsu Nishino apprenticed at one of Japan's renowned kaiseki restaurants, then spent five years working with celebrated chef Nobu Matsuhisa in Los Angeles before coming to Seattle and opening Nishino, on the fringes of moneyed Madison Park. The soothing space is decorated with spare, Japanese elegance. In the open kitchen and in the adjacent sushi bar, Eastern traditions meet Western bravado in a felicitous fashion. The voluptuous assortment of fresh seafood on display is fashioned into striking arrangements: raw, pale pink albacore tuna may anchor a crown of taro chips or support a dollop of lumpfish caviar and a drop of edible liquid gold. Look to the fresh sheet for memorable flavor combinations, such as pan-seared halibut cheeks with shiitake mushrooms and spinach in a luxurious butter sauce laced with bits of sea urchin, lemon, soy, and mirin. If ankimo (monkfish liver) is available, don't be squeamish; it tastes like foie gras from the sea. More than two dozen sushi items are listed on the menu, and while you can certainly opt for tempura or teriyaki, you would miss much of the sheer joy of dining at Nishino. *$$$; AE, MC, V; no checks; dinner Mon–Sat; full bar; reservations recommended; map:GG6* &

Noble Court / ★★

1644 140TH AVE NE, BELLEVUE; 425/641-6011

A few years under steady management, including the same head chef and the same dim sum master, have allowed Bellevue's Noble Court to elevate itself among the elite of Northwest Chinese restaurants. Witness the hordes waiting an hour or more on Sundays for the area's most popular dim sum. Observe a parade of critters being plucked from fresh tanks just inside the door—Dungeness crab, Alaskan king crab, lobster, spot prawns, turtles—and then undergoing expert transformation to the plate for big-time expense-account dinners. Grab a table by the windows if you can, so you can look out on a small, charming creek (instead of a dining room in need of freshening). Adventures into hot pots and sizzling platters seldom go unrewarded. Ask for a translation of the menu and you might discover the only place for blocks around with decent snake soup. *$$; AE, MC, V; no checks; lunch, dinner every day; full bar; reservations accepted; map:GG2* &

ObaChine / ★★

1518 6TH AVE; 206/749-9653
Wunderchef Wolfgang Puck is as famous for his multitude of chic restaurants as for his chic frozen pizzas. Now he's part of the local lingo, having brought ObaChine number two (the first lives in Beverly Hills, the third in Phoenix) into the megawatt Meridian complex. There's a small, less-conspicuous satay bar downstairs, but the action's above, in the oversize dining room dominated by an exhibition kitchen, Asian art and artifacts, and entirely too much purple. We give the nod to Puck's interesting, well-executed taste-of-Asia fare: crisp lamb samosas and shiitake-filled pot-stickers; moist, tea leaf–baked ten-spice salmon; exotic, colorful side dishes and desserts that never get short shrift; and an appealing, Northwest-heavy wine list. Tables along the far wall may prove too close together for comfort for the business-lunchers who flock here by day. *$$; AE, DC, MC, V; no checks; lunch Mon–Sat, dinner every day; full bar; reservations recommended; map:J5* &

Pagliacci Pizza / ★

426 BROADWAY E (AND BRANCHES); 206/324-0730
It's human nature: we tend to take our institutions for granted. When it comes to pizzerias, this is a mistake. We get distracted by the herbed dough at one new pizza joint; by the wacky toppings (barbecue sauce and dried apricots?) at another; by the elaborate piercings on the staff at a third. Meanwhile, Pagliacci waits for us like a faithful old dog, thumping its tail on its Formica floor when we come crawling back. All Pagliacci locations offer the same simple yet eternal lure: thin-and-tangy cheese pizzas. Their tasty crusts are the result of thorough research by the owners, who ultimately settled on Philadelphia-style. The true test of this exceptional crust is the original cheese pizza, which is unadorned except for a light, fresh tomato sauce and mozzarella. Served hot from the oven, it's hard to beat. Skip the salads and go straight to the cheesy tomato source—Pagliacci has several variations of "primo" pies. This place is

about pizza, and that's it. You can take out from all Pagliacci locations, or eat in at the Capitol Hill, Lower Queen Anne, and University District branches. Comfortable, echoing, and sometimes hectic, they're all fine places for a solo meal. A phone call to Pagliacci's central delivery service (206/726-1717) will get you delivery from the closest outlet. *$; MC, V; local checks only; lunch, dinner every day; beer and wine; reservations not accepted; map:HH7* &

The Painted Table / ★★★

92 MADISON ST (ALEXIS HOTEL); 206/624-3646
Chef Tim Kelley exhibits a deft touch with meat and fish, but it is the vegetables that truly distinguish this sexy, two-tiered, art-hung, high-ceilinged, wood-paneled-and-pillared room. Relationships with regional organic growers yield inventive, jazz-riff matchmaking: potato-*prune* gratin (it works!), Japanese eggplant paired with poblanos (!), parsnip/Granny Smith hash, or puréed celery root sidling up to sautéed asparagus and crisped morels. This celebration of the greengrocer almost, but not quite, overshadows a vanilla bean–marinated veal chop or a huckleberry-sauced Muscovy duck. Kelley honed his craft in New York at highly regarded Vong and Bouley, but it is here in one of Seattle's best boutique hotels that he has made his mark. *$$$; AE, DC, DIS, MC, V; local checks only; breakfast, dinner every day, lunch Mon–Fri; full bar; reservations recommended; map:L8* &

Palace Kitchen / ★★★

2030 5TH AVE; 206/448-2001
The latest Tom Douglas invention marries a palatial open kitchen and a serious bar scene in a dramatic setting that's as casual as it is sophisticated. Whether you're seated at the enormous tile-topped bar (where martinis come in individual mini-shakers), or in a wooden booth, a storefront banquette, or the glassed-in private room (all with a view of the action—of which there is plenty), you can eat and drink yourself into ecstatic oblivion. Make a meal of finger foods without spending a fortune: fat, spicy, grilled chicken wings; crisp-fried, semolina-coated anchovies; house-made sopressata sausage; a killer cheese plate. Up the ante and order one of the night's applewood-grilled specials—spit-roasted meat, poultry, or whole grilled fish. Seafood gets special treatment here, as does dessert. You'll recognize your favorites from the Dahlia Lounge and Etta's Seafood (see reviews); this is the dessert kitchen for all of Douglas's restaurants. The informative wine list is the most entertaining in town. *$$; AE, DC, DIS, MC, V; checks OK; dinner every day; full bar; reservations recommended; www.tomdouglas.com; map:H6* &

Palisade / ★★
Maggie Bluffs / ★

2601 W MARINA PL (ELLIOTT BAY MARINA); 206/285-1000 (PALISADE), 206/283-8322 (MAGGIE BLUFFS)
Inside, with a waterfall and a seawater tidal pool (complete with marine life), tropical-looking plants and trees, chandeliers festooned with glass balls, and a player piano perched on a ledge over the bar, Palisade might be mistaken for the Hyatt Regency on Maui. Outside, beyond the Elliott Bay Marina to the grandstand view of the city and Sound, it's definitely Seattle. Step over the cobblestone bridge into the expansive dining area, where there's not a bad seat in the house. The vast menu highlights contemporary grilling, searing, and rotisserie cooking styles for a variety of fish, meat, and poultry. Order the pupu platter and you'll sample most of the appetizers; try the shellfish chowder and you'll be rewarded with a velvety broth crowded with veggies and bites of crab and shrimp. Imaginative entrees favor sweet-and-sour glazes and Polynesian-inspired creations. Consider a simple fish preparation—perhaps an applewood-grilled escolar, a mild, moist Fijian white fish both succulent and sweet. Finish with a trio of burnt-cream custards flavored in turn with classic vanilla, rich chocolate, and Grand Marnier.

Downstairs is the burger bar, Maggie Bluffs, whose simple, straightforward atmosphere—with food to match (big burgers with shoestring fries, fish 'n' chips, and salads)—offers a respite from the South Pacific schmaltz. *$$$/$; AE, DC, DIS, MC, V; checks OK (Palisade), local checks only (Maggie Bluffs); lunch Mon–Sat, dinner every day, brunch Sun (Palisade), breakfast Sat–Sun, lunch, dinner every day (Maggie Bluffs); full bar; reservations recommended (Palisade); reservations accepted (Maggie Bluffs); map:GG8* &

Panos Kleftiko / ★★

815 5TH AVE N; 206/301-0393
Panos Marinos is the heart and soul (and host/chef) of this traditional Greek taverna in a small, cozy storefront a few blocks north of Seattle Center. Come with a clutch of friends and cram your table with mezedes or "little dishes" (there are 32 choices, priced from $1.50 to $8), several servings of warm pita bread (the best we've had anywhere), and a glass or three of retsina. Everything's tasty, but we especially love the melanzanesalata (a cold salad of roasted eggplant, tomatoes, and herbs), the hummus, the baked kalamata olives, and the spicy meatballs. Arrive early if you have tickets to a show; Panos encourages lingering and doesn't take reservations. *$; MC, V; local checks only; dinner Mon–Sat; beer and wine; reservations not accepted; map:B4*

Pecos Pit BBQ / ★★

2260 IST AVE S; 206/623-0629

It's open only for weekday lunch—but oh, what a lunch. This pit stop south of the Kingdome and the baseball stadium is worth a trip in order to give yourself over to sheer, carnivorous indulgence. Step up to the window and order your fun-on-a-bun: a sliced beef brisket, pork, Pecos beef, ham, or link sandwich. Ask them to "spike it" and you'll get a link tucked into your already meat-filled treasure. Choose from mild, medium, or hot sauce, but be warned: hot means *hot*. Be sure to order a side of spicy baked beans before heading off to claim a picnic table. *$; no credit cards; no checks; lunch Mon–Fri; no alcohol; reservations not accepted; map:II7* &

Philadelphia Fevre Steak & Hoagie Shop / ★

2332 E MADISON ST; 206/323-1000

Ask any expat Philadelphian and they'll tell you: it's not Pat's Steaks, but, as they say in the City of Brotherly Love, "What's it to yez?" Still, the cheesesteaks and hoagies at this Madison Valley luncheonette are the closest thing to the real McCoy around here. And if you sit at the counter listening to wisecracking grillmeister Renée LeFevre's David Brenneresque accent while reading *Philadelphia Magazine*, you'll get more Philly flavor than you bargained for. Renée will grill up a pile of thinly sliced rib-eye steak with onions, add some white American cheese and hot cherry peppers if you like, and serve it up on an Italian roll. Eat it the way you should, with a basket of french fries and a TastyKake, and you'll learn the real reason Rocky Balboa had to run up and down the steps at the Philadelphia Art Museum. *$; AE, MC, V; no checks; lunch, early dinner Mon–Fri; beer only; reservations not accepted; map:GG6* &

Pho Bac / ★

1314 S JACKSON ST; 206/323-4387

This oversize shack is crowded and funky, serving nothing but pho—the classic everyday dish of Vietnam. You won't need a menu, and you won't have to wait long for a bowl of the fragrant, herb-infused beef stock topped with paper-thin slices of raw beef that cook through as you slurp up the rice noodles nesting in the bottom. Order either a large ($5.50) or small ($4.50) portion, and garnish it from a plate of fresh basil, bean sprouts, jalapeño, and lime that arrives alongside the steaming bowls. Customize your soup to suit your fancy with fish sauce, chile sauce, and hoisin kept in squeeze bottles on the table. *$; no credit cards; no checks; lunch, dinner every day; no alcohol; reservations not accepted; map:HH6*

Phoenecia at Alki / ★★

2716 ALKI AVE SW; 206/935-6550
Hussein Khazaal's fans (whose devotion verges on the cultish) have followed him from one off-the-beaten-path location to another. Finally, he and they have a site worthy of his talents. At this, Phoenecia's third incarnation, the ocher-sponged walls seem to glow with Mediterranean sunshine. The standard hummus and baba ghanouj are here, but then it's off on pan-Mediterranean explorations: saffron-and-pine-nut risotto with shellfish; Moroccan eggplant with penne and tomatoes; excellent, inventive, thin-crust pizza; several versions of the most fragrant marinated lamb you've ever tasted; and a mariner's ransom of exquisite seafood. To round it all off you may choose, appropriately, between espresso and Turkish coffee, and between tiramisu and *chaibyaat*, a pistachio pastry with rose petals, lavender, and orange. Call before you go, however, as who knows if the restaurant will move again. *$$; MC, V; no checks; dinner Tues–Sun; beer and wine; reservations accepted (recommended on weekends); map:II9* &

Piecora's / ★★

1401 E MADISON ST; 206/322-9411
We know people who drive across town just to sit down to one of Piecora's oversize thin-crust pies and dream of New York. You'll know you've come to the right place when you see that damsel of the dispossessed, Lady Liberty, dressed in neon and hoisting a pizza above a crowded storefront. At this busy neighborhood joint decorated with New York subway maps and other Big Apple kitsch, delivery drivers run in and out, the din can reach epic proportions, and pizza tossing is a fine art. Some 32 toppings are available on pizzas sold by the pie, the half pie, or the slice. Pastas, calzones, sandwiches, and generous salads, too. Pizza is served until midnight on weekends. *$; MC, V; checks OK; lunch, dinner every day; full bar; reservations accepted; map:HH6*

The Pink Door / ★★

1919 POST ALLEY (PIKE PLACE MARKET); 206/443-3241
The low-profile entrance (simply a pink door on Post Alley) underscores the speakeasy ambience of this Italian trattoria just steps from the Pike Place Market. In winter, the dining room grows noisy around a burbling fountain. Come warmer weather, everyone vies for a spot on the trellis-covered terrace with its breathtakingly romantic view of the Sound.

Inside or out, the arty, under-30 set who call the place home might be happily noshing on garlicky black-olive tapenade and quaffing tumblers of wine from the reasonably priced, mostly Italian list. The menu features hearty, generously portioned pastas, a daily risotto, excellent rack of lamb paired with mascarpone mashed potatoes, and a lusty seafood-filled cioppino. Inventive salads are composed of mostly organic local produce. There's often live music (and sometimes a tarot card reader) in the evenings. *$$; AE, MC, V; no checks; lunch, dinner Tues–Sat; full bar; reservations recommended; map:J8*

Place Pigalle / ★★⯪

81 PIKE ST (PIKE PLACE MARKET); 206/624-1756

This pretty little bistro offers picture-postcard views of Puget Sound, warm, professional service, and astonishingly ambitious French-North-west-Italian cooking from a tiny kitchen whose crew must choreograph every movement. Hidden away in Pike Place Market, Place Pigalle is the perfect spot to sip an eau-de-vie, lunch with a friend, or engage in a romantic dinner à deux. Ask for a window table and order something as simple as onion soup gratinée (beefy broth, silky onions, chewy Gruyère), or as sophisticated as roulade of duck confit (preserved duck, goat cheese, and butternut squash rolled in pasta). Avoid the cassoulet with its undercooked beans, nearly invisible lamb bits, and—emblematic of the kitchen's sometimes inappropriate inventiveness—incongruous citrus-peel garnish. On sunny days, a small deck attracts those anxious to catch every ray, but the inside tables have the advantage of being in servers' sight lines. The little bar is ideal for dining solo. *$$$; AE, DC, MC, V; no checks; lunch, dinner Mon–Sat; full bar; reservations recommended; map:J8*

Plenty Fine Foods / ★★

1404 34TH AVE; 206/324-1214

This was initially a neighborhood grocery/deli, but so many people stood around eating without bothering to go home that owner Jim Watkins added some tables and voilà!—a restaurant was born. Folks come to this whimsically decorated storefront because they get what they want: elegant food that happens to be good for you. Beautifully arranged groceries line the shelves of the center room, and refrigerator cases dominate the main dining room. The menu, which changes weekly, always includes vegetarian options and features Watkins's signature red beans and rice as well as chicken and fish entrees. The crowning glory of the resplendent dessert case: chocolate cake—huge, moist, and frosted just right. *$$; DC, MC, V; local checks only; lunch every day, dinner Mon–Sat; beer and wine; reservations accepted (recommended on weekends); map:HH6* &

Pon Proem / ★

3039 78TH AVE SE, MERCER ISLAND; 206/236-8424

Homey touches warm up a weary little Thai dining room at the south end of the main Mercer Island business district. The owner herself sewed the seat covers and changes them seasonally. Linen napkins fan out from water glasses, which get topped off after just about every sip. At the start of lunch hour the staff lights incense for the Buddha, then proceeds to honor him with their work until closing: service can be as crisp as the stir-fried pea pods. Stir-fries like the *gai pahd met ma muang* have better balance than a gymnastics team, thanks to three kinds of soy sauce along with chili paste, veggies, and chicken. We like the little things, such as the petite cup of homemade chicken soup at lunch, and the desserts: sticky rice with mango or bread pudding. Respect the star system; four stars is *really* spicy here. *$; AE, DIS, MC, V; Mercer Island checks only; lunch Mon–Fri, dinner every day; beer and wine; reservations accepted; map:II4* &

Pontevecchio / ★★

710 N 34TH ST; 206/633-3989

If Federico Fellini had lived to discover Fremont, he would have been a regular at Pontevecchio, where on some evenings you might have to wait until the couple dancing the tango finishes so you can get to your table— one of only about a dozen in the place. Owner Michele Zacco has the heart of an impresario and the soul of an artist. He simmers the best tomato sauce in the city (Mama's recipe) for about six hours and then ladles it over toothsome ravioli. His antipasti platter is a carnival of flavors; his panini are fresh, overstuffed jewels. Though the menu seldom varies, the entertainment does. You might find yourself listening to Puccini while enjoying capelli d'angelo alla Norma (broiled eggplant and tangy ricotta over angel hair pasta), or forking tender veal marsala to the beat of a samba. It's all a little zany and a lot of fun. *$$; MC, V; checks OK; lunch every day, dinner Mon–Sat; beer and wine; reservations recommended; map:FF8*

Ponti Seafood Grill / ★★★

3014 3RD AVE N; 206/284-3000

Ponti, tucked almost under the Fremont Bridge, might inspire dreams of the Mediterranean, with its canalside perch, stucco walls, red-tiled roof, and elegantly understated dining rooms, but executive chef Alvin Binuya borrows from an array of ethnic flavors (with more than a passing nod to Asia). One of the first in Seattle to create what some call "fusion" cuisine, Binuya still performs cross-cultural magic with combinations such as seared ahi in a ginger-jolted soy and sake sauce with coconut rice cake and cucumber-wasabe aioli. Thai curry penne (with broiled scallops, Dungeness crabmeat, spicy ginger-tomato chutney, and basil chiffonade) is a long-running favorite, but savvy diners will turn to the fresh sheet for the most exciting offerings of the day: grilled sea bass with tomatillo sauce; a stew of lobster and mussels in coconut broth flavored with cilantro pesto; or red-wine risotto with halibut cheeks, artichoke, asparagus, and chard. Alvin's mom, Victoria, does the desserts here; her fruit pies are a joy. Dine outdoors in warm weather on balconies overlooking the boat traffic on the canal and the joggers and bikers on the path below. *$$$; AE, DC, MC, V; local checks only; lunch, dinner every day, brunch Sun; full bar; reservations recommended; mnger@ponti. com; www.ponti.com; map:FF8* &

Provinces Asian Restaurant & Bar / ★★

201 5TH AVE S, EDMONDS; 425/744-0288

Years ago, the thought of a pan-Asian restaurant was too much for many monoethnic eaters. But today, the idea is accepted even in the suburban town of Edmonds—where a serene and decidedly older crowd enjoys a range of Asian cuisine in an attractive, dimly lit dining room set in a quaint shopping mall. We like the friendly, efficient service, the occasional dish of sweet-and-spicy broccoli stems brought to the table gratis, and the Bangkok hot-and-sour soup—served in a cast-iron pot brimming with large prawns, bay shrimp, fresh scallops, and straw mushrooms, fragrant with lemongrass and large enough to feed four. The Cantonese-style lobster is served with shellfish and vegetables and flavored with salty Chinese black beans. The huge portion of Mongolian ginger beef is a touch sweet, but pleasantly potent with ginger and garlic. The abbreviated lunch menu, including humongous bowls of udon noodle soup, is a bargain and a half. The adjoining cocktail lounge—where folks meet to bend an elbow, smoke a cigarette, and make merry—is decidedly more boisterous, though that doesn't seem to bother the teetotalers sipping their green tea in the dining room. A sister restaurant, Shallots Asian Bistro (see review), opened in 1997 in Belltown. *$$; AE, DC, DIS, MC, V; local checks only; lunch Mon–Sat, dinner every day; full bar; reservations accepted* &

Queen City Grill / ★★☆

2201 1ST AVE; 206/443-0975

Though a polite fellow manipulating a velvet rope frequently needs to control traffic into this chic saloon, it's not because the food's uniformly terrific. That can be hit-and-miss, though when it's a hit, you feel it's worth the chance. It was not always so, evidence that success breeds complacency. Not that the regulars who pack the place would agree. A delicious and impeccable caesar salad might be followed by tepid grilled vegetables, but the accommodating, intimate service and welcoming atmosphere distract your attention from food flaws and temper any disappointments. Our advice: stick with the seafood. The big fish sign outside signifies that Queen City's a fish house, and that's what it does best. Gilled meats sometimes linger on the heat too long, as the overworked cooks struggle to keep up with demand. There's smoking at the bar and up front at a half-dozen linen-draped tables. Polished booths line one side of this deep, narrow space, affording little sanctuary. All in all, however, this is a classy, convivial space in which to enjoy a nosh. *$$; AE, DC, MC, V; checks OK; lunch Mon–Fri, dinner every day; full bar; reservations recommended; robair@seanet.com; map:G8* &

Raga / ★★

555 108TH AVE NE, BELLEVUE; 425/450-0336

In a town disproportionately blessed with good Indian restaurants, Raga stands out. The menu fairly spans that great subcontinent, with its varied regional approaches to food, from robustly flavored to combustibly seasoned. For a time, the Raga dining experience varied dramatically in overall quality. Owner Kamal Mroke opened a second restaurant on Queen Anne, and both places suffered from diffused attention. But he sold the Seattle place and now manages the Bellevue locale himself. Once again everything, from the teardrop-shaped naan to the tamarind-coconut curries to the richly golden lamb *methi*, is outstanding. The rooms, shaded in cool blue, look more contemporary American than Indian, but the wonderful food leaves no doubt. *$$; AE, DC, DIS, MC, V; local checks only; lunch, dinner every day; full bar; reservations accepted (recommended on weekends); map:HH3* &

Ray's Boathouse / ★★☆

6049 SEAVIEW AVE NW; 206/789-3770

With its peerless, unabashedly romantic view of Shilshole Bay and the Olympics beyond, Ray's is the place for waterfront dining favored by tourists and locals alike. The restaurant has rebounded after a rough patch when it suffered from management upheavals and a fire that necessitated an extensive renovation. Fine food and attentive service once again characterize this Seattle landmark—and it looks better than ever. Executive chef Charles Ramseyer is capable of knocking your socks off with steamed Penn Cove mussels awash in a creamy Thai-style lemon-grass-and-curry broth, king salmon glazed with cherries and petite sirah, and what may be the world's best version of kasu black cod, marinated in sake lees. The award-winning wine list, always strong in Northwest varietals, is broadening to embrace the globe. A moderately priced, more casual menu—lingcod fish 'n' chips, rock shrimp and crab cakes, silky chowder—is offered for lunch as well as dinner upstairs in the deck-rimmed cafe, where the bar is especially popular at happy hour. When the sun shines, expect the restaurant to be slammed; a prime-time reservation in the dining room may take weeks to secure, and the cafe may have a wait of an hour or more. *$$$; AE, DC, DIS, MC, V; local checks only; lunch, dinner every day; full bar; reservations recommended (dinner only), reservations not accepted in the cafe; Rays@rays.com; www.rays.com; map:EE9* &

Red Mill Burgers / ★★

312 N 67TH ST; 206/783-6362

1613 W DRAVUS ST; 206/284-6363

When Babe and John Shepherd were schoolkids in Seattle, they often hung out at the Red Mill—an old diner-style restaurant. Thirty years after the old Red Mill served its last meal, the brother-and-sister team opened their tiny, namesake Red Mill Burgers in a corner of an old brick building on Phinney Ridge. Within weeks they were attracting crowds of burger worshipers who came for one of their 18 varieties. Within months, they expanded into an adjoining space to accommodate the hordes. This is not a fast-food joint, but the wait is worth it, as you'll see when you sink your teeth into a burger topped with thick slices of pepper bacon, anointed with a smoky house-made mayo, and sandwiched inside a big, warm bun with the freshest of lettuce and tomatoes. Those who eschew foods that moo will be pleased by the array of vegetarian and chicken offerings (try the verde chicken burger with roasted Anaheim peppers and Jack cheese). Everyone will love Babe's killer onion rings dipped in a cornmeal batter laced with thyme, cumin, and cayenne. Top it all off with a Creamsicle-flavored malt or a milk shake. *$; no credit cards; local checks only; lunch, dinner Tues–Sun; no alcohol; reservations not accepted; map:EE8; map:FF8* &

Ristorante Buongusto / ★★

2232 QUEEN ANNE AVE N; 206/284-9040

When Anna and Salvio Varchetta opened their intimate Queen Anne restaurant in 1990, their brother Roberto was in the kitchen, and the menu clung closely to the family's Neapolitan roots. The current chef, however, draws inspiration from up and down the Italian peninsula. Familiar dishes are executed extremely well: rigatoni in a basil-flecked, cream-kissed tomato sauce is heavy with sausage; butter finishes a sauce of mushrooms and marsala wine covering thin, tender veal; sautéed squid is lightly dressed in oil, lemon, and herbs; and the house-made ravioli may be stuffed with spinach and ricotta and lavished with pesto. Antipasti change daily and make good use of an array of organic vegetables. With a cozy fire flickering on the frescoed terra-cotta walls and mellow jazz wafting through the low arches that divide the dining room, Buongusto is a sure bet for romance. Order a bottle of wine from the wide-ranging list of mostly Italian selections, and you are likely to be holding hands long before you take the last bite of a beguiling tiramisu. In fine weather, a small patio allows for dining alfresco. *$$; AE, DC, MC, V; no checks; lunch Tues–Fri, dinner every day; full bar; reservations accepted; map:GG7*

Ristorante Machiavelli / ★★

1215 PINE ST; 206/621-7941
There seems to be an Italian restaurant on every corner in town, but few corners attract as many happy campers as Pine and Melrose. Machiavelli isn't big on decor, and the menu may look slightly standard at first glance—reminiscent of the old family-style Italian-American spots—but on closer inspection, this is the real thing, at pleasingly moderate prices. The use of chicken liver in the lasagne signals a chef with true Italian roots. The carbonara's not overwhelming, but rather a skilled toss of pasta, Parmesan, and pancetta, and the gnocchi has a sterling reputation. The pizza here is a skinflint's dream: plate-size with a thin, breakaway crust and enhanced with a couple of good ingredients. The staff is skilled in keeping customers happy and keeping food on the table, striking the right balance between unobtrusive and affable to keep your meal upbeat. *$$; MC, V; no checks; dinner Mon–Sat; full bar; reservations not accepted; map:J2* &

Ristorante Paradiso / ★★

120-A PARK LANE, KIRKLAND; 425/889-8601
Tucked amidst Kirkland galleries, Ristorante Paradiso is a small work of art in itself—one that offers not only a little romance but surprisingly sophisticated Italian fare as well. Much of owner/chef Fabrizio Loi's menu has remained constant from its 1991 debut. Openers include a beautifully arranged plate of grilled vegetables for two or a generous bowl of fresh, perfectly cooked mussels and clams in a wine-based broth so good you'll scoop up every drop. There's a range of meat dishes, including a delicate saltimbocca, and a long list of pastas. We like the cannelloni gratinati—lovely pasta crepes stuffed with a delicate mix of ground veal, chicken, and mozzarella and served with two sauces (one red, one white). A great selection of wines, featuring many Italian labels, is priced from the mid-teens and up. *$$; AE, DC, DIS, MC, V; checks OK; lunch Mon–Fri, dinner every day; beer and wine; reservations recommended; map:EE3* &

Rover's / ★★★⯪

2808 E MADISON ST; 206/325-7442
Chef Thierry Rautureau, who began his culinary apprenticeship in the French countryside at age 13, is Seattle's answer to Jacques Pepin—a handsome elf with a warm wit, a world of personality, and an inspired hand in the kitchen. His warmly decorated restaurant is a small house tucked into a garden courtyard in Madison Valley. Dinners here are marvelously sauced, classically French-inspired treatments of not-strictly-Northwest fare. Rautureau's forte is seafood, and he's adept at finding the best-quality ingredients. It may feel a tad fussy and expensive, but the three prix-fixe ménus de dégustation are served with a generous hand.

Maine lobster, steamed and served shell-less with a Périgord truffle sauce, will be savored with each mouthful. Tender pink slices of venison in a dark green peppercorn-and-Armagnac sauce taste surprisingly delicate. Expect ever-professional service, and expect sticker shock when perusing the carefully chosen wine list. Dining in the courtyard, weather permitting, is an enchanting experience. *$$$; AE, DC, MC, V; checks OK; dinner Tues–Sat; beer and wine; reservations required; www.rovers-seattle.com; map:GG6*

Roy St. Bistro / ★★☆

174 ROY ST; 206/284-9093

Situated on a quiet, tree-lined Lower Queen Anne street just a short meander from Seattle Center, this place has all the unpretentious warmth and charm of an English village dining room. Owner Patrick Conlan is, in fact, an ex-Londoner, as well as a former waiter, who brings a lot of polish to the front of the house and often tends the bar himself. The kitchen is in equally good hands. The menu puts a creative spin on classic British and Northern European fare with dishes like ostrich pie filled with chestnuts and root vegetables in a dense wine sauce or hefty prime rib under a blanket of creamy mushroom gravy. Fish of the day may be baked in parchment or grilled. Roast chicken might arrive suffused with lemon and rosemary, or with a touch of ginger on a bed of mushroom-and-spinach duxelles. For starters, try the hazelnut-studded lamb pâté or the steamed Penn Cove mussels in a broth kissed with Pernod. Conlan has composed a thoughtful wine list and will expertly walk you through it. A cheese plate and a glass of port make a very proper finish. *$$; MC, V; no checks; lunch Mon–Fri, dinner every day; full bar; reservations recommended; map:A6* ♿

Roy's / ★☆

1900 5TH AVE (WESTIN HOTEL); 206/256-7697

Honolulu-based celebrity chef Roy Yamaguchi has parlayed the vertical-food, fusion-crazed early '90s into a Pacific Rim chain of glamorous restaurants bearing his name. He fetched up on our shore just as the vertical-food fad was fading and local chefs were improving on the fusion idea. If he's paying attention, he will discover he's stranded in time at this all-day hotel dining room. Still, when the kitchen isn't dizzily spinning the globe, some good food can be found here. Avoid playing the wide-eyed rube for earnest servers and stick with simple preparations like beef short ribs and uncomplicated, beautifully cooked fish and grilled meats. *$$$; AE, DC, DIS, MC, V; local checks only; breakfast, lunch, dinner every day, brunch Sat–Sun; full bar; reservations accepted; map:I6* ♿

Ruby's on Bainbridge / ★

4569 LYNWOOD CENTER RD, BAINBRIDGE ISLAND; 206/780-9303
Maura and Aaron Crisp turned this location next door to the island's only movie theater into a mini–destination restaurant. It's a steamy, garlicky little place a hobbit might love—just casual enough for the locals, just sumptuous enough for weekend guests and daytrippers. The menu changes often, but you'll encounter entrees such as fettuccine tossed with wild mushrooms, swordfish dressed in soy and ginger, and pork tenderloin with a raspberry reduction. *$$; MC, V; checks OK; lunch Tues–Sun, dinner every day, brunch Sat–Sun; beer and wine; reservations accepted (recommended on weekends)*

Saigon Bistro / ★★☆

1032 S JACKSON ST; 206/329-4939
Light, airy Saigon Bistro is a cut above the many other cafes found along Jackson Street's Little Saigon. The open kitchen lends the room life, and this may be Seattle's only Vietnamese restaurant with a view—albeit one of the Duwamish corridor. The menu's many options reflect the Southern Vietnamese style of cookery, and everything here is prepared with care. A signature dish is *bun mang vit*, the apotheosis of soup and salad: a light soup of noodles in duck stock on one side, and a duck and cabbage salad with sweet, pungent ginger sauce on the other. Eggplant hot pot and *oc* (snail) soup are also standouts. Many dishes can be ordered with cold noodles, with noodles in fragrant broth, or with roll-your-own rice pancakes served with an array of fresh herbs. *$; MC, V; no checks; breakfast, lunch, dinner every day; beer and wine; reservations accepted; map:HH6* &

Saleh al Lago / ★★★

6804 E GREENLAKE WAY N; 206/524-4044
Saleh Joudeh is a native of the Middle East who left his heart in central Italy twentysome years ago. Self-taught and earnest about his restaurant, Joudeh has put out some of the most consistently good central Italian food in Seattle here at Green Lake since 1982. The two-tiered, peach-hued destination dining place is more popular with Seattle's moneyed muckamucks than with the city's beautiful trend-seekers (who may find the room too bright, the menu too traditional). But what Saleh al Lago might lack in excitement, it makes up for in execution. The menu is steadfast and true—as is the staff. You're not likely to find a better plate of calamari than this lightly floured version sautéed with lemon, garlic, and parsley. Risotto is done to chewy perfection here, perhaps with a rich red sauce and bits of filet mignon or with chicken, arugula, and Gorgonzola. Try the sautéed Provimi veal with its delicate quattro formaggi sauce, or

the nutmeg-tinged house-made spinach-and-cheese ravioli. Bored with tiramisu? Think again before you pass up Saleh's. *$$$; AE, DC, MC, V; checks OK; dinner Mon–Sat; full bar; reservations required; map:EE7* ⅄

Salish Lodge / ★★⯪

6501 RAILROAD AVE SE, SNOQUALMIE; 425/888-2556
Chefs come and go, but two things remain constant in the dining room of this luxurious lodge and spa that sits squarely above Snoqualmie Falls, about 45 minutes east of Seattle: the sweeping view across fir-clad mountains, and sommelier Randall Austin, who presides knowledgeably over the extensive cellar of international wines. William Belickis, a creative young chef who arrived in the spring of '98, shows promise but needs to find his footing. While the Salish has long been justly famous for its traditional country breakfast, the dinner menu offers comfort and sophistication that exactly suits the mood of the darkly romantic dining room. A gentle curry seasons rack of lamb; plum sauce moistens flavorful, if fatty, Muscovy duck breast paired with delicate herbed spaetzle; 75-year-old balsamic vinegar sweetens seared foie gras and poached peaches. We especially liked roasted quail in its saucy duet of glazed carrots and port wine, and seductive seared ahi, bathed in coconut and lime and pillowed on fragrant basmati rice. Both dried-out Oregon rabbit on a bed of chewy Egyptian wheat and characterless smoked trout on field greens disappointed. The very formal service leans toward the pretentious, but then this is a restaurant where the least expensive dinner entree—a plate of linguine with baby vegetables and portobellos—costs $24. The same pasta is half the price on the lunch menu—a relative bargain, especially when you consider there's no extra charge for the view. *$$$; AE, DC, MC, V; checks OK; breakfast, lunch, dinner every day; full bar; reservations recommended; www.salish.com* ⅄

Salute of Bellevue / ★★

10134 MAIN ST, BELLEVUE; 425/688-7613
Seattle ristorante pioneer Raffaele Calise opened the first Salute in 1984, a place now owned by his ex-wife. The menu at his newer, highly popular Old Bellevue location pretty much duplicates that at the old place, meaning that good Italian, which has endured for centuries in Italy, can make it for decades, anyway, in Western Washington. The basil-cream sauce on al dente linguine and chicken virtually sings a verse of "Volare." In the spicy mix of tomato, caramelized onion, Parma prosciutto, and fresh basil in a rigatoni amatriciana, one hears a spritzy "That's Amore." Chew on a pizza; the crust is chewy. Sip a vino; choices abound, including many Italians. Try to hear in a place with a terra-cotta floor, oilclothed tables, wood-beamed ceiling, see-through fireplace, and virtually nothing to absorb sound. It looks and feels as though a trattoria was abducted

from Calise's native Isle of Ischia and plopped down a few blocks south of Bellevue Square. *$$; AE, DC, MC, V; local checks only; lunch, dinner every day; beer and wine; reservations recommended; map:HH3* &

Salvatore Ristorante Italiano / ★☆

6100 ROOSEVELT WAY NE; 206/527-9301
What packs this place is food and amore. OK, the former—like over-salted pizza—can let you down. But the latter never fails. Salvatore Anania loves the Southern Italian food of his native Basilicata, and he loves his patrons. If they're stuck in line, he'll seat them in a small ante-room, bring them a glass of red, and get them started with antipasti. Servers follow his lead. They're never less than attentive, even when the kitchen falls behind and they're on a dead run. We suggest starting with one of the thin-crust pizzas but passing on the lackluster salads. Then consult your server on specials, or order spicy, satisfying penne put-tanesca. *$$; DIS, MC, V; checks OK; dinner Mon–Sat; beer and wine; reservations not accepted; map:EE6* &

Sanmi Sushi / ★★

2601 W MARINA PL, SUITE S (AT ELLIOTT BAY MARINA); 206/283-9978
Misao Sanmi was a Buddha-like presence behind a few well-known sushi bars before he opened his own Sanmi Sushi next door to the giant Palisade. Sit in the serene, sunny dining room and view the pleasure craft docked in the marina, or head directly to the sushi bar, where Sanmi presides over a fine view of some great-looking fish. The menu features a lengthy list of appetizers, including glistening, salty-sweet, black cod kasuzuke (also available as an entree) and marvelous albacore tuna, seared, sliced, and resting atop vinegar-dressed onions. A number of soups, combination dinners (with raw fish or cooked meat and seafood components), oodles of Japanese noodles, and grilled meats and fish round out the menu. Bring your appetite to lunch and order the makunouchi bento to sample a superb array of Sanmi's finest treats. *$$; AE, MC, V; no checks; lunch Mon–Fri, dinner every day; full bar; reservations accepted; map:GG8* &

Santa Fe Cafe / ★★

2255 NE 65TH ST; 206/524-7736
5910 PHINNEY AVE N; 206/783-9755
Santa Fe's New Mexican menu provides a welcome respite from the Tex-Mex and Jalisco-centered Mexican food that pervades the Seattle area. These sibling cafes serve beautifully conceived, though simple, chile-based fare. Start with the silky garlic custard or the creamy artichoke ramekin and marry that with a red-chile beer (Full Sail Amber Ale spiked with chile peppers). Then move on to lip-smacking entrees running the gamut from pork tamales to spicy enchiladas to chicken-filled crepes—all sauced memorably. If your meal doesn't come with posole—flavorful

Southwestern hominy—ask for some on the side. Desserts include such standouts as banana flan, tequila sherbet, and bread pudding. *$$; AE, MC, V; local checks only; lunch Tues–Fri (65th St), lunch Sat–Sun (Phinney Ave), dinner every day; full bar; reservations recommended; map:EE6; map:EE7 &*

Sazerac / ★★★

1101 4TH AVE; 206/624-7755
The Mardi Gras mood at Sazerac, chef Jan Birnbaum's tribute to his Louisiana homeland, encourages excess. There's something about those dizzy chandeliers, the bright colors, the plush purple booths, and the lavish cocktails that renders you defenseless. The menu entices shamelessly. Appetizers truly tease: two grilled scallops bedded on shaved fennel and radish under a pesto drizzle leave you begging for more. Entrees such as the big, bold, tomato-sauced pork porterhouse cuddling up to "soft and sexy" grits, or tuna in a seductive shellfish broth redolent of lemon and thyme, leave no hope for restraint. You'll enjoy too much the jolt of sherry-laced cayenne mayonnaise over a shapely crab-and-rock-shrimp cake, not to mention the musky aroma of warm raclette oozing around a thick, savory sausage. And if you think that's tempting, wait until you hit the gooey chocolate pudding cake flaunting its pitcher of cream. The only problem with Sazerac is that you get full long before you want to stop eating. *$$$; AE, DC, DIS, MC, V; no checks; breakfast, lunch, dinner every day; full bar; reservations recommended (required for dinner Thurs–Sat); map:K6 &*

Sea Garden / ★★
Sea Garden of Bellevue / ★★

509 7TH AVE S; 206/623-2100
200 106TH AVE NE, BELLEVUE; 425/450-8833
The name says it all: the best efforts are put into anything that comes from the sea—particularly if it has spent its last minutes in the live tank up front. Neither of these places is anything fancy, but we've always been enamored of Sea Garden's ability to keep such consistently excellent seafood so reasonably priced. Expect subtle Cantonese fare, the tamely spiced stuff we all enjoyed before we developed our culinary crush on fiery Sichuan or Hunan food. Choose lobster or crab and they'll bring it snapping mad in a bucket to your table for inspection. Minutes later it arrives, perfectly turned out, chopped into tender pieces and served with a consistently finger-lickin'-good black bean sauce, or a refreshing ginger and green onion sauce. Big, succulent sea scallops populate a plate with honey-glazed walnuts. Naturally sweet spot prawns burst with flavor. The extensive menu offers plenty of vegetarian options, plus exotics like jellyfish, sea cucumber, or fish maw. Larger

parties fill the somewhat dreary upstairs room. Open late every day.

In 1994 Sea Garden moved east in a big way. Rather than settling into used digs—as do many of the Seattle eateries branching into Bellevue and the Eastside—the owners, an extended family, built from the ground up. It's not a grand place, but it is smart and bright. Service at both restaurants ranges from adequate to exasperating. *$/$$; AE, DC, MC, V; no checks; lunch, dinner every day; full bar; reservations accepted (large parties only); www.chinesecuisine.com; map:R6; map:HH3* ♿

Seattle Catch Seafood Bistro / ★★☆

460 N 36TH ST; 206/632-6110
The massive, mirror-backed, 1920s-era mahogany bar, decorative stained glass, ornate wrought-iron table legs, and glass chandeliers conspire to set a stylish tone—despite the bare tile floors and wood tabletops at this Fremont eatery specializing in seafood with a Sicilian soul. Five kinds of fish usually anchor the daily fresh sheet, each one grilled to perfection with little more than a brush of olive oil, pepper, and herbs. Pastas are often served still sizzling in the skillet; among them is a huge and satisfying linguine fra diavola (crab, calamari, shrimp, scallops, mussels, and clams in a robustly seasoned tomato sauce). Braised greens are deftly handled; they may turn up alongside sautéed scampi or next to crunchy, garlic-and-herb-flecked risotto cakes. The gently priced wine list is a work in progress; a number of glass pours are available. A handful of beers is available on tap. *$$; MC, V; checks OK; lunch Mon–Fri, dinner every day, brunch Sun; beer and wine; reservations accepted (large parties only); jlevine@aa.net; www.aa.net/seattlecatch; map:FF8* ♿

Serafina / ★★

2043 EASTLAKE AVE E; 206/323-0807
Perhaps it's the low dark ceiling. Perhaps it's the predominantly black-clad crowd. Perhaps it's the little stage from which a revolving lineup of musicians offers up Afro-Cuban, Latin, and jazz. Perhaps it's the low-key, relaxed staff who run Serafina like a collective of friends. Whatever the chemistry, this romantic, candlelit, slightly ramshackle bistro feels like a Greenwich Village spot. As it's owned by two ex–New Yorkers, that's no coincidence. The rustic Italian-accented menu eschews slick. And if you have to wait for your meal, that just means it'll come piping hot direct from the stove. No one objects to the delay, as everyone's mellowed out over glasses of red while achieving various stages of intimacy. Though the menu changes three times yearly, you can usually count on excellent grilled lamb chops. Full-flavored pastas come in generous portions. Serafina fills and refills, as couples drop by for late coffee and dessert to stretch out their evening of conversation and handholding. *$$; MC, V; checks OK; lunch Mon–Fri, dinner every day; full bar; reservations recommended; map:GG7* ♿

Shallots Asian Bistro / ★★☆

2525 4TH AVE; 206/728-1888

Among the town's pan-Asian options, none are so likable as this intimate bistro. Dark wood booths, elaborately folded napkins, tasteful Asian art, and a shrub-lined patio compose an ambience so agreeable it's worth the journey to the edge of Belltown's sizzling scene. Happily, the food rises to the occasion. It's mostly Chinese, with an intriguing mix of Thai, Vietnamese, Cambodian, Japanese, and Korean dishes adding allure; everything arrives precisely cooked in generous, well-priced portions. Satays and satay roll appetizers, for example, come as meal-size portions along with a tiny, fragrant bowl of rice and a miniature salad. Lunch choices include a Pacific platter of wok-seared seafood and fresh vegetables in a rich, garlicky sauce. If you're timid, order Sichuan garlic pork. But why not try rock-candy-gingered rabbit, or French Cambodian New York Steak salad, or anything simmered in a *lu* pot? *$$; DC, DIS, MC, V; checks OK; lunch, dinner every day; beer and wine; reservations recommended; map:E7* &

Shamiana / ★★

10724 NE 68TH ST, KIRKLAND; 425/827-4902

Not strictly an Indian restaurant, Shamiana counts among its influences Bangladesh, Kenya, and Pakistan. Thence its "India and Beyond" subtitle, which mirrors the childhood experiences of the owners, a brother-sister team, Tracy and Eric Larson, who spent their youth as foreign service kids. Now they recreate the experience for diners from Kirkland and beyond. Vegetarians fare well here with choices aplenty, and the menu marks dishes made sans dairy products. The spicing in various curries and other entrees is bold, and if you order hot, you'd better be prepared for hot. A fine meal can be made simply of bread and soup: heavenly naan, especially the garlic variety with its brush of garlic-coriander butter and dipping sauce of orangish, cumin-flavored raita; and out-of-this-world mulligatawny—a warmly spiced, rich red brew with chicken and lentils. Desserts deserve mention, especially a cool mango yogurt mousse topped with a golden crown of mango purée. The lunch buffet special rates "best buy" in what has become a veritable Kirkland institution. *$; AE, DC, MC, V; checks OK; lunch Mon–Fri, dinner every day; beer and wine; reservations accepted; map:EE3* &

Shanghai Garden / ★★☆
Shanghai Café / ★★☆

524 6TH AVE S (AND BRANCH); 206/625-1689
12708 SE 38TH ST, BELLEVUE; 425/603-1689

Shanghai Garden owner/chef Hua Te Su caters to a largely Chinese clientele in this very pink restaurant in the International District. Mr. Su (as he is respectfully known) attracts diners from every Chinese province with regional dishes that change seasonally. The vast menu is filled with exotica such as black-moss-and-bamboo-fungus soup, sautéed hog maw, and fish-head casserole. Come prepared to be wowed by anything made with pea vines or with the chef's special hand-shaved noodles. The vivid tendrils of the sugar pea plant resemble sautéed spinach, and you'd never imagine they'd cook up this tender and clean-tasting, especially when paired with plump shrimp. The noodles, shaved off a block of dough (either rice, corn, or barley green), are the main ingredient in a dozen different dishes. Try them in what we're sure will be the best chow mein you'll ever eat. This might be the only Chinese restaurant in town where desserts should not be missed. Shanghai Garden has a second branch in Issaquah (80 Front St N; 425/313-3188), where Su's menu has attracted its own local following. And there's a smaller (yet still pink) version in the Factoria area of Bellevue, under the direction of Su's brother, Ping Fu Su. We are witnessing the creation of an empire based on the hand-shaved noodle. *$; MC, V; no checks; lunch Mon–Fri, dinner every day (Seattle and Issaquah), lunch, dinner every day (Bellevue); beer and wine (Seattle and Bellevue), full bar (Issaquah); reservations accepted; map:R7; map:JJ2*

Shiro's / ★★★

2401 2ND AVE; 206/443-9844

Seattle's best-known sushi chef, Shiro Kashiba, sold his legendary Nikko restaurant after 20 years, moved it to fancy digs in the Westin Hotel, presided there for a year, then retired. Briefly. In 1995, to the delight of legions of fans, he opened Shiro's. Graced with a blond hardwood sushi bar, linen-draped tables, and the presence of the master, this immaculate, simply decorated Belltown storefront was an immediate hit. Though the small menu offers full-course dinner entrees as well (tempura, sukiyaki, and teriyaki with accompanying rice, salad, and miso soup), it's the sushi that commands full sensual attention: this is the most lustrously gleaming fish you'll see in this town, and you'd do best to heed the call. *$$$; AE, MC, V; no checks; dinner every day; full bar; reservations recommended; map:F8* ♿

Shuckers / ★★

411 UNIVERSITY ST (FOUR SEASONS OLYMPIC HOTEL); 206/621-1984
There's an oddly mixed clientele at masculine, high-ceilinged yet intimate Shuckers: power-lunching suits, families from the hotel eating with their kids, and people dining blissfully alone. The helpful staff caters to all, with swift, businesslike service for the first; crayons, orange juice, and a plate of maraschino cherries for the second; and a friendly word and plenty of attention for solos. Shuckers celebrates seafood, from a broad selection of oysters on the half shell—or perfectly fried—to salmon to whatever else is fresh. If you like fish grilled rare, tell them, and it will be so. For value, turn your attention to chalkboard specials like pan-fried Arctic char wrapped in cornmeal. Otherwise the expense-account prices are extortionate. Those bumpy muffins in the bread basket are Irish soda bread, and they're addictive, especially with one of the chowders. Crème brûlée here boasts a stellar reputation. *$$–$$$; AE, DC, DIS, JCB, MC, V; no checks; lunch Mon–Sat, dinner every day; full bar; reservations recommended; map:L6* &

Si Señor / ★★☆

2115 BELLEVUE-REDMOND RD, REDMOND; 425/865-8938
The cuisines of Peru and the northeastern Mexican city of Monterrey influence much of the originality on this menu. Though you can order the usual south-of-the-border standbys, why miss out on the exotica? *Lomo de almendra* is marinated pork loin in a deliciously dark and almond-flavored sauce; seco, a Peruvian lamb or beef dish, comes sauced with a blend of cilantro and onions. Devilishly hot and spicy *camarones a la diabla* are prawns sautéed with mushrooms in a complex, deep-red sauce. A dinner-size appetizer, *anticuchos*, will astound those frustrated by skimpy little sticks of Thai satay; here you get a platter with baked potatoes flanking skewers laden with flat slabs of tender, marinated, charred beef heart (don't balk: if you didn't know it, you'd never guess). The staff is lively and lighthearted. A mariachi band accompanies dinner on Wednesdays and Fridays. *$; AE, MC, V; checks OK; lunch, dinner every day; full bar; reservations accepted; map:EE1* &

Siam on Broadway / ★★☆
Siam on Lake Union / ★

616 BROADWAY E; 206/324-0892
1880 FAIRVIEW AVE E; 206/323-8101
Among Seattle's multitude of Thai restaurants, tiny Siam on Broadway wins the popularity contest, hands down. Working the woks and burners in a tiny open kitchen fronted by counter seating, a quartet of women move with utmost grace, portioning meats and vegetables, dipping into salty potions. They produce, among other flavorful dishes, what might be the city's best *tom kah gai*—the chicken soup spicy with chiles, sour

with lemongrass, and soothed with coconut milk. The menu doesn't stray far from the Bangkok standards, but the dishes created by the deft hands in the kitchen are distinctive. Sit at the counter and enjoy the show or wait for one of only 15 tables in the back.

You won't have to wait at Siam on Lake Union, a newer, larger outpost. Nor will you have to search for a parking space (they've got a private lot). Though good, the food here doesn't quite live up to its Broadway sibling's. *$; AE, DC, MC, V; checks OK; lunch Mon–Fri, dinner every day; beer and wine (Broadway), full bar (Lake Union); reservations accepted; map:GG7*

Sisters European Snacks / ★

1530 POST ALLEY (PIKE PLACE MARKET); 206/623-6723

Show up early in the morning for an egg sandwich or a German pastry and you'll see sisters Aruna, Mariam, and Nirala Jacobi chopping, stirring, and simmering ingredients in preparation for what will inevitably be a busy day. Their colorful shop, with a counter facing out on busy Post Alley, occupies what may be the brightest corner of Pike Place Market. It's a very pretty, very girly place, with the amiable siblings chattering back and forth in their native German and legions of lunchers arriving for sandwiches and for soups that originate from all over the globe— from silky African peanut to Hungarian mushroom to exotic Indian dal. The Jacobis create focaccia sandwiches with such ingredients as Roma tomatoes, baked eggplant, Black Forest ham, and assorted cheeses (fontina, feta, mozzarella, and cream cheese). After stuffing, the focaccia is grilled to crisp, melting perfection and served with a small salad. *$; no credit cards; local checks only; breakfast, lunch every day; no alcohol; reservations not accepted; map:J8*

Six Degrees / ★★☆

7900 E GREEN LAKE DR N; 206/523-1600

Standing-room-only-boisterous at night, cheerful and subdued at lunch, Six Degrees achieves the owners' lofty goals of reinventing the British pub and the American tavern. They wanted natural light, bright colors, entertaining and flavorful food, and a buoyant, welcoming attitude. And they got it all—plus an upstairs art gallery. When locally renowned chef Emily Moore arrived a year after opening and began tweaking the fare, they also got just the creative, no-holds-barred approach they needed. Not everything works ideally. But with wild boar ribs; thick onion rings (served on a peg); a smoky pork-loin sandwich with caramelized onion, melted fontina, and sweet-hot cherry sauce; crisp shrimp cakes with mustard sauce; and rotisserie chicken glazed with honey mustard—well, who'd be churlish enough to complain? *$$; AE, DC, DIS, MC, V; local checks only; lunch, dinner every day; beer and wine; reservations not accepted; map:EE7* &

A LITTLE ROMANCE

There's no disputing that Seattle is a romantic city, from its lush landscapes and moody, unpredictable weather to its cozy coffeehouses and charming cafes. For lovers who find their sense of amour heightened and honed by a fine meal, a spectacular view, or both, the city has no shortage of romantic locales in which to do some serious wooing—or maybe even pop the question, if they're so inclined. Below is a sampling of places that have the proven power to put us in the mood for love:

Andaluca Ensconced at street level below downtown's Mayflower Park Hotel, this intimate eatery, with its burnished wood booths and warm, sophisticated decor, offers bold, Mediterranean-inspired cuisine that fairly bursts with passionate flavor. The heavenly desserts will send you floating off in a haze of delight.

Chez Shea Fans of this dining room tucked high above the Pike Place Market swear it's the most romantic spot in the city. And indeed, it's hard to imagine a more quintessentially Seattle scene than a white linen–clad table for two near an open clerestory window, with the salt breeze wafting in and a view of ferries slicing through Elliott Bay.

On a Ferry Whether you're returning from an afternoon of exploring Bainbridge Island or a multiday trip to the Olympic Peninsula via Bremerton, the most thrilling part of the journey home is approaching Elliott Bay at sunset or at dusk. Nothing is more romantic than standing at the rail of the ferry's outdoor deck, wrapped in each other's arms for warmth (or just because), watching the city skyline, sparkling as if set with jewels, move ever closer as the deepening purple of the sky is reflected in the water below. If there's a moon, you'll swoon.

Avenue One Perhaps as close to Paris as Seattle is apt to get, this bistro offers year-round romance, including a sidewalk cafe in balmy weather and dining in cozy warmth around a roaring fireplace in winter. Traditional, simply prepared French specialties dominate the menu, and the views of Elliott Bay from the back of the dining room are bound to inspire hand-holding, if not impromptu smooching.

Mona's Occupying a low-slung storefront in an unassuming Green Lake neighborhood, Mona's is at the top of the list for many couples celebrating special occasions—or those seeking to create them. Weekend jazz beckons diners into the lounge for a nightcap and a bit of tantalizing, postprandial flirting.

Bandoleone If spice is an apt metaphor for sexual excitement, Bandoleone serves up a tempting recipe for romance. Sip a margarita and snack on traditional Latin American dishes such as empanadas and posole, all of which pack a pepper-infused heat that will bring roses to your cheeks and passion to your mind. Grab a table on the deck in warm weather for a truly langorous tropical feeling.

Space Needle Restaurant Cliché it may be, but for couples in the advanced throes of ardor, the Space Needle has proven to be the setting of more declarations, promises, and proposals than most of us would guess. Maybe it's the altitude, the unbeatable views, or the effect of the restaurant's low-speed revolutions on those already made dizzy by love . . .

Campagne Fans of country-French style love Campagne for its welcoming, white-linen atmosphere and its courtyard setting that seems miles away from the nearby bustle of Pike Place Market. Linger for hours here over the heavenly cassoulet, smoked seafood dishes, and authentic steak and pommes frites. Secure a tiny table in the quiet bar for the utmost in romance; you can order from the dining menu here as well.

Snoqualmie Falls The rush of the water, the pounding of the falls, the light touch of spray on your face—what could be more romantic? Only a weekend at the Salish Lodge, where you'll feast on fabulous meals, be pampered in the luxurious spa, and be near the falls the entire time. (The lodge claims to hosts some 400–500 honeymoons a year, not to mention more than 1,500 anniversary celebrations, 70-plus weddings, and—if hotel press releases are to be believed—40 marriage proposals every Valentine's Day.)

Marco's Supperclub Anything goes at Marco's, the destination of choice for hip-and-trendy singles and couples looking for a satisfying meal in an atmosphere that exemplifies casual, freewheeling romance: no cares, no worries, just good food and excellent company. Everyone's so intent on their own scene, no one's apt to notice a stolen kiss or two across the table.

Washington Park Arboretum You can get lost in the 200 acres of this sprawling public park. Plan for a picnic, stroll along Azalea Way, or duck into the Japanese Garden.

— Jo Brown

The Slip / ★★☆

80 KIRKLAND DR, KIRKLAND; 425/739-0033

 The name refers to the Kirkland Marina, just a few paces away; and this is truly just a slip of a place, bragging of being the smallest full-service restaurant in Washington. When it's nice enough to dine on the patio, though, there's room for more than your average basketball team. Out there you can fire up one of the Slip's fine cigars and sip a choice single-malt or sour mash. Creative burgers include a homemade veggie version chock-full of mushrooms and bulgur. The Kirkland shrimp burger, our favorite, gets swabbed with a wasabe-touched mayo—as do fingers, plate, napkin, and so on, since it inevitably falls apart on the first bite. Ditto the veggie burger. Black bean chili never tasted so good, thanks to fresh salsa, yes, but thanks even more to a dose of Jack Daniels. Creole prawns make their own fat statement—first-rate finger food. And the fries get roasted, not fried, so you can toast your health as you dip fist-fuls into the Slip's own smoky, spicy ketchup. *$; AE, DC, DIS, MC, V; local checks only; lunch, dinner every day, breakfast Sat–Sun in summer; full bar; reservations not accepted; map:EE3* &

Snappy Dragon / ★★☆

8917 ROOSEVELT WAY NE; 206/528-5575

Judy Fu is a one-woman Chinese noodle factory and wokmeister extra-ordinaire whose quiet, competent elegance pervades the kitchen at this quaint North End house-turned-restaurant. Fu cooked professionally for others for over 25 years before opening her own restaurant in 1993; diners who frequented Panda's before it became Pandasia will remember her as the stately flour-smudged head chef, ever rolling out handmade noodles in the open kitchen. Here, with the help of her son and daughter-in-law—who manage the phone, the floor, and a line of cooks, and help her keep pace with a busy take-out and delivery trade—Fu turns out those famous homemade noodles, rolled and cooked to order; a sampling of authentic clay hot pots; well-executed versions of the standard wokked-up chicken, pork, beef, and vegetable dishes; and some of the city's finest mu-shu. Outstanding appetizers include *jiao-zi* (boiled meat-filled dumplings with a fragrant dipping sauce) and a delicate green-onion pancake (think Chinese focaccia). Big bowls of comforting soups star Fu's thick, tender noodles. *$; AE, DC, MC, V; local checks only; lunch Mon–Sat, dinner every day; full bar; reservations accepted (large parties only); map:DD7* &

Sostanza Trattoria / ★★★

1927 43RD AVE E; 206/324-9701

Lorenzo Cianciusi is the latest in a succession of talented chef/proprietors (Dominique Place and Erin Rosella preceded him) to make the farthest end of Madison Park's tony commercial strip a prime dining destination. Except for the addition upstairs of a full bar and skylighted dining room that opens onto a flower-rimmed balcony with a peekaboo view of Lake Washington, Sostanza Trattoria looks much as it did when it was simply called Sostanza—Tuscan yellow walls, exposed wood beams, and big brick fireplace. Cianciusi presents Northern Italian specialties with simple, straightforward flair. In dishes such as fresh pappardelle tossed with veal and portobellos in a barolo cream sauce, pancetta-wrapped quail bathed in Chianti demiglace, woodsy wild mushroom risotto sweetened with marsala, and rustic Tuscan bean soup, Lorenzo comes close to magnificent. Distinctive Italian bottlings join a smattering of domestic favorites on the limited but well-chosen wine list. *$$; AE, MC, V; checks OK; dinner Mon–Sat; full bar; reservations recommended; map:GG6* &

Spazzo Mediterranean Grill / ★★

10655 NE 4TH ST, BELLEVUE; 425/454-8255

It's a sign of our age that downtown Bellevue's rustic Mediterranean restaurant resides atop a tower of steel and glass. But then, Spazzo's not really that rustic. A showy part of the Schwartz Brothers empire, it exudes a certain sophistication, a lot of polish. It draws a mixed crowd, including singles in the bar and dates in the dining room. The menu supposedly draws from wherever in the Mediterranean the olive tree grows—from Turkey to Portugal. A local pioneer in popularizing tapas, Spazzo kicks out 30 or more varieties of these little appetizer plates, meant to be shared. Order a couple, order a couple more, and so on until you're full. More traditional dining is available as well, with pastas, stews, and a few other entrees. The quality can vary widely—delicious baked goat cheese for spreading on bread, dreary fried cauliflower unhappy with its mint, cinnamon, and tahini. In general, though, the place looks great, with loopy light fixtures and Matisse-inspired murals, and the dining experience is fun—which translates in Greek to "spasso." *$$$; AE, DIS, DC, MC, V; checks OK; lunch Mon–Fri, dinner every day; full bar; reservations recommended; map:HH3* ⅋

Still Life in Fremont Coffeehouse / ★

705 N 35TH ST; 206/547-9850

Fremont's favorite coffeehouse is a Seattle classic: a big, steamy space with a wall of windows, mismatched tables and chairs, a big '40s radio, and Dick Powell and June Allyson's old coffee table. Add good art and—remember these?—good vibes. Still Life smacks of the '60s, when hanging out required only a good book and a bowl of soup. Indeed, the soups are stunning: thick purée of curried split pea and sweet potato, or perhaps parsnip and celery root. The short sandwich menu is now overshadowed by the growing list of specials: wild-rice salad studded with smoked turkey, veggies, and hazelnuts; a hefty polenta square topped with tomato, red pepper, olives, and pepper Jack; an artichoke pie. Or sip a coffee or a cup of chai and nosh on a sweet. Service is your own. *$; no credit cards; local checks only; breakfast, lunch, dinner every day; beer and wine; reservations not accepted; map:FF7* ⅋

Streamliner Diner / ★

397 WINSLOW WAY, BAINBRIDGE ISLAND; 206/842-8595

First pit stop up from the ferry dock, this crowded little diner changes owners about every three years. Locals don't seem to mind. They sit around swilling coffee (no espresso here!) for hours on end, chasing morning into afternoon. Do these people have jobs? How can they afford their expensive sneakers? However they pull it off, the lackadaisical vibes generated by relaxed islanders make the Streamliner a ferry-ride destination for mainlanders. The grub mostly remains within diner boundaries, with a few effete touches like tofu scramble, quiche, and Cajun mayo on the meat loaf sandwich. The signature dish, potatoes deluxe, rises above kitchen-sink cooking through the inclusion of fresh spinach. The fried-egg-and-bacon sandwich earns local renown. Don't miss a big slice of fruit pie baked by a local woman. But resist the "Warm-'er-up?" temptation; nuking this flaky crust into a soggy mass ought to be a gross misdemeanor. *$; no credit cards; checks OK; breakfast every day, lunch Mon–Sat; no alcohol; reservations not accepted &*

Swingside Cafe / ★★

4212 FREMONT AVE N; 206/633-4057

After a brief closure for repairs and remodeling, the little Swingside Cafe reopened with higher ceilings and an improved kitchen, but the same cozy, intimate appeal. Owner/chef Brad Inserra (he's the guy working his buns off in the absurdly small kitchen) produces a world of big flavors and an always inventive menu. The hearty stews, sautés, and pasta dishes of his Pittsburgh-Sicilian provenance are spiced with unpredictable North African, Creole, and nouvelle-American accents. The brown Moroccan tamarind sauce melts in the mouth; tangy seafood dishes sing of the sea. Everything's rich, delicious, and amply portioned; don't overorder or you may have to be carried home. Desserts are a sometime thing, depending on who's supplying. As for atmosphere, you've probably forgotten eating out could be as simple, casual, and friendly as this. *$$; MC, V; local checks only; lunch Tues–Sat, dinner Tues–Sun, brunch Sun; beer and wine; reservations accepted (large parties only); map:FF8* &

Szmania's / ★★★

3321 W MCGRAW ST; 206/284-7305

It's worth wending your way into the heart of Magnolia to eat at Szmania's. Ludger and Julie Szmania (pronounced "Smahn-ya") opened their comfortably modern restaurant in 1990, and now it's one of the city's most sought-out dining spots. Remodeled to stunning effect in 1997, its coolly elegant decor is the equal of anything downtown. Twelve seats rim the open kitchen where German-born Ludger puts a continental gloss on Northwest ingredients to create such wide-ranging dishes as Jaegerschnitzel with spaetzle and horseradish-brushed mahi-mahi in lobster-and-shiitake sauce. Servings are generous, and the Szmanias know it; many entrees are offered in half portions. Expect strong flavors that work well together—such as New York steak in peppercorn sauce with balsamic onions and a goat cheese–potato pancake—and occasionally some that don't, like a salty and overpowering kasu Chilean sea bass in a soy and ginger vinaigrette. Take note of the loveliest array of vegetables ever to garnish a plate and of the succulent house-smoked seafood. For dessert, look no further than the saffron-banana semifreddo gateau in a puddle of caramelized banana-rum sauce for a sweet and satisfying finale. *$$; AE, DC, MC, V; local checks only; lunch Tues–Sat (closed for lunch in summer), dinner Tues–Sun; full bar; reservations recommended; map:FF8* &

Tandoor / ★★

5024 UNIVERSITY WAY NE; 206/523-7477

A small storefront with a shadowed back room of exceptional neatness and gentle, gracious service, Tandoor serves mostly Northern Indian fare, with an emphasis on tandoori-style cooking. But avoid that—with the exception of the tandoor-baked breads like naan and paratha. Marinating fish, fowl, and meat for long periods and then cooking them at high temperature invariably results in drying them out or ruining their texture. Select from the vegetarian menu or from among the many non-tandoori choices. Bhuna lamb, for example, marries tomatoes, mushrooms, onions, ginger, garlic, yogurt, and a host of those mysterious "Indian spices" into a savory union. Eggplant bharta typifies the Indian vegetarian artistry. Eggplant is roasted, mashed, then sautéed with onions—it's like a dish from a fantasy Thanksgiving dinner. Or journey south for any of a number of dishes that include coconut milk. Finish with an authentic Indian dessert, despite the temptation of mango ice cream. *$$; AE, DIS, MC, V; local checks only; lunch, dinner every day; beer and wine; reservations accepted; map:FF6* &

Taqueria Guaymas / ★☆

1622 SW ROXBURY ST (AND BRANCHES); 206/767-4026

Ethnic oases often seem to be found near gritty industrial centers. This one's in White Center, south of Harbor Island's once-thriving steel and flour mills—a 15-minute drive from downtown, but a world away from the city's less authentic yupperias. The fare here is as simple and working class as the decor: a small lunch counter and picnic tables for those who aren't ordering to go; a fridge full of beer; and a television blaring Spanish soap operas. Tacos, burritos, and other reliables come jazzed up with options like tongue, tripe, or brains, or with the usual chicken, beef, and pork for the less adventuresome. Huge prawns are featured in dishes such as *coctel de camarones*, a spicy, gazpacho-style blend of prawns, avocado, tomatoes, and cilantro; or in platters of *camarones al mojo de ajo*, where the wondrous crustaceans swim in melted butter and chopped garlic (order by the half-pound). On weekends, try the hangover special, *menudo* (tripe soup). Sample the daily thirst-quenchers ladled from big glass jugs: melon juice, rice water, or a tamarind drink. A trio of outposts can be found in West Seattle, Lynnwood, and Renton—but this one is the real McCoy. In addition, two slightly more upscale, quick-service siblings of Taqueria Guaymas are at Green Lake and on south Capitol Hill (in the

QFC), under the name Tacos Guaymas. *$; no credit cards; checks OK; lunch, dinner every day; beer only; reservations not accepted; map:LL8* &

Thai Ginger / ★★

3717 128TH AVE SE, BELLEVUE; 425/641-4008

16480 NE 74TH ST (REDMOND TOWN CENTER), REDMOND; 425/558-4044

On finishing the namesake entree at this little charmer wedged in the heart of that vast morass known as Factoria, you'll likely say, "Man, that was a lot of ginger!"—but it's good. Considerable energy went into converting a former sub sandwich shop into a cozy, comfortable place where rattan-frame, "leather"-clad cushioned chairs invite lingering. So too does the kitchen counter, where books on Thailand compete for your attention with the chattering conclave of cooks, kicking out simply wonderful dishes practically before they are ordered. That means if you want pacing, you must order incrementally. Choice bites include good old red curry with its orange/vermilion coconut sauce sopped up by forkfuls of fragrant jasmine rice, and cashew chicken with a chile paste–spiked sauce that adds wonderful piquancy to the veggie/nut/chicken sauté. *Tod mun* fish cakes can be marred by excess grease, and a pedestrian peanut sauce does not complement the excellent satay sticks. But black rice pudding will end any meal on a sweet note. A branch recently opened in Redmond Town Center. *$; DIS, MC, V; checks OK; lunch, dinner every day; beer and wine; reservations accepted (large parties only); map:II2; map:EE1* &

Thai Thai / ★★

11205 16TH AVE SW; 206/246-2246

Right smack-dab in the middle of no-man's land—between White Center and Burien—stands the whitewashed building of Thai Thai. This popular restaurant has been holding forth for more than a decade, serving the same great food at amazing prices. The decor is perfunctory at best, but regulars come from as far away as Issaquah to treat themselves to the best phad Thai and Panang curry in the Puget Sound region. Go there more than a couple of times, and owner Sam Sudthaya will start greeting you by name. Perennial customer favorites include the intense soups, *larb gai, yum neau,* and anything made with peanut sauce (one of the few peanut sauces in town actually pounded out from scratch). Thai Thai is one of the precious few places that don't use prefab sauces and powders, and the difference is striking. Chances are you'll be overwhelmed by the 100-plus items on the menu, so choose a combination dinner, a multi-course option that's a steal at around 10 bucks a head. If you go this route, make sure you nab one of the two massive rosewood tables with matching chairs—enormous and intricately carved, these behemoths will make you feel like presiding Thai royalty. *$; MC, V; no checks; lunch Mon–Fri, dinner Mon–Sat; beer and wine; reservations accepted (large parties only); map:MM8* &

Theoz / [unrated]

1523 6TH AVE; 206/749-9660

Theoz, which opened in early 1997 in the historic Decatur Building, occupies a space notable for its graceful architectural elegance: high ceilings, a sweeping staircase, sea green walls, and a burnished wood bar. It's a sea of tranquility that belies the soap-opera goings-on below stairs. Though opening chef Emily Moore received mostly rave reviews for her eclectic "ring of fire" cuisine, she departed abruptly after less than a year. The toque was passed briefly to Michael Felsenstein, who had worked under Moore, and then to John de Boer, who decamped to open Yakima Grill (see review), run by the same team who brought you Theoz. Enter Earl Ray Hook ("just call me Joe"), who seemed determined to de-Moore-alize Theoz and give it a French twist. Hook's year and a half working at Lampreia (see review) showed in the clarity of flavors and the simplicity of many of his preparations, such as pan-seared foie gras splashed with Armagnac and drizzled with reduced balsamic vinegar or the cast-iron pot–roasted chicken with pommes frites. At press time, however, another Lampreia alum, Chet Wallenstein, has taken the helm and appears to be continuing the French theme. Don't touch that dial. *$$$; AE, DC, DIS, MC, V; local checks only; lunch Mon–Fri, dinner Mon–Sat; full bar; reservations accepted; map:J5* &

Third Floor Fish Café / ★★★

205 LAKE ST S, KIRKLAND; 425/822-3553

This upstairs beauty has evolved over the past few years into one of the region's best restaurants. One reason is general manager Doug Guiberson, a 20-year Canlis veteran who knows how to make things click. It doesn't hurt that every table in this mahogany-accented, shades-of-pastel room affords a drop-dead view west across Lake Washington. Despite the Third Floor's name, it's not strictly a fish house, and the menu includes entrees such as an impressive chicken roasted in a sweet garlic crust. But the fish is marvelous, ranging from an appetizer of big grilled prawns in an irresistible lobster sauce to charred ahi to pan-seared swordfish. Side dishes get equally expert treatment: one entree might be served with a ginger-jolted, orange-curry couscous, another with a pearly Israeli couscous redolent of apple, clove, and smoky bacon. The pastry chef, too, deserves your attention. An increasingly ambitious wine program and a lively piano bar complete the scene. *$$$; AE, DIS, DC, MC, V; local checks only; dinner every day; full bar; reservations recommended; map:EE3* &

13 Coins Restaurant / ★

125 BOREN AVE N; 206/682-2513

18000 PACIFIC HWY S; 206/243-9500

It'll take a lot more than 13 coins to pay for the privilege of sinking into one of the humongous booths or sitting in one of the high-backed leather counter seats and watching the polished short-order cooks at this three-decade-old Seattle dining institution. But who can resist the opportunity to choose from a menu so varied (with breakfast, sandwiches, pasta, fish, and meat dishes) and so perfectly dated (with eggs Benedict, fettuccine alfredo, and a complimentary antipasti plate)? Especially when it's all available any time of the day or night, every day of the week. Around-the-clock dining and ample portions have made this pair of restaurants popular for many years (helped by the fact that they occupy neighborhoods—near the *Seattle Times* building and the airport, respectively—with little competition). If you crave sweetbreads at 3am, these are the places to go. *$$; AE, DC, MC, V; checks OK; breakfast, lunch, dinner every day (all day); full bar; reservations accepted (large parties only); map:F3; map:OO6* &

Three Girls Bakery / ★

1514 PIKE PL (PIKE PLACE MARKET); 206/622-1045

Stop by any day around noon, and the crowd around Three Girls' L-shaped lunch counter will likely be three hungry locals and a couple of displaced New Yorkers deep. Sandwiches don't get a whole lot better than this, and "whole" is the operative word here, 'cause there ain't no halves, as the hardworking, wisecracking architects of meat-and-cheese will gladly tell you. There's soup—nothing fancy, but filling and hot—and a meat loaf sandwich like Mother used to make. On those depressing gray days, a trip to the Market for a bowl of spicy chili—served up by one of the most efficient counter staffs in town—will surely cure what ails you. Order bakery fixings at the take-out window—a loaf of pumpernickel or Russian rye, an apple fritter, perhaps a rugalach or three, and the best cheese croissants in the state, according to some. The restaurant closes at 5:30pm, the bakery at 6pm. *$; MC, V; local checks only; breakfast, lunch every day; reservations not accepted; no alcohol; map:J8*

Tosoni's / ★★

14320 NE 20TH ST, BELLEVUE; 425/644-1668

One of the Eastside's enduring treasures, Tosoni's is known to its many loyal regulars simply as "Walter's place." They know that the humble strip-mall exterior belies the Old World delights awaiting inside, where chef Walter Walcher and a sous chef work the open kitchen, presiding over a small booth-lined room filled with antique-looking cabinets and armoires. The menu tends toward continental (Walcher hails from Austria but feels more kinship with Northern Italy). Meat eaters have kept the garlic lamb—tender strips sautéed in olive oil, heavily garlicked, and smartly peppered— on the menu for 12 years. Meanwhile, vegetarians always have a choice option or two, often constructed around various wild fungi, a Walcher favorite. It's sort of like sitting in an old friend's dining room with a view to the kitchen, where one can watch the chef arrange bounty plate by plate, even if the garlic mashed spuds arrive at the table tepid. *$$$; AE, MC, V; checks OK; dinner Tues–Sat; beer and wine; reservations recommended; map:GG2* &

Trattoria Mitchelli / ★

84 YESLER WAY; 206/623-3885

Good enough, they say, is never good enough. Well, guess what, they're wrong again. Dany Mitchell has earnestly built himself an empire of restaurants that serve good-enough Italian food: Angelina's Trattoria in West Seattle and Stella's Trattoria in the University District. Mitchell alone has provided Seattle with places where you can host a lively impromptu party in the bar or restaurant at almost any time of night (a late-night menu is served Tuesday through Saturday till 4am). Yes, the food is usually mediocre, but that's not really the point. Think of it instead as dependable food, some of it quite good, such as the ravioli in butter and garlic, the pizzas, anything made with veal (usually fresh and tender), and breakfasts of Italian frittatas. Besides, mediocrity never had a more appealing bohemian backdrop than the original trattoria in Pioneer Square. *$; AE, DIS, MC, V; local checks only; breakfast, lunch, dinner every day; full bar; reservations accepted; map:EE8* &

Triangle Lounge / ★

3507 FREMONT PL N; 206/632-0880

Once a triangular hipster tavern, now remodeled into a triangular hipster lounge, the Triangle lies at the center of Fremont's self-styled Center of the Universe scene, a reminder of the old, raucous Fremont that is fast disappearing as prosperity brings prettification to the no-longer-isolated district. The triangular dining room, decorated by conspicuously three-sided artwork, still opens onto a narrow, festively lit patio in the shape of . . . a triangle. At the opposite end is the lounge. A long bar dominates, along with a neon sign proclaiming "Prescriptions." Service is flaky (OK, hung over). But the food isn't bad. Charbroiled lamb burgers, grilled-chicken-and-hummus pitas, pastas, and pizzas all come out better than the setting would suggest. *$; AE, MC, V; no checks; lunch, dinner every day; full bar; reservations not accepted; map:FF8*

Tulio / ★★★

1100 5TH AVE (HOTEL VINTAGE PARK); 206/624-5500

Tulio's neighborhood Italian charm belies its busy downtown hotel location. Downstairs, where most of the action takes place, white-draped tables are packed in tightly, the sweet scent of roasted garlic hangs in the air, and a wood-burning oven and an open kitchen make the ever-lively room even livelier. An upstairs dining room allows space for larger parties. Service is swift, knowledgeable, and attentive, and with chef Walter Pisano in charge, your meal is always in good hands. His bruschetta mista (a mix of breads, marinated mushrooms, goat cheese, tapenade, and tomatoes tossed with pine nuts and currants) and the calamari fritti (enough spicy fried squid to feed a navy) will start things off right. The artful and very fresh *primi* (first courses), such as the smoked-salmon ravioli tart with a lemon cream sauce, pique the palate. Roasted and grilled cuts of meat and fish round out the dinner menu, while thin-crust pizzas and cheesy calzones add a casual note to the lunch offerings. Breakfast is a welcome respite from typical hotel fare. *$$; AE, DC, MC, V; local checks only; breakfast, lunch, dinner every day; full bar; reservations recommended; map:L6* &

22 Fountain Court / ★★

22 103RD AVE NE, BELLEVUE; 425/451-0426

The former Azaleas Fountain Court, long a favorite of the romantic and the expense-account blessed, has undergone a change of ownership, a change of direction (now upward), and a change of name. Inside the converted clapboard house, three distinct dining rooms boast tasteful, comfortable decor. Outside, the fountain court in back beckons, a delightful, private respite from the clamor and clank of downtown Bellevue. Another, smaller fountain in front gurgles near a couple of lawn tables. Salads soar, beautifully dressed, while the kitchen kicks out a perfect mango salsa—a little chile, a little cilantro to bring out the best of a fillet of wild king salmon. Huge scallops, when available, come seared on the outside, succulent inside. Meats meet the needs of carnivore business folk at power dinners—a well-sauced beef fillet and juicy prime rib. The wine list is not extensive but offers a number of choices in the $20s as well as some higher-priced vintages. *$$$; AE, MC, V; local checks only; lunch Mon–Fri, dinner Mon–Sat; full bar; reservations recommended; map:HH3* &

Two Bells Tavern / ★★☆

2313 4TH AVE; 206/441-3050

Belltown's starving artists tried not to tell anyone about the excellent, cheap burgers on sourdough at the funky Two Bells, but word got out and now the tavern is packed all the time with an eclectic crowd joining in common worship of the burger. It's big and juicy, smothered in onions and cheese, served on a sourdough roll with your choice of sides, including a rich, chunky potato salad. Another favorite with the Bells gang is the hot beer-sausage sandwich. Satisfying isn't the half of it—this food is so full of flavor and freshness and goes so well with the beer that you don't care about getting mustard all over your face. Food is served till 10pm (11pm on weekends), but the tavern stays open till 2am. *$; AE, DIS, MC, V; no checks; lunch, dinner every day; beer and wine; reservations accepted (large parties only); map:G7* &

Union Bay Cafe / ★★☆

3515 NE 45TH ST; 206/527-8364
In this softly lit Laurelhurst storefront, folks are as likely to be celebrating a birthday or an anniversary as stopping in for a relaxing dinner after a hard day's work. Chef/owner Mark Manley often leaves his kitchen to welcome guests and discuss dishes. His ever-changing menu is small and perceptively conceived; performance never wavers. Keep a watchful eye for any appetizer made with mushrooms. A starter of Mediterranean mussels, scented with basil and ginger and smoothed with a touch of cream, proves that while his menu leans toward Italian, Manley can do Asian, too. Meats are handled with particular care, as evidenced by slices of venison sauced with chanterelles and huckleberries. Fresh fish and seasonal produce are well respected, and you'll find vegetarian options at every meal. A reasonable wine list offers first-rate choices by the glass. For dessert—anything, from the bread pudding to a crisp made with apples and bourbon-soaked cherries. The bill is the final pleasure. A small courtyard allows room for outdoor seating. *$$; AE, DC, DIS, MC, V; checks OK; dinner Tues–Sun; beer and wine; reservations recommended; map:FF6* &

Union Square Grill / ★☆

621 UNION ST; 206/224-4321
The Union Square Grill has run through a lot of schticks: first a French brasserie, then a steak house, then a clubby steak house complete with the maître d' you were supposed to have known for years. Today, it's simply a dependable steak house. There is an undeniably hearty, masculine, yet somehow glitzy feel to the handsome dining room, with its dark wood, yellow light, and oversize antique advertising posters. At lunchtime the place is a sea of businessfolk, all of whom seem to be negotiating that last detail of a very important deal. The evening crowd varies, and usually includes theatergoers taking advantage of a well-executed pre-theater menu. As for the standard menu, only a curmudgeonly vegetarian could feel disappointed. Beef, in its many guises, is invariably a fine choice; the kitchen is less successful when venturing into grilled-halibut-over-wilted-spinach territory. For those nostalgic for the tableside histrionics of the '70s, a caesar salad is a must. Unrelentingly well intentioned service is sometimes less sophisticated than you'd expect. Award-winning pastry chef Laura Jeffards produces a surprisingly light cheesecake with a delicate graham cracker crust. The bar is a favorite downtown watering hole, thanks to a flashy selection of martinis and the

availability of a full menu. *$$$; AE, DC, DIS, JCB, MC, V; local checks only; lunch Mon–Fri, dinner every day; full bar; reservations recommended; map:K5* &

Waters, A Lakeside Bistro / ★★☆

1200 CARILLON POINT (WOODMARK HOTEL), KIRKLAND; 425/803-5595
An attractive room in the lower level of the Carillon Point Woodmark Hotel, looking out across an emerald lawn to Lake Washington and beyond, Waters has only treaded water the last few years, never quite living up to its potential. True, on a warm day there's nowhere on the Eastside we'd rather sit than the patio, with its beautifully crafted wooden deck furniture. But the hotel management hasn't made the same commitment to excellence as at neighboring Yarrow Bay Grill (see review). Fusion dishes can be hit or miss, such as a piece of mahi-mahi overworked with passion-fruit glaze and basil-mango relish. So we recommend sticking to more forthright fare, along with anything starring wild salmon. Can't miss with the bistro meat loaf and accompanying garlic mashed spuds and mushroom gravy (they'll give you the recipe). Excellent sandwiches and burgers can be had at lunch. *$$; AE, DC, MC, V; checks OK; breakfast, lunch every day, dinner Tues–Sat; full bar; reservations recommended; map:FF3* &

Wild Ginger Asian Restaurant and Satay Bar / ★★★

1401 3RD AVE; 206/623-4450
Wild Ginger is wildly popular. Basking in the glow of much national attention are owners Rick and Ann Yoder, whose culinary vision—inspired by time spent in Southeast Asia—has left a lasting impression on the Seattle restaurant scene. Just as the restaurants and markets of Bangkok, Singapore, Saigon, and Djakarta offer a wide range of multi-ethnic foods, so does Wild Ginger, bringing together some of the best dishes from these Southeast Asian cities. At the mahogany satay bar, order from a wide array of sizzling skewered selections: simple seared slices of sweet onion and Chinese eggplant, or tender Bangkok boar basted with coconut milk. Wherever you sit, indulge in the succulent Singapore-style stir-fried crab, fresh from live tanks and redolent of ginger and garlic; mildly hot, slightly sweet beef curry from Thailand; or *laksa*, a spicy Malaysian seafood soup whose soft, crunchy, and slippery textures and hot and salty flavors encompass everything good about Southeast Asian cookery. Great live jazz makes this the city's most happening scene on Monday nights. The Yoders recently moved the restaurant to significantly larger digs in the Mann Building (Third Avenue and Union Street), which they've been restoring for several years. *$$; AE, DC, DIS, MC, V; no checks; lunch Mon–Sat, dinner every day; full bar; reservations recommended; map:J7* &

Wildfire Ranch BBQ / ★

317 NW GILMAN BLVD, ISSAQUAH; 425/392-1334
The cook here once worked at what is now Relais, a fine French restaurant, so you can expect a tad more attention to nuances of taste. Nuances of barbecue? Well, there's a spicy carrot slaw and occasionally blue cornbread spiked with jalapeño and sun-dried tomato. Maybe the spud salad hints more of Dijon than of mayo. The spiced, roasted pumpkin seeds prove addictive (and are a bargain snack at 75 cents for a cupful). But meats are the main attraction—chewy ribs or tender bird, bulky pork, or beef brisket sandwiches you can't hold together however hard you try. If you want extra sauce, they've got it, plus a rack of hot sauces for an extra mule kick. Service could use a kick too, but in nice weather we're in no hurry. The walls literally roll up, garage-door style, so hanging out and sipping a frosty root beer becomes a pleasant diversion. And patio eating is a bit like a rural Texas picnic right in the middle of quaint Gilman Village. *$; MC, V; local checks only; lunch, dinner every day; beer and wine; reservations not accepted* &

Yakima Grill / ★★

612 STEWART ST (WESTCOAST VANCE HOTEL); 206/956-0639
Seattle's first self-styled "nuevo Latino" restaurant aspires to bring the Latin cookery of Mexico, Cuba, Spain, and South America to the cutting edge. The new dining room in the WestCoast Vance Hotel (it replaced Salute in Città) was still finding its footing in the weeks before we went to press, but our first bites were promising. A long list of hot and cold tapas leads off the menu: we liked the poblano chile stuffed with quinoa and jazzed with pickapeppa sauce, but we swooned over *ceviche verde* (buttery sea bass marinated in lime and tequila). Main courses range from portobello mushroom fajitas to rum-marinated salmon to chile-and-maple-glazed pork tenderloin. The mood is Mexican cantina: sundrenched yellow and spruce green walls, Mission-style arches, natural pine beams overhead, and terra-cotta underfoot. Sip quality tequilas and rums at the bar under a lazily spinning ceiling fan. Service feels a little inexperienced. *$$; AE, MC, V; checks OK; breakfast, lunch, dinner every day; full bar; reservations accepted; map:I5* &

Yanni's Greek Cuisine / ★★

7419 GREENWOOD AVE N; 206/783-6945
One of the brightest spots in Seattle's neighborhood ethnic dining scene is one of its best Greek restaurants. The place exudes the humble comforts of a Greek taverna. The deep-fried calamari appetizer is meal-size, with tender, perfectly fried squid and a side of pungent skordalia for dip-

ping. That and a horiatiki salad—a heaping mound of tomatoes, cucumbers, kalamata olives, peppers, romaine, and feta cheese—can make a complete dinner for two, along with good pita. The moussaka is especially good, each layer distinct, yet the whole a pillow of richly blended flavors, and we know people who swear by the spit-roasted chicken (which is also available for take-out). *$; MC, V; checks OK; dinner Mon–Sat; beer and wine; reservations recommended (weekends only); map:EE8* ⅙

Yarrow Bay Grill / ★★★
Yarrow Bay Beach Café / ★★

**1270 CARILLON POINT, KIRKLAND; 425/889-9052 (GRILL);
425/889-0303 (CAFE)**

A pair of sibling restaurants, one stacked atop the other, boast gorgeous Lake Washington views. Upstairs, the tony grill ranks in the upper echelon of Eastside dining spots, thanks to the reliable creativity of chef Vicky McCaffree and consistent management. A recent small addition and general updating make the understated, sophisticated room more attractive, while deck dining affords sweeping views westward across Lake Washington, past marina-moored boats that cost more than most houses. On the plate, McCaffree likes to assemble influences as diverse as Southwest, Northwest, Mediterranean, and Asian. An apple cider–gewürztraminer sauce covers sea-fresh scallops. Risotto flavored with lobster stock holds sea bass, salmon, and prawns. Sake and ginger flavor a salmon fillet, along with shiitake–pickled ginger butter. The grill has become a waterfront destination restaurant.

Downstairs, the Beach Café is a lively spot, rivaling neighboring Cucina! Cucina! on the scene scale. Knock a few bucks off the upstairs prices and sample a jazzed-up, rotating, United Nations menu—now Turkey, then Chile, followed by Morocco, and so on—under the direction of chef Cameon Orel, along with a stable roster of sandwiches, nibbles, and meat or fish entrees. The bar scene is clamorous, and in warm weather the fun spills out onto a lakeside patio. *$$–$$$/$$; AE, DC, DIS, MC, V; checks OK; lunch Mon–Fri, dinner every day, brunch Sun (Grill); lunch, dinner every day (Café); full bar; reservations recommended; map:FF3* ⅙

Zeek's Pizza / ★★

41 DRAVUS ST (AND BRANCHES); 206/285-6046

The original Zeek's—known for its absurd pizza toppings and too-nice-to-be-for-real staff of pizza-throwers, salad-makers, and money-takers—is tucked into an unattractive strip mall between Seattle Pacific University and the Fremont Bridge. In 1995, young pizza impresarios Doug

McClure and Tom Vial's busy pizza parlor gave rise to a second (much bigger) Zeek's on Phinney Ridge (6000 Phinney Ave N; 206/789-0089; map:EE7), and a third has now opened in Belltown (419 Denny Way; 206/448-6775; map:D7). Don't hesitate to order the Thai One On, a pizza doused with the makings of phad Thai: chunks of chicken, slivers of carrot, crunchy mung bean sprouts, and fresh cilantro atop a spicy hot peanut sauce that'd do a satay proud. Purists may lean toward the Frog Belly Green, with basil pesto, Roma tomatoes, and whole-milk mozzarella layered over a very white, slightly doughy crust with an olive oil glaze. Then there are the weird-but-wonderful Texas Leaguer (with barbecued chicken, red onion, and cilantro) and the El Nuevo Hombre (with salsa, refried beans, green peppers, and fat slices of jalapeño). Order by the slice (lunch only) or the pie, to eat in or take out. Good, huge, inexpensive salads, too. *$; MC, V; checks OK; lunch, dinner every day; beer and wine; reservations accepted; map:FF8* &

Zula / ★

916 E JOHN ST; 206/322-0852

Mixing and toasting his 14 secret spices in this homey East African restaurant just steps away from Broadway, Deabesai Yemane has created a culinary niche popular with both native Ethiopians and the Broadway set. Everything arrives on a sharing platter, to be plucked up with *injera*— the soft, sour flatbread that serves as spoon and fork. Try the spicy chicken with greens (bearing in mind that "spicy" as described on this menu does not refer to the heat quotient). This complex dish is served with lettuces and *alitcha*—a tender, tasty cabbage and potato dish. *Zegnie*—a stew featuring your choice of beef, lamb, or chicken—is one hot little number, so ask for a side of soothing homemade cottage cheese. Also good is the vegetarian platter with spicy lentils, *alitcha*, carrots, greens, and yellow split peas; everyone will appreciate the warm, accommodating service. *$; MC, V; local checks only; dinner every day; full bar; reservations accepted; map:GG6*

LODGINGS

LODGINGS

Downtown/Seattle Center

Alexis Hotel ★★★

1007 1ST AVE; 206/624-4844 OR 800/426-7033

When the Sultan of Brunei showed up in Seattle on business, this is where he stayed. And if it's good enough for one of the richest men in the world, you'll probably like it too. The Alexis is a gem carved out of a lovely turn-of-the-century building in a stylish section of downtown near the water-front. You'll be pampered here with Jacuzzis or real-wood fireplaces in some of the suites, and nicely insulated walls between rooms to ensure privacy. Request a room that faces the inner courtyard; rooms facing First Avenue can be noisy, especially if you want to open your window. A 1995 renovation turned the adjacent Arlington Suites into additional guest rooms, bringing the total number of rooms to 109, but the Alexis retains its intimate, boutique-hotel feel. We especially love the bright mix of patterns and colors in the newer rooms. For a splurge, book one of the new spa suites: the bathroom—complete with a deep Jacuzzi—is as big as some hotel rooms. Amenities include complimentary morning tea and coffee, evening wine tasting (5:30–6:30pm), a morning newspaper of your choice, shoeshines, and a guest membership in the nearby Seattle Club ($15 per day). There's a steam room that can be reserved just for you, and an Aveda spa, where you can have such treatments as massages and facials (or request an in-room massage, if you prefer). The Painted Table serves innovative Northwest cuisine (see Restaurants chapter); the Bookstore Bar is a cozy, if smoky, nook in which to enjoy a libation and a light meal (see Bars, Pubs, and Taverns in the Nightlife chapter). *$$$; AE, DC, JCB, MC, V; checks OK; www.alexishotel.com; map:L8* &

Best Western Executive Inn ★

200 TAYLOR AVE N; 206/448-9444

The lobby of this cheerful motor inn is welcoming, with a gas fireplace and rustic twig furniture. Spacious rooms are done up in mauves and teals (try for a room with a view of the Space Needle). There's no charge for children under 18, and the parking is free. Proximity to the Monorail at Seattle Center and a free downtown shuttle from the inn make the location feasible even without a car. The inn has a spa and workout room, as well as an informal restaurant and lounge. *$$; AE, DC, MC, V; checks OK; www.usa.nia.com/bwexec; map:F5* &

Best Western Pioneer Square Hotel ★★

77 YESLER WAY; 206/340-1234 OR 800/800-5514

Regentrification is the name of the game along this lovely block in Pioneer Square, and this (shhh: you'd never know) Best Western property offers just that. Renovations have transformed a formerly seedy hotel into a handsome, comfortably appointed, moderately priced lodging—a boon for travelers intent on staying in the heart of Seattle's old town among galleries, bookstores, boutiques, restaurants, and nightclubs. In each guest room you'll find rich, elegant cherry-wood furniture and two armoires (one to use as a closet—since the former closets have been transformed into spacious bathrooms—and one for the TV). There's a small sitting alcove in these surprisingly quiet rooms (the hotel is in close proximity to the busy Alaskan Way Viaduct). Quibbles? The front-desk staff could use some polish, and the complimentary continental breakfast may be pretty picked over if you sleep past 7:30am. The neighborhood may not suit timid travelers, but for those willing to embrace the urban melting pot, this is a great choice. *$$; AE, DC, DIS, MC, V; no checks; info@pioneersquare.com; www.pioneersquare.com; map:N8* &

Camlin Hotel [unrated]

1619 9TH AVE; 206/682-0100 OR 800/426-0670

Built in 1926 by two bankers who embezzled the funds necessary to raise this 11-story property, the Camlin has survived its colorful past to become a sort of grande dame in the northeast corner of downtown (not far from the Convention Center and the Paramount Theatre). Unfortunately, the last time it was remodeled was in the mid-1980s, and it's definitely due for some sprucing up. (Plans to extensively remodel the interior have been announced and are set to begin in 1999.) Although its conference facilities are limited, the Camlin appeals to the business traveler, with large rooms that have small sitting/work areas, spacious closets, and spotless bathrooms; those with numbers that end in 10 boast windows on three sides. Just avoid the Cabanas—they're small and dreary and for smokers—and the room service, which can be quite slow. The top-floor Cloud Room comprises a dining room serving continental cuisine with Northwest accents, as well as a retro-chic cocktail-and-piano bar favored by both locals and out-of-towners (see Bars, Pubs, and Taverns in the Nightlife chapter). *$$; AE, DC, DIS, MC, V; checks OK; www.camlinhotel.com; map:I4*

Cavanaugh's on Fifth Avenue ★☆

1415 5TH AVE; 206/971-8000 OR 800/325-4000

Even though this 20-story tower was converted from an office building into a hotel in the mid-1990s, it's still rather characterless and utilitarian. Most of the 297 guest rooms are unremarkable in decor and amenities, providing either king- or queen-size beds, televisions tucked into armoires,

147

coffeemakers, hair dryers, and modem ports; most of the standard rooms also provide honor bars and vanity counters outside the bathrooms. If you plan to spend much time in your room, it might be worthwhile to step up to one of the suites, which offer separate parlors, better views of downtown or the Sound, and bathrobes. (A Presidential Suite even comes equipped with a fireplace and a dining room that seats six.) Rooms higher up are best for people who might be troubled by noise along hectic Fourth and Fifth Avenues. The fifth-floor Terrace Garden Restaurant serves Northwest cuisine in a light-filled space or (when the weather cooperates) on an outdoor terrace, and schedules light jazz on Wednesday, Thursday, and Friday nights. More fun (despite its abundance of nattering TV sets) is the Elephant & Castle, a fairly tame British-style pub and restaurant below the lobby that dishes up fish and chips, bangers and mash, and meat pies, in addition to American burgers. Underground parking is available, as is 24-hour room service. *$$$; AE, DC, DIS, MC, V; checks OK; www.cavanaughs.com; map:J6* &

Claremont Hotel ★★☆

2000 4TH AVE; 206/448-8600 OR 800/448-8601
Travelers from all over keep the Claremont heavily booked year-round. The location can't be beat: three blocks from Pike Place Market, a block and a half from Westlake Center and the Monorail. Built in 1926 as an apartment hotel, the Claremont has recently completed renovations that began in the early 1990s. Guest rooms offer either one king- or queen-size bed or two double beds, as well as a sitting area and bathrooms of white tile and marble. Junior Suites are still bigger, with granite wet bars, while Executive Suites have separate living rooms and bedrooms. For longer stays, a few rooms with kitchens are available. All rooms provide robes, hair dryers, irons and ironing boards, two-line phones with computer data ports, and voice mail. Upper floors boast views of downtown and the Market. Check out the elegant two-story ballroom during your stay. On the ground floor, you'll find Assaggio Ristorante, an excellent and lively Northern Italian eatery (see Restaurants chapter). *$$; AE, DC, DIS, MC, V; no checks; claremont@travelbase.com; www.travelbase. com/destinations/seattle/claremont; map:H6* &

Crowne Plaza ★★☆

1113 6TH AVE; 206/464-1980 OR 800/227-6963
This hotel bends over backward for the repeat and corporate visitor. The top "Executive Floors" are corporate, comfortable, and very clean, with decor that includes marble bathroom floors, blond wood, and dark accents. Business travelers taking advantage of "club-level" services receive a lot of individual attention in addition to free papers, a lounge, complimentary breakfast, and evening hors d'oeuvres (for just a $25 upgrade). Lower-floor guest rooms are spacious, if not especially visually

appealing. The lobby and lounge don't have a lot of charm, reminding you that this is a former Holiday Inn that's gone upscale. There is a full range of meeting facilities, and the location is convenient: right off the freeway and about four blocks from the Convention Center. *$$$; AE, DC, MC, V; checks OK; cplaza@wolfenet.com; map:L5* &

Four Seasons Olympic Hotel ★★★★

411 UNIVERSITY ST; 206/621-1700 OR 800/821-8106
Elegance is yours at Seattle's landmark hotel, where grand borders on opulent, and personal around-the-clock service means smiling maids, quick-as-a-wink bellhops, and a team of caring concierges who ensure your every comfort. Luxury extends from the 450 handsome guest rooms and suites tastefully furnished with period reproductions (executive suites feature down-dressed king-size beds separated from an elegant sitting room by French doors) to the venerable Georgian Room (see Restaurants chapter), where the talents of the kitchen, the decorum of liveried waiters, and the strains of a grand piano create a fine-dining experience you won't soon forget. Enjoy afternoon tea in the Garden Court or relax in the solarium spa and pool (where a licensed masseuse is on call). The hotel even goes out of its way for kids, right down to a teddy bear in the crib and a stepstool in the bathroom. There are several elegant meeting rooms and fine shops in the retail spaces off the lobby. The hotel's prices are steep, especially considering there are few views, but this is Seattle's one world-class contender. *$$$; AE, DC, DIS, MC, V; checks OK; www.fourseasons.com; map:L6* &

Hampton Inn & Suites ★☆

700 5TH AVE N; 206/282-7700 OR 800/426-7866
An easy stroll away from Seattle Center and the numerous eateries scattered about Lower Queen Anne, this efficient and surprisingly friendly facility offers 198 rooms, most with balconies. Standard rooms include individually controlled heating and air conditioning, hair dryers, irons and ironing boards, and voice mail. One-bedroom and two-bedroom suites also provide multiple televisions and small kitchen units. Decor doesn't get much beyond old-fashioned British hunting prints on the walls, but most of the folks who stay here don't seem to spend much time in their rooms anyway. A complimentary continental breakfast is served each morning, and there's plenty of free below-ground parking. *$$$; AE, DC, DIS, MC, V; no checks; www.hampton-inn.com; map:A4* &

Hotel Edgewater ★★

PIER 67, 2411 ALASKAN WAY; 206/728-7000 OR 800/624-0670
Alas, you can't fish from the famous west-facing windows of this waterfront institution anymore. You can, however, still breathe salty air and hear the ferry horns toot. The lobby and the rooms have a rustic tone,

with stained white pine and overstuffed chairs, plaid bedspreads, and lots of duck-motif kitsch and antler art. It's like a lodge on a busy (and sometimes noisy) Northwest waterfront, but with a reputable restaurant (the Restaurant at the Hotel Edgewater, whose cruise ship–style Sunday brunch is a veritable extravaganza), the Mudshark Bar, and an uninterrupted view of Elliott Bay, Puget Sound, and the Olympic Mountains. Waterside rooms have the best views but can get hot on summer afternoons. At the moment, the Edgewater remains the only hotel on the waterfront, allowing it to command prices approaching outrageous. It's a short walk to the recently developed Bell Street Pier (Pier 66), with restaurants, the Odyssey Maritime Discovery Center, and an overpass for easier access to nearby Pike Place Market. $$$; AE, DC, DIS, JCB, MC, V; checks OK; www.edgewaterhotel.com; www.noblehousehotels.com; map:F9 &

Hotel Monaco ★★★

1101 4TH AVE; 206/621-1770 OR 800/945-2240

The connection between Seattle and Greece may be a stretch; nevertheless, the Monaco, with its bright, Mediterranean look, is proving itself a welcome addition to Seattle's hotel scene. The domed lobby—with its nautical mural of dolphins playing in the Aegean Sea circa 2000 B.C., white marble floors, and images of steamer trunks—evokes another travel era altogether. No bland decor here: every one of the 189 rooms is decorated boldly in a blend of eye-popping stripes and florals that may strike some as busy and others as utterly charming. As at many local hotels, views take a back seat (this used to be a nondescript telephone-company switching center); service and design are the big pluses for tourists and business travelers alike (there are 6,000 square feet of meeting space). Those who insist on a view should request south-facing rooms on floors 6 through 11, and those who insist on bringing their pets, may. (If you don't have a pet, consider asking about the loaner goldfish.) Next to the hotel is the popular Southern-inspired Sazerac restaurant (see Restaurants chapter). The Monaco is part of the popular Kimpton Group hotel chain. $$$; AE, DC, DIS, MC, V; checks OK; www.monaco-seattle.com; map:L6 &

Hotel Vintage Park ★★★

1100 5TH AVE; 206/624-8000 OR 800/624-4433

Part of the San Francisco–based Kimpton Group, the Vintage Park is a personable, well-run, classy downtown hotel with genuinely attentive service. There are two kinds of rooms: those facing inward and those facing outward (the exterior rooms tend to have a little more space, but forget about a view). Unfortunately, the Vintage Park is located near a busy I-5 entrance ramp, and soundproofing seems to help only on the upper floors. The hotel's only suite (recently renovated) takes up the entire

THE GREENING OF SEATTLE

In the wake of the Klondike gold rush of 1897–99, as Seattle was booming, city commissioners realized they needed a comprehensive plan for urban development, one that included a unified strategy for the creation of urban parks. Wisely, in 1902 they turned for guidance to the Olmsted Brothers landscaping firm of Massachusetts, founded by Frederick Law Olmsted Sr. (creator of the Boston park system and design supervisor of New York's Central Park) but by then under the management of his sons, Frederick Law Olmsted Jr. and John Charles Olmsted.

It was John Olmsted who dealt most with the Seattle project, coming out to survey the city and then creating a plan that integrated natural areas with commercial and residential ones—a true expression of the "City Beautiful" ideas then popular across the nation. Among the firm's principal intentions for Seattle was to provide a park or playground within one mile of every home. Unfortunately, much of the best land here had already been scooped up by business and industry, and government had to exercise its broad powers of condemnation to acquire barely developed or undevelopable land wherever possible. Seattle voters helped the cause, passing bond issues in 1906, 1908, and 1910 to implement the Olmsteds' plans.

A 20-mile string of Olmsted parklands and landscaped boulevards eventually reached north and west from the Bailey Peninsula (rechristened Seward Park) on Lake Washington to Fort Lawton (today's Discovery Park) in Magnolia. Beacon Hill, Green Lake, Woodland and Volunteer Parks, and the Mount Baker neighborhood were all eventually influenced by the Olmsteds' visions. So were Seattle's far northern reaches, where the firm designed the lush Highlands subdivision in 1909 for local business barons such as airplane manufacturer William E. Boeing and mill owner Charles D. Stimson. In that same year, the Olmsteds created the site plan for the Alaska-Yukon-Pacific Exposition—some of whose buildings and features afterward became part of the University of Washington campus. There were only a few occasions when the firm's beautification proposals failed, mostly due to lack of financing.

Today, Seattle is praised for its 5,000 acres of parks—and the Olmsted Brothers are often credited with saving this city from the willy-nilly growth of other less forward-thinking cities.

—J. Kingston Pierce

top floor and gives a fun twist to elegance. Everywhere else, the hotel has carried its "vintage" theme to the limit: rooms named after wineries, burgundy upholstery, and green-and-maroon bedspreads. All rooms have fax machines and direct high-speed Internet access, as well as robes, hair dryers, irons and ironing boards, and phones in the bathrooms. There's lightning-fast 24-hour room service from the hotel's Italian restaurant, Tulio (see Restaurants chapter). The hotel provides coffee in the morning; there's complimentary fireside wine-tasting in the lobby from 5:30 to 6:30pm, and complimentary port is served there from 9:30 to 10pm. *$$$; AE, DC, DIS, MC, V; checks OK; www.hotelvintagepark.com; map:L6* &

Houseboat Hideaway [unrated]

MULTIPLE LOCATIONS (MAIL: 2226 EASTLAKE AVE E, SEATTLE 98102); 206/323-5323

A stay on one of these floating hideaways could be the quintessential Seattle experience. You're moored on sparkling south Lake Union, with unencumbered lake vistas and all the comforts of home. Houseboat Hideaway is a family-owned and -operated rental company providing overnight houseboat accommodations on European-style canal barges. All are fully furnished and have kitchen or kitchenette, but this is, first and foremost, a make-yourself-at-home-in-Seattle private marine hideaway. Prices range from $155 to $195 per night for two. *$$$; AE, MC, V; checks OK; map:A1*

Inn at Harbor Steps ★★

1221 1ST AVE; 206/748-0973 OR 888/728-8910

Open since 1997, this Four Sisters property is the second in the Northwest (Whidbey Island's Saratoga Inn was the first), offering the California-based chain's hallmark country-inn ambience in a decidedly urban setting. Tucked into the swanky high-rise commercial-and-condo complex at Harbor Steps, the inn is both intimate and elegant, catering to the business or holiday traveler with 20 rooms overlooking a garden courtyard. Each has tasteful furnishings, a fireplace, king or queen bed, wet bar, fridge, and sitting area; deluxe rooms include spa tubs. Among the many amenities are 24-hour concierge/innkeeper services, complimentary evening hors d'oeuvres and wine, and a breakfast buffet. Guests have access to an indoor pool, sauna, Jacuzzi, exercise room, and meeting room. *$$$; AE, DC, MC, V; checks OK; www.foursisters.com; map:K8* &

Inn at the Market ★★★☆

86 PINE ST; 206/443-3600 OR 800/446-4484

The setting—perched just above the fish, flower, and fruit stalls of Pike Place Market, with a heart-stopping sunset view over Elliott Bay and the Olympic Mountains—is definitively Seattle and unsurpassed. This small (65 rooms and suites) hotel features first-class personalized service coupled with fine cuisine at the adjacent French Country restaurant, Campagne (see Restaurants chapter). Guests may choose from beautifully furnished rooms with views of the city, the Market, the courtyard, or the bay; even some side rooms enjoy big views. Oversize bathrooms are equipped with hair dryers and fluffy bathrobes. Floor-to-ceiling windows open to the breeze off the Sound and the sounds of the Market below. Stroll through the Market in the early morning as vendors set out their wares, then return to this intimate yet spacious inn for your complimentary coffee or room-service breakfast ordered from Bacco in the courtyard. In-room dinners come from Campagne. *$$$; AE, DC, DIS, MC, V; checks OK; www.innatthemarket.com; map:I8* &

Inn at Virginia Mason ★

1006 SPRING ST; 206/583-6453 OR 800/283-6453
The Inn at Virginia Mason works hard to let the public know it's not just a place for friends and family of patients at Virginia Mason Medical Center. The location is convenient to the Convention Center yet offers respite from the downtown bustle (if not from ambulance sirens). The standard rooms are on the small side, although comfortably and tastefully furnished, but the suites ($135–$200) are fairly priced for what you get. Try for the one on the top floor, with a fireplace in the living room, bar, TVs, and a behind-the-city view of Puget Sound. The pleasant Rhododendron Restaurant is available for meals, but you're also an easy walk from downtown shops and restaurants. *$$$; AE, DC, MC, V; checks OK; map:L3* &

Madison Renaissance Hotel ★★

515 MADISON ST; 206/583-0300 OR 800/278-4159
This large hotel at the southeast edge of downtown successfully conveys a sense of warmth and intimacy. The lobby is tasteful and uncluttered, upstairs hallways are softly lit, and the rooms are elegantly furnished, with lots of marble and wood; most offer great city views. Avoid rooms on the freeway side; although the windows are soundproofed, the hum of traffic still seeps in. Guests enjoy complimentary coffee and morning newspapers and a rooftop pool, and some rooms include free in-town tranportation. The pricey Club Floors offer exclusive check-in privileges, concierge services, hors d'oeuvres and a continental breakfast at the Club Lounge, a library, and the best views. Prego, the restaurant on the 28th floor, offers a fine selection of seafood to complement the view. *$$$; AE, DC, MC, V; checks OK; www.renaissancehotels.com; map:M5* &

Marriott Residence Inn–Lake Union ★☆

800 FAIRVIEW AVE N; 206/624-6000 OR 800/331-3131
It's not quite on the lake; rather, it's across busy Fairview Avenue. Still, the 234 rooms, half of which are one-bedroom suites boasting lake views (request one on the highest floor possible), are spacious and tastefully decorated, and some have fully outfitted kitchenettes. Continental breakfast and evening dessert are presented in the lobby—a light, plant-filled courtyard with an atrium and a waterfall. The hotel has no restaurant,

but plenty of the lakeside eateries across the street allow guests to charge meals to their rooms. Amenities include meeting rooms, lap pool, exercise room, sauna, and spa. *$$$; AE, DC, DIS, MC, V; checks OK; www.residenceinn.com; map:D1* &

Mayflower Park Hotel ★★

405 OLIVE WAY; 206/623-8700 OR 800/426-5100
Step out of the heart of the downtown shopping district and into the coolly elegant lobby of this handsomely renovated 1927 hotel. On one side of the lobby sits Oliver's (a perfectly civilized spot for a perfect martini) and on the other is Andaluca (see Restaurants chapter), an upscale experiment combining Northwest and Mediterranean themes. Rooms are small, still bearing charming reminders of the hotel's past: lovely Oriental brass and antique appointments; large, deep tubs; thick walls that trap noise. Suites are tastefully decorated and offer comfortable sitting areas and private sleeping quarters with king-size beds. Modern intrusions are for both better and worse: double-glazed windows in all rooms keep out traffic noise, but many rooms have undistinguished furnishings. The slightly bigger deluxe rooms have corner views; ask for one on a higher floor, or you may find yourself facing a brick wall. *$$$; AE, DC, MC, V; checks OK; mayflower@seanet.com; map:I6* &

Pacific Guest Suites [unrated]

VARIOUS LOCATIONS (MAIL: 411 108TH AVE NE, BELLEVUE 98004); 425/454-7888 OR 800/962-6620

Pacific Guest Suites rents condos in Seattle, Bellevue, Redmond, Everett, and Renton. Most of the locations have amenities such as swimming pools, fitness centers, fireplaces, Jacuzzis, and weekly maid service. Ideally suited to long-term business stays, the condos are also perfect for families on vacation, as the minimum stay is only three days (although the nightly rate drops the longer you stay). *$$; AE, DC, DIS, MC, V; checks OK; reservations@pgsuites.com*

Pacific Plaza ★

400 SPRING ST; 206/623-3900 OR 800/426-1165
The midsize Pacific Plaza offers a welcome respite from astronomical downtown hotel prices. For those who care more about location and budget than amenities, this is the perfect place. Rooms start at under $100, even in summer, and include irons and ironing boards, in-room movies, and voice mail; select rooms also have coffeemakers. Rates include a generous continental breakfast. The ambience brings to mind a good budget hotel in a European city: long hallways; simple, comfortable rooms; and small, clean bathrooms. A recent $650,000 renovation spruced up paint, wallpaper, carpeting, and bedspreads. Light sleepers may choose to stay elsewhere, as the Pacific Plaza is not air-conditioned,

and opening the windows invites traffic noise. *$$; AE, DC, DIS, MC, V; no checks; www.usa.nia.com/pacificplaza; map:L6*

Paramount Hotel ★★

724 PINE ST; 206/292-9500 OR 800/426-0670
The Paramount, which opened in 1996, is yet another feather in the cap of the WestCoast hotel chain. Located kitty-corner from the theater that shares its name, it's convenient to the Convention Center and midtown shopping. Step inside: the cozy faux-library look of the lobby (think: arty hunting lodge with grand fireplace) is in keeping with the hotel's intended "European chateau" ambience. The Paramount's modest size—146 guest rooms, two small meeting rooms, and a tiny fitness center—will appeal to those who eschew megahotels. Standard guest rooms are prettily appointed, though rather small, as are the bathrooms. Consider splurging for an "executive" room, whose corner location means a bit more space and whose bathroom boasts a whirlpool tub. The adjoining restaurant, Blowfish (see Restaurants chapter), home to a robata bar and a wall of pachinko machines, joined Seattle's growing pan-Asian restaurant roster in 1997 and is a trendy nightspot. *$$$; AE, DC, DIS, JCB, MC, V; checks OK; www.westcoasthotels.com/paramount; map:J4* &

Pensione Nichols ★

1923 1ST AVE; 206/441-7125
Its location is the best feature of Pensione Nichols: it's perched just above Pike Place Market. Some of the rooms face First Avenue and can be quite noisy; although the other rooms don't have windows, they do have skylights and are much quieter. Ten guest rooms ($60 single, $85 double) share four bathrooms. The large common room at the west end of the third floor has a gorgeous view of the Market's rooftops and Elliott Bay beyond; it's here that the bountiful breakfast—including fresh treats from the Market—is served. Unusual antiques abound (the Nicholses also own the N. B. Nichols antique store in Post Alley, which doubles as the daytime entrance to the inn). Also available: two wonderful suites with private bath, full kitchen, bedroom alcove, and a living room with that great view ($160 each). *$; AE, MC, V; checks OK; map:H8*

Sheraton Seattle Hotel and Towers ★★½

1400 6TH AVE; 206/621-9000 OR 800/325-3535
Seattle's Sheraton is an 840-room tower rising as a sleek triangle, the Convention Center in its shadow. It, too, aims at the convention business, so the guest rooms are smallish and standard, and much emphasis is placed on the meeting rooms and the restaurants. There's a lobby lounge and oyster bar; the casual Pike Street Cafe, known for its 27-foot-long dessert spread; and Schooners Sports Pub (complete with large-screen TVs, Northwest microbrews, and accompanying pub fare). The

fine-dining restaurant, Fullers, is an oasis of serenity adorned with fine Northwest art (see Restaurants chapter). Service is quite efficient. Convention facilities are complete, and the kitchen staff can handle the most complex assignments. Discriminating business travelers can head for the upper four VIP floors (31–34), where a hotel-within-a-hotel offers its own lobby, concierge, and private lounge, and you'll find considerably more amenities in the rooms (which are, however, the same size as the less expensive ones). The top-floor health club is open to guests of the entire hotel and features a heated pool and a knockout city panorama. *$$$; AE, DC, MC, V; checks OK; www.sheraton.com; map:K5* &

Sixth Avenue Inn ★

2000 6TH AVE; 206/441-8300 OR 800/648-6440
Catering to tourists and conventioneers, this sprightly motor inn is done up in blues and tans, and some of the rooms have brass beds. You'll find less street noise on the east side. Service is professional and friendly. There's room service, a restaurant, free parking, and a good location, with nearby retail on one side of the hotel and movie theaters on the other. *$$; AE, DC, MC, V; checks OK; map:H5*

Sorrento Hotel ★★★☆

900 MADISON ST; 206/622-6400 OR 800/426-1265
Occupying a corner just east of downtown in Seattle's First Hill neighborhood, the Sorrento is an Italianate masterpiece that first opened in 1909, was remodeled in 1981, and has recently completed a makeover for the millennium, adding top-notch service touches such as fax machines, in-room voice mail, and a small on-site exercise facility. The 76 rooms are decorated in muted good taste, with slightly Asian accents. We recommend the extravagantly large 08 series of suites, in the corners. Suites on the top floor make elegant quarters for special meetings or parties—the showstopper being the 2,000-square-foot, $1,500-a-night penthouse, with a grand piano, patio, Jacuzzi, view of Elliott Bay, and luxurious rooms. A comfortable, intimate fireside lobby lounge is a civilized place for taking afternoon tea or sipping cognac while listening to jazz piano or classical guitar. Chef Brian Scheehser serves Mediterranean cuisine at the manly Hunt Club (see Restaurants chapter). Complimentary town car service will take guests throughout downtown. Some travelers may find the Sorrento's location—five blocks uphill from the heart of the city—inconvenient, but we find it quiet and removed. *$$$; AE, DC, DIS, MC, V; checks OK; sorrento@earthlink.net; www.hotelsorrento.com; map:M4* &

Warwick Hotel ★

401 LENORA ST; 206/443-4300 OR 800/426-9280
The Warwick is part of an international chain that aims its pitch at the corporate traveler; unfortunately, the result is somewhat characterless. Rooms are large and comfortable, though, with floor-to-ceiling windows (reserve a room above the sixth floor for a great view) and marble bathrooms. The pool in the health club is shallow and too short for laps, but a spa and sauna will help you unwind. If you've got the bucks, splurge for the Queen Victoria Suite, with its elegant appointments and panoramic view (good for private parties, too). The hotel's restaurant, Liaison, has decent service and good, if unimaginative, food. As at most downtown hotels, you pay for parking, but there's 24-hour courtesy van service for downtown appointments. The Warwick is one of the few city hotels that allow small pets (ask first). *$$$; AE, DC, MC, V; checks OK; www.warwickhotel.com; map:H6* &

WestCoast Plaza Park Suites ★★

1011 PIKE ST; 206/682-8282 OR 800/426-0670
For better or for worse, this suites-only hotel is steps away from the Convention Center. Each room is commendably spacious (even the studios), with a living room and kitchenette, and the formerly muted furnishings are gradually undergoing a jazzy, plum-hued update. Some rooms have fireplaces, while others have whirlpool tubs. Expect all the amenities of a full-service hotel: conference rooms, exercise rooms (sauna and Jacuzzi, too), and laundry and valet service. Personal needs are gladly met—from groceries to an extra phone line for your modem. There's no restaurant, but an extensive continental breakfast is included; eat in the dining room or take it up to your suite, as you wish. There's even a shop in the lobby that stocks frozen dinners to pop in your microwave. The Plaza Park is great for corporate clients on long-term stays or families on vacation who want a little room to spread out (and an outdoor pool for the kids). *$$$; AE, DC, MC, V; checks OK; www.westcoasthotels.com; map:K3* &

WestCoast Roosevelt Hotel ★

1531 7TH AVE; 206/621-1200 OR 800/426-0670
Gone is the grand skylit lobby that so distinguished the Roosevelt when it first opened its doors in 1930; the space is now inhabited by Von's Grand City Cafe (serving sandwiches, steaks, fish—and especially martinis). The new hotel lobby is low-ceilinged and cramped, but elsewhere the Roosevelt's Art Deco sensibilities have been somewhat preserved. The hotel's 20 stories have been reconfigured for the contemporary traveler, but studios are still almost comically small. The deluxe rooms are a better choice, with adjoining sitting areas; the 13 suites each contain a Jacuzzi and a separate sitting area. Sixteen floors are now nonsmoking. Considering its proximity to the Convention Center and the shopping district,

the Roosevelt's prices—$105 to $220—are decent, but the service could be more polished. *$$–$$$; AE, DC, DIS, MC, V; checks OK; www.westcoasthotels.com/roosevelt; map:J5* &

WestCoast Vance Hotel ★

620 STEWART ST; 206/441-4200 OR 800/426-0670
Here's another WestCoast mission to save a forgotten downtown hotel. Most of the decade-old restoration, it seems, was focused on the lobby—making for a very pretty entrance. The rooms are small and spartan, and are showing serious signs of wear: carpet stains, scuff marks, and the occasional chipped paint. Standard rooms, at $99–$140 for a double, are no bargain, as there's barely enough room to swing a cat (the bathrooms are shoehorned into former closets; claustrophobics should shower elsewhere). Still, the location is nice and convenient. The north-facing rooms above the fifth floor are best, with a view toward Queen Anne and the Space Needle. Room service comes from the Latin restaurant downstairs, Yakima Grill (see Restaurants chapter). *$$–$$$; AE, DC, MC, V; checks OK; vancehotel@sprintmail.com; www.westcoasthotels/vance.com; map:H5*

Westin Hotel ★★☆

1900 5TH AVE; 206/728-1000 OR 800/WESTIN-1
The Westin's twin cylindrical towers may be called corncobs by the natives, but they afford spacious rooms with superb views, particularly above the 20th floor. The size of the hotel (896 rooms and 48 suites) contributes to some lapses in service, however: we can attest to long lines for check-in and occasional difficulties getting attention from the harried concierge staff. Convention facilities, spread over several floors of meeting rooms, are quite complete. There's a large pool and an exercise room. On the top floors are some ritzy, glitzy suites. The location, near Westlake Center and the Monorail station, is excellent, as are meals at Nikko, a Japanese restaurant on the premises (see Restaurants chapter). Another fine-dining establishment, Roy's Seattle, is also in the hotel. *$$$; AE, DC, MC, V; checks OK; www.westin.com; map:H5* &

Capitol Hill

Bacon Mansion ★★

959 BROADWAY E; 206/329-1864 OR 800/240-1864
Built by Cecil Bacon in 1909, this Tudor-style mansion is now a fine bed and breakfast, with lovingly restored woodwork and tastefully furnished common areas. Seven rooms in the main guest house (five with private baths) are appointed with antiques and brass fixtures. The top of the line is the Capitol Room, a huge suite on the second floor with a sunroom,

fireplace, four-poster bed, and view of the Space Needle. The basement Garden Room (which stays pleasantly cool in summer) has 8-foot ceilings and a kitchenette. The Carriage House, a separate two-story building, is appropriate for a small family or two couples. Proprietor Daryl King is an enthusiastic, friendly host. Smoking is allowed outside. *$$; AE, MC, V; checks OK; baconbandb@aol.com; www.site-works.com/ bacon/; map:GG6*

Bed and Breakfast on Broadway ★

722 BROADWAY AVE E; 206/329-8933
Conveniently located just one block north of the popular Broadway strip of shops, restaurants, and theaters is this distinctive house featuring beautiful stained-glass windows, hardwood floors, and Oriental rugs. Hosts and proprietors Russel Lyons—whose original paintings are on display throughout—and Don Fabian invite guests to make themselves at home in one of the four spacious rooms, all with private baths. The Penthouse has a private deck lined with well-tended flower pots. A formal sit-down breakfast is included. *$$; AE, MC, V; checks OK; www.chcs.com/bbonbroadway; map:GG6*

Capitol Hill Inn ★

1713 BELMONT AVE; 206/323-1955
This is one of the most conveniently located B&Bs in the city—within walking distance of the Convention Center and Broadway shops and restaurants (as long as you don't mind hills). Unfortunately, you give up any charm of a neighborhood for this convenience, but the 1903 Queen Anne–style home is itself a lovely place. It's run by pleasant mother-daughter team Katie and Joanne Godmintz, who live on the premises and who restored the inn down to its custom-designed wall coverings, period chandeliers, carved wooden moldings, and sleigh and brass beds. There are four rooms upstairs (two with full baths, two with toilets and sinks and a shower down the hall) and two rooms downstairs in the daylight basement (with private bath, fireplace, and Jacuzzi). *$$; MC, V; checks OK; www.capitolhillinn.com; map:HH6*

Gaslight Inn and Howell Street Suites ★★☆

1727 15TH AVE; 206/325-3654

Praised by repeat guests and bed-and-breakfast owners alike, the Gaslight is one of the loveliest, most reasonably priced, and friendliest B&Bs in town. Trevor Logan, Steve Bennett, and John Fox have polished this turn-of-the-century mansion into a 10-guest-room jewel. Five rooms have private baths, two have fireplaces, and each is decorated in a distinct style—some contemporary, some antique, some Mission. Outside are two sundecks and a large heated swimming pool.

The Howell Street Suites next door (six full and one studio) are outfitted with wet bars, coffeemakers, microwaves and refrigerators, wineglasses, fruit, and flowers. Targeted at businesspeople, the suites also offer phones, fax availability, off-street parking, maid service, and laundry facilities. One suite takes up the entire top floor, offering a spectacular view of downtown and the Olympic Mountains. Unlike the other suites, which are decorated with classic antiques, this one has modern furnishings and a one-of-a-kind art glass chandelier. There's a garden area between the two houses. No pets, kids, or smoking (you may light up outdoors, though). *$$; AE, MC, V; checks OK; www.gaslight-inn. com; map:HH6*

Hill House Bed and Breakfast ★★★

1113 E JOHN ST; 206/720-7161 OR 800/720-7161
The special touches and personal service from innkeepers Herman and Alea Foster are what make the Hill House memorable. What with fresh flowers in all guest rooms, down comforters in pressed cutwork duvet covers, crisp cotton sheets, and handmade soaps, you may find it hard to even leave your room. But be sure you do, as you won't want to miss Herman's exceptional two-course gourmet breakfasts, with entrees such as smoked salmon omelets and walnut bread French toast, cooked to order and served on china and crystal. This elegantly restored 1903 Victorian, located in the heart of historic Capitol Hill, offers guests a choice of seven beautifully decorated rooms, five with private baths. *$$$; AE, DIS, MC, V; checks OK; hillhouse@foxinternet.net; www.foxinternet. net/business/hillhouse; map:GG6*

Mildred's Bed and Breakfast ★★

1202 15TH AVE E; 206/325-6072
This large, double-turreted turn-of-the-century Victorian is the ultimate setting for traditional, caring B&B hospitality. All three guest rooms have private baths, TV/VCRs, queen-size beds, writing desks, and comfortable seating. Special touches at Mildred's include coffee and juice delivered to your room a half hour before a full breakfast is served. The home has been beautifully maintained in its original style, with natural wood throughout and a wraparound front porch just perfect for sipping tea and watching the world go by. If you feel more like taking a stroll, historic 44-acre Volunteer Park, home to the Seattle Asian Art Museum, is just across the street. *$$; AE, MC, V; checks OK; www.mildredsbnb. com; map:GG6*

Roberta's Bed & Breakfast ★★

1147 16TH AVE E; 206/329-3326
Roberta is the gracious, somewhat loquacious lady of this Capitol Hill house near Volunteer Park and a few blocks from the funky Broadway

district. The front porch is a soothing spot to while away a couple of hours, and inside it's lovely: refinished floors throughout, an old upright piano, and a large rectangular dining table and country-style chairs. Of the five rooms, the Hideaway Suite (the entire third floor)—with views of the Cascades from the window seat, skylight windows under the eaves, a sitting area with a futon sofa and a small desk, and a full bath with a tub—is our favorite. Others prefer the Peach Room with its antique desk, bay window, love seat, and queen-size oak bed. Early risers will enjoy the Madrona Room, with its morning sun and private bath. (Of the five rooms, four have private baths, and the fifth has its own bath right across the hall.) In the morning, Roberta brings you a wake-up cup of coffee, then later puts out a smashing, full, meatless breakfast. No children or smoking. *$$; MC, V; checks OK; roberta@robertas.com; www.robertas.com/; map:GG6*

Salisbury House ★★

750 16TH AVE E; 206/328-8682
A welcoming porch wraps around this big, bright, turn-of-the-century Capitol Hill home, an exquisite hostelry on a tranquil residential street near Volunteer Park. Glossy maple floors and lofty beamed ceilings lend a sophisticated air to the guest library (with a chess table and a fireplace) and the living room. Up the wide staircase and past the second-level sunporch are four guest rooms (one with a lovely canopied bed, all with queen-size beds and down comforters) with full baths. The lower-level suite has a private entrance, fireplace, refrigerator, and whirlpool tub, making it a perfect home base for longer stays. Breakfast is taken in the dining room or on the sunny terrace. Classy, dignified, nonsmoking, and devoid of children (under 12) and pets, the Salisbury is a sure bet in one of Seattle's finest neighborhoods. *$$; AE, MC, V; checks OK; sleep@ salisburyhouse.com; www.salisburyhouse.com/; map:HH6*

University District/North End

Chambered Nautilus ★★

5005 22ND AVE NE; 206/522-2536
This blue 1915 Georgian colonial in a woodsy hillside setting in the University District offers six airy guest rooms beautifully furnished with antiques. All have private baths (though one bath is a few steps outside the bedroom door), and four open onto porches with tree-webbed views of the Cascades. All rooms have robes, desks, flowers, reading material, bottled water, and resident teddy bears in case you forget your own. This location, just across the street from graduate student housing and a few blocks from Fraternity Row, can get noisy during rush. Other times, though, it's surprisingly quiet. Innkeepers Joyce Schulte and Steve Poole

A STAR WAS BORN HERE

What do stripper **Gypsy Rose Lee** and golfer **Fred Couples** have in common? Their common link to clubs isn't the answer; both were born in Seattle.

Many other celebrities have at one time or another called the Seattle area home, including a respectable number of writers: **E. B. White,** who penned *Charlotte's Web*, was fired from his reporting job at the *Seattle Times* after nine months. Playwright **Eugene O'Neill** lived here when he won the Nobel Prize for literature in 1936. **Mary McCarthy** (*The Group*) was born here in 1912, and her parents died in the flu epidemic of 1918. Playwright **August Wilson** is a current resident, as are writers **Sherman Alexie**, **David Guterson**, **J. A. Jance**, **Ann Rule**, and **Robert Fulghum**, who taught art at the private Lakeside School. Mystery writer **Earl Emerson** lives in North Bend but works at the Seattle Fire Department. Poet **Theodore Roethke** taught at the University of Washington; poet **David Wagoner** still does, as do writers **Shawn Wong** and **Charles Johnson**.

Seattle can also claim a number of internationally known visual and performing artists. The raspy-voiced Broadway vet **Carol Channing** (*Hello, Dolly*) was born here. Dancer/choreographer **Mark Morris** graduated from Seattle's Franklin High and taught dance at the University of Washington. **Robert Joffrey**, founder of New York's Joffrey Ballet, was born in Seattle. Cartoonist **Lynda Barry** got her start in the pages of the UW's *Daily*; **Hank Ketcham**, creator of *Dennis the Menace*, spent a year at the UW before heading south to Los Angeles and a job with Disney; and *Far Side* creator **Gary Larson** lives here. Glass artists **Dale Chihuly** and **Ginny Ruffner** and painter **Jacob Lawrence** are also all longtime Seattle residents.

Of course, the town is famous for its collection of resident musicians. Saxophonist **Kenny G** has a home here, as do **Ann and Nancy Wilson** of the rock band Heart, plus various members of the alternative rock bands **Pearl Jam**, **Alice in Chains**, and **REM**. Jazz giants **Quincy Jones**, **Ernestine Anderson**, **Diane Schuur**, and **Ray Charles** at one time made their homes, as well as their music, here. **Jimi Hendrix**, who died of a drug overdose in 1970, is buried at Renton's Greenwood Memorial Park, and Nirvana's **Kurt Cobain** committed suicide in his Seattle home in 1994.

Small-screen stars with Seattle connections include **Dawn Wells** ("Mary Ann" from *Gilligan's Island*), **Josie Bissett** (the *Melrose Place* actor owns a pottery paint studio in Bellevue Square), **John Corbett** and **Cynthia Geary** of *Northern Exposure*, who own clubs in Seattle, and **John Ratzenberger** ("Cliff Claven" of *Cheers*), who lives on Vashon Island. Many actors—ranging from **Patrick Duffy** (*Dallas*), **Richard Karn** (*Home Improvement*), and **Kyle MacLachlan** (*Twin Peaks*) to **Kate Mulgrew** (*Star Trek: Voyager*) and **Julia Sweeney** (*Saturday Night Live*, *It's Pat*)—first studied drama in Seattle.

Before she became a star of the silver screen in the 1930s (and the subject of the 1983 film *Frances*, starring Jessica Lange), UW grad **Frances Farmer** cleaned rooms at Seattle's Olympic Hotel. **Dyan Cannon** grew up in West Seattle and studied anthropology at the UW before she became a flight attendant and met (and later married and divorced) Cary Grant. Martial arts great **Bruce Lee** (buried beside his son, Brandon, at Capitol Hill's Lake View Cemetery) was a student when he met his wife at the UW. Twenty years before falling in love with Julia Roberts's prostitute-with-a-heart-of-gold character in *Pretty Woman*, **Richard Gere** apprenticed at the Seattle Repertory Theatre. One of the city's best-known resident actors, **Tom Skerritt** (*Top Gun*, *Picket Fences*), calls Capitol Hill home. And film directors **Cameron Crowe** (*Jerry Maguire*), **Richard Donner** (*Lethal Weapon*), and **Alan Rudolph** (*Afterglow*) have homes in or around Seattle. Crowe's Seattle connection includes being the spouse of native rocker Nancy Wilson.

Of course, just like any family, every city has its black sheep whom it would just as soon forget. At the top of Seattle's most *un*wanted list is **Ted Bundy**; the serial killer started his murderous spree here, where he also majored in psychology, of all things, at the UW and even worked for the Seattle Crime Prevention Committee. He was executed in Florida 1989.

— Shannon O'Leary

serve a full breakfast and complimentary afternoon tea and cookies. A spacious public room, meeting facilities, a library of 2,000-plus volumes, and an enclosed porch/reading room with soothing chamber music round out this tasteful inn. Make prior arrangements for kids under 8. No smoking. *$$; AE, MC, V; checks OK; www.chamberednautilus.com; map:FF6*

College Inn Guest House ★

4000 UNIVERSITY WAY NE; 206/633-4441

With the glorious grounds of the University of Washington practically at your doorstep, you can excuse a little noise (there's a cafe and pub on the premises) and the dormlike quality of the toilet and bathing facilities (separate-sex, rows of showers, down the hall). Housed in the upper three floors of a renovated 1909 Tudor building that appears on the National Register of Historic Places, the College Inn is designed along the lines of a European pension: it's devoid of TV and radio (though all rooms have phones). Each of the 25 guest rooms offers a sink, a desk, and a single or double bed. The best of the lot even have window seats. A generous continental breakfast (included in the bargain rates) is served upstairs in the communal sitting area. *$; MC, V; checks OK; c-inn@speakeasy.org; www. speakeasy.org/collegeinn; map:FF6*

Edmond Meany Hotel ★★☆

4507 BROOKLYN AVE NE; 206/634-2000 OR 800/899-0251
Named in honor of a popular University of Washington professor and Seattle promoter, designed by renowned architect Robert C. Reamer (who also did downtown's exquisite Skinner Building and a couple of grand hotels in Yellowstone National Park), and constructed where once stood the home of "Big Bertha" Landes, Seattle's first and only woman mayor, this 15-story tower was the Pacific Northwest's largest suburban hotel when it opened in 1931. With its 70th birthday approaching, the Meany has undergone a $5 million renovation that not only enhanced its Art Deco detailing, renewed the elegance of its lobby (check out the terrazzo flooring), and freshened up its guest rooms, but even gave this landmark back its original name (after years of being known as the Meany Tower Hotel). The octagonal-tower design allows every one of the 155 guest rooms (about half of which contain king-size beds) a bay window with a view—some better than others—and those on the south side are sunny. You're one block from shopping on the Ave and two blocks from the University campus. Pleiades Restaurant and Lounge (serving Northwest cuisine) is open for breakfast, lunch, and dinner, and there's live jazz there on Thursday and Friday nights. Eddie's News Café, facing N 45th Street, is a boon for early risers whose appetite for newspapers and magazines matches their appetite for muffins and espresso. *$$; AE, DC, DIS, MC, V; checks OK; www.meany.com; map:FF7* &

Edmonds Harbor Inn ★

130 W DAYTON ST, EDMONDS; 425/771-5021 OR 800/441-8033
Strategically located near the Edmonds ferry and train terminals, this inn is an attractive choice for a night in this charming, waterside Seattle suburb. It features 61 large rooms (with views, unfortunately, of the surrounding business park rather than the picturesque Sound), oak furnishings, continental breakfast, and access to the athletic club just next door. If you're traveling with youngsters in tow, the rooms with modern kitchenettes, coupled with the inn's extremely reasonable rates, will be particularly appealing. Get directions—the place is near the harborfront, but a little difficult to find in the gray sea of new office and shopping developments. *$$; AE, DC, MC, V; checks OK; nwcinns@seanet.com; www. nwcountryinns.com;* &

Lake Union B&B ★★★☆

2217 N 36TH ST; 206/547-9965

Simply walking through the gate and into the peaceful backyard garden of Janice Matthews's Lake Union B&B invites you to relax and leave your cares at the door. In fact, leave your shoes too, and sink into the white cloud of carpet throughout this modern, three-story house near Gas Works Park. The three rooms have Lake Union views, TV/VCRs, telephones, fluffy bathrobes, queen-size beds, and carefully ironed sheets. You can truly pamper yourself in the romantic penthouse suite with its panoramic-view solarium (check out the telescope), fireplace, private bath, and enormous Jacuzzi. The sauna in the bathroom downstairs has piped-in music. Matthews, a former restaurateur, gladly prepares private dinners on request. *$$$; no credit cards; checks OK; map:FF7*

University Inn ★★⯪

4140 ROOSEVELT WAY NE; 206/632-5055 OR 800/733-3855
This is a bright, clean, well-managed University District establishment. Rooms in the newer south wing are more spacious; some have king-size beds, and all contain irons and ironing boards. North-wing rooms are more standard, with shower stalls in the bathrooms (no tubs). Some have small balconies overlooking the heated outdoor pool and hot tub. All rooms offer voice mail, small safes, and data modem ports. Other amenities include a complimentary continental breakfast, free morning paper, small fitness room, and free off-street parking. Extended-stay rooms are available. The entire hotel is nonsmoking. *$$; AE, DC, DIS, MC, V; checks OK; univinn@aol.com; www.universityinnseattle.com; map:FF7* &

Bainbridge Island

The Buchanan Inn ★

8494 NE ODDFELLOWS RD, BAINBRIDGE ISLAND; 206/780-9258 OR 800/598-3926
First-time innkeepers Ron and Judy Gibbs have added a touch of sophistication to this beautifully-renovated Odd Fellows Hall built in 1912. Located in one of Bainbridge Island's most picturesque and sunny neighborhoods, the four-bedroom B&B touts suites so luxe the Odd Fellows would be ecstatic convening here today. Rooms have private baths and king- or queen-size beds, and gas fireplaces are an option in two of the rooms. If you prefer to leave your jammies on during the breakfast hour, you can request a continental breakfast basket be brought to your room. (If you're the more sociable type, a complete gourmet breakfast is served in the formal dining room.) Just a short stroll away are Fort Ward State Park and the beach—and it's just a few steps to the rustic cottage where a bubbling hot tub awaits. Pets and children under 16 are not allowed unless the entire inn is reserved. *$$–$$$; AE, DIS, MC, V; checks OK; jgibbs@buchananinn.com; www.buchananinn.com*

Eastside

Bellevue Club Hotel ★★★

11200 SE 6TH ST, BELLEVUE; 425/454-4424 OR 800/579-1110
The hotel at the Bellevue Club (an athletic facility) surely gives the Hyatt Regency a run for its money, especially among well-heeled business travelers. Each of the 67 rooms is beautifully decorated, featuring striking modern furnishings and pieces by Northwest artists. The oversize limestone-and-marble bathrooms are absolutely fabulous, complete with spalike tubs and separate shower stalls. The lovely garden rooms open onto private patios. Other rooms overlook the five tennis courts. The extensive athletic facilities available to hotel guests include an Olympic-size swimming pool; indoor tennis, racquetball, and squash courts; and aerobics classes. *$$$; AE, MC, V; checks OK; www.bellevueclub.com; map:HH3* &

Bellevue Hilton ★★

100 112TH AVE NE, BELLEVUE; 425/455-3330 OR 800/BEL-HILT
With every amenity in the book, the Bellevue Hilton is the best bet on the Eastside's hotel row. Rooms are tastefully done in warm colors. Amenities include use of a nearby health-and-racquet club, free transportation around Bellevue (within a 5-mile radius), complimentary room service (until midnight), a Jacuzzi, a sauna, a pool and exercise area, cable TV, and two restaurants. Working stiffs will appreciate the modem hookups and desks in every room; computer, fax machine, and copy machine are also available. *$$$; AE, DC, MC, V; checks OK; www.hilton.com; map:HH3* &

Holly Hedge House ★★

908 GRANT AVE S, RENTON; 425/226-2555
This deliciously comfortable 1901 cottage for two, which sits high above I-405's S-curves, has been beautifully updated. The sunroom in front looks out over the Renton Valley clear to the Cascades (the room won an award from *Country Inns Bed and Breakfast* magazine). The backyard features a wide deck, gazebo-enclosed hot tub, lawn, and garden; and guests have private use of the proprietor's kidney-shaped pool next door. Inside there's a sitting room with gas fireplace and a collection of videos and CDs. A white-pine queen-size bed dominates the bedroom, and the kitchen is equipped for cooking as well as eating. Choose between a continental breakfast or a you-bake gourmet affair. *$$$; MC, V; checks OK; holihedg@nwlink.com; www.nwlink.com/~holihedg; map:MM2*

Hyatt Regency at Bellevue Place ★★
900 BELLEVUE WAY NE, BELLEVUE; 425/462-1234 OR 800/233-1234
The Hyatt Regency is just one part of Kemper Freeman's splashy, sprawling retail-office-restaurant-hotel-health club complex called Bellevue Place. The 382-room hotel with 24 stories (the highest in Bellevue) offers many extras: pricier Regency Club rooms on the top three floors, two big ballrooms, several satellite conference rooms, use of the neighboring Seattle Club (for a $7 fee), and a restaurant, Eques, serving Pacific Rim cuisine—pasta, steak, and seafood. The best view rooms are on the south side above the seventh floor. *$$$; AE, DC, MC, V; checks OK; www.hyatt.com; map:HH3* &

La Residence Suite Hotel ★
475 100TH AVE NE, BELLEVUE; 425/455-1475 OR 800/800-1993
Conveniently located across from some of the region's best shopping (Bellevue Square), this 24-room facility is a homey alternative to commercial superhotels on the Eastside. There's leather furniture in the living rooms; two phones in each room, with free local calls; and a fax and copy machine (at no charge) for business use. Rooms have kitchens, separate bedrooms, and large closets, making the hotel popular for longer stays (there's no minimum stay, and rates drop after eight days). Laundry facilities and free parking. *$$$; AE, DC, MC, V; checks OK; www.laresidencehotel.com; map:HH3* &

Residence Inn by Marriott–Bellevue ★★★
14455 NE 29TH PL, BELLEVUE; 425/882-1222 OR 800/331-3131
A quiet cluster of suites just off Highway 520 in east Bellevue, the Eastside version of the Residence Inn feels more like a condominium complex than a hotel. Well suited to business travelers, yet also great for families, this may very well be the Eastside's best-kept lodging secret. All suites have fireplaces and full kitchens with separate living rooms and bedrooms; a complimentary continental breakfast is provided in the main building. The complex has an outdoor pool, three spas, and a sports court, and passes to a nearby health club are provided. Additional guest amenities include laundry facilities and a complimentary van shuttle within a 5-mile radius of the hotel. They'll even do your grocery shopping for you. Travelers with smaller budgets might try the moderately priced basic hotel rooms next door at the Courtyard by Marriott, 425/869-5300. *$$$; AE, DC, DIS, MC, V; checks OK; www.marriott.com; map:GG2* &

Pacific Guest Suites [unrated]
VARIOUS LOCATIONS (MAIL: 411 108TH AVE NE, BELLEVUE 98004); 425/454-7888 OR 800/962-6620
See listing under Downtown/Seattle Center lodgings in this chapter.

Shumway Mansion ★★

11410 99TH PL NE, KIRKLAND; 425/822-0421

This four-story historic home, built in 1909, was moved to Kirkland's Juanita Bay to escape the wrecking ball. Now it's a gracious bed and breakfast with an equal emphasis on seminars and receptions. The eight guest rooms are furnished with antiques and stuffed animals (some might find the latter a bit cloying); public rooms overlook the bay, just a short walk away, and the lower parking lots. Common areas are charmingly decorated with period furnishings and decorative details. The ballroom downstairs, often used for weddings or special meetings, opens onto a flowering patio in summer. A full breakfast, offering something for everyone (including dieters) is served in the dining room on linen-covered tables. Guests can use the Columbia Athletic Club a block away at no charge. Children over 12 are welcome. No pets or smoking. *$$; AE, MC, V; checks OK; www.shumway/nwpages.com; map:DD3* &

Woodmark Hotel ★★★

1200 CARILLON POINT, KIRKLAND; 425/822-3700 OR 800/822-3700

On the eastern shore of Lake Washington, this hotel claims the title of the only lodging actually on the lake. From the outside, it resembles a modern office building, but on the inside one encounters the soft touches of a fine hotel: 100 plush rooms (the best have lake views and the sounds of geese honking and ducks quacking) with fully stocked minibars and refrigerators, terrycloth robes, oversize towels, and service (from laundry to valet) to match. You'll get a complimentary newspaper and a chance to "raid the pantry" for late-night snacks and beverages. Downstairs on the lake level there's a comfortable living room with a grand piano and a well-tended fire. The hotel has its own restaurant, Waters, A Lakeside Bistro, featuring Northwest cuisine and an appealing terrace with a sumptuous view (see Restaurants chapter). Check out the nearby specialty shops (including a luxury day spa), or rent a boat from the marina. Business travelers may take advantage of extra amenities such as a pager for off-site calls or a cellular phone. Parking access is a bit of a maze. *$$$; AE, DC, MC, V; checks OK; www.thewoodmark.com; mail@thewood mark.com; map:EE3* &

Airport Area

Doubletree Hotel Seattle Airport ★★

18740 PACIFIC HWY S; 206/246-8600 OR 800/222-TREE

Formerly the Red Lion Hotel, this gargantuan structure now boasts the increasingly prominent logo of the Doubletree Hotel chain. With 838 rooms and 12 suites, this lodging makes conventioneers comfortable. The east-facing rooms have views of the Cascades. Diners have a choice of three full restaurants, and two lounges provide evening entertainment such as dancing, televised sports, and interactive video. Additional services include around-the-clock airport shuttle and room service. Despite the hotel's enormous size, guests feel just a little more at home when they're greeted with freshly baked chocolate chip cookies—a Doubletree tradition. *$$$; AE, DC, DIS, JCB, MC, V; checks OK; www.double treehotels.com; map:PP6* &

Doubletree Suites/Doubletree Inn ★

16500 SOUTHCENTER PKWY, TUKWILA; 206/246-8220 OR 800/DBL-TREE
The Doubletree, fixed between I-5 and the Southcenter shopping mall, is two hotels. The handsome luxury suites ($99–$166) include such amenities as refrigerators and small wet bars. Southeast-facing rooms have views of Mount Rainier. There's an indoor heated pool, Jacuzzi, and a sauna on the premises; the outdoor pool is across the street in a secluded courtyard at the Doubletree Inn, the older, more plebeian sibling. The woody Northwest lobby of the Inn is nice, but rooms here ($69–$121) are somewhat average; avoid the north-facing ones, which hum with the sounds of I-5. Service is quite friendly. *$$; AE, DC, MC, V; checks OK; www.dbltrehotls.com; map:OO5* &

Holiday Inn Select ★★

1 S GRADY WAY, RENTON; 425/226-7700 OR 800/521-1412
A spirited, friendly staff gives this average midrise, corporate-oriented hotel some personality, and a recent multimillion-dollar renovation has brought the place aesthetically up to date. Business travelers may enjoy the executive rooms on the fifth and sixth floors, where coffee and a continental breakfast are served in the concierge lounge. There are two restaurants on-site. Guest services include a 24-hour airport shuttle, or, if you spend the night before you leave from the airport, you can park here free while you're away. *$$; AE, DC, DIS, MC, V; no checks; map:NN4* &

Seattle Airport Hilton Hotel ★★

17620 PACIFIC HWY S; 206/244-4800 OR 800/HILTONS
In this streamlined four-winged building camouflaged by trees and plantings, the Seattle Airport Hilton manages to create a resort atmosphere along an airport-hotel strip. The 178 plush, larger-than-standard rooms (at posh prices) are set around a landscaped courtyard with pool and indoor/outdoor Jacuzzi; they feature desks and computer hookups, irons and ironing boards, and coffeemakers. An exercise room and numerous meeting and party rooms are available. So is a 24-hour business center, complete with fax, copy machine, computer, and laser printer. The Great American Grill serves breakfast, lunch, and dinner. A planned $53 million redevelopment project, scheduled to be completed in the third

quarter of 2000, will add more than 200 new rooms, an adjoining health club, and a standalone state-of-the-art conference center. *$$$; AE, DC, DIS, JCB, MC, V; checks OK; www.hilton.com; map:PP6* &

Seattle Marriott at Sea-Tac ★★

3201 S 176TH ST; 206/241-2000 OR 800/228-9290

Business travelers (and folks who prefer to spend a night near the airport rather than fight traffic to catch an early-morning flight) will appreciate the swift, courteous service at this 452-room megamotel about a block from the airport strip. The lobby, with its warm Northwest motif, opens into an enormous covered atrium complete with indoor pool and two Jacuzzis. There's also a sauna and a well-equipped exercise room. A casual dining room offers all the usual hotel fare, from sandwiches to steaks. Why bother with a standard room? For slightly higher rates, more spacious, handsomely appointed suites are available on the concierge floor. These include such amenities as higher-quality linens, robes, turn-down service, hair dryers, irons and ironing boards, and access to a lounge that serves continental breakfasts and nightly nibbles. *$$$; AE, DC, MC, V; checks OK; www.marriott.com; map:PP6* &

WestCoast Sea-Tac Hotel ★

18220 PACIFIC HWY S; 206/246-5535 OR 800/426-0670

Meeting facilities at this WestCoast outpost can handle up to 200 people; an outdoor pool, Jacuzzi, and sauna accommodate everyone who stays in the bright rooms. Terrycloth robes, morning newspapers, and mini-refrigerators are available in 32 limited-edition suites. All rooms contain hair dryers and coffeemakers. Guests are treated to free valet parking for seven days. (A slightly less upscale WestCoast Gateway hotel across the street caters handily to the business traveler; 18415 Pacific Highway S, 206/248-8200.) *$$$; AE, DC, DIS, MC, V; checks OK; www.westcoasthotels.com/seatac; map:PP6* &

Wyndham Garden Hotel ★

18118 PACIFIC HWY S; 206/244-6666

You can't get much closer to the airport than this. Attractive styling inside, warm wood paneling in the lobby lounge, and an inviting library and fireplace make the Wyndham Garden a bit classier than your standard airport hotel. Accommodations include 180 guest rooms with writing desks and 24 suites with coffeemakers and hair dryers. Room service (from 6 to 10pm daily) and meeting space are available. *$$$; AE, DC, DIS, MC, V; checks OK; www.wyndham.com; map:PP6* &

EXPLORING

EXPLORING

Top 25 Attractions

1) PIKE PLACE MARKET

Pike St to Virginia St on Pike Pl; Information: 206/682-7453 If cities have souls, then Pike Place Market is Seattle's. The Market that now sells an abundance of foods and wares—everything from seafood and sheep's-milk cheese to garden shrubs and slug souvenirs—opened as an experiment on August 17, 1907, in response to the demands of angry housewives who were tired of exorbitant food prices padded by middlemen. Bringing farmers and consumers together proved immensely successful, and soon fishmongers and shopkeepers joined the farmers' wagons along Pike Place. The Market has had its ups and downs, but after nearly a century of operation, it is still a boisterous bazaar.

Despite relentless gentrification of the area, this oldest continuously operating farmers market in the United States still prides itself on being an incubator for small businesses—"the biggest mom-n-pop store in town." National and regional chain stores or franchise businesses aren't allowed in (except, of course, for Starbucks, which opened its very first store at the Market in 1971). About 125 local farmers have permits to sell their produce at day stalls; more than 200 permanent businesses operate here year-round; and about 200 registered craftspeople and artists come here to entice passersby with their handmade goods (Market guidelines prevent infiltration of anything mass-produced).

The people of the Market are really its main attraction—old sea dogs who reminisce about the Market's lusty past; friendly produce and fish vendors who bark encouragingly at shoppers; street musicians, puppeteers, and mimes who turn street corners into stages. The way to "do" the Market is to spend an unstructured day meandering its crannies, nibbling from its astonishing variety of ethnic and regional foods, browsing the shops, watching the crowds. If you visit before 9am, you can observe the place come alive as the farmers set up; in spring and summer, shopping is best done (once most of the farmers have come) in the early morning hours. In the off season, vendors are less harried and you can talk to them about what's in season and how to cook it, and really get a feel for the Market community.

The official entrance is at the corner of First Avenue and Pike Street, at the **INFORMATION BOOTH** (1st Ave and Pike Pl; 206/682-7453), where you can pick up a map and some advice on sights, or just a self-guided-tour pamphlet. (The booth doubles as a day-of-show, half-price ticket outlet, Ticket/Ticket, Tuesday–Sunday, noon–6pm.) **READ ALL ABOUT IT** (206/624-0140), the Market's newsstand and official gossip

TOP 25 ATTRACTIONS

1) Pike Place Market
2) Pioneer Square
3) Hiram H. Chittenden Locks
4) Space Needle & Seattle Center
5) Seattle Asian Art Museum
6) Smith Tower
7) Museum of Flight
8) Seattle Art Museum
9) Odyssey, the Maritime Discovery Center
10) Waterfront
11) Monorail & Westlake Center
12) Woodland Park Zoo
13) Klondike Gold Rush National Historical Park
14) Elliott Bay Book Company
15) Burke Museum of Natural History and Culture
16) Volunteer Park
17) Pacific Science Center
18) Fishermen's Terminal
19) Seattle Aquarium
20) Nordstrom & REI
21) Boeing Plant Tour
22) Washington Park Arboretum
23) Spirit of Washington Dinner Train
24) Gas Works Park
25) Green Lake

station, anchors this busy corner, as does **DELAURENTI'S SPECIALTY FOODS** (206/622-0141), Seattle's landmark Italian deli with an eye-opening array of olive oils, cheeses, and imported meats, a substantial wine selection, and some of the city's best breads. To the south is the **SOUTH ARCADE**, home to the modern-looking shops and condos that have spread forth from the 7-acre Market Historic District (created by voters in 1971). Walking west, down the covered corridor, past artists' stalls and vegetable stands, you'll come to the elbow of the L-shaped Market. This is the start of the **MAIN ARCADE**—the famous neon Pike Place Market sign and clock are just above you—and home to the big bronze pig named **RACHEL** (a good spot for meeting a friend). The produce vendors called "highstallers" display beautifully arranged (don't touch) international produce. Farmers at the low stalls sell seasonal, regional produce—local berries, sweet onions, Washington apples—direct from the farm. In the midst of this is a Market institution: the **ATHENIAN INN** (206/624-7166), a smoky, working-class cafe that's been the favorite haunt of Market old-timers since 1909 (and was one of the settings for 1993's *Sleepless in Seattle*). The down-home food is okay, but the real draws are the marvelous view of Elliott Bay and the long beer list.

Engraved floor tiles throughout the Market were part of a fundraising project in 1986, when a $35 donation bought anyone a wee bit of immortality. The Main Arcade also has two labyrinthine levels below the street, where you can find **GOLDEN AGE COLLECTABLES** (206/622-

9799), which features a wonderful trove of new and vintage comic books and more; the **MARKET MAGIC SHOP** (206/624-4271), where you might catch owners Darryl Beckman and Sheila Lyon demonstrating a bit of legerdemain; and **MISTER E BOOKS** (206/622-5182), offering a range of titles but specializing in first-edition mysteries.

In summer, the artists' and craftspeople's tables stretch along the Main and North Arcades from Pike Place to Virginia Street and **VICTOR STEINBRUECK PARK**, the splash of green that marks the northern border of the Market (see Parks and Beaches in this chapter). Across Pike Place, you'll discover shops and ethnic eateries—including the one that started it all, the original **STARBUCKS**—leading to a shady courtyard in the back, where covered tables are set out for **EMMETT WATSON'S OYSTER BAR** (206/448-7721), a folksy seafood joint named in honor of the longtime Seattle journalist and raconteur.

If you take a short detour here, up the wooden stairs to **POST ALLEY,** you'll find two Seattle restaurant gems: **THE PINK DOOR** (206/443-3241), a funky, likable trattoria with terrific summertime porch seating, and **KELLS** (206/728-1916), a rough-hewn Irish pub and restaurant. Follow Post Alley south now to where it meets Pike Place at the **SANITARY MARKET** (so named because horses were not allowed inside); you'll pass Peter Lewis's wonderful **CAFE CAMPAGNE** (206/728-2233), just below the stylish, 65-room **INN AT THE MARKET** (206/443-3600), Pike Place Market's only sizable hotel. In the next block you'll go by the see-and-be-seen sipping bar at **SEATTLE'S BEST COFFEE** (SBC) (206/467-7700) and the entrance to an array of shops and eating places—including a fine regional gift seller, **MADE IN WASHINGTON** (206/467-0788)—in the somewhat more sterile arcade of the **POST ALLEY MARKET BUILDING**.

Across the street from the highstallers you'll also encounter **TOTEM SMOKEHOUSE** (206/443-1710), where you can pick up smoked salmon (or arrange to have it shipped). **LE PANIER** (206/441-3669) is a French bakery on the corner, and wafts of garlic pour out of nearby **CUCINA FRESCA** (206/448-4758). Stop by **PIROSHKY PIROSHKY** (206/441-6068) for a savory pastry. **SEATTLE GARDEN CENTER** (206/448-0431) stocks many difficult-to-find bulbs and seeds as well as a wide array of gardening books. **SUR LA TABLE** (206/448-2244) is a nationally acclaimed cook's emporium.

Inside the Sanitary Market is an atmospheric, chaotic jumble of produce stands and eating places, including the **PIKE PLACE MARKET CREAMERY** (206/622-5029), which sells delicious dairy goods; **JACK'S FISH SPOT** (206/467-0514), purveyor of steaming cups of cioppino from an outdoor bar; and **THREE GIRLS BAKERY** (206/622-1045), this city's best sandwich counter.

Just to the south is the last building in the historic stretch: the **CORNER MARKET,** a picturesque structure of careful brickwork and

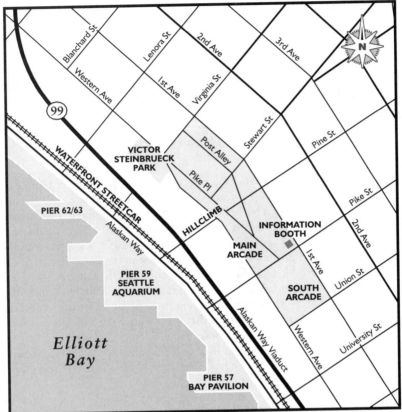

PIKE PLACE MARKET

arched windows that houses produce and flower stalls. A couple of restaurants are hidden in its upper reaches: the tiny **MATT'S IN THE MARKET** (206/467-7909), a cozy perch from which to enjoy an oyster po' boy or a candlelit seafood dinner; and **CHEZ SHEA** (206/467-9990), perhaps the most romantic nook in town, with an adjoining bistro/bar called **SHEA'S LOUNGE**, open most evenings till just after midnight. Post Alley continues on the south side of Pike Street, as it dips down below street level and passes the classy, dimly lit Italian restaurant **IL BISTRO** (206/682-3049) and the **MARKET THEATER** (206/781-9273), home to an improvisational comedy–theater troupe.

A steep but well-landscaped cascade of stairs, known as the **HILL-CLIMB CORRIDOR**, connects the Market (at Western Avenue) with the waterfront below. Among the shops hugging this incline are two very different furniture showplaces: **KASALA** (1505 Western Ave; 206/623-7795), which specializes in high-style home and office furniture, and the

CHICKEN & EGG STORE (1426 Alaskan Way; 206/623-6144), full of beds and sofas made from peeled logs.

It's almost impossible to get a parking space on congested Pike Place—local regulars don't even try—so either come here by bus or splurge for a space in the spiffy 550-slot parking garage on Western Avenue, with its elevator that opens directly into the Market (some merchants help defray the cost by giving out parking stamps, free with purchase, so be sure to ask). Alternatively, try one of the lots a little farther down Western or along First Avenue to the north. *Every day; information@pikeplacemarket.org; www.pikeplacemarket.com; map:J8–I8*

2) PIONEER SQUARE

Jackson St to Columbia St along 1st Ave No place better represents Seattle's long and quirky history than does Pioneer Square. Located just south of the modern business district, this neighborhood has undergone several transformations. It started out as the site of a Native American village, then was settled by white pioneers in 1852, and grew into the city's original downtown before being razed in the Great Fire of 1889. Although rebuilt according to more architecturally coherent—and less flammable—standards, Pioneer Square fell into a lengthy decline after 1900, when the town's center started to move north. By the 1960s, the area had become so run-down that conservative city officials proposed leveling it to make room for new office buildings and parking lots. Fortunately, wiser heads fought to save the Square. Banks chipped in with incentive loan programs for businesses, and Pioneer Square was made the city's first historic district.

Today, that district encompasses almost 90 acres, making it one of the most extensive "old towns" in the nation. It's a busy place filled with bookstores, art galleries, gift stores, antique shops, and nightclubs. Lawyers, architects, and media folk dominate the work force. Though the robust economy of recent years seems to have reduced the number of panhandlers on these sidewalks, homeless transients are still drawn here by a preponderance of missions (and park benches).

Seattle's earliest intersection, at First Avenue and Yesler Way, is home to triangular **PIONEER PLACE PARK**, which became a major landmark after the 1889 fire. It is adorned with a Victorian iron-and-glass pergola (a holdover from the days of trolley cars) and a totem pole—a replica of a Tlingit Indian work stolen by Seattle burghers during an 1899 visit to Alaska. Facing the park is the **PIONEER BUILDING**, designed by Elmer Fisher, a prolific Scotsman who established the architectural vernacular of post-fire Seattle, synthesizing his Victorian philosophies about facades with the weighty Romanesque Revival look. The building houses offices, a maze of antique shops on the lower level, and the headquarters of the **UNDERGROUND TOUR**, a touristy subterranean prowl through the

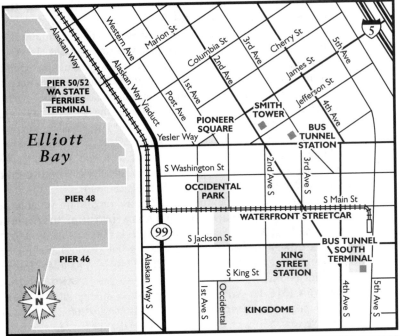

PIONEER SQUARE

original streets of downtown (see Walking Tours under Organized Tours in this chapter).

Diagonal **YESLER WAY** doesn't look much different from other thoroughfares nowadays. But in the mid-19th century it was covered with small, greased logs, and trees cut in the Seattle hills were dragged down that avenue to feed pioneer Henry Yesler's waterfront sawmill. It quickly became familiar as "skid road," a nickname (often mangled into "skid row") that was used as an insult in the early 20th century to describe inner-city neighborhoods that (like Pioneer Square) had fallen on hard times. Just across Yesler from Pioneer Place is **MERCHANTS CAFE** (109 Yesler Way; 206/624-1515), Seattle's oldest restaurant. To the west, you'll find a tasty breakfast or late-night dinner at **TRATTORIA MITCHELLI** (84 Yesler Way; 206/623-3883), an unofficial Pioneer Square landmark, open every day—and most days until 4am. **AL BOCCALINO** (1 Yesler Way; 206/622-7688) is a wonderful nook for a romantic (and pricier) Italian meal.

First Avenue is the main, tree-lined artery through the historic district, intersected by streets that terminate at the waterfront a block west (best chance for parking in this area is under the Alaskan Way Viaduct;

bring quarters for the meters). Heading south you'll see the **NEW ORLEANS RESTAURANT** (114 1st Ave S; 206/622-2563), a Creole/Cajun eatery known for its Dixieland and R&B acts as well as the mint juleps concocted in its bar, and **NORTHWEST FINE WOODWORKING** (1st Ave S and S Jackson St; 206/625-0542), with its continually changing exhibits of exquisite handcrafted furniture and sculptures. **FIREWORKS GALLERY** (210 1st Ave S; 206/682-8707) offers beautifully made pottery, jewelry, and other handicrafts. On the same block is the **GRAND CENTRAL ARCADE**. Opened in 1879 by entrepreneur (and later Washington governor) Watson C. Squire, the structure housed Seattle's first real theater. Rebuilding after the '89 blaze, Squire converted it into a hotel. It now contains two levels of upscale retail, including the excellent **GRAND CENTRAL BAKING COMPANY** (214 1st Ave S; 206/622-3644).

Immediately across from the Grand Central on S Main Street is the interesting and unusual **KLONDIKE GOLD RUSH NATIONAL HISTORICAL PARK**, and at First Avenue S and S Main Street is the renowned **ELLIOTT BAY BOOK COMPANY** (see separate listings in this chapter). Next door, **BOWIE AND COMPANY** (314 1st Ave S; 206/624-4100) handles rare and out-of-print books and does efficient book searches. **GRAND CENTRAL MERCANTILE** (316 1st Ave S; 206/623-8894), a quality kitchen emporium, and the whimsical **WOOD SHOP** (320 1st Ave S; 206/624-1763), an imaginative toy shop with great stuffed animals, are a couple of other worthy stops along this stretch.

OCCIDENTAL AVENUE SOUTH is a sun-dappled, brick-lined pedestrian walkway studded with galleries. On the first Thursday of every month, this mall—indeed, all of Pioneer Square—fills up with art- (and scene-) appreciators who turn out for **FIRST THURSDAY GALLERY WALKS**, when galleries stay open late to preview new shows (see "Art Appeal" box). If your feet get tired, pause for a nosh at the chic, high-character Italian coffee bar **TORREFAZIONE ITALIA** (320 Occidental Ave S; 206/624-5847). Occidental Avenue S segues into **OCCIDENTAL PARK**, a Northwest attempt at a Parisian park setting with cobblestones and trees. The international feeling is enhanced by the occasional horse-drawn buggy or rickshaw-like pedicab that breezes by. A more unusual park is tucked into a corner at Second Avenue and S Main St: **WATERFALL GARDENS**, where an artificial waterfall spills over large rocks in a cool urban grotto (see Parks and Beaches in this chapter).

Looking south, it's impossible to miss Seattle's largest sports stadium, the **KINGDOME** (4th Ave S and S King St; 206/296-3128). Hailed by some as fine Brutalist design, maligned by many as an oversized cement orange-juice squeezer, the Kingdome is slated for demolition and replacement by a new Seahawks football stadium to complement the new baseball stadium rising next door. **F. X. MCRORY'S STEAK, CHOP AND**

OYSTER HOUSE (419 Occidental Ave S; 206/623-4800) is still the restaurant and watering hole of choice for gamegoers. Just north of the Kingdome is King Street Station (2nd Ave S and S aMain St). With its striking clocktower, the station opened for business in 1906 and stil receives Amtrak trains. West on King Street is **MERRILL PLACE**, Pioneer Square's high-rent district. Once Schwabacher's Hardware, the revitalized building conceals an enclave of apartments and **IL TERRAZZO CARMINE** (411 1st Ave S; 206/467-7797), an esteemed Italian restaurant with a romantic bar and a terrace overlooking a fountain—the perfect place to wind-up a Pioneer Square tour. Map:O9–M8

3) HIRAM M. CHITTENDEN LOCKS

3015 NW 54th St; 206/783-7059 Talk of digging a navigable canal between the fresh water of Lakes Washington and Union and the salt water of Puget Sound began shortly after Seattle's pioneers arrived in the 1850s. However, debates over the best location for such a waterway and searches for financing delayed the start of work until 1911. And there were still numerous engineering challenges ahead: the biggest was the design and construction of locks near the canal's western end, which could control the difference in water levels between the Sound and the much higher Lake Washington. (In the end, the latter was lowered by 9 feet, exposing new property and interfering with salmon migrations.) Not until 1917 was the 8-mile-long **LAKE WASHINGTON SHIP CANAL** dedicated, and another 17 years would pass before it was officially declared complete. In 1936, the Corps of Engineers named the locks in honor of Major Hiram M. Chittenden, who had supervised the canal project.

Today, more than 100,000 pleasure and commercial boats per year go through the canal and what are colloquially known as the "Ballard Locks." Couples and families trot down to watch this informal regatta as it works its way through the "water elevator." The descent (or ascent) takes 10 to 25 minutes, depending on which of the two locks is being used. Particularly good people-watching is available during Seafair in July, when boats filled with carousing men and women crowd the locks, impatient to get through.

Across the waterway, in **COMMODORE PARK**, the falls generated by a **FISH LADDER** entice struggling salmon each year, the sleek creatures bound for spawning grounds in Lake Washington and Cascade mountain streams. You can watch the fishes' progress from a viewing area with windows onto the ladder: salmon in summer (peak viewing for sockeye is in early July) and steelhead in winter. With the salmon come the playful but controversial sea lions, who know a prime dining spot when they see one—much to the chagrin of salmon conservationists.

Call the **VISITORS CENTER** for times of tours (daily in summer, weekends only during the rest of the year); there's also an interesting exhibit that explains the use and building of the locks. The green lawns and tree-lined waterside promenade of the park, along with the impressive rose display at the **CARL S. ENGLISH JR. BOTANICAL GARDENS** (see Gardens in this chapter), make grand backdrops for summer picnics. *Free; every day 7am–9pm; map:FF9*

4) SPACE NEEDLE & SEATTLE CENTER

Between Denny Way and Mercer St, 1st Ave N and 5th Ave N; 206/684-8582 This 74-acre park north of downtown, at the base of Queen Anne Hill, is the legacy of the 1962 Century 21 Exposition—Seattle's second world's fair (after the 1909 Alaska-Yukon-Pacific Exposition on what is now the University of Washington campus) and one of the few such extravaganzas to turn a profit and leave a permanent facility behind. Today it's the arts and entertainment hub of this city, hosting such popular annual events as the Northwest Folklife Festival (Memorial Day weekend), the Bite of Seattle (mid-July), and Bumbershoot (Labor Day weekend). (See Calendar of Events in the Planning a Trip chapter.)

Seattle Center has recently seen extensive (and expensive) new construction and improvements. The Pacific Science Center underwent a major renovation, new theater space has been opened, and the tepee-ish old Coliseum—home to circuses, concerts, and the Seattle Thunderbirds hockey team—was renamed **KEYARENA** and expanded in 1995. There are further changes in the works. In the year 2000, billionaire Paul Allen (Bill Gates's former partner at Microsoft) is planning to open his $60 million, 110,000-square-foot **EXPERIENCE MUSIC PROJECT** (325 5th Ave N; 425/450-1997; www.experience.org) on the Center's east side.

Some 9 million visitors wash through the Center every year, they come primarily for a 43-second, 520-foot elevator ride. New York City has its Empire State Building. San Francisco has the Golden Gate Bridge. And Seattle has . . . a flying saucer on a tripod? Actually, the **SPACE NEEDLE** (206/443-2111) looks a lot like George Jetson's cloud-level apartment building, if that sounds any better. This 605-foot tower was the chief attraction at Seattle's 1962 world's fair, and it remains the most widely recognized symbol of the city.

Legend has it that the Needle (originally called the "Space Cage") began as a doodle sketched on a cocktail napkin by world's fair chairman Eddie Carlson. Architects John Graham Sr., Victor Steinbrueck, and John Ridley later translated that into what at the time was considered a futuristic concept in metal and glass. When King County commissioners refused to fund the project, a private corporation stepped in and completed the work in an astonishing eight months, at a cost of $4.5 million. (The structure is still privately owned.) Anchored to terra firma by almost

6,000 tons of concrete, the tower was built to withstand winds of up to 200 miles per hour and has already survived one major earthquake (in 1965) unscathed. The ride up provides panoramic views on clear days as well as a mini-history lesson, all for $9 ($4 kids, $8 seniors). *Every day; spaceneedle@digital-sherpas.com; www.spaceneedle.com; map:B6* &

The **SPACE NEEDLE RESTAURANT** (206/443-2150), at 500 feet, revolves 360 degrees every hour (thanks to two gearboxes equipped with one-horsepower motors), giving diners and slow sippers in the bar panoramic views of Puget Sound, the Olympic Mountains, and the city center. Restaurant patrons ride the elevator free of charge.

Visitors to Seattle Center who arrive with kids next head for the dinosaurs and dynamos at the **PACIFIC SCIENCE CENTER** (see separate listing in this section). Chances are they'll also visit the **FUN FOREST** (206/728-1585), a small-scale amusement park near the Space Needle that contains a Ferris wheel, a wild river ride, a roller coaster, and an indoor pavilion offering laser tag and video games. Ride tickets—purchased individually or in discounted packs—are available at booths within the Forest. *The Fun Forest is open Mon–Thurs noon–11pm (June 1– Labor Day only), and Fri–Sat noon–midnight, Sun noon–10pm (year-round).*

For more sophisticated youth entertainment, there's the **SEATTLE CHILDREN'S THEATRE**, with two stages—the 485-seat Charlotte Martin Theatre and the smaller Eve Alvord Theatre—on which are performed plays that have a bit more intensity than you might expect from kids' fare (see Theater in the Performing Arts chapter). Meanwhile, adults enjoy the performing arts at a string of other stages arranged along Mercer Street at the Center's northern edge. The striking, neon-adorned **BAGLEY WRIGHT THEATRE** is home to the Seattle Repertory Theatre (call 206/443-2210 to arrange for a free tour of the theater, September–May). The Rep's old digs, the **INTIMAN PLAYHOUSE**, currently houses the Intiman Theatre, while the **OPERA HOUSE** accommodates the Seattle Opera and Pacific Northwest Ballet.

If you'd rather hang out and do nothing much on a sunny summer day, that's certainly possible at the **INTERNATIONAL FOUNTAIN**, a huge landmark near the Center's center, where enormous jets of water shoot from a metal dome into the sky, sometimes synchronized with music and lights. Just to the north is the **NORTHWEST CRAFT CENTER** (206/728-1555), displaying a variety of pottery, crafts, paintings, and jewelry for sale; to the south is the **FLAG PLAZA**, with flags commemorating all 50 states. Should you grow hungry, stop in at the nearby **CENTER HOUSE** (206/684-8582), a cavernous structure with a vast selection of ethnic fast food and populated by conventioneers, pre-adolescents looking to be seen, and senior citizens. On the lower level of the Center House is the world-class **CHILDREN'S MUSEUM** (see Museums in this chapter).

There is no admission charge to get onto the Seattle Center grounds (except during a few major festivals such as Bumbershoot), but parking can be a problem. The cheapest lots are on the east side. For events at the Opera House, Mercer Arena, and Intiman Playhouse, the covered parking garage directly across Mercer Street from the Opera House affords easy access, but the egress can be maddeningly slow on busy nights. One way to avoid the problem is to take the **MONORAIL** from downtown—a 90-second ride (see separate listing in this section) that drops you off at the Center House. (The Monorail stops running at 11pm, however, so you may have to hail a cab back downtown after a late show.) *Seattle Center: every day; www.seattlecenter.com; map:B6* &

5) SEATTLE ASIAN ART MUSEUM

1400 E Prospect St, Volunteer Park; 206/654-3100 The Seattle Asian Art Museum is exquisite. With the opening of the downtown Seattle Art Museum in 1991, this original building (designed in Moderne style by Seattle architect Carl F. Gould) was renovated to serve as the home for the museum's extensive Asian art collections. Built in 1931 by Richard Fuller and his mother, Margaret E. MacTavish Fuller, the museum first housed their 1,700-piece collection of Asian art before growing into a more eclectic institution. Now the carefully lit galleries once again hold sacred images—the Buddha in perfect meditation, a monk at the moment of enlightenment, the Hindu deities Siva and Parvati rapt in divine love— the kind of art that draws you away from daily obsessions, that soothes the mind and expands the soul. In addition to old favorites from the collection—such as the 17th-century Japanese crow screens and the Fullers' array of elaborate *netsuke*—don't miss the ancient Chinese funerary art and the collection of 14th- to 16th-century ceramics from Thailand. An Educational Outreach Gallery also has been added, with hands-on displays. The **KADO TEAGARDEN** serves Asian teas and fresh pastries, and the Asian Art Library, downstairs near the tearoom, is available for public use. Admission charge for adults and children 12 and older; everyone is admitted free on the first Thursday and Saturday of each month. (Admission tickets also may be used for entry to SAM downtown—see separate listing in this section—within a week of purchase.) *Tues–Wed, Fri–Sun 10am–5pm; Thurs 10am–9pm; www.seattleartmuseum. org; map:GG6* &

6) SMITH TOWER

506 2nd Ave; 206/682-9393 Against the picket fence of skyscrapers that currently make up Seattle's skyline, the Smith Tower looks almost puny. Yet when it was first opened in the summer of 1914, this 42-story (522-foot) terra-cotta-and-steel spire was the tallest building west of the Mississippi. It remained the highest in Seattle until 1969, when the old

Seattle-First National Bank Tower (now the 1001 4th Avenue Building), climbed to 50 stories, or 609 feet. (The 605-foot Space Needle, finished in 1962, was also taller than the Smith Tower but doesn't usually count in the record books since it wasn't a "building" per se.) Even now, though, the Smith Tower is considered the most beloved of this city's cloud-kissing edifices.

It's the legacy of New Yorker Lyman C. Smith, an armaments manufacturer turned typewriter magnate who visited Seattle in 1909 and decided that this town had potential for commercial growth. Wanting to benefit from that growth, Smith commissioned the architectural firm of Gaggin & Gaggin, based in Syracuse, New York, to design an office structure both distinctive and tall enough that it wouldn't be exceeded in Seattle during his lifetime. He got exactly what he'd ordered, if not what he'd intended; Smith died before his skyscraper was finished. Not long afterward, the city's commercial and governmental heart began moving aggressively north, out of what was then "downtown" (today's Pioneer Square), leaving the Smith Tower on the sidelines until Pioneer Square was "rediscovered" in the 1960s.

Though it is undergoing a multi-million-dollar renovation in 1999, the Smith Tower will retain what are reportedly the West Coast's only manually operated elevators—eight brass-caged beauties. Its 35th-floor **CHINESE ROOM**, an elaborate space that's popular for weddings, is surrounded by an observation deck where visitors can take in some magnificent views of downtown for a couple of bucks. *Every day, 10am–5pm; map:O7* &

7) MUSEUM OF FLIGHT

9404 E Marginal Way S; 206/764-5720 You don't have to be an aviation buff to enjoy the sheer physical spectacle of 20 full-size airplanes— including a 40,000-pound B-17—suspended from the ceiling of a stunning six-story glass-and-steel gallery. The Museum of Flight, located 10 miles south of Seattle, is notable for its expansive galleries, its sophisticated design, its impressive collection, and its unique location at a working airfield. Though it's often referred to informally as "the Boeing Museum of Flight," this institution has no formal affiliation with Boeing—the aircraft-manufacturing behemoth and mainstay of the Northwest economy—apart from its location at Boeing Field and its origination in the **RED BARN**, which was Boeing's humble first home in 1910 and now sits adjacent to the main museum structure.

The museum takes you from the early legends of flying through the history of aviation, from pioneering stages to the present, with special emphasis on Pacific Northwest flight—military, commercial, and amateur. The collection includes a replica of the Wright brothers' original glider; a 1917 Curtiss Jenny biplane; a Douglas DC-3; a 707 version of

Air Force One; Apollo and Mercury space capsules; and the 98-foot Lockheed A-12 Blackbird, the fastest plane ever built (it has flown coast to coast in 67 minutes). The museum has a variety of workshops, films, tours, and special programs. Children especially enjoy the hangar with three explorable planes, and hands-on learning areas with paper airplanes, boomerangs, and other toys that fly. Admission charge for adults and children 5 and older; free on the first Thursday evening of each month, 5–9pm. *Mon–Wed, Fri–Sun 10am–5pm; Thurs 10am–9pm; map:NN6* &

8) SEATTLE ART MUSEUM

100 University St; 206/654-3100 Because of its central downtown location, its bold design (by renowned American architect Robert Venturi), and the presence of sculptor Jonathan Borofsky's 48-foot mechanical **HAMMERING MAN** at its First Avenue entrance, the Seattle Art Museum (SAM) rarely fails to attract attention. Since it opened at its present location in 1991, local residents, well-known architects, and eminent international art authorities have all weighed in with either praise or criticism.

SAM has always been known as an excellent regional museum notable for its Asian collections. Now, with 145,000 square feet of space (though only a third of it is actually gallery space) and many new acquisitions, its focus is worldwide, with particular emphasis on Asian, African, and Northwest Coast Native American art. Each gallery is especially tailored to complement the collections—for example, dark, dramatically lit rooms for the ceremonial works of Africa and the Northwest Coast; tall ceilings with ornate moldings for European decorative arts; and white loftlike spaces for New York School paintings. The **JAPANESE GALLERY** features an authentic bamboo-and-cedar teahouse, where a Japanese master performs the tea ceremony for small groups of visitors two or three times a month (reservations required). A big **SPECIAL EXHIBITIONS GALLERY** houses periodic traveling shows, an occasional in-house exhibit, and events geared to mass audiences, such as the 1998 *Leonardo Lives* exhibit, built around a notebook of script and sketches by Leonardo da Vinci now owned by Microsoft mogul Bill Gates. A lecture room and a 300-seat auditorium lend themselves to talks, films, music, and dramatic performances; there's a fully equipped art studio for children's and adult classes, and a good cafe. The **MUSEUM STORE** is excellent.

On Thursday evenings SAM stays open late, with refreshments, live music, poetry readings, and performances scheduled each week. Admission charge for adults and children over 12; everyone admitted free on the first Thursday of each month. (Admission tickets also may be used for entry to the Seattle Asian Art Museum in Volunteer Park—see separate listing in this section—within a week of purchase.) *Tues–Wed, Fri–Sun 10am–5pm, Thurs 10am–9pm; www.seattleartmuseum.org; map:K7* &

9) ODYSSEY, THE MARITIME DISCOVERY CENTER

2205 Alaskan Way, Pier 66; 206/374-4000 Seven piers north of the Seattle Aquarium sits a complementary museum that shifts the focus from water life to shore life. Odyssey is an interactive museum celebrating the natural and commercial uses of Seattle's marine environment, with exhibits that allow visitors to experience simulated kayaking, fishing, or freighter navigation. Geared toward kids but entertaining for adults too, the educational center emphasizes technology, human interactions with the marine environment, and an overall "you-are-there" exhibit feel. The local touch is laced with humor, as a Ken Griffey Jr. baseball glove "travels" from Midwestern leather hide to South Korea for tanning, and the Philippines for stitching, before finally returning to the United States. Admission charged. *Sun–Wed 10am–9pm, Thurs–Sat 10am–5pm (July–Aug); every day 10am–5pm (Sept–June); www.ody.org; map:G9* &

10) WATERFRONT

S Main St to Denny Way along Alaskan Way Once a busy commercial area, noisy with the thrum of steam-powered trading vessels and the clatter of trains hauling goods to markets north and south, Seattle's waterfront today is mostly a tourist boardwalk bordered by kitschy souvenir shops, harbor-tour operations, and fish 'n' chips counters. Since the 1950s, it has been separated from the rest of the city by the ugly Alaskan Way Viaduct (Highway 99) running high overhead. However, construction of the **BELL HARBOR INTERNATIONAL CONFERENCE CENTER**, a new maritime museum, and a $27 million **WORLD TRADE CENTER** and hotel around Pier 66 were all calculated to draw more visitors and maybe even locals to this still-working harbor.

The best way to explore the waterfront is to walk in one direction and then hop aboard the **WATERFRONT STREETCAR** (206/553-3000) for the return trip. These vintage wood-trimmed trolleys, imported from Australia and restored by volunteers, make non-narrated, 20-minute trips from Pier 70 south along Alaskan Way, then through Pioneer Square to the International District. Streetcars operate daily, with extended hours in summer. The fare is $1 ($1.25 during rush hours); kids' fare is 75¢ and senior/disabled fare is 25¢.

The nonindustrial waterfront is anchored at **PIER 48** (foot of Main St) and the pergola of the **WASHINGTON STREET PUBLIC BOAT LANDING**. The waterfront side of the pier has an excellent interpretive display of this harbor's history, and periscopes offer grand seaward views. Look along this space (and directly north and south) for a thought-provoking art project/exhibit about the conflicting issues of waterfront development. Pier 48 also plays host every fall to the Northwest Bookfest (206/378-1883), which brings booksellers and publishers together with writers for a weekend of readings, panel discussions, and exhibits of new titles (see Calendar of Events in the Planning a Trip chapter).

North on Alaskan Way is the city's main ferry terminal, **COLMAN DOCK** (foot of Marion St at Pier 52), where boats depart for Bremerton, Bainbridge Island, and (for foot passengers only) Vashon Island (see By Ferry under Getting Around in the Lay of the City chapter).

At **PIER 54** are a couple of Seattle's most endearing landmarks. **YE OLDE CURIOSITY SHOP** (206/682-5844), established in 1899, is a mecca for trinket junkies or for anyone who wants to commemorate his or her Seattle visit with a keepsake rubber slug or a polychromatic seashell, a piece of Native American art, or maybe a shrunken head. Co-owner Andy James says that his secret to stocking this emporium is to "buy what you love, and buy what you hate. . . . The things we really do well with are those that you see and really fall in love with, or those that you look at and you think you wouldn't buy in a thousand years." **IVAR'S ACRES OF CLAMS** (206/624-6852), with its breezy outdoor fish bar (attracting more than a few hungry seagulls), was the first in a local chain of seafood eateries created by notorious raconteur, Seattle booster, friend to artists, and ace fish hustler Ivar Haglund.

WATERFRONT PARK, at Pier 57, offers boardwalks and elevated levels to give visitors a fine perspective both on Elliott Bay and on the Seattle cityscape. Adjacent to the park is a plaque that recalls the gold rush's beginning here in 1897, when the steamer *Portland* arrived at the former Pier 58 with the first news that gold had been discovered in the Klondike.

Past Pier 59 and the **SEATTLE AQUARIUM** (see separate listing in this section) is **PIER 66/BELL STREET PIER,** which includes the International Conference Center, a marina (with short-term public moorage available), several restaurants that take advantage of splendid views out over the Sound, and **ODYSSEY, THE MARITIME DISCOVERY CENTER** (see separate listing in this section). The Port of Seattle, once headquartered at Pier 66, has moved to Pier 69, where it has joined the **VICTORIA CLIPPER** (see By Ferry under Getting Around in the Lay of the City chapter, or Victoria in the Day Trips chapter) in a huge white whale of a building. Next door is **PIER 70,** a picturesque barnlike structure with some shops.

Finally comes **MYRTLE EDWARDS PARK** (see Parks and Beaches in this chapter), which winds back into more working piers (you'll often see container ships and auto carriers docked back here) and a huge grain elevator that has become a waterfront landmark. Keep walking north through **ELLIOTT BAY PARK** and you'll come to a public fishing pier. Farther north, this path leads to **ELLIOTT BAY MARINA** and the glitzy **PALISADE** restaurant (2601 W Marina Pl; 206/285-1000), although this last is more conveniently reached by car from Magnolia. *Map:O9–A9*

11) MONORAIL & WESTLAKE CENTER

400 Pine St; 206/441-6038 (Monorail) 206/287-0762 or 206/467-1600
Few places speak more clearly of Seattle's commercial complexity or the
determination of its leaders to preserve the energy of downtown than
does the glass-and-steel **WESTLAKE CENTER**. Developed by the Rouse
Company, a Maryland-based designer of "festival marketplaces"
 (including Boston's revitalized Faneuil Hall and Portland's Pioneer
Place), this shopping mall spikes up from what used to be a major
streetcar hub. Since the 1950s, the property had been a battleground
where architects (who wanted to create a commodious urban commons
on the site) faced off against merchants (who wanted to retain the land
for retail). In the late '80s an uneasy compromise was finally struck,
giving over most of the site to a retail arcade and office building but
establishing a triangular portion on the south end as Westlake Park.

Across Pine Street (once closed to traffic, but reopened in 1997 by
public vote), Westlake Park hosts Seattle artist Robert Maki's *Westlake
Star Axis/Seven Hills*, which includes a pink granite column, a granite-
framed waterfall, and a granite arch from which public speeches are
sometimes made. Red, gray, and white granite paving blocks (arranged
in a weaving pattern familiar from Salish Indian baskets) tie this open
space across Pine Street to the mall. Though low on landscaping, the park
is high on citizen occupation. Warm afternoons attract a diverse mix of
businesspeople on lunch breaks, street musicians, teenagers milling
around trying to define "cool," and stentorian preachers telling the
world exactly where it's gone wrong.

Three of the mall's four retail levels are occupied by upscale chain
stores, as well as some local/regional enterprises. The top floor is dominated by fast-fooderies, serving everything from pizza to Thai food to hot
dogs on a stick. *Weekdays 9:30am–9pm, Sat 9:30am–8pm, Sun 11am–
6pm; map:I6* &

The top floor of Westlake Center is also the location of one of two
stations for the **MONORAIL**. Way back in 1910, a local inventor named
W. H. Shephard suggested that the city construct an elevated monorail
network to reduce traffic on its streets. But not until Seattle hosted the
1962 world's fair was a monorail erected here. Although it cost $3.5 mil-
lion at the time, it was basically just a space-age gimmick (built by
Sweden's Alweg Rapid Transit Systems) that shuttled tourists between
downtown and the fairgrounds at what's now Seattle Center. Yet it was
so popular that even after the fair closed down, the city continued to
operate the Monorail. It still carries about 40,000 riders annually
(making it one of the world's few profitable rapid-transit operations).
The trains travel 1.3 miles (a 90-second ride) between Westlake Center
and Seattle Center. Tourists are the principal users—except during Bumbershoot and the Folklife Festival (both guaranteed to fill parking lots

around Seattle Center), when many city residents prefer to park downtown and hop the Monorail to the festivities. Watching the Monorail speed by above 5th Avenue (especially at night, when neon light bleeds across the trains' silver sides) can be a futuristic experience. Riding the train, though, can be less exciting—especially on hot summer days, when the sun threatens to bake passengers inside the big-windowed cars. Trains depart Westlake and Seattle Center every 15 minutes, and the fare is $1.25 one way for adults, and 50¢ one way for kids and seniors. (Double the price for a round-trip ticket.) *Weekdays 7:30am–11pm, weekends 9am–11pm; map:I6* &

12) WOODLAND PARK ZOO

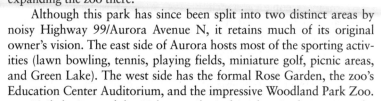

5500 Phinney Ave N; 206/684-4800 Guy Phinney was a tall, beefy Nova Scotian of British descent who, in the late 1880s, used the money he'd made peddling Canadian land to buy a huge forested tract north of downtown Seattle (along the ridge that today carries his name). This property he turned into something approximating an English country estate, complete with flower garden, dance pavilion, bicycle racetrack, and menagerie. Phinney then opened his "park" to the public, on the condition that visitors not bring in guns or liquor and that they not disturb his animals (including a bear named Bosco). A few years after its creator died in 1893, the estate was purchased by the city, which in 1909 began expanding the zoo there.

Although this park has since been split into two distinct areas by noisy Highway 99/Aurora Avenue N, it retains much of its original owner's vision. The east side of Aurora hosts most of the sporting activities (lawn bowling, tennis, playing fields, miniature golf, picnic areas, and Green Lake). The west side has the formal Rose Garden, the zoo's Education Center Auditorium, and the impressive Woodland Park Zoo.

Hailed as one of the 10 best zoological gardens in the country, the Woodland Park Zoo has evolved over the last couple of decades from a traditional animals-behind-bars facility into one that provides lifelike re-creations of natural habitats ("bioclimatic zones" in zoo lingo). Among these habitats are a grassy **AFRICAN SAVANNA** populated with giraffes, zebras, and hippos that wallow merrily in their own simulated mud-bottomed river drainage (the lions, though nearby, enjoy their own grassland); the **TEMPERATE FOREST,** with a marsh and swamp for waterfowl and waders; **TROPICAL ASIA,** with its **ELEPHANT FOREST**—4.6 acres that include an elephant-size pool, an Asian forest, and a replica of a Thai logging camp and Thai temple (this last serving as the elephants' nighttime abode); and the **TRAIL OF VINES,** an adjoining 2.7-acre exhibit that takes visitors on an imaginary voyage through India, Malaysia, and Borneo with its display of orangutans, siamang apes, Malayan tapirs, and lion-tailed macaques. The **TROPICAL RAIN FOREST** explores the woodland's multiple layers, from the floor to a domed canopy where tropical birds fly freely overhead. It is home to 20,000 plant species and more than 50 exotic animal species. After the Rain Forest, visit one of the heavily planted **LOWLAND GORILLA ENCLOSURES** concealing a brooding troop of adults and their precocious offspring. The **NORTHERN TRAIL** introduces visitors to three cold, rugged regions of the North, with brown bears, wolves, bald eagles, and mountain goats. Interspersed with these exhibits are less-inspired leftovers from the 1950s (the feline house, for instance), which await updates of their own. Coming renovations include Australasia, featuring animals from Australia and New Zealand.

On a tamer scale, the renovated **FAMILY FARM** (located in the Temperate Forest) is a wonderful place for human youngsters to meet the offspring of other species. The **RAIN FOREST CAFE** is an indoor-outdoor food court (and a great place to throw a birthday party); you might not love the food, but the kids, no doubt, will. Admission charge for adults and children 2 and older.

The zoo also offers a rich schedule of family programming, including orientation walks, classes, special events, and lectures. Its popular **ZOO-TUNES CONCERTS** series, held outdoors on summer evenings for more than 15 years, draws from a panoply of renowned musicians. Ticket prices range from $8 to $10 (206/615-0076). *9:30am–6pm (March 15–Oct 14); 9:30am–4pm (Oct 15–March 14); www.zoo.org; map:FF7* &

13) KLONDIKE GOLD RUSH NATIONAL HISTORICAL PARK

117 S Main St; 206/553-7220 "Seattle has gone stark, staring mad on gold," reported the *New York Herald* after the steamship *Portland* docked at Elliott Bay on July 17, 1897, bearing 68 ragged prospectors and what local newspapers claimed was a "ton of gold" (it was actually closer to *two* tons) collected from tributaries of northwestern Canada's Klondike River. Within a week, bank clerks, barbers, ferry pilots, and preachers from all over town had turned in their resignations and sailed to the southeast Alaskan coast, from which rugged mountain trails and turbulent rivers would lead them inland to Canada's Yukon and Dawson City, at the heart of the Klondike Valley. They were followed by tens of thousands more folks anxious to find their fortunes during North America's last great frontier adventure: the Klondike Stampede.

It's said that only about 4,000 people actually panned or dug up gold during that epic rush. But Seattle certainly profited by selling supplies to the hordes of northbound miners. And much of the gold that eventually flushed through this city stayed here, along with many of the prospectors themselves. By the time the stampede began to wane in 1899, Seattle was busily shedding its raw woolliness to become the Northwest's urban showcase.

Those wild times are still celebrated at this Pioneer Square "park"—really a storefront museum, the southernmost unit of the National Park Service's Klondike gold rush historical sites. (Other units are the town of Skagway and the famous Chilkoot Trail, both in southeast Alaska.) Myriad black-and-white photographs and films show steamers leaving Seattle docks in 1897 and '98, all crowded with would-be Croesuses. Exhibits highlight the use of placer-mining equipment, the plentiful photographic coverage of the Klondike rush, and the decisive role newspapers played in spreading word of that subarctic mother lode. There's even a set of gold scales once owned by George Washington Carmack, the first man to stake a claim on the Klondike's richest tributary. Perhaps the most unusual display, though, shows the 2,000 pounds of provisions—from crates of evaporated apples and cans of coffee and condensed milk, to winter clothing and equipment for cooking and mining—that Canada's North-West Mounted Police required each prospector to have in tow upon entering the Yukon. *Free; every day 9am–5pm; www.nps.gov/klgo; map:O8* &

14) ELLIOTT BAY BOOK COMPANY

101 S Main St; 206/624-6600 Since opening in 1973, Seattle's premier bookstore has never stopped growing beyond the boundaries of its original rough-hewn one-room shop in Pioneer Square. Today it still offers a relaxed, literary atmosphere, but you may need a map to navigate your way around. The children's section has expanded to fill a large area of the store. Travel has its own high-ceilinged room, filled with not only guidebooks but also maps, atlases, volumes of travel essays, and foreign-language references. The crime-fiction and mysteries department offers one of the best selections in the city. Regardless of your favorite niche, you're likely to find *something* interesting among Elliott Bay's 150,000 titles. Service is smart and efficient; employees will field any question, and they'll even wrap and send all your gift purchases. If you just can't wait to begin reading your new books, drop into the basement cafe for soups, sandwiches, and, of course, coffee.

The store's free quarterly newsletter, *Elliott Bay Booknotes,* publishes book reviews and staff recommendations, profiles authors, and announces recent paperback releases. Readings and signings, drawing the nation's premier authors—out-of-towners like Amy Tan and Norman Mailer to local stars such as David Guterson and Charles Johnson—take place six days a week (see Literature in the Performing Arts chapter). There's no charge for these, but tickets are often required to ensure seating. A schedule of pending author appearances is printed on your purchase receipt. Kids' readings take place the first Saturday morning of each month. *Mon–Sat 10am–11pm, Sun noon–6pm; queries@elliottbay book.com; www.elliottbaybook.com/ebbco; map:O8*

15) BURKE MUSEUM OF NATURAL HISTORY AND CULTURE

17th Ave NE and NE 45th St, University of Washington; 206/543-5590
Fans of the Burke in its previous incarnation, back when it was an eccentric treasure trove of dusty artifacts, aren't yet convinced that its recent remodeling was wise. They pooh-pooh the addition of cast dinosaur skeletons and a "walk-through volcano" as shameless come-ons to folks who'd rather watch *Jurassic Park* than, say, a public-TV special about Earth's multi-million-year evolution. Yet there's no arguing with the fact that crowds (including many children) are showing up again to see what the Burke has to offer.

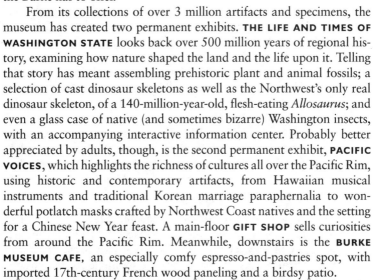

From its collections of over 3 million artifacts and specimens, the museum has created two permanent exhibits. **THE LIFE AND TIMES OF WASHINGTON STATE** looks back over 500 million years of regional history, examining how nature shaped the land and the life upon it. Telling that story has meant assembling prehistoric plant and animal fossils; a selection of cast dinosaur skeletons as well as the Northwest's only real dinosaur skeleton, of a 140-million-year-old, flesh-eating *Allosaurus*; and even a glass case of native (and sometimes bizarre) Washington insects, with an accompanying interactive information center. Probably better appreciated by adults, though, is the second permanent exhibit, **PACIFIC VOICES**, which highlights the richness of cultures all over the Pacific Rim, using historic and contemporary artifacts, from Hawaiian musical instruments and traditional Korean marriage paraphernalia to wonderful potlatch masks crafted by Northwest Coast natives and the setting for a Chinese New Year feast. A main-floor **GIFT SHOP** sells curiosities from around the Pacific Rim. Meanwhile, downstairs is the **BURKE MUSEUM CAFE**, an especially comfy espresso-and-pastries spot, with imported 17th-century French wood paneling and a birdsy patio.

The museum is named in honor of Judge Thomas Burke (1846–1925), a chief justice of the Washington State Supreme Court who was greatly responsible for convincing Minnesota railroad tycoon James J. Hill to establish the western terminus of his Great Northern line at Seattle, thus winning for the city in 1893 a long-sought transcontinental train connection. Designed by James J. Chiarelli, the museum has occupied its present location since 1962. The large killer whale sculpture at the main entrance was carved by Bill Holm and installed in 1985. Admission charge for adults and students; free to children 5 and under, members, and UW students/staff. *Mon–Wed, Fri–Sun 10am–5pm, Thurs 10am–8pm; www.washington.edu/burkemuseum; map:FF6* &

16) VOLUNTEER PARK

15th Ave E and E Prospect St; 206/684-4075 Mature trees, circling drives, grassy lawns, and lily ponds make this the most elegant of Seattle's parks—as stately as the mansions that surround its 48 acres. Designed by the distinguished Olmsted Brothers firm of Massachusetts and dedicated to Seattleites who fought in the Spanish-American War, Volunteer Park graces the top of Capitol Hill and offers sweeping views of the Space Needle, the Sound, and the Olympic Mountains.

At the north end of the main concourse lies the elaborate 1912 **VOLUNTEER PARK CONSERVATORY** (near 15th Ave E and E Galer St; 206/684-4743), boasting three large greenhouse rooms filled with flowering plants, cacti, and tropical flora. It's open (no charge) to the public; step inside for a quick trip to the tropics, complete with the humidity. At the conservatory's entrance, don't miss the Monument to William H. Seward, the U.S. Secretary of State who purchased Alaska dirt cheap from the Russians in 1867. Created by New York artist Richard Brooks for Seattle's 1909 Alaska-Yukon-Pacific Exposition, the statue was supposed to be installed here only temporarily, awaiting a move to Seward Park. But 90 years later, it still hasn't moved. Traipse a bit farther north from the conservatory and you'll hit **LAKE VIEW CEMETERY,** containing the graves of numerous Seattle pioneers as well as those of father-son martial-arts stars Bruce and Brandon Lee.

At the other end of Volunteer Park's main concourse is an old 75-foot **WATER TOWER,** which the hardy can climb for a splendid view of the city and the Olympics. The Seattle Asian Art Museum is also located here (see separate listing in this section). *Map:GG6*

17) PACIFIC SCIENCE CENTER

200 2nd Ave N, Seattle Center; 206/443-2880 A cluster of six white buildings around shallow pools and graceful, 110-foot white arches, the Science Center was originally designed as part of the 1962 world's fair by Minoru Yamasaki, the architect responsible for the inverted-pencil Rainier Square tower downtown (as well as New York City's twin-towered World Trade Center). Since then, some 30 million people have trooped through here to see hands-on science and math exhibits for school-age children as well as traveling shows aimed at all age groups. There are enough excellent displays, films, and demonstrations to keep a family occupied for most of a day.

One of several permanent exhibits, **DINOSAURS: A JOURNEY THROUGH TIME** introduces five roaring robotic creatures from Earth's Mesozoic period, including a flesh-eating *Tyrannosaurus rex* and a three-horned, herbivorous *Triceratops*. In the Tech Zone, children can play virtual basketball, hang-glide through a virtual city, and match wits with a robot. The Science Playground offers a kid-friendly introduction to physics. Girls and boys learn why a hot air balloon rises; speak into a 72-foot-long echo tube to experience the delay between the transmission and the receipt of a sound; and are invited to throw their fastest pitch and have it measured by a radar gun. Outside the center, they can take aim with a water cannon or explore their center of gravity on the High Rial Bike. Admission charge for adults and children 2 or older; members and disabled persons are admitted free. *Mon–Fri 10am–5pm, Sat–Sun 10am–6pm; www.pacificsciencecenter.com; map:C7* ♿

An **IMAX THEATER** (206/443-IMAX) boasts a six-channel surround-sound system and a 35-by-60-foot screen on which viewers can thrill to experiences such as a trip to Alaska or a climb up Mount Everest. Admission charge (combination IMAX-Science Center tickets are available). *Shows most afternoons every day, evenings Thurs–Sat* ♿

18) FISHERMEN'S TERMINAL

3919 18th Ave W; 206/728-3395 A most authentic tourist attraction, this working terminal is the busiest of its kind in the North Pacific. Built in 1913, it was one of the Port of Seattle's first facilities and is now home base to some 700 commercial fishing vessels (ranging in length from 30 to 300 feet), most of which head north into Alaskan waters. The terminal sits on protected Salmon Bay, the last stretch of the Lake Washington Ship Canal before it reaches the Hiram M. Chittenden Locks and meets the waters of Puget Sound.

Head out to the crowded piers to inspect hundreds of gillnetters and crab boats that make up the Northwest's most active fleet. Look also for trollers (they're the ones with two tall poles stuck straight up in the air) and the big factory processors, on which fish are cleaned at sea. This freshwater terminal is an optimal choice for fishers, since their boats are protected from the corrosion and other problems associated with salt-water storage.

Revamped in 1988, the terminal includes new docks, a large public plaza (with interpretive panels detailing the development of the local fishing industry), and the **SEATTLE FISHERMEN'S MEMORIAL**, a bronze-and-concrete pillar created by Seattle sculptor Ron Petty to honor local fishers lost at sea during the 20th century. Chinook's at Salmon Bay (206/283-4665) offers tasty seafood dishes and a splendid view of the waterway; or try its annex next door for quick fish 'n' chips. At Wild Salmon Fish Market (1900 W Nickerson St; 206/283-3366), only feet from the boats, you can purchase fresh seafood for dinner. Time your visit with an incoming fishing boat and you might get an even fresher catch. *Every day; map:FF8*

19) SEATTLE AQUARIUM

Pier 59, 1483 Alaskan Way; 206/386-4320 Two parts of this waterfront aquarium have long earned the most attention. The Underwater Dome is a 400,000-gallon fish tank that surrounds visitors, their heads aswivel as they try to take in the myriad king salmon, reef sharks, snapper, and other colorful Puget Sound and Pacific Ocean inhabitants whisking by.

And in the topside tanks, seals and sea otters act especially clownish at feeding times. The recently added Watersheds exhibit, however, may draw its own following with its playful pair of river otters.

A functioning salmon ladder explains the life cycle of Northwest salmon. Children enjoy the Discovery Lab, where they can handle sea stars and hermit crabs, and the Marshroom, with tadpole tanks and a 40-foot interactive freshwater marsh mural. Admission charge for adults and children 3 and older; nonresidents pay more. *Memorial Day through Labor Day, 10am–7pm; after Labor Day to before Memorial Day, 10am–5pm; www.seattleaquarium.org; map:J9* &

The adjacent **OMNIDOME THEATRE** (206/622-1868) is a dramatic cinema-in-the-round, featuring *The Eruption of Mount St. Helens* and other Omnimax spectacles. Admission charge (combination Omnidome/ Seattle Aquarium tickets are available). *12 shows daily beginning at 10am; www.imaxtheatre.com/seattle/index.htm* &

20) NORDSTROM & REI (RECREATIONAL EQUIPMENT INC.)

Nordstrom, 500 Pine St; 206/628-2111; REI, 222 Yale Ave N; 206/223-1944 Whether you're a fashion maven or an incurable gearhead, you can worship at the cash-register altars of the city's two premier shopping destinations. Both opened impressive new flagship stores here in recent years—garnering front-page coverage in city newspapers, with store diagrams to boot!

In 1998 locally grown retail giant **NORDSTROM** opened its shining new department store across the street from its old location (the new building was once the flagship for the defunct Frederick & Nelson chain). Now it has a whopping five spacious floors to showcase its clothes, shoes, accessories, cosmetics, fine jewelry, and fabled customer service. Special attractions of the new Nordy's include the Northwest's only Chanel boutique, a full-service day spa, and a complimentary wardrobe consulting service; besides the customary cafe, exclusive to the Seattle flagship store is the Nordstrom Grill, featuring fresh market seafood. And the shoes: 150,000 pairs (including hard-to-find sizes: 3AAAAA to 14EE for women) are spread among five departments. Appropriately enough for a store that first made its mark in shoe leather, Nordstrom has installed glass cases around the store displaying 70 examples of footwear, ranging from turn-of-the-century ankle boots to 1970s ankle-challenging platform shoes. *Mon–Sat 9:30am–9pm, Sun 10am–7pm; www.nordstrom-pta.com; map:J5*

At **REI**, the nation's largest consumer co-op (51 stores nationwide, just over two million members), you'll find basically everything you need for mountaineering, backpacking, camping, cross-country skiing, biking, and other outdoor pursuits. Seattle's high-visibility two-level location just off I-5 features a 65-foot indoor climbing pinnacle, mountain bike and hiking test paths, a rain simulator in which to try out the latest Gore-Tex, a children's play area, a deli/cafe, and a wide assortment of items and brands. The store is an excellent source for anything made of fleece, as well as maps, trail food, and outdoor books. The trip planning office of the Forest Service's Outdoor Recreation Information Center is also located here (206/470-4060)—buy a pair of hiking boots and then find out the best place to break them in that day.

Anyone can shop here, but members (who pay only $15 to join) receive at least a 10 percent yearly dividend on their purchases. Founded in 1938 by a group of Seattle mountaineers who wanted to import European equipment, the co-op was presided over for years by Everest conqueror Jim Whittaker, and it is still staffed by knowledgeable outdoorspeople. The flagship is constructed largely out of recycled building materials and features many playful accents: clocks in the shape of Swiss Army watches, climbing-axe door handles, and a river-rock fireplace, to name a few. Many lectures, events, and courses take place here; call for a current schedule. Rentals at good prices, too. Smaller branches are in Bellevue, Federal Way, and Lynnwood. *Mon–Fri 10am–9pm, Sat 9am–7pm, Sun 11am–6pm; www.rei.com; map:H1*

21) BOEING PLANT TOUR

Tour Center, Hwy 526, Everett; 206/544-1264 or 800/464-1476 An engineer and the son of a Michigan timber baron, William E. Boeing first became fascinated with flying in 1910. Ninety years later, despite some rough going, the company he created has become one of the world's aerospace giants. Boeing's magnitude is well reflected in the dimensions of its **MAIN AIRPLANE ASSEMBLY BUILDING**, adjacent to Paine Field in Everett, 30 miles north of Seattle. With almost 300 million cubic feet of space, this is the world's largest building by volume, big enough to make even 747s and 777s look small inside.

Public tours of the facility and surrounding areas of Boeing's Everett plant have been conducted for some 30 years and remain popular. Lasting about 1 hour and 15 minutes, these escorted jaunts begin at the Tour Center with a short video presentation about Boeing airplanes and other products. Participants are then loaded onto a bus and taken to the assembly building, where a balcony gives them an exciting view of planes under construction. From there, the bus wheels out to the Flight Line, where a variety of jets are nearing completion. Tours are conducted Monday through Friday. A limited number of tour tickets are sold at the Tour Center for same-day use, beginning at 8:30am every day; during summer, visitors line up for tickets as early as 7am, so get there early too. From May through October, tickets can all vanish by noon. You may pick up tickets for any of six tours each day, but your party must be nine or fewer. (Schools and groups of 10 or more have to make reservations.

There's no charge for school groups, but other group tours pay $10 per person.) Children must be at least 50 inches tall, and visitors may not carry babies on the tour. No cameras are allowed on company property. Boeing began charging admission for the tours in 1999: $5 adults, $3 children under 16 and seniors; cash only. *Mon–Fri; everett.tourcenter@ boeing.com; www.boeing.com/companyoffices/aboutus/tours*

22) WASHINGTON PARK ARBORETUM

2300 Arboretum Dr E (at Lake Washington Blvd); 206/543-8800 Year-round, Washington Park Arboretum is as full of people as it is of trees. Naturalists and botanists rub elbows with serious runners and casual walkers, for this 200-acre public park (set aside as urban wilderness in 1904 and developed beginning in the 1930s) doubles as a botanical research facility for the nearby University of Washington. The Arboretum stretches from Foster Island, just off the shore of Lake Washington, through the Montlake and Madison Park neighborhoods, its rambling trails screened from the houses by thick greenbelts. More than 5,000 varieties of woody plants are arranged here by family. (Pick up maps or an illustrated guide at the visitors center if you want to find specific trees.)

From spring through autumn, the Arboretum's **JAPANESE GARDEN** (1502 Lake Washington Blvd E; 206/684-4725) is well worth a visit. Just off Lake Washington Boulevard E, which winds north-south through the park, this authentic garden was constructed in 1960 under the direction of Japanese landscape architect Juki Iida. Several hundred tons of rock hauled from the Cascades were incorporated into the design, as were stone lanterns donated by the city of Kobe and a **TEAHOUSE** sent by the governor of Tokyo, where tea ceremonies were performed even before the surrounding garden was completed. Nowadays visitors stroll winding paths, admiring trees and shrubs pruned as living sculptures. The graceful **CARP POND**, spanned by traditional bridges of wood and stone and lined with water plants, is home to countless ducks, herons, and muskrats. Though the original teahouse was destroyed by vandals years ago, it has since been replaced, and the tea ceremony is still performed on the third Saturday of the month, April–October, at 1:30pm by members of the Seattle branch of the Urasenke Foundation. The Japanese Garden is open daily at 10am, March–November; closing time varies seasonally. Admission charge for adults and children over 5. Guided tours are available by arrangement for a fee. Call for event schedules and operating hours.

Just across the road to the north runs **AZALEA WAY,** a wide, grassy thoroughfare that winds through the heart of the Arboretum. (No recreational running is permitted on this popular route.) Always pleasant, Azalea Way is magnificent in April and May, when its blossoming shrubs are joined by scores of companion dogwoods and ornamental cherries.

Drop in on the **JOSEPH A. WITT WINTER GARDEN**, especially from November through March. The Winter Garden focuses on plants that show distinctive seasonal bark, winter flowers, or cold-season fruit to attract birds. Side trails lead through the Arboretum's extensive **CAMELLIA AND RHODODENDRON GROVES** (the latter collection is world famous).

Follow Azalea Way to the copper-roofed **GRAHAM VISITORS CENTER** (2300 Arboretum Dr E; 206/543-8800), where you can find maps and Arboretum guides as well as horticulture-related books, gifts, and informational displays. On weekends beginning at 1pm, guided Arboretum tours begin at the center, which is open 10am–4pm daily. The Arboretum also hosts an annual spring plant sale each April and a fall bulb sale each October. *Every day; wpa@u.washington.edu; weber.u. washington.edu/~wpa/; map:GG6* &

23) SPIRIT OF WASHINGTON DINNER TRAIN

625 S 4th St, Renton (Renton to Woodinville); 425/227-RAIL or 800/876-RAIL It's not exactly the Orient Express, but the Spirit of Washington Dinner Train definitely has its attractions for diners who crave a bit of nostalgia and adventure with their meal. At downtown Renton's **SPIRIT DEPOT** (625 S 4th St), you and your fellow passengers board a train composed of Depression-era railcars and engines, all immaculately restored. From there, you're whisked north on a 45-mile, 3¾ round trip along the eastern shore of Lake Washington to Woodinville (all the while following Burlington Northern tracks used by freight trains six days a week). Among the highlights of the excursion is when the train passes over Bellevue's **WILBURTON TRESTLE**—at 102 feet high and 975 feet in length, the longest wooden trestle still in use in the Northwest. For the best views, pay a $10 premium to secure seats in one of the three dome cars. And it isn't just the scenery that travelers will remember. Meals served on board are much better than you might expect! When you make your reservation for a ride, you choose one of four entrees. (A separate children's menu has options for kids who crave nothing more complicated than a hamburger or a slice of pizza.) Service is attentive without being overbearing. Cocktails are available.

If the meal and the gentle rocking of the coach don't put you to sleep, visit the **COLUMBIA WINERY** at the route's northern end. Take a 45-minute tour of the winery or simply retire to its tasting room for samples of fine Northwest vintages. And take that nap on the way back south.

During the summer, trains run once daily (6:30pm) and twice on weekends (noon and 6:30pm Saturday, 11am and 5:30pm Sunday). There is no Monday train during the winter (October through May). Dinner guests pay $59 for regular seating, $69 for dome seats. Lunch is $49 for regular seating, $59 for dome seats. For those who like to dress up and play games, the train runs "Murder Mystery Trains" on select weekdays year-round ($74 per person including dinner). From November through April, children 12 and under ride—and eat—for no charge when accompanied by an adult. *Every day (June to Sept); Tues–Sun (Oct to May); map:NN3–CC2* &

24) GAS WORKS PARK

N Northlake Way and Meridian Ave N; 206/684-4075 What do you do when the piece of property with the grandest skyline and lakeside view in the city is dominated by a greasy old gas-processing plant? You turn it into a park, of course. Gas Works Park, in the Wallingford neighborhood, represents urban reclamation at its finest. A quarter-century after the Seattle Gas Company plant shut down here in 1956, landscape architect Richard Haag re-created the industrial eyesore as one Seattle's most delightful greenswards, with a high grassy knoll for kite flying, a large picnic shelter (call 206/684-4081 to reserve space), a wonderful play barn, and a multitude of front-row spots from which to watch sailboats bounce around on Lake Union. Climb the grassy knoll to enjoy a huge mosaic **SUNDIAL** (created by artist Charles Greening) and a view of the downtown towers just 2 miles south. Against a sky full of dancing kites, the brooding works look solidly handsome. The threat of lurking soil pollutants, which once closed the park, has been ruled out, provided you don't eat the dirt. (Parents with toddlers beware.) Cutting east from Gas Works is the **BURKE-GILMAN TRAIL**, a wonderful 12½-mile biking and jogging path that winds clear up to Lake Washington's northern edge (see Bicycling under Outdoor Recreation in the Recreation chapter). *Map:FF7*

25) GREEN LAKE

Between E Green Lake Dr N and W Green Lake Dr N; 206/684-4075 When the sun shines and the joggers, tanners, and in-line skaters muster en masse, the greenbelt around Green Lake looks like a slice of Southern California that's been beamed to the temperate Northwest. Even on dreary days, the recently refurbished 2.8-mile paved inner circuit around the lake is likely to be crowded. For less competition (but more car exhaust fumes), runners can try the 3.2-mile unpaved outer loop. No less a personage than President Bill Clinton has been known to run here (accompanied by a phalanx of Secret Service agents) when he's in town. On any given day, however, you're much more likely to spot couples circling the water in intense conversation—some of them looking distinctly pained. So many love affairs have broken up during Green Lake strolls that many Seattleites cringe at the very thought of visiting there with their paramours.

What is now the center of Seattle's exercise culture is the remnant of a large glacial lake that was well on its way to becoming a meadow when the pioneers arrived. In the 1880s, land surrounding the lake was promoted to "suburban" home builders. But by 1910, construction there had been curbed under a comprehensive city beautification scheme created by John C. Olmsted, nephew and stepson of the famous American landscape designer Frederick Law Olmsted. The younger Olmsted proposed that Green Lake's water level be lowered by 7 feet, exposing more waterfront property to parkland development. City burghers went along with the plan—only to realize, too late, that by filling in the shoreline and diking off natural streams that had fed Green Lake for centuries, they were inviting the water's stagnation. Despite improvements in drainage since the 1960s, bathers still complain of "swimmer's itch."

The lake offers enjoyable sailing and windsurfing, as well as great people-watching—it draws a microcosm of the city's humanity, much as Central Park does in New York. If you'd rather watch birds, they're around too, from Canada geese to red-winged blackbirds to the occasional bald eagle. Although the tennis courts, soccer field, indoor pool and recreation center, outdoor basketball court, baseball diamond, pitch-and-putt golf course, boat rental, thriving commercial district, and considerable car traffic around the lake make it feel like an urban beach resort, you can usually find one or two grassy patches for a picnic. There's a well-equipped kids' playground on the northeast side.

Limited parking can be found in three lots: the northeast lot (Latona Ave N and E Green Lake Way N, the most crowded), the northwest lot (7312 W Green Lake Way N), and the south lots (5900 W Green Lake Way N). *Map:EE7*

THE MARKET IN THE MORNING

If you are an early riser—or if you're willing to be one for one day—give yourself a treat by visiting the Pike Place Market in the morning. As the sun rises over Puget Sound, the tourists and shoppers are few, and the bustle is all business.

The sound of trucks rumbling along the cobblestones fills the air. Everything moves to an invisible choreographer's command, as workers fill formerly empty stalls with fresh vegetables, fruit, fish, and flowers. The aromas of baking bread and steaming coffee beans waft from Le Panier Very French Bakery. People of many ages and persuasions perch on stools at the Athenian Inn, lingering over the day's second or third cup of joe.

The melting ice of yesterday is tossed out onto the street, and new ice is poured to bed freshly caught salmon and halibut. Apples, beans, and potatoes are stacked in perfect pyramids. Tables fill with crafts both homely and handsome. The metal gates are lifted. The Market is open.

— *Barbara Spear*

Neighborhoods

DOWNTOWN AND BELLTOWN

Between 1st Ave and 9th Ave, Yesler Way and Battery St Seattle's commercial district has shifted over time. Before 1900, most government and business offices huddled in Pioneer Square (see Top 25 Attractions in this chapter), at the south end of today's downtown. After the Great Fire of 1889, crowding in that historic district and the search for cheaper real estate drove the city's expansion northward.

Today's **RETAIL CORE** lies basically between Third and Sixth Avenues from Stewart to University Streets. It's anchored by two big department stores—the **BON MARCHÉ**, at Fourth Avenue and Pine Street, and the new flagship **NORDSTROM**, occupying the former Frederick & Nelson building at Fifth Avenue and Pine Street—as well as two upscale malls. **WESTLAKE CENTER** resides at Fourth and Pine (see Top 25 Attractions in this chapter) and airy **PACIFIC PLACE**, which opened in 1998, sits two blocks east at Sixth Avenue and Pine Street. Along Fifth Avenue you'll also find that stylish dealer in men's and women's clothes, **BANANA REPUBLIC** (1506 5th Ave), housed in a beautiful terra-cotta edifice that used to be the Coliseum Theater, and hometown favorite **EDDIE BAUER** (1330 5th Ave), where you can pick up sturdy outdoor wear, chic casual clothing, and even household furniture.

Paralleling Pine Street is Pike Street, and at Seventh Avenue and Pike are housed **GAME WORKS**, a video game emporium-cum-restaurant; **NIKETOWN**, a mammoth Nike sportswear store; and **PLANET HOLLY-WOOD**, the ubiquitous celebrity-studded eatery. (Also in the same structure is the Meridian 16 multiplex cinemas—see also Film in the Performing Arts chapter.) Colorful smaller shops line Fourth and Fifth Avenues south to **RAINIER SQUARE** (4th Ave and Union St), an elegant three-story atrium at the base of **RAINIER TOWER**, a modernist box of a building that's balanced atop a tapered 12-story pedestal. Across University Street to the south is the **FOUR SEASONS OLYMPIC HOTEL** (4th Ave and University St), the noble grand dame of Seattle hostelries, opened in 1924 and now girded with boutiques of international pedigree. High tea in the Olympic's **GARDEN COURT** (206/621-1700) makes a civilized break for shoppers.

Construction downtown seems to have abated some, after a flurry of building that began in the 1980s. To see the results of that boom, you need only look up: downtown Seattle bristles with skyscrapers. All hope to outshine their neighbors—but few stand out in terms of architectural quality. The **1201 THIRD AVENUE BUILDING** (formerly known as the Washington Mutual Tower), designed by the New York firm of Kohn Pedersen Fox, is a postmodern confection with a stair-stepped profile

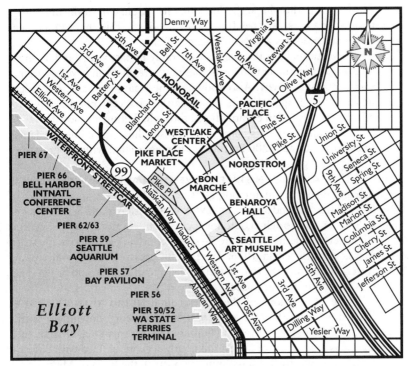

DOWNTOWN AND BELLTOWN

reminiscent of the Empire State Building's and a covering of pink granite that seems to glow at sunset. **CITY CENTRE** (5th Ave and Pike St) boasts a somber gray-blue hue and a light-filled lobby that contains freestanding architectural ornaments, engaging chandeliers, and delightful glass sculptures. Three floors of exclusive shops provide excellent browsing, and the **PALOMINO** bistro tastefully drapes over both sides of the third-floor escalator. The tallest building downtown—but also one of the least attractive—is the 76-story **COLUMBIA CENTER**, about six blocks south at Fourth Avenue and Columbia Street. (For a grand view, visit its observation platform on the 73rd floor. Check in with the security desk in the lobby; $3.50 adults, $1.75 children and seniors, weekdays only.) More interesting are some older towers, such as the **COBB BUILDING** (4th Ave and University St), an elegant 11-story brick-and-terra-cotta structure finished in 1910, and the Art Deco, 26-story **SEATTLE TOWER**, completed in 1929 (3rd Ave and University St).

Walk west along University to reach **BENAROYA HALL** (between 3rd and 2nd Aves), the distinctive new home of the Seattle Symphony, and the **SEATTLE ART MUSEUM** (between 1st and 2nd Aves; see Top 25

Attractions in this chapter). North on First Avenue from the museum is
PIKE PLACE MARKET (see Top 25 Attractions in this chapter), popular
with both shoppers and people watchers.

First Avenue has upscaled considerably in past years, and its shopping and entertainment opportunities now stretch north beyond Virginia
Street into BELLTOWN. Also known as the Denny Regrade, this neighborhood was proposed as the site of Seattle's civic center in the early 20th
century, but that plan eventually fell through. Belltown is noted now for
its hip restaurants, bars, shops, and music clubs, including the famed
CROCODILE CAFE (2200 2nd Ave), often associated with the growth of
Seattle "grunge" music.

The WASHINGTON STATE CONVENTION AND TRADE CENTER (8th
Ave and Pike St), a mammoth, glass-enclosed building, sprawls atop 12
lanes of freeway and adjoins FREEWAY PARK (6th Ave and Seneca St), one
of Seattle's most original outdoor spaces. This extraordinary park forms
a lid over thundering Interstate 5—a feat of urban park innovation when
it was constructed in 1976. Here, amid grassy plateaus and rushing
waterfall canyons, the roar of traffic seems to disappear, and brown-bag-
gers find rejuvenating solace.

Five bus stations of the underground METRO TRANSIT TUNNEL
opened in late 1990 to ease Seattle's menacing downtown traffic
problem. From the Convention Center to the International District, each
station is a showcase of underground urban glamour lined with different
kinds of public art (from sculpture to poetry), the fruits of Metro's $1.5
million arts program. *Map:F5–N5 and F9–N9*

INTERNATIONAL DISTRICT

S Weller St to S Washington St, between 4th Ave S and 12th Ave S
The history of white treatment of Asians in Seattle is not a pleasant one.
But you wouldn't know that to look at this peaceful and unpretentious
neighborhood southeast of Pioneer Square. Seattle's International District is a collection of distinct ethnic communities (the Chinese have their
own newspapers and opera society, the Japanese have a theater) and a
cohesive melting pot (a community garden, museum, and neighborhood
playground are shared by all). The influx of Southeast Asian immigrants
and refugees in recent decades has only served to enrich the city's historical mix of Chinese, Japanese, Filipinos, and Koreans and given the "I.
D." a new vibrancy.

A centerpiece of the neighborhood is the vast emporium called UWA-
JIMAYA (519 6th Ave S; 206/624-6248), the closest thing this city has to
a real Japanese supermarket/department store. Inside, the tile-roofed
building is a playground for the Asian gourmet, with huge tanks of live
fish and rare imported produce. A cooking school here is well regarded
throughout the region, and the market's second level houses KINOKU-

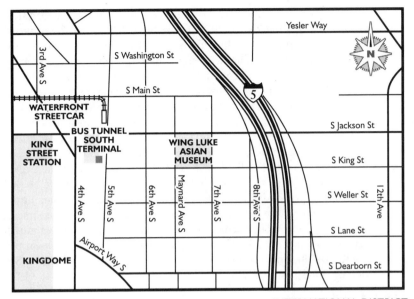

Yesler Way

3rd Ave S

S Washington St

S Main St

5

WATERFRONT
STREETCAR

S Jackson St

BUS TUNNEL
SOUTH
TERMINAL

KING
STREET
STATION

WING LUKE
| ASIAN |
MUSEUM

S King St

4th Ave S

5th Ave S

6th Ave S

Maynard Ave S

7th Ave S

8th Ave S

S Weller St

12th Ave

S Lane St

Airport Way S

KINGDOME

S Dearborn St

INTERNATIONAL DISTRICT

NIYA (206/587-2477), a branch of the largest Japanese bookstore chain in the United States. To get an idea of the engaging contrasts of the International District, drop in at tiny **HOVEN FOODS** (502 6th Ave S; 206/623-6764), which, in much humbler fashion, sells excellent fresh tofu and soybean milk.

If you'd rather have somebody else prepare all of the intriguing food-stuffs available in this district, note that a traditional Chinese breakfast can be had at **HOUSE OF DUMPLINGS** (512 S King St; 206/340-0774). Or try **HOUSE OF HONG** (409 8th Ave S; 206/622-7997), a bit farther east, for dim sum. **SHANGHAI GARDEN** (524 6th Ave S; 206/625-1689) offers the cuisines of varying regions of China and what many consider the best Chinese food the city has to offer.

On Seventh Avenue is the **WING LUKE ASIAN MUSEUM** (407 7th Ave S; 206/623-5124), named after the first person of Asian ancestry elected to public office in Washington. With rotating exhibits and a permanent display of photographs, the museum sensitively chronicles the experience of early Asian immigrants to the West Coast (see Museums in this chapter). Across Jackson Street to the north is the main Japanese district, where you'll find a real Japanese pre–World War II five-and-dime, the **HIGO VARIETY STORE** (604 S Jackson St; 206/622-7572), presided over for the last half-century by the Murakami family. This is also where many of the I. D.'s Japanese restaurants are clustered, including **BUSH GARDEN**

(614 Maynard Ave S; 206/682-6830) and the tiny, inexpensive **KORAKU** (419 6th Ave S; 206/624-1389). North on Sixth Avenue are the **NIPPON KAN THEATRE** (628 S Washington St; 206/467-6807), known for its annual Japanese Performing Arts Series, and **KOBE TERRACE PARK**, with a noble stone lantern from Seattle's Japanese sister city of Kobe. Here, too, you'll get a splendid view of the district, including the **DANNY WOO INTERNATIONAL DISTRICT COMMUNITY GARDENS** (206/624-1802). Built in the late 1970s, the gardens were parceled out to low-income elderly inhabitants of the district, who tend their tiny plots with great pride.

East of here on Jackson, the International District takes on a Vietnamese air. **VIET WAH** (1032 S Jackson St; 206/328-3557) has an excellent selection of fresh and packaged foods at very low prices, and it boasts the most comprehensive selection of Chinese and Southeast Asian ingredients in town. Seattle has a well-deserved reputation for fine Vietnamese restaurants, and this is where you'll find many of them: **HUONG BINH** (1207 S Jackson St; 206/720-4907), **THANH VI** (1046 S Jackson St; 206/329-0208), and **A LITTLE BIT OF SAIGON** (1036-A S Jackson St; 206/325-3663). *Map:HH7*

CAPITOL HILL

Along Broadway, from E Roy St to E Pine St, and along 15th Ave E, from E Denny Way to E Mercer St Along the spine of Capitol Hill lies **BROADWAY**, Seattle's answer to the effervescent spirit of San Francisco's Castro Street. At one time a victim of urban decay, Broadway has experienced a dramatic revival in recent decades, establishing itself as a haven for black clothes and pierced body parts; Seattle's unofficial gay district; and one of the only areas of town where sidewalks are still busy after 10pm.

The southern end of the district is at Harvard Avenue E and E Roy Street, home to the **HARVARD EXIT** (807 E Roy St; 206/323-8986), one of Seattle's foremost art-film theaters, and the **DELUXE BAR AND GRILL** (625 Broadway E; 206/324-9697), crowded with folks hungering after burgers and microbrews and an absence of chichi decor. Just across the boulevard, Thai fanciers will find sufficiently tongue-searing dishes at **SIAM ON BROADWAY** (616 Broadway E; 206/324-0892). Capitol Hill's free-stepping spirit is perhaps best expressed in Jack Mackie's inlaid bronze *Dancers' Series: Steps* offbeat public art that appears at intervals as you walk south along Broadway, inviting strollers to get in step with the tango or the foxtrot.

Vintage and imported fashion, books, and home accessories are the focus of Broadway's best stores. **BROADWAY MARKET** (between Republican and Harrison Sts; 206/322-1610), featuring a florist, clothing and card shops, a movie complex, and the futuristic, vegetarian **GRAVITY BAR** (206/325-7186), is an imposing symbol of the continuing million-dollar

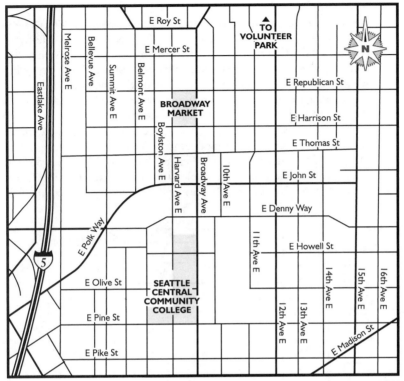

enfranchisement of this once-funky street. **RETROVIVA** (215 Broadway E; 206/328-7451) purveys fashions that encourage us to show our kitschy, retro sides. On the other side of Broadway are a well-stocked newsstand, **STEVE'S BROADWAY NEWS** (204 Broadway E; 206/324-7323), and a handsomely eclectic bookstore, **BAILEY/COY BOOKS** (414 Broadway E; 206/323-8842). The southern end of the strip is marked by a second excellent movie house, the **EGYPTIAN** (801 E Pine St; 206/323-4978).

Capitol Hill's other main drag is the slightly less flamboyant **15TH AVENUE EAST**. Lined with shops and eateries, it is particularly notable for two terrific businesses: **CITY PEOPLE'S MERCANTILE** (500 15th Ave E; 206/324-9510), a great general store with a healthy, earthy bent; and **COASTAL KITCHEN** (429 15th Ave E; 206/322-1145), a loud, fun diner-cum-grillhouse with kickin' flavors from coastal regions worldwide. Several blocks farther north on 15th Ave E, **VOLUNTEER PARK** drapes its grassy lawns among the stately mansions of north Capitol Hill (see Top 25 Attractions in this chapter). *Map:HH6–GG6*

QUEEN ANNE

Along Queen Anne Ave N, from Denny Way up the hill to W McGraw St
Seattle's Queen Anne is divided into two districts—Upper and Lower—
joined by "the Counterbalance," the part of Queen Anne Avenue that
climbs up the steep south slope and owes its nickname to the days when
weights and pulleys helped haul streetcars up that incline.

LOWER QUEEN ANNE is anchored by Seattle Center (see Top 25
Attractions in this chapter). The area also boasts some good restaurants:
within a few blocks' radius you can eat Mediterranean, Middle Eastern,
Japanese, Thai, or Mexican food. Seattle Center and KeyArena events,
along with **TOWER BOOKS** (20 Mercer St; 206/283-6333), open daily till
midnight, and the neon-Deco triplex **UPTOWN CINEMAS** (511 Queen
Anne Ave N; 206/285-1022), disgorge patrons to fill up late-night

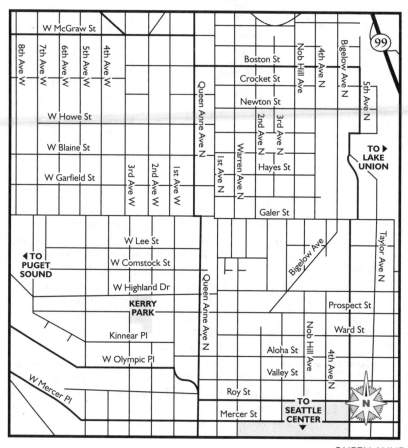

QUEEN ANNE

espresso and dessert spots or to take in the congenial bar scene at **T. S. MCHUGH'S RESTAURANT & PUB** (21 Mercer St; 206/282-1910). Move up the hill and the area becomes more residential. **UPPER QUEEN ANNE** seems to be the territory of the big, expensive view house (and it is), but look closely: there are smaller, more modest bungalows and cottages among the condos. Big attractions up here are the grand old-money mansions, many of them spread along **HIGHLAND DRIVE**—once considered the finest address in all of Seattle, home to newspaper owners, timber barons, and bankers. On a clear day, stop at **KERRY PARK** (3rd Ave W and W Highland Dr), which affords a smashing outlook (especially at sunrise) over downtown, Elliott Bay, the Space Needle, and even hide-and-seek Mount Rainier. Farther west is **BETTY BOWEN VIEWPOINT** (named in memory of one of the local art scene's great patrons), providing another perspective on Seattle's beauty: Puget Sound, West Seattle, the ferries, and the islands.

Queen Anne Avenue N is dominated by restaurants. The **5 SPOT** (1502 Queen Anne Ave N; 206/285-7768) is rich in attitude and does a thriving business in flavorful American regional cuisines; **PARAGON BAR & GRILL** (2125 Queen Anne Ave N; 206/283-4548) tends to be more stylish and serves traditional American dishes with elegant or seasonal twists; the often-noisy **HILLTOP ALEHOUSE** (2129 Queen Anne Ave N; 206/285-3877) concentrates on pub grub and its wide array of beers. But a few other enterprises deserve attention, too, including **QUEEN ANNE AVENUE BOOKS** (1629 Queen Anne Ave N, Suite 101; 206/283-5624), strong on fiction and children's lit; **A & J MEATS AND SEAFOODS** (2401 Queen Anne Ave N; 206/284-3885), offering a diverse selection of basic cuts and pre-prepared meals; and the tempting **MCGRAW STREET BAKERY** (615 W McGraw St; 206/284-6327). *Map:GG7*

BALLARD

Along NW Market St and Ballard Ave NW Ballard began as an industrial burg, full of sawmills, shingle mills, and shipyards, and it has retained its distinctive character ever since (despite its annexation by the City of Seattle in 1907). Much of its current flavor derives from the hordes of Scandinavians who flocked to the shores of Salmon Bay looking for work at the turn of the last century. Traces of the Nordic life show up in the "Velkommen to Ballard" mural at Leary Avenue NW and NW Market Street and the neighborhood's unofficial slogan of affirmation: "Ya Sure, Ya Betcha."

Its ethnic history is also apparent along NW Market Street, Ballard's main commercial hub. **NORSE IMPORTS SCANDINAVIAN GIFT SHOP** (2016 NW Market St; 206/784-9420) has more trolls than you would know what to do with and lots of jokes at the expense of lutefisk and Danish drivers, and **OLSEN'S SCANDINAVIAN FOODS** (2248 NW

BALLARD

Market St; 206/783-8288) sells homemade specialties and imported foods with tastes (and names) that celebrate their foreign roots. The **NORDIC HERITAGE MUSEUM** (3014 NW 67th St; 206/789-5707) displays textiles, tools, and photos from the old country and Ballard long ago (see Museums in this chapter).

BALLARD AVENUE NW, an Historic Landmark District since 1976, gives you an idea of how this area looked a century ago. It's a fun place to stroll, inviting peeks into aged storefronts that now contain woodworkers and cabinetmakers. Most prominent along here is the **BALLARD CENTENNIAL BELL TOWER** (Ballard Ave NW and 22nd Ave NW), a cylindrical, copper-topped monument holding a 1,000-pound brass bell that was saved from Ballard's 1899 City Hall, which stood on this corner until it was torn down after a severe earthquake in 1965. Nearby **BURK'S CAFE** (5411 Ballard Ave NW; 206/782-0091) is one of the brightest spots in the Ballard dining scene, known for its Cajun and Creole eats. Farther down the street, **CONOR BYRNE** (5140 Ballard Ave NW; 206/784-3640) schedules weekends of traditional Irish music. If you're looking for a wider variety of tunes—from blues to rock to reggae—try the **BALLARD FIREHOUSE** (5429 Russell Ave NW; 206/784-3516), a converted 1908 fire station.

One good way to get a feel for this area is to take a tour with the **BALLARD HISTORICAL SOCIETY** (206/782-6844). Call for reservations and information, or pick up a copy of the self-guided walking tour at the **BALLARD CHAMBER OF COMMERCE** (2208 NW Market St, Suite 100; 206/784-9705) or area merchants. *Map:FF8*

FREMONT/WALLINGFORD

North of the Lake Washington Ship Canal, along Fremont Ave N, and east along N/NE 45th St There's an endearing funkiness to Fremont, the self-proclaimed "Center of the Universe." Once a seedy area, this Seattle district has undergone a tremendous renaissance. Some residents contend that this success will be detrimental, that the development of new office buildings here—including those housing **ADOBE** software company's Seattle headquarters—will ruin the neighborhood's character. But so far, those fears seem unrealized.

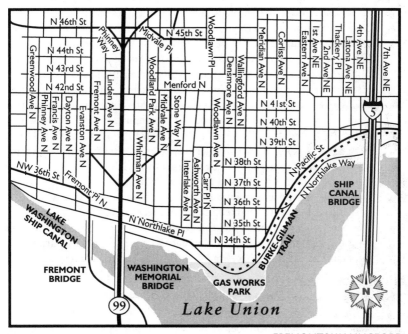

FREMONT/WALLINGFORD

Fremont boasts the city's most popular—and populist—sculpture, People Waiting for the Interurban (Fremont Ave N and N 34th St), which locals revel in decorating year-round. It also claims one of the most unusual art pieces, the Fremont Troll (under the north end of the Aurora Bridge), as well as one of its most controversial, a huge statue of Vladimir Lenin (Fremont Pl N and N 36th St) that only emphasizes Fremont's independent nature. And of all the parades that occur in Seattle annually, the most enjoyable may be Fremont's **SOLSTICE PARADE** in June, packed with mondo-bizarro floats and the occasional nude bicyclist.

Streets here are filled with highly browsable antique, secondhand, and retro-kitsch stores with names such as **THE DAILY PLANET** (3416 Fremont Ave N; 206/633-0895), **DELUXE JUNK** (3518 Fremont Pl N; 206/634-2733), and **GLAMORAMA** (3414 Fremont Ave N; 206/632-0287). If you're looking for even more reasonably priced castoffs, as well as new arts and crafts, and enough tie-dyed wear to outfit a third Woodstock gathering, stop by the **FREMONT SUNDAY MARKET**, open Sundays from May till Christmas and occupying a couple of large parking lots on N 34th Street, between Fremont and Phinney Avenues. Stroll the pleasant park strip along the **LAKE WASHINGTON SHIP CANAL** to the **TROLLEYMAN**, Redhook Ale's comfortable brewpub.

To the east lies Wallingford, a more conventional but no less ingenuous sort of place—"the James Garner among Seattle neighborhoods," as one local magazine put it. While Fremont caters mostly to young singles, Wallingford is full of young marrieds—so full, in fact, that locating streetside parking there can be a nightmare. Most of the businesses hug N 45th Street. **WALLINGFORD CENTER** (N 45th St and Wallingford Ave N; 206/632-2781) is an old public school gentrified into a warren of restaurants and jewelry, clothing, and bookstores. Farther east, you'll find **WIDE WORLD BOOKS** (1911 N 45th St; 206/634-3453), a great resource for both real adventurers and armchair travelers; the very Irish **MURPHY'S PUB** (1928 N 45th St; 206/634-2110); **JITTERBUG** (2114 N 45th St; 206/547-6313), a wonderfully relaxed eatery with a pan-ethnic menu ranging from all-American burgers to a Moroccan-French lentil stew; and **DICK'S DRIVE-IN** (111 NE 45th St; 206/632-5125), a Seattle classic serving up both some of the best French fries in town and a parking lot full of watchable families and teens in lust.

Several blocks south of all this commercial hubbub rests **GAS WORKS PARK**, a pleasant greensward on the edge of Lake Union that is particularly popular with kite fliers (see Top 25 Attractions in this chapter). *Map:FF7*

GREENWOOD/GREEN LAKE

Along Greenwood Ave N/Phinney Ave N, from N 85th St to N 65th St, and east to Green Lake People who've lived in Greenwood for a while say it's "like Wallingford before it became so popular." Once considered a far-northern suburb of Seattle, barely connected to downtown by a rattling municipal streetcar line, Greenwood remains more family-oriented than commercial, with a preponderance of secondhand stores. But since about the mid-1980s it has been attracting many younger residents and the diversity of restaurants they crave.

The neighborhood's most interesting stretch runs south from N 85th Street along Greenwood Avenue N. **PELAYO ANTIQUES** (8421 Greenwood Ave N; 206/789-1333) is slightly more expensive than some secondhand dealers, but it also carries some of the broadest selections in the neighborhood. (A second Pelayo outlet is at 7601 Greenwood Ave N; 206/789-1999.) The **PIG'N WHISTLE** (8412 Greenwood Ave N; 206/782-6044) is a cozy pub and eatery whose menu offers fine ribs and ample sandwiches (try the savory halibut po' boy). If you want to revisit your childhood through vintage comic books, step next door to sumptuously stocked **ROCKET COMICS & COLLECTIBLES** (8408 Greenwood Ave N; 206/784-7300). For a dollop of attitude with your latte, there's **DIVA ESPRESSO BAR** (7916 Greenwood Ave N; 206/781-1213). The comfort-food craze rules at **PETE'S EGGNEST** (7717 Greenwood Ave N; 206/784-5348), featuring hefty sandwiches, Greek specials, and tasty omelet breakfasts all day. **YANNI'S** (7419 Greenwood Ave N; 206/783-6945) is

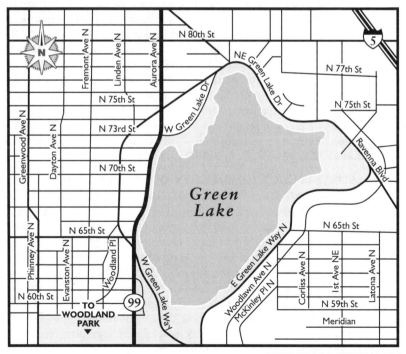

GREENWOOD/GREEN LAKE

one of the top Greek restaurants in the city, for good reason, but it's usually quieter than either **CARMELITA** (7314 Greenwood Ave N; 206/706-7703), which dispenses much-better-than-average vegetarian meals, or the **74TH STREET ALE HOUSE** (7401 Greenwood Ave N; 206/784-2955), known for its chicken sandwiches and spicy soups. **TERRA MAR** (7200 Greenwood Ave N; 206/784-5350) sells handmade clothing, masks, and folk art from national and international makers.

Greenwood Avenue N becomes Phinney Avenue N at N 67th Street, which is also where you'll find **RED MILL BURGERS** (312 N 67th St; 206/783-6362), attracting crowds with its wide selection of juicy burgers. And weekends rarely fail to cause a lineup of breakfast aficionados outside **MAE'S PHINNEY RIDGE CAFE** (6412 Phinney Ave N; 206/782-1222). Continue south on Phinney, and you'll hear the trumpeting of elephants and cackling of wild birds that signals your approach to the **WOODLAND PARK ZOO** (see Top 25 Attractions in this chapter).

East of Greenwood, the Green Lake area is busy with runners as well as patrons of the many businesses that ring the water. On the lake's east side, **SALEH AL LAGO** (6804 E Green Lake Way N; 206/524-4044) has been putting out consistently good Italian meals since 1982. Less formal but no less a culinary institution is **SPUD FISH 'N' CHIPS** (6860 E Green Lake Way; 206/524-0565), wrapping up orders of flaky fish and greasy fries for people who want to eat by the lake or watch an amateur softball game at one of several nearby fields. **GREGG'S GREENLAKE CYCLE** (7007 Woodlawn Ave NE; 206/523-1822) carries a wide range of bicycles and in-line skates for sale, but also rents wheels to fair-weather athletes. At small **LAKESIDE PLAZA** (7900 E Green Lake Dr N), **GUIDO'S PIZZERIA** (206/522-5553) thrives with its array of spicy thin- and thick-crust pies, while **ED'S JUICE AND JAVA** (206/524-7570) proves that just about any fruit or vegetable can be blended or puréed into a healthful libation. If you're into savory hand-meals, try the paella wrap at **WORLD WRAPPS** (206/524-9727). *Map:EE7*

UNIVERSITY DISTRICT (UNIVERSITY OF WASHINGTON)

UW Visitor Information Center: 4014 University Way NE; 206/543-9198 Just 15 minutes north from downtown on the freeway, the 694-acre University of Washington campus is the center of a vital and diverse community as well as the Northwest's top institute of higher learning. The university was founded in 1861 on a plot of land downtown (on University St) and moved to its present site in 1895. In 1909, the campus played host to Seattle's first world's fair—the Alaska-Yukon-Pacific Exposition—and inherited from that not only some grand buildings, but infrastructural improvements to support the neighborhood's growth. The "U-District" is now one of the city's most vibrant, youth-oriented areas. The university's **MAIN ENTRANCE** is on NE 45th Street at 17th

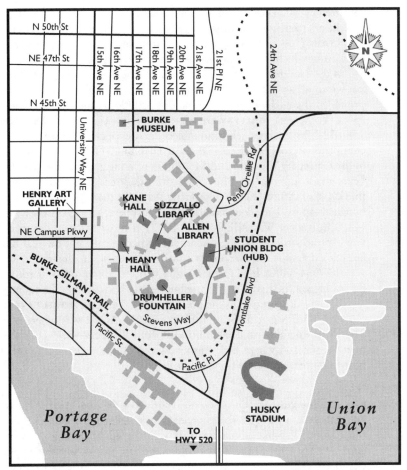

UNIVERSITY DISTRICT

Avenue NE opposite **GREEK ROW**, a collection of stately older mansions inhabited mostly by fraternities and sororities. Just inside that entrance, to the right, is the **BURKE MUSEUM OF NATURAL HISTORY AND CULTURE**, displaying Native American artifacts and natural-history exhibits (see Top 25 Attractions in this chapter). Wander south past the Burke on Memorial Way to see **DENNY HALL**, the oldest building on campus (circa 1895) and the source of the hourly chimes that can be heard ringing throughout the district. Continuing south, you'll find **CENTRAL PLAZA**— aka "Red Square"—a striking marriage of Brutalist architecture with Siena's town square. Most noteworthy there is **SUZZALLO LIBRARY** (206/543-9158), the UW's main research library, with a Gothic exterior and stained-glass windows, as well as its modern **ALLEN LIBRARY** addition (donated by Microsoft co-wizard Paul Allen). Walk on between Suzzallo and the adjacent administration building, and you'll reach **DRUMHELLER FOUNTAIN** ("Frosh Pond"), a pleasant stopping point among rose gardens, from which (on a clear day, anyway) you can see Mount Rainier.

If the university is the brains of this district, **UNIVERSITY WAY NE**, known to all as "The Ave," is its nerve center. Though chain stores are prominent here, there are still some distinctly local and often eccentric spots. **FOLK ART GALLERY/LA TIENDA** (4138 University Way NE; 206/632-1796) carries select art objects and exotic crafts from several continents. Across the street is the **BIG TIME BREWERY AND ALEHOUSE** (4133 University Way NE; 206/545-4509), offering good sandwiches and beers made on the premises. Just off the street in an alley you'll find **CAFE ALLEGRO** (4214½ University Way NE; 206/633-3030), serving excellent espresso in a counterculturish atmosphere, and **BULLDOG NEWS** (4208 University Way NE; 206/632-6397), a browser's paradise where you can flip leisurely through hundreds of periodicals. But the real bibliophile's dream is the **UNIVERSITY BOOK STORE** (4326 University Way NE; 206/634-3400), in perpetual rivalry with the Harvard Co-op for the title of biggest, best, and most varied university bookshop in the country.

Finally, since you're in the area, drop by the **BLUE MOON TAVERN** (712 NE 45th St). A half-dozen blocks off the Ave, it was where poet Theodore Roethke—and later novelist Tom Robbins—held court for many years, and where Jack Kerouac (according to legend) and other beats did their inimitable thing. *Map:FF6*

BELLEVUE

East of Lake Washington, between 100th Ave NE and 156th Ave NE, NE 12th St and Main St To many Seattleites, Bellevue symbolizes everything they don't like about Eastside suburbs—political conservatism, cookie-cutter houses, and a lack of community history. But this largest city on the other side of Lake Washington now rivals Seattle for its downtown skyline of hotels and office towers. And though Bellevue does seem to be mostly about shopping (one of the city's most recognizable landmarks is **BELLEVUE PLACE**, a hotel, restaurant, and chichi shopping complex downtown), little pockets of livability can be found among the malls. Past the drive-through espresso stands and parking lots full of BMWs are parks, streets lined with small shops, and a surprising variety of ethnic foods—all of which can be enjoyed without setting foot in Bellevue Square.

This is not to say there's no reason to visit the square itself. With more than 200 shops and eateries, the constantly metamorphosing **BELLEVUE SQUARE** (NE 8th St between Bellevue Way NE and 110th Ave NE; 425/454-8096) is the proverbial one-stop-shopping center and a focus for the community. Some people even show up there on weekday

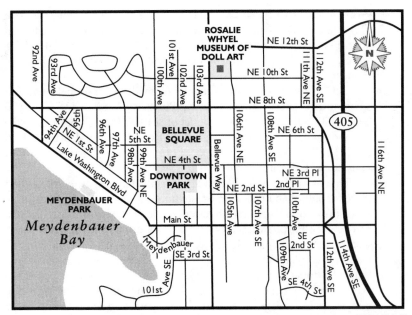

mornings just to walk for exercise. Along with fashion outlets, fast-food-eries, and shops selling home decorations, the square hosts the **BELLEVUE ART MUSEUM** (301 Bellevue Square; 425/454-3322) on its top floor. The museum mounts rotating exhibits of local and national artists, from the avant-garde to the traditional. An adjoining gift shop offers some truly unusual buys. (Current plans call for BAM to move to a new three-story facility across the street from the shopping center by the year 2001.) On nice days you can conclude a visit to Bellevue Square with a walk through **DOWNTOWN PARK**, a 19-acre site in the heart of the shopping district and across the street from Bellevue Square. There you'll find a 240-foot-wide, 10-foot-high waterfall, a canal enclosing a 5-acre meadow, and a 28-foot-wide promenade, fine for strolling with or without the kids.

Art-fair lovers shouldn't miss the **PACIFIC NORTHWEST ARTS AND CRAFTS FAIR** (held the last weekend in July at Bellevue Square), which attracts thousands of visitors and hundreds of artists from throughout the West. It is said to be the largest crafts fair in the Northwest, and local legend holds that it never rains on the weekend of the fair (Eastsiders plan weddings and barbecues accordingly).

OLD BELLEVUE (Main St between Bellevue Way NE and 100th Ave NE) isn't much when it comes to historic districts hereabouts. The city's main shopping district before Bellevue Square was built in the 1940s, it's now just a quiet street lined with specialty shops and restaurants.

COCINA DEL PUERCO (10246 Main St; 425/455-1151), a cafeteria-style Mexican cafe, is fine for an informal lunch or dinner. For a more formal atmosphere, try **22 FOUNTAIN COURT** (22 103rd Ave NE; 425/451-0426), a restaurant of romantic Old World elegance in an old Bellevue residence.

Before leaving this part of town, you might want to make two last stops: at **UNIVERSITY BOOK STORE** (990 102nd Ave NE; 425/632-9500 or 206/632-9500), the Eastside outlet of Seattle's famed store (minus the textbook and buy-back options); and the Rosalie Whyel Museum of Doll Art (1116 108th Ave NE; 425/455-1116), with its diverse selection of dolls, teddy bears, and miniatures.

East of town, out SE Eighth Street, is **KELSEY CREEK PARK**, a good place for suburban kids to get a taste (albeit a tame one) of the country. A demonstration farm offers up-close contact with pigs, horses, chickens, and rabbits. Further east lies **CROSSROADS SHOPPING CENTER** (intersection of NE 8th St and 156th Ave NE; 425/644-1111), a midsize mall where the emphasis shifts from shopping to community events and ethnic foods. Visitors can play a game of chess (with giant chess pieces) at the giant board painted on the floor, or choose from the menus of a growing number of ethnic eateries. Almost nobody passes up a visit to **THE DAILY PLANET** (425/562-1519), one of the best newspaper and magazine stands in the area. And every Friday and Saturday night, Crossroads sponsors free live musical entertainment—featuring some of the area's most talented musicians playing anything and everything, from jazz to polka (Thursday nights are open mike, for those who dare). *Map:HH3–HH1*

KIRKLAND

East of Lake Washington, between NE 116th St and Carillon Point This town was supposed to be "the Pittsburgh of the West"—or at least that was the dream shared in the late 19th century by Leigh S. J. Hunt, publisher of the *Seattle Post-Intelligencer*, and Peter Kirk, an English industrialist. They were convinced that an iron-and-steel works could thrive on Moss Bay, just east of Seattle across Lake Washington. However, in 1893, after only a few buildings and homes had been raised in the area, the nation was struck by its worst financial depression. All that remains of Kirkland's campaign to become Pittsburgh are a few handsomely refurbished historical structures, such as the **PETER KIRK BUILDING** (620 Market St) and the **JOSHUA SEARS BUILDING** (701 Market St).

Kirkland today is a friendly, low-profile Eastside town that hugs Lake Washington and offers more public access to the water than any other city on the lake's shores. One of the best ways to experience the lake is with a visit to **JUANITA BAY PARK** (access is off Market Street just south of Juanita Drive). Nature tours are offered the first Sunday of every month beginning at 1pm. These naturalist-led tours point out the great

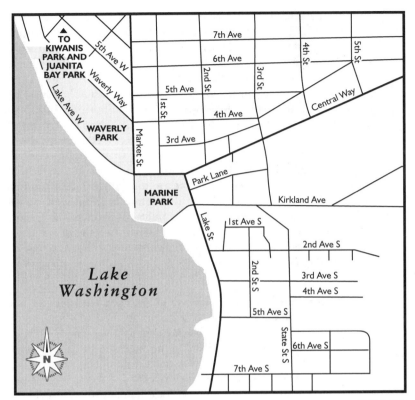

KIRKLAND

blue herons, owls, turtles, beavers, and other varieties of wildlife that inhabit these natural wetlands and marshes. For more solitary strolling, try **ST. EDWARDS STATE PARK** (take Market Street north and head west on Juanita Drive), a densely forested park with a variety of trails that lead down to lakefront beaches.

A more urban tour of the town might begin at the **KIRKLAND ANTIQUE GALLERY** (151 3rd St; 425/828-4993), a fun stop for antique aficionados, with more than 80 dealers selling everything from antique tin toys to Depression-era glass. Not far away is **DANISH-SWEDISH ANTIQUES** (207 Kirkland Ave; 425/822-7899) and, next door, the **DAKOTA ART STORE** (209 Kirkland Ave; 425/827-7678), with wonderful art supplies and gifts for artists. If you'd rather look at art than create it, tour the many **ART GALLERIES** in the downtown area: Foster/White Gallery (126 Central Way; 425/822-2305); Howard Mandeville Gallery (120 Park Lane; 425/889-8212); Kirkland Arts Center (620 Market St; 425/822-7161); and Park Lane Gallery (130 Park Lane; 425/827-1462).

When you need to nourish your body instead of your soul, try **CAFE DAVINCI'S** (89 Kirkland Ave; 425/889-9000), popular with the socializing 20-something crowd. In summer, the east wall of the restaurant is rolled up, creating an open-air cafe. A quieter choice for lunch or dinner is the Northern Italian **RISTORANTE PARADISO** (120-A Park Lane; 425/889-8601), serving incredibly good breads and pastas. For smashing lake views, try **ANTHONY'S HOMEPORT** (135 Lake St; 425/822-0225) or the **THIRD FLOOR FISH CAFE** (205 Lake St; 425/822-3553).

CARILLON POINT, south of downtown proper, is a luxury waterfront complex that includes the **WOODMARK HOTEL** (1200 Carillon Point; 425/822-3700 or 800/822-3700), specialty shops, waterfront walkways, paths, and benches. **YARROW BAY GRILL** (1270 Carillon Point; 425/889-9052) features fancy food at fancier prices, while downstairs the **YARROW BAY BEACH CAFÉ** (425/889-0303) offers simpler fare. Fortunately, the best thing about Carillon Point is free: the view. Enjoy a walk around the grounds, or rent a paddleboat and get your exercise on the lake. *Map:EE3*

REDMOND

East of Lake Washington, between NE 60th St and NE 124th St, and 132nd Ave NE and 164th Ave NE Pioneers in the late 19th century seemed to have had some trouble making up their minds about a moniker for this farming settlement in the Sammamish Valley, east of Kirkland. For a while the town was called Salmonberg, for the dog salmon that swam so plentifully in its rivers and creeks. Later it was known as Melrose, after a prominent local homestead, but the burg's name was finally changed to Redmond in honor of Luke McRedmond, the first mayor and postmaster of the community.

Surely, McRedmond would have a tough time recognizing his little hamlet these days, what with the infestation of corporate headquarters for **MICROSOFT** and **NINTENDO** and the phenomenal growth that those and other high-tech businesses have engendered.

Like Bellevue, Redmond has a bustling downtown shopping mall: **REDMOND TOWN CENTER** (near NE 74th St and 164th Ave NE; 425/867-0808), with more than 50 stores and the **REDMOND TOWN CENTER CINEMAS** arranged around plazas and a large open space used for musical performances. But this city offers some more distinctive delights, as well— especially **MARYMOOR PARK** (6046 W Lake Sammamish Pkwy NE; 206/296-2966). Located south of downtown, Marymoor comprises 522 acres of playfields, running and horseback-riding trails, tennis courts, an interpretive nature trail, and even a 45-foot climbing wall (crowded on weekends). This is also where you'll find the **MARYMOOR VELODROME**

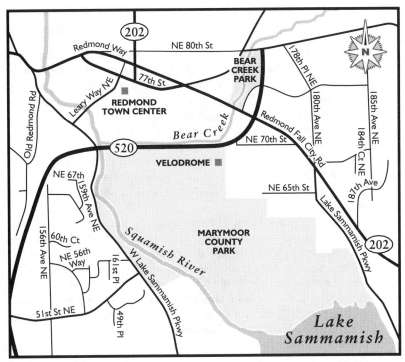

REDMOND

(2400 Lake Sammamish Pkwy; 206/675-1424), a 400-meter oval bicycle-racing track that attracts championship riders from around the country as well as picnickers who come to watch the spoked wheels go round and round. (Spectators pay $3 to attend Friday-night races.) For a less-active diversion, check out the **CLISE MANSION**, built by Seattle businessman John Clise in 1904 as an Eastside hunting lodge. Today, that brown-shingled retreat contains the **MARYMOOR MUSEUM** (425/885-3684), which recalls the area's history in exhibits focusing on dairy farming, Native American habitations, and turn-of-the-century village life. Every Fourth of July weekend, the park hosts a **HERITAGE FESTIVAL** featuring ethnic foods, crafts, and music.

From Marymoor, the **SAMMAMISH RIVER TRAIL** stretches for 10 miles to Bothell, north of Kirkland. It's a flat but circuitous route ideal for fair-weather bicyclists, runners, and skaters who enjoy views of the surrounding mountains, slow-moving livestock, and even a few wire sculptures of cows. *Map:EE1–FF1*

Museums

Artworks are so liberally sprinkled throughout Seattle that you'll find it hard to avoid going past, through, or over some of them—whether murals, sculptures, decorated manhole covers, artist-designed gateways, plazas, or bus stops. The sheer quantity of **PUBLIC ART** is mostly due to a groundbreaking 1973 city ordinance that calls for 1 percent of certain capital improvement funds to be spent on art. King County, Washington State, and corporate and private donors have also contributed to the collection, with works by contemporary artists from the Northwest and elsewhere. The best guide to this museum-without-walls is the Seattle Arts Commission's *A Field Guide to Seattle's Public Art*, available at most local bookstores.

The art ranges widely in form, style, and personality—from traditional metal monuments to environmental pieces so subtly integrated into their settings they almost disappear. In the former category, few public sculptures have enjoyed as much unbridled affection as Richard Beyer's *People Waiting for the Interurban* (1979) in Fremont—the gray, huddled band of cast-aluminum trolley riders (Fremont Ave N and N 34th St; map:FF7) whose distinctly homely figures have become a symbol of the neighborhood. Other additions to the landscape have gotten cooler receptions. Michael Heizer's *Adjacent, Against, Upon*, three massive hunks of granite sitting next to, leaning on, and lying atop three mammoth chunks of concrete, was the subject of a loud public outcry over "spending tax dollars on rocks" when it was installed at Myrtle Edwards Park (Alaskan Way and Bay St; map:B9) in 1976 but is now an accepted part of the waterfront. And some artworks bring out the vehement loyalty of Seattleites. In 1987, when Seafirst Bank announced the sale of Henry Moore's 11-ton bronze bone forms, *Three-Piece Sculpture: Vertebrae* (1968) (1001 4th Ave Plaza; map:M6), to a Japanese investor, the art community roared in protest and the sale was blocked. Eventually, Seafirst donated the work to the Seattle Art Museum with the proviso that it remain in its present location for 100 years.

Undoubtedly the most riveting landmark downtown is Jonathan Borofsky's towering black *Hammering Man* (1992) (100 University St; map:K7), a four-story figure whose motorized arm and hammer is set to pound four beats a minute, commemorating—so the artist intends—the city's workers. *Hammering Man* made a big impression when he arrived to guard the doorway of the new downtown Seattle Art Museum, crashing to the pavement just as he was being craned into place. The present piece, completely refabricated, might well be called *Hammering Man II*.

The biggest art project to date is the Metro transit bus tunnel (map:I3–J6) and its terminals (opened 1990), which, with a $1.5 million art budget, employed dozens of artists in its design and appointments, from plazas to murals, benches, and clocks. Buses traveling through the 1.3-mile tunnel stop at all five stations (International District, Pioneer Square, University Street, Westlake Center, and Convention Place) frequently every day except Sundays, when the tunnel is closed.

BELLEVUE ART MUSEUM (BAM) / Bellevue Way NE and NE 8th St, Bellevue Square, Bellevue; 425/454-3322 Sitting atop a slick shopping mall, BAM doesn't always transcend the general ambience; but for the most part it has created its own niche with exhibits that favor Northwest artists, craftspeople, and craft traditions from around the world. The museum will move from its shopping center site to a new $23 million facility across the street in 2001, and the new space will feature three exhibition galleries, as well as classrooms for hands-on art-making and lots of interactive activities. BAM officials won't yet comment on any new direction the exhibit schedule may take, except to mention the influence of technology—a nod to the museum's wealthy Eastside neighbor, Microsoft. Recent shows have ventured bravely into foreign territory: artists whose prime concerns are social and political instead of decorative. BAM sponsors the massively popular Pacific Northwest Arts and Crafts Fair at Bellevue Square each July. Admission to the museum is $3 adults, $2 seniors and students, free for kids under 12. Tuesdays are free for everyone. *Every day; www.bellevueart.org; map:HH3*

BURKE MUSEUM OF NATURAL HISTORY AND CULTURE / 17th Ave NE and NE 45th St, University of Washington; 206/543-5590 See Top 25 Attractions in this chapter.

CENTER FOR WOODEN BOATS / 1010 Valley St; 206/382-2628 You can sail away with the exhibits at the Center for Wooden Boats, which has its own little harbor at the southern tip of Lake Union. This maritime museum, kept afloat financially by private donations and a contingent of volunteers, celebrates the heritage of small craft before the advent of fiberglass. Of the 75 vintage and replica wooden rowing and sailing boats in the collection, more than half are available for public use. Admission is always free. Rentals range from $10 to $25 an hour. Lessons in sailing, traditional woodworking, and boatbuilding are offered for all ages. *Wed–Mon; www.eskimo.com/~cwboats; map:D1*

THE CHILDREN'S MUSEUM / Center House, Seattle Center; 206/441-1768 Located on the fountain level of the busy Seattle Center House, the Children's Museum has tripled in size since its opening. It's an imaginative learning center that stresses participation, with hands-on activities and exploration of other cultural traditions, and houses a number of permanent features, including a play center, a mountain, and a global village with child-size houses from Japan, Ghana, and the Philippines. The variety of special programs—Mexican folk dancing, Native American games, Chinese storytelling, Japanese kitemaking—is impressive. The Imagination Station features a different artist every month guiding activities with various materials. The Discovery Bay exhibit is geared to infants and toddlers. Admission is $4 adults, $5.50 kids 12 and under; annual family memberships are $48–$100. *Every day; www.thechildrens museum.org; map:B6*

FRYE ART MUSEUM / 704 Terry Ave; 206/ 622-9250 This once-stodgy museum, known for sentimental 19th-century German salon paintings from the collection of late Seattleites Charles and Emma Frye, underwent a dramatic expansion and remodel in 1997. Since reopening, it's become a lively hub of activities, with poetry readings, chamber music, and other performances in addition to frequently changing exhibits. A new director has chosen a more liberal view of the museum's commitment to figurative art. Shows can be as diverse as the metaphorical paintings of Norwegian artist Odd Nerdrum, the art of Russian ballet dancer Vaslav Nijinsky, or a tribute—in words and imagery—to National Poetry Month. Admission is always free. *Every day; www.fryeart.org; map:N3*

HENRY ART GALLERY / 15th Ave NE and NE 41st St, University of Washington; 206/543-2280 After a major expansion project that quadrupled its size, the Henry is working to forge a new identity that lives up to its exemplary past. Although it hasn't yet re-created the furor caused by the Ann Hamilton and James Turrell installations in the early '90s, the new Henry is mounting some provocative shows, with a bent toward installations, video, and unusual media. The permanent collection—especially strong in photography—now has a showcase in the original galleries. Additions to the museum include an outdoor sculpture court, a 150-seat auditorium, a cafe (the food is pre-fab), and an education center for children. Admission is $5 adults, $3.50 seniors, free for UW students and faculty. *Tues–Sun; www.henryart.org; map:FF6*

MUSEUM OF FLIGHT / 9404 E Marginal Way S; 206/764-5720 See Top 25 Attractions in this chapter.

MUSEUM OF HISTORY AND INDUSTRY (MOHAI) / 2700 24th Ave E; 206/324-1125 The rambling, amiable MOHAI is a huge repository of Americana, with artifacts pertaining to the early history of the Pacific Northwest. There's a 1920s Boeing mail plane, an exhibit about the great Seattle fire of 1889 (it started in a gluepot on the waterfront), and a hands-on history of the fishing and canning industry in the Northwest. There are antique cars, lace- and bustle-decked gowns, and a half-dozen immense wooden female beauties—and one masculine counterpart—

who once rode the prows of ships in Puget Sound. Locally oriented exhibits change throughout the year. Admission is $5.50 adults, $3 seniors and children 6–12, $1 children 2–5, free for kids 2 and under. *Tues–Sun; www.historymuse-nw.org; map:FF6*

NORDIC HERITAGE MUSEUM / 3014 NW 67th St; 206/789-5707 Established in a stately restored schoolhouse, the Nordic Heritage Museum focuses on the history of Nordic settlers in the United States, with exhibits of maritime equipment, costumes, and photographs, including an Ellis Island installation. Periodic traveling exhibits have included a show of 18th-century Alaskan and Northwest Coast Native artifacts from the National Museum of Finland, as well as artworks by contemporary Scandinavian artists—all shown in some of the loveliest gallery space in town. The building also houses a language school and a music library. Holidays bring ethnic festivals. Admission is $4 adults, $3 seniors and students, $2 children 6–18, under 6 free. *Tues–Sun; nordic@ intelistep.com; www.nordicmuseum.com; map:EE9*

ODYSSEY, THE MARITIME DISCOVERY CENTER / 2205 Alaskan Way, Pier 66; 206/374-4000 See Top 25 Attractions in this chapter.

ROSALIE WHYEL MUSEUM OF DOLL ART / 1116 108th Ave NE, Bellevue; 425/455-1116 Housed in a pink confection of a building near Bellevue Square, this privately owned museum opened in 1992 and was an instant hit in the insular world of doll collecting. Don't be put off by that. Anyone with an eye for beauty and fine craftsmanship, or with a fascination for the evolution of totems, effigies, miniatures, and all manner of playthings, will be entranced by this eclectic group of multicultural objects. You'll find more than 3,000 dolls, including everything from ancient Egyptian burial charms to extravagantly outfitted porcelain princesses—not to mention a few of their modern, mass-produced counterparts. A gift shop with a pricey selection of new and antique toys caters to collectors. Admission is $6 adults, $5.50 seniors, $4 children 5–17, under 5 free. *Every day; www.dollart.com/dollart; map:HH3*

SEATTLE ART MUSEUM / 100 University St; 206/654-3100 See Top 25 Attractions in this chapter.

SEATTLE ASIAN ART MUSEUM / 1400 E Prospect St, Volunteer Park; 206/654-3100 See Top 25 Attractions in this chapter.

WING LUKE ASIAN MUSEUM / 407 7th Ave S; 206/623-5124 Named after Seattle's first Chinese-American city councilman, this lively little museum in the International District is devoted to the Asian American experience in the Northwest. Particularly moving is the small exhibit of photographs and artifacts relating to the internment of Japanese-Americans during World War II. Changing exhibits are devoted to Chinese,

Korean, Filipino, Vietnamese, and Laotian peoples and their often difficult meetings with the West. Admission is $2.50 adults, $1.50 students and seniors, 75 cents children, kids under 5 free. Free on Thursdays. *Tues–Sun; www.wingluke.org; map:R6*

Galleries

Seattle's main gallery scene—art, crafts, and Native American—is concentrated in the historic Pioneer Square district, with additional galleries sprinkled to the north along First Avenue, especially in the vicinity of the downtown Seattle Art Museum. One good way to get to know many of them is to roam with the crowd in and around Pioneer Square on the first Thursday evening of each month (about 6pm to 8pm), when new shows are previewed (see "Art Appeal" box).

CAROLYN STALEY FINE PRINTS / 314 Occidental Ave S; 206/621-1888 The specialty here is fine old prints, including Japanese *ukiyo-e* woodblock prints, antique maps, and botanical prints. Staley also hosts occasional book-art shows. *Tues–Sat; map:O9*

CENTER ON CONTEMPORARY ART (COCA) / 65 Cedar St; 206/728-1980 COCA's mission is to provide a venue for outer-edge art, especially performance and installation works that would otherwise have little chance for survival in the marketplace. With yet another change of leadership in the works, COCA's direction, even its survival, is hard to predict. Recent exhibits have included an assortment of UFO-related art and memorabilia and a show of giant mechanized sculptures by Japanese artist Kenji Yanobe. A few traditional shows are scheduled as well, such as the cluttered salon-style Northwest Annual. *Call for event info and hours; map:E8*

DAVIDSON GALLERIES / 313 Occidental Ave S; 206/624-7684 Geared to traditional tastes, Davidson shows landscapes and figurative works by contemporary Northwest painters, interspersed with shows by Russian, Czech, and Chinese artists. The back gallery features contemporary printmakers from around the world. Upstairs, check out the antique print department, with loads of work on file, as well as rotating shows of everything from Blake illustrations to Indian miniature paintings. *Tues–Sat; map:O8*

ELLIOTT BROWN GALLERY / 619 N 35th St, Suite 101; 206/547-9740 Owner Kate Elliott has been involved with the Pilchuck School and its glass art almost from the school's beginning in 1971. Now she has a gallery, tucked unobtrusively in a Fremont back alley, where she uses her connections in the glass world to line up shows by top international artists. One highlight of her roster was the first solo West Coast show of famed Czech glass artists Stanislav Libensky and Jaroslava Brychtova. *Tues–Sat; map:FF8*

FOSTER/WHITE GALLERY / 123 S Jackson St; 206/622-2833 Foster/White showcases paintings, sculpture, and ceramics—usually abstract and decorative—by Northwest artists living and dead. The gallery, which moved in 1999 to a new Pioneer Square location, is also one of the major local dealers in contemporary glass by Pilchuck School stars, most notably Dale Chihuly. An Eastside outpost is located in downtown Kirkland (126 Central Way; 425/822-2305; map:EE3) and another, strictly devoted to glass, is housed in the City Centre Shops (5th Ave and Pike St; 206/340-8025; map:K5). *Every day; map:O8*

FRANCINE SEDERS GALLERY / 6701 Greenwood Ave N; 206/782-0355 In judicious operation since 1966, Seders represents some venerable members of Seattle's art community, including Jacob Lawrence, Gwen Knight, Robert Jones, and Michael Spafford. New additions to the stable include generous numbers of minority artists, among them painters, sculptors, and assemblagists. *Tues–Sun; map:EE7*

G. GIBSON GALLERY / 122 S Jackson St, 2nd floor; 206/587-4033 Gibson opened her cozy upstairs space in 1991, providing a much-needed venue for contemporary photography—by both well-known Americans and adventurous young Northwesterners. *Tues–Sun; map:O9*

GREG KUCERA GALLERY / 212 3rd Ave S; 206/624-0770 One of the city's top gallery owners, Kucera maintains a carefully chosen stable of artists, many with national reputations. He has a great eye for emerging talent but also shows editioned works by established blue-chip artists. Recent shows have featured prints by Frank Stella, Robert Motherwell, and Helen Frankenthaler. One thematic exhibit each year addresses a touchy topic: sex, religion, politics. The gallery has recently relocated to this new space in the same neighborhood. *Tues–Sun; map:O7*

GROVER/THURSTON GALLERY / 309 Occidental Ave S; 206/223-0816 In the heart of the gallery district, Grover/Thurston gained considerable status when it picked up one of the region's most popular artists, Fay Jones, just before her 1997 retrospective at the Seattle Art Museum. Otherwise, the gallery's focus veers toward the decorative. *Tues–Sat; map:O8*

KIRKLAND ARTS CENTER / 620 Market St, Kirkland; 425/822-7161 In a historic brick building near the waterfront, this publicly funded center puts on several shows each year by Puget Sound–area artists. A variety of art classes are open to children and adults. *Mon–Fri; map:EE3*

THE LEGACY / 1003 1st Ave (Alexis Hotel); 206/624-6350 Northwest Native American works, some antique but most created by contemporary practitioners deeply devoted to reviving tribal traditions, are the

ART APPEAL

Leave it to health-conscious Northwesterners to favor an athletic form of art appreciation.

The **First Thursday Gallery Walk**, centered in downtown Seattle's historic Pioneer Square, began in 1982, when a few gallery owners were looking to drum up traffic. Today the monthly walk is an arts staple, with crowds of art lovers checking out the dozens of galleries scattered around the square, which stay open for extended hours, 6–8pm. The Seattle Art Museum bolstered the turnout when it joined the walk and waived its admission price on Thursday evenings.

As much a social spectacle as an artistic exercise, the walk is a bonanza for people-watchers—the event draws an eclectic mix of types. It's also a notorious way for Seattle's single sophisticates to meet. The only hitch in the walk is that it's now so popular that parking can be a problem. To avoid driving in circles, head for where most cars don't. Just a four-block walk from the galleries, in the International District east of Fourth Avenue S on Main and Jackson Streets, is that rarest of conditions, free on-street parking. Or try the metered parking (no charge after 6pm) beneath the Alaskan Way Viaduct, or the relatively inexpensive open parking lots off Occidental Square in nearly every direction. Or ditch the car—and potential headaches—and hop a Metro bus; rides are free within the downtown core till 7pm.

Copies of *Art Guide Northwest*—a comprehensive guide filled with maps and listings of the region's art galleries, museums, and special events—are available in many Pioneer Square galleries and bookstores.

Looking to replicate the success of the downtown art parade, in 1997 the Capitol Hill neighborhood started the **Capitol Hill Arts Orbit** on the first Saturday of the month, 1–6pm. Orbit maps are available at the Robbie Mildred Gallery in the Broadway Market (401 Broadway E; 206/325-5228) or Portage Bay Goods (1121 Pike St; 206/622-3212).

Galleries, working studios, and public art (such as the giant troll lurking at the foot of the Aurora Bridge) are part of Fremont's **Art About** walk on the second Saturday of the month, 1–5pm. Maps are available at the Marvin Oliver Gallery (N 35th St and Fremont Ave N; 206/633-2468); more information is available from the Fremont Chamber of Commerce (206/633-0812).

On the Eastside, the **Kirkland Art Walk** takes in several closely packed galleries and some pretty quirky public art (a coyote riding the back of a cow, for example) on the second Thursday of the month, 5–9pm. Free four-hour parking is available at the Kirkland Library (808 Kirkland Ave).

— *Shannon O'Leary*

focus here: elaborately hand-carved wooden masks (originally important in Northwest Coast winter festivals), bentwood boxes, silver work, button blankets, baskets, and prints. *Mon–Sat; map:L8*

LINDA HODGES GALLERY / 410 Occidental Ave S; 206/624-3034 Hodges shows contemporary paintings, and occasionally photography and sculpture, by artists from Seattle, Portland, and other Northwest burgs. The art ranges from fantasy to realism, with the biggest draw being the zany, countrified mythology of adored Eastern Washington painter Gaylen Hansen. *Tues–Sun and by appointment; map:O8*

LISA HARRIS GALLERY / 1922 Pike Pl, Pike Place Market; 206/443-3315 Amid the jostling crowds of the Market, this small upstairs gallery can be an oasis of calm. Harris favors expressionistic landscape and figurative works, with several Bellingham artists forming the core of her stable. *Every day; map:I8*

MARTIN-ZAMBITO FINE ART / 721 E Pike St; 206/726-9509 These two guys from the East Coast know more about the obscure corners of Northwest regionalism than almost anybody. And they're on a mission: to bring recognition to overlooked early artists of the area, especially women—such as photographer Myra Wiggins, whose work attracted international attention in the early 1900s and then disappeared in the shifting tides of art history. *Tues–Sat; map:K1*

NORTHWEST CRAFT CENTER / Seattle Center; 206/728-1555 Ceramics is the focus here, in solo or small group shows that change monthly. There are also wood items and jewelry. *Every day (Memorial Day–Labor Day, Thanksgiving–Jan 1); Tues–Sun (Jan 1–Memorial Day, Labor Day–Thanksgiving); map:A7*

NORTHWEST FINE WOODWORKING / 101 S Jackson St (and branches); 206/625-0542 This cooperatively owned gallery offers one-of-a-kind tables, desks, chairs, cabinets, sideboards, screens, boxes, and turned bowls, all by local craftspeople. An Eastside gallery is in Kirkland (122 Central Way; 425/889-1513; map:EE3), and a third branch is located in Post Alley (1602 Post Alley; 206/441-4015; map:I8). *Every day; map:O8*

SACRED CIRCLE GALLERY OF AMERICAN INDIAN ART / Daybreak Star Cultural Arts Center, Discovery Park; 206/285-4425 A profit-making arm of the United Indians of All Tribes Foundation, this top-notch gallery features contemporary paintings, prints, and sculptural pieces, always reflecting tribal heritages, by a broad selection of Native American artists from the United States and Canada. *Every day; map:FF9*

SEAFIRST GALLERY / 701 5th Ave, 3rd floor; 206/585-3200 Founded in 1993, the nonprofit gallery grew out of a merger between Seafirst and Security Pacific banks that absorbed the innovative Security Pacific gallery. Seafirst is not a sales gallery and doesn't represent any particular artists; however, it hosts seven to eight shows a year, primarily in conjunction with other arts and civic organizations. *Mon–Fri; map:N6*

SNOW GOOSE ASSOCIATES / 8806 Roosevelt Way NE; 206/523-6223 In 1993 Snow Goose changed ownership and moved from a display room in a private home to a new gallery space filled with art and artifacts of Alaskan and Canadian Eskimos and Northwest Coast Indians. Annual shows include the fall exhibit of prints by Inuit artists from Cape Dorset on Baffin Island. Snow Goose has been in operation for almost 30 years. *Tues–Sat; map:DD7*

WILLIAM TRAVER GALLERY / 110 Union St; 206/587-6501 Pilchuck School glassworks are always on view at Traver, which hosts an annual Pilchuck glass show in December. The stunning second-story space at First Avenue and Union Street, near the Seattle Art Museum, showcases paintings, sculptures, photographs, ceramics, and assemblages, mostly by local artists. *Tues–Sun; map:K7*

WOODSIDE/BRASETH GALLERY / 1533 9th Ave; 206/622-7243 You'll find strictly Northwest fare in the city's oldest gallery (founded in 1962): paintings by Mark Tobey, William Ivey, Morris Graves, Paul Horiuchi, and a varying selection of midcareer artists. *Tues–Sat; map:J4*

Gardens

Mild and moist of climate, the maritime Northwest ranks among the world's best places for gardening. The native flora are both abundant and varied, including towering Douglas firs and tiny calypso orchids, spectacular rhododendrons that set the mountain trails ablaze in May, and the subtle greenery of maidenhair ferns. Not surprisingly, Seattle is a green city. Corporate headquarters are swathed in gardens, and tiny urban yards spill down sidewalk strips into vacant lots and traffic circles. Dramatic container gardens encircle tall office buildings, baskets dripping with flowers decorate windows and lampposts, and community gardens, called P-Patches, beautify otherwise unused city property. Downtown rooftops and terraces are green with gardens. Freeway Park drapes the midcity interchanges with verdant curtains of ivy, the incessant roar of the traffic obscured by whispering stands of bamboo. The University of Washington's campus is rich with trees; pick up the Brockman Memorial Tree Tour pamphlet for a small fee at the bus shelter across from Anderson Hall. Volunteer Park on Capitol Hill boasts magnificent specimen trees and a splendid Victorian conservatory overflowing with flowers.

Here are some of the area's outstanding gardens, most of which may be visited without charge.

BELLEVUE BOTANICAL GARDEN / 12001 Main St, Bellevue; 425/452-2750 Although this garden opened only in 1992, it has quickly become a popular year-round destination. Walking up the steps to the entrance, visitors are greeted by a cleverly designed water feature that is both visually striking and pleasing to the ear. The Shorts Visitor Center houses a gift shop and provides maps and seasonally appropriate descriptions of the gardens. The Botanical Garden, which sits on 36 acres within Wilburton Hill Park, contains several smaller display gardens. To the east of the visitors center is the Waterwise Garden, which features descriptive signage detailing numerous techniques to conserve water; specially selected plants are well labeled to provide ideas for the home gardener. The Alpine Garden, added in 1992, has a generous display of flora found in rocky alpine settings (visitors are asked not to sit or climb on the rocks). The half-mile trail that rings the Botanical Garden winds past several other gardens, including the Yao Japanese Garden, the entrance to which is framed by a traditional covered wooden gate. Inside the gate is a well-executed garden incorporating modern and traditional Japanese features. The trail continues on to the Perennial Border—a 20,000-square-foot mixed planting of perennials, bulbs, trees, shrubs, and grasses that is maintained entirely by Northwest Perennial Alliance weekend volunteers.

The garden has special events throughout the year—a Mothers' Day Open House, plant sales, and its largest event, Garden d'Lights. A holiday light festival that extends from late November through early January from 4 to 10pm nightly, Garden d'Lights often includes music or other happenings. The light displays re-create real flowers: a wisteria arbor, sunflowers, climbing roses, rhododendron blossoms. Docents are available Saturday and Sunday noon–4pm, March through October, and group tours can be arranged by calling 206/451-3755. No pets, bicycles, or skateboards are allowed in the garden. Admission is free. *Every day 7:30am–dusk (visitors center 10am–4pm); www.ci.bellevue.wa.us/Parks /wburton.htm; map:HH3*

BLOEDEL RESERVE / 7571 NE Dolphin Dr, Bainbridge Island; 206/842-7631 Since the late 1980s, this 150-acre Bainbridge Island estate has been open to the public on a limited basis. The manse, which overlooks Puget Sound, is now a visitors center where interpretive material is available to guide one's walk through the property. The parklike grounds contain a number of theme gardens, including a Japanese garden with cloud pruned pines, a Zen sand garden, and a moss garden full of intriguing native plants. Nature trails lead through native woods and wetlands. A small pond attracts birds in increasing numbers as its plantings mature. Not a place for a family picnic or a romp with the dog. Reservations for entrance are required (and limited; call well in advance during the busy spring months). Guided tours can be arranged for groups, and many of the trails are wheelchair accessible (the reserve has two sturdy wheelchairs available for public use; call ahead). Admission is $6 adults, $4 seniors, students, and children 5–12. Children under 5 are free. *Wed–Sun 10am–4pm; www.bloedelreserve.org/* &

CARL S. ENGLISH JR. BOTANICAL GARDENS / Hiram M. Chittenden Locks; 3015 NW 54th St; 206/783-7059

One of the region's great horticulturists, Carl English made Seattle a horticultural hot spot earlier in the century through his plant- and seed-collecting efforts. Here one can explore 7 acres of gardens containing more than 500 species of plants, including those that made up English's personal arboretum. Rare ornamental trees and shrubs from all over the temperate world are underplanted with flowering plants in similarly rich variety. The English gardens are worth a visit even in winter, when the tapestry of bark and berry and the perfume of winter-flowering plants will brighten the grayest day. In summer the Seattle Fuchsia Society's display garden enlivens the spacious lawns, where one can picnic and watch the boats make their way through the lock systems that connect Lake Washington to Puget Sound. A summer band concert series and special theme family events, such as Scandinavian Day, provide further entertainment on the weekends. Guided tours of the locks, fish ladder, and garden are held daily in summer (June 1–September 30) and on weekends during the rest of the year; special in-depth tours can be arranged. (See Hiram M. Chittenden Locks under Top 25 Attractions in this chapter.) Admission is free. *Every day 7am–9pm; www.nps.usace.army.mil/opdiv/lwsc/garden.htm; map:FF9*

THE HERBFARM / 32804 Issaquah–Fall City Rd, Fall City; 25 miles east of Seattle; 425/784-2222 or 800/866-4372

This country herb nursery has grown into a thriving family business offering herbs living and dried as well as a multitude of herbal products and herb-related gifts. Hundreds of herbs are grown on the premises, and some 17 herbal theme gardens demonstrate their looks in the garden setting. A mature herb garden holds culinary and medicinal herbs as well as flowers for drying. Among the themes are a fragrance garden, a cook's garden, a pioneer garden of herbs common a century or so ago, and a plot holding plants mentioned in the writings of Shakespeare. Tours of the gardens and greenhouses are offered on spring and summer weekends (or by appointment for groups). Annual events include herbal-crafts classes and workshops, and a variety of seasonal festivals. Picnickers are always welcome. An intimate, nationally renowned restaurant provided cooking demonstrations and meals based on the Northwest's bounty and the gardens' harvest here for years until a fire in 1997 destroyed the main building. At press time, plans to rebuild were still tentative. Admission is free but there is a charge for tours. *Mon–Fri 10am–6pm, Sat–Sun 9am–6pm (April–Sept); every day 10am–5pm (Oct–March); herborder@aol.com; www.theherbfarm.com*

KUBOTA GARDENS / 55th Ave S at Renton Ave S; 206/725-5060 This Japanese garden tucked away in the Rainier Beach neighborhood is a surprising oasis, home to such exotics as dragon trees. Begun in 1927 by Fujitaro Kubota, a self-taught gardener, the grounds first served as his private residence and as a nursery and display garden for the Kubota Gardening Company. The garden is now owned by the city of Seattle and cared for by a nonprofit organization. The large area encompasses many styles, from traditional Japanese garden to expansive lawns perfect for picnicking. The grounds are laced with winding paths that open onto ethereal views framing the many artfully trained pines and pruned plantings. A number of benches provide places for quiet contemplation. The north-central area of the garden is the site of the Necklace of Ponds, a network of waterfalls and ponds with a recirculating water system. Many beautiful stone and wooden bridges span the water and provide interesting perspectives of the garden. Admission is free, and free tours are available on the last Saturday and Sunday of each month at 10am, starting in the parking lot; tours can also be arranged at any time for groups of eight or more. The Kubota Gardens Foundation holds plant sales in May and September which are open to the public. *Every day dawn to dusk; map:MM4*

PACIFIC RIM BONSAI COLLECTION / Weyerhaeuser Way S (Weyerhaeuser Company), Federal Way; 253/924-5206 The corporate headquarters of America's biggest timber business also houses a pair of significant plant collections, both open to the public (see also next listing). Frequently changing exhibits showcase the diminutive gems of the bonsai collection, including a 1,000-year-old dwarf Sierra juniper, tiny pines, and a mature sequoia—usually among the tallest of trees—a mere 3 feet in height. Many of the plants are displayed in pots, but some are arranged in complex landscapes or miniature forests (children find these very appealing). On alternate Sundays at 1pm, mid-April to mid-October, professional bonsai artists demonstrate pruning, propagation, and caretaking techniques. Basic bonsai care lectures are offered the second Saturday of the month at 1pm, June–September. Tours are Sunday at noon or by appointment. Admission is free. *Sat–Wed 11am–4pm (June–Feb), Fri–Wed 10am–4pm (March–May); www.weyerhaeuser.com/bonsai/default.htm* &

RHODODENDRON SPECIES BOTANICAL GARDEN / Weyerhaeuser Way S (Weyerhaeuser Company), Federal Way; 253/661-9377 The Rhododendron Species Foundation's plantings encompass the largest, most comprehensive collection of rhododendron species and hybrids in the world. This is as much a preserve as a garden—more than 60 of the over 500 species growing here are endangered in the wild. The foundation's goals—the preservation, distribution, and display of rhododendrons—are met through research and education programs. A pair of study gardens are open throughout the year, so visitors can observe the rhododendron family's changing beauties through the seasons; though most are spring bloomers, others peak in winter or in summer, and many deciduous species take on magnificent fall foliage color. Ferns, an ideal companion plant, are well represented, and the foundation hopes that in time this collection, too, will rank among the world's most complete. The foundation has assembled a collection of gardens on its 22 acres, including a wonderful Alpine Garden with many representative plantings. The garden has a gift shop and plant sale pavilion. This is not a garden for picnicking or pets. Admission March–October is $3.50 adults; $2.50 per person for students, seniors, and tour groups; free to children under 12 and school groups. Free to all November–February. *Sat–Wed 11am–4pm (June–Feb), Fri–Wed 10am–4pm (March–May); rsf@halcyon.com; www.halcyon.com/rsf/2RHSPE.html*

SEATTLE TILTH DEMONSTRATION GARDENS / 4649 Sunnyside Ave N (Good Shepherd Center); 206/633-0451 Urban gardeners find a world of practical assistance at the Tilth gardens on the grounds of Wallingford's Good Shepherd Center. Admission is free, and self-guided instructional walks lead visitors through the gardens and an impressive array of composting units. Travel at your own pace, absorbing information from the explanatory signs provided at each step. The thriving gardens are tended organically and are kept healthy through natural pest controls and environmentally sound horticultural practices. One Tilth program trains master composters who take their skills to the community, teaching apartment dwellers and homeowners alike how to deal constructively with yard and kitchen wastes (schoolkids especially love learning to make and maintain worm bins). Edible landscaping is a specialty here, but many of the 1,200 plants grown are also ornamental (including edible flowers). A lovely dry border showcases perennials, shrubs, and bulbs that tolerate drought, pollution, and other urban challenges.

This midcity oasis of living greenery serves everyone from raw beginners interested in learning how to prepare soil and sow carrots to advanced gardeners who trade heritage vegetable seeds or rare border plants. Numerous workshops and classes are offered. Tilth activities also include a spring plant sale at the end of April. The **CHILDREN'S GARDEN**, east of the demonstration gardens, lets young green thumbs practice organic and sustainable gardening too. The west end of the garden houses the Good Shepherd P-Patch. (The **SEATTLE P-PATCH PROGRAM**, a community gardening program, was begun in 1973 and is one of the largest in the country. All P-Patch sites are organic and provide gardening space for families and individuals throughout Seattle. For information on visiting one of the 38 sites, call the Seattle P-Patch Program, 206/684-0264.) *Every day; www.speakeasy.org/~tilth/; map:FF7*

UNIVERSITY OF WASHINGTON MEDICINAL HERB GARDEN / Stevens Way at Garfield Lane, University of Washington; 206/543-1126 First established in 1911 by the UW School of Pharmacy on a single acre, the Medicinal Herb Garden currently occupies a little more than 2 acres on the University of Washington campus and is reported to be the largest such garden in the Western Hemisphere. It serves as an accurate specimen garden for botanists, herbalists, medics, and gardeners. (It is not meant to provide medical information, however, and none is posted.) The garden displays more than 600 species and is divided into seven areas running west to east. The first "room," the Cascara Circle, on the western end, is guarded by a pair of carved monkeys and is graced by a pleasant stream planted with iris. This naturalistic area provides a nice contrast to the formal beds to the east. The latter are filled with a vast collection of herbs, well labeled with scientific and common names and the geographical area in which the plant is found, offering a wonderful opportunity to view plants cultivated and used by people throughout the world for centuries. A centrally located office displays a map of the garden and gives descriptions of each "room." Admission is free, and free tours are available the second Sunday of every month at noon, May through October. In-depth tours can be arranged by appointment for groups of 10 or more for a fee of $5 per person. The garden is located across from the Botany Building and extends east to Rainier Vista. *Every day; www.nnlm.nlm.nih.gov/pnr/uwmhg/; map:FF6*

WASHINGTON PARK ARBORETUM / 2300 Arboretum Dr E (at Lake Washington Blvd); 206/543-8800 See Top 25 Attractions in this chapter.

WOODLAND PARK ROSE GARDEN / 5500 Phinney Ave N; 206/684-4863 Seattle's premier rose garden offers gardeners a chance to evaluate the regional performance of several hundred kinds of roses. Two acres of permanent plantings hold some 5,000 shrubs, both old-fashioned varieties and modern hybrids. Newest of all are the unnamed roses grown each year in the Seattle Rose Society's trial beds. Here likely candidates are tested for two years; the best of the bunch will become All-America Rose Selections. The Seattle Rose Society offers rose care and pruning demonstrations in the appropriate seasons (call the garden for information). Admission is free. *Every day; www.zoo.org/VirtualTour/rose_garden.htm; map:EE7*

Parks and Beaches

In 1884, Seattle pioneers David and Louisa Denny donated to the city a 5-acre plot of land at what is now the corner of Denny Way and Dexter Avenue N, and Seattle had its first park. Since then, the park system has grown to more than 5,000 acres, many of them designed by visionary park planners John Charles Olmsted and Frederick Olmsted Jr. (sons of New York's Central Park mastermind, Frederick Law Olmsted). Seattle's parks range from the classical (Volunteer Park) to the recreational (Green Lake) to the wild (Discovery Park) to the ingenious (Gas Works Park). At last count there were 397 parks and playgrounds in the city of Seattle alone; the following are the best. To find out more about any of them, call the appropriate parks agency: Washington State Parks (general information 800/233-0321; Parks Department headquarters in Olympia 360/902-8500; camping reservations 800/452-5687); King County (206/296-4232); Seattle (206/684-4075); Bellevue (425/452-6885); Issaquah (425/837-3300); Kirkland (425/828-1218); Mercer Island (206/236-3545); or Redmond (425/556-2300).

ALKI BEACH / Along Alki Ave SW, Duwamish Head to 63rd Ave SW
This 2½-mile strip of West Seattle beach is the spot where, in 1851, Seattle's original white settlers established their first homesteads. (The Native American word alki meant "by and by," which the pioneers borrowed to describe their raw settlement as "New York-Alki," a place that might someday grow into the West's foremost city.) Now the beach has many faces, depending on the season. It's cool and peaceful in the fall, stormy in winter. But the summer months are when this sandy strand really becomes active, with volleyballers demonstrating their spiking prowess, picnickers vying for space at public tables, and young women sashaying about in bikinis that may never come close to the water but rarely fail to make a splash with teenaged male gawkers.

Despite the usually teeth-rattling temperatures of Puget Sound, Alki Beach has been a popular hangout for the last century. A private natatorium (indoor swimming pool) was installed here in 1905. In 1907, famed German carousel maker Charles I. D. Looff (creator of Coney Island's first carousel) built Luna Park, a 10-acre amusement center, on Duwamish Head at the north end of this strip. For the next 11 years, Seattleites were entertained by Luna Park's thrill rides, arcades, and much-advertised "longest bar on the bay." Though those particular attractions have disappeared, you can walk, jog, bike, or blade along the paved path that runs beside the waterfront to find a miniature **STATUE OF LIBERTY** (61st Ave SW and Alki Ave SW), erected by the Boy Scouts in 1952, as well as the Coast Guard's automated and tourable **ALKI POINT LIGHT STATION** (3201 Alki Ave SW) at the tip of the point. The scenic extension of Alki Beach continues southward along Beach Drive past windswept **ME-KWA-MOOKS PARK** and on to Lincoln Park (see listing in this section). Views over the Sound are especially good from Duwamish Head and the lighthouse. If you grow hungry gazing, stop by the **ALKI HOMESTEAD RESTAURANT** (2717 61st Ave SW; 206/935-5678), a 1904 log cabin eatery that serves filling plates of 1940s food, the specialty of the house being pan-fried chicken with mashed potatoes and green beans—just like your grandmother might have made. *Map:II9* ⓑ

BOTHELL LANDING / 9919 NE 180th St, Bothell; 425/486-3256, ext 4377 This quaint little community park across the Sammamish River from the Sammamish River Trail offers rolling green lawns for family picnics and Frisbee throwing, an amphitheater (with Friday-evening concerts in summer), a historical museum housed in a turn-of-the-century frame building, and an adult day center. Canoes and small boats can tie up at the public pier. There is limited parking at the site itself; a parking lot at 17995 102nd Avenue NE, on the south side of the river, has additional spaces. *Map:BB2*

BRIDLE TRAILS STATE PARK / 116th Ave NE and NE 53rd St, Kirkland; 425/455-7010 As its name suggests, this 480-acre park is a densely wooded equestrian paradise laced with horse trails (one links up with Marymoor Park) and even an exercise ring. Though you may feel like an alien if you come to do anything but ride (even the private homes in the area all seem to have stables), the park also has picnic sites. Warning: The overgrowth is so dense that it's easy to get lost on the trails; also, for obvious reasons, watch where you step. *Map:FF2*

CAMP LONG / 5200 35th Ave SW; 206/684-7434 West Seattle's Camp Long, run by the Seattle Parks and Recreation Department, has a variety of broader functions: as a meeting/conference facility (a lodge holds 75 people in its upper room and 35 in the basement); an in-city outdoor experience for family or group use (10 rustic bunk-bed-equipped cabins sleep up to 12 people at $30 a cabin—make reservations at least two weeks in advance); or simply a 56-acre nature preserve. The park also offers interpretive programs, perfect for school or Scout groups, and family-oriented nature programs on weekends. The lodge and cabins feature 1930s-style log architecture. Climbers can sharpen their skills on a climbing rock and a simulated glacier face. *Map:JJ8*

CARKEEK PARK / NW Carkeek Rd and 9th Ave NW Carkeek Park is 186 acres of wilderness in the northwest corner of the city. Forest paths wind from the parking lots and two reservable picnic areas (206/684-4081) to the footbridge spanning the railroad tracks, and then down a staircase to the broad beach. (Use caution around the tracks; trains run frequently through the park, and you may not hear them clearly.) Grassy meadows (great for kite flying), picnic shelters, and pretty, meandering Piper's Creek are other good reasons to relax here. *Map:DD8*

CHISM BEACH PARK / 1175 96th Ave SE, Bellevue One of Bellevue's largest and oldest waterfront parks, Chism sits along the handsome residential stretch south of Meydenbauer Bay. There are docks and diving

235

boards for swimmers, picnic areas, a playground, and a large parking area above the beach. *Map:HH4*

DISCOVERY PARK / 3801 W Government Way Formerly the site of Seattle's Fort Lawton Army base, this densely foliated Magnolia wilderness has been allowed to revert to its pre-metropolitan natural order. At 513 acres, it is full of variety and even a little mystery—in 1982 a cougar was discovered in the park, and no one knew how it got there or how long it had roamed free. Self-guided interpretive nature loops and short trails wind through thick forests, along dramatic sea cliffs (where powerful updrafts make for excellent kite flying), and across meadows of waving grasses. The old barracks, houses, and training field are the few vestiges of the Army's presence. Discover the park's flora and fauna yourself, or take advantage of the scheduled walks and nature workshops conducted by park naturalists. On weekends, the park offers free guided walks and, in spring and fall, bird tours—call ahead to check the schedule, or stop by the visitors center (east parking lot, near Government Way entrance to park, 206/386-4236). Groups can also arrange their own guided walks. Check the tall trees frequently; there's often a bald eagle in residence.

Two well-equipped kids' playgrounds are here, along with picnic areas, playfields, tennis and basketball courts, and a rigorous fitness trail. The network of trails is a favorite among joggers; the 2.8-mile Loop Trail circles the park, passing through forests, meadows, and sand dunes. **DAYBREAK STAR CULTURAL ARTS CENTER** (206/285-4425) sponsors Native American activities and gallery exhibits of contemporary Indian art in the Sacred Circle Gallery. **WEST POINT LIGHTHOUSE**, built in 1881, is the oldest lighthouse in the Seattle area. *Map:FF9*

DOWNTOWN PARK / 10201 NE 4th St, Bellevue; 425/452-6881 See Bellevue under Neighborhoods in this chapter.

FAY BAINBRIDGE STATE PARK / 15446 Sunrise Dr NE, Bainbridge Island; 206/842-3931 About a 15-minute drive from the Winslow ferry dock on Bainbridge Island, Fay Bainbridge is a smallish (17-acre) park known for its camping areas and views of Mount Rainier and Seattle. The log-strewn beach has pits for fires; other features include a boat launch, horseshoe pits, and two kitchen shelters. It's a popular stop for cyclists on their way around the hilly isle.

FREEWAY PARK / 6th Ave and Seneca St See Downtown under Neighborhoods in this chapter.

GAS WORKS PARK / N Northlake Way and Meridian Ave N; 206/684-4075 See Top 25 Attractions in this chapter.

GENE COULON BEACH PARK / 1201 Lake Washington Blvd N, Renton; 425/235-2560 This arboreal park on the shore of Lake Washington is the prize of Renton's park system. It has won national awards for the arresting architecture of its pavilion and restaurant concession (an Ivar's Fish Bar), but is best loved for the beach. Log booms around the swimming area serve as protective barriers for wind surfers. Well-signed paths wind through well-labeled plantings. Don't miss the floating picnic area. *Map:MM3*

GOLDEN GARDENS / North end of Seaview Ave NW Alki Beach's spiritual counterpart to the north, Golden Gardens teems with tanning humanity on summer weekends. A breezy, sandy beach, nearby boat ramp, beach fire pit, and the pretty—and cold—waters of Shilshole Bay are the biggest lures, although fully half of the park's 88 acres lie to the east of the railroad tracks along the wooded, trail-laced hillside. The marina here is home to a small village of sailboats. *Map:EE9*

GREEN LAKE / E Green Lake Dr N and W Green Lake Dr N; 206/684-4075 See Top 25 Attractions in this chapter.

HING HAY PARK / S King St and Maynard Ave S Hing Hay Park (the Chinese words mean "pleasurable gathering") is a meeting and gathering place for the International District's large Asian community. From the adjacent Bush Hotel, an enormous multicolored mural of a dragon presides over the park and the ornate grand pavilion from Taipei. A great place to get a feel for the rhythms of International District life. *Map:Q6*

KELSEY CREEK PARK / 13204 SE 8th Pl, Bellevue See Bellevue under Neighborhoods in this chapter.

KERRY PARK AND VIEWPOINt / 3rd Ave W and W Highland Dr See Queen Anne under Neighborhoods in this chapter.

KIRKLAND WATERFRONT / Along Lake Washington Blvd, Kirkland A string of parks, from Houghton Beach to Marina Park at Moss Bay, lines the shore of Kirkland's beautiful Lake Washington Boulevard. Kids feed the ducks and wade (only Houghton Beach and Waverly Beach have lifeguards); their parents sunbathe and watch the runners lope by. This is as close to Santa Cruz as the Northwest gets. *Map:DD4*

LAKE SAMMAMISH STATE PARK / 20606 SE 56th St, Issaquah; 425/455-7010 The sprawling beach is the main attraction of this state park at the south end of Lake Sammamish. Shady picnic areas, grassy playfields, and volleyball courts are excellent secondary draws. Large groups must reserve day-use areas—the place can be overrun in summer. Issaquah Creek, fine for fishing, runs through the park's wooded area.

LAKE WASHINGTON PARKS / From Madison Park at E Madison St and 43rd Ave E to Stan Sayres Memorial Park at 3800 Lake Washington

Blvd S This string of grassy beachfronts acts as a collective backyard for several of the neighborhoods that slope toward Lake Washington's western shore. Bicycle Saturdays and Sundays take place in the summer, when the route from Colman Park to Seward Park is closed to cars from 10am to 6pm. **MADISON PARK**, the site of an amusement park and bathing beach in the early 1900s, has shed its vaudeville image and is now a genteel neighborhood park, with a roped-in swimming area and tennis courts. If you head west on E Madison Street and turn left onto Lake Washington Boulevard, you'll wind down to meet the beach again, this time at **MADRONA PARK** (Lake Washington Blvd and Madrona Dr), a grassy strip with a swimming beach, picnic tables, a (summer-only) food concession, and a dance studio. Farther on is **LESCHI PARK** (Lakeside Ave S and Leschi Pl), a nicely manicured city park that occupies the hillside across the boulevard. It offers great views of the Leschi Marina and the dazzling spinnakers of sailboats, as well as a play area for kids. Another greenbelt, **COLMAN PARK** (36th Ave S and Lakeside Ave S), also with a play area, marks the start of the seamless strip that includes **MOUNT BAKER PARK** (Lake Park Dr S and Lake Washington Blvd S), a gently sloping, tree-lined ravine; the hydroplane racing mecca—once a marshy slough, now a manicured park and spectator beach with boat launches—called **STAN SAYRES MEMORIAL PARK**; and the lonely wilderness peninsula of **SEWARD PARK** (see listing in this section). *Map:GG5–JJ5*

LINCOLN PARK / Fauntleroy Ave SW and SW Webster St Lincoln Park, a 130-acre jewel perched on a pointed bluff in West Seattle, offers a network of walking and biking paths amid grassy forests, picnic shelters (call 206/684-4081 to reserve), recreational activities from horseshoes to football to tennis, and expansive views of the Olympic Mountains from seawalls and rocky beaches. There are tide pools to be inspected and beaches to roam, and the kids will delight in the playground equipment. Don't miss the (heated) outdoor saltwater **COLMAN POOL** (summer only), which began as a tide-fed swimming hole. When you're finished at the park, walk next door to the Fauntleroy ferry dock and take a pleasant 15-minute ferryboat ride to Vashon Island. *Map:LL9*

LUTHER BURBANK PARK / 2040 84th Ave SE, Mercer Island Luther Burbank's undulating fields and endless land-and-lake recreational areas occupy a good chunk of the northern tip of Mercer Island and make it the Eastside's favorite family park. There are picnic areas, barbecue grills, a swimming area, nicely maintained tennis courts, an outdoor amphitheater for summer concerts, a first-rate playground, several playing fields, docks for boat tie-ups (the haunt of sun-worshiping teens in summer), and green meadows that tumble down to the shore. When the main beach is crowded, head north toward the point to find a lonelier picnic spot. Parking is plentiful. *Map:II4*

MAGNUSON PARK / Sand Point Way NE and NE 65th St This 194-acre park fronts Lake Washington just southeast of now-closed Sand Point Naval Station, with a mile of shoreline, a boat launch, a playing field, and six tennis courts. Adjacent to the north is the National Oceanic and Atmospheric Administration (NOAA), where you'll find a series of unique artworks along the beach. One sculpture, the *Sound Garden*, is fitted with flutelike aluminum tubes that create eerie music when the wind blows. The site is open every day from dawn to dusk and is a hauntingly wonderful spot to sit on a blue whale bench, listening to the wailing wind chimes and watching the sun come up over Lake Washington. *Map:EE5*

MARYMOOR COUNTY PARK / 6046 W Lake Sammamish Pkwy NE, Redmond 206/296-2964 See Redmond under Neighborhoods in this chapter.

MYRTLE EDWARDS PARK / Alaskan Way between Bay St and W Thomas St Myrtle Edwards and adjacent Elliott Bay Park provide a front lawn to the northern section of downtown. This breezy and refreshing strip is a great noontime getaway for jogging (the two parks combined form a 1.25-mile trail), picnicking on benches that face Puget Sound, or just strolling. Parking at the Pier 70 lot just south of Myrtle Edwards is at a premium, but the waterfront streetcar stops nearby. *Map:B9*

NEWCASTLE BEACH PARK / 4400 Lake Washington Blvd S, Bellevue This Bellevue park takes full advantage of its waterfront location with a fishing dock, swimming area, and bathhouse facility (complete with outdoor showers). Walking paths—including a three-quarter-mile loop—weave throughout the 28 acres, and a wildlife area offers the chance to see animals and birds in their natural habitat. *Map:JJ3*

RAVENNA PARK / 20th Ave NE and NE 58th St This steep woodland ravine strung between residential districts north of the University District is a lush sylvan antidote to the city around it. At the west end is Cowen Park (University Way NE and NE Ravenna Blvd), with tennis courts and play and picnic areas. Trails along burbling Ravenna Creek lead to the eastern end of the park and more picnic areas, tennis courts, and playing fields, plus a wading pool. The whole expanse is a favorite haunt of joggers, as is Ravenna Boulevard, the gracious, tree-lined thoroughfare that defines its southern flank and leads west to Green Lake. *Map:EE6*

SCHMITZ PARK / SW Stevens St and Admiral Way SW Just south of West Seattle's Alki Beach is this 53-acre virgin nature preserve, full of raw trails through thickly wooded terrain. The largest western red cedars and hemlocks here are likely to be about 800 years old—seedlings when Richard the Lionhearted was leading his troops on the Third Crusade. It's a marvelous place for contemplation and nature study. No playgrounds, picnic areas, or other park amenities. *Map:II9*

SEWARD PARK / Lake Washington Blvd S and S Juneau St This majestic wilderness, occupying a 277-acre knob of land in southeast Seattle, gives modern Seattleites an idea of what the area must have looked like centuries ago. At times the park is imbued with a primal sense of permanence, especially on misty winter days when the quiet of a solitary walk through old-growth Douglas fir forest is broken only by the cries of a few birds. But at other times—hot summer Sundays, for instance—Seward turns into a frenzy of music and barbecues. You can drive the short loop road to get acquainted with the park, past the bathhouse and beach facilities; **SEWARD PARK ART STUDIO** (206/722-6342), which offers classes in the arts; some of the six picnic shelters (call 206/684-4081 for reservations); and some of the trailheads, which lead to the fish hatchery, to the outdoor amphitheater, and into the forest preserve. Cyclists and runners can make an even better loop on the scenic 2.5-mile lakeside trail encircling the park. *Map:JJ5*

VICTOR STEINBRUECK PARK / Western Ave and Virginia St Pike Place Market's greatest supporter and friend is the namesake of this splash of green at the north end of the Market. With the Alaskan Way Viaduct right below, the park can be quite noisy during peak traffic hours. It also tends to be a favorite hangout for street people. Despite those caveats, the park's grassy slopes and tables make a fine place for a Market picnic, and the view of the blue bay and ferry traffic is refreshing. *Map:H8*

VOLUNTEER PARK / 15th Ave E and E Prospect St; 206/684-4075 See Top 25 Attractions in this chapter.

WASHINGTON PARK ARBORETUM / 2300 Arboretum Dr E (at Lake Washington Blvd); 206/543-8800 See Top 25 Attractions in this chapter.

WATERFALL GARDENS / 2nd Ave S and S Main St (northwest corner); 206/624-6096 How many downtowns can boast a park with a 22-foot crashing waterfall, even an artificial one? The waterfall in this tiny Pioneer Square park was built to honor the United Parcel Service, which started in this location in 1907. It does crash (this is no place for quiet conversation), and the benches fill up by noon on weekdays, but the park makes for a marvelous little nature fix in the middle of a busy urban day. *Map:O8*

WATERFRONT PARK / Pier 57 to Pier 61 on Alaskan Way A park that spans three piers between the Aquarium and Pier 57 provides a break from the bustling activity of the rest of the waterfront. The park contains a tree-encircled courtyard, raised platforms with telescopes for a view of the bay and islands, plenty of benches, and—strange for a park in this town—nary a blade of grass. *Map:J9*

WOODLAND PARK / 5200 Green Lake Way N; 206/684-4075 This 188-acre park abuts Green Lake on one side and has Aurora Avenue running through the middle. On the west side are the rose garden and Woodland Park Zoo (see Top 25 Attractions in this chapter). On the east are playfields, picnic areas, lawn bowling, and tennis courts. *Map:EE7*

Organized Tours

There's always more to the city than meets the eye, and tours are one way to scratch the surface of the metropolis and see what makes it tick. Clearly fun for visitors, a tour is also a great chance for locals to learn something new about their hometown—an angle they may never have considered. (For instance, all environmentally inclined Seattleites should take a tour of a lumber mill, to see the other side of the story.) You can tour the **BOEING PLANT** (206/544-1264) to see the source of one of the city's major employers and economies (see Top 25 Attractions in this chapter). Tours can be as informational as one of the **SEATTLE ARCHITECTURAL FOUNDATION'S VIEWPOINTS TOURS** (206/667-9186), which examine the mix of art and architecture throughout the city; as colorful as Jeri Callahan's specially tailored **DISCOVER HOUSEBOATING** (206/322-9157) tours-by-water of Lake Union's quirky houseboat neighborhoods; or as delicious as the **TASTE OF THE NORTHWEST CHEF'S TOUR** (206/340-6710), where for $65 you can cruise the stalls and shops of Pike Place Market with chef Tim Kelley from the Alexis Hotel's Painted Table, then sit down to a Northwest-inspired lunch (complete with Northwest wines) at the arty hotel restaurant. Every other year in late April/early May, the **SEATTLE ART MUSEUM** (206/654-3198) sponsors a walk through the lofts and studios of some of the city's artists—a great way to poke into creative lives. When selecting your tour of the city, call ahead; some excursions are by reservation only.

AIR TOURS

KENMORE AIR / 950 Westlake Ave N; 6321 NE 175th St, Kenmore; 425/486-1257 or 800/543-9595 The largest seaplane operator in the area, Kenmore Air has a fleet of 20 planes that make scheduled and charter flights around Puget Sound and to Victoria, British Columbia, from seaports on Lake Union and north Lake Washington. A one-way passage to the San Juan Islands is $85 per person on a scheduled flight ($95 July 1–Sept 6), or $267 for a charter for one to three people. A 2-hour round-trip scenic flyover of the San Juans is $45 per person; or sign up for a spring or summer day-trip package (including lunch and ground transportation on San Juan Island) for $125. Round-trip all-day excursions to Victoria are $145 per person. The company also offers a 20-

minute city tour (which originates from the Lake Washington location only) for $140 for three passengers, $170 for six. Be sure to call ahead; several tours are available on a day-of-flight basis only, and advance reservations are required for other trips. *www.kenmoreair.com; map:GG7; map:BB5*

SEATTLE SEAPLANES / 1325 Fairview Ave E; 206/329-9638 or 800/637-5553 Seattle Seaplanes does its main business in charters to Canadian fishing camps, but also offers a 20-minute exhaustive airborne tour of Seattle (University of Washington, Lake Washington, Kingdome, the waterfront, Magnolia, the Locks, Shilshole, Green Lake, and back to Lake Union) for $42.50 per person. Consider taking a flight to and from majestic Mount Rainier ($280 for one to four passengers, $315 for five), Mount St. Helens ($560 for one to four passengers), or the San Juan Islands ($371 for one to four passengers). Call for reservations. *www.seattleseaplanes.com; map:E1*

SOUND FLIGHT / Renton Municipal Airport, 243 W Perimeter Rd, Renton; 425/255-6500 Up to 20 passengers can arrange their own pilot-narrated floatplane tours of Seattle, Mount Rainier, the San Juan Islands, Mount St. Helens, or the North Cascades. Prices (from $79 to $200 per person) depend on the number of people and extent of the tour. *Map:MM4*

BOAT TOURS

In the water-locked city of Seattle, it's only natural that water-borne travel is one of the best ways to get a look at the Puget Sound area. Besides customizing your own tour via one of 29 **WASHINGTON STATE FERRIES** (206/464-6400; www.wsdot.wa.gov/ferries)—seven of which leave from downtown's Colman Dock 71 times daily en route to Bainbridge Island, Bremerton, or Vashon Island—there are a boatload of boat tours available. (See By Ferry under Getting Around in the Lay of the City chapter.)

ARGOSY CRUISES / Piers 54, 55, and 57; 1200 Westlake Ave N; 206/623-1445 or 800/642-7816 Scheduled tours departing from Lake Union include daily, year-round, 1-hour narrated cruises along the Seattle waterfront and Elliott Bay ($14.50); 2½-hour tours through the Hiram M. Chittenden Locks and Lake Washington Ship Canal ($24.75); and a 2-hour Lake Washington excursion ($19.75), featuring peeks at the pricey palaces surrounding the lake—including the 40,000-square-foot Xanadu that Microsoft CEO Bill Gates has erected. Saltwater sport-fishing trips on Puget Sound waters are available year-round (for about $80), and, May through September, the 40-knot *Seattle Rocket* zips passengers about the Sound for half an hour ($11). On the Eastside, Argosy offers seasonal 1½-hour cruises around Lake Washington ($19.75) that depart from the Kirkland City Dock. Charters for private parties or special events are available for groups of 10 to 400. *www.argosycruises.com; map:L9–K9; map:A1*

**EMERALD CITY CHARTERS (LET'S GO SAILING) / Pier 56 (north side);
206/624-3931** A 70-foot custom-built former racing sloop, the *Obsession* cuts through Elliott Bay waters May 1 to October 15. Star of the movie *Masquerade* (along with Rob Lowe and Meg Tilly), the yacht can comfortably carry up to 49 passengers, who should count on packing their own meals for the scheduled 1½-hour trips that leave at 11am, 1:30pm, and 4pm daily. Cost for day cruises: $20 adults, $18 seniors, $15 children 12 and under. A 2½-hour sunset sail leaves between 6 and 7pm daily and costs $35 adults, $32 seniors, and $28 children 12 and under. Private charters are also available year-round. Call to check on sailing times and availablility. *obsession@afts.com; map:K9*

MOSQUITO FLEET SAN JUAN ORCA CRUISES / 1724 W Marine View Dr, Everett; Cap Sante Marina, Float D, Space 0, Anacortes; 425/252-6800 or 800/325-ORCA Whale-watching cruises leave daily from Everett and Anacortes June–September, and on a limited basis during April, May, September, and October. The 9½-hour cruises are narrated by a naturalist, who lectures on orcas (and identifies their pods) as well as on other marine life and San Juan maritime history. Depending on the time of year, tickets range from $29.50 to $79. Call for reservations. *www.whalewatching.com.*

RIDE THE DUCKS OF SEATTLE / 5th Ave N and Broad St; 206/441-DUCK or 800/817-1116 for reservations See Seattle's sights by land *and* sea aboard amphibious vehicles (aka "ducks"). The refurbished World War II landing craft are piloted by Coast Guard–certified sea captains who motor visitors about the streets of downtown, Pioneer Square, and Fremont before launching into the waters of Lake Union for tours past Seattle's houseboats and glass artist Dale Chihuly's studio. The 90-minute rides are $20 adults, $15 kids 12 and under. The ducks take off hourly throughout the year from the northeast corner of Fifth and Broad (across from the Space Needle). Drop by the ticket booth, located between the Needle and the Monorail, or call for reservations; private duck tours are also available. *www.ridetheducksofseattle.com; map:C6*

SAILING IN SEATTLE / 2000 Westlake Ave N; 206/298-0094 The cozy 33-foot sailboat *Whoodat* cruises around Lake Union's waterfront for 2½ hours every evening as the sun sets for $45 per person; an all-day trip through the locks and around Puget Sound costs $100 per hour for up to six people; and a 5-hour tour of Lake Washington comes with views of the University of Washington and Bill Gates's estate for $55 per person. The *Whoodat*, which carries a maximum of six passengers, sails year-round. *www.sailing-in-seattle.com; map:A1*

SPIRIT OF PUGET SOUND CRUISES / 2819 Elliott Ave, Pier 70; 206/674-3500 for reservations It's clear that these professionals have floating entertainment figured out. The 600-passenger luxury ship sails daily (depending on availability) for 2-hour lunch and 3-hour dinner tours of the Sound in a style akin to that of a deep-sea cruise liner: with a full-service restaurant, entertainment, and dancing. Lunch cruises run $30–$35, dinner cruises $55–$60. *www.spiritcruises.com; map:D9*

TILLICUM VILLAGE TOUR / Pier 55; 206/443-1244 A Northwest tourist staple, this 4-hour narrated voyage from downtown Seattle to nearby Blake Island (reputedly the birthplace of Seattle's namesake, Chief Sealth) has been operating for more than 35 years. The highlight of the hyped-up look at Northwest Indian culture is a salmon bake and a Native American dance ($50.25). (Also accessible from Bremerton; see Day Trips chapter.) *www.tillicumvillage.com; map:L9*

MOTOR TOURS

GRAY LINE OF SEATTLE / 4500 W Marginal Way SW; 206/624-5813 This popular bus touring service offers several choice trips: Mount Rainier

SEATTLE MICROBREWERIES

Although coffee is the beverage most often associated with Seattle, some residents would urge that we throw off that tired stereotype and proclaim the city's official beverage to be beer. Not the colorless, characterless, watery beer produced in Milwaukee, but noble ales, refreshing lagers, and fortifying porters that are full-bodied, frothy, and bursting with flavor—the sort produced by Seattle's smaller craft breweries, the numbers of which have grown by leaps and bounds in recent years.

Once the region's most famous microbrewer, Redhook can no longer claim that title, as it currently sells more than 100,000 barrels annually—well over the 15,000-barrel limit that defines the term. The company, founded in 1981, now produces Ballard Bitter, Redhook ESB, and six other varieties from breweries in Woodinville and Portsmouth, New Hampshire. Its beers are now sold nationwide, and although Redhook's popularity hasn't abated around these parts, the granddaddy of microbrews has plenty of company these days. Craft-brewery tours and tastings have become a recreational activity of their own; here's a sampling of local beermeisters and tour info.

Redhook Ale Brewery Redhook has two Puget Sound–area breweries: Redhook Ale Brewery and Trolleyman Pub in Fremont (3400 Phinney Ave N; 206/548-8000) and Redhook Ale Brewery and Forecaster's Public House (14300 NE 145th St, Woodinville; 425/483-3232). Tours at the Woodinville brewery only are offered daily, on the hour, from noon to 5pm. Cost is $1 per person, and includes beer samples and a souvenir glass.

Pyramid Breweries (1201 1st Ave S; 206/682-3377) Formerly Hart Brewing, this expansive pub and brewing operation near the Kingdome and the new Safeco stadium

(summer only, $49 per person); the Boeing plant ($38 per person; see Top 25 Attractions in this chapter); the popular Seattle city tours ($36 for 7 hours or $26 for 3 hours); overnighters to Victoria, British Columbia, and more. Free pickup at several downtown hotels. *www.seattleonline. com/grayline/; map:JJ8*

PRIVATE EYE ON SEATTLE MYSTERY AND MURDER TOUR / Windsor and Hatten Legal Investigations; 206/622-0590 Grizzled gumshoe Windsor Lincoln Olson weaves his blood-red van in and out of some of Seattle's most notorious crime scenes—from the International District, site of the Wah Mee Club massacre, to downtown alleys such as one at Fifth Avenue and S Jackson St, where the 70-plus Olson reveals the mystery of the "unclaimed" head. Be advised, this is not an excursion for children or squeamish adults. Cost for the 1½-hour macabre adventure is $20 per person; group discounts are available. *www.privateeyetours.com*

SEATTLE TOURS / 206/768-1234 Ballard's Locks and downtown shops as well as Fremont, Alki Beach, the floating bridges, and more are on the itineraries for these 3-hour minicoach tours. Custom-designed coaches hold up to 20 people, and cost is $32 per person. Closed December 15 through February. *home.sprynet.com/sprynet/seattletours*

offers free tours and tastings of the popular Pyramid ales Monday through Friday at 2pm and 4pm and on weekends at 1, 2, and 4pm. A mere $2 buys you a souvenir glass.

Maritime Pacific Brewing Co. (1514 NW Leary Way; 206/782-6181) The makers of the popular Flagship Red Ale, the dark, delectable Nightwatch, and other specialty brews offer tours of their Ballard brewery every Saturday in the early afternoon. There's a tap room too, called the Jolly Roger.

Pike Brewing Co. (1432 Western Ave; 206/622-3373) The makers of the celebrated Pike Place Ale have a nice, new brewing facility and pub near the edge of Pike Place Market. Tours are available by reservation.

Seattle Brewers (530 S Holden St; 206/762-7421) One of the area's smaller brewers produces Alki Ale and Seattle Stout, as well as a selection of seasonals. Belly up to Jerry's Jungle Bar for a pint, or ask for a tour of the facilities. The pub is open only until 7pm on weekdays and is closed on weekends.

Brew Hops Tours (2403 Dexter Ave N, Suite 3; 206/283-8460) Here's a way to quaff to your heart's content without having to worry about driving. Three-hour lunch or dinner tours include transportation to several area breweries and tours of the facilities, a pub-food meal, and tastings of more than a dozen locally brewed ales. The price includes a glass and other souvenirs to take home. Tours begin at Pyramid Breweries, and are offered by advance reservation Tuesday through Sunday from noon to 3pm and from 5 to 8pm. — Jo Brown

SHOW ME SEATTLE / 206/633-CITY Colorfully decaled vans hit the usual Seattle hot spots—downtown, the Seattle Art Museum, the International District—and do drive-bys of the city's more distinctive neighborhoods, including Fremont, Green Lake, and Queen Anne. The *Sleepless in Seattle* houseboat on Lake Union is an oft-requested stop. Cost is $32 per person; reservations required. *www.pugetsound.com/fauntleroy/office/ agents/loop/showme/index.html*

TRAIN TOURS

SPIRIT OF WASHINGTON DINNER TRAIN / 625 S 4th St, Renton; 425/227-RAIL or 800/876-RAIL See Top 25 Attractions in this chapter.

WALKING TOURS

BILL SPEIDEL'S UNDERGROUND TOUR / 610 1st Ave; 206/682-4646 These tours are mostly one story down—the level of the city before it was rebuilt after the great fire of June 6, 1889. (Poor drainage at the old, lower level made the higher streets imperative.) It's all pretty cornball, but you'll get a salty taste of the pioneers' eccentricities and some historical insights, with plenty of puns from the guides. The tours begin at Doc Maynard's Public House in Pioneer Square and run 1½ hours. Tour times vary seasonally. Cost is $7 adults, $6 seniors, $5.50 students 13–17 or with college ID, and $2.75 children 6–12. Call ahead for reservations. *www.undergroundtour.com; map:N8*

CHINATOWN DISCOVERY / 206/236-0657 Humorous Seattle native Vi Mar conducts four walking tours of the International District, providing a historical and cultural perspective that, in some cases, comes with a meal. For instance, the Chinatown by Day tour features a six-course dim sum lunch; the nighttime tour is an eight-course affair. Reservations required. Rates for adults range from $9.95 to $34.95, and for children from $6.95 to $19.95. Group rates are available. *www.seattlechamber. com/chinatowntour*

SEATTLE WALKING TOUR / 206/885-3173 This 2-hour tour led by local author Duse McLean concentrates on the architecture and history of downtown. The $15 tours begin outside Westlake Center (400 Pine St) on Wednesdays and Thursdays at 5:30pm and Saturday at 10:30am, June–September. *dusem@aol.com; map:I6*

SEE SEATTLE WALKING TOURS / 425/226-7641 Catering to those with no time to waste finding Seattle's favorite sights on their own, Terry Seidler conducts several walking tours through Pike Place Market, the waterfront, Pioneer Square, and other downtown points of interest. Custom tours are available for groups, including mystery and scavenger hunts (perfect for parties or corporate groups). Typical cost is $10–$15 per person. *walking@see-seattle.com; www.see-seattle.com*

SHOPPING

SHOPPING

Shopping Areas and Malls

DOWNTOWN SEATTLE

Stroll along Seattle's downtown sidewalks and they seem to vibrate with the sound of credit cards charging and ATMs humming. Not so long ago, however, the downtown core was in danger of becoming a retail ghost town. Following a national trend, the supremacy of the suburban shopping malls—with their acres of free parking and covered sprawls of shops—had gone unchallenged by the big city.

Seattle sparked its downtown retail reversal of fortune with a battery of big-name superstores. Today, amid first-rate restaurants, cafes, and theaters, nearly every corner sports an A-list retailer. **BANANA REPUBLIC**, located in the historic Coliseum movie theater building, dresses up the northeast corner of Fifth Avenue and Pike Street; the **WARNER BROS. STUDIO STORE** is on Fifth between Pike and Pine Streets; **NIKETOWN**, a three-story tabernacle of sneakers and sportswear, dominates the northeast corner of Sixth Avenue and Pike Street; **THE ORIGINAL LEVI'S STORE** fits into the Meridian shopping/entertainment complex on Sixth between Pike and Pine; and the trendy clothing store **OLD NAVY** recently dropped anchor at the former I. Magnin building on the corner of Sixth and Pine.

The biggest and brightest jewels in downtown's commercial crown are the new side-by-side flagship **NORDSTROM** store and **PACIFIC PLACE** shopping center, which opened for business in 1998. Joined at the hip by a glass walkway that stretches over Sixth Avenue, they are an irresistible shop-till-you-drop combination.

As the saying goes, nothing succeeds like success. Seattle now boasts one of the healthiest downtown retail cores in the country, and shopping has become as irresistible a tourist attraction as doing the Space Needle.

And the retail growth spurt hasn't been restricted to the city's center. Occupying prime waterfront real estate on First Avenue, **HARBOR STEPS**, across from the Seattle Art Museum, is a twin-tower development of high-rise residences and high-end retail, from stylish florists and home stores, such as **THREE FURIES** and **FORTE**, to eateries, such as the **WOLFGANG PUCK CAFE**. Harbor Steps will double its empire with the addition of two more retail/residence towers by 2001. (See also Downtown under Neighborhoods in the Exploring chapter.)

THE BON MARCHÉ / 3rd Ave and Pine St; 206/506-6000 The last of the true department stores downtown, the Bon has been fulfilling shoppers' clothing and household needs in its present location for more than 100 years. The store's annual hoisting of its 3,600-bulb Holiday Star signals the start of the holiday season. *Every day; map:I6*

CITY CENTRE / 1420 5th Ave; 206/622-6465 (cinemas only) FAO Schwarz's giant sculpture teddy bear welcomes shoppers into this urban mall featuring a collection of ritzy retailers, ranging from upscale clothier Barneys New York to equally upscale footwear purveyor Joan & David. To sweeten the appeal there's also a movie theater, the posh Palomino Euro-bistro, and 1,100 underground parking spots. *Every day; www.seattlecitycentre.com; map:J5*

NORDSTROM / 500 Pine St; 206/628-2111 See Top 25 Attractions in the Exploring chapter.

PACIFIC PLACE / 600 Pine St; 206/405-2655 Inside a 12,000-square-foot skylit atrium, Pacific Place shelters a wealth of retailers (nearly one-third of them new to the Northwest): Tiffany & Co., Cartier, J Crew and J. Peterman, Ann Taylor, Barnes & Noble, Restoration Hardware, Pottery Barn, Williams-Sonoma Grande Cuisine. To ease shopper headaches, the center has 1,200 underground parking spaces, several strength-sustaining restaurants, and a state-of-the-art 11-screen cinema, fashioned after a Northwest lodge, that caps the complex. Every day; www.pacificplaceseattle.com; map:J5

RAINIER SQUARE / 1335 5th Ave The sleek two-level home-furnishings store Z Gallerie sets the tone for this stylish shopping center, whose retailers also include Eddie Bauer and Brooks Brothers. Every day; map:K6

WESTLAKE CENTER / 400 Pine St; 206/287-0762 Four floors of mall within a 26-story high-rise are packed with more than 80 shops. Westlake offers the full range of top-of-the-line retailers, from the arty (Fire-Works) to the aromatic (Godiva Chocolatier). An upper-level food court has more than 18 eateries. Boasting the city's largest lighted Christmas tree, Westlake is particularly appealing during the holidays. Every day; map:I6

HISTORIC DISTRICTS

Let yourself be taken in by the unaffected charm of the **PIKE PLACE MARKET** (1st Ave between Pike and Virginia Sts; every day; map:J8–I8), arguably the most unusual shopping area in town. This is the spot for food—mainly fresh produce and seafood—and fun: the fish-throwing antics of the crew at Pike Place Fish are a perennial crowd-pleaser. It's like a carnival every day here, with street performers competing for the attention of shoppers, who meander in and out of the Market's labyrinthine passageways and arcades packed with vintage apparel, antiques, arts, and crafts. Recent years have also brought an upscale overspill of shops, as the neighboring **SOUTH ARCADE** (1st Ave between Pike and Union Sts; map:J8) marches southward along First Avenue.

Another egress from the Market is via an appealing lineup of retail along the **PIKE MARKET HILLCLIMB** (Pike St to Pier 59; map:J8) toward the **WATERFRONT** (Alaskan Way from Pier 52 to Pier 70; map:M8–D9).

Here, during summer months, tourists outnumber the seagulls hanging about the piers, most of which have been converted into colorful emporiums that stock typical touristy items (does anyone really need a "Sleeveless in Seattle" tank?), but there are a couple of quirkier offerings. Alfred Hitchcock would be quite at home in Pier 54's **YE OLDE CURIOSITY SHOP** (100 years old, in fact), which counts an authentic mummy and assorted real stuffed animals and birds among its bizarre decorations. The **BAY PAVILION** on Pier 57 has its own arcade, complete with a replica of a 1910 wooden carousel.

PIONEER SQUARE (between 2nd Ave and the waterfront, from Cherry to King Sts; map:N8) is where Seattle got started in 1852; now the area boasts the Northwest's most prestigious concentration of art galleries and a dizzying proliferation of cafes, bars, and shops. The square combines upscale condominiums, office space, and retail in many of its elegantly restored brick buildings. You'll encounter a number of Oriental rug stores, as well as at least three good bookstores, including the Elliott Bay Book Company. For more details on Pioneer Square and Pike Place Market, see also Top 25 Attractions in the Exploring chapter.

Historic areas farther afield in the greater Seattle area have also been recast as shopping districts. **GILMAN VILLAGE** (exit 17 off I-90, Issaquah; 425/392-6802; every day) is a minitown of shops and restaurants, most in 19-century-style structures connected by charming boardwalks. Stores feature high-end merchandise and the glorious backdrop of the Cascade foothills. Edmonds's historic offering, **OLD MILLTOWN** (201 5th Ave S, Edmonds; 425/771-4515, every day), is another collection of quaint shops. **COUNTRY VILLAGE** (exit 26 off I-405, Bothell; 425/483-2250; every day; map:AA3) in Bothell offers a hearty mix of shops offering country gifts and home decorations.

NEIGHBORHOODS

THE AVE (University Way NE from NE 41st St to NE 50th St; map:FF6), running just west of the University of Washington campus, features a concentration of book, record, and ice cream stores, plus some interesting boutiques and ethnic restaurants. Though its student/bohemian flavor is being gradually erased by a combination of deadbeat culture, encroaching panhandlers, and advancing chain stores, the retail blocks still yield some good browsing, and the shopping district is slowly spreading north.

Once a sleepy shopping spot, **UNIVERSITY VILLAGE** (NE 45th St and 25th Ave NE; 206/523-0622; every day; map FF6), down the 45th Street viaduct from the UW campus, has seen an explosion of new retail. Home to especially good gourmet and specialty food stores, the open-air shopping center, whose expansion began in 1995 with an Eddie Bauer branch and a gargantuan Barnes & Noble, has grown to include branches of Pottery Barn and Restoration Hardware (an impossibly tempting home accessory and furnishing store) as well as the spendy Sundance Catalog Company Store and the large-scale gardening store Molbak's.

Two neighboring districts also serve university folk with good shopping: **ROOSEVELT** (Roosevelt Way NE from NE 55th St to NE 70th St; map:EE6), a strip offering stereo stores, vintage-clothing shops, and diverse restaurants; and **WALLINGFORD** (along N 45th St from Stone Way N to Latona Ave NE; map:FF7). Wallingford, with a refurbished and converted school building, **WALLINGFORD CENTER** (1815 N 45th St; every day; map:FF7), as its showpiece, caters to its constituents with funky gift shops and quirky, slightly "alternative" retail (an erotic bakery, for instance, as well as the city's first condom store).

South of Portage Bay and the Ship Canal, head for Capitol Hill's **BROADWAY** (E Pine St to E Roy St; map:GG6), center of Seattle's punk universe and the best see-and-be-seen shopping scene in town. Vintage clothing, chic apparel, espresso, and housewares dominate, as do a multitude of restaurants. Five blocks east is the neighborhood commercial district of **15TH AVENUE EAST** (E Denny Way to E Mercer St; map:HH6), which embodies the homegrown, untrendy element of Capitol Hill's collective personality: mom-and-pop businesses, a health-food grocery, consignment shops, and several small bookstores. South of here, E Madison Street intersects 15th Avenue E on its way from downtown to **MADISON PARK** (along E Madison St from McGilvra Blvd E to 43rd Ave E; map:GG6). Here, the lakeside shopping/restaurant enclave reflects the family orientation and upward mobility of the neighborhood. Closer to downtown is **MADISON VALLEY** (along E Madison St from Martin Luther King Jr. Way to 32nd Ave E; map:GG6), a pleasant, upscale, and highly browsable retail pocket that attracts the landed gentry from the nearby Washington Park and Broadmoor residential districts.

Increasingly giving Capitol Hill a run as the city's new center of cool, **BELLTOWN** (1st and 2nd Aves, between Blanchard St and Denny Way; map:G8–D8) has supper clubs that chummily mix with billiards halls and nightclubs. Retail offerings range from vintage clothing and record stores to ultramodern gift and home-furnishing shops. Being hip can be a transitory experience, however; businesses here have a habit of disappearing faster than Internet startups. And, much as in Pioneer Square and on Capitol Hill, among the retro retail, cafes, and condos you'll find panhandlers and the homeless.

To the north is **QUEEN ANNE HILL** (map:GG8), whose lower slopes around Queen Anne Avenue N and Mercer Street are studded with shops and restaurants. Seattleites are rediscovering the many good restaurants at the top of the hill, and new retail establishments are cropping up everywhere. Past the northern slope of Queen Anne Hill and across the Lake

Washington Ship Canal lies **FREMONT** (Fremont Ave N and N 34th St; map:FF7), a funky neighborhood known to its residents as the "Republic of Fremont" and noted for antique-and-kitsch stores, retro boutiques, and some of the city's better pubs. West of Fremont lies **BALLARD** (map:EE8). Famous locally for its Scandinavian population and its excruciatingly slow drivers (not coincidentally, there's a large senior population), the neighborhood somehow manages to bridge the gap between hip restaurants, clubs, and galleries and Old World antiques and bakeries. Finally, Eastsiders in search of the neighborhood shopping experience head for **OLD BELLEVUE** (Main St at Bellevue Way NE; map:HH3), where traditional shops on flower-lined streets cater to the carriage trade; or the **KIRKLAND WATERFRONT** (along Lake Washington Blvd NE from 2nd Ave S to Central Way; map:EE4), a stretch of retail and art galleries hugging the shore of Moss Bay. (See also Neighborhoods in the Exploring chapter.)

EASTSIDE MALLS

Although downtown Seattle may be in the midst of a retail renaissance, the Eastside invented shopping mall know-how, and it's home to the standard-setter for the region: Bellevue Square.

Smaller Eastside malls include **KIRKLAND PARK PLACE** (exit 18 off I-405, Kirkland; 425/828-4468; every day; map:EE3); **FACTORIA MALL** (exit 10 off I-405, Bellevue; 425/641-8282; every day; map:II3); **TOTEM LAKE MALL** (124th St exit off I-405, Kirkland; every day; map:CC3); and **CROSSROADS SHOPPING CENTER** (NE 8th St and 156th Ave NE, Bellevue; 425/644-1111; every day; map:HH1). With its mix of retail, restaurants (24 international eateries), live music, a giant chessboard, and a 12-screen cinema, Crossroads earns its nickname of "the Eastside's living room."

BELLEVUE PLACE / 10500 NE 8th St, Bellevue; 425/453-5634 Bellevue Square developer Kemper Freeman is also the name behind the sparkling Bellevue Place, with 20 high-end shops—including couture wear at Helen's (Of Course)—and a number of excellent restaurants, some of which occupy the dramatic glass-walled Wintergarden atrium. *Mon–Sat; map:HH3*

BELLEVUE SQUARE / NE 8th St and Bellevue Way NE, Bellevue; 425/454-8096 One of the best malls of its kind in the nation, glittering Bellevue Square offers a sunny, spacious interior, the Big Three department stores (Nordstrom, the Bon, and J. C. Penney), and an ever-expanding coterie of exceptionally high-quality shops ranging from FAO Schwarz and Pottery Barn to Guess? and Banana Republic. *Every day; map:HH3*

REDMOND TOWN CENTER / 16495 NE 74th St, Redmond (off SR 520 at W Lake Sammamish Pkwy); 425/867-0808 The newest kid on the shopping-mall block is the chichi Redmond Town Center. Dubbed by its operators a "lifestyle center," the open-air mixed-use mall has an impressive array of retail—AKA Eddie Bauer, The Gap, Z Gallerie—and restaurants, plus an eight-screen movie complex. Every day; map:FF1

OTHER MALLS

NORTHGATE MALL / off I-5 at the Northgate exit; 206/362-4777 Northgate had the distinction (or shame, depending on your opinion of malls) of being the first mall in the nation when it opened in 1950. Now thoroughly modern (since a 1997 facelift), the mall has the full complement of stores, including a Nordstrom and a Bon Marché, as well as an excellent food court. *Every day; map:DD7*

Northgate's south-end, climate-controlled counterpart is **SOUTHCENTER MALL** (off I-5 at Southcenter mall exit, Tukwila; 206/246-7400; every day; map:OO5). Just south of Southcenter, at the **PARKWAY SUPERCENTER** (17300 Southcenter Pkwy, Tukwila; every day; map:OO5), every store, from Old Navy to Shoe Pavilion, deals in discounted merchandise.

Other suburban shopping action can be found at the discount megamall **SUPERMALL OF THE GREAT NORTHWEST** (1101 Supermall Way, Auburn; 253/833-9500; every day), at **SEA-TAC MALL** (320th St exit off I-5, Federal Way; 253/839-6150; every day), and at **ALDERWOOD MALL** (Alderwood Mall exit off I-5, Lynnwood; 425/771-1211; every day).

Shops from A to Z

ANTIQUES/VINTAGE/RETRO

ALMOST ANTIQUES / 6019 15th Ave NW; 206/783-5400 A modest Ballard storefront with a scrolly sign on the side of the building, Almost Antiques has room after room of gilt mirrors, tapestried love seats, lamps, and dining sets. Lots of quality furnishings in mahogany, maple, walnut, and cherry. There's crystal, china, sterling, and quality flatware, too. *Every day; map:EE8*

ANTIQUE IMPORTERS / 640 Alaskan Way; 206/628-8905 Direct importing from Denmark and occasionally from England (each item hand-selected by the store's buyers) ensures that the stock of pine and oak furniture and stained glass is of excellent value and respectable quality. High-ish prices; mostly standard items, with a few rare finds, including some interesting cast-iron pieces. New shipments arrive often. *Every day; map:M8*

ANTIQUE LIQUIDATORS / 503 Westlake Ave N; 206/623-2740 Without a doubt this is the largest antique store in town, with 22,000 square feet of sales and storage space. New merchandise arrives constantly to meet the high demand for practical furnishings (mostly Danish and English; lots of chairs and drop-leaf tables). Browsing among the antique kitchen accessories is great rainy-day fun. Endless variety and good prices, but don't expect perfect quality. *Every day; map:D2*

THE CRANE GALLERY / 104 W Roy St; 206/622-7185 Crane is highly respected in the business for its fine Asian antiques and artifacts. Paintings, ceramics, bronzes, ivory, jade, and furniture from the Orient are museum quality—and priced accordingly. *Tues–Sat; map:GG7*

DAVID WEATHERFORD ANTIQUES AND INTERIORS / 133 14th Ave E; 206/329-6533 ▪ 1200 2nd Ave; 206/233-0796 A Capitol Hill mansion provides a resplendent showplace for exquisite 18th-century English and French furniture, as well as Oriental rugs, porcelain, screens, and art glass. A resident design team advises clients on integrating antiques gracefully with their present furnishings. The downtown location in the Washington Mutual Tower specializes in commercial collections. *Mon–Sat; www.davidweatherford.com; map:HH6; map:L7*

DELUXE JUNK / 3518 Fremont Pl N; 206/634-2733 Not to be taken too seriously, Deluxe Junk is trashy, exuberant, and kitschy, specializing in furnishings and housewares from the '50s. The clothes, from the 1930s through the 1960s, have—if not grace—a lot of style, and the stock rotates seasonally (heavy tweed coats and handmade sweaters in winter, cool cotton shirts and straw hats in summer). This former funeral parlor also has lots of space for other funky goodies and collectibles. *Every day; map:FF7*

DIRTY JANE'S / 1530 Melrose Ave; 206/682-9890 A garden-collectibles store, Dirty Jane's looks like the flower shop your grandmother loved, decorated with fresh, blooming lilies, irises, and daisies. Vintage pottery— a specialty here—antique patio tables, chaise longues, and cupboards come from the Midwest. *Every day; www.aa.net/dirtyjanes/; map:I2*

EILEEN OF CHINA / 624 S Dearborn St; 206/624-0816 Those looking for Asian opulence will find it at this large International District store stocked with Chinese antiques that make a statement: a $68,000 cloisonné elephant trunk, 6-foot-tall Chinese vases, grand armoires, and hand-painted screens. *Every day; map:R7*

FREMONT ANTIQUE MALL / 3419 Fremont Pl N; 206/548-9140 Mark Salo lets the community of Fremont shape the contents of his antique store in the basement of the Fremont Building. The results? It's more a place for collectibles than for antiques. There are 60 to 70 dealers, with vintage clothing and toys, dinnerware and appliances from the 1950s, Oriental rugs, and even a little bit of the real stuff here and there. *Every day; map:FF7*

FRITZI RITZ / **3425 Fremont Pl N; 206/633-0929** All the clothes are labeled with the decade in which they were produced—that's what makes this store so great. With racks of dresses, skirts, shoes, slacks, and handbags, plus a well-stocked jewelry case, Fritzi Ritz is a favorite among hard-core vintage shoppers. *Every day; map:FF7*

GREG DAVIDSON ANTIQUE LIGHTING / **1020 1st Ave; 206/625-0406** It's dark inside Greg Davidson's cavernous antique lighting store. All the better to get the feel of the warming glow that shines through the graceful shade of a Tiffany-Handel lamp. A handful of fine furnishings set off a collection of mostly American fixtures, standing and desk lamps, and chandeliers. Whether your fuel of choice is gas, kerosene, or electricity, Davidson (who can be found wiring and repairing in the recesses of the shop) has an expert eye for Arts and Crafts and Victorian pieces. *Every day; map:L8*

HONEYCHURCH ANTIQUES / **1008 James St; 206/622-1225** John Fairman runs this excellent shop, which has a second location in Hong Kong—thus it has the largest selection of 19th-century Japanese and Chinese furniture in the Northwest. The store's attraction lies in its tasteful blend of Asian fine art, folk art, and furniture with a reputation for integrity and quality that is well deserved. The shop puts on bimonthly shows of early Chinese ceramics and Japanese wood-block prints. *Tues–Sat; map:O3*

ISADORA'S ANTIQUE CLOTHING / **1915 1st Ave; 206/441-7711** Laura Dalesandro's shop is distinguished by her understanding of, and passionate attention to, every period of clothing from the 1900s to the 1950s. And there's no "filler." The museum-quality clothing at Isadora's is elegant and truly stunning, including gowns and tuxedos. *Every day; map:I7*

JEAN WILLIAMS ANTIQUES / **115 S Jackson St; 206/622-1110** A distinctive collection of French, English, and American 18th- and 19th-century furnishings is showcased in this commodious Pioneer Square storefront. Handsome fireplace mantels, mirrors, and other classic accent pieces fill the crannies. You can also get French and English handmade reproductions here at half the cost of genuine antiques. *Mon–Sat; www.jeanwilliams antiques.com; map:O9*

LE FROCK / 317 E Pine St; 206/623-5339 Le Frock is like an older sister's full closet—lots of stuff you like and a couple of things you might not. There's a healthy complement of men's clothes, but the women's selection is better: dresses, skirts, vests, shoes—all in good condition. Prices are moderate but fair. You need a certain amount of imagination to shop the bargain balcony, but the price is definitely right. *Every day; map:K2*

MADAME & COMPANY / 1901 10th Ave W; 206/281-7908 The people at Madame & Company treat vintage clothing with respect, knowledge, and love—a fact recognized by collectors, shoppers, and Hollywood costumers, all of whom frequent the store. Mother/daughter owners Carol and Deborah Winship carry inventory up to the 1940s (though the store is heavier on pre-1920s clothing). Lingerie and evening wear are thoughtfully restored before being marked for sale. Check out the lace yardage, collars, buttons, and hats, or just indulge yourself in a highly satisfying browse. *Tues–Sat; bridal by appointment only; map:GG8*

N. B. NICHOLS AND SON / 1924 Post Alley, Pike Place Market; 206/448-8906 The sign in Post Alley sums it up: "Antiques, Fine Imported Objects, Extraordinary Junk." From 11th-century B.C. Egyptian antiquities to English garden figurines, this store stocks the junk of the world. Don't expect to find flawless treasures; do expect an interesting conglomeration of European, Asian, and African Old World things—some truly lovely. *Tues–Sat; map:I8*

PARTNERS IN TIME / 1332 6th Ave; 206/623-4218 This downtown location offers antique pine furniture imported from England, Austria, Germany, and Holland. Also Asian carpets, Japanese porcelain, and other collectibles. *Every day; map:K5*

PELAYO'S / 7601 Greenwood Ave N; 206/789-1999 ▪ 8421 Greenwood Ave N; 206/789-1333 Pedro Pelayo specializes in Danish country pine furniture from the 19th and 20th centuries, as well as pieces from England and central Europe. Scandinavian crockery, bric-a-brac, wine jugs, and benches can be found, along with brass and copper accessories and more than 100 Russian items. When the owner ran out of room in his original Greenwood Avenue location, he found more space just down the street—thus two stores with the same name. *Every day; map:EE8*

PRIVATE SCREENING / 3504 Fremont Pl N; 206/548-0751 There are so many clothes on the racks that your arm gets tired pushing dress after dress to the side. Everything's in excellent condition; if you can't find it here, you might not find it anywhere. And since they've got great stock, you may as well get a "new" pair of shoes and a porkpie hat to go with that vintage suit. *Every day; map:FF7*

REHEAT / 2326 2nd Ave; 206/374-0544 Make this your first stop for vintage kitchen goods. Owner Maria Sanchez has carried wares from Ernie's in San Francisco and Brennan's in New Orleans as well as from local eateries. The martini glass is a popular favorite here. *Mon–Sat; map:F7*

RETROVIVA / 1511 1st Ave (and branches); 206/624-2529 A funky shop with men's and women's clothing (new and used) and accessories from every era, Retro Viva is your best bet when you need a leopard-skin bra from the 1960s. Jewelry—some costume, some collector's—fills the display cases. Clothing is well priced, and customers are told if a piece is damaged. Other stores are on Broadway (215 Broadway E; 206/328-7451; map:GG7) and the Ave (4515 University Way NE; 206/632-8886; map:FF6). *Every day; map:J7*

RHINESTONE ROSIE / 606 W Crockett St; 206/283-4605 Rhinestone Rosie rents, buys, and sells an exceptionally large and complete inventory of rhinestone treasures in all colors, shapes, and sizes. Her specialty is buying broken pieces of jewelry and repairing them herself before selling them for low prices. Hers is the only store on the West Coast with a rhinestone repair service; if you have lost a stone out of a favorite piece, she can probably find a replacement for you. *Tues–Sat; map:GG8*

RUBY MONTANA'S PINTO PONY / 1623 2nd Ave; 206/443-9363 The five-and-dime of vintage objects, Ruby Montana sells wonderfully awful things that you just can't live without. Ruby specializes in collectibles and popular culture must-haves from the '40s and '50s: kidney-shaped sofas, lava lamps, marlin and moose heads to hang on walls. She's also got the largest salt-and-pepper-shaker selection on the West Coast. A treasure trove of vintage '70s and '80s smaller merchandise includes note cards, lamps, clocks, and other novelties. Postcards galore and dinnerware, too. *Every day; luckydog@rubymontana.com; www.rubymontana.com; map:I7*

SEATTLE BUILDING SALVAGE / 202 Bell St; 206/448-3453 This store's got everything including the kitchen sink. Redecorating your home? Here's your Mecca. Rummage through vintage claw-foot tubs, light fixtures, doors, and chandeliers, plus locks and doorknobs, from Art Deco to Arts and Crafts designs. *Tues–Sat; map:G8*

STUTEVILLE ANTIQUES / 1518 E Olive Way; 206/329-5666 Marshall Stuteville brings to his shop an impressive collection of Georgian period furniture as well as Continental and American pieces. The authenticity of every item, including the smaller silver and porcelain items, is evident. He also offers a restoration service. *Tues–Sat, and by appointment; map:HH6*

TWO ANGELS ANTIQUES / 1527 Western Ave; 206/340-6005 Steve Glueck and Sally Maryatt's exceptional shop is a veritable art museum. Whimsical, creative window displays will draw you inside. Once you're in, the fabulous furnishings and objets d'art are further proof that serious antiques—even extraordinarily expensive, museum-quality treasures such as a pair of 15th-century angels, or a string of period chairs hanging carefully from the high ceiling—can be fun, too. *Mon–Sat; map:J8*

VINTAGE VOOLA / 705 E Pike St; 206/324-2808 This is not one of those stuffed-to-the-rafters vintage shops; it feels instead like an eccentric friend's personal collection of retro furniture, clothing, and accessories. The dresses are in perfect condition, as are the hats. There's a rack of eye-catching drapes in bright colors, carefully cleaned and hung—someone smart knew they'd be back in style someday. *Every day; map:K1*

APPAREL

ANN TAYLOR / 1420 5th Ave, City Centre (and branches); 206/623-4818 Classic, reliable, timeless career fashions—and relatively afford-able, too, especially if you watch the sales. It's the place to go for luxurious fabrics, accessories, and fine footwear from the custom-shoe salon. The downtown store has a consistently good selection of petite sizes. Other branches are at Pacific Place, Bellevue Square, Redmond Town Center, University Village, and Alderwood Mall. *Every day; map:J5*

ARDOUR / 1115 1st Ave; 206/292-0660 Whimsy, fun, and utter femi-ninity characterize the women's apparel in this small boutique, located a few blocks down from the Seattle Art Museum. Dresses in shimmering, sensuous silks spell summer here, with cozy sweaters, soft Ts, and pants rounding out the fall and winter offerings. There's also bridal and evening wear, as well as distinctive bath products, heartbreakingly deli-cate lingerie, and accessories. This brand of romance, like many others, typically comes at a high price. *Every day; map:L8*

BCBG / 600 Pine St, Pacific Place; 206/447-3400 ▪ Bellevue Square, Bellevue; 425/454-7691; Parisian designer Max Azria fills his studio-style boutiques with merchandise that drapes, feels, and wears as though it had come from a fashion house in his native city, but retails at prices more realistic for the young professional woman. Here you'll find suits and semiformal cocktail dresses in polyacetates, cashmeres, and silks that especially flatter a tall, curvier silhouette. Azria creates one of the most consistently stunning and sought-after holiday collections in town, high-lighting neutrals with seasonal accents. *Every day; map:J5; map:HH3*

BANANA REPUBLIC / 1506 5th Ave (and branches); 206/ 622-2303 Banana Republic's expansive downtown location—a multimillion-dollar revamp of the former Coliseum Theater—carries the classic Irish linens, cotton twill chinos, and leather bomber jackets that have distinguished its men's and women's clothing lines since the beginning. These days there's a fresh new emphasis on tailored European-style suiting, and semiformal evening wear too. Head to the University Village store for a less frenetic shopping experience. Branches are in University Village (206/525-5560; map:FF6) and Bellevue Square (425/453-0991; map:HH3). *Every day; map:J6*

BARNEYS NEW YORK / 1420 5th Ave, City Centre; 206/622-6300 Kudos to Barneys for forever banishing the myth that every Seattleite's closet holds 75 percent denim and 25 percent flannel. Showcasing dozens of internationally acclaimed, ready-to-wear lines rarely found off Madison Avenue or Rodeo Drive, this split-level miniature department store features Prada and Jil Sander for women and Armani, Paul Smith, and Prada for men. Too taxing to your credit card? Scope out Barneys' in-house line, featuring exclusive, tasteful suiting and sportswear collections modeled after designer offerings but with much more palatable price tags. And don't forget to pop by in early January and July, when the incoming spring and autumn lines prompt alluring markdowns of 30 to 50 percent on existing merchandise. *Every day; map:J5*

BETSEY JOHNSON / 1429 5th Ave; 206/624-2887 Until Jean-Paul Gaultier opens a boutique on Seattle's Fifth Avenue, the city's most fashionably daring women will continue to count on Betsey Johnson to keep the light and playful in their wardrobes. The operative word is *whimsical*, as expressed through vibrant maize-painted walls, paisley-printed furnishings, and merchandise racks packed with sequined bandeau tops, faux-fur outerwear, and flirty baby-doll dresses. Whether you're in for a night of serious clubbing or glamorous posing with plenty of attitude, Betsey J is the best preparatory stop. *Every day; map:J5*

BONNEVILLE'S OF GIG HARBOR / 114 Lake St, Kirkland; 425/822-7002 Beauty and a sure sense of style pervade Bonneville's, both in ambience and in merchandise. Colorful and unusual scarves; sequined, beaded, or appliqued tops; and tons of accessories are displayed side by side with Oriental carpets, antique wood furniture, silk flowers, and Japanese parasols. Truly lovely stuff. *Mon–Sat; map:EE3*

BROOKS BROTHERS / 1335 5th Ave; 206/624-4400 ▪ Bellevue Square, Bellevue; 425/646-9688 Brooks Brothers' famous conservative lines of men's casual and dress fashions are well geared to this city's climate. Tremendous depth of inventory, a fine special-order system, two terrific sales a year (two weeks in June and the week after Christmas), and gracious service amid sedate surroundings are the store's trademarks. Some good women's lines in among the button-downs. A growing line of casual wear and big and tall sizes, too. *Every day; map:K6; map:HH3*

BUTCH BLUM / 1408 5th Ave; 206/622-5760 ▪ University Village; 206/524-5860 William "Butch" Blum and Kay Smith-Blum have created an oasis for Seattle's most stylish men, showcasing high-end, on-the-rise, fashion-forward designers such as Yohji Yamamoto, Calvin Klein, and Zegna. Subdued neutrals have characterized recent lines, but the consistent polish of the pieces is what really sets the tone. The new University Village store carries similar quality sans the suits. *Mon–Sat (downtown); every day (University Village); map:FF6; map:K6*

DAKOTA / 2025 1st Ave (and branches); 206/441-3177 These locally owned boutiques showcase several local women's designers, including Iris Singer, Ingenuity, and Christopher Blue, who are best known for their neutral tones and forgiving sihouettes in sizes 4 to 14. Look for more urban-inspired lines too, including the popular Big Star jeans. Those mourning the closure of NYC-based designer Joan Vass's specialty shop in Westlake Center need look no further, as Dakota carries an ample selection of her line throughout the year. A selection of Neal's Yard Remedies aromatherapy treatments contributes to the warm, casual ambience here. Branches are in Bellevue Square (425/462-1677; map:HH3) and Redmond Town Center (425/882-1882; map:FF1). *Every day; map:H8*

DAVID LAWRENCE / 1318 4th Ave; 206/622-2544 ▪ Bellevue Square, Bellevue; 425/688-1699 Frustrated by a lack of variety in men's upper-end specialty stores locally, David Blackham and Larry Strong opened the first David Lawrence shop in Bellevue Square in 1994. Ensuing success brought a downtown Seattle branch a year later, stocked with edgier designer options. Both stores are anchored in the fine men's suiting lines and sportswear of Versace, Hugo Boss, and Donna Karan's gold label. The stores' smaller dimensions and personable salespeople make shopping here a less intimidating experience than at some comparable retailers, with no sacrifice of high style or quality. *Every day; map:K6; map:HH3*

DEREK ANDREW STORE / 2001 4th Ave; 206/448-8696 From the outside, you might easily mistake this loft-style boutique in Belltown for a day spa. Mr. Andrew's tactile, brushed cotton apparel within can be found in the likes of Saks Fifth Avenue and Neiman-Marcus in other major cities, but only Seattle has direct access to his private studio and latest lines of women's and men's casual daywear separates and accessories. If he is not on the sales floor alongside his helpful staff, he's most likely upstairs laboring away on his latest collection. *Every day; map:H6*

DESIGN PRODUCTS CLOTHING / 208 1st Ave S; 206/624-7795 Sumptuous sweaters, casual pants and skirts, and an outstanding array of blouses offset softly tailored apparel at Design Products Clothing. This snazzy boutique in Pioneer Square also carries a limited selection of accessories, including lovely filmy scarves, and some local designer clothing, including Deliane Klein's. *Mon–Sat; www.seattlesquare.com/ designproducts; map:O8*

DITA BOUTIQUE / 1525 1st Ave, Suite 2; 206/622-1770 Dita's has a wide array of innovative silhouettes from a diverse array of sources, ranging from European labels to relaxed pieces by Texan designer Kathleen Sommers. Here, 20- and 60-year-olds shop side by side; the selections are rooted in style, not age. Service is expert and friendly. *Every day; map:J7*

THE FORUM MENSWEAR / 95 Pine St; 206/624-4566 A fashionable guy's paradise near Pike Place Market, with an outstanding selection of moderate-to-expensive suits and accessories. Lines include Jhane Barnes, Henry Grethel, and sleek Italian designs from Tallia Uomo and Genetti. European ties and accessories finish the look. *Every day; map:I8*

HELEN'S (OF COURSE) / 1302 5th Ave; 206/624-4000 ▪ Bellevue Place, Bellevue; 425/462-1400 Fashions from the pages of *W* fill these venerable marble showcases, with labels from the world's haughtiest couture houses (Oscar de la Renta, Escada Boutique). Here, seasoned saleswomen minister to longtime clients, some of Seattle's worldliest—and wealthiest—fashion mavens. *Mon–Sat; map:K6; map:HH3*

J CREW / 600 Pine St, Pacific Place; 206/652-9788 ▪ Bellevue Square, Bellevue; 425/451-2739 Inventive window displays, soft lighting, and easy navigation are the hallmarks of J Crew stores, adding up to a shopping experience that's just as pleasant as mail-ordering from the company's phenomenally successful catalogs. Lightweight linens, cottons, and silks dominate the men's and women's spring and summer offerings, while heavier jackets, suits, and sweaters of durable wool blends make the autumn and winter collections indispensable to the store's low-key yet style-conscious clientele. *Every day; map:J5; map:HH3*

JAEGER / 1427 5th Ave; 206/622-4627 Yet another high-end newcomer to downtown, Jaeger seeks to drape the fashion-conscious woman who eschews trends. The studio-boutique is meticulously laid out to best display the line's trademark high-quality suits, sportswear, and cocktail dresses, all with their accompanying high price tags. Jaeger's seasonal offerings provide a certain thread of consistency, making a purchase from this store a wardrobe investment that will pay off for many seasons to come. *Mon–Sat; map:J5*

LES AMIS / 3420 Evanston Ave N; 206/632-2877 This intriguing boutique offers pure romance in the heart of funky Fremont. Here you'll find one-of-a-kind dresses, blouses, sweaters, and skirts in natural fibers, with delightful details such as unusual buttons and inventive stitching. Characterized by a certain whimsy and daring, these are clothes that will make the wearer stand out in a crowd, subtly. Numerous baskets stashed here and there hold silky and lacy lingerie, and there's a nice selection of socks, bags, and other accessories. Bath products, delicate bead jewelry, and selected baby items, too. *Every day; map:FF8*

LOCAL BRILLIANCE / 1535 1st Ave; 206/343-5864 Local Brilliance showcases West Coast designers, including owner Renata Tatman, so you can get originals at fairly affordable prices. A smattering of accessories, including jewelry, belts, and scarves, rounds out the thoughtfully chosen selection. *Every day; map:J7*

LOEHMANN'S / 1423 4th Ave; 206/223-4222 ▪ 3620 128th Ave SE, Bellevue; 425/641-7596 This women's off-price clothing store has it all—casual, business, and party wear, lingerie, coats, accessories, and plenty of shoes—all new. There are name brands and good deals, but you have to hunt a little. Selection changes often, so if at first you don't succeed. . . . *Every day; map:J6; map:II2*

MARIO'S OF SEATTLE / 1513 6th Ave; 206/223-1461 An ambitious store remodel and the addition of a new Hugo Boss specialty boutique have helped Mario's earn its reputation as Seattle's most reliable purveyor of Boss and Giorgio Armani. Other lines include Dolce & Gabbana, Calvin Klein, and TSE. The retail space is spacious and inviting, the staff courteous and skilled. Custom-tailored shoes and special orders on exclusive European merchandise, too. *Every day; map:J5*

NANCY MEYER / 1318 5th Ave; 206/625-9200 With about as much square footage as the walk-in closets of some of its patrons, this eclectic boutique manages to stock a surprising selection of the finest designer and imported lingerie. The tasteful luxury displayed here has made it a favorite among the physically and fiscally fortunate. *Mon–Sat; map:K6*

NELLY STALLION / 1622 Queen Anne Ave N; 206/285-2150 Original, elegant, savvy. Nelly's buyer prowls the garment district of New York and flies the finds to this stunning shop before anyone else in Seattle has them. Consequently, Nelly Stallion has won the hearts of the area's most stylish, who look upon the annual sales as seasonal must-attend events. High points are the beautiful separates, pretty lingerie, and vintage fashions. *Mon–Sat; map:GG8*

NUBIA'S / 1507 6th Ave; 206/622-0297 ▪ 4116 E Madison St; 206/325-4354 These stores are the namesake of the affable and knowledgeable owner, who considers them a labor of love. Nubia's Colombian roots show up in her eclectic inventory; she weaves a theme of Latin, Asian, and American styles with relaxed sophistication. The best natural textiles and a certain boldness distinguish the garments, whether knit sweaters and skirts or elegant silk pieces fashioned by Nubia herself. Accessories, scarves, and designer jewelry complement the clothing. *Mon–Sat; map:J5; map:GG6*

PARAGON / 2200 1st Ave; 206/448-9048 Funky but chic, and decidedly hip. Before Max Azria's BCBG specialty store made its way to Bellevue and Seattle, this was the only place you could find his line with reliability. It may be a bit cluttered, but this established Belltown independent boutique mixes the pricey and trendy better than the competition. Second-best fun shoe selection in town, next to John Fluevog, just down the street in the Market. *Every day; map:H8*

TOTALLY MICHAEL'S / 521 Union St; 206/622-4920 Part of the Seattle clothing scene since 1971, the experienced and friendly owners, Michael Smith and Carol Baldwin, carry exciting clothing for sophisticates at work (beautifully tailored suits and separates), at play (relaxed, oh-so-chic casuals), and after dark (evening and party dresses). You'll find local designers represented along with Hind & Malee and Tamotsu. *Mon–Sat; map:K5*

URBAN OUTFITTERS / 401 Broadway E; 206/322-1800 Located on Capitol Hill, miles away in spirit from the loftier pretensions of downtown retailers, Urban Outfitters attracts the youthful and urbane in search of streetwise, on-the-rise, mostly American designers. The relatively puny price tags have been known to reflect merchandise quality, producing occasional grumbles from regular customers, but the goods turn over quickly—and whether the latest trend is an Asian-inspired slip dress or a retro striped ski sweater, you're sure to find it here. The store has earned its reputation of catering to waifish frames for a reason: its junior-size cuts leave little selection for voluptuous and vertically blessed women of size 12 or larger. *Every day; map:GG6*

WHAT'S THAT? / 8117 161st Ave NE, Redmond; 425/881-3034 Owner Lenoir Perara specializes in dressing women in moderately priced alternative clothing, with accessories to complement the looks. Suits have softer lines here, and casual clothes are chosen with a creative flair. Perara has a keen eye for fashion, and she obtains her stock from all over the world. *Mon–Sat; map:EE1*

ZEBRACLUB / 1901 1st Ave; 206/448-7452 Finally shedding its reputation for loud, silkscreen-printed logo sweatshirts, Zebraclub has developed into a reliable club kids' haven—although we've also seen a smattering of silver-haired folks shopping happily for jeans alongside the ravers. Look for good selections of the ultra-hip Reactor, Replay, and Energie sport lines for men and women—not to mention the city's largest selection of Diesel clothing. *Every day; map:I7*

BAKERIES

A PIECE OF CAKE / 514 S King St; 206/623-8254 Adored for its light, fresh, fruit-filled sponge cakes (mango is the best), this immaculate bakery is well worth a stop when you're in the vicinity. The International District favorite also bakes napoleons, éclairs, and Black Forest cakes, as well as authentic Chinese pastries. *Wed–Mon; map:R6*

BAGEL OASIS / 2112 NE 65th St (and branches); 206/526-0525 This is the bagel shop that transplanted Easterners rave about. Boiled before they are baked, the bagels are crisp-skinned outside and chewy inside, as authentic as you'll find this side of the Mississippi. No gimmicks here; the bagels come in traditional flavors, from salt to sesame seed to pumpernickel, along with a big, oniony bialy. The noshing crowd also hangs out for full breakfasts and generously filled bagel sandwiches. Branches are in Fremont (462 N 36th St; 206/633-2676; map:FF7) and Juanita (11606 98th Ave NE, Juanita; 425/823-5404; map:DD3). *Every day; map:EE6*

BOULANGERIE / 2200 N 45th St; 206/634-2211 At this authentic French bakery you can count on excellent crusty loaves, buttery croissants, and heavenly brioches. The *seigle noix*—a dense, light rye bread with walnuts—is superb with cheese, which is sold here as well. The place bustles, but service is quick. The full range of Boulangerie goodies are also available at the Queen Anne and Admiral Thriftway stores. *Every day; map:FF7*

CREDENZIA VILLAGE BAKERY / 10 Mercer St; 206/284-4664 A new entry in the artisan bakery category, Credenzia features a large, gas-burning, flying saucer–shaped oven designed by its owner. The three oversize breads—Romana, Campagna (sourdough), and Rustica (wheat germ)—offer long-lived crusty texture and loads of flavor. One loaf will serve a party, but you can also purchase them by the half or quarter loaf. The hearty cakes, especially the Budapest coffee cake—laden with sour cream, cinnamon, and nuts—and the just-tart-enough lemon are perfect partners to the carefully prepared coffee or tea served here. Credenzia also offers imaginative salads, house-made soups, sandwiches, and pizzettas at lunch, with a selection that changes daily. *Every day; map:A7*

THE CRUMPET SHOP / 1503 1ST AVE, Pike Place Market; 206/682-1598 Any resemblance to an American version of an English muffin here is purely coincidental. These English griddle cakes are made from a yeasted batter, using no fat, sugar, butter, or cholesterol. Get yours toasted, with butter and jam, and the crumpet's hole-y surface will catch every last drip of topping. Or try them as a sort of open-faced sandwich with tomatoes and ricotta or "green eggs and ham" (with pesto). *Every day; map:J8*

THE CRUSTY LOAF / 2123 Queen Anne Ave N; 206/282-5623 Here's one bakery that delivers on what its name promises. A recent addition to

Seattle's artisan bread brigade, it sells its own crisply crusted breads, bread sticks, and rolls. Large windows open onto the street and spread the smell of baking deliciously throughout the neighborhood; just try to walk by without going in. The selection changes daily, but some favorites such as the rosemary–sea salt and the Kalamata olive loaves are worth an extra detour to Queen Anne Hill. *Every day; map:GG8*

DESSERT WORKS / 6116 Phinney Ave N; 206/789-5765 Everything here is made to order, and you must place your order by noon the day before, but you can't miss with such tempting treats as white coconut cake, pecan caramel tart, or the strawberry bagatelle made with layers of white velvet cake and strawberries in white chocolate mousse. The simple-seeming cookies are especially delicious—special enough to make an accomplished home cook try to pass them off as his/her own. *Tues–Sat; map:EE7*

THE EROTIC BAKERY / 2323 N 45th St; 206/545-6969 The name says it all—this naughty but nice bakery makes cakes for special occasions like men's and women's stag parties, anniversaries, or other (truly!) memorable celebrations. White or chocolate cakes are topped off with buttercream frosting and a marzipan sculpture of usually private body parts. Although they are usually purchased for their appearance, the cakes taste pretty good, too. *Every day; map:FF7*

GRAND CENTRAL BAKING COMPANY / 214 1st Ave S; 206/622-3644 The craze for Italian rustic bread started here, and this is still one of the best of the specialty bakeries. Thanks to raves from local and national publications and the abiding high quality of the baked goods, legions of fans stop by to pick up their daily bread. The classic is the Como loaf, a moist-inside, super-crusty-outside loaf of Italian-style bread. The savory rosemary rolls and soft, doughy potato bread are also not to be missed. Grand Central does a brisk lunch business with sandwiches on the same fine breads, and also offers scones and other pastries. *Mon–Sat; map:O8*

GREENWOOD BAKERY / 7227 Greenwood Ave N; 206/783-7181 Big sister to Ballard Baking Company, this modest bakery is a neighborhood institution with a fiercely loyal clientele and a bustling trade, especially on weekend mornings. The natives are friendly, though, so there's no reason to let a long (but usually fast-moving) line intimidate you. The fruit tart with Grand Marnier custard is a favorite, and the award-winning sourdough *pain au levain* is an excellent excuse to order a sandwich. Cookies are small and traditional; pastries border on decadent. *Every day; map:EE7*

HOFFMAN'S FINE PASTRIES / 226 Park Place Center, Kirkland; 425/828-0926 June and Ed Hoffman's tiny, six-table bakery makes up in quality what it lacks in size. Buttery croissants, oh-so-tender scones, cookies, and Danishes fill the cases. Their specialty cakes have earned them local renown, especially the Princess Torte—a surprisingly light concoction of sponge cake, Bavarian cream, raspberry filling, and bright green marzipan icing. *Every day; map:EE3*

JOHN NIELSEN PASTRY / 520 2nd Ave W; 206/282-3004 Nielsen's is the kind of bakery-cum-coffee-shop that you don't find often anymore. This marvelous, old-fashioned favorite has authentic Danish pastries, petits fours, butter cookies, and specialty cakes at great prices. Don't miss the kringle, and come early for a breakfast pastry, hot from the oven. *Mon–Sat; map:GG8*

LA PANZANELLA / 1314 E Union St; 206/325-5217 Ciro Pasciuto started making his naturally fermented rustic Italian bread a few years back, and could hardly keep up with the demand. Now his retail shop on Capitol Hill offers not only his famous "Ciro bread" but also Italian pastries, seasonal fruit tarts, and small pizzas, panini, and crostini appetizers to take out. The weekday lunches, where a cross section of Seattle citizens meets to break bread and debate everything from food to politics to art, are legendary. *Mon–Sat; map:HH7*

LARSEN BROTHERS DANISH BAKERY / 8000 24th Ave NW; 206/782-8285 The best Scandinavian bakery in town, Larsen's also offers many of its baked goods at most QFC stores. Quality is high, with moderately priced Danish pastries, coffee cakes, kringles (large, pretzel-shaped puff pastries with almond paste in the center), light cookies, and great breads, particularly the eight-grain and the Swedish rye. *Every day; map:EE8*

LE FOURNIL / 3230 Eastlake Ave E, Suite A; 206/328-6523 This soupçon of Paris transplanted to Eastlake may look like a scrupulously clean American storefront with glass-fronted cases, but look closer. These goods are the real thing, baked by Frenchman Nicolas Paré. You'll find irresistibly buttery croissants and brioches as well as authentically delicious baguettes, decadent napoleons, éclairs, and other lovely-to-see, delightful-to-consume pastries. *Tues–Sat; map:GG7*

LE PANIER VERY FRENCH BAKERY / 1902 Pike Pl, Pike Place Market; 206/441-3669 Drawing Market visitors into its doors with some of the most enticing aromas in town, Le Panier doesn't disappoint with the flavors of its baked goods. Its hearth ovens turn out fine baguettes; decorative *epis*; unusual breads (notably the onion and the hazelnut); heavenly amandine croissants; fruit tarts; and flavorful *feuilletées* (puff pastry pockets with savory or sweet fillings), especially those filled with spinach and tomatoes. Treat yourself to a croissant and coffee, and perch in the front window for a great view of all the action at Pike Place Market. *Every day; map:J8*

MACRINA BAKERY & CAFÉ / 2408 1st Ave; 206/448-4032 See review in Top 200 Restaurants chapter.

MCGRAW STREET BAKERY / 615 W McGraw St; 206/284-6327 Loyal Queen Anne residents and patrons from other neighborhoods flock here for what many believe are some of the best pastries around. The friendly, helpful employees make everyone feel like a regular, and the variety of old kitchen tables provide comfortable seating. Not to be missed: the marionberry coffee cake, chocolate cinnamon Danish, and pecan shortbread. Great coffee and lattes make this an early-morning must-stop for commuters, and it's also a great neighborhood place to while away the afternoon over a sandwich. *Every day; map:GG8*

60TH STREET DESSERTS / 7401 Sand Point Way NE; 206/527-8560 Although for years it has been primarily a wholesaler to many of Seattle's better restaurants, the bakery has recently opened a retail outlet. Here you can find its superb tarts, cheesecakes, and tortes, some in small sizes or by the slice. The desserts change seasonally and include marionberry cheesecake, Bavarian apple torte, and a lovely selection of cookies. Any desserts deemed less than perfect are sold as seconds for a fraction of the price. *Mon–Fri; map:EE5*

BODY CARE

AVEDA LIFESTYLE STORE / Westlake Center (and branches); 206/623-0766 The wildly popular brand of skin and hair care products is sold in dozens of salons in the Seattle area, but these shops carry the largest selections of the more than 700 Aveda lotions, potions, shampoos, and treatments made from flower and plant essences. You'll also find home-related goods such as natural cleaning solvents and "air care" products, as well as healthy-lifestyle workshops and other services. The First Avenue location offers spa services too. Branches are downtown (1007 1st Ave; 206/628-9605; map:L8) and in Bellevue Square (425/454-1375; map:HH3). *Every day; www.aveda.com; map:I6*

THE BODY SHOP / Northgate Mall (and branches); 206/440-9378 These shops—which originated in the U.K. and launched a revolution in the natural skin-care industry—carry a vast variety of lotions, shampoos, fragrances, and makeup, all using natural ingredients. The company is legendary for its commitment to the environment and its opposition to animal testing, while its products pamper exquisitely. *Every day; www.the-body-shop.com; map:DD7*

GARDEN BOTANIKA / Westlake Center (and branches); 206/624-8292 Three environmentally concerned Northwest natives began this skin- and body-care company in late 1990, and there are now over 100 stores nationwide (with 8 in the greater Seattle area). No animal products, no controversial animal testing, no petroleum products, and minimal packaging. *Every day; map:I6*

THE HERBALIST / 2106 NE 65th St; 206/523-2600 The Herbalist—located in a storefront one block away from PCC in Ravenna—stocks all kinds of natural body-care supplies, including essential and massage oils, natural cosmetics, vitamin supplements, and a variety of herbs to cure, clean, and calm. A good selection of books and potpourri supplies, too; service is friendly and helpful. *Every day; map:FF6*

PARFUMERIE ELIZABETH GEORGE / 1424 4th Ave; 206/622-7212 First, Elizabeth George tests your skin's pH content; then she matches the right fragrance to your skin and helps you learn to wear it. She's spent over 10 years at her craft, purveying one of the top lines of designer-matched scents (less expensive copies of the originals) and specializing in custom and hard-to-find perfumes. Beautiful atomizers and a line of lotions and bath products. *Mon–Sat; map:J6*

PARFUMERIE NASREEN / 1005 1st Ave, Alexis Hotel; 206/682-3459 Fittingly situated off the lobby in the Alexis Hotel, Parfumerie Nasreen is the only all-perfume store in the city, stocking close to 400 different fragrances, many from exotic lands, in all price ranges. *Mon–Sat; map:L8*

THE SOAP BOX / 4340 University Way NE (and branches); 206/634-2379 A fragrant emporium of perfumed soaps, bath oils, lotions, unique and beautiful imported items from all over, and other novelties for the bath. You can always find a gift here; they'll mix any scent you like into a lotion, oil, or bubble bath brew. There's a branch in Pike Place Market, as well as one in West Seattle and one in Kirkland. *Every day; map:FF6*

TENZING MOMO & CO. / 93 Pike St, Pike Place Market; 206/623-9837 If you get past the thick cloud of incense that lingers in the doorway of this small Pike Place Market shop, you'll discover a serious natural apothecary. Herbal body-care products line the shelves, and the staff is extremely knowledgeable about the properties (and mysteries) of the dozens of varieties of herbs, tinctures, and elixirs they carry, including natural remedies for PMS, dandruff, athlete's foot, or whatever ails you. *Mon–Sat; map:J8*

BOOKS AND PERIODICALS

ALL FOR KIDS BOOKS AND MUSIC / 2900 NE Blakeley St, Suite C; 206/526-2768 In this jam-packed store near University Village, classics and classics-to-be are given equal attention. All for Kids seems to embrace the evolving concept of interactive children's books, stocking plenty of kits, tapes, and activities as well. There's a music or reading event every day, except in August. *Every day; map:FF6*

BAILEY/COY BOOKS / 414 Broadway E; 206/323-8842 Bailey/Coy offers a wide spectrum and an eclectic mix, well suited to the Broadway crowds: fiction and literature (including mystery and sci-fi), poetry, lesbian and gay studies, women's studies, and philosophy. Look here also for coffee-table books, child care, gardening, cooking, and a good selection of literary magazines. *Every day; map:GG7*

BARNES & NOBLE BOOKSELLERS / 626 106th Ave NE, Bellevue (and branches); 425/451-8463 The selection is generally excellent (though the staff is not generally knowledgeable), and the store does a good job of showcasing local authors. Twelve branches in the Seattle area include a new one in Pacific Place. The University Village location rivals St. Peter's for size and sheer overwhelmingness, and B&N even has the courage to put chairs and tables right next to the magazine racks. Starbucks cafes come attached. *Every day; www.barnesandnoble.com; map:HH3*

BEATTY BOOKSTORE / 1925 3rd Ave; 206/728-2665 Among the largest general used-book stores in Seattle, Beatty has a huge inventory that includes one of the best bibliography sections on the West Coast. Excellent regional, art, philosophy, and cookbooks, too. They pay well for the used books they buy, ask fair prices for the books they sell, and are knowledgeable about their inventory. *Mon–Sat; map:I6*

BEYOND THE CLOSET BOOKSTORE / 518 E Pike St; 206/322-4609 Filling an important niche in the community, Beyond the Closet carries all manner of new and used books both by gay and lesbian authors and on gay or lesbian subjects—from the political to the everyday to the explicit. The fiction section is notable for the lesser-known authors and books from small presses, though it also carries best-sellers if they're appropriate. *Every day; beyondtc@aol.com; map:K1*

BORDERS BOOKS & MUSIC / 1501 4th Ave (and branches); 206/622-4599 The large general inventory is enhanced by a wide and varied Northwest section and a sensible, comfortable store layout. After choosing this week's good read, head upstairs to the music section and browse through the impressive array of CDs. The store also features regular events and signings and a small cafe. Branches are in Redmond (16549 NE 74th St; 425/869-1907; map:EE2) and Tukwila (17501 Southcenter Pkwy; 206/575-4506; map:OO5). *Every day; www.borders. com; map:J6*

BOWIE & COMPANY BOOKSELLERS / 314 1st Ave S; 206/624-4100 Here you'll find the oldest and rarest books in town (dating as far back as 1475). M. Taylor Bowie, known for his outstanding collection of antiquarian books, also stocks a wide range of out-of-print books, maps, and west-of-the-Mississippi ephemera. Items range from $5 to $70,000. A catalog is issued frequently for mail orders. Appraisals are available (informal ones are free of charge), as is a good book-search service. *Every day; bowiebks@isomedia.com; map:O9*

BULLDOG NEWS AND FAST ESPRESSO / 4208 University Way NE; 206/632-6397 ▪ Broadway Market; 206/322-6397 Between 1,800 and 2,700 publications are stocked at the indispensable Ave newsstand: periodicals, foreign magazines, and newspapers. They also sell espresso to sip while you browse. The second branch is a kiosk in the heart of the Broadway Market. *Every day; map:FF6; map:GG6*

CHAMELEON / 514 15th Ave E; 206/323-0154 If you're lucky, you'll get to hear owner Al Frank practicing jazz riffs on his upright piano as you browse through his carefully chosen collection of used books. The once-general stock has begun to lean toward the rare and antiquarian, and includes a fine selection of volumes on art and architecture, science and medicine, and illustrated books, among others. Sets, fine bindings, books on books, and first editions, too. Fair prices for trades. *Every day; afrank9@ibm.net; www.abebooks.com/home/chameleon/; map:GG6*

CINEMA BOOKS / 4753 Roosevelt Way NE; 206/547-7667 A specialty bookstore located beneath a movie theater could sell only one thing: film-related books. You'll also find magazines, screenplays, posters, stills, and technical books for filmmakers. Truly a movie-lover's paradise. *Mon–Sat; map:FF6*

DAVID ISHII, BOOKSELLER / 212 1st Ave S; 206/622-4719 This small, crowded Pioneer Square shop features discriminatingly selected books reflecting the tastes and interests of the proprietor. David Ishii's eclectic collection of used, out-of-print, and scarce books is the region's largest on these subjects. Ishii is also Seattle's fly-fishing and baseball guru, and baseball fans can even buy Everett AquaSox tickets here. *Every day; map:O8*

EAST WEST BOOK SHOP / 1032 NE 65th St; 206/523-3726 Based on the East West store in Palo Alto, Seattle's version is a good place to thumb through alternative and off-the-wall books by authors who are either crazy or geniuses, and sometimes a bit of both. One of the most comprehensive Jungian psychology selections in town. Friday-night speakers' forums focus on topics ranging from spiritual healing to near-death experiences. *Every day; ew@halcyon.com; www.ewbookshop.com; map:EE7*

ELLIOTT BAY BOOK COMPANY / 101 S Main St; 206/624-6600 Seattle's favorite bookstore offers a marvelous maze of books in which to browse, excellent service, and one of the most respected reading series in the country. Undoubtedly a best place. See Top 25 Attractions in the Exploring chapter. *Every day; queries@elliottbaybook.com; www.elliottbay book.com/ebbco/; map:O8*

FILLIPI BOOK AND RECORD SHOP / 1351 E Olive Way; 206/682-4266 A store in which to lose yourself, Fillipi has a superb stock of used and rare books, records, and sheet music that is constantly being updated. The store can get virtually anything. Prices, however, tend to be higher than elsewhere in the city. *Tues–Sat; map:HH7*

FLORA & FAUNA BOOKS / 121 1st Ave S; 206/623-4727 This Pioneer Square basement offers the largest selection of books on natural history, gardening, and the life sciences you'll find anywhere on the West Coast, possibly in the country. New, used, and rare books—it's all here, aardvarks to zinnias, in more than 25,000 titles. Buy or sell. *Mon–Sat; map:N8*

FREMONT PLACE BOOK COMPANY / 621 N 35th St; 206/547-5970 Located in the heart of this now-trendy grass-roots neighborhood, Fremont Place is a small, bright bookstore anchored in its tight community. New and contemporary fiction, women's studies, gay and lesbian literature, and regional books are the areas of emphasis, along with a small but well-chosen children's section. Tags with good recommendations from staff members are subtly pasted to the shelves. The store also showcases a selection of colorfully painted T-shirts. *Every day; fremontbks@aol.com; map:FF8*

THE GLOBE BOOKS / 5220 University Way NE; 206/527-2480 You'll find a broad selection (new and used) in the humanities (especially literature and reference books) and a growing section of natural-science books in this U-District bookstore. Don't be intimidated by the specialized inventory; this is a wonderfully unstuffy place and a real labor of love. Browse through the antique maps and replicas, too. Trades are welcome. *Tues–Sun; map:FF6*

HALF PRICE BOOKS RECORDS MAGAZINES / 4709 Roosevelt Way NE (and branches); 206/547-7859 No evasiveness here. Half Price sells used and new books at, well, half price. They will also buy your used books, and there's someone on call at all hours to price them. There's a large selection of classical literature, as well as a huge line of discounted new and used software. Branches in Bellevue, Tukwila, and Edmonds. *Every day; hpv27@foxinternet.net; www.halfpricebooks.com; map:FF7*

HORIZON BOOKS / 425 15th Ave E (and branches); 206/329-3586 Don Glover has been buying and selling used books from his nook-and-cranny shop on 15th Avenue E since 1971, offering an emphasis on literature, criticism, history, mystery, and philosophy. His second store (6512 Roosevelt Way NE; 206/523-4217; map:EE7) is well stocked, neatly laid out, and eminently browsable, and a third location is now open in Greenwood (8570 Greenwood Ave N; 206/781-4680; map:EE7). *Every day; map:GG6*

ISLAND BOOKS / 3014 78th Ave SE, Mercer Island; 206/232-6920 A good general bookstore with a lot of personal service from knowledgeable staff. Besides a fine assortment of children's books, nice touches for kids include a playhouse and story hours on Saturdays throughout the year. Owner Roger Page has added a small but growing section of carefully chosen used books. Gift wrapping and domestic shipping are additional free services. *Every day; islandbooks@seanet.com; map:II4*

KINOKUNIYA BOOKSTORE / 519 6th Ave S (above Uwajimaya); 206/587-2477 Upstairs at Seattle's largest Asian grocery store, Uwajimaya, is an extraordinary landscape of Japanese books and magazines comparable in size to many English-language bookstores in town. There's a great selection of books in English, too—mostly by Japanese authors or on Japanese subjects—spanning a variety of topics, including alternative medicine, travel, language (tapes too), fiction, children's books, and cookbooks. *Every day; map:Q7*

LEFT BANK BOOKS / 92 Pike St, Pike Place Market; 206/622-0195 From buttons to bumper stickers to books, variety is the rule in this cooperatively run, alternative bookstore in the Corner Market building. The emphasis is on politics of a reddish hue; there are also good new and used sections on social science, contemporary poetry, fiction, gay and lesbian studies, and philosophy. *Every day; leftbankbooks@leftbankbooks.com; www.leftbankbooks.com; map:J8*

M COY BOOKS / 117 Pine St; 206/623-5354 Michael Coy takes bookselling seriously, and he's crafted his retail business into a fine art. He has a talent for suggesting other titles that will interest you (discuss them over a latte at the espresso bar in back). The Pine Street store (one block east of Pike Place Market) carries a spectrum of books, with an emphasis on contemporary literature, photography, art, gardening, and interior and graphic design. *Every day; map:J8*

MADISON PARK BOOKS / 4105 E Madison St; 206/328-7323 On a corner in the cozy Madison Park neighborhood, this pleasant, roomy shop with a patient and helpful staff is a good choice for browsing new titles. There's a nice array of large-format coffee-table volumes, with a concentration on art and photography, and cookbooks and garden books are well represented. Kids' selections are thoughtfully chosen. *Every day; map:GG6*

MAGUS BOOKSTORE / 1408 NE 42nd St; 206/633-1800 If you can't find a used book here, it probably doesn't exist. A staple in this student-dominated neighborhood, Magus carries everything from classical literature to engineering; it has a large science-fiction selection and tons of Cliff Notes, as well as a poetry section that would do any new-book store proud. *Every day; www.magusbks.com; map:FF6*

MISTER E BOOKS / Pike Place Market, lower level; 206/622-5182 This Pike Place Market shop specializes in mystery (hence the name), fantasy, horror, and signed editions by the likes of Ray Bradbury, Harlan Ellison, and Maurice Sendak. Authors' signings and lots of kids' books, as well as hard-to-find collectors' volumes and an eclectic array of LPs, too. *Every day; misterE@misterE.com; map:I8*

OPEN BOOKS—A POEM EMPORIUM / 2414 N 45th St; 206/633-0811 The store's subtitle says it all. Owners Christine Deavel and John Marshall are both poets, the editors of *Fine Madness* magazine, and devoted to their craft. If you're not a dedicated poetry reader when you go in, volume after volume of new, used, and out-of-print poetry (as well as poetry on tape) just might convert you. Quiet and inviting, Open Books hosts readings, and an adjoining wine bar increases the allure of reading and contemplation. Obscure poets are here, as well as classics and contemporary greats, but Deavel and Marshall are not too proud to carry *Poetry for Cats. Tues–Sat; map:FF7*

PARKPLACE BOOKS / 348 Park Place Center, Kirkland; 425/828-6546 Co-owner Ted Lucia is a book rep who decided to open his own account. He and his wife, Kathi, own this general bookstore that pays close attention to children's books, mystery, and fiction. Open and airy and impeccably organized, the store also has a friendly staff worthy of a book rep's knowledge. *Every day; map:EE3*

PETER MILLER ARCHITECTURAL AND DESIGN BOOKS AND SUPPLIES / 1930 1st Ave; 206/441-4114 In an elegantly spare space, Peter Miller's shop carries not only the best local selection of new, used, and out-of-print architectural books (one of few such specialized outlets in the country) but also a collection of European and Japanese gadgets and drafting supplies. Ask about the catalog. *Every day; pmb@msn.com; www.petermiller.com; map:I7*

QUEEN ANNE AVENUE BOOKS / 1629 Queen Anne Ave N; 206/283-5624 Its selection fits into a cozy space, but the staff at this pleasant neighborhood shop more than make up for the squeeze with their intelligence, good recommendations, and overall geniality. Special orders are handled quickly and efficiently. *Every day; map:GG8*

READ ALL ABOUT IT INTERNATIONAL NEWSSTAND / 93 Pike St, Pike Place Market; 206/624-0140 An enormous selection of local, national, and international papers and magazines is displayed at this colorful newsstand in Pike Place Market (across from DeLaurenti Specialty Food Markets). A Market institution with a jolly staff. *Every day; map:J8*

SEATTLE MYSTERY BOOKSHOP / 117 Cherry St; 206/587-5737 Bill Farley set up his subterranean store in Pioneer Square in 1990 with a shivering collection of thrillers. The whodunit crowd will love this well-thought-out, well-laid-out shop. From the latest releases to Sherlock Holmes, from a clever display of first-in-a-series to out-of-print editions, you'll find them here. Today's most popular mystery writers often drop in for signings. *Every day; staff@seattlemystery.com; map:N8*

SECOND STORY BOOKS / 1815 N 45th St (Wallingford Center); 206/547-4605 A terrific little general bookstore with excellent children's, regional, and fiction sections. Ask about joining the rental library, or come for an autograph party. Good displays draw you in, and big, comfy armchairs invite you to stay. *Every day; map:FF7*

THE SECRET GARDEN CHILDREN'S BOOKSHOP / 6115 15th Ave NW; 206/789-5006 The Secret Garden is the oldest exclusively children's bookstore in the city, and in its big Ballard location it continues to grow, with expanded parenting and children's nonfiction sections. The selection is fine here; special events (musical performances, classes, signings, and the occasional reading) are entertaining. The Secret Garden is involved in literacy efforts, with programs for teachers and parents and book fairs for local schools. *Every day; map:EE8*

SHOREY'S BOOKSTORE / 1109 N 36th St; 206/633-2990 Shorey's, one of the world's largest general antiquarian bookstores, has been in existence since 1890 and has an inventory now numbering over a million items. You can find everything here, from 95-cent paperbacks to $10,000 rare printings, as well as historic pamphlets. The staff conducts effective searches for out-of-print titles. *Every day; shorey@serve.net; www. shoreybooks.com/shorey; map:FF7*

STEVE'S BROADWAY NEWS / 204 Broadway E; 206/324-7323 ▪ 3416 Fremont Ave N; 206/633-0731 Steve Dunnington's news nook on Broadway has become a newshound's source for current issues of periodicals, from regional magazines to Australian dailies. No back issues. The Broadway shop is open every day from 8am until midnight; Steve's Fremont News closes at 10pm (11pm on weekends). *Every day; map:GG7; map:FF7*

TOWER BOOKS / 20 Mercer St; 206/283-6333 ▪ 10635 NE 8th St, Bellevue; 425/451-1110 Russ Solomon's chain is not exactly a chain— since part of the selection is bought locally. Tower has an outstanding computer-book selection and an excellent general-book selection, with a bias toward genres: mysteries, sci-fi, and sports. Open until midnight every day of the year, even holidays. *Every day; www.tower.com; map:A7; map:HH3*

TWICE SOLD TALES / 905 John St (and branches); 206/324-2421 What
began as a one-room shop on Capitol Hill's John Street (luring in bus-
stop customers with racks of 50-cent books and a sign reading "You can
always catch the next bus") has overflowed into the store next door and
three other (separately owned) locations. No musty stacks of old science
texts here; the shelves offer a generous collection of fiction, poetry,
cooking, and more—interspersed with cartoons, cat humor, and pop philosophy. The stores are known for fair prices when buying books, though
this is reflected in the retail prices, which some people feel are high.
Things are never dull at the John Street location: a bubble machine runs
constantly out a front window, cats stroll overhead on specially designed
highways that bridge the tall bookcases, and the owner (and her
employees) are opinionated and loud. Branches are in the U-District
(1311 NE 45th St; 206/545-4266; map:FF6) and Fremont (3504 Fremont Ave N; 206/632-3759; map:FF7). *Every day; tst@twicesoldtales.
com; www.twicesoldtales.com; map:GG7*

**UNIVERSITY BOOK STORE / 4326 University Way NE (and branches);
206/634-3400** The largest bookstore in Washington also happens to be
the largest college bookstore in the United States. The UW's primary
bookstore has a vast selection (especially the gardening, arts, and design
departments) that is a bit overwhelming at first. Don't hesitate to ask for
help: customer service goes beyond expected boundaries, with free book
shipping, gift wrapping, and parking validation; and in the rare event
that your title is not in stock, staff will promptly special-order it. But
browse on your own, too, especially the large remaindered section. The
store often sponsors large events or readings (see Literature in the Performing Arts chapter) in conjunction with the university, and if you want
a computer, a camera, or a stuffed Husky dog dressed in purple and gold,
you'll find them here, too. The smaller branch across the lake in Bellevue
(990 102nd Ave NE, Bellevue; 425/632-9500; map:HH3) does not carry
textbooks or offer the buy-back service; it does carry an extensive general literature and children's selection. In 1995 a branch opened downtown (1225 4th Ave; 206/545-9230; map:K6; Mon–Sat). Catering to
corporate Seattle, it features an awesome selection of business and computer titles. *Every day; bookstor@u.washington.edu; www.bookstore.
washington.edu; map:FF6*

WESSEL & LIEBERMAN BOOKSELLERS / 121 1st Ave S; 206/682-3545
Beyond books for reading, there are books for collecting. This high-
quality shop specializing in first-edition fiction, Western Americana
(especially Northwest and Native American history), and books on
books quickly became a favorite among Seattle book collectors, thanks
to the personal attention of Mark Wessel and Michael Lieberman. In an
increasingly electronic age, it's exciting to see due respect given to the

craft of making books. And Wessel & Lieberman's presentations of books as art objects—miniature books, take-apart books, books in cigar-box covers, and a rotating exhibit of artists' books—give bibliophiles yet another reason to visit often. *Mon–Sat; www.wlbooks.com; map:N8*

WIDE WORLD BOOKS AND MAPS / 1911 N 45th St; 206/634-3453 All of the employees are seasoned wanderers, so advice on specific trips and travel in general is part of the service. Aside from a vast array of travel books, you'll find a complete range of accessories, including globes, maps, language tapes, a passport photo service, and luggage. The serene Teahouse Kuan Yin next door is the perfect place to contemplate future journeys. *Every day; travel@speakeasy.org; www.travelbooksandmaps. com; map:FF7*

CANDY AND CHOCOLATE

BERNARD C CHOCOLATES / 128 Central Way, Kirkland (and branches); 425/822-8889 These sleek gems showcase the renowned Belgian-style Callebaut chocolates, made by Bernard's Calgary confectionery. Sauces, baking supplies, and ice cream bars, too. Bernard himself occasionally travels to Kirkland to conduct candy-making classes at the shop. Additional branches are in downtown Seattle (1420 5th Ave, City Centre; 206/340-0396; Mon–Sat; map:J5) and Bellevue (205 Bellevue Way NE; 425/462-1777; Mon–Sat; map:HH3). *Every day; map:EE3*

CHOCOLAT / Bellevue Square, Bellevue; 425/452-1141 Specializing in fine European chocolates that make your mouth water just to look at them, this chocolate cafe sells mostly Belgian and French brands, including Neuhaus and Teuscher, as well as coffees and teas. *Every day; map:HH3*

THE CONFECTIONERY / University Village; 206/523-1443 A Candyland of treats gleaned from around the world. Chocolates from Fran's, Dilettante, Joseph Schmidt, and Baker's, plus Valrhona and Perugina bars, licorice, gummies, Jelly Bellies, hard candies, taffy, and kosher, plus low-cal and sugarless candies. Fun selection of gift tins, bags, and piñatas. *Every day; map:FF6*

FRAN'S CHOCOLATES / 2805 E Madison St (and branches); 206/322-6511 If you regard chocolate as one of the four basic food groups, you won't want to miss this temple of the beloved delectable. In addition to Fran Bigelow's famous hand-dipped candy, there's baking chocolate of the highest quality and simply scrumptious ice cream in a seasonal array of flavors. Branches are in Bellevue (10305 NE 10th; 425/453-1698; every day; map:HH3) and University Village (206/528-9969; every day; map:FF6). *Tues–Sat; map:GG6*

GODIVA CHOCOLATIER / **Westlake Center; 206/622-0280** ■ **Bellevue Square, Bellevue; 425/646-8837** These are the only shops in the Northwest devoted exclusively to Godiva—the chocolate as rich in cachet as in calories. Chocolate sauces and espresso as well. *Every day; www.godiva. com; map:I6; map:HH3*

THE SWEET ADDITION / **Gilman Village, Issaquah; 425/392-5661** It's licorice heaven, but dozens of chewy, gummy, hard, or sugarless candies tempt shoppers just as much. Look for Portland's Moonstruck truffles here, plus other fine chocolates. The Addition also serves homespun pies, towering cakes, and soup/salad/sandwich–style lunches. *Every day*

TEUSCHER / **410 University St, Four Seasons Olympic Hotel; 206/340-1747** Coffee, tea, and rich, creamy, Swiss chocolates everywhere. You won't think there's anything else to life. *Mon–Sat; map:K6*

CHILDREN'S CLOTHING

BOSTON STREET / **1815 N 45th St, Wallingford Center (and branches); 206/634-0580** Snazzy duds for stylish kids sizes 0 to 14. Much of the clothing here is locally made and one of a kind, including pretty smocks and tiny jean jackets. Boston Street also carries the colorful Cotton Caboodle label and pint-size accessories and umbrellas. Great gifts for your favorite niece or nephew. Some of the best baby duds around. Other branches are at Northgate Mall (206/366-9802; map:DD7) and Redmond Town Center (16515 NE 74th St, Redmond; 425/895-0848; map:FF1). *Every day; map:FF7*

FINE THREADS / **Redmond Town Center; 425/558-5888** Here you'll find a good selection of classic, high-quality boys' and men's clothing (Fine Threads carries sizes for males ages 4 to 104). This is where to shop for his first suit—if you are willing to pay a man's price. *Every day; map:FF1*

FLORA AND HENRI / **1215 1st Ave; 206/749-0004** The catchphrase here is "pure and simple," and it certainly seems to fit: the spare, studiolike store displays orderly rows of simply sophisticated cotton clothing for children from newborn to twelve years old. Prices are high—which is to be expected in return for such details as hand-stitching. Definitely for the child who must have everything, from heartbreakingly lovely 100 percent cotton batiste dresses to tailored overcoats nicer than anything inhabiting most adult Seattleites' closets. *Every day; www.florahenri. com; map:K8*

THE KIDS CLUB / **Crossroads Shopping Center, Bellevue; 425/643-5437** ■ **University Village; 206/524-2553** These two stores feature colorful (if slightly expensive) children's and infants' clothes and shoes. They also have an abundance of baby paraphernalia, from car-seat covers to bottle warmers to snugglies. The Crossroads location, which is larger and has a better selection, even has a kiddie hair salon (the Hair Chair) to keep the kids occupied while Mom shops (the University Village store has a big TV with videos running to accomplish the same purpose). *Every day; map:HH1; map:FF6*

LI'L PEOPLE / Westlake Center; 206/623-4463 ■ Bellevue Square, Bellevue; 425/455-5967 Whimsy and comfy cottons prevail here. Charming and practical reversible-print jumpers, overalls, sweet little sweaters, and inventive headgear, including a great selection of sun and just-for-fun hats. *Every day; map:I6; map:HH3*

ME 'N MOM'S / 5514 24th Ave NW; 206/781-4827 Relocated to Ballard from Roosevelt Square, this shop carries both consignment and new merchandise, including the Flapdoodles line of 100 percent cotton playwear. Sizes 0 to 14, with an emphasis on sizes 6x and under. The store also carries maternity wear. *Every day; map:FF8*

RISING STARS / 7404 Greenwood Ave N; 206/781-0138 This charming shop suits its Greenwood neighborhood just fine, offering kids' clothing fashioned mainly by local designers—some who live and work mere blocks away. You'll find an eclectic selection of pajamas, hand-knit sweaters, and cotton casuals for boys and girls, plus lots of stuffed animals, books, and other amusements, too. *Every day; map:EE8*

THE SHOE ZOO / University Village (and branches); 206/525-2770 The kids' shoe store to use if you want comprehensive selection with salespeople who really pay attention to your child. They specialize in old-fashioned service (they keep a file of kids' previous purchases so you don't have to remember your child's shoe size in a particular brand every time), with a good selection of everything from Buster Browns for dress-up to the latest version of kid-Teva's. Branches are at Gilman Village (755 NW Gilman Blvd, Issaquah; 425/392-8211) and Redmond Town Center (7325 164th Ave NE, Redmond; 425/558-4743; map:FF1). *Every day; map:FF6*

COFFEE AND TEA

CAFFÈ D'ARTE / 1625 2nd Ave; 206/728-4468 When the Cipolla family moved from Italy to Seattle in the 1970s, they missed the aromas and flavors of their native country. Unable to find exactly what they were looking for in a cup of espresso, they decided to do it themselves, and have since produced award-winning cups, named after various regions of Italy (Firenze, Parioli, Capri, Taormina, Fabriano, and Velletri), each boasting different, full flavors, blended and roasted according to rigid artisan traditions. *Mon–Sat; www.caffedarte.com; map:I7*

CAFFÈ VITA / 813 5th Ave N (and branches); 206/285-9662 See Coffee, Tea, and Dessert in the Nightlife chapter.

MARKET SPICE / 85-A Pike Pl, Pike Place Market; 206/622-6340
Market Spice, famous for its namesake orange spice blend tea, also offers
teas in more than 50 flavors. Scoot under the Market clock and turn left
past the flying fish to find a surprising boutique that's simply jammed
with aromatic goodies. In addition to selling tea, it's also a good source
for hundreds of different spices from all over the world, including hard-
to-find items and well-priced familiars, and for a wide selection of coffee
beans. *Every day; map:J8*

**PEGASUS COFFEE / 131 Parfitt Way SW, Bainbridge Island; 206/842-
6725 ▪ 711 3rd Ave; 206/682-3113** Both the original Pegasus on Bainbridge and the downtown shop receive about 20 freshly roasted varieties
of coffee daily. They have an expanded tea selection and offer home-
baked goods, too. Pegasus coffees can be found in local retail stores such
as Larry's Markets. *Mon–Fri (downtown); every day (Bainbridge);
map:N7*

**PERENNIAL TEA ROOM / 1910 Post Alley, Pike Place Market; 206/448-
4054** Get away from Seattle's coffee mania and enter a place where tea
is king—or is that queen? The Perennial Tea Room sells more than 60 tea
varieties plus infusers, kettles, cozies, and tea-centric books. For the
largest selection of teapots (from the British Isles as well as Asia, and an
impressive collection of handcrafted pots by Northwest artisans), look
no further. Many of the pots are whimsical, proof of the shop's abiding
mission to share the fun of tea. *Every day; map:I8*

**SEATTLE'S BEST COFFEE (SBC) / 1530 Post Alley, Pike Place Market
(and many branches); 206/467-7700** Here's a great alternative to Starbucks overload. The branch in Pike Place Market is a good place to sit,
catch your breath from shopping, and watch the passing crowd. Other
outlets are stylish spots for socializing and sipping Seattle's trademark
beverage. A large local roaster (originally named Stewart Brothers
Coffee), SBC roasts its beans on Vashon Island. The stores also sell mugs
and other coffee accoutrements. *Every day; www.seabest.com; map:J8*

**STARBUCKS / 1912 Pike Pl, Pike Place Market (and many, many
branches); 206/448-8762** Boasting more than 1,500 stores in the United
States, Canada, and around the world, Starbucks can be credited with
establishing Seattle as the notorious coffee-swilling town that it is. Good
blends and varietals (nearly 50 of them) are the reason, though some
claim the beans are overroasted (Starbucks' lightest roast is reportedly
two times darker than other roasters' darkest). You'll also find the best
in brewing accessories, several imported teas, and coffee by the cup. And
don't forget that hot-weather favorite, the Frappuccino. A few branches
serve sandwiches (made out-of-house); most offer various sweets and
breakfast breads. The flagship store in Pike Place Market, although it has

no seating, is a veritable shrine for the coffee lover. *Every day (most stores); map:J8*

THE TEA CUP / 2207 Queen Anne Ave N; 206/283-5931 If Seattle's endless hyperbolic talk of coffee makes you yearn for a cuppa, make a beeline for the Tea Cup. It serves more than 100 different teas (including a tea latte), all of which can be purchased in bulk as well. Sippers can linger at one of the two tables, or, on a nice day, sit outside on the benches and observe the bustle of Queen Anne. Also available are an excellent assortment of teapots and kettles, along with cozies, cups, spoons, and strainers. *Every day; map:GG8*

TEAHOUSE KUAN YIN / 1911 N 45th St; 206/632-2055 See Coffee, Tea, and Desserts in the Nightlife chapter.

TORREFAZIONE ITALIA / 320 Occidental Ave S (and branches); 206/624-5847 For authentic Italian coffee, Torrefazione is the place. Maybe it's the beautiful Deruta demitasse in which it's served, but there's definitely something special about a shot of Torrefazione espresso. Offering a dozen or so delicious decaffeinated and regular blends of his own design, Umberto Bizzarri carries on the tradition that he learned from his father in Perugia. In addition to the charms of the coffees, named for Italian cities, this Pioneer Square bar offers some of the city's best people-watching. Branches are in Rainier Square (1310 4th Ave; 206/583-8970; map:K6) and downtown (622 Olive Way; 206/624-1429; map:I5). *Every day; www.titalia.com; map:P8*

TULLY'S COFFEE / 4036 E Madison St (and branches); 206/329-6659 A young, Northwest-based coffee company, Tully's is expanding rapidly, going toe-to-toe with many Starbucks locations. What differentiates Tully's coffee from other coffees is the roasting—mild but not too light, yielding a strong cup that won't knock you over. Most stores offer a variety of sweets and panini sandwiches, and the walls are filled with shelves of cups and coffeemakers. The ginger peach tea (served hot or cold) makes a cooling summertime treat. *Every day; map:GG6*

ETHNIC MARKETS AND SPECIALTY FOODS

A & J MEATS AND SEAFOODS / 2401 Queen Anne Ave N; 206/284-3885 Regarded as the best in town, A & J Meats offers a grand array of top-quality basic cuts, including superb lamb and beef, as well as great specialty items. The owners make all their own wieners and lunch meats (both pure beef), chicken cordon bleu, stuffed pork chops, meat loaves, and sausages of all types (including fruit-spiked varieties). They also do their own applewood smoking. Wonderful selection, wonderful service. *Tues–Sun; map:GG8*

BAVARIAN MEAT DELICATESSEN / 1920 Pike Pl, Pike Place Market; 206/441-0942 German is definitely spoken here in the north end of Pike Place Market, where you'll find a large selection of sausages—from bratwurst to knockwurst—along with deli meats, cheeses, and German and other Northern European specialty foods. There's also a small array of gifts. *Mon–Sat; map:I8*

BEACON MARKET / 2500 Beacon Ave S; 206/323-2050 A large, full-line Asian grocery store with row after row of canned and dried foods from Taiwan, Thailand, the Philippines, Japan, Korea, and Singapore. The produce section is good, with offerings like long beans and green papayas. Look for interesting species at the smallish seafood counter (lionfish, golden thread fish). Tilapia and catfish swim in the live tank (and you can't beat that for freshness). Reasonable prices draw customers from all over the area. *Every day; map:II6*

BRITISH PANTRY LTD. / 8125 161st Ave NE, Redmond; 425/883-7511 Whether you are a homesick Brit or simply a devotee of the best of the U.K., this cheerful outpost of civility is a good destination. It stocks must-haves like mushy peas, pork pies, curries, Fortnum & Mason teas, biscuits, and the like. A tearoom/restaurant and an English gift shop with items such as British Christmas crackers complete the picture. *Every day; map:EE1*

BORRACCHINI'S BAKERY AND MEDITERRANEAN MARKET / 2307 Rainier Ave S; 206/325-1550 People have been thronging to this Rainier Valley institution for years for the good selection of (and even better prices on) imported Italian foods and wines. There are fresh and frozen pastas, deli meats and cheeses, and, of course, the famous bakery. Tens of thousands of birthdays, retirements, and anniversaries have been celebrated with a Borracchini's sheet cake. The process is straightforward: you choose the cake (white, chocolate, banana, or carrot), the filling (lemon, raspberry, custard, mocha, or one of four others), and the message, and the expert decorators do the rest. *Every day; map:II6*

BRIE & BORDEAUX / 2227 N 56th St; 206/633-3538 Brie & Bordeaux prides itself on offering an astonishing range of cheeses, especially from such locals as Sally Jackson and specialists like Neal's Yard, all cut to order. The shop even maintains a "nursery" for ripening cheese to the peak of perfection. This small shop also offers a thoughtful array of wines not typically found in grocery stores, specially selected to complement food. The knowledgeable staff will, if you like, guide you to a great wine to partner your cheese selection. The bistro is open for lunch and dinner weekdays and for brunch on weekends. *Tues–Sun; map:EE7*

CASCIOPPO BROTHERS ITALIAN MEAT MARKET / 2364 NW 80th St; 206/784-6121 Seattle's only Italian meat market, a longtime Ballard tradition, carries several lines of imported Italian specialty foods. The Italian sausage is spicy and excellent (it's the choice of many Italian restaurants in town), and some customers consider the homemade pepperoni the hottest in the world. The pastrami, though not exactly Italian, is famous as the best in the city. *Every day; map:EE8*

COST PLUS IMPORTS / 2103 Western Ave (and branches); 206/443-1055 This large import store (part of a California-based chain) has a little of everything—rattan furniture, glass storage jars, faux Italian pottery, corn-shaped candles. It also offers some good deals on tea, coffee, spices, and hard-to-find gourmet packaged goods such as the bread mixes from Bette's Ocean View Diner in Berkeley. The wine prices are also very good, but you need to know what you want—there's no one on hand to offer assistance. Besides the downtown Seattle store, branches are in Lynnwood, Bellevue, and Tukwila. *Every day; map:H8*

CUCINA FRESCA / 1904 Pike Pl, Pike Place Market; 206/448-4758 When you just don't feel like cooking, or when you want to supplement your meal with some flavorful sides, this is a hip, attractive source for lunch or dinner to go. Try some of the potato-and-roasted-onion ravioli, a towering slice of lasagne, or the thickly sliced roasted eggplant with mint and olive oil. Good fresh noodles are always available, some with alluring flavors such as red pepper or lemon. Prices are somewhat spendy. *Every day; map:I8*

DELAURENTI SPECIALTY FOOD MARKETS / 1435 1st Ave, Pike Place Market; 206/622-0141 ▪ 317 Bellevue Way NE, Bellevue; 425/454-7155 A Market anchor for more than 50 years, DeLaurenti is a popular source for international foodstuffs, mostly Mediterranean, and is nearly as well known for its great service. The narrow aisles are dense with canned goods, olives, olive oils, imported pasta, and truffles. The deli is noted for its excellent meats, and the Market location has over 160 kinds of cheese. Bakers love the imported chocolates and dried fruits. The wine department is known for its Italian labels and good selection. The baked-goods department features breads from some of the area's best bakers, although most are marked DeLaurenti. The Bellevue location has less of everything, but it's still well stocked with wonderful imported food and wine. *Mon–Sat; map:J8; map:HH3*

DON & JOE'S MEATS / 85 Pike St, Pike Place Market; 206/682-7670 Located under the clock in the Main Arcade, Don & Joe's is the best butcher in the Market, and many shoppers contend that they offer the best meat in town. Their smoked ham, fresh turkeys, and lamb chops are superb. Lamb's tongue, sheep's head, sweetbreads, and tripe can be yours, too. They'll even give your veal tenderloin the "mother-in-law treatment"—

tenderizing it with the flat side of a cleaver. Don't be put off by the crowd at the counter; service is friendly and speedy. *Mon–Sat; map:J8*

EL MERCADO LATINO / 1514 Pike Pl, Pike Place Market; 206/623-3240 This tiny store in the Sanitary Market is well stocked with the fresh and preserved ingredients of Caribbean, South American, Spanish, Creole, and Thai cuisines. Its front boasts a greengrocery stocked with vegetables and fruits. Chiles are a specialty, with six to eight fresh varieties and more dried and canned. Many hard-to-find spices, dried edible flowers, beans, and fruit drinks, too. The staff is very friendly—bring your recipe along for extra help. *Every day; map:J8*

FISCHER MEATS AND SEAFOODS / 85 Front St N, Issaquah; 425/392-3131 An Issaquah institution since 1910, this is the place to go for chicken—it's delivered fresh daily, as is the seafood. Fischer also makes its own German, Italian, potato, and smoked sausages, as well as beef and turkey jerky. Good, old-fashioned service. *Mon–Sat*

GEORGE'S SAUSAGE AND DELICATESSEN / 907 Madison St; 206/622-1491 A true Polish grocery with a faithful clientele. Come here for Hungarian peppers, Polish sauerkraut, pickled vegetables, mustards, preserves, juices, and candies. George's own authentic kielbasa, blood sausage, and potato salad are made in the back. Reasonable prices, friendly service. *Mon–Sat; map:M4*

HUSKY DELI / 4721 California Ave SW; 206/937-2810 A true Seattle jewel, this is a wonderful deli and market that's been in the West Seattle Junction since the 1930s. The Miller family sets a high standard, offering only the best-tasting foods. There's a wide array of fancy mustards, dressings, crackers, and candies. They also boast some of the greatest homemade ice cream in the city, a whopping 40 flavors, offered by the cone or the half gallon. The large, hand-dipped Husky milk shakes are not to be missed. Premium cold cuts and cheeses, plus some scrumptious sandwiches and salads to go. There's a small lunch bar and sidewalk seating. Catering, too, at very reasonable prices. *Every day; map:KK9*

THE INCREDIBLE LINK / 1511 Pike Pl, Pike Place Market; 206/622-8002 The name may sound like hype, but Jimi Dorsey and his extended family make sausages that actually live up to it. Their Pike Place Market sausage kitchen (you can watch the preparations through the glass-front window in the heart of the Market) adjoins the small retail shop. These incredible links have no nitrates, preservatives, fillers, MSG, or meat by-products and include incendiary Louisiana hot links, chorizo, and English bangers, among others. For those who just say no to red meat, there are links made with seafood, chicken, or turkey (and a veggie version complete with fruit, rice, sunflower seeds, and tofu). Jimi and crew will even custom-make sausage to your specifications. Try a grilled sausage sandwich and you won't have to be convinced to take home a pound or two. The owners plan to open a second location on the Eastside sometime soon. *Every day; map:J8*

KOSHER DELIGHT / 1509 1st Ave; 206/682-8140 You don't have to keep kosher to appreciate the offerings at Kosher Delight. The charming, friendly owner, Michel Chriqui, runs a sparkling *glatt* (the highest rating) kosher deli. Customers can nosh on several kinds of knishes, lox, bagels, kosher tofu "cream cheese," and other eat-in fare. Closed on the Sabbath. *Sun–Fri; map:J7*

LARRY'S MARKETS / 10008 Aurora Ave N (and branches); 206/527-5333 A supermarket that's really a high-style specialty market, Larry's is a treasure. If you're looking for something unusual, especially if it's au courant, you'll likely find it here. Vast selection, excellent service, and top quality are the rules. In addition to regular supermarket offerings, there's organic produce, lots of ethnic foods and spices, a line of Oriental macrobiotic products, and a Biofoods section with natural and organic foods, created by owner Larry McKinney and his family. The Queen Anne store has an exemplary meat-and-seafood counter. The cheese selection runs from 200 to 400 varieties, depending on the store. Queen Anne, Totem Lake, and Bellevue have temperature-controlled wine rooms; Bellevue offers cooking classes. Branches are in North Seattle, Queen Anne, Totem Lake, Bellevue, and Sea-Tac. *Every day; map:DD7*

THE MEXICAN GROCERY / 1914 Pike Pl, Pike Place Market; 206/441-1147 When it's time to move beyond tacos and burritos, you'll find all the necessary Mexican ingredients in this tidy little store in the Market's Soames-Dunn Building. Chicharrones, mole, Mexican chocolate, corn husks, and more than a dozen kinds of dried chiles are available here, along with Mexican canned goods and fresh salsas. The grocery's own La Mexicana fresh tortillas come in corn, flour, organic blue corn, or red chile flavors. Call ahead for uncooked hominy for posole and masa dough for tamales. *Every day; map:J8*

OLSEN'S SCANDINAVIAN FOODS / 2248 NW Market St; 206/783-8288 Whether or not you are familiar with Scandinavian foods, this sparkling Ballard shop is worth a trip to the neighborhood. Owned by the Olsen family for nearly 30 years, it has more than lefse, lingonberries, and lutefisk. They make their own Scandinavian cold cuts and pickled herring, and import cheeses, cod balls, Swedish caviar pastes, soup and pudding mixes, and more. Just-baked Scandinavian cookies and fragrant cardamom rolls are specialties. *Every day; map:FF8*

ORIENTAL MART / 1506 Pike Pl, Pike Place Market; 206/622-8488 This is a very good place to find basic ingredients for Filipino, Korean, Indonesian, Vietnamese, Chinese, and Japanese cooking. The staff, mostly from the Philippines, are always glad to help with recipes. The lunch counter has inexpensive Filipino lunches, like adobo chicken, and suman—a rice dessert wrapped in banana leaves. Located in the Corner Market (enter where you see the jumping paper slugs). *Every day; map:J8*

PACIFIC FOOD IMPORTERS (PFI) / 1001 6th Ave S; 206/682-2022 A genuine treasure trove for the savvy foodie, this is the retail outlet for Seattle's biggest wholesale importer. Great deals on European cheeses, meats, dried pastas, bulk beans and lentils, and spices. The selection of Greek and Italian olive oils is extensive, and no one can beat the prices here on bulk feta or kalamata olives (bring your own lidded container and they'll add brine to preserve your purchase). Decor is early warehouse; service is friendly. Be mindful: meats, cheeses, and olives have a 1-pound minimum; meats and cheeses are sold unsliced (PFI doesn't have a slicer). Come early on Saturdays; the checkout lines can be long, and closing time is 2pm. *Tues–Sat; map:II7*

PACIFIC MARKET / 12332 Lake City Way NE; 206/363-8639 A real find for those who love the fragrant complexities of Persian cuisine. New owner Shawn Moghaddam stocks her store with pussy-willow water, sour-grape juice, dried limes, pomegranate molasses, Persian teas—and a lot more you won't find anywhere else. A deli case offers Bulgarian feta cheese, mortadella, and dolmades (stuffed grape leaves). Persian breads, cookbooks, music, and videos from before and after the Iranian revolution, too. *Every day; map:CC6*

PASTA & CO. / University Village (and branches); 206/523-8594 The oft-imitated Pasta & Co. is one of Seattle's favorite take-out joints, as well as a dependable source for olive oil, balsamic vinegar, and other European-style foodstuffs. Marcella Rosene's fresh pastas, sauces, salads, and entrees usually taste as wonderful as they look. Choose from the healthy-style quinoa and other whole grain salads, or go for broke with the robust lasagne, cheese-filled tortellini, and cream-based sauces. Branches are located downtown in the 1001 4th Avenue Plaza, on Queen Anne, on Capitol Hill, and in Bellevue. *Every day; map:FF6*

PIKE PLACE MARKET CREAMERY / 1514 Pike Pl, Pike Place Market; 206/622-5029 Locals come here for exceptional dairy foods and eggs. You'll find Russian yogurt, kefirs, goat and soy milk products, rich heavy cream, unsalted butter, and ice creams. They also sell naturally colored aracauna chicken eggs, fresh duck and quail eggs, and more. Located in the Sanitary Market. *Every day; map:J8*

QUALITY CHEESE / 1508 Pike Pl, Pike Place Market; 206/624-4029 Peerless quality and a superb selection distinguish this old-fashioned cheese shop, which has been in the Corner Market since World War II. Owner Shirley Linteau hand-selects her cheeses from the United States and Europe, and champions local handmade varieties like Sally Jackson's goat's-milk cheeses. Friendly staff members will cordially let you taste as you make your choice. *Every day; map:J8*

SCANDINAVIAN SPECIALTY PRODUCTS / 8539 15th Ave NW; 206/784-7020 Its space may be small, but this shop stocks an incredible array of imported Scandinavian vegetables, jams, fish, cheeses, coffees, and flatbreads. The broad selection attracts customers from all over the United States. One wall is dense with Norwegian and Swedish candies and chocolates. Owners Ruby and Herb Anderson make authentic Norwegian meat rolls and sausages, and fresh fish pudding. Quality and cleanliness are tip-top; Herb is a former food inspector for the Department of Health. At Christmas, look for traditional treats. They even have marzipan pigs. *Mon–Sat; map:EE8*

SEATTLE SUPER SMOKE / 2454 Occidental Ave S; 206/625-1339 Seattle Super Smoke caught on so feverishly with Seattle palates that it had to move to much larger quarters. Its main business is wholesale, but you can also buy this deeply smoky, alderwood-redolent poultry and meat from a retail deli. The barbecue sauce is a fine accompaniment. *Mon–Fri; map:II7*

THE SOUK / 1916 Pike Pl, Pike Place Market; 206/441-1666 ▪ 11730 Pinehurst Way NE; 206/367-8387 This esoteric Market store provides a tremendous inventory of Middle Eastern and Indian delicacies: dal and lentils in every color, bulghur sold by coarseness, unusual flours, spice pastes, and lots of chutneys. The shop may be tiny, but the array of ingredients is dazzling. It's a good idea to know what you're looking for; the staff are not always much help. There's also a store in Pinehurst. *Every day; map:J8; map:DD6*

TSUE CHONG (ROSE BRAND) COMPANY INC. / 801 S King St; 206/623-0801 This understated Chinese noodle shop offers high-quality fresh and dried noodles as well as steamed noodles for frying, slim soup noodles, and fresh wontons and gyoza wrappers. They also bake 11 flavors of fortune cookies—and you can custom-order fortunes. *Mon–Sat; map:R5*

UWAJIMAYA / 519 6th Ave S; 206/624-6248 ▪ 15555 NE 24th St, Bellevue; 425/747-9012 The cornerstone of the International District, this large supermarket sells all kinds of Asian foods—as well as a lot of other stuff, from small electrical appliances (rice cookers, woks) and housewares to gifts and makeup. The real distinctions, though, are its wide variety of canned goods, its depth of choice (one aisle is wholly devoted to rice), its fresh shellfish tanks, and its produce department. You'll find fresh geoduck, live prawns and crabs, bitter melons, water chestnuts, and all the makings for sushi. Service is quite knowledgeable. The Bellevue store has a fine Asian bakery case. Both branches have in-store cafes with Asian food for eating in or carrying out. *Every day; map:Q7; map:GG1*

VIET WAH SUPERMARKET / 1032 S Jackson St; 206/329-1399 If you can stand a little funkiness, this is truly one of the best Chinese and Southeast Asian grocery stores in town. You'll find all the ingredients you need (and you'll no doubt be seduced by the vast variety of things you don't need) to stock an estimable Asian pantry. A simply amazing assortment of produce and fresh seafood, and a butcher shop, too (the chicken is so cheap it's nearly free). There's a Chinese herbal pharmacy near the entrance. *Every day; map:HH7*

WELCOME SUPERMARKET / 1200 S Jackson St; 206/329-7044 Welcome Supermarket is the real thing, an authentic International District grocery with a broad array of Asian greens and fruit and a low-priced selection of rice, including bags of Thai black sticky rice. It also offers seafood and canned goods. *Every day; map:HH6*

FLORISTS AND NURSERIES

BAINBRIDGE GARDENS / 9415 Miller Rd NE, Bainbridge Island; 206/842-5888 A country nursery with a fine selection of woody plants, Bainbridge Gardens has theme gardens for herbs, perennials, grasses, water plants, and shade plants. There's also a well-stocked garden gift shop. The restored Harui Memorial Garden (begun in 1908, abandoned during World War II) showcases bonsai trees, and a nature trail loops through native woods. In November and December, you can reserve a wreath-making machine (no fee) and fabricate your own Northwestern holiday gifts (there's UPS service on site as well). A small outdoor cafe offers beverages, snacks, and light lunches. *Every day*

BALLARD BLOSSOM / 1766 NW Market St; 206/782-4213 Family-run since 1927, Ballard Blossom offers a cheerful profusion of fresh flowers, silk flowers, dried flowers, potted plants, and gift items. The friendly staff can send many selections anywhere in the world, while personally chosen arrangements can be delivered areawide. *Mon–Sat (open Sun in Dec); www.ftd.com/ballardblossom; map:FF8*

BAY HAY AND FEED / 10355 Valley Rd, Bainbridge Island; 206/842-2813 A funky storefront that has served the Rolling Bay neighborhood of Bainbridge Island for more than a century, Bay Hay and Feed carries a great selection of farm- and garden-related toys, gifts, books, and clothing. The small nursery is ably staffed and offers a full range of edible and ornamental plants, including some collector's treasures. Rustic lawn furniture, hand tools, and unusual clay pots are specialties. *Every day*

CAPITOL HILL FLOWER AND GARDEN / 300 15th Ave E; 206/325-5068
You can order exquisite, deceptively simple, Oriental-type arrangements at this family-owned business, maybe with orchid and tuberose and curly willow; or something loose and airy in English country garden style, with unusual greenery and fewer flowers, base price $20. Something else? Just ask. A good selection of potted plants lines the floor. Deliveries to greater Seattle and worldwide. *Every day; map:HH6*

CHASES DOWNTOWN FLORIST / 1201 3rd Ave; 206/625-9500 This small shop in the Washington Mutual Tower does distinctive, classy arrangements in French country style. Exotic flowers are a specialty. There's always a large selection on hand: you can order 300 roses on the spur of the moment, and they'll say, "No problem." Chases carries a few gift items, seeds, and potted plants as well. Arrangements from $25, areawide and worldwide delivery. *Mon–Fri, and Sat by appointment; map:K7*

CITY FLOWERS INC. / 1191 2nd Ave (and branches); 206/622-6760 City Flowers' gorgeous arrangements follow French country and English garden styles, often including wildflowers, but with no mums, no carnations, and nothing cutesy. You'll find a few cards and potpourris at the tiny downtown shop, and more gifts at the stores in Bellevue (10500 NE 8th St, Bellevue; 425/454-0882; Mon–Sat; map:HH2) and on Capitol Hill (123 Broadway E; 206/323-7943; every day; map:GG7). Arrangements from $22; areawide and worldwide delivery. *Mon–Fri; www.cityflowers.com; map:L7*

CITY PEOPLE'S GARDEN STORE / 2939 E Madison St (and branches); 206/324-0737 An urban nursery for the serious gardener and a delight to walk through, City People's offers not only plants (though the selection of both garden plants and houseplants is very good here) but gifts, garden tools, books, furniture, ornaments, and a full-service florist's shop, with English garden–style arrangements or any other style you might ask for. Areawide and worldwide delivery. Additional branches carry more housewares, clothing, and hardware and fewer nursery items; these are located on Capitol Hill, in Fremont, and on Sand Point Way NE. *Every day; map:GG6*

CRISSEY FLOWERS AND GIFTS / 2100 5th Ave; 206/448-1100 First opened in the 1890s (and bearing the Crissey name for the past 50 years or so), this is surely the oldest established florist in the city, specializing in English garden–style arrangements and the tropical hi-style—a synthesis of Dutch and Japanese traditions, base price $25. From private dinner parties to corporate galas, weddings to wakes, this is a full-service florist that does everything with excellence, delivering areawide and worldwide. *Mon–Sat; www.ftd.com/crissey; map:H6*

ENCHANTED GARDEN / 1524 Pike Pl, Pike Place Market; 206/625-1205
Open only a couple of years, Enchanted Garden has made its mark with highly unusual and beautiful plants—orchids, bromeliads, cacti, succulents. You can find a vellerigera here—a large, fuzzy, red and gold hanging bloom (mistaken by some for a creature)—or a fern curl as large as a shepherd's crook. Artist-trained designers mix tropical, garden, and wildflowers into lush, inspiring creations. Deliveries within greater Seattle. *Every day; map:I8*

MARTHA E. HARRIS FLOWERS AND GIFTS / 4218 E Madison St; 206/568-0347 The florist shop is way at the back, past fine accessories, jewelry, and accent pieces for the home. Expect extravagant, dramatic, bountiful arrangements from Martha Harris, whose Euro-Northwest style is not of the arrange-by-numbers sort: each is an original. Parties and weddings are her specialties, and she maintains a bridal registry. Deliveries within greater Seattle and worldwide. *Every day; map:GG6*

MEGAN MARY OLANDER FLORIST / 222 1st Ave S; 206/623-6660 Loose, elegant arrangements in the European country garden style characterize this little shop in Pioneer Square. Border perennials and wildflowers are often included among the hothouse beauties, all of which can be bought by the stem (the pleasant staff offers expert advice and assistance if you need it). Olander also carries a pretty assortment of containers that display exuberant bouquets to advantage, as well as French ribbon, dried wreaths, and tussy-mussies. Weddings and corporate accounts are specialties, but walk-ins are welcome. Deliveries areawide and worldwide. *Mon–Fri, and Sat by appointment; map:O8*

MOLBAK'S GREENHOUSE AND NURSERY / 13625 NE 175th St, Woodinville (and branches); 425/483-5000 Lavish holiday displays bring visitors here in droves, but Molbak's is an attraction any time of year for those who love to drink in the scent of growing things amid the sounds of water and singing birds. This is rich ground for the novice and the expert gardener, both of whom will find plenty to explore among the hundreds of houseplants and the full range of outdoor plants (everything from trees to ground covers). Molbak's also offers gifts, a Christmas shop, a garden store, and distinctive floral designs. Branches are in University Village (206/754-6500; map:FF6) and Pike Place Market (Seattle Garden Center; 1600 Pike Pl; 206/448-0431; map:I8). *Every day; map:BB2*

PIKE PLACE FLOWERS / 1st Ave and Pike St, Pike Place Market; 206/682-9797 Here you'll find contemporary, original, and tropical hi-style arrangements (and no carnations or pompoms). You can buy bunches of flowers for as little as $2 and arrangements for $15 and up ($30 minimum on deliveries, areawide or worldwide). Staff are enthusiastically helpful. *Every day; map:J7*

PIKE PLACE MARKET / Pike Place Several of the market stalls carry generous, imaginative arrangements of locally grown flowers, fresh and dried, at very low prices. Great to brighten your hotel room. Containers are utilitarian. Cash and carry. *Map:J8*

SWANSON'S NURSERY AND GREENHOUSE / 9701 15th Ave NW; 206/782-2543 A riot of exuberant color greets you at Swanson's. With 5 acres of display gardens that are a joy to wander through, this excellent full-service nursery includes uncommon plants of all kinds. Perennials are a specialty, but in every category, from trees and shrubs through ground covers to houseplants, Swanson's emphasizes choice offerings over sheer quantity. A cafe in the gift shop offers light meals and espresso amid European garden tools, books, knickknacks, and handsome planting containers. *Every day; garden@swansonsnursery.com; www.swansonsnursery.com; map:DD8*

WELLS-MEDINA NURSERY / 8300 NE 24th St, Medina; 425/454-1853 The perennial-lover's favorite nursery, regionally famed for depth and variety, this is also the place to buy choice shrubs—the selection of rhododendrons and Japanese maples is unmatched in the area. Look here for unusual vines, bulbs, and ground covers as well, and check out the long demonstration border (newly redesigned). The excellent plant range and prices are complemented by a knowledgeable and helpful staff. *Every day; map:GG4*

YOUNG FLOWERS / 1111 3rd Ave; 206/628-3077 Mark Young keeps this busy downtown corner exciting with knockout displays of fresh and unusual flowers. Most of the arrangements here are natural in style, European in flavor; if you want drama, charm, spunk, or sheer romance, just ask—he can do that, too. Buy by the stem, and the staff will gladly share tips on assembling your own floral creations. Base price for arrangements is $35. No weddings, but they handle lots of parties and corporate accounts. Fair prices and lovely products, fully guaranteed. Area deliveries, plus wire service throughout the United States and Canada. *Mon–Fri; map:L7*

FURNITURE

CAPE COD COMFYS / 114 N 36th St; 206/545-4309 In this small Fremont shop you'll find comfortable cedar resort furniture that actually works well indoors, too. Owner Dwight Jacobson makes the low-slung Adirondack chairs—the ultimate in casual reclining, with their wide, flat arms perfect for holding a tall, cold drink and a book on a balmy summer day. Child-size chairs are available too. The shop also sells sturdy hammocks for slinging between two trees in the shade. *Every day; map:FF7*

CHICKEN & EGG STORE / 1426 Alaskan Way; 206/623-6144 Besides the peeled Douglas fir rocking chairs, benches, and beds made by Chicken & Egg (whose profits from the log furniture line go to nonprofit organizations, including the Children's Trust Program), the store has plenty of Northwest-originated home furnishings and accessories, as well as Pendleton blankets, specialty foods, and jewelry. There's a lot of square footage in which to browse. *Every day; map:K8*

DEL-TEET FURNITURE / 10308 NE 10th St, Bellevue; 206/462-5400 Del-Teet's Bellevue showroom sports an emphasis on classic-contemporary Northwest items in addition to its stock of gifts and accessories. Furniture can be custom-made here, and an interior design service is provided. *Every day; map:HH3*

KASALA / 1505 Western Ave; 206/623-7795 ▪ 1014 116th Ave NE, Bellevue; 425/453-2823 Kasala emphasizes moderate prices and modern, space-conscious lifestyles. Its collection includes contemporary, trendy European home accessories—with an emphasis on lighting systems—plus glassware, gift items, and furniture. *Every day; map:J8; map:HH3*

MASINS / 220 2nd Ave S; 206/622-5606 ▪ 10245 Main St, Bellevue; 425/450-9999 Talk about staying power: the Masin family has been in the business more than 70 years and have been selling furniture from this Pioneer Square location since the late '30s. This traditional store's extensive showrooms display the full range of classic furnishing styles from such names as Stickley, Henredon, Drexel-Heritage, and Karastan. The proficient staff offer free in-home consultations. *Every day; www.masins. com; map:O8; map:HH3*

MODELE'S HOME FURNISHINGS / 1006 Western Ave; 206/287-9942 Why buy new when you can buy honestly priced preowned furniture that looks this good? Stock changes weekly (if not more often) and moves quickly as buyers get hip and the client base continues to grow. Occasional new pieces are also displayed, along with preowned carpets and artwork. A small, artful stock of new home accessories (table linens, vases, and candles among them) makes for good browsing. *Every day; map:L8*

PENNSYLVANIA WOODWORKS / 17705 140th Ave NE, Woodinville; 425/486-9541 Many of the pieces here are individually made by the Amish; they're simple, traditional designs in solid woods (no veneers). Prices reflect the handcrafting. If the store doesn't have what you want, the pleasant sales staff will be happy to place a special order. Admire the Amish-made quilts and rugs, and don't leave without buying a little trinket (say, a candleholder or a kitchen hook) fit for the slimmer purse. *Every day; map:BB1*

GIFTS/HOME ACCESSORIES

BELLE PROVENCE / **Country Village, Bothell; 425/483-4696** Tucked inside quaint Country Village is this spirited and artful shop. Antique-reproduction jewelry, Hungarian porcelain, unusual children's books, and fragrant European toiletries line the shelves and give both collectors and browsers a shopping experience abundant with possibilities. *Every day; map:AA3*

THE BEST OF ALL WORLDS / **523 Union St; 206/623-2525** This downtown shop is crowded with fine and esoteric stuff for the home: wrought-metal birdcages, tapestry pillows, sumptuous and unusual tabletop accessories, French flatware, and linens from all over the world. A nice eye for detail distinguishes the merchandise here as something special. *Mon–Sat; map:K6*

BITTERS CO. / **513 N 36th St; 206/632-0886** It looks much like a fashionably restored garage, but sisters Amy and Katie Carson have turned this stylishly simple space (named for their mother, whose maiden name was Bitters) into a classic Fremont showplace that they liken to an eclectic general store. Scouring the world, the United States, and their adopted city in a well-honed, no-chotchkes-need-apply fashion, they stock their store with antique tools and buttons, ceramic wares, weathered wood furnishings, artistic textiles, jewelry, and other pretties. *Tues–Sun; map:FF8*

BIZANGO / **759 N 80th St; 206/784-7455** ▪ **1811 Queen Anne Ave N; 206/285-0693** Visitors will find every inch of these eye-popping stores well used: walls are lined with vivid objets d'art, Mexican masks, clocks, and magnets, while countertops and tables spill over with journals, folk art items, homemade soaps, frames, and candles. The focus here is on fun and wacky hand-created items, made by local, national, and international artisans. *Every day; map:EE7; map:GG8*

BOW WOW MEOW TREATORIA / **1415 N 45th St; 206/545-0740** ▪ **7508 164th Ave NE, Redmond, Redmond Town Center; 425/556-9899** As the name implies, this store is every pet's and every pet-lover's dream. The Wallingford branch is housed in a converted bungalow, and stocks its Sit Stay Deli with freshly made, nutritious pet treats—sampling by your four-legged friend is certainly encouraged. Additional rooms are filled with greeting cards, jewelry, mugs, T-shirts, frames, and clocks, all featuring the irresistible likenesses of cats and dogs. Pet gear and natural grooming and health care products are also available. The Redmond branch carries almost all of the same merchandise in a slightly less appealing space. *Every day; map:FF7; map:EE1*

BUYING NATIVE AMERICAN ART

The history of this area's native peoples is inextricably woven into the fabric of the city of Seattle. One of the richest expressions of the traditions of the Northwest Coast tribes, including those from British Columbia and Alaska, is through their art and art objects. Purchasing an antique Haida mask or a contemporary Tlingit blanket is a wonderful way to take home a piece of the region's soul—much more satisfying than T-shirts and cheap souvenirs, and more rewarding as the years go by.

Although collecting is an individual pursuit, as is the creation of the art itself, here are a few rules of thumb to think about as you shop.

Do your homework. To many collectors, this is the most enjoyable part of the whole experience—even better than actually making a purchase. Visit museums—both the Seattle Art Museum and the Burke Museum have excellent Northwest Coast collections. Buy art books or check them out from the library, and peruse the galleries. Eventually, you'll become familiar with the distinct styles of particular regions and groups, and you'll be able to identify examples of the types of art that speak to you.

Make sure it's authentic. Whether the piece you choose is contemporary or antique, ensure it's authenticity by asking the dealer for the artists's name and tribal affiliation, and getting the information in writing. A good dealer will have this information on hand and will be eager to tell you about the background of each piece he or she sells. If the dealer doesn't know, you may want to contact the tribe and ask yourself before making a purchase.

Shop within your price range. Consider purchasing a moderately priced contemporary mask or carving rather than an antique piece, which could well run into four or five figures. Be realistic about what you can spend, and be honest with the dealer so that he or she can help you find what you want.

Get the story behind the art. Once you find a piece you like, take time to learn the meaning behind the symbolism of the design. All Native American art springs from story and narrative; the more you know about a piece, the more value and meaning it will hold for you. Again, a good dealer will be enthusiastic about relaying the origin of each piece of art.

Buy only what you love. Purchasing art as an investment is a proposition best left to dealers with vast resources. It's better to buy a piece you really love on its own merits than to buy with the hope that it will go up in value. Choose a piece you'll want to live with and enjoy for a long time.

— Jo Brown

BURKE MUSEUM STORE / University of Washington; 206/685-0909
Housed inside the Burke Museum at the northwest corner of the UW campus, the gift store follows the museum's lead. Browse the selection of Northwest Coast Native American art, silkscreen prints, basketry, and wooden boxes, and don't miss the geological specimens and dinosaur replicas. *Every day; map:FF6*

BURNT SUGAR / 604 N 34th St; 206/545-0699 This sunny, colorful Fremont store stands out among several newly opened shops that cleverly combine vintage furnishings and accessories with imaginative contemporary pieces. Funky suitcases from the '40s, chrome kitchen tables, well-loved cabinets, and old school desks are accented with lushly colored candles, frames, cheery linens, and bright dishes. If your home needs that retro touch, this is the place to find it. *Every day; map:FF8*

CRACKERJACK CONTEMPORARY CRAFTS / 1815 N 45th St, Wallingford Center; 206/547-4983 Showcasing many local artists, Crackerjack, which holds a central position in classy Wallingford Center, is a gift buyer's paradise. Candles, wooden boxes, whimsical dishes, aromatic soaps, and finely crafted jewelry and hats find a home here. The store also stocks a delightful array of pet items. *Every day; map:FF7*

DESIGN CONCERN / 1420 5th Ave, City Centre; 206/623-4444 An eclectic array of items fills this sleek, contemporary, two-level store, but all share at least one feature: unique, functional, topnotch design. Pens and desktop accessories, handcrafted jewelry, watches, leather goods, and housewares and glassware from around the world make browsing a pleasure here. *Every day; map:J5*

DOMUS / Bellevue Square, Bellevue; 425/454-2728 Bellevue Square's best housewares store carries an extremely well chosen stock—wineglasses, linen towels, jewelry, note cards, furniture, china, aprons, cutlery. Affordable, with a sleek, modern inclination. There's also a bridal registry. *Every day; map:HH3*

EGBERT'S / 2231 1st Ave; 206/728-5682 You'll rarely see the same thing twice at this Belltown address, but you can be assured of finding creative, fine-quality items all the time. An Italian leather chair sets off a Scandinavian dining table in light wood; jewelry from around the world approaches museum quality; African art mixes with folklore-inspired bronzes. There is even some clothing thrown in for good measure. The potpourri style is executed quite successfully by owner Jim Egbert, whose eclectic tastes run the gamut from whimsical to functional. *Mon–Sat; map:G8*

EXPLORE MORE STORE / Pacific Science Center, Seattle Center; 206/443-2870 Don't let the educational benefits of browsing here deter you from a visit—it's fun, too. The shop ties in with the Pacific Science

Center exhibits, so you'll find minerals, astronomy paraphernalia, dinosaur items, and other science-related toys and books for children. The collection of crystals is extensive—and affordable, compared with those of the New Age specialty stores. *Every day; map:C7*

FIREWORKS GALLERY / 210 1st Ave S (and branches); 206/682-8707 No old grandmom gifts here; if it's clever, quirky, and fun, this shop probably has it. FireWorks displays a compelling array of ceramics, glass, and other handcrafted wares—from the wild and whimsical to the elegantly functional. A browse through the store is your best introduction to the work of choice local artisans as well as outside talent. Great offbeat jewelry, fiber art, and woodwork. A lot of fun at Christmas (there's tree-trimming stuff like you've never seen). Other branches are at Westlake Center, Bellevue Square, and University Village. *Every day; map:O8*

FOX PAW / 160 Winslow Way W, Bainbridge Island; 206/842-7788 With her assortment of artwork, jewelry, books, photo frames, note cards, linens, and lace, owner Linda Allen has created an eclectic place to shop. Esoteric music and exceptional gifts, clothing galore, and home furnishings. *Every day*

FRANK AND DUNYA / 3418 Fremont Ave N; 206/547-6760 Quirky Frank and Dunya are the owners' departed dogs, and their likenesses perpetually, cheerfully greet all comers. The store is filled with handmade furniture, unique jewelry, whimsical artwork, and accessories—nearly all crafted locally. Everything here is a character piece—overwhelmingly so. Expensive, and well worth it. *Every day; map:FF7*

GARGOYLES / 4550 University Way NE; 206/632-4940 A gothic mood prevails in this small, candlelit shop specializing in—guess what?—gargoyles. The statuary comes from artists all over the country (some local), and a few sweet-faced angels are thrown in for good measure. Candleholders, shelf brackets, fountains, and statues of all sizes are available in a wide variety of weights and finishes. Truly remarkable (if spooky) stuff. *Every day; map:FF6*

GREAT JONES HOME / 1921 2nd Ave; 206/448-9405 French and American primitive items for the home fill this airy, expansive store. The owners make monthly jaunts to the Midwest and cart back one-of-a-kind treasures like aged cabinets, small shelves, and old farm tables, all wearing the faded, chipped paint that points to their years of use and care. Small wooden frames, handmade cards, heavenly scented candles, vintage American pottery, and slipcovers and bedding round out the offerings. Ulysses and Dexter, the owners' Jack Russell terriers, love to greet visitors and help point them in the direction of the designer pet items display. *Every day; map:I7*

KEEG'S / 10575 NE 12th St, Bellevue; 425/635-0655 Keeg's supplies all the pricey necessities for modern living: glassware, leather accessories, contemporary lighting, rugs, flatware, tables and chairs, and more, including wrapping paper and note cards. *Every day; map:GG3*

MADE IN WASHINGTON / 1530 Post Alley, Pike Place Market (and branches); 206/467-0788 And everything is—from crafts and local books to foodstuffs and wine. The selection is vast. You can assemble gift packages for friends who have the misfortune to live anywhere else. *Every day; map:J8*

MARKET GRAPHICS / 1935 1st Ave; 206/441-7732 From Leonardo da Vinci to Pop art, Market Graphics carries contemporary and classic art reproductions. The shop offers museum posters, black-and-white photographic reproductions, framing, and small gift items. The helpful owners provide special service to businesses decorating with posters. *Every day; map:I7*

MUSEUM OF FLIGHT STORE / 9404 E Marginal Way S; 206/764-5720 A barnstorm of aviation books: general, space, military, and literary. Models and posters are geared to all ages, from small plastic planes for kids to fairly complex airplane models for adult hobbyists. There's also a small outlet at—where else?—Sea-Tac Airport. *Every day; map:LL6*

NIDO / 1920½ 1st Ave; 206/443-1272 Pairing unusual antiques with contemporary items, Andrea Stuber-Margelou has a knack for putting together an eclectic collection of one-of-a-kind home accessories. You'll find body-care products, architectural artifacts, handcrafted jewelry, candles, and Victorian and chic European furniture side by side here. Definitely not for the budget-conscious. *Mon–Sat; map:I7*

NORTHWEST DISCOVERY / Bellevue Square, Bellevue; 425/454-1676 ■ ELEMENTS GALLERY / 10500 NE 8th St, Bellevue; 425/454-8242 Northwest Discovery is an Eastside showcase for local artists' work, featuring a fine woodwork collection of boxes, cribbage boards, and mirrors as well as tapestries, pottery, and wall art. Porcelain, silver, gold, and beaded jewelry are of distinctive design and reasonably priced. Elements Gallery displays handblown glass and jewelry in a gallery-like atmosphere. Owner Bonnie Altenburg is the spouse of Michael Altenburg, who owns Northwest Discovery. *Every day; map:HH3*

PHOENIX RISING / 2030 Western Ave; 206/728-2332 Maureen Pierre's Phoenix has risen steadily near the north end of Pike Place Market since she opened her fine crafts gallery in 1989. Her forte is carefully chosen and beautifully displayed functional art (glass, ceramics, jewelry, and even a few handcrafted furnishings), works that have garnered the shop national acclaim and make for original gifts. A full complement of

Northwest artists is represented. Though you can spend a bundle for a bauble, 25 percent of the stock is in the $50-and-under range. *Every day; map:H8*

PORTAGE BAY GOODS / 1121 Pike St; 206/622-3212 Combine good taste with do-good environmental and social awareness and you've got this warmly inviting shop, where you might browse comfortably for an hour among the crafts and handmade items. Much of the stock here is made from recycled materials or bought from international cooperatives, and it's all beautifully displayed on recycled wooden pallets: Spanish pottery, English pewter, Scottish yarns. On dreary days, the store's in-house espresso stand hits the spot. *Every day; map:J2*

POTTERY BARN / 600 Pine St, Pacific Place; 206/621-0276 ■ University Village; 206/522-6860 Specializing in tabletop and living-space accoutrements for the modern home, this stylish chain showcases stenciled cotton rugs, bold vases, a panoply of glass and stemware, garden accents, and frames—all practical, classy, and affordable to boot. Formerly in the City Centre building, the store moved to expanded quarters in Pacific Place in 1998. *Every day; map:J5; map:FF6*

RAGAZZI'S FLYING SHUTTLE / 607 1st Ave; 206/343-9762 Wondrous finds can be made here. This contemporary wearable-crafts gallery in Pioneer Square specializes in handsome, hand-woven clothing, as well as jewelry crafted from a wide range of media, including paper, glass, ceramics, and beads. A great place to find a gift. *Every day; map:N8*

SUNDANCE CATALOG COMPANY STORE/ University Village; 206/729-0750 A feast for the senses awaits those who enter Sundance, an offshoot of Robert Redford's Utah-based Sundance catalog and resort. This is the company's flagship store, and no expense was spared here in creating a rustic, American West ambience. The walls are made of rock quarried in Utah, and the supporting wood beams were salvaged from old barns. Aromatic dried flowers and herbs cultivated at Sundance Farms; distinctive Southwestern and antique-reproduction jewelry; stylish, durable clothing; handcrafted home accessories; gourmet salsas and jams—all evoke a feeling of endless horizons and sunny blue skies that Seattleites can only dream of on winter days. *Every day; map:FF6*

THREE FURIES / 1211 1st Ave; 206/442-9705 Three Furies is not (fortunately) owned by three terrible winged goddesses from Greek mythology. Instead, this artful, affordable shop offers winged angel statuary, unusual books and cards, personal care items, a multitude of lovely frames, small lamps, and a number of interesting crafts and seasonal surprises. *Every day; map:L8*

THE WEED LADY / 122 4th Ave S, Edmonds; 425/775-3800 Set in an old-fashioned house off the main street, this shop is fragrant with potpourris, dried everlastings, and soaps. The owner is especially creative with dried floral arrangements and does outstanding custom work for weddings and special occasions (ask to see her photo album). The Weed Lady offers seasonal classes in floral design, and her garden in the back of the store is a quiet oasis among the low-key bustle that is Edmonds. *Every day*

THE WELL MADE BED / University Village (and branches); 206/523-8407 Talk about the stuff that dreams are made of. Elegant dreams. Comfortable dreams. Expensive dreams. But when you consider that you spend a third of your life between the sheets, shelling out bucks for good bedding makes all the sense in the world. Sheets, pillow slips, comforters, dust ruffles, and custom-fitted or ready-made duvets are sold by staff who are eager to provide you with individual attention. They can special-order bed linens from any American manufacturer. Eastside branches are in Bellevue (990 102nd NE; 425/455-3508; map:HH3) and Redmond (Redmond Town Center; 425/881-1524; map:FF1). *Every day; map:FF6*

YE OLDE CURIOSITY SHOP / 1001 Alaskan Way, Pier 54; 206/682-5844 This "world-famous" Seattle attraction (since 1899) is a novelty stop for residents as well as tourists. It's a veritable kitsch museum, housing a remarkable collection of Northwest Indian and Eskimo art, ivory, and soapstone, plus imports, totem poles, and other curios. Weird and wonderful things are to be found among the souvenir junk, such as shrunken heads from the Jivaro tribe of South America. *Every day; map:L9*

Z GALLERIE / 1331 5th Ave, Rainier Square; 206/749-9906 ■ 16548 NE 74th St, Redmond Town Center, Redmond; 425/867-1588 A lot like Pottery Barn without the ubiquitous catalog, Z Gallerie offers tastefully displayed and surprisingly affordable home furnishings and decorative items geared toward upwardly mobile professionals. An abundance of worthy gift items, including chenille pillows and throws, beaded-shade lamps, and wrought-iron candleholders, supplements a smaller yet well-chosen selection of sofas, chairs, tables, and other furniture. Linens, tableware, and framed prints, too, as well as window treatments and sleek bath accessories. *Map:K6; map:FF1*

ZANADIA / 1815 N 45th St, Wallingford Center; 206/547-0884 Zanadia carries a wide range of contemporary, reasonably priced kitchen and lifestyle accessories, as well as rugs, clocks, mirrors, magazine racks, picture frames, and other can't-do-withouts. Lots of seasonal stuff and a good selection of furniture, too. The store recently created an addition to house even more goodies; it's located directly below the original store in the Wallingford Center basement. *Every day; map:FF7*

HEALTH FOOD STORES

CENTRAL CO-OP GROCERY / 1600 E Madison St; 206/329-1545 For 20 years, this Capitol Hill independent co-op has offered bulk foods, organic produce, and a wide range of macrobiotic products. The quality is consistently high, and the assortment of products in many specialty health categories is the best in town. It is an excellent source for special dietary needs (salt-free, sugar-free, wheat-free, and other alternatives). Nonmembers are welcome but pay a slightly higher price. *Every day; map:GG6*

THE GRAINERY / 13629 1st Ave S, Burien; 206/244-5015 It's not exactly a working mill, but this Burien store will grind your grain into flour. There's a large selection of whole grains, or you can purchase flours in bulk. You'll find beans, raw honeys, and vitamin and mineral supplements, as well as flour grinders, juicers, and bread machines. The very friendly staff is ready to offer help when you need it. *Mon–Sat; map:OO7*

MARLENE'S MARKET AND DELI / 31839 Gateway Center Blvd S, Federal Way; 253/839-0933 Marlene's has been a full-service market/deli/health-food store in south King County for going on 30 years. It offers organically grown produce, bulk grains, spices, natural cosmetics and body-care products, vitamins, herbs, and books. A natural-foods deli and bakery adjoins the store. *Every day*

NATURE'S PANTRY / 10200 NE 10th St, Bellevue (and branches); 425/454-0170 The Eastside's finest and most comprehensive natural foods store features all-organic produce, groceries, vitamins, natural cosmetics, and a sit-down deli/bakery with whole-grain baked goods. The Crossroads Shopping Center store (425/957-0090; map:HH1) has a state-of-the-art juice bar and there's a Mercer Island branch as well (7611 SE 27th St; 206/232-7900; Mon–Sat; map:II5). *Every day; map:HH3*

PCC NATURAL MARKETS / 6504 20th Ave NE (and branches); 206/525-1450 Formerly Puget Consumers' Co-op, PCC has evolved from an established co-operative into a full-line natural foods grocery store. Up to 10,000 people join the co-op each year, but nonmembers can shop here, too (though they pay a surcharge). Produce, much of it organic, is centrally displayed, and each store carries more than 200 whole foods available in bulk. PCC has a wide range of vitamins and supplements, packaged goods, frozen foods, beer and wine, and additive- and chemical-free meats, all at competitive prices. All stores have delis that offer heat-and-eat entrees, salads, desserts, sauces, and fresh pastas in addition to meats and cheeses; branches are located in several neighborhoods, including Green Lake, Fremont, Kirkland, and West Seattle. Each store also has a wine department and a small selection of gift items. *Every day; map:EE7*

RAINBOW GROCERY / 409 15th Ave E; 206/329-8440 The neighborhood grocery natural-style, this folksy little market features natural food products and healthy cosmetics at competitive prices. Much of the produce is organic, and the fine dairy department offers hormone-free milk and several varieties of cheese—some rennet-free. Great, friendly service. *Every day; map:HH6*

JEWELRY

ALVIN GOLDFARB JEWELER / 305 Bellevue Way NE, Bellevue; 425/454-9393 The owner learned his trade as a gemologist at Friedlander, his wife's family's business. Today Alvin Goldfarb provides unerring personal attention and quality. Many of Bellevue's affluent won't go anywhere else. *Mon–Sat; map:HH3* &

BEN BRIDGE / 1432 4th Ave (and branches); 206/628-6800 The best place for diamonds is Ben Bridge, in the same downtown location since 1912. The diamonds range from inexpensive to expensive, and service is informative. Mountings are fairly traditional, but custom design work is offered. *Every day; map:K6* &

CARROLL'S FINE JEWELRY / 1427 4th Ave; 206/622-9191 Carroll's, in business for more than a century, sparkles with unusual finds from all over the world; it's one of the loveliest and most fascinating gem stores in Seattle. You might discover an antique silver picture frame or a set of antique Oriental gaming pieces. There's also a classy selection of watches, rings, bracelets, necklaces, and gemstones. *Mon–Sat; map:K6*

CARTIER / 600 Pine St, Pacific Place; 206/389-6505 Right next door to Tiffany in Pacific Place, Seattle's first Cartier store carries Hermès-style scarves, watches, and sunglasses, as well as fine jewelry and some leather goods. *Every day; map:J5*

FACÈRE JEWELRY ART / 1420 5th Ave, City Centre; 206/624-6768 Proprietor Karen Lorene, one of the city's leading authorities on antique jewelry, specializes in Victorian jewelry art here in this small space on the main level of City Centre. Along with exquisite old pieces, some dating from the late 18th century, she offers a beautifully displayed collection of Art Deco rings, as well as contemporary works by local designers and jewelry artists from around the country. *Every day; www.facerejewelryart.com; map:J5*

FOX'S GEM SHOP / 1341 5th Ave; 206/623-2528 If there really were a diamond as big as the Ritz, here's where you'd find it. Fox's is an elegant shop with stiff prices. The specialties: glittering gemstones and dazzling diamonds. You dress up to shop here. The gift section has silver for all occasions and a large selection of clocks. Fox's carries gems from

Tiffany's as well as Cartier and Mikimoto pearls and jewelry. *Mon–Sat; www.fox's.com; map:K6*

GEM DESIGN JEWELERS / 14310 NE 20th St, Suite B, Bellevue; 425/643-6245 Owners Shauna and Richard Miller specialize in original and custom designs and stone remounting. They also have a nice line of earrings, gold necklaces, and individual colored stones, diamonds, and pearls. *Tues–Sat; map:GG2*

GOLD & SILVER SHOP / 526 1st Ave N; 206/284-2082 ▪ Bellevue Square, Bellevue; 425/462-8202 Traditional to ultramodern jewelry is fabricated in-house here. Diamonds are an especially good value because the shop buys directly from contacts in Israel. Gemstones, too. *Tues–Sat; map:A7; map:HH3*

GOLDMAN'S JEWELERS / 1521 1st Ave; 206/682-0237 Goldman's carries exciting, state-of-the-art jewelry, much of it made by local artists. Expect to find unusual gems and colored stones, custom and artist inlay work, and an extensive clock selection. Goldman's ships all around the world. *Mon–Sat; map:J7*

MICHAEL FARRELL, JEWELER / 324 15th Ave E; 206/324-1582 ▪ 5420 Sand Point Way NE; 206/524-8848 This friendly shop is always full of clients buying or admiring the excellent selection of vintage watches. There's an impressive collection of sterling silver hollowware, as well as vintage American costume jewelry, some signed by the designer. The store also does custom repairs. *Mon–Sat; map:HH6; map:FF5*

PHILIP MONROE JEWELER / 519 Pine St; 206/624-1531 The top of the line when it comes to custom jewelry (which makes up 95 percent of its business), this small shop has an air of restrained elegance. Occasionally the lovely selection of unusual and antique jewelry gets hung from the arms of exquisite Oriental figurines. Antiques and art objects, too. *Mon–Sat; map:J5*

SOMETHING SILVER / Westlake Center (and branches); 206/621-7800 If you're looking for something silver, look no further. Owners Cheri and Tony Swan have meticulous eyes for exquisitely cut stones set into silver only, from rings to necklaces to bracelets to charms. And check out the walls—the Gustav Klimt re-creations are by Seattle's Smash Designs. Branches are in University Village (206/523-7545; map:FF6) and Bellevue Square (425/462-5261; map:HH3). *Every day; map:I6*

TIFFANY & CO. / 600 Pine St, Pacific Place; 206/264-1400 They don't serve breakfast, but Seattle's first Tiffany's store in downtown's sparkling new Pacific Place has all the diamonds, gold, and other jewelry a girl could want. *Every day; www.tiffany.com; map:J5*

TURGEON RAINE JEWELERS / 1407 5th Ave; 206/447-9488 Norman Turgeon and Jerry Raine have some of the finest custom and designer jewelry in town. From the new classics (like tension-set diamonds) to the old (modern twists on antique pieces), you'll find something to please. Don't let the elegant digs and the guard at the door scare you off: they welcome all comers, and the personable sales staff will make you feel at home among the precious baubles, bangles, and beads. Expensive? Sure. Worth it? Indeed. *Mon–Sat; www.turgeonraine.com; map:J5*

MUSIC (CDS, RECORDS, AND TAPES)

BOP STREET RECORDS & TAPES / 5512 20th Ave NW; 206/783-3009 This hole-in-the-wall Ballard record shop bulges at the seams with its selection of jazz, blues, and rock vinyl. A few used CDs, 78s, and cassettes are hanging around, but Bop Street's main draw is its inventory consisting of approximately 120,000 albums and 100,000 45s. Most of the inventory is housed in a nearby warehouse, which belies the overcapacitated appearance of the shop itself. If you feel a bit overwhelmed by the massive stock spilling off shelves onto boxes on the floor, 19-year owner Dave Voorhees is more than willing to help you navigate the chaos. *Mon–Sat; map:EE8*

BORDERS MUSIC / 1501 4th Ave (and branches); 206/622-6799 Despite its size and national status, Borders Music has remained one of Seattle's best-kept secrets, with the best selection, stock, and layout of any store in the area. From the most obscure world music titles to ultra-rare imports to *Billboard* chart-toppers, Borders has it all. You can usually listen before you buy because each section has its own listening station stocked with staff picks and new releases. Branches are in Redmond (16549 NE 74th St, Redmond Town Center; 425/869-1907; map:EE1) and Tukwila (17501 Southcenter Pkwy; 206/575-4506; map:OO5). *Every day; www.bordersstores.com; map:K6*

BUD'S JAZZ RECORDS / 102 S Jackson St; 206/628-0445 Hidden away in an underground Pioneer Square location, Bud's is a jazz-lover's dream come true. Since 1982, Chicago refugee and jazz buff Bud Young has hosted Seattle's only jazz, all-jazz, and nothing-but-jazz store. It has one of the most extensive inventories in the country, with around 15,000 titles in all—making it the biggest of its kind west of Chicago. Surrounded by framed photographs of the jazz greats, musicians argue over the unlisted sidemen on old Charlie Parker records, and Bud (who's almost always on duty) keeps an exhaustive jazz library for settling such arguments. The free search service has a great track record. *Every day; map:O9*

**CELLOPHANE SQUARE / 4538 University Way NE (and branches);
206/634-2280** Thanks to a reliable base of empty-pocketed college students, Cellophane Square maintains Seattle's most extensive selection of used rock CDs. The store's three branches pay top dollar for good-condition used CDs. Good news for you reclusive types: Cellophane Square's Web site lets you download the entire inventory so you can do all your shopping from the comfort of your desk chair. The same goes for selling or trading in your old CDs—just email your lists to the store and the staff will take it from there. Branches are in Bellevue (322 Bellevue Way NE; 425/454-5059; map:HH3) and on Capitol Hill (130 Broadway E; 206/329-2202; map:GG6). *Every day; music@cellophane.com; www. cellophane.com; map:FF6*

DELICIOUS MUSIC / 1015 E Pike St; 206/328-7112 The "it" place for new-school vinyl collectors, Delicious Music is into its third year in Capitol Hill's burgeoning Pike-and-Pine district. Minimal decor matches the relatively sparse selection: the stock here is geared strictly towards lovers of techno in all its permutations. But even if you're not a DJ or a seeker of rare wax, don't pass up this place, as its selection of DJ mix tapes, its flyers, and its knowledgeable staff make it a good source of information for all things techno. *Every day; map:HH6*

FALLOUT RECORDS, BOOKS & COMICS / 1506 E Olive Way; 206/323-BOMB If you're into punk rock and you have only one stop on your record-shopping tour, this should be it. If you're not into punk, well, you might feel out of place should you randomly stroll into this joint. But take a chance, because you could run into the next Kurt Cobain while browsing this small-but-well-known location. Fallout has vinyl (true to punk's roots), some CDs, and a staff who, while not particularly friendly, know every obscure independent/punk label, band, and recording ever made. One side of the store is devoted to music, the other to indie-press books and comics (we're not talkin' Marvel here). Doing its part to compete with the pervasive Ticketmaster, Fallout also sells tickets to a few indie rock shows. *Tues–Sun; map:GG6*

GOLDEN OLDIES / 201 NE 45th St (and branches); 206/547-2260 Entering the dilapidated Wallingford building that is home to Golden Oldies, one gets the distinct impression that time has stopped for this shop alone. It has more records than other formats, and of those, most are 45s. Golden Oldies even sells adapters so you can head straight home with your 45 and plop it on your turntable (assuming you still have one) with no delay. Well organized—CDs by genre and vinyl by artist, with a catalog stetching back to 1910—the store will buy, sell or trade almost anything recorded since 1900. There are seven branches total, in Bellevue, Renton, Everett, Tacoma, and elsewhere in Washington. *Every day; oldies@ix.netcom.com; www.goldenoldiesrecords.com; map:FF7*

ORPHEUM / 618 Broadway E; 206/322-6370 Orpheum is known among locals as the best alternative to the Tower Records–style stores for new releases in modern and indie rock, jazz, techno, and dance. It carries a few rarities and boxed sets, but the main draw tends to be the upstairs, mainly vinyl, loft, where DJs of all flavors converge to battle over new and used hip-hop, R&B, techno, and house records. *Every day; map:GG6*

RETROSPECT RECORDS / 1524 E Olive Way; 206/329-1077 Over its 18-year tenure on Capitol Hill, Retrospect has become known as one of the best places to snag rock vinyl recordings of all kinds. New, used, rare, 45s, 12-inch, 7-inch—Retrospect has it all, plus a great punk rock section, new and used CDs, some cassettes, and a pretty decent 99-cent record bin. If you, like many, discarded your turntable when CDs came on the scene, Retrospect usually has a few used ones for sale. With its selection of unusual posters, T-shirts, and collector's items such as books, magazines, concert-ticket stubs, and picture discs, this is truly a place for the voracious rock consumer. Enthusiastic and knowledgeable employees make it a great store to get lost in for a while. *Every day; www.retrospectrecords.com; map:GG6*

RUBATO RECORDS / 136 105th Ave NE, Bellevue; 425/455-9417 Lots of tapes, used CDs, and vinyl in this shop tucked away in a downtown Bellevue back alley. A really good place to find mid-'80s alternative and pop albums that never made it onto CD. *Every day; map:HH3*

SILVER PLATTERS / 9560 1st Ave NE (and branches); 206/524-3472 Silver Platters reputedly has the country's largest selection of compact discs—virtually everything on the market. There's also a sizable selection of laser videodiscs. Branches are in Bellevue (14603 NE 20th St; 425/643-3472; map:GG2) and Tukwila (16935 Southcenter Pkwy; 206/575-3472; map:OO5). *Every day; map:DD7*

SINGLES GOING STEADY / 2219 2nd Ave; 206/441-7396 Who says punk rock is dead? For two years now, Singles Going Steady has been doing its part to make sure it's alive and kicking in Seattle. With an impressive selection of vinyl, CDs, T-shirts, patches, buttons, studded belts, collars, and armbands, plus posters by modern graphic-art hero Lindsey Kuhn to boot, this record store has truly cornered the market on punk collectibles. Ex-punkers take note: the shop will take your old gear off your hands and they'll pay top dollar for it, too. *Every day; map:G7*

SUB POP MEGA MART / 1514 Pike Pl, Pike Place Market; 206/652-4356 Now in its Pike Place Market digs, this one-stop shop for all things Sub Pop continues a well-chronicled tradition of indie-rock retail. The store's name is a tongue-in-cheek jab at the corporate rock industry that its namesake label built an empire in spite of; the Mega Mart is actually a small, highly specific music store, and everything sold here is in some way related to the label, if not on the label itself. So, yes, you'll find the usual grunge suspects here (read: Nirvana and friends), but the mart also stocks the work of artists who got their start at Sub Pop, such as L7, and dispenses all kinds of label-related paraphernalia—stickers, T-shirts, hats, and the like. Impress the staff by not asking any Nirvana-related questions. *Every day; www.subpop.com; map:J8*

TOWER RECORDS / 500 Mercer St (and branches); 206/283-4456 The antithesis of quaint, mom-and-pop-style record stores, Tower Records is a behemoth of a chain. But if you're looking for a specific title, you're more likely to find it here than in the smaller, independently owned shops. The classical selection is almost unrivaled, the hits are always in stock, and, best of all, the stores are open 'til midnight seven days a week. Also in the U-District (4321 University Way NE; 206/632-1187; map:FF6) and Bellevue (10635 NE 8th St; 425/451-2557; map:HH3). *Every day; map:B4*

WALL OF SOUND / 2237 2nd Ave; 206/441-9880 If you're looking for the latest *Billboard* chart-toppers, this probably isn't the shop for you. You're in luck, however, if you're in search of off-the-beaten-path CDs and records falling roughly into the world, jazz, or electronica categories. The key word here is "eclectic"—in fact, it's the most common filing category in the store. From French hip-hop to Peruvian percussion, Wall of Sound's inventory offers a virtual round-the-world tour by ear. The store is divided into two parts: one side houses all the CDs, while the vinyl rests on the other (a shared space with the Mag Daddy magazine store). The store has listening stations, too, where you can relax with the store cat while sampling possible purchases. *Every day; map:G7*

OUTDOOR GEAR

ALPINE HUT / 2215 15th Ave W (and branches); 206/284-3575 Alpine Hut is a great place to find good deals on all kinds of ski gear in winter or wet suits, mountain bikes, and bike wear in summer. The owner is friendly and the store aims to please. *Mon–Sat; map:GG8*

C. C. FILSON CO. / 1555 4th Ave S; 206/622-3147 One of the few Seattle businesses around since the turn of the (20th) century, Filson sells rugged wearables that are enjoying something of a rebirth since the opening of a retail store just south of downtown. Heavy wool jackets and vests, canvas hunting coats, oil-finish hats, and wool pants are the style here. The original C. C. Filson sold clothes to the men headed north to Alaska during the gold rush, and today's clothes are still attractive and tough— not necessarily in that order (one jacket style, the Cruiser, hasn't been much changed since Filson designed and patented it in 1914). Complete line of handsome luggage (including gun bags), too. At Filson they take themselves rather too seriously, but after more than 100 years in business, why shouldn't they? *Mon–Sat; www.ccfilson.com; map:R9*

CROSSINGS / 921 Fairview Ave N; 206/287-9979 ■ Carillon Point, Kirkland; 425/889-2628 Though the emphasis here is on sailing, these crew outfits work nicely for almost any kind of boating endeavor. The outerwear keeps you dry on deck, and the natural-fiber fabrics keep you dapper. Landlubbers and water fiends alike will appreciate the handsome collection of general outerwear for both men and women. *Every day; www.crossings-crew.com; map:D1; map:EE3*

THE CROW'S NEST / 1900 N Northlake Way, Suite 155; 206/632-3555 This large marine hardware store specializes in yachting accessories, clothing, foul-weather gear, and hardware. *Every day; www.crowsnest.com; map:FF7*

DAVID MORGAN / 11812 Northcreek Pkwy N, Suite 103, Bothell; 425/485-2132 Here is where you buy those functional Koolah Australian riding coats. Also look for British ordnance survey maps, C. C. Filson clothing (the prime outdoorwear made in Seattle), Akubra hats, and Welsh woolens. Everything for the well-heeled hunter or all-purpose outdoorsman, plus Celtic and Northwest Coast Native American jewelry. *Mon–Sat; www.davidmorgan.com; map:BB4*

EASY RIDER / 15666 W Valley Hwy, Tukwila; 425/228-3633 The largest West Coast manufacturer of canoes and kayaks (in business for more than 25 years), Easy Rider offers its complete line of 50 different styles factory-direct to the public. Factory pickup offers good savings on first-quality boats, with even better savings on seconds. There are whitewater, lake, saltwater, all-purpose, family, and hunting styles in 12½-foot to 22½-foot lengths. *Mon–Tues, Thurs–Sat; www.easyriderkayaks.com; map:NN5*

EDDIE BAUER / 1330 5th Ave (and branches); 206/622-2766 Once Seattle's very own, Eddie Bauer is now a national chain (owned by Spiegel Inc.) with a reputation to match. You used to shop here for fine goose-down sleeping bags, comforters, and pillows, but now you come for outdoor fashion: goose-down jackets, vests, and parkas, along with shorts, rugby shirts, and other sportive ensembles. All are very high quality, dependable, and pricey. In addition, Eddie Bauer's 200 stores sell some backpacking equipment, sports accessories, knives, sunglasses, and shoes. The downtown store's lower level is devoted to the company's latest venture: furniture, bedding, and home accessories. Branches are in most malls; outlet stores are in Auburn and Silverdale. *Every day; www.eddiebauer.com; map:K6*

ELLIOTT BAY BICYCLES / 2116 Western Ave; 206/441-8144 Intimidating to novices, Elliott Bay is the Cadillac of bike stores. It's regarded as something of a pro shop: it sells bikes to cyclists who know what they're doing and do enough of it to justify the high prices. Among its other attributes, the shop is home base for Bill Davidson, a nationally known frame builder, whose latest designs include custom titanium frames. *Every day; www.elliottbaybicycles.com, www.davidsonbicycles.com; map:H9*

FAST LADY SPORTS / University Village; 206/522-2113 Fast Lady has the most complete selection of women's clothing and footwear for running, cycling, swimming, and aerobic workouts in the Seattle area. The friendly staff dispense accurate information and advice. Other branches are in Kirkland (5 Lake St; 425/889-9433; map:EE3) and Redmond Town Center (425/558-7856; map:FF1). *Every day; www.fastladysports.com; map:FF6;*

FEATHERED FRIENDS / 119 Yale Ave N; 206/292-2210 These are the top-of-the-line down products in the city; the shop's Gore-Tex and down clothes have been leading climbing expeditions for years. It specializes in sporting goods, sleeping bags (made to order), and climbing equipment, and also sells bedding and comforters. *Every day; www.featheredfriends.com/; map:H1*

GREGG'S GREENLAKE CYCLE / 7007 Woodlawn Ave NE (and branches); 206/523-1822 Gregg's is a high-volume, high-pressure Seattle institution, perhaps (at least initially) by virtue of its Green Lake location. With such a large inventory, it can handle the entire family: kids' bikes, all-terrain bikes, and Japanese-, Italian-, and American-made racing cycles, along with Seattle's largest collection of touring bikes. Because of its sheer volume, it's the best first stop when you're hunting for a bicycle. If you do buy from Gregg's, you'll get good follow-up service. The Green Lake location has a large clothing and accessories department and rents bikes, roller skates, in-line skates, and snowboards. Branches are in Bellevue (145 106th Ave NE, Bellevue; 425/462-1900; map:HH3) and North Seattle (Aurora Cycle; 7401 Aurora Ave N; 206/783-1000; map:EE7). *Every day; www.greggscycles.com; map:EE7*

IL VECCHIO / 140 Lakeside Ave; 206/324-8148 Visually, George Gibbs's bicycle shop in Leschi looks more like an art gallery than a bike shop. The award-winning Weinstein-designed store is minimalist in appeal—there are very few bikes here—and maximalist in quality (and price): Italian racers, De Rosa, Fondriest, and Pinarello, and American-made Landshark. Proper frame fit is a certainty. In addition to the road and racing bicycles, the shop sells top components and cycling apparel. *Tues–Sat and by appointment; map:HH6*

ISSAQUAH SKI AND CYCLE / 975-G Gilman Blvd, Issaquah; 425/391-7547 The Issaquah area's full-service neighborhood bike shop (which offers ski rental and ski clothing as well) upholds its reputation as the place to go for mountain bikes (a selection of road bikes is available, too). Back when it was known, in its original location, as Mercer Island Cyclery, it was credited with starting the mountain-bike craze in this area. The shop is small, so you're always bound to be talking to one of the owners—enthusiastic cyclists who are eager to help. *Every day*

MARINER KAYAKS / 2134 Westlake Ave N; 206/284-8404 Mariner kayaks are considered by many sea kayakers as some of the best in the world. Shop owners, brothers, and kayak designers Cam and Matt Broze are always available to talk the finer points of hull shape and function. Opinions run strong here, but all are well founded on years of paddling experience. Matt developed the modern paddle float used for rescues and has written numerous articles on sea-kayaking skill and safety. In addition to the Mariner line, which includes kayaks for sea touring and the outer coast surf, Mariner Kayaks sells the Seda, Nimbus, and Feather-craft lines, Lightning and Epic paddles, and everything else you need to get out on the water. *Tues–Sat; map:GG7*

MARLEY'S SNOWBOARDS AND SKATEBOARDS / 5424 Ballard Ave NW; 206/782-6081 If you aren't enthusiastic about snow-boarding when you walk into this darkish, subterranean store, you will be by the time you walk out. Co-owner Ian Fels, a skier who took up snowboarding 10 years ago and never looked back, is a friendly, talkative guy who can tell you anything you need to know about getting radical or getting started. Marley's carries top brands that cover the price range from reasonable to jaw-dropping. There's a wide selection of those baggy, comfortable clothes that are de rigueur for snowboarders. In summer the emphasis switches to skateboards. *Every day; map:FF8*

MARMOT MOUNTAIN WORKS / 827 Bellevue Way NE, Bellevue; 425/453-1515 Marmot outfits the skier, backpacker, and mountaineer with cross-country skis, packs, tents, boots, crampons, ice axes, and more—all for sale or rent. Prices for outerwear are some of the highest around; however, deals can be found on some ski accessories, such as climbing skins for the backcountry. An excellent selection of climbing hardware. *Every day; www.premier1.net/~marmot/; map:HH3*

MCHALE PACKS / 29 Dravus St; 206/281-7861 Mountaineer Dan McHale has been designing backpacks for professional climbers since 1971, and his expertise is renowned here among experts and weekend trailhounds alike. The store and workshop near the Ship Canal cater to serious backcountry skiers and hikers, with a full line of rucksacks and internal-frame packs, including the Bayonet, a popular large-capacity design that converts to accommodate smaller loads for day trips. McHale's packs are built with comfort in mind and customized to ensure proper fit. *Tues–Fri and by appointment; www.aa.net/mchalepacks; map:FF7*

THE NORTH FACE / 1023 1st Ave; 206/622-4111 A well-known name in backpacking equipment design, North Face also carries down clothing and bags, outdoor apparel, and skiwear. The store has every guidebook imaginable to plan your mountaineering trip. The feeling here is of a yuppified REI (and prices are high, high, high), but that doesn't mean the store isn't serious about products and service. *Every day; map:L8*

NORTHWEST OUTDOOR CENTER / 2100 Westlake Ave N; 206/281-9694 When you see a kayak on Lake Union, it most likely came from here. Right on the lakefront, NWOC is the easiest place to try out or rent a variety of kayaks—a must if you are thinking of buying. A full-service paddling shop, NWOC carries sea and whitewater kayaks, gear, and accessories. Check out the range of paddling courses—from navigation to how to roll to river rescue—for beginning and advanced paddlers. Enthusiastic staff, excellent instruction. *Every day; www.nwoc.com; map:GG7*

PACIFIC WATER SPORTS / 16055 Pacific Hwy S; 206/246-9385 A landbound spot on the Pacific Highway S strip is an unlikely location for this burgeoning water-play shop. Here, advanced and novice paddlers outfit themselves with the boat (canoe, sea kayak, or whitewater kayak) and the suit (wet or dry). The shop features the full line of Lee Moyer–designed Pacific Water Sports sea kayaks, as well as boats by Necky, Current Designs, Dagger, Perception, Valley, and more. Excellent instruction ranges from canoe basics to intensive whitewater excursions. Exceptionally friendly service and advice. Rentals, too. *Mon–Sat; pwskayaks.com; map:OO6*

PATAGONIA / 2100 1st Ave; 206/622-9700 It's all sleek-wood glamour and high-quality outdoor fashion at this handsome retail outlet. Here at Seattle's own Patagucci Central, you'll feel like a million bucks in Synchilla and Capilene fleece, and you'll be oh-so-politically-correct in your made-with-only-organically-grown-cotton garments. Tyke sizes, too. In fashion colors, built for comfort and style and made to last—with price tags to prove it. Great book selection. Staff is well versed in local environmental issues and eager to talk. *Every day; www.patagonia.com; map:H8*

PATRICK'S FLY SHOP / 2237 Eastlake Ave E; 206/325-8988 Fishing enthusiasts think of this shop as the premier source of information on area fly-fishing and fly-tying. As well they should: this is the oldest fly shop in the state, having been around for more than 50 years. Patrick's offers workshops as well as friendly, old-fashioned fishing stories and advice. *Every day; map:GG7*

R & E CYCLES / 5627 University Way NE; 206/527-4822 Owners Dan Towle and Estelle Gray specialize in hand-built Rodriguez frames (the original "R" in "R & E"), tandems, racing bikes, and wheel building. The owners also operate Seattle Bike Repair (5601 University Way NE; 206/527-0360; map:EE7). The shop opens at noon, but is open mornings and after hours by appointment. *Every day in summer, Tues–Sun in winter; www.rodcycles.com; map:FF6*

REI (RECREATIONAL EQUIPMENT INC.) / 222 Yale Ave N (and branches); 206/223-1944 See Top 25 Attractions in the Exploring chapter.

RECYCLED CYCLES / 1011 NE Boat St; 206/547-4491 An idea whose time has come. At Recycled's pleasant Boat Street location, old bikes are taken in, cleaned up, given new parts where necessary, and put back on the market. Though the focus is on mountain, road, and 10-speed bikes, no bike is too old, specialized, or goofy-looking—even old Schwinn beaters, track bikes, or bikes that Mary Poppins would have liked. *Every day; www.recycledcycles.com; map:FF6*

RICKY YOUNG SURFBOARDS / 17 102nd Ave NE, Suite B, Bellevue; 425/453-2346 Yes, there's surfing in Washington (and Oregon). Ricky Young, a nationally ranked surfer in the '60s, is the sport's top local promoter and adviser. Young manufactures and sells his own line of boards for both short- and long-board surfers (accessories and rentals, too). This is a *real* surf shop. *Mon–Sat; map:HH3*

SEATTLE ATHLETIC AND EXERCISE / 842 NE Northgate Way; 206/364-5890 ■ 294 Bellevue Way NE, Bellevue; 425/453-2006 Look here for everything from 1-pound weights to $7,000 exercise machines, including exercise mats, rowing machines, treadmills, and other high-quality exercise equipment. They'll train you to use your new purchase, too. *Every day; www.seattle2000.com; map:DD7; map:HH3*

SECOND BOUNCE / 513 N 36th St; 206/545-8810 Expertly filling the new and used outdoor equipment niche, Second Bounce carries a wide range of quality gear for climbing, mountaineering, cycling, paddling, and general camping. The shop is folksy, with excellent help, and owners know their business, carrying the right products at bargain prices. Buy, sell, trade, and consign. *Every day; www.secondbounce.com; map:FF8*

SNOWBOARD CONNECTION / 604 Alaskan Way; 206/467-8545 No fancy neon ski outfits here, just the latest in equipment and accessories for this growing downhill craze. Boards by K2 and Gnu (and perhaps a dozen other companies), tuning, and great advice from shredheads who really know the sport; T-shirts, boots, and basic, functional warm clothing, too. Also skateboards and surfboards. New products arrive daily. *Every day; map:N8*

SUPER JOCK 'N JILL / 7210 E Green Lake Dr N; 206/522-7711 Sportsmedicine clinics and doctors send their patients here for proper shoe fitting. These salespeople know their merchandise and understand the mechanics of running and power walking. A podiatrist is in the store once a week to answer questions and help with problems. The selection of other merchandise (running gear, bathing suits) is smaller, but often this is the one place in town to carry a specific item. It is also a good source on races, fun runs, routes, and training. *Every day; jocknjill.com/ sjj; map:EE7*

SWIFTWATER / 4235 Fremont Ave N; 206/547-3377 This little Fremont storefront specializes in rafts and inflatable kayaks. They'll rent you one, sell you one, or help you organize a trip on one. These guys know their rivers. *Mon–Sat in summer; Mon–Tue, Thurs–Sat in winter; map:FF7*

URBAN SURF / 2100 N Northlake Way; 206/545-9463 This upscale shop across from Gas Works Park offers a flashy selection of the latest windsurfing, in-line skating, surfing, and snowboarding equipment and apparel. In-line skate rentals. Shop talk is lively and informative. *Every day; www.urbansurf.com; map:FF7*

WARSHAL'S SPORTING GOODS / 1000 1st Ave; 206/624-7300 A downtown dinosaur, Warshal's has been holding down the corner of First and Madison forever. You come here for virtually any sporting-goods need, along with unadvertised discounts, hunting and fishing licenses, and a fine selection of darkroom supplies and photography equipment. The regular-Joe atmo appeals in this high-gloss part of town. *Mon–Sat; map:M8*

WEDGWOOD CYCLE / 8507 35th Ave NE (and branches); 206/523-5572 Challenging Gregg's hegemony in the new-bike market, Wedgwood now has three locations—the old Wedgwood location, a store in Ballard (5601 24th Ave NW; 206/784-7273; map:FF8), and a new shop in Issaquah (660 NW Gilman Blvd; 425/557-5425). Prices here are reasonable (more so than in other parts of town), and the staff are friendly and knowledgeable. Wedgwood carries good brands such as Marin and Gary Fisher, as well as parts and accessories (including the spiffy Timbuktu bags that bike messengers favor). *Every day; www.wedgwoodcycle.com; map:EE6*

WEST MARINE PRODUCTS / 6317 Seaview Ave NW; 206/789-4640 ■ 1000 Mercer St; 206/292-8663 West Marine has a well-established reputation as a sailing-equipment supplier, with a full line of marine supplies for powerboats and sailboats, and accessories for both: binoculars, winches, line (for sails or for tying up), outboards, dinghies, sports boats up to 12 feet, and more. *Every day; www.westmarine.com; map:EE9; map:D2*

WILEY'S WATER SKI SHOP / 1417 S Trenton St; 206/762-1300 Wiley's sells water skis out of a garagelike South End store. Wet suits, dry suits, slalom skis, ropes, life preservers, wakeboards, and inner tubes complete the selection. The staff will custom-make bindings for customers. A large selection of waterskiing equipment for kids is available too. *Mon–Sat; www.wileyski.com; map:LL6*

WRIGHT BROTHERS CYCLE WORKS / 219 N 36th St; 206/633-5132 You can have reliable bike repairs done here or, for a small fee, join this cooperative and do your own bike maintenance with Wright Brothers' tools and space. Owner Charles Hadrann and his staff are known for wheel building, informative repair classes, and good advice. There's an ever-growing selection of tires, and prices on parts are fair. *Tues–Sun in summer; Tues–Sat in winter; map:FF7*

SEAFOOD

CITY FISH / 1535 Pike Pl, Pike Place Market; 206/682-9329 Great quality and consistently knowledgeable service have earned City Fish its reputation and faithful clientele. This Main Arcade purveyor does a brisk business in local fish and shellfish, and also offers some exotics like Louisiana crawfish. Dungeness crab and line-caught king salmon are specialties. Overnight shipping to anywhere in the country. *Every day; map:J8*

JACK'S FISH SPOT / 1514 Pike Pl, Pike Place Market; 206/467-0514 Point to a Dungeness crab or an oyster in the tank, and Jack's crew will pluck it and clean or shuck it on the spot. This fine seafood shop has the only live-shellfish tanks in the Market, with loads of live crabs, clams, lobsters, and oysters. They smoke their own salmon, run a walk-up oyster bar, and have great fish 'n' chips and clam chowder. *Every day; map:J8*

MUTUAL FISH COMPANY / 2335 Rainier Ave S; 206/322-4368 Consistently the most highly regarded fish purveyor in town, Mutual Fish is where many of the city's best restaurants buy their seafood, and it's easy to see why. Top quality and a dazzling selection are the result of the undivided attention of the Yoshimura family. Fresh tanks are full of several types of local oysters and crabs, and the seafood cases present the best from the West and East Coasts. Seattleites are pleased to find mahi-mahi, tilefish, Maryland soft-shell crabs (in season), and other exotics. Prices are good, and they'll pack for air freight or carry-home. *Mon–Sat; map:II6*

PIKE PLACE FISH / 86 Pike Pl, Pike Place Market; 206/682-7181 Duck, here comes a flying fish! Although this show is highly entertaining, you can also secure a salmon that hasn't taken a flyer over the cheering crowd. There's a good selection of fresh fish and shellfish, plus smoked

BUT IS IT FRESH?

To impress guests and family with a grand seafood dinner, start with a great fish. The quality of the seafood you purchase has more effect on your cooking success than the method of preparation, so be sure your catch is freshly caught! Here are some hints from the experts about how to make sure the fish you buy is fresh.

Begin by following your nose: A fish stall or seafood shop should have an aroma like the sea. If it smells fishy, go elsewhere for your purchase.

Next, use your eyes. A fresh fish will appear shiny, almost sparkling, with clear, protruding eyes and a firm texture. The most flavorful Northwest salmon are chinook and sockeye. Chinook, the most prized variety of Pacific salmon, is also usually the largest—with black spots on its tail and back, and flesh ranging in color (depending on the time of year) from very pale pink to almost red. Sockeye are smaller, with deeper-colored flesh and silvery skin.

Also look at the sanitation conditions at the fish counter. Whole fish should be covered with fresh ice. Steaks and fillets should be in refrigerated cases, placed in trays that rest on ice.

Once you pick out your future meal, it's your responsibility to make sure your purchase stays cold until you're ready to cook it. If you're traveling or not heading home directly, ask the fishmonger to package your fish in ice. Many Seattle-area fish sellers will pack seafood for a flight home or ship it for you.

— *Barbara Spear*

and kippered seafood, and some local rarities like the homely geoduck (a must-see for tourists). Pike Place Fish will pack and ship for the traveler. It's hard to miss this stand—it's usually surrounded by an ogling, cheering crowd of onlookers. Located in the Main Arcade, next to the bronze pig. *Every day; www.gourmetworld.com/ks01/Kspike.htm; map:J8*

PORT CHATHAM PACKING COMPANY / 632 NW 46th St (and branches); 206/783-8200 People flock here for wild Alaskan seafood that's been smoked to satiny perfection. For years Port Chatham has been turning out some of the best alderwood-smoked salmon anywhere, as well as supplying an eye-popping array of smoked shellfish, trout, gourmet seafood baskets, and caviar. The Ballard location is off the beaten track, but there are enough branches in downtown Seattle (and nearby cities) to take care of your gift needs for the next decade. Phone orders and shipping are no problem. Kosher. *Mon–Sat; map:FF8*

QUEEN ANNE THRIFTWAY / 1908 Queen Anne Ave N; 206/284-2530 ■ West Seattle Admiral Thriftway; 2320 42nd Ave SW; 206/937-0551 When food dignitaries come to town, they head here. At the Queen Anne store, fish guru Rick Cavanaugh runs one of the best seafood departments in the United States (Julia Child orders from him): pristine stock and 20 to 30 kinds of fish and shellfish, from here and all over. He's also usually the first local to score the highly sought after Copper River salmon, available only for a limited time each spring. Savvy cooks call ahead to tailor their menus to what's in that day. Special orders welcome; free packing for travel. The recently remodeled West Seattle Thriftway carries on the same fine tradition, with a stunning service counter. *Every day; map:GG8; map:II9*

SEATTLE CAVIAR COMPANY / 3147 Fairview Ave E; 206/323-3005 When it comes to caviar, Betsy Sherrow, owner of this Lake Union caviar importer, offers only the best. Sherrow sells the finest beluga, osetra, and sevruga caviar from the Caspian Sea, in addition to Northwest fresh American malossol caviar and all the froufrou accoutrements of serious roe-eating (such as pretty mother-of-pearl spoons and caviar *presentoirs*). Want to impress your friends and business associates? She gladly arranges beautiful gift packages, and even handles shipping. *Mon–Fri and by appointment; map:GG7*

UNIVERSITY SEAFOOD & POULTRY CO. / 1317 NE 47th St; 206/632-3900 Good prices and impeccable quality are the hallmarks of Dale Erickson's U-District fish market. The selection includes salmon, halibut, and lingcod, plus seasonal treats such as local sturgeon. An amazing array of caviars, from flying fish to Columbia River sturgeon to beluga. Hard-to-find game birds, free-run chickens, and the freshest eggs. Prices are not posted but, surprisingly enough, are in line with supermarket prices. The fishmongers at the counter are friendly, and are all good cooks with recipes to share. *Mon–Sat; map:FF6*

WILD SALMON SEAFOOD MARKET / 1900 W Nickerson St; 206/283-3366 With personal service and fresh-from-the-docks seafood, Wild Salmon has a lot to offer. In addition to tanks filled with live lobster, oysters, clams, and mussels, this small seafood specialist sells good-looking fish fillets, steaks, and whole fish and shellfish from its large service counter. Crab cakes and salmon cakes are usually available—all you need to do is cook them through for a great entree. *Every day; map:FF8*

SHOES

BALLY OF SWITZERLAND / 1218 4th Ave, Four Seasons Olympic Hotel; 206/624-9255 Bally's white marble entryway and beige interior are forbidding: a cathedral for shoes. But the staff are friendly and the merchandise is superb. For women: midcalf horsehair boots in addition to office wear and dressy heels suitable for an evening at the ballet. For men: Euro-style low boots, casual tasseled loafers, and dressier leathers. Velvet scarves, golf sweaters, and briefcases are a few of the other expensive items. *Mon–Sat; map:L6*

CHURCH'S ENGLISH SHOES / 520 Pike St, Suite 101; 206/682-3555
Church's offers an enticing selection of proper English men's shoes. A variety of textures (woven, alligator) and styles (loafers, two-tones) punctuate the perfect-for-the-fancy-office footwear (in brown, black, and cream leathers). Also, more casual weekend wear from Clark's of England. Prices are not scaled for the budget-conscious. *Every day; map:J5*

CLOG FACTORY / 217 1st Ave S; 206/682-2564 This Pioneer Square joint has been selling the famed Scandinavian shoe for which the store is named for more than 20 years. Wooden and rubber clogs—some meticulously handcrafted—are the only shoes sold here. (Some come from Germany and Austria.) *Mon–Sat; map:N8*

DUNCAN AND SONS BOOTS AND SADDLES / 541 1st Ave S; 206/622-1310 In business since 1898, this family-run boot shop carries more than 30 styles of Western boots for men, women, and children. Prices run from $90 to $350. Most of the boots are handmade in Texas. *Mon–Sat; map:P9*

ENZO ANGIOLINI / Bellevue Square, Bellevue; 425/450-5582 These Italian leather women's shoes are in step with the latest trends, at remarkably reasonable prices. Careful attention to details—like the leather buttons and colors (the chocolate brown is beautiful)—make Enzo Angiolini elegant as well as fashionable. Leather picture frames, belts, and bags, too. *Every day; map:HH3*

JOAN & DAVID SHOES / 1420 5th Ave, City Centre; 206/624-2427 Expensive and irrefutably stylish, a pair of Joan & David shoes makes a perfect investment. From white-and-silver summer sandals to black silk opera shoes to smart leather boots, the shoes are oh-so-appropriate yet wear like minor jewels. A tasteful selection of bags and accessories and a few pieces of elegant clothing complement the shoes. Watch for the twice-yearly sales. *Every day; map:J5*

JOHN FLUEVOG SHOES / 1611 1st Ave; 206/441-1065 Pink patent leather, platform Mary Janes, square toes, and flared heels—Fluevog's footwear is some of the hippest in town. The Canadian owner does the designs; the shoes are made in England, Poland, Mexico, and Spain. For dance-club divas and daring souls. *Every day; seattle@fluevog.ca; www.fluevog.com; map:I7*

M. J. FEET'S BIRKENSTOCK STORE / 1514 Pike Pl, Pike Place Market (and branches); 206/624-2929 This is where you get those sturdy Birkenstock sandals in all colors and styles. The cheerful shops carry a lot of jazzy socks and tights by Hue, plus a small selection of clothing.

They're also good places to get hard-to-find, beautiful Ellington school bags. Great repair service, too. Other branches are on the Ave (4334 University Way NE; 206/632-5353; map:FF6) and in Bellevue Square (425/646-0416; map:HH3). *Every day; mjfeet@aol.com; www.thebirkenstockstore.com; map:J8*

MAGGIE'S SHOES / 1927 1st Ave; 206/728-5837 Maggie journeys to Italy and picks out the latest from the country that knows fine legs deserve fine footwear. She also carries Argus, a nice French-made shoe. Subtle browns, blacks, deep blues, and creams; brushed suede; and elegant buttons and straps make Maggie's women's and men's shoes most desirable. Quite reasonable prices. *Every day; map:I7*

OUTSIDE SHOES / 2025 1st Ave; 206/441-1182 Upscale European walking shoes seduce even the most fashion-savvy shoe snobs after they slip one foot into these cushiony soles. This shop carries 25 lines, mostly from Northern Europe. *Mon–Sat; map:H8*

SAN MARCO / 1509 6th Ave; 206/343-9138 Shoes are displayed as art at San Marco—carefully placed atop wavy pieces of plastic and fake rock. Such artful attention is warranted: the women's shoes (and the small selection of men's shoes) are daring and glamorous. Strappy, shiny pieces from Petra, deeply colored, soft suede Arche shoes, and DKNY footwear can be counted on. The employees are stylish and kind. Watch for the end-of-summer and end-of-winter sales. *Every day; map:J5*

THE WOOLLY MAMMOTH / 4303 University Way NE; 206/632-3254 ▪ Annex: 4309½ University Way NE; 206/547-3192 This University District shop has outfitted generations of students of both genders with sturdy, rainproof walking shoes and durable backpacks. The Woolly Mammoth mostly carries comfortable brands such as Rockport, Bass, and Timberland, the stylish yet sensible White Mountain label, and clogs for women. A second store up the street, called the Annex, carries trendier stuff—Doc Martens, Converse, and the like. *Every day; map:FF6*

SPECIALTY SHOPS

ARCADE SMOKE SHOP / 1522 5th Ave; 206/587-0159 Originally sited in the basement arcade of long-closed department store Frederick & Nelson's, this extensive shop occupies a hard-to-find basement venue next to a teriyaki joint. Trip down the stairs to view the lacquered wooden humidors, the rotating stands of Zippo lighters, the wall stacked with pipes (briarwood, amber root, many by Dunhill) and the long glass counters of smooth cigarette and bulbous cigar cases made from leather, silver, and pewter. Cigars line the shelves of a separate, glass-walled room, while pipe tobacco blends fill hefty glass jars. The shop also sells hammered pewter and silver hip flasks, and thoughtfully provides Vicks cough drops. *Mon–Sat; map:J6*

DUSTY STRINGS / 3406 Fremont Ave N; 206/634-1662 In 1977, Ray and Sue Mooers heard the light, dancing tones of a hammered dulcimer performance at the Folklife Festival and fell in love. They learned to play, and then to make, the trapezoidal wooden boxes, and started selling their dulcimers in 1979. The music splashing onto Fremont's main drag today comes from their underground factory and retail store, expanded in 1991 from a small 1982 original. Only carefully crafted hammered dulcimers and lever harps (as opposed to the classical pedal harp) are produced in the factory, but Dusty Strings also sells high-quality guitars (many by Taylor), banjos, fiddles, mandolins (hourglass-shaped "mountain" and banjo-looking "walkabout" versions), hand drums, concertinas, and flutes. One room is devoted entirely to music, in sheet, lesson book, video, and CD form. Celtic, folk, bluegrass, traditional, and jazz musicians form the customer base, but if you ever wanted to learn Japanese shakuhachi flute or Hawaiian slack-key guitar, this is the place to look. *Mon–Sat; map:FF7*

LOVE PANTRY / 10333 Aurora Ave N; 206/523-5683 No murk or trenchcoats here. A bright, airy space with well-labeled items and friendly salespeople welcomes the timid to a sex shop focused more on lighthearted variety than on serious equipment. Racks of skimpy negligees, thongs, and zip-front boxers blend with videos, greeting cards, how-to books and statuary of questionable aesthetic merit. The dominatrix selection is small but entertaining, as are the shelves of prosthetic gadgets. Jokey treats, including boxes of salacious pasta, candles, and fortune cookies, give social gatherings that useful soupçon of vulgarity. *Every day; map:DD7*

METSKER MAPS / 702 1st Ave; 206/623-8747 ■ 14150 NE 20th St, Bellevue; 425/746-3200 Shiny posters of satellite-image maps, thick Atlas Gazetteers, folding maps of Lebanon in German—if you can conceive the navigating need, Metsker's probably has the solution. Shelves display a staggering assortment of travel guides, with a generous emphasis on the Northwest. Globes, including one that lights up, sit underneath reproduction posters of antique maps and prints. Map tacks are boxed by color, and laminated Mac field guides, handy for flora and fauna identification on beach walks or mountain hikes, are hidden in a corner. The truly intrepid can purchase trail park passes for hikes into Washington's national forests. *Mon–Sat; map:N8; map:GG2*

MICHAEL MASLAN HISTORIC PHOTOGRAPHS POSTCARDS & EPHEMERA / 214 1st Ave S; 206/587-0187 A teeny shop in the little Pioneer Square mall that houses Grand Central Bakery, Michael Maslan opens up for browsing as his whimsy takes him. Catch him open, and the whimsy is indeed enchanting: vintage lithographs of jungle scenes, faded portraits of stiff-lipped Victorians, and endless postcards from every location and era of the past century. The walls are covered with vintage maps, photographs, and posters, mostly elegant samples from the era of shipboard travel or kitschy ads from the post–World War II airline boom. Prices range from extremely reasonable to heirloom level. *Mon–Fri and infrequent weekend openings; map:O8*

THE RUBBER TREE / 4426 Burke Ave N; 206/633-4750 The tree festooned with drooping red, yellow, and green prophylactics is one of Seattle's better examples of urban window painting, and the vivid shelves of the Rubber Tree are just as visually arresting. Latex, skin, ribbed, flared, colored, flavored, Japanese, Swedish—the condom is marketed here with boundless enthusiasm. Walls are plastered with advice and informational fliers, reminders of the shop's parent, Zero Population Growth. Bumper stickers, T-shirts, pins, better-sex and love-your-body books fill the extra space between the colorful rows of condoms and lubricants. For diehards, the counter displays include nylon condom carriers and glycerine soaps with the little latex rings embedded inside. *Mon–Sat; map:FF7*

SCARECROW VIDEO / 5030 Roosevelt Way NE; 206/524-8554 The rare, the obscure, and the just plain weird have pride of place at this comprehensive, winding two-floor store. Scarecrow's immense collection of videocassettes, DVDs, and laserdiscs is catalogued not just by New Releases and Top Rentals but by director (alphabetically), place of origin ("Balkan States") and unusual category (animé, blaxploitation, experimental, and so on). A revolving selection of new and used films is on sale at any given time, boosted by yearly blowouts and enhanced by a knowledgeable staff that not only orders in-print movies but will search for out-of-print flicks as well. VCR (both American and PAL, a European VHS format) players and DVD players are available for nightly rental for under $10. There's even an espresso stand by the door for late-night video marathon fueling. *Every day; map:FF7*

SILBERMAN/BROWN STATIONERY / 1322 5th Ave; 206/292-9404 Long windows with gleaming displays lead into a two-tiered, low-ceilinged shrine to pens, paper, and the desk. Rows of richly colored pens and shelves of fine stationery are just the beginning; handcrafted silver pen sheaths (to mask an unsightly ballpoint), floral painted stamp dispensers and flat silver business card cases are just a few of the elegant items attractive for their very lack of necessity. An ordering service can produce engraved announcements or invitations in (with luck) just a few days. Monogrammed stationery, seals and colored sticks of sealing wax, photo frames, tooled leather photo albums, Limoges porcelain pillboxes, and a Civil War chess set round out the eclectic, seductive wares. *Mon–Sat; map:K6*

TOYS

AMERICAN EAGLES / 12537 Lake City Way NE; 206/440-8448 The largest hobby shop in the country specializes in historical hobbies and model railroads. Owner Michael Edwards stocks more than 87,000 different items, including a regiment of 22,000 miniature soldiers, and lots and lots of models. *Mon–Sat; map:CC6*

ARCHIE MCPHEE / 2428 NW Market St; 206/297-0240 Contemporary kitsch at its wacky best. Home to glow-in-the-dark dinosaurs, rubber slugs, and the famous boxing nun puppets, Archie McPhee's is a great place to stock up on cheap toys and party favors or just to browse the memorable catalog. Plenty of grown-ups confess shameful inclinations to losing themselves among the windup toys and bendable plastic creatures. A long-time institution on Stone Way, Archie's recently moved to beautiful Ballard. *Every day; map:FF8*

THE DISNEY STORE / Westlake Center (and branches); 206/622-3323 A place that drives parents Disney. Nonstop patter from multiple video screens playing the latest Walt Disney clips. The G-rated clerks also sell Disney-inspired gadgets and garb. Kids love the sing-along tapes featuring songs from Disney hits. Other stores are at Southcenter (206/241-8922; map:OO5) and Bellevue Square (425/451-0540; map:HH3). *Every day; map:I6*

DON'S HOBBIES / 2943 NE Blakeley St; 206/525-7700 A gold mine for the hobbyist, Don's has radio-controlled boats, model airplanes, motorized race cars, and American and European electric trains in all the usual gauges. Models of all kinds and system toys by Fischer, Brio, and more draw a faithful clientele from all over. *Mon–Sat; map:FF6*

EASTSIDE TRAINS / 217 Central Way, Kirkland; 425/828-4098 Trains, trains, and more trains. The business chugged along for years out of the owner's home. Now it's full speed ahead in its Kirkland retail location. For train lovers young and old, this is a shop like no other, where you'll find train-related shirts, hats, and videos, too. *Mon–Sat; map:EE3*

FAO SCHWARZ / 1420 5th Ave, City Centre (and branches); 206/442-9500 ■ Bellevue Square, Bellevue; 425/646-9500 From the mechanical clock tower—a two-story-high, singing, prancing toy sculpture that greets you at the door—to the animal-stuffed jungle room with its talking tree, the preschool area with toddler toys to interest one and all, and the Barbie room (every five-year-old's fantasy, a very pink display of all the Barbie dolls and accessories ever made), it's clear why FAO is the biggest toy show in town. The staff is so earnest and cheerful that you'll wonder whether they're watching a video of Tom Hanks in *Big* during their coffee breaks. The Bellevue Square store, as befits its mall location, is slightly less ostentatious. *Every day; map:J5; map:HH3*

FANTASTIC GAMES AND TOYS / 3333 184th St SW, Mervyn's Plaza, Lynnwood; 425/775-4871 Fantastic specializes in miniature gaming and role-playing games. Your one-stop shop for Dungeons and Dragons–type games. *Every day*

GREAT WINDS KITE SHOP / 402 Occidental Ave S; 206/624-6886 Kites of all kinds live in this friendly Pioneer Square shop. It's a whimsical and wonderfully colorful place where you can also get kite-making kits, wind socks, boomerangs, and plenty of good advice from a well-seasoned, experienced staff. *Every day; map:P9*

THE GREAT WIND-UP / 93 Pike Pl, Pike Place Market; 206/621-9370 For the kid in every adult. The Great Wind-Up is full of every kind of windup (collectible tin items, too) and battery-operated animated toy imaginable (you can hear the whirring and chirping from a few doors away). Home to everyone's favorite nostalgia toys: Slinky, Sea Monkeys, Pez, and Gumby. In the Economy Market Atrium. *Every day; map:J8*

IMAGINATION TOYS / 1815 N 45th St, Wallingford Center; 206/547-2356 ■ 2236 NW Market St; 206/784-1310 A great source for wonderful, well-made toys by Brio, Gund, and the ever-popular Lego, this family-run store also carries activity toys by Playmobil, train sets, games, and puzzles. They feature a wide assortment of musical instruments ranging from ukuleles to keyboards, too. *Every day; map:FF7; map:FF8*

MAGIC MOUSE / 603 1st Ave; 206/682-8097 Top-of-the-line toys, chosen by a "professional child," fill the shelves of this marvelous Pioneer Square store: Steiff animals, Corolle dolls, Brio wooden train sets, and Märklin electric trains. The stuffed-animal collection includes over 100 styles of teddy bears alone. There's a selection of developmental baby and preschool toys, art supplies, games and puzzles, kids' books, windup toys, stocking stuffers, and literally hundreds of different decks of cards. *Every day; map:N8*

PINOCCHIO / 4540 Union Bay Pl NE; 206/528-1100 Pinocchio features puzzles, interactive play media (such as Playmobil), nature-exploring aids (binoculars and science workbooks), a wide variety of paints (non-toxic watercolors and tie-dyeing kits), and Ty toys (stuffed animals by the makers of Beanie Babies). Books in stock are geared more toward adults reading bedtime stories to the little 'uns than toward older children who read on their own. *Every day; map:FF6*

TERI'S TOYBOX / 526 Main St, Edmonds (and branches); 425/774-3190 Teri Soelter's small shop in downtown Edmonds is chock-full of wonderful stuff. It's a great place to gift-shop (ask for wrap and they'll gladly tuck your purchase into a gaily beribboned gift bag). Collectible dolls are handsomely displayed, and you're sure to find something for every kid on your list: art and jewelry-making supplies, educational toys, stuffed animals, building blocks, kiddy carpenter's tools, cassette tapes and CDs, and more. There are two other Toybox's as well: one in Kirkland (356 Kirkland Park Pl; 425/828-9121) and one in University Village (206/526-7147; map:FF6). *Every day*

THINKER TOYS / 10610 NE 8th St, Bellevue; 425/453-0051 This small but discriminating shop—which has moved down the block to a jazzy converted vintage gas station—has an intelligently chosen, upper-end inventory. There's a little bit of everything: kites, games, trains, dolls, books, 3-D puzzles. Kids of all ages will go bonkers in the mind-boggler section. *Every day; map:HH3*

TOP TEN TOYS / 104 N 85th St; 206/782-0098 Both parents and kids love the sections of toys devoted to the youngest and most demanding—the toddler area, the infant area, and the "2's" area. This one-of-a-kind store is filled to the rafters with goodies. Look for the trike and wagon room, the jungle gym equipment, and the unexciting but most necessary Safety First line for parents (featuring electrical-outlet covers and cabinet safety locks). *Every day; map:EE8*

TREE TOP TOYS / 1717 N Bothell Way, Lake Forest Park Town Center; 206/363-5460 Tree Top aims directly for a child's imagination, with a supply of dress-up clothes such as sequined ballerina outfits and Robin Hood garb. Cooking texts offer cultural education with recipes featuring ethnic foods, but the main draw is a giant Brio train that promises to fascinate children long past the necessary shopping visit's allotted time. *Every day; map:BB5*

WOOD SHOP TOYS / 320 1st Ave S; 206/624-1763 Since 1972, Wood Shop Toys has provided well-crafted, sturdy wooden toys by Pacific Northwest artisans, stocked side by side with imported European items including pull toys, dolls, and trucks, as well as old-fashioned board games. The Folkmanis puppets it stocks come in wonderful animal shapes, and look like mere stuffed animals until a child's hand slipped inside brings them to life. *Every day; map:O9*

WINE AND BEER

BRIE & BORDEAUX See Ethnic Markets and Specialty Foods in this chapter.

CITY CELLARS FINE WINES / 1710 N 45th St; 206/632-7238 Recently purchased by longtime employees Sarah Griffin, Michael Herndon, and Rafer Nelsen, City Cellars continues its tradition of carrying specialty food items and a wide selection of European—especially Italian—wines. The Bungalow Wine Bar and Cafe is now the sole focus for former City Cellars owners Jeff Treistman and Polly Young. Located seven blocks east (2412 N 45th St), it's open until late evening Tuesday through Saturday for appetizers, desserts, and tastings by the glass (with more than 60 selections from which to choose). *Every day; map:FF7*

ESQUIN WINE MERCHANTS / 2700 4th Ave S; 206/682-7374 In its location on 4th Avenue S and Lander Street, Esquin continues its founding goal of finding the best values for the money. Monthly specials reflect the best wines from all regions at some of the best prices in town. The owner seeks out the special or unique, occasionally acquiring wines no one else has. The French, Italian, Australian, and American selections are all good. You'll find close to 500 labels, case discounts, free twice-weekly tastings, and outstanding sales. Many choices in the $5 to $15 range. *Every day; map:II7*

LA CANTINA WINE MERCHANTS / University Village; 206/525-4340 ■ **10218 NE 8th St, Bellevue; 425/455-4363** Although they're under separate ownership, both stores are exactly what a small specialty shop is all about. Owners are knowledgeable, and by getting to know their regular customers are able to make suggestions based upon the customers' tastes. With an emphasis on French bottlings, this is the shop for fine Burgundies and Bordeaux. The Bellevue store offers discounts through its buying club. *Every day (University Village); Mon–Sat (Bellevue); map:FF6; map:HH3*

LARRY'S MARKETS / 10008 Aurora Ave N, Oak Tree Village (and branches); 206/527-5333 True to Larry's gourmet mission, the wine sections are among the largest in any Seattle-area grocery store. The Northwest selection is particularly extensive. Larry's also has an aggressive direct-import program that provides good values but has limited the depth of its California and European selections. When it comes to microbrews, Larry's has the gamut, all of them available chilled and ready to drink. *Every day; map:DD7*

LIBERTY MALT SUPPLY CO. / 1419 1st Ave, Pike Place Market; 206/622-1880 Though this is primarily a supplier for home brewmeisters, Liberty Malt Supply also sells a broad array of craft beers and microbrews, both local and national, as well as a big selection of specialty European beers. *Mon–Sat; map:J7*

LOUIE'S ON THE PIKE / 1926 Pike Pl, Pike Place Market; 206/443-1035 This all-purpose grocery store, at the north end of Pike Place Market, has an extensive collection of wine and beer, especially the local stuff from small producers. Although service is at a premium—that is, there isn't much—the prices can be good enough that you won't care. *Every day; map:J8*

MCCARTHY & SCHIERING WINE MERCHANTS / 6500 Ravenna Ave NE; 206/524-9500 ■ **2209 Queen Anne Ave N; 206/282-8500** Dan McCarthy (at Queen Anne) and Jay Schiering (at Ravenna) actively seek out the newest and most promising producers from Europe and the United States. Come here to discover the rising stars in the wine world. Regular Saturday afternoon in-store tastings, a knowledgeable staff, and a special rate for "Vintage Select" club members add appeal. A good place to find a rare bottle. California and the Northwest are as well represented as France. *Tues–Sat; map:GG8; map:EE6*

PETE'S WINES / 58 E Lynn St; 206/322-2660 ▪ 134 105th Ave NE, Bellevue; 425/454-1100 Owner George Kingen has finally given in and let his surprising little store be listed in the phone book by what it really offers. For years it was called Pete's Supermarket, a definite misnomer, since any grocery stock is dwarfed by the vast array of wine overflowing into the store's narrow aisles. The store has the best deals in town on champagne, and also offers good values on Northwest, California, French, and Italian wines. The roomy Bellevue shop (Pete's Wines Eastside) is devoted solely to wine, with the same good prices and special-order service. *Every day; map:GG7; map:HH3*

PIKE & WESTERN WINE MERCHANTS / 1934 Pike Pl, Pike Place Market; 206/441-1307 If you think of Pike Place Market as one big grocery store, think of Pike & Western as its wine section. Although this is still one of the best places to learn about Northwest wines, Pike & Western boasts a staff knowledgeable about wines from the rest of the world, too. They make a concerted effort to offer the best values and are especially adept at helping shoppers match wines to the dinner ingredients they've purchased elsewhere in the Market. Owner Michael Teer uses his knowledge of wine and food to help some of the city's best restaurants craft their wine lists. *Every day; map:J8*

QUEEN ANNE THRIFTWAY / 1908 Queen Anne Ave N; 206/284-2530 ▪ West Seattle Admiral Thriftway; 2320 42nd Ave SW; 206/937-0551 Seattle-area grocery stores have developed amazingly large cellars, and this superlative independent is one of the best. Its purchase and upgrading of two other Thriftways (Admiral in West Seattle and Queen Anne in Tacoma) show the store's commitment to fine food and wine. Wine manager Jeff Cox oversees an ever-changing selection including many of the current hits. In addition, Thriftway carries more than 100 varieties of beer, including an extensive selection of microbrews. *Every day; map:GG8; map:II9*

PERFORMING ARTS

PERFORMING ARTS

Theater

What a difference a few years can make. Not that long ago, the mainstream Seattle theater scene was in the doldrums, while "the fringe," housed in lofts, basements, and the back rooms of bars, was exploding with talent and promise. Today, those with more conventional tastes in theater (and theaters) can expect work just as lively, just as innovative, but *far* more polished at the three big "mainstream" houses: the Seattle Rep, A Contemporary Theatre, and the Intiman.

The fringe continues to be lively too, however. The climax of the fringe year comes in early spring (anywhere from late February to early April), with the annual **SEATTLE FRINGE THEATRE FESTIVAL**: literally hundreds of shows presented in a dozen or more venues over three exhausting weeks. Some of the work is, naturally, amateurish if not sophomoric. But over the years Seattle's FringeFest has become a popular spot to try out new work intended to go on the road to the continent-spanning Canadian fringe theater circuit, and even to the mother of all fringe festivals, Edinburgh.

Outside festival time, the Seattle fringe scene is calmer, with usually only four to six companies presenting work at any one time. The Seattle daily newspapers do a pretty good job of covering the fringe, but the most critical and informed reviews and listings are likely to be found in the two city weeklies. Consult *Seattle Weekly* for a more audience-friendly, consumerist approach, *The Stranger* for a highly partisan, artist-oriented angle.

Among the smaller companies with established track records, look for the following (in alphabetical order). **ANNEX THEATRE** (1916 4th Ave; 206/728-0933; map:I6) is a collective enterprise where the performer is king and the energy often raises the roof. **HOUSE OF DAMES** (no permanent space; 206/720-1729) creates luminous, mysterious music-theater works in unconventional settings. **ONE WORLD THEATRE** (www.sewerscape.com/oneworld/; no phone) spends most of its time on the road but is well worth a visit when it makes one of its rare appearances in its hometown. **PRINTER'S DEVIL THEATRE** (no fixed abode; 206/860-7163) is given to new work by emerging playwrights, presented in stunningly visualized productions. Don't be put off by the flippant sound of **THEATER SCHMEATER** (1500 Summit; 206/324-5801; map:K2) and **A THEATRE UNDER THE INFLUENCE** (Union Garage, 1418 10th Ave; 206/720-1942; map:HH6): both perform a wide variety of material from deep to wacky, including most of the sparse productions of classic plays to be seen hereabouts. The **UNIVERSITY OF WASHINGTON SCHOOL OF DRAMA** (three theaters on campus; 206/543-4880; map:FF6) sometimes presents first-rate productions directed by jobbed-in big-name professionals and featuring students from the school's Professional Actor Training Program. Other productions are all-student work—some terrific, others less so; inform yourself before you go.

ON THE BOARDS (1st Ave W and Roy St; 206/217-9888; map:GG8) occupies an intermediate position between fringe and establishment—and between the arts of theater and dance as well (see Dance in this chapter). It's here you'll see both cutting-edge performance art from around the world (Japan, Croatia, Belgium, England, you name it) and new creations by Seattle-based artists, which in their turn will be hitting the international avant-garde road.

The theater establishment proper—those companies that operate in one way or another under the rules of Actors Equity and other theater unions—has suffered losses in recent years, as two companies have folded completely and another has withdrawn from active production. But despite the endemic pressures of rising costs and loss of government support, the "big kids" continue to thrive and even expand their activities.

A CONTEMPORARY THEATRE (ACT) / 700 Union St; 206/292-7676 A prominent star on the Seattle theater scene, ACT boasts a gorgeous facility containing three strikingly different performance spaces, an energetic artistic director (Gordon Edelstein), and a year-round program featuring some of the finest talent drawn from Seattle's pool of resident actors (as well as the occasional big name such as Julie Harris and Alan Arkin). During the Christmas holidays ACT presents its own adaptation of Dickens's *A Christmas Carol*, eagerly attended by Seattleites of three generations. *www.acttheatre.org; map:K4* &

CABARET DE PARIS / Crêpe de Paris restaurant, Atrium Level, Rainier Square; 206/623-4111 The brainchild of singer-comedian-impresario David Koch, this modest stage in a downtown French restaurant is a showcase for the brightest musical-comedy talents in town. The repertory mixes original revues (like the often-revived, tourist-targeted Seattle satire *Waiter, There's a Slug in My Latte*) with zany fantasias that put pop standards into unaccustomed settings (often with new words, as in the recent *The Carpeters: Uncomfortably Close to You*). You can buy a ticket for the show only, order the full meal-and-entertainment package, or just have a drink and/or dessert during the show. The food is adequate if not inspired, and reasonably priced. *Map:K6* &

EMPTY SPACE THEATRE / 3509 Fremont Ave N; 206/547-7500 Seattle's oldest "alternative theater" is now housed in the funky, '60s-retro Fremont neighborhood, and under author-director Eddie Levi Lee its programming has adapted to match its setting. You might see a straight-ahead classic like Steinbeck's *Of Mice and Men*, a loony original (like *Wuthering! Heights! The! Musical!*), or a mock-horror melodrama based on the tales of Edgar Allan Poe. The whole Fremont neighborhood is a year-round street fair/block party: plan to have a bite and tip a brew or two after the show at one of the too-numerous-to-mention brewpubs within a block or two of the theater. *www.seattlesquare.com/emptyspace; map:FF8* &

5TH AVENUE THEATRE / 1308 5th Ave; 206/625-1900 Sharing the same artistic management as Houston's Theater Under the Stars, the 5th Avenue specializes in revivals of mainstream Broadway musicals, with the occasional new Broadway touring show thrown in to sweeten the mix for subscribers. Also playing are new and original musicals that the management hopes will make it to Broadway (*Jekyll and Hyde* is one recent example). Not the most adventurous house in town (though the theater recently mounted a knockout production of Stephen Sondheim's legendary "flop" *Follies* as a labor of love), but the 30,000 or so sub-scribers don't seem to mind. *www.5thavenuetheatre.org; map:L6* &

INTIMAN THEATRE / Intiman Playhouse, Seattle Center; 206/269-1901 For a few years Intiman ruled the scene here, taking its *Kentucky Cycle* to Broadway for a Pulitzer, presenting the local premiere of *Angels in America*, getting the pick of serious new drama from New York and London. Now that ACT and the Seattle Rep are back in shape, Intiman has some competition for material, but the season lineup still includes plenty of high-powered drama, and the theater's newly refurbished lobby is twice as comfortable as it used to be. *www.seattlesquare.com/intiman; map:A6* &

MOORE THEATRE / 1932 2nd Ave; 206/443-1744 See Paramount Theatre below. &

PARAMOUNT THEATRE / 911 Pine St; Information: 206/443-1744, Tickets: 206/292-ARTS (Ticketmaster) Jointly managed with the Moore Theatre by the nonprofit Seattle Landmark Association, the Paramount plays host to Broadway tours, pop headliners of all descriptions, and community events as well. Remodeled to the tune of $30 million and

---

TICKET ALERT

Tickets to many local performing arts events are available from **Ticketmaster** (various locations around town; 206/292-ARTS) or at **Ticket/Ticket** (401 Broadway E; map:GG6; and 1st and Pike; map:J7; 206/324-2744), which sells half-price, day-of-show tickets to theater, music, comedy, and dance performances.

equipped with one of the first hydraulic seating systems to be installed in the United States, the 3,000-seats-plus hall can be converted with a flick of a switch into a flat-floor rock venue or banquet facility in less than half an hour. The 1,100-seat Moore, on a corner near the Pike Place Market, is far funkier but perfectly suited to the more venturesome acts presented there: magician-comedians Penn & Teller, *Tap Dogs*, the rock musical *Rent*, and so on. You can buy tickets to Moore and Paramount shows only through Ticketmaster or in person at the Paramount box office. *soldout@theparamount.com; www.theparamount.com; map:J3* &

SEATTLE CHILDREN'S THEATRE / Charlotte Martin Theatre, Seattle Center; 206/441-3322 Challenging Minneapolis's Children's Theater Company in size and prestige, SCT presents as many as 10 beautifully mounted productions a year for young and family audiences, most of them world premieres commissioned from leading playwrights and based on both classic and contemporary children's literature. With only three evening performances a week (the rest are daytime performances, sold to school groups), seats can be hard to come by, but they're worth the effort. *www.sct.org; map:C7* &

SEATTLE REPERTORY THEATRE / Bagley Wright Theatre, Seattle Center; 206/443-2222 The oldest (est. 1963) theater in town, under artistic director Sharon Ott, is firmly in place as the flagship of the local scene. With a reputation for lavish physical productions to live up to, the Rep always provides something to dazzle the eye, but under Ott the mind and heart get a workout as well. Shows like Mary Zimmerman's gorgeously unconventional *Notebooks of Leonardo da Vinci* and the two-person avant-mime revue *Le Cirque Invisible* are as likely to turn up on the 800-seat mainstage as is a revival of Oscar Wilde's *An Ideal Husband* or Shaw's *Pygmalion*. More intimate productions play the Leo K. Theatre, a little jewel of modern stage design. *www.seattlerep.org; map:A6* &

VILLAGE THEATRE / 303 Front St N, Issaquah; 425/392-2202 Off the beaten path for visitors but worthy of mention is the Village Theatre, based in the Cascade-foothills town of Issaquah. The Village specializes in musicals, new and old, famed and obscure. Thanks to the abundant pool of professionally trained (but nontheatrically employed) actors in the area, their production standard is remarkably high. *www.vt.org* or *www.speakeasy.org/ concierge/village/index.html* &

Classical Music and Opera

Over the past decade, Seattle has built a thriving classical music scene appropriate to a cultured cosmopolitan city. The symphony and opera are firmly on the national map, and chamber music is a local passion.

Excellent early music and choral music groups abound. Several musicians of national and international reputation make their homes here and share their musical expertise generously. Seattle is also a regular stop for major performers on tour.

The city's concert-venue options expanded dramatically in 1998 when the Seattle Symphony moved from the Opera House to its new downtown home, Benaroya Hall, which has a main auditorium (2,500 seats) and a recital hall (540 seats). Acoustically, both performing spaces have proved to be live and clear, with good sound and balance from bass to treble. Of the city's other **VENUES**, both sightlines and sound are respectable in almost any performance hall, and fair to good in the many churches used for performance.

BELLE ARTE CONCERTS / Meydenbauer Center Theater, 11100 NE 6th St, Bellevue; and other venues; 425/454-2410 The 17-year-old Belle Arte Concerts in Bellevue presents five chamber music concerts per season. Under musical director Heidi Lehwalder, the quality of performance has risen to high levels, with national and even international groups appearing along with the best that the Northwest has to offer. Recent performers include pianist André-Michel Schub and the Vermeer String Quartet. Lehwalder has encouraged adventurous programming and broadened a generally classical format to include some jazz. Here's your chance to hear top performers in a smaller setting. *info@bellearte. org; www.bellearte.org; map:HH3* &

THE BRIDGE ENSEMBLE / Various venues; 206/633-2428 A piano quartet, the Bridge Ensemble (with members bridging three continents) has risen fast to join the cream of Seattle's chamber music groups. Polished performances and insightful interpretations are its hallmark, particularly in contemporary and 20th-century Russian music, though its well-designed programs also include classics. It performs about four concerts a season. *ksigers@aa.net; www.thebridgeensemble.com*

EARLY MUSIC GUILD / Various venues; 206/325-7066 The Early Music Guild is credited with making Seattle a center of historically informed early music performance. EMG's popular International Series comprises five concerts of medieval, Renaissance, Baroque, or classical music, and features top international players and ensembles, both instrumental and vocal. The fine Recital Series, with three concerts, highlights performers whose art is best presented in an intimate venue, such as lutenist Jakob Lindberg. EMG also gives concert assistance to many small early music groups performing in the area, including the Medieval Women's Choir and the Benevolent Order for Music of the Baroque. *emg@halcyon.com; www.halcyon.com/emg/*

INTERNATIONAL CHAMBER MUSIC SERIES / Meany Theater, University of Washington; 206/543-4880 or 800/859-5342; TDD: 206/616-8574 The popular six-concert International Chamber Music Series, presented by the University of Washington and with some concerts now co-presented by Seattle's venerable Ladies Musical Club, brings to town the best of the nation's chamber music ensembles (and an occasional group from abroad), with an emphasis on string quartets and trios. The Emerson String Quartet is a frequent visitor. *www.meany.org; map:FF6* &

MOSTLY NORDIC CHAMBER MUSIC SERIES AND SMÖRGÅSBORD / Nordic Heritage Museum, 3014 NW 67th St; 206/789-5707 Started in 1996 under the auspices of the Nordic Heritage Museum Foundation, Mostly Nordic presents five concerts per season, one for each of the Scandinavian countries. Contemporary and classical chamber music from Denmark, Finland, Iceland, Norway, and Sweden, performed by local and occasionally Scandinavian musicians, is followed by an authentic smörgåsbord that's included in the ticket price. *nordic@intelistep.com; www.nordicmuseum.com; map:EE9* &

NORTHWEST CHAMBER ORCHESTRA / Benaroya Recital Hall, 200 University St; 206/343-0445 Just past its 25th anniversary, NWCO, one of the region's few professional chamber orchestras, continues to flourish under the management of Louise Kincaid and the musical leadership of Adam Stern. The orchestra's focus is chamber music of the 17th to 20th centuries, performed on modern instruments with attention to appropriate performance practices. It's moving up these days to more distinguished soloists, such as pianist Jon Kimura Parker and flutist Eugenia Zuckerman. NWCO presents seven subscription concerts (with four repeated on the Eastside) and five Showcase chamber music concerts at Benaroya Recital Hall; three "Music in the Park" afternoon concerts at the Seattle Asian Art Museum in Volunteer Park; and occasional special performances. A child under 17 is admitted free with a ticket-buying adult. *nwco@wolfenet.com; map:K7* &

PRESIDENT'S PIANO SERIES / Meany Theater, University of Washington; 206/543-4880 or 800/859-5342; TDD: 206/616-8574 The University of Washington brings to town current pianists of international stature, such as Garrick Ohlsson, plus occasional recent prize-winners in a five-concert recital series, and usually a sixth special concert as well. *www.meany.org; map:FF6* &

SEATTLE BAROQUE ORCHESTRA / St. Stephen's Episcopal Church, 4805 NE 45th St; 206/675-1805 Seattle Baroque Orchestra was founded in 1994 and, under the leadership of baroque violinist Ingrid Matthews and harpsichordist Byron Schenkman, its accomplishments have exceeded all expectations. Visiting soloists of national and international caliber, such as soprano Ellen Hargis, join the brilliant young ensemble in historically informed performances, exploring familiar and unfamiliar literature of the era with panache. Four concert pairs are presented between fall and spring. *jmendels84@aol.com; www.halcyon.com/emg/; map:FF5* &

SEATTLE CHAMBER MUSIC FESTIVAL / Lakeside School, 14050 1st Ave NE; 206/283-8808 Founded by University of Washington cello professor Toby Saks, this popular monthlong series in July showcases local and international talent. The performances are spirited, ofttimes exceptional, and almost always sold out. Grace notes include pre-performance dining on the lawn (bring a picnic or buy a catered meal) and a minirecital before each concert. Programming tends to the tried-and-true, but more adventurous works are gradually creeping in, and the recitals feature the performers' own choices (often rarely heard pieces). The acoustics in St. Nicholas Hall are only so-so, but for a gracious summer evening, you can't do better. In 1999, the festival began a one-week run in January; the winter program is held at Benaroya Hall. *scmf@aol.com; www.scmf.org; map:CC7* &

SEATTLE CHAMBER PLAYERS / Benaroya Recital Hall, 200 University St; 206/367-1138 An unusual grouping of flute, clarinet, violin, and

FESTIVAL CITY

Once upon a time the only festival Seattle was known for was Seafair. Nowadays you'd be hard pressed to find a resident who even comprehends why we ever worshiped airplane engines in boats. As the rest of Seattle's arts and cultural scene has grown, so has the number of music festivals, and now there's more noise in the air than turbine engines.

Bumbershoot (206/281-8111) is the biggest and best of Seattle's arts festivals, and though it's more than strictly a music festival, its music programming has been called some of the best in the nation. About the only festival that rivals it in number and quality of musical acts is the New Orleans Jazz and Heritage Festival. Bumbershoot is held Labor Day weekend at Seattle Center, and lineups are usually announced a month in advance. Ticket prices have been inching up over the past several years, but it's still the region's best bargain.

Northwest Folklife Festival (206/684-7300) is the area's second-biggest festival and attracts folk acts from all over the world. Folklife is currently still free, and its open-door policy is both good and bad: the event is family-friendly, but it's also crowded. Most of the acts playing Folklife are up-and-coming performers, since the budget usually doesn't allow paying high fees. The festival takes place every Memorial Day weekend.

cello, Seattle Chamber Players adds guests and high-quality out-of-town soloists, as needed, to perform 19th-century, contemporary, and newly commissioned chamber music with style and imagination. Pianist Anton Nel is a frequent visitor. A three-concert series (usually in fall, winter, and spring) is repeated outside the city. *paultaub@dbug.org; map:K7* &

SEATTLE MEN'S CHORUS / Benaroya Hall, 200 University St; 206/323-2992 Dennis Coleman, who directs the 20-year-old, 180-member gay chorus, is one of the best choral conductors in this city of choirs. The chorus is one of the country's busiest, with about 30 appearances a year at various events and a subscription series of three concerts: an always-sold-out family-fun holiday concert in December, a popular-music spectacular in the summer, and a spring show that varies in content. Performers who have recently come to Seattle under SMC's presenting arm, Emerald City Arts, include Armistead Maupin and sisters Liz Calloway and Ann Hampton Calloway. *info@seattlemenschorus.org; www. seattlemenschorus.org; map:K7* &

SEATTLE OPERA / Opera House, Seattle Center; 206/389-7676 Sellout audiences have come to expect fresh and innovative productions from Seattle Opera, one of the country's leading companies under Speight Jenkins, general director since 1983. Seattle Opera mounts a program of five full-scale operas every season, from cherished familiars to the adventurous and unusual—among them a lavish summer production that draws an international audience. Major artists like Ben Heppner and Jane

The latest addition to Seattle's festival lineup may be the best: **WOMAD (World of Music and Dance)** (206/281-7788). This world music festival had its first full U.S. debut at Redmond's Marymoor Park in August 1998 and is scheduled for that venue through 2002. The festival pulls in ethnic music, art, and dance from all over the globe.

Seattle also boasts a number of outdoor concert series that continue annually. The **Pain in the Grass** series of free shows at Seattle Center (most Friday nights in summer) have been raising headbangers for years now. One Reel (the organization behind Bumbershoot and WOMAD) also puts on **Summer Nights at the Pier** (206/281-8111), a series of pop-rock outdoor concerts at Pier 62/63. Outdoor shows at **Chateau Ste. Michelle** (14111 NE 145th St, Woodinville; 425/488-3300) remain popular with their mix of pop and acoustic sounds, and the last few years have also seen a series of mostly folk concerts at Woodland Park Zoo, called **Zoo Tunes** (206/684-4800), during the summer. Free downtown lunchtime concerts are also offered during the summer as part of the **Out to Lunch** series (206/623-0340). Consult local newspapers' entertainment guides for what's happening this year.

— *Charles R. Cross*

Eaglen are heard here in their prime. A new production of Wagner's *Ring* cycle (a signature event regularly performed here) appears in August 2001. *www.seattleopera.org; map:B5* &

SEATTLE SYMPHONY / Benaroya Hall, 200 University St; 206/215-4747 The excellent, 95-year-old Seattle Symphony works hard to serve the city. With the opening of its own home— the splendid Benaroya Hall downtown—in 1998, it can look now to a new level of artistic progress unhampered by the trials of rented space. As well as its 18 pairs of mainstream season subscription concerts under longtime music director Gerard Schwarz and guest conductors, the orchestra performs shorter series packaged for every kind of music lover: from pops to light classics to Baroque, from performances for children to programs for older adults to concerts with insightful commentary by the conductor, plus a distinguished artist series with stars such as Jessye Norman. The new Benaroya Recital Hall hosts a chamber music series, and one for young and emerging artists. The symphony has a busy outreach program with special concerts in many area communities. *www.seattlesymphony.org; map:K7* &

SEATTLE YOUTH SYMPHONY / Benaroya Hall, 200 University St; 206/362-2300 One of the premier youth orchestras in the country, the Seattle Youth Symphony is reaching new heights of performance under conductor Jonathan Shames, who became music director in 1994. The talented young musicians give three usually dazzling concerts, plus a benefit performance, during the winter season. Five feeder orchestras train a large number of younger musicians. *info@syso.org; www.syso.org; map:K7* &

TUDOR CHOIR / St. Mark's Cathedral, 1245 10th Ave E; 206/675-1805 In a few short years, the chamber-sized Tudor Choir has established itself as an a cappella choir in the best English tradition, of the same type and virtually on the same level as the Tallis Scholars. Under conductor Doug Fullington, the choir specializes in English church music of the late Renaissance and today's mystical composers. It performs a four-concert series, plus an American shape-note concert in August and a noteworthy Handel's *Messiah* with Seattle Baroque Orchestra and national soloists at Christmas. *tudor@scn.org; www.scn.org/arts/tudorchoir; map:GG7* &

WORLD MUSIC AND THEATRE / Meany Theater, University of Washington; 206/543-4880 or 800/859-5342; TDD: 206/616-8574 A fascinating University of Washington series, World Music and Theatre features seven famous ethnic performing-arts groups from around the world, such as the Throat Singers of Tuva and Cubanismo! *www.meany. org; map:FF6* &

Dance

In past years, Seattle suffered a nasty trade imbalance in dance, losing Merce Cunningham, Robert Joffrey, Trisha Brown, and Mark Morris to New York and beyond. But now the city has become one of the more interesting regional dance centers (and Morris himself makes almost annual visits to the UW World Dance Series at Meany Theater, while the others return occasionally). The wealth of distinctive choreographers who have sprung from local series to gain national attention (Pat Graney, Llory Wilson, aerialist Robert Davidson), as well as the supply of talented long-legged women in the city's ballet company, has led New York critics to request the recipe for our drinking water. A whole series of independent choreographers and dancers ebbs and flows here, and at the moment the flow is strong. Though money is short, the scene is vital and lively, and the ability to self-produce a casual, low-tech concert helps to keep talent living and working in the city.

ON THE BOARDS / 100 W Roy St; 206/217-9888 Plugged into David White's National Performance Network in New York City, On the Boards produces and presents cutting-edge works that merge dance, music, theater, and visual media. In 1998 it moved from the ancient, funky Washington Hall Performance Gallery (where wheelchairs had to be carried up the stairs) into A Contemporary Theatre's former building near Seattle Center. Renovated to be a state-of-the-art center for contemporary performance, it seats 275–500 for the mainstage (according to the requirements of any individual show) and 100 in the studio theater. The sellout New Performance Series (October to May) brings in internationally known contemporary artists like Anne Teresa De Keersmaeker, Meredith Monk, and Ron Brown, plus local greats such as Pat Graney and Robert Davidson, and rising stars like 33 Fainting Spells. Every six weeks, year-round, 12 Minutes Max showcases five to seven short performances of new and experimental work by regional composers, choreographers, and playwrights, while the Northwest New Works Festival, which runs for several weekends in late spring, presents longer, more polished versions of similar work. Special events take place in summer. *otb@ontheboards.org; www.ontheboards.org; map:GG8* &

PACIFIC NORTHWEST BALLET / Opera House, Seattle Center; 206/292-2787 Under the guidance of artistic directors Kent Stowell and Francia Russell, former dancers with New York City Ballet, PNB has earned recognition as one of the top five regional companies in America. Fueled by a strong, well-staged selection of classic and rare Balanchine repertory (and, recently, an extraordinary and successful season of new works to celebrate its 25th season), an average five-show PNB season also features

335

large-scale classical works and story ballets by director Stowell, and contemporary offerings by the likes of Val Caniparoli, William Forsythe, Nacho Duato, and Mark Dendy. Most Augusts, the company presents two fun, family-oriented, outdoor performances at Chateau Ste. Michelle. Its holiday-season *Nutcracker* is superb for all ages, thanks to sets by Maurice Sendak and an excellent reserve of young PNB school students. *marketing@pnb.org; www.pnb.org; map:B5* &

WORLD DANCE SERIES / Meany Theater, University of Washington; 206/543-4880 or 800/859-5342; TDD: 206/616-8574 Six major dance groups are brought in every year as part of Meany Theater's World Dance Series, and each year the programming seems to get more complete and thrilling. The October-through-May series always includes such tried-and-true top draws as the Merce Cunningham Dance Company, the Alvin Ailey American Dance Theater, or the Paul Taylor Dance Company. There's usually one wilder card thrown into the mix, such as the Ballet Philippines. And homeboy Mark Morris has taken to showing up here for several seasons running. *www.meany.org; map:FF6* &

Film

Seattle doesn't really have a film scene yet—not in the sense of a thriving culture of regional filmmakers placing the city on the pop culture map as surely as the grunge movement once made Seattle an alternative-rock mecca. But while we're still waiting for our Rain City version of Quentin Tarantino to emerge, Seattle continues to enjoy its longtime reputation as an outstanding place for those who love watching film and video. A wonderfully layered exhibition circuit—consisting of venerable old movie houses, numerous film festivals, avant-garde events, and defiantly marginal cinema activities—has grown in the last dozen years, giving the local arts scene added density and texture.

Certainly the area has its share of prefab multiplex theaters in the heart of the city as well as the 'burbs, but among these are a few classy and comfortable first-run movie palaces. The **UPTOWN CINEMA** (511 Queen Anne Ave N; 206/285-1022; map:A8 &) is a fine place with three roomy theaters near Seattle Center. Cineplex Odeon's **CITY CENTRE CINEMA** (Sixth Ave and Union St; 206/622-6465; map:K5 &), on the top floor of a handsome shopping complex, has two spacious houses with excellent presentation and nice proximity to Seattle's downtown core.

A pair of boutique multiplex theaters that belong to the Seven Gables/Landmark chain show select fare from Hollywood mixed with the best of independent and foreign cinema for discriminating audiences. One of these, the **BROADWAY MARKET** (425 Broadway E; 206/323-0231; map:K1 &), is on Capitol Hill, and the other, the **METRO** (NE 45th St and

Roosevelt Way NE; 206/633-0055; map:FF7 &), is on the west end of the University District. But Seven Gables/Landmark is better known for a cluster of mostly single-screen, older film houses, rich in character and memories, strategically spread over Seattle's neighborhoods. Capitol Hill's **HARVARD EXIT** (807 E Roy St; 206/323-8986; map:GG6; downstairs theater &, but not upstairs), with its huge lobby and stately air, was founded ages ago by a pair of eccentric film fans. Also on Capitol Hill is the **EGYPTIAN** (801 E Pine St; 206/323-4978; map:HH6 &), in a former Masonic temple. The **GUILD 45TH** (2115 N 45th St; 206/633-3353; map:FF7 &) in Wallingford is actually two neighboring theaters, where one can usually find the latest Henry James adaptation. The small, dreamy **SEVEN GABLES** (the anchor of the theater chain, 911 NE 50th St; 206/632-8820; map:EE7) makes for a very pleasant experience—even more so when the scent of delicious sauces from the Italian restaurant downstairs comes wafting up. Two University District theaters complete the Landmark circle: the single-screen **NEPTUNE** (1303 NE 45th St; 206/633-5545; map:FF6 &) and the three-screen **VARSITY** (4329 University Way NE; 206/632-3131; map:FF6).

Downtown multiplexes include the **MERIDIAN 16 CINEMAS** (1502 7th Ave; 206/223-9600; map:J5 &) and **GENERAL CINEMAS** at Pacific Place (600 Pine St; 206/652-2404; map:J5 &).

A handful of local theaters participate in Seattle's biggest annual cinema event: the **SEATTLE INTERNATIONAL FILM FESTIVAL** (SIFF). A quarter-century old and now the biggest film fest in the United States (in its number of film presentations, guest appearances, and special programs), SIFF is a springtime juggernaut that might seem overwhelming at a casual glance. But a seasoned, polished staff at Cinema Seattle— SIFF's nonprofit umbrella organization—has made the event simple to understand and navigate. Though it takes place in May and June, you can get information on the festival at any time by calling Cinema Seattle (206/324-9996) or by logging on to www.seattlefilm.com/cinemaseattle. That same Web site contains information on the organization's year-round activities as well, including the outstanding **WOMEN IN CINEMA FILM FESTIVAL**, which usually takes place in January; the **EASTSIDE INTERNATIONAL FILM FESTIVAL** in October; and the unique **SCREEN-WRITERS SALON** series, held July through April, which presents live readings of new scripts, sometimes with the participation of noted actors such as Tom Skerritt, Ned Beatty, and Peter Horton, on alternate Mondays at the Alibi Room (85 Pike St; 206/623-3180; map:J8).

Seattle also enjoys another cinematic tradition in the all-season film programs of the **SEATTLE ART MUSEUM** (100 University St; 206/654-3100; map:K7 &). Curated for almost 30 years by the film department's founder, Greg Olson, each of SAM's quarterly series usually focuses on the work of a renowned actor or director (Jimmy Stewart, Alfred Hitchcock) or on a theme such as French comedy or American film noir. Frequent short programs are featured as well: a few weekends of Yasujiro Ozu, an evening of David Lynch.

The roots of Seattle's thriving art-house scene are in the tiny, 30-year-old **GRAND ILLUSION CINEMA** (NE 50th St and University Way NE; 206/523-3935; map:FF7 &). These days, the newly remodeled Grand Illusion is the centerpiece of ambitious plans by the Northwest Film Forum to present worthy small films that have fallen through mainstream distribution cracks, while simultaneously encouraging Seattle filmmakers through patronage, education, and exposure. Learn more about this conspiracy of goodwill through www.wigworld.org (email: wigworld@nwlink.com).

Another essential institution outside mainstream film exhibition is **911 MEDIA ARTS** (117 Yale Ave N; 206/682-6552; map:H2 &), which always has a busy schedule of documentaries and experimental work, open screenings where anyone can show work in progress to an opin-

SEATTLE CINÉ

Tom Hanks probably did as much as Bill Gates to draw the world's attention to Seattle when he helpfully pointed out the city's location on a map in the 1993 film *Sleepless in Seattle*. Not since Elvis Presley strutted his stuff around the Space Needle in his 1963 musical *It Happened at the World's Fair* had the city been so singularly featured in a feature.

It might not seem like that big a deal, but the impact of such cinematic contributions cannot be underestimated. Not only did the film boost tourism (Tom Hanks's quaint Seattle houseboat is a must-see on most city tours) and sales of tourist paraphernalia (from coffee mugs to T-shirts), but its title has spawned countless similar catchphrases (a national story on local unmarrieds, for example, was inevitably titled "Single in Seattle").

Most films made here haven't excited quite the hoopla of *Sleepless*, but Seattle is no newcomer to the screen—she got her SAG card back in the 1930s, when the Wallace Beery and Marie Dressler movie *Tugboat Annie* was shot here. Sometimes the city has had a starring role. The seamier side of Seattle's streets is on display in *Cinderella Liberty* (1973), the James Caan/Marsha Mason love story between a sailor and a call girl. The Space Needle makes a dizzying assassination site in *The Parallax View* (1974) starring Warren Beatty. *Frances*, the 1981 film with Jessica Lange, offers a Seattle double-shot: not only was it filmed here, but the tortured real-life actress Frances Farmer grew up here. The University of Washington is one of the stops for the deadly Theresa Russell character in *Black Widow* (1986), co-starring Debra Winger. Sylvester Stallone and Antonio Banderas try to off each other on the streets of Seattle (including a car chase

ionated audience, and classes and workshops in all aspects of production. A full schedule can be viewed at www.911media.org (email: info@ 911media.org).

Loads of interesting fringe film and video activities take place in Seattle, and many of these groups have found strength in numbers by forming the **SEATTLE INDEPENDENT FILM AND VIDEO CONSORTIUM,** a clearinghouse of information. The SIFVC has also become a network for interdisciplinary showcases, as seen in its annual Satellites event, where such organizations as Independent Exposure (an excellent monthly showcase of experimental pieces) and Evolution Engine (a gallery space for film, video, and other visual arts) curate programs with common themes. SIFVC member activities are best explored through www.lightlink. com; or email joel@speakeasy.org and request a full listing of monthly goings-on.

Summer brings an unusual but popular film happening: the **FREMONT OUTDOOR CINEMA** (600 N 34th St at the U-Park lot at Evanston Ave N; 206/282-5706; map:FF8 &), where movies (from *The Godfather* to *Wayne's World*) are projected onto a big wall while patrons sit in a parking lot and watch. Do people actually go to these things? You bet. And in costume. Even more offbeat is the "back porch summer series" at **LINDA'S TAVERN** (707 E Pine St; 206/325-1220; map:J2 &) on Capitol Hill.

The other cinema phenomenon that has hit Seattle in a big way in the last few years has been the rise of specialized festivals. Not a month goes by when at least one Asian American, African, Polish, Jewish, gay and lesbian, Native American, Irish, or children's film fest doesn't kick off with opening night fanfare. The best way to keep up with the dizzying festival circuit is to read arts listings in local publications.

along the Alaskan Way viaduct) in the 1995 film *Assassins*. The city doubles as moody "Rain City," where Kris Kristofferson and Genevieve Bujold explore the mysteries of love, in *Trouble in Mind* (1985). Seattle looks gritty in the lounge singer/piano player love story *The Fabulous Baker Boys* (1989), with Michelle Pfeiffer and Jeff Bridges, and grungy in *Singles* (1991), with Bridget Fonda and Matt Dillon. (Even grungier is Doug Pray's 1996 documentary *Hype*.)

At other times Seattle is a mere bit player. In *The Hand That Rocks the Cradle* (1991), Rebecca De Mornay stalks her suburban family with little attention paid to local landmarks. Demi Moore sexually harasses Michael Douglas in *Disclosure* (1994), with only brief glimpses given of ferries and downtown. The city has even starred in absentia: in *Stakeout* (1987), with Richard Dreyfuss, one shot of what is purported to be the downtown Seattle Police Department is actually a locale in Vancouver, British Columbia.

— *Shannon O'Leary*

Literature

Seattle is one of the most bookish cities in the country (home even to the "world's largest bookstore," Internet bookseller Amazon.com), so it's small wonder that this town practically percolates with options when it comes to all things literary. In fact, the writer traffic in and out of the city seems at times heavier than the tourist trade. Be it thoughtful readings by literary sophisticates or the fast-and-furious give-and-take of poetry slammers, nearly every literary urge can be satisfied in this metropolis.

BUMBERSHOOT / Seattle Center; 206/281-8111 This popular music-and-arts festival brings the author elite to Seattle for Labor Day weekend. In addition to its Literary Arts programs offering readings, performances, poetry slams, and panel discussions with world-class authors, the festival's long-running Bookfair boasts the largest West Coast concentration of small presses, which come from around the country to promote and sell their collections of fiction, poetry, nonfiction, hand-set letterpress books, and 'zines. *www.bumbershoot.org; map:C6* &

JACK STRAW WRITERS' PROGRAM / 4261 Roosevelt Way NE; 206/634-0919 Every year a different local writer curates this reading series of original works by Puget Sound writers that takes place in April and May. Previous curators include Rebecca Brown and Charles Mudede. Readings are held at Jack Straw Productions or the Henry Art Gallery. There's a suggested $5 donation, but the program chapbook is free. *joan@jackstraw.org; www.jackstraw.org; map:FF6*

LITERARY BUS TOUR OF SEATTLE; 360/385-4925 Members of Seattle's literati act as tour guides on this road romp to the homes and haunts of some of the city's notable writers. One stop on the tour (held once each fall and spring) is the Seward Park home of the late poet Denise Levertov. A seat on the bus costs $60–$80 and includes a gourmet box lunch. Proceeds benefit Port Townsend's nonprofit publisher Copper Canyon Press. *www.ccpress.org*

NORTHWEST BOOKFEST / Washington State Convention and Trade Center; 206/378-1883 Every fall more than 25,000 bibliophiles crowd inside at this love-in for the book. Authors reading at past fests include Tobias Wolff, Doris Kearns Goodwin, Pam Houston, Tom Robbins, Joyce Carol Oates, and Anita Hill. Younger readers are given their due as well, with an array of hands-on activities—such as book making, a storyteller's stage, and plenty of costumed fictional characters. And what would a book festival be without books? Hundreds of main- and small-stream titles are for sale at more than 200 booths. Admission to the fest, held for two days toward the end of the fall, is free, though a donation is encouraged. Proceeds benefit Pacific Northwest literacy organizations. *nwbook-fest@speakeasy.org; www.speakeasy.org/nwbookfest; map:K4* &

RICHARD HUGO HOUSE / 1634 11th Ave; 206/322-7030 Named in honor of the late Seattle poet Richard Hugo, this newly renovated 1908 fourplex on Capitol Hill hosts writing classes, readings, and other literary programs. A variety of groups call Hugo home: the Rendezvous Reading Series showcases new work, fall through spring; the Sketch Club Series, founded and hosted by local writer Rebecca Brown, presents groups of guest writers reading original works, fall through spring; and some years the Seattle Poetry Festival is held here in April. Hugo's annual literary celebration, held for three days in October, features a full schedule of readings, writers' panels, and outside activities (one year there was a bus tour of Richard Hugo's stomping grounds as well as a softball game). Most events at Hugo are free or low-cost and are held on the main floor, which also has a cafe and a library stocked with more than 500 magazines. *admin@hugohouse.org; www.hugohouse.org; map:HH6* &

SEATTLE ART MUSEUM / 100 University St; 206/654-3100 The visual arts give way to the literary when the city's foremost museum presents Poetry After Hours every first and third Thursday night of the month. Admission is $6, which also includes access to the museum exhibits until 9pm. The series focuses on emerging contemporary American poets, often from Seattle. *www.seattleartmuseum.org; map:K7* &

SEATTLE ARTS & LECTURES / 5th Avenue Theatre, 1308 5th Ave; 206/621-2230 At the top of the local literary feeding chain is this evening lecture series, founded in 1987, which runs from September through May. Whether it be an evening of witty exchanges between a panel of top-drawer writers or strictly a solo affair, the lecturers always manage to surprise (resident writer Sherman Alexie caused a minor sensation with his assertion that writers peak at 25). The list of SAL guests reads like a veritable who's who of great modern writers—ranging from John Updike and William Styron to Toni Morrison and Joan Didion. Sometimes the source of the best moments is the postlecture audience question-and-answer period. The lectures are held in the highly ornamental 5th Avenue Theatre (so ornate, in fact, that one writer confessed it was the first time he'd been frightened by a ceiling). Tickets for the seven-event series range from $75 to $95; individual tickets cost $15–$18 and are half-price for students, though be warned: some nights, they can be as hard to come by as Sonics playoff tickets. *sal@seattleartsandlectures. org; www.seattleartsandlectures.org; map:L6* &

SEATTLE PUBLIC LIBRARY, WASHINGTON CENTER FOR THE BOOK / Central Library, 1000 4th Ave; 206/386-4650 or 206/386-4184 Not a lot of shushing goes on at Seattle libraries, where book happenings are as commonplace as book carts. The central library downtown hosts manifold readings, book discussion groups, lectures, and workshops by national and local writers through its Washington Center for the Book, an affiliate of the Center for the Book at the Library of Congress. The library's "If All of Seattle Read the Same Book" program (running through the year 2000) brings readers together with the center's writer-in-residence for three days in the fall and winter. A monthly Writers Salon (held fall though spring) attracts guest speakers from all literary walks—ranging from writers and agents to editors and publishers. One of the center's most lively productions is its fall Living History Series, a lineup of chautauqua-style evenings where scholars play the roles of historical characters.

A number of local groups provide erudite escapes at neighborhood branches throughout the city as well. The long-running "It's About Time Writers' Reading Series" (206/527-8875) makes room for poets and writers of all experience levels every second Thursday evening of the month at the University District branch (5009 Roosevelt Way NE). Easily the best book buy in town, all library offerings are free. *www.spl.org; map:*M6 &

ELLIOTT BAY BOOK COMPANY / 101 S Main St; 206/624-6600 Elliott Bay is a local literary landmark with a well-deserved national reputation for spotting talent: Amy Tan gave one of her first public readings here, as did Sherman Alexie. Since 1984, daily (often twice-daily) readings by authors of national caliber—ranging from Raymond Carver to Terry McMillan—have drawn book lovers down into the belly of the brick-and book-lined Pioneer Square store. The bulk of Elliott Bay's offerings are free; on rare occasions, typically for special benefit events, tickets cost $5–$10. See also Top 25 Attractions in the Exploring chapter. *www.elliottbaybook.com/ebbco/; map:*O8

A multitude of other Seattle and Eastside bookstores (see Books and Periodicals in the Shopping chapter) also vie for visiting authors for readings and signings. Among the heavyweights are the **UNIVERSITY BOOK STORE** (4326 University Way NE; 206/634-3400; www.bookstore.wash ington.edu; map:FF6) and **BARNES & NOBLE BOOKSELLERS** (University Village; 206/517-4107; map:FF6), which presents the Seattle Love of Life Poets Reading Series every first and third Monday night. On the smaller side, **BAILEY/COY BOOKS** (414 Broadway E; 206/323-8842; map:HH6) caters to the alternative Capitol Hill crowd and holds several readings per month; Wallingford's **OPEN BOOKS: A POEM EMPORIUM** (2414 N 45th St; 206/633-0811; map:FF7) also offers a first-rate reading series.

Filling out the literary landscape are dozens of bars, coffeehouses, and cafes. In downtown's Pioneer Square district, the city's poets take aim at each other every Wednesday at the **OK HOTEL** (212 Alaskan Way S;

206/621-7903; map:O9) during the Seattle Slam. There's a $3–$4 cover charge to slam or be slammed. And screenwriters work out the bugs in their scripts at the Cinema Seattle **SCREENWRITERS SALON** (206/324-9996; kathleen@seattlefilm.com; www.seattlefilm.com/cinemaseattle), at the Alibi Room or the Market Theatre (1428 Post Alley; map:J8; see also Film in this chapter). Admission is around $5, but audience members are encouraged to put in more than their two cents during read-throughs. The Alibi also hosts a **DIRECTORS' SALON** (206/441-5661; www.directorssalon.com) on alternate Sundays at 7pm, where actors, directors, and audience members collaborate on a single scene. A $4 donation is suggested.

On Capitol Hill, **HABITAT ESPRESSO** (202 Broadway E; 206/329-3087; www.ahern.org/habitat; map:HH6) serves up organic coffee and tea as well as an open-mike poetry night on Monday nights. (Reflecting Seattle's altruistic nature, the Habitat is one of the country's few non-profit cafes—donating all proceeds to local social service organizations.) Vegan fare is on the menu and poetry on the walls, which are covered with literary murals, at the **GLOBE CAFÉ** (1531 14th Ave; 206/324-8815; map:HH6). The Globe is home to the venerable Red Sky Poetry Theater group, which has been around for decades and gathers to perform on Sunday nights. The Globe's Salon Poetry Series appeals to the Hill's younger set on Tuesdays nights.

Belltown bustles with arty atmosphere and literary venues. The gaudy '60s decor of the **SIT & SPIN** cafe (2219 4th Ave; 206/441-9484; map:G6) conceals a back room with an open-mike night on the first Wednesday of the month. If the poetry gets too abstract, there's always the practical distraction of washing a load of clothes at the cafe's laundromat.

Another excellent means of tracking literary happenings about town is **WORDSCAPE** (206/675-1668; wrdscape@speakeasy.org). The free monthly guide is available at most of the above-mentioned venues.

NIGHTLIFE

Nightlife by Features

ALTERNATIVE
Ballard Firehouse
The Breakroom
Colourbox
Crocodile Café
DV8
OK Hotel
The Old Firehouse
RKCNDY
Re-Bar
Showbox
Sit & Spin
Velvet Elvis
Vogue

BLUES
Bohemian Cafe
Central
Dimitriou's Jazz Alley
Doc Maynard's Public
  House
Fenix Underground
Larry's Greenfront
New Orleans Restaurant
Old Timer's Café
Scarlet Tree

CABARET
The Pink Door

CELTIC
Conor Byrne's Public
  House
Kells
Murphy's Pub
Owl 'n' Thistle

COCKTAIL LOUNGES
The Backdoor (Ultra)
  Lounge
Baltic Room
Capitol Club
Cloud Room
Fireside Room
The Nitelite
Tini Big's Lounge
Vito's Madison Grill

COMEDY
Comedy Underground
Giggles

COUNTRY
Riverside Inn

Timberline
Tractor Tavern

DANCING/DANCE
  FLOORS
ARO.space
The Backdoor (Ultra)
  Lounge
El Gaucho's Pampas
  Room
Fenix Underground
Garden Court
Neighbours
Re-Bar
Romper Room
Showbox
Timberline
Tractor Tavern
Vogue

DRINKS WITH A VIEW
Adriatica
Cloud Room
Leschi Lakecafe
Mudshark Bar
Pescatore Fish Café
The Pink Door
  (deck only)
Ray's Café
Roanoke Inn
Salty's on Alki
Shea's Lounge
Space Needle

FOLK/ACOUSTIC
Bohemian Café
Fiddler's Inn
Four Angels Coffeehouse
Grateful Bread Café
Honey Bear Bakery
Latona By Green Lake
Madison's Cafe & Music
  House
Owl 'n' Thistle
Paragon Bar and Grill
Shark Club
Tractor Tavern
Velvet Elvis
Zoka Coffee Roaster and
  Tea Co.

GAY/LESBIAN BARS
ARO.space

Neighbours
Re-Bar
R Place
Timberline
The Wild Rose

JAZZ
Baltic Room
Dimitriou's Jazz Alley
El Gaucho's Pampas Room
Elysian Brewing Co.
Latona By Green Lake
New Orleans Restaurant
OK Hotel
Old Timer's Café
Paragon Bar and Grill
Romper Room
Velvet Elvis

OUTDOOR SEATING
Axis
Belltown Pub
The Bookstore . . . A Bar
Brooklyn Seafood, Steak,
  & Oyster House
Deluxe Bar and Grill
Fiddler's Inn
Harbour Public House
J&M Cafe and Cardroom
Kells
Kirkland Roaster &
  Alehouse
Leschi Lakecafe
Linda's Tavern
Nickerson Street Saloon
Old Timer's Café
Pescatore Fish Café
The Pink Door
Pioneer Square Saloon
Ray's Café
Red Door Alehouse
Roanoke Inn
Salty's on Alki
Triangle Lounge
Wedgwood Alehouse

PIANO BARS
Baltic Room
Cloud Room
Fireside Room
Mudshark Bar

POOL TABLES/ BILLIARDS

Belltown Billiards
Blue Moon Tavern
The Breakroom
The Buckaroo
College Inn Pub
Comet Tavern
The Duchess Tavern
Dynamite Lounge
Eastlake Zoo
Fenix Underground
Garage
Grady's Montlake Pub
and Eatery
Linda's Tavern
Nickerson Street Saloon
The Old Pequliar
Owl 'n' Thistle
Red Onion Tavern
Roanoke Inn
Shark Club
Temple Billiards
211 Billiard Club

PUBS/ALEHOUSES

The Attic Alehouse and
Eatery
Belltown Pub
Big Time Brewery and
Alehouse
College Inn Pub
Conor Byrne's Public
House
Cooper's Alehouse
Elysian Brewing Co.
Forecaster's Public
House
Grady's Montlake Pub
and Eatery
Hale's Brewery and Pub
Harbour Public House
Hilltop Alehouse
Hopvine Pub
Issaquah Brewhouse
Kells
Kirkland Roaster &
Alehouse
Latona By Green Lake
McMenamins Pub &
Brewery
Murphy's Pub
Nickerson Street Saloon
The Old Pequliar
Old Town Alehouse
Pacific Inn Pub

Red Door Alehouse
Red Onion Tavern
The Roost
74th Street Alehouse
Six Arms Brewery and
Pub
Trolleyman Pub
Two Bells Tavern
Wedgwood Alehouse

REGGAE/SKA/ WORLDBEAT

Ballard Firehouse
Fenix
Fenix Underground
New Orleans Restaurant
OK Hotel

ROCK

Ballard Firehouse
The Breakroom
Central
Crocodile Café
DV8
Dynamite Lounge
Gibson's Bar & Grill
Jimmy Z's
Madison's Cafe & Music
House
RKCNDY
Romper Room
Showbox
University Sports Bar
and Grill
Velvet Elvis

ROMANTIC

Adriatica
Baltic Room
Dimitriou's Jazz Alley
El Gaucho's Pampas
Room
Fireside Room
Garden Court
Il Bistro
The Pink Door
Shea's Lounge

SMOKE-FREE

Belltown Pub
Fiddler's Inn
Four Angels Coffeehouse
Hale's Brewery and Pub
Hilltop Alehouse
Latona by Green Lake
McMenamins Pub &
Brewery

Nickerson Street Saloon
Old Town Alehouse
Trolleyman Pub
Virginia Inn

SPORTS BARS

Big Time Brewery and
Alehouse
Cooper's Alehouse
The Duchess Tavern
F. X. McRory's Steak,
Chop, and Oyster
House
The Roost

SWING

Dynamite Lounge
Fenix
Showbox

UNDERAGE/NO ALCOHOL

DV8
The Old Firehouse
RKCNDY
Velvet Elvis

Nightlife by Neighborhood

BAINBRIDGE ISLAND
Harbour Public House

BALLARD/SHILSHOLE
Ballard Firehouse
Conor Byrne's Public
House
Hale's Brewery and Pub
Hattie's Hat
The Old Pequliar
Old Town Alehouse
Pescatore Fish Café
Ray's Cafe
Tractor Tavern

BELLTOWN
Axis
Belltown Billiards
Belltown Pub
Crocodile Café
El Gaucho's Pampas
Room
Five Point Café
Frontier Room
Lava Lounge
Queen City Grill
Two Bells Tavern
211 Billiard Club

CAPITOL HILL
ARO.space
Baltic Room
B&O Espresso
Bauhaus Books and
Coffee
The Breakroom
Café Dilettante
Caffe Vita
Capitol Club
Coffee Messiah
Comet Tavern
Deluxe Bar and Grill
Elysian Brewing Co.
Four Angels Coffeehouse
Garage
Green Cat Cafe
Hopvine Pub
Joe Bar
Linda's Tavern
Neighbours
R Place
Roanoke Park Place
Tavern

Six Arms Brewery and
Pub
Vogue
The Wild Rose

DOWNTOWN
(see also Belltown and
Pike Place Market)
The Bookstore . . . A Bar
Brooklyn Seafood, Steak,
& Oyster House
Cloud Room
Dimitriou's Jazz Alley
Fireside Room (more
like Pill Hill/Cap)
Garden Court
Gibson's Bar & Grill
McCormick & Schmick's
McCormick's Fish House
and Bar
Mudshark Bar
The Nitelite
Palomino
RKCNDY
Re-Bar
Showbox
Shuckers
Sit & Spin
Timberline
Union Square Grill
Virginia Inn
Vito's Madison Grill

EASTLAKE
Eastlake Zoo
Lousia's Bakery & Café

FREMONT
The Buckaroo
Nickerson Street Saloon
(across bridge)
Red Door Alehouse
Simply Desserts
Triangle Lounge
Trolleyman Pub

GREEN LAKE
Latona by Green Lake
The Urban Bakery

**GREENWOOD/PHINNEY
RIDGE**
74th Street Alehouse

ISSAQUAH
Adriatica
Honey Bear Bakery
Issaquah Brewhouse
Lake Forest Park
Lake Union
The Roost

KIRKLAND
Da Vinci's
Dynamite Lounge
Kirkland Roaster &
Alehouse
Shark Club

LAKE CITY
Cooper's Alehouse

LESCHI
Leschi Lakecafe

**MADISON
PARK/MONTLAKE**
The Attic Alehouse and
Eatery
Grady's Montlake Pub
and Eatery
Red Onion Tavern

MERCER ISLAND
Roanoke Inn

MERIDIAN
Honey Bear Bakery
Zoka Coffee Roaster and
Tea Company

PIKE PLACE MARKET
Alibi Room
Il Bistro
Kells
The Pink Door
Procopio Gelateria
Shea's Lounge

PIONEER SQUARE
The Backdoor (Ultra)
Lounge
Bohemian Café
Central
Colourbox
Comedy Underground
Doc Maynard's Public
House
Fenix

Fenix Underground
F. X. McRory's Steak,
   Chop, and Oyster
   House
J&M Cafe and Cardroom
Larry's Greenfront
New Orleans Restaurant
OK Hotel
Old Timer's Café
Owl 'n' Thistle
Pioneer Square Saloon
Temple Billiards
Velvet Elvis

QUEEN ANNE
Caffe Appassionato
Caffe Ladro
Caffe Vita
Hilltop Alehouse
McMenamins Pub &
   Brewery
Mecca Café
Paragon Bar and Grill
Romper Room
Tini Big's Lounge
Uptown Espresso and
   Bakery

RAVENNA
Scarlet Tree

REDMOND
The Old Firehouse

SEATTLE CENTER
DV8
The Famous Pacific
   Dessert Company
Space Needle

TUKWILA
Riverside Inn

UNIVERSITY DISTRICT
Big Time Brewery and
   Alehouse
Blue Moon Tavern
Cafe Allegro
College Inn Pub
The Duchess Tavern
Espresso Roma
Giggles
Grand Illusion

WALLINGFORD
Murphy's Pub
Pacific Inn Pub
Teahouse Kuan Yin

WEDGWOOD
Fiddler's Inn
Grateful Bread Café
Wedgwood Alehouse

WEST SEATTLE
Madison's Cafe & Music
   House
Salty's on Alki
Uptown Espresso and
   Bakery

WOODINVILLE
Forecaster's Public
   House

349

NIGHTLIFE

Music and Clubs

One of the greatest ironies about the Seattle music scene of the late '80s—the scene that spawned Pearl Jam, Nirvana, Soundgarden, and Alice in Chains—was that bands had nowhere to play. Most of those famous bands struggled to find gigs, and many times they played in unusual settings (Nirvana's biggest Seattle gig before getting signed was at an old parking garage that used to sit near Stewart Street and Denny Way).

It was only after Seattle received international attention that the local club scene started to shine, with the opening of such famous clubs as the Crocodile and Moe. By that time, many of the biggest Seattle bands had moved to arenas. Still, ever since 1991 the region has been crawling with new bands that represent what locals call "the second wave of grunge," and the city has been crawling with clubs. The club scene today reflects larger and more diverse musical influences: world music, jazz, and dance play as big a role as hard and alternative rock.

Even though there are more—and better—Seattle clubs than ever, competition and quickly changing tastes affect booking policies and club operations. Clubs go out of business or change formats as fast as restaurants, so always call ahead before you head out. Today's jazz club could be tomorrow's taco stand, and, given enough time, your parking garage could become the next hot spot that launches a new form of music to be heard around the world.

Though we've listed phone numbers and days open for most of these places, be aware that you won't always get a person on the phone and hours are often erratic. Also, most clubs don't take checks. For current listings, check the local daily newspapers (weekend goings-on listings appear on Thursday or Friday), *Seattle Weekly* or *The Stranger* (the city's alternative weeklies, which come out on Thursday), *The Rocket* (the city's biweekly music publication), or the online entertainment guide Seattle Sidewalk (www.seattle.sidewalk.com).

ARO.SPACE / 925 E Pike St; 206/320-0424 Even with the arty new name and the arty new decor, locals will call this place "the old Moe" for years to come. Still, no one will confuse the acts playing the new joint with those at the old: where Moe mixed grunge and funk, ARO.space (the initials stand for Arts and Revolution Organization) mixes industrial dance music with industrial dance music. Occasionally other genres show up (the club booked Vanilla Ice during its first month of operation), but if you're not into dance music, you'll want to avoid ARO.space. Moe attracted a mixed crowd—white, black, gay, straight—while so far ARO.space is decidedly white and gay. Not only is smoking allowed, but the joke on opening night was that this would be the first Seattle club where smoking would be required by all in attendance. *Full bar; AE, MC, V; no checks; Tues–Sun; map:L1*

BALLARD FIREHOUSE / 5429 Russell Ave NW; 206/784-3516 Chances are if you want to see some rock dinosaurs at work—from Night Ranger to Missing Persons—they'll be playing the Firehouse. The booking is a little more adventuresome, however, when it comes to blues, reggae, ska, or the occasional foray into punk. The venue itself is a classic: it's got a great dance floor and a nice outdoor porch, and it's intimate enough that you can see the band from anywhere in the club. The only time you'll want to avoid this club—other than when Night Ranger is booked—is on a hot August night, when the place can live up to its name. *Full bar; AE, MC, V; no checks; every day; map:FF8*

BALTIC ROOM / 1207 Pine St; 206/625-4444 This may be the closest thing Seattle has to a hip lounge, so don't come here in your jeans and flannels. The Baltic Room started in 1997 in a spot formerly known as Kid Mohair. It's co-owned by Linda Derschang, of the Capitol Club and Linda's Tavern, so it's guaranteed to be cutting edge. Live music here is mostly piano jazz, but the atmosphere is always worth the visit. *Beer and wine; MC, V; no checks; every day; map:J2*

BOHEMIAN CAFÉ / 111 Yesler Way; 206/447-1514 This club has been a fixture in Pioneer Square for years and usually books blues or folk acts. The club's layout is unusual, with an upstairs and a downstairs (the band plays downstairs by the window). *Full bar; AE, DIS, MC, V; no checks; Mon–Sat; map:N8*

THE BREAKROOM / 1325 E Madison St; 206/860-5155 This former auto shop is the latest hot club on Capitol Hill and now one of the premier venues for local rock bands. It doesn't book music every night—usually it attracts a pool-playing, beer-drinking crowd—but on music nights it's packed. Bring your earplugs, don't wash your hair, and have a good time. *Beer and wine; no credit cards; no checks; every day; map:HH6*

CENTRAL / 207 1st Ave S; 206/622-0209 The "new" Central is not to be confused with the Central circa 1981 (country rock central) or the Central 1988 (grunge central). The format is back to sweet blues, with an occasional pop-rock band for good measure. *Full bar; AE, MC, V; local checks only; every day; map:O8*

COLOURBOX / 113 1st Ave S; 206/340-4101 This Pioneer Square club is one of the few in the area that consistently books alternative rock and supports local bands. It's one of the best places to see up-and-coming bands before they get too famous. The downside is that the club itself is essentially a cement cavern, and though that might have been great for launching the Beatles' career, it makes the acoustics here less than ideal. The venue itself is rumored to be slated for demolition, so check it out while you can. *Beer and wine; MC, V; no checks; every day; map:O8*

COMEDY UNDERGROUND / 222 S Main St; 206/628-0303 For a decade and a half, this Pioneer Square basement has been Seattle's top comedy club. It's also the only club in town that has comedy every night of the week. On weekends you can still expect a significant wait when the talent is big enough. The club can be hard to find for novices: it's called the Comedy Underground because it's underneath Swannie's restaurant. *Full bar; AE, DC, MC, V; checks OK; every day; www.comedyunder ground.com; map:P8*

CROCODILE CAFÉ / 2200 2nd Ave; 206/441-5611 It can't hurt a club when the owner is married to a member of R.E.M., but then Stephanie Dorgan (married to Peter Buck) has been one of the most competent club owners in Seattle for a long time (and before Buck came into the picture). The Croc continues to thrive because it has a combination of great booking, ranging from local favorites to national rock, folk, and blues artists, ideal sound, and a perfect location (in the center of Belltown, convenient for everything but parking). Though the club actually began after the Seattle music scene of the late '80s had already developed, it's now the stuff of legend: it's been the site for gigs by Nirvana, Mudhoney, Mad Season, and others. The only downside to the Croc comes from its continued popularity; most shows are crowded, and during the past two years those throngs have taken to talking constantly, which can be annoying for anyone wanting to hear the music. Chatterers should head to the back of the club, where a separate cocktail lounge is always the place to find the latest hot gossip about the Northwest rock scene. There's even a restaurant at the Croc, though you'll have to eat your food in the middle of a loud, smoky club. The cover charge is very affordable unless the act is a national name. *Full bar; MC, V; no checks; every day; map:G7*

DIMITRIOU'S JAZZ ALLEY / 2033 6th Ave; 206/441-9729 John Dimitriou's venue is not just the best jazz club in Seattle, it's one of the best in the nation. His reputation brings in international-caliber talent, and the club itself is perfectly designed—you can hear and see from every seat. During the past year, Dimitriou has added more blues acts to his bookings, and local artists frequently play during the week. The cover can be expensive, and there are drink minimums on weekends. You can guarantee yourself a seat by going early for dinner, although the food is not quite as good as the jazz. *Full bar; AE, MC, V; checks OK; every day; www.jazzalley.org; map:H5*

DOC MAYNARD'S PUBLIC HOUSE / 610 1st Ave; 206/682-4649 This longtime Pioneer Square blues club attracts a young, frat-like crowd for

THE SEATTLE SOUND

Downtown Kansas City doesn't have slaughterhouses anymore, but people still order a Kansas City cut of steak. It's a similar situation with Seattle and "grunge": the only true grunge bands were ones that barely registered on the cultural radar back in the late '80s (including Blood Circus, Tad, and the Fluid—the last not even from Seattle). By the time Nirvana, Soundgarden, and Alice in Chains were making international headlines, their music was far more rock than true grunge. But that didn't stop everyone from calling it grunge—and in the early '90s record stores in Europe had entire sections devoted to the genre, while fashion designers were talking about their new grunge lines.

Tags are usually meant to define a small, true sound. Unfortunately, they end up being applied to larger cultural landscapes, which is why most Seattle musicians cringe when asked about grunge. Ten years after the first grunge bands came and went, the term still gets kicked around to describe anything loud, distorted, and slow, which these days works for only a handful of young bands.

Seattle's music scene is actually far more diverse than most surveys would suggest, including large factions of heavy metal fans, experimental noise bands, hip-hop aficionados, and even a thriving Christian rock scene. These days there is no definable "Seattle sound," though experimental jazz and hip-hop are making big inroads, and many local bands with large followings now explore the fusion between funk and rock. The "sound" of a city is usually defined by the style of bands at the hottest clubs; but Seattle has so many different clubs that are happening at any one time that it's impossible to suggest that just one dominates.

Rock is still popular in Seattle nightclubs, and many bands work within the garage-rock confines first explored in these parts by the Sonics and the Wailers in the early '60s. The more things change in music, the more they stay the same. You can see Zeke or the Makers and you'll be seeing both a bit of the past and a taste of the future. Most bands that develop large followings (Pearl Jam, for example) end up watering down their sound so much that it's best to call it rock or pop, but it's certainly nothing as pure as grunge.

So if you want to see a grunge band, you'd better set your time machine for 1988, close your eyes, put in your earplugs, and turn up the amps.

— Charles R. Cross

most events. It's a very intimate space—in one of the oldest buildings in Seattle—and if the lineup is one you like, it's a great place to see a show. It is not the sort of place you'd want to go just to hang out or talk, unless your idea of talking is getting hit on by a Delta Chi. *Full bar; MC, V; no checks; Fri–Sat; map:N8*

DV8 / 131 Taylor Ave N; 206/448-0888 If you're 20 or older, you'll feel old at DV8, since the club caters to the underage crowd. No alcohol is served, but bookings can be intoxicating, with many alternative rock acts (think Foo Fighters, Breeders) making this their venue of choice. This is always one of the loudest places to hear a show, so bring your earplugs and go early. Because of the very young crowd, it's not unusual for DV8 shows to start at 6pm and be over by 9pm. *No alcohol; open only when shows are booked; map:D6*

DYNAMITE LOUNGE / 15 Lake St, Kirkland; 425/822-3474 Believe it or not, the Eastside now has a club that could give its urban counterparts a run for their money. That club is the swank Dynamite Lounge. With a performance area equal in size to the bar area (both ample), Dynamite is a perfect place to catch a live band or dance the night away at weekly swing events. Not to neglect sports-inclined patrons, this place also has a foosball table, darts, a couple of pool tables, and five TV screens tuned to the sports channels. *Full bar; AE, MC, V; checks OK; every day; map:EE3*

EL GAUCHO'S PAMPAS ROOM / 90 Wall St; 206/728-1140 The Pampas opened in early 1998 below the El Gaucho restaurant. Like its upstairs neighbor, it attracts a dressed-up crowd, but here the draw is the upscale jazz (and dancing) rather than the juicy steaks. *Full bar; AE, DC, MC, V; checks OK; Fri–Sat; www.elgaucho.com; map:F8*

FENIX / FENIX UNDERGROUND / 315 2nd Ave S; 206/467-1111 The two Fenix clubs took over a couple of tired Pioneer Square venues and have made the music refreshing and up-to-date. The only negative is that even when the clubs book the weirdest avant-garde acts, they seem to pull in a largely frat crowd. (One recent addition is a tattoo parlor, so if you get really drunk you can have the name of your house put on your butt.) The Underground tends to book more reggae, blues, and funk, while the aboveground Fenix lately has been the center of the ska and big-band scenes, with acts like the Royal Crown Revue getting the crowd jitterbugging. The club also occasionally has booked hip-hop and rap—one of the few Seattle venues to do so successfully. A recent addition is the midlevel cigar bar and pool hall. *Full bar; AE, DIS, MC, V; no checks; every day; home.earthlink.net/~fenixinc; map:P8*

FOUR ANGELS COFFEEHOUSE / 1400 14th Ave; 206/329-4066 Four Angels brings to Capitol Hill something it was desperately missing: a place to hear acoustic folk music. The club opened in the spring of 1998, and the lineup has been top-notch right from the start. Music is on weekends, irregularly, so check the schedule. *Beer and wine; no credit cards; checks OK; every day; map:HH6*

GIBSON'S BAR & GRILL / 116 Stewart St; 206/448-6369 For years this club was known only for its stiff drinks and the fact that someone once got killed there. It's now known for its stiff drinks and for on-the-rise punk and hard rock bands. They were drinking there anyway, so they figured why not play? *Full bar; AE, MC, V; no checks; every day; map:I8*

GIGGLES / 5220 Roosevelt Way NE; 206/526-5653 Though the comedy scene in general has had its ups and downs (and lately it's mostly been down), Giggles has endured the swings and has consistently brought some of the best touring acts to town. Located in the University District, it draws a younger crowd than the Comedy Underground. *Full bar; MC, V; no checks; Thurs–Sun; map:FF7*

GRATEFUL BREAD CAFÉ / 7001 35th Ave NE; 206/525-3166 The name suggests you'll hear only "Dark Star," but this little Wedgwood bakery has turned into the city's best folk club. It's tiny, though, so get there early. Shows are held irregularly; call the Seattle Folklore Society (206/782-0505) to check the schedule. *No alcohol; no credit cards; local checks only; every day; map:EE6*

LARRY'S GREENFRONT / 209 1st Ave S; 206/624-7665 This place is a dive that gives you the feeling that most people go to Larry's for the drinks (stiff) rather than the blues bands (loose), yet this club has the best blues bookings in Pioneer Square. *Full bar; AE, DC, DIS, MC, V; checks OK; every day; map:O8*

MADISON'S CAFE & MUSIC HOUSE / 3803 Delridge Way SW; 206/935-2412 Madison's began in 1995 as one of the first local clubs to book the growing number of singer/songwriters who aren't quite folk and aren't quite rock. It also boasts a decent cafe. It's somewhat hard to find (take the Delridge Way exit from the West Seattle Bridge) but worth the trip. Entertainment is booked only on weekends. *Beer and wine; DC, DIS, MC, V; checks OK; every day; map:KK8*

NEIGHBOURS / 1509 Broadway E; 206/324-5358 For a couple of decades, Neighbours has been *the* neighborhood gay dance spot on Capitol Hill. In the last few years, the club has become more diverse, with more lesbian and straight women showing up (and sometimes dancing with their shirts off). The music—which is always canned—is disco and Top 40. "Everybody dance now. . . ." *Full bar; no credit cards; no checks; every day; map:HH6*

NEW ORLEANS RESTAURANT / 114 1st Ave S; 206/622-2563 The New Orleans is one of the best venues in Pioneer Square because the owners support a booking policy that goes with the food: spicy, exotic, and classy. You'll find good Creole cuisine in the kitchen and zydeco, jazz, and blues in the showroom. *Full bar; AE, MC, V; local checks only; every day; map:N8*

OFF RAMP / 109 Eastlake Ave E; 206/652-9900 This space was known as the Off Ramp, then it was shuttered for two years, then it was Sub Zero, and now it's back to being the Off Ramp. Not much else has changed, however. It still books up-and-coming alternative rock and hard rock bands (recent bookings include Day Glo Abortions, Christ Driver, and Thorazine), and though it rarely attracts national touring acts, this is a great place to see bands on the way up (or down). *Full bar; no credit cards; no checks; every day; map:H1*

OK HOTEL / 212 Alaskan Way S; 206/621-7903 This Pioneer Square nightspot is world renowned, if only because it was featured in the movie *Singles*. But despite its reputation, it's hard to find for first-timers: it's west of First Avenue S, on Alaskan Way S, essentially underneath the Viaduct. The eclectic mix of alternative rock bands, reggae groups, jazz artists, and divas makes it worth the trip. The club has music both in the back room and in the bar, and regular poetry slams on Wednesdays. Historical note: Nirvana debuted "Smells Like Teen Spirit" here in 1991. *Full bar; MC, V; no checks; Mon–Sat; map:O8*

THE OLD FIREHOUSE / 16510 NE 79th St, Redmond; 425/556-2370 Not to be confused with the Ballard Firehouse, this Redmond venue is an all-ages hot spot where teenagers go to hear alternative rock. There's no alcohol, but soda will cost you only 50 cents, and the bands playing here are some of the best in the region. Just because it allows underage kids doesn't mean hip adults have to skip it. Shows, when they are scheduled, are Fridays and Saturdays. *No alcohol; no credit cards; no checks; every day; map:EE1*

OLD TIMER'S CAFÉ / 620 1st Ave; 206/623-9800 Jazz and blues seven nights a week are the draw here, along with a full bar and a classic Pioneer Square wood-and-brass decor. *Full bar; AE, MC, V; no checks; every day; map:N8*

OWL 'N' THISTLE / 808 Post Ave; 206/621-7777 This Irish pub is hidden two blocks off the waterfront, just north of Pioneer Square, and it's worth the walk. The bookings usually are Celtic folk bands. There's also a small pool room and a comfortable dining area up front. *Full bar; AE, DIS, MC, V; no checks; every day; www.teleport.com/~dgs1300/owlthistle.html; map:M8*

PARAGON BAR AND GRILL / 2125 Queen Anne Ave N; 206/283-4548 This is the hottest club on Queen Anne—though at the moment that's not saying much. It tends to attract a young "fake-tan" crowd, but the music is usually decent jazz or folk. *Full bar; AE, DC, MC, V; local checks only; every day; map:GG7*

RE-BAR / 1114 Howell St; 206/233-9873 Re-Bar books live music only once a week, but it does attract musicians, who either hang out in the bar or get funky and dance. Thursday is Queer Disco night, as it has been for years, though the crowd is always sexually diverse. The DJs here are top-notch. *Beer and wine; no credit cards; no checks; every day; map:I2*

RIVERSIDE INN / 14060 Interurban Ave S, Tukwila; 206/244-5400 Put your shit-kickers and your mud-flaps on before you head to the River-side: it's the closest thing the Seattle area has to a honky-tonk. It's got live music seven nights a week, and dancing lessons (two-step, line, and so on) early in the evening. Y'all come back now. *Full bar; AE, DIS, MC, V; checks OK; every day; map:OO5*

RKCNDY / 1812 Yale Ave; 206/667-0219 Even without the vowels this club has garnered an international reputation, though many out-of-towners don't know that you simply call it "rock candy." The club recently underwent an ownership change, but the music bookings remain all-ages and are always alternative or hard rock. The new owners promise some remodeling—yet with future development in the area looming, it's doubtful this club will see the millennium. The crowd comes early and in packs. Most shows sell out, so plan ahead for tickets. There's no booze here, so if you must liquor up, head over to the Off Ramp beforehand. *No alcohol; no credit cards; no checks; open only when shows are booked; map:H1*

ROMPER ROOM / 106 1st Ave N; 206/284-5003 The Presidents of the United States of America actually played a few gigs here early in their career, though the lineup these days is usually jazz, funk, or frat rock. *Full bar; MC, V; no checks; Mon–Sat; romper@speakeasy.org; map:A7*

SCARLET TREE / 6521 Roosevelt Way NE; 206/523-7153 The Scarlet Tree may be best known as a place where you can get a hard drink at 6am (and don't think people aren't in there), but it also consistently draws crowds for the hard-driving blues bands it books. *Full bar; AE, MC, V; local checks only; every day; map:EE7*

SHARK CLUB / 52 Lakeshore Plaza, Kirkland; 425/803-3003 This club, known locally as "The Shark," draws a mostly Bellevue crowd who want a little dose of Seattle rock in Kirkland. The last few years have brought more adventuresome bookings and even Seattle folk singer Gerald Col-lier. The venue itself is well designed, and it's a good place to see a show if you can handle the beer buddies next to you. *Full bar; AE, DIS, MC, V; no checks; every day; map:EE3*

SHOWBOX / 1426 1st Ave; 206/628-3151 The Showbox has had more lives than any hepcat, but its latest incarnation may be the one that gets remembered the longest. This former bingo parlor, then punk rock club, then comedy club, and now concert hall is one of the most popular rooms in town. It mixes national touring acts (Elvis Costello, Paul Westerberg, Semisonic) with local alternative rock and dance bands, so it's always hopping. The club features regular dance nights (presently Pomade and Electrolush) that pull in fans from all corners of the Northwest to dance and be seen. It's reminiscent of a European club, and, as at a hip nightspot in Madrid, expect young crowds, walls of smoke, and mostly black clothes. On weekends, swingers take over the place for Zoot Suit Sundays, with live bands every other week. *Full bar; MC, V; no checks; Tues–Sun; map:K7*

SIT & SPIN / 2219 4th Ave; 206/441-9484 Sit & Spin once was simply a laundromat that also had a coffee shop. Then it became a cafe, and now it's also a nightclub. Why anyone would want to wash their clothes in the middle of a nightclub is hard to answer, but you'll find a brave few folding their panties at 1am. This club is tiny, but it's also a fun place to see bands; it is intimate enough that you won't be more than 20 feet away from the stage, and the booking keeps the crowd young and energetic. One recent bill had this stellar lineup: Tad, Family Sex, Jackpot, and Tot Finder. If you know any of these bands, you're probably already hanging out here. *Full bar; no credit cards; no checks; every day; map:G7*

TIMBERLINE / 2015 Boren Ave; 206/622-6220 Shake a leg to country and western music at this lively, popular gay and lesbian disco. Don't know how to two-step? Show up Tuesdays or Wednesdays and they'll teach you for free, and give you line-dancing lessons as well. Swing lessons are on Thursdays (also free, although there is a $1 cover all nights), and weekend nights are strictly country and western. You can shake your thang on Sunday afternoons to classic '70s disco (a Seattle tradition) while sipping draft beers for under a buck. *Beer and wine; no credit cards; no checks; Tues–Sun; map:G3*

TRACTOR TAVERN / 5213 Ballard Ave NW; 206/789-3599 Since the closing of the venerable Backstage in 1997, the Tractor has been the hottest spot in Ballard, if not the hottest club in the city—at least when it comes to roots rock. The club's bookings are diverse but always a little left of mainstream, whether they be alternative country acts (Jimmie Dale Gilmore) or alternative folk acts (the ever-popular Paperboys). *Beer and wine; no credit cards; local checks only; Tues–Sun; map:FF8*

VELVET ELVIS / 107 Occidental Ave S; 206/624-8477 This Pioneer Square haunt is best known for being an all-ages venue, but the booking is surprisingly eclectic, and almost always worth a shot. The club was the first venue the Foo Fighters played in Seattle, though most shows these days are more in the folk vein (Elliott Smith, Mary Lou Lord). The Velvet Elvis is also nearly perfect for jazz. Unfortunately, the *Kerouac: The*

Essence of Jack one-man show (which played for years) ended its run in early 1999. It will be missed. *No alcohol; MC, V; checks OK; open only when shows are booked; map:O8*

VOGUE / 1516 11th Ave; 206/443-0673 The Vogue moved out of gentrified Belltown in 1999 and its latest incarnation resides on Capitol Hill. Nirvana, Soundgarden, and Tad all had early shows here, but its been years since the club offered live bands. Now the music is always from DJs, though the Vogue can still be a fun alternative, particularly on "fetish night." *Beer and wine; MC, V; no checks; every day; map:H8*

Bars, Pubs, and Taverns

ADRIATICA / 1107 Dexter Ave N; 206/285-5000 Although its Lake Union view was sacrificed to what passes for progress in this changing neighborhood, Adriatica remains an oasis at the top of an endless staircase. The mood is still romantic, the martinis excellent, and the wine list adventuresome. A late-night menu of savory Mediterranean fare and midweek jazz make this restaurant's bar a reliable stop on the sophisticate circuit. *Full bar; AE, MC, V; checks OK; every day; map:B2*

ALIBI ROOM / 85 Pike St, Pike Place Market; 206/623-3180 Opened and owned by local Hollywood types (including the ubiquitous Tom Skerritt), the Alibi was concepted as a watering hole for Seattle indie filmmakers, complete with a script-reading series and film-related decor. On weekends, the nicely restored space hidden in cobblestoned Post Alley is packed with drinkers of the hip and single variety, film literacy not required. Lunch and dinner menus offer sandwiches and seafood. Weekend disco downstairs is geared toward the very young and peppy. *Beer and wine; MC, V; no checks; every day; map:J8*

THE ATTIC ALEHOUSE AND EATERY / 4226 E Madison St; 206/323-3131 From Madison Park old-timers to fresh-faced UW grads, everyone comes to the Attic for a good selection of microbrews, Guinness on tap, and consistently tasty nightly dinner specials. *Beer and wine; AE, MC, V; checks OK; every day; map:GG6*

AXIS / 2214 1st Ave; 206/441-9600 Delectable snacks and an endless parade of well-dressed (or badly dressed, depending on your point of view) professionals make the lounge at Axis one of Belltown's liveliest. Order a glass of wine from the thoughtfully chosen list, and indulge in some deep-fried pickles—if you can find a table. *Full bar; AE, DC, MC, V; no checks; every day; map:G8*

THE BACKDOOR (ULTRA) LOUNGE / 503 3rd Ave; 206/622-7665 This Pioneer Square bar, tucked at the top of steep stairs next to the Yesler

Way bus tunnel station, has become the darling of the *Swinger's* set. The kitschy decor is a gas, if you're the type who can actually relax in a replica of Uncle Al's rumpus room circa 1966 (complete with Aunt Jaynie's hand-knit afghan pillows). DJ dancing on weekends, and nightly martini specials. *Full bar; AE, DIS, MC, V; no checks; Mon–Sat; map:O7*

BELLTOWN BILLIARDS / 90 Blanchard St; 206/448-6779 Belltown Billiards is a mishmash: part high-tech bar and dance floor, part high-class pool hall, part high-gloss Italian restaurant. But everyone is having too much fun to mind the confusion. The food takes a back seat on weekend nights, when the crowds descend and the crush of bodies turns pool into a true spectator sport. *Full bar; AE, MC, V; no checks; every day; map:G8*

BELLTOWN PUB / 2322 1st Ave; 206/728-4311 Pile into a spacious booth, admire the wooden scull rowing overhead, and sip micros to your heart's content, but leave the Marlboros at home: there's no smoking here at the Belltown—unless you can snag one of the few outdoor tables in summer. Some choice appetizers make lingering easy; try the steamed mussels with Italian sausage, and soak up the broth with the tasty focaccia. *Full bar; AE, MC, V; no checks; every day; map:G8*

BIG TIME BREWERY AND ALEHOUSE / 4133 University Way NE; 206/545-4509 Antique beer ads clutter the walls at the U-District's most popular alehouse, where the brews are made on the other side of the wall. The place is hopping with students and faculty, some burrowed into booths with piles of books, others looking for love or entertaining visiting friends and colleagues. The front room is nonsmoking; in the back there's a shuffleboard game, though it's the off-the-floor variety. *Beer and wine; MC, V; no checks; every day; map:FF6*

BLUE MOON TAVERN / 712 NE 45th St It's seedy, it's smoky, and it's beloved: when this lair of legends and gutter dreams appeared to be in the path of the wrecking ball, a cry of protest went up, books on its shady history were quickly printed, and demonstrations were organized. A yearlong battle with developers produced a 40-year lease and a collective sigh of relief from the neighborhood pool players, Beat ghosts, living poets, and survivors of the U-District's glory days. Tom Robbins put in his time in this crusty joint, and no wonder; the graffiti-covered booths are filled with strange characters who seem to be in search of a novel. Blue Moon funds the literary journal *Point No Point* and holds an annual poetry and fiction contest. *Beer and wine; no credit cards; no checks; every day; map:FF7*

THE BOOKSTORE . . . A BAR (ALEXIS HOTEL) / 1007 1st Ave; 206/382-1506 The front bar of the Alexis Hotel is a great rainy-day hangout for sipping coffee or cognac. Books line the shelves, and there's a wide selection of magazines and newspapers; or you can simply watch the passersby scurrying down First Avenue. The Bookstore is popular with the business crowd as well as hotel guests, and you may spot an out-of-town Hollywood star or two on occasion. The food is fab (you can order from the menu of the Painted Table, the Alexis's excellent restaurant, as well), and anchovy lovers can partake of the city's most intense caesars. The bartenders are chatty, making the atmosphere amiable even for the less literarily inclined. *Full bar; AE, DC, DIS, MC, V; checks OK; every day; map:L8*

BROOKLYN SEAFOOD, STEAK, & OYSTER HOUSE / 1212 2nd Ave; 206/224-7000 If you're looking to meet a lawyer, this is the place: after work, the Brooklyn crawls with suits. On summer weekends tourists replace lawyers, oohing and aahing at the fresh oyster selection. There's plenty of seating at the wraparound bar and a good choice of beers, although this is more of a single-malt Scotch crowd. *Full bar; AE, DIS, MC, V; checks OK; every day; map:K7*

THE BUCKAROO / 4201 Fremont Ave N; 206/634-3161 Upper Fremont's legendary roadhouse sports one of the city's finest displays of neon—the lassoing cowboy out front. The helmet rack is always full, as bikers from miles around pile in for a brewski and a game of pool. One doesn't come here for MENSA meetings, though. The place can get a bit rowdy; women heading out for an evening alone might better drink elsewhere. *Beer and wine; no credit cards; checks OK; every day; map:FF7*

CAPITOL CLUB / 414 E Pine St; 206/325-2149 Seattle's own Casbah, this stylish second-floor den is a favorite with hip young professionals, who crowd the outdoor terrace and cozy up at candlelit tables with martinis and plates of Middle Eastern noshes, including fragrant olives, pita, and hummus. The restaurant occupies the main level, and its adjacent Blue Room serves as an intimate gathering place for special occasions, but the comfortable yet exotic bar is the place to make the scene. *Full bar; AE, MC, V; no checks; every day; map:J2*

CLOUD ROOM (CAMLIN HOTEL) / 1619 9th Ave; 206/682-0100 Kitty-corner from the Paramount, this dark, clubby place is a great spot for pre- or post-show sipping. The piano bar seems straight out of New Jersey. The well-mixed drinks are strong and expensive, and you can count on the tickler of the ivories to know "our song." No views of the water—those have been obscured by surrounding buildings for decades. Nonetheless, the rooftop terrace is a pleasant spot to while away an evening, with city lights atwinkle. (The future of this hot spot is uncertain, as it may be renovated out of existence during the Camlin's planned remodeling.) *Full bar; AE, DIS, MC, V; local checks only; every day; map:I4*

COLLEGE INN PUB / 4006 University Way NE; 206/634-2307 The dark, cozy basement of the College Inn is the closest thing hereabouts to a campus rathskeller, since any such is strictly verboten at the university a block away. Students who've reached the age of majority drink microbrewed ales by the pitcher, attack mounds of nachos, play pool (free on Sunday) to loud music, and convene for more serious symposia in the private room in back. *Beer and wine; MC, V; no checks; every day; map:FF6*

COMET TAVERN / 922 E Pike St; 206/323-9853 The scruffy Comet is a Capitol Hill institution, packed on the weekends with ripped-jean types of both genders who keep the pool tables and dartboards in active use. It's smoky, rowdy, and sometimes smelly, although nobody seems to care, and the graffiti are among the most inspired in the city. *Beer and wine; no credit cards; no checks; every day; map:L1*

CONOR BYRNE'S PUBLIC HOUSE / 5140 Ballard Ave NW; 206/784-3640 The former site of the long-beloved Owl has aged into the most authentic-feeling Irish pub in town, where the Guinness flows freely, loosening the silver tongues of the (real and pseudo) Irishmen sitting at the bar. Celtic music on weekends. *Beer and wine; MC, V; checks OK; every day; www.conorspub.com; map:FF8*

COOPER'S ALEHOUSE / 8065 Lake City Way NE; 206/522-2923 A mecca for serious brew lovers and home to postgame soccer and rugby bacchanals, this neighborhood pub aims to please in a straightforward, no-nonsense manner. Patrons can opt for darts or for sports on TV, but the beer's the main thing, and Cooper's offers 26 taps, most of them dispensing Northwest microbrews. The Ballard Bitter–battered fish 'n' chips are terrific. *Beer and wine; MC, V; no checks; every day; map:EE7*

DA VINCI'S / 89 Kirkland Ave, Kirkland; 425/889-9000 Formerly known as "the cruisiest bar in Kirkland," Da Vinci's has cleaned up its act with a renovation and is now worthy of sharing its moniker with the Renaissance Man. The various collages and murals are a 21st-century nod to their namesake. The crowd has tamed down a bit to make way for a hipper, more subdued set. In summer, regulars perch on high stools by the open-walled street side of the place to watch passersby. Hungry? The adjoining Cafe Da Vinci cooks up some mean Italian fare. *Full bar; AE, DC, DIS, MC, V; checks OK; every day; map:EE3*

DELUXE BAR AND GRILL / 625 Broadway E; 206/324-9697 The time-honored Deluxe is where the more mainstream Broadway boulevardiers go for stuffed baked potatoes and electric iced teas. The bar is often crammed, although the retractable wall in front lets you sit on the sidewalk in nice weather and watch the steady stream of passersby. Nightly drink specials. *Full bar; AE, DIS, MC, V; no checks; every day; map:GG6*

THE DUCHESS TAVERN / 2827 NE 55th St; 206/527-8606 This is the kind of neighborhood tavern that former university students remember fondly decades after graduation. Today's Duchess has cleaned up its act considerably, it's more open and airy than in the past, and there are 20 beers on tap (more than half are microbrews). The darts, the pool table, and the '60s rock make it the perfect place to stop for a pitcher after the game. The pizza is remarkably tasty. *Beer and wine; AE, MC, V; local checks only; every day; map:FF6*

EASTLAKE ZOO / 2301 Eastlake Ave E; 206/329-3277 One of the city's most venerable and beloved neighborhood tavs, the Zoo is equally popular with young pool hustlers and older barflies, including regulars who've made this their home away from home for more than two decades. Plenty to do besides drink beer: play pool, shuffleboard, darts, or pinball (no video games). Free pool until 5pm. *Beer and wine; no credit cards; no checks; every day; map:GG7*

ELYSIAN BREWING CO. / 1211 E Pike St; 206/860-1920 This spacious Capitol Hill club is best known for its beer (excellent, and brewed on the premises), but it's also become a live music venue on Saturday nights for jazz and other genres. *Beer and wine; MC, V; no checks; every day; www.elysianbrewing.com; map:HH6*

F. X. MCRORY'S STEAK, CHOP, AND OYSTER HOUSE / 419 Occidental Ave S; 206/623-4800 There's plenty of Old World charm here, as well as more Gilded Age bravura and bourbon than you can imagine. F. X. McRory's is a favorite among the town's professional athletes. Fresh oysters and a solid beer collection, too. Go with a Seattle Prep grad who talks sports—loudly. *Full bar; AE, DC, DIS, MC, V; checks OK; every day; map:P9*

FIDDLER'S INN / 9219 35th Ave NE; 206/525-0752 Opened in Wedgwood in 1995, this affiliate of the Latona by Green Lake pub has the look and feel of a log cabin in the woods. It's a one-room, nonsmoking establishment, with picnic tables set on an outdoor patio. There's acoustic music on weekends. *Beer and wine; MC, V; checks OK; every day; map:DD6*

FIRESIDE ROOM (SORRENTO HOTEL) / 900 Madison St; 206/622-6400 The clubby lounge in the lobby of the Sorrento evokes a leisurely world of hearthside chats in overstuffed chairs, an unrushed perusal of the daily newspaper, a hand of whist. Most pleasant for a late-evening drink, particularly on Thursday through Saturday nights, when the piano accompanies the music of many and varied conversations. Appetizers are available until midnight. *Full bar; AE, DIS, MC, V; checks OK; every day; map:M4*

FIVE POINT CAFÉ / 415 Cedar St; 206/448-9993 Stuffed fish on the wall, nuts in the chairs, rocks in the jukebox—you never know what you'll find here, except extra-strong drinks that have minimal impact on your wallet. With a friendly clientele that ranges from bluehairs and gays to suburban babes and Rastafarians, the place—despite its divey decor and perma-nicotined walls—gives hope that world peace may be achievable after all. *Full bar; AE, MC, V; no checks; every day; map:E7*

FORECASTER'S PUBLIC HOUSE / 14300 NE 145th St, Woodinville; 425/483-3232 The bustling, cheery pub at Redhook's Woodinville brewery is a hub for tourists and Burke-Gilman Trail cyclists in warm weather, and a cozy spot for beer- and food-lovers of all stripes to linger in winter. Take a tour of the brewery, or just enjoy several Redhook varieties while munching on appetizers or heartier sandwiches and seafood entrees. Live music is played on Friday and Saturday nights. *Beer and wine; AE, MC, V; checks OK; every day; map:BB1*

FRONTIER ROOM / 2203 1st Ave; 206/441-3377 Don't wear your Sunday best here: jeans are de rigueur. Partiers pile into booths in the shacklike bar or gather at tables in the dark back room, which is lit with Christmas lights. You can turn gray before a server arrives, so go up to the bar for your drinks, which, once in hand, are painfully strong. Despite (or perhaps because of) its skanky vibes and general seediness, it's one of Belltown's most action-packed spots. *Full bar; MC, V; no checks; every day; map:H8*

GARAGE / 1130 Broadway; 206/322-2296 Just what Seattle needed—another pricey pool hall. Fortunately, this one's oozing with amiable character and outfitted with 18 good tables plus plenty of neon in the bar. Local celebrity owners include Pearl Jam's Mike McCready. Come during happy hour for $2 beer and $3 well drinks, and order a designer pizza or a plate of fries. Cigar smokers are free to light up. *Full bar; AE, MC, V; no checks; every day; map:M1*

GRADY'S MONTLAKE PUB AND EATERY / 2307 24th Ave E; 206/726-5968 Grady's is a convivial neighborhood pub, comfortable and clean. Come for the good selection of micros on tap and the food, which is a cut above the usual pub fare, but stay away on Husky game days unless you're a diehard fan. Nonsmokers beware. *Beer and wine; MC, V; local checks only; every day; map:GG6*

HALE'S BREWERY AND PUB / 4301 Leary Way NW; 206/782-0737 This gleaming, spacious brewpub, a showcase for locally renowned Hale's ales, also serves as an oasis of sophistication in the Fremont-Ballard industrial neighborhood. Grab a booth, or bring along enough of the gang to fill one of the long tables in the high-ceilinged back room, where live music is performed on weekend nights. Nine varieties of Hale's pour year-round, including Moss Bay Extra and Celebration Porter, as well as a selection of rotating seasonal varieties. Salads, sandwiches, and nicely crafted pizzas make up the menu, and smoking is permitted outdoors only. *Beer only; MC, V; checks OK; every day; map:FF8*

HARBOUR PUBLIC HOUSE / 231 Parfitt Way SW, Bainbridge Island; 206/842-0969 This friendly pub on Bainbridge's Eagle Harbor is an easy stroll from the ferry dock. In winter it's cozy and amber-lit; in summer, sunlight slants through loft windows and onto the airy waterside deck. There's a connoisseur's selection of lagers and ales along with a broad list of wines, ports, and sherries. And there's an enlightened menu of food, from traditional pub fare to pasta. *Beer and wine; MC, V; local checks only; every day*

HATTIE'S HAT / 5231 Ballard Ave NW; 206/784-0175 Deep in the heart of Scandinavian Ballard is Hattie's Hat, home of Aunt Harriet's Room and its massive back bar brought 'round the Horn at the turn of the century. Although the place has been gentrified considerably, thanks to new owners and its inevitable discovery by the ever-restless hip crowd, it manages to retain the alluring seediness of a classic saloon—as well as a goodly number of thirsty fishermen. There's live music in the back room a couple of times a month. *Full bar; MC, V; local checks only; every day; map:FF8*

HILLTOP ALEHOUSE / 2129 Queen Anne Ave N; 206/285-3877 The 74th Street Ale House's sister establishment atop Queen Anne shares many of its excellent qualities: a healthy selection of beers, tasty pub food, and a convivial atmosphere, making the Hilltop a great contribution to the neighborhood. *Beer and wine; MC, V; checks OK; every day; map:GG7*

HOPVINE PUB / 507 15th Ave E; 206/328-3120 Another seedy tavern transformed into a clean pub featuring lots of microbrews. There are hop vines stenciled and sculpted on the walls, wooden booths and tables stained in bright colors, and a smoking area in back. With pizza on the menu and acoustic music a couple of nights each week, this is a welcome addition to the Capitol Hill neighborhood. *Beer and wine; MC, V; checks OK; every day; map:GG6*

IL BISTRO / 93-A Pike St, Pike Place Market; 206/682-3049 The amber lights cast a romantic glow that's ideal for a secret rendezvous in this sloping bar, tucked beneath the Market where cobblestoned Pike Street dips and turns. A busy after-work place, it's also a magnet for nocturnal sorts—from artists to jet-setters and restaurateurs—who gather around marble tables or perch at the bar, eating caesar salads, sipping well-crafted martinis, and chatting through the night. Think of the second-hand smoke as an evil that's necessary to the European-style ambience. *Full bar; AE, DC, MC, V; no checks; every day; map:J8*

ISSAQUAH BREWHOUSE / 35 W Sunset Way, Issaquah; 425/557-1911
Denizens of Issaquah have been reeling in disbelief for several years
now—could it be true that a deep-Eastside location such as theirs could
really boast its own authentic brewhouse? As the six on-site brewed ales
will attest, it is true. And they're not half bad, either. Bullfrog is a tasty
wheat ale with hints of citrus and honey, while the Swamp Water Stout
covers the other end of the spectrum with its dark, coffeelike finish. The
only marked difference between Issaquah Brewhouse and its cousins
across Lake Washington is that the room is filled with crying children
instead of smoke. *Beer and wine; MC, V; checks OK; every day*

J&M CAFE AND CARDROOM / 201 1st Ave S; 206/292-0663 Pioneer
Square's beloved historic saloon has a long front bar, plus another in the
former cardroom that you can escape to when the crowds get thick, as
well as a decent menu of hofbrau sandwiches and burgers. Sold and saved
from eviction in 1995, the J&M is the place to meet someone before or
after a sporting event—if the packs of roaring fraternity brothers don't
drive you away. *Full bar; AE, DC, MC, V; no checks; every day; map:O8*

KELLS / 1916 Post Alley, Pike Place Market; 206/728-1916 Rousing
sing-alongs to live Celtic music boom throughout the licensed pub side
of this Irish restaurant Wednesday through Saturday. Good coddle, good
soda bread. *Full bar; AE, MC, V; local checks only; every day; map:I8*

**KIRKLAND ROASTER & ALEHOUSE / 1111 Central Way, Kirkland;
425/827-4400** Serving microbrews since long before the rest of the Eastside caught on, the Kirkland Alehouse is entering its second decade of
operations with no signs of slowing. The bar celebrates its raison d'être—
the dispensing of quality beer—in its decor. Beer barrels, taps, and bottles line walls covered with microbrew-label murals. Everything seems to
shout of beer. Why resist? *Full bar; AE, DC, MC, V; checks OK; every
day; map:EE3*

LATONA BY GREEN LAKE / 6423 Latona Ave NE; 206/525-2238 The
Latona is a light, woody, microbrew-and-cheese-bread-lovers kind of
place, a favorite with its residential neighbors and lake lizards alike.
Things can get cozy in this small but thankfully smoke-free space, which
seems more expansive due to high ceilings. Service is extra friendly and
accommodating. Most Thursday through Sunday evenings, the pub
hosts local jazz and folk musicians. *Beer and wine; MC, V; local checks
only; every day; map:EE7*

LAVA LOUNGE / 2226 2nd Ave; 206/441-5660 This long, skinny Belltown bar sports a tiki-hut theme in spades, from lava lamps to velvet
paintings of bare, busty maidens. Don't expect any froufrou drinks with
little umbrellas, however; this is a beer bar (beers are available both bottled and on tap). A standard stop on the Belltown watering-hole circuit,

it's a great place to meet friends, grab a booth, and get down to serious gabbing and gulping. Pinball and shuffleboard provide added amusement, along with Wednesday-night live music. *Beer and wine; MC, V; no checks; every day; map:G8*

LESCHI LAKECAFE / 102 Lakeside Ave S; 206/328-2233 Ah, the sporting life. The Lakecafe serves the jogging-sailing-cycling constituents of the Leschi neighborhood with a vast selection of beers and booze. It's best in summer, when the umbrellas in the courtyard shade the hottest tables around Lake Washington. *Full bar; AE, DC, DIS, MC, V; local checks only; every day; map:HH6*

LINDA'S TAVERN / 707 E Pine St; 206/325-1220 There might be a stuffed buffalo head over the bar, a wagon-wheel chandelier, and other Wild West decor, but Linda's ain't no place to go two-steppin'. The crowd here is a multiethnic mix of Gen-Xers, with a smattering of just plain folks. They all come to drink or play pool to the strains of alternative music blaring from the stereo, to watch films on the back porch in summer, or to listen to DJ music (Tuesday and Sunday nights). Everyone is made to feel welcome—and that's another nice alternative. *Beer and wine; no credit cards; no checks; every day; map:GG6*

MCCORMICK & SCHMICK'S / 1103 1st Ave; 206/623-5500 Bankers like it because it looks like a bank. Dark-stained mahogany and beveled glass provide just the right atmosphere for stockbrokers and lawyers sipping Irish coffees and stiff well pours. Good downtown location; great happy-hour and late-night specials on both drinks and snacks. *Full bar; AE, DC, DIS, JCB, MC, V; no checks; every day; map:L8*

MCCORMICK'S FISH HOUSE AND BAR / 722 4th Ave; 206/682-3900 Polished wood and brass, stand-up counters, and fresh oysters make this the closest thing to a high class San Francisco bar. McCormick's crawls with attorneys and bureaucrats after 5pm, as well as tourists in season. Excellent meal deals at happy hour. *Full bar; AE, DC, DIS, JCB, MC, V; no checks; every day; map:N6*

MCMENAMINS PUB & BREWERY / 200 Roy St; 206/285-4722 This brewpub—Seattle's first venture for the Portland-based McMenamin brothers—has settled quite nicely into its Lower Queen Anne neighborhood, hosting local residents and Seattle Center visitors alike with characteristic low-key amiability. There's a great selection of McMenamins brews, plus a seasonal representation of other local micros. Great fries and other reasonably priced pub grub, and the place is smoke-free. *Beer and wine; AE, DIS, MC, V; no checks; every day; map:A6*

MECCA CAFÉ / 526 Queen Anne Ave N; 206/285-9728 The narrow bar alongside this cafe was formerly home to many a geriatric drinker. The

367

clientele is now young, cool, and prone to take advantage of the hit-heavy jukebox in the corner. Dark and snug, this hideaway lined with cardboard coasters can barely hold a dozen, but it's a festive place to end a rollicking night on Queen Anne. *Full bar; AE, MC, V; no checks; every day; map:GG7*

MUDSHARK BAR (HOTEL EDGEWATER) / 2411 Alaskan Way, Pier 67; 206/728-7000 It's hard to go wrong when you've got the city's premier waterfront view, and all of the tables here are good ones. The atmosphere is cozy and lodgelike, and there's music on Tuesdays through Saturdays in the piano bar up front, where customers request—and sometimes sing—their favorites. *Full bar; AE, DC, DIS, MC, V; checks OK; every day; map:H9*

MURPHY'S PUB / 1928 N 45th St; 206/634-2110 As Irish pubs go, Murphy's is a pretty classy place (fireplace, antiques, and stained glass). Wallingfordians and others pile in to play darts (real, of course, not electronic) or to catch the Wednesday open mikes and weekend Celtic music. The 'tenders are kindly, the comfort food tasty. More than a dozen local brews and stouts are poured on draft, and there's a nice collection of single-malt Scotches and single-barrel bourbons, but no well drinks. It's a zoo on St. Paddy's day. *Beer and wine; AE, MC, V; local checks only; every day; map:FF7*

NICKERSON STREET SALOON / 318 Nickerson St; 206/284-8819 Alas, the legendary burgers that made the former tenant at this site (the 318) famous are no more, but you can enjoy a wide selection of beers on tap (including some lesser-known varieties) and some decent pub grub. The place has been cleaned up and the outdoor seating is nice—but we still miss those 318 burgers! *Beer and wine; AE, MC, V; no checks; every day; map:FF7*

THE NITELITE / 1920 2nd Ave; 206/448-4853 A favorite of the hip young bar-hopping crowd, the Nitelite could well be the king of kitschy Seattle lounges. The original decor is from the '40s, with a mind-bending compendium of objects spanning the decades through the '70s. The place was used as a set in the movie *Dogfight* in 1991, and most of the props were kept firmly in place. Check out the train set encased in plastic under the bar. Cheap beer specials, stiff martinis, and syrupy libations for the Captain Crunch crowd are what's pouring. *Full bar; no credit cards; no checks; every day; map:I7*

THE OLD PEQULIAR / 1722 NW Market St; 206/782-8886 It's part scruffy tavern, part Old English pub, and the folks on the Ballard bar circuit seem to eat it up. Play pool, shoot some darts, listen to live music, or test your brainpower at the Tuesday-night quiz contests. There's always a congenial crowd quaffing microbrews and imports. Just snag a table in the comfy pub corner and you're set. *Beer and wine; AE, DIS, MC, V; no checks; every day; map:FF8*

OLD TOWN ALEHOUSE / 5233 Ballard Ave NW; 206/782-8323 The Old Town evokes the look of Old Ballard, with an ornate antique bar and icebox, exposed-brick walls, and old black-and-white photos. Guinness fans will like Monday night's $2.50 pints; Tuesdays are devoted to live jazz. The Ballard Wedge sandwiches are tasty—and the fries that come alongside are out of this world. Smoke-free. *Beer and wine; MC, V; local checks only; every day; map:FF8*

PACIFIC INN PUB / 3501 Stone Way N; 206/547-2967 Should you come for the brew (half a dozen on tap, a couple of dozen in bottles and cans) or for the fab cayenne-spiked fish 'n' chips? Most regulars enjoy both at this Wallingford workingman's mainstay. Old-timers know the PI's owner, Robert Julien, as the wonderful singing bartender at long-gone-but-not-forgotten Jake O'Shaughnessy's. *Beer and wine; MC, V; local checks only; every day; map:FF7*

PALOMINO / 1420 5th Ave, City Centre; 206/623-1300 It's still one of the most dramatic spaces in town: three stories high above the City Centre atrium, with gorgeous glass light fixtures and a handsome bar. It's a great spot for an after-work or post-cinema cocktail, and if you're hungry, the Gorgonzola cheese fries are a hit, as are the wood-fired pizzas. *Full bar; AE, DC, DIS, MC, V; checks OK; every day; map:J5*

PESCATORE FISH CAFÉ / 5300 34th Ave NW; 206/784-1733 The former site first of Hiram's at the Locks and then of a different Pescatore with an Italian focus, this latest version still has what Seattleites and their visitors seem to crave most: outdoor seating with a view of the water. Throw in the added interest of boat traffic coming through the locks and a nice selection of appetizer plates with the emphasis on seafood, and you're in the Emerald City version of heaven. *Full bar; AE, DC, DIS, MC, V; checks OK; every day; map:FF9*

THE PINK DOOR / 1919 Post Alley, Pike Place Market; 206/443-3241 We know it's kitschy, but imbibing blue martinis on the prettiest rooftop terrace in town while nibbling antipasti to the accompanying strains of accordion music happens to be one of our weaknesses. A variety of musical acts come by in the evenings, including multipersonalitied cabaret singer Julie Cascioppo, who does Liza Minnelli better than Liza Minnelli. *Full bar; AE, MC, V; no checks; Tues–Sat; map:J8*

PIONEER SQUARE SALOON / 77 Yesler Way; 206/628-6444 This is one of the few bars in Pioneer Square that doesn't offer live music—and thus doesn't slap on a cover. The clientele ranges from slackers to corporate types, the taped tunes are good, and there's a dartboard in the back. In summer, the patio tables—where you can survey the tourists wandering by—are packed. Between the kindly bartenders, the good (and cheap) wines by the glass, and the unaffected air, this could be the best spot in the city for making new friends. Poetry readings on Thursdays. *Beer and wine; AE, DC, MC, V; no checks; every day; map:N8*

QUEEN CITY GRILL / 2201 1st Ave; 206/443-0975 Fluted lights, flowers, and a rosy glow that bathes the room make this one of Belltown's classiest options. On weekends it gets packed with artists, yuppies, and off-duty bartenders pretending they're in New York or San Francisco; we much prefer Queen City on weeknights, when sitting at the curved bar can be quietly lovely. *Full bar; AE, DC, DIS, MC, V; no checks; every day; map:G8*

RAY'S CAFÉ / 6049 Seaview Ave NW; 206/789-3770 One visit to the jammed view-deck cafe atop Ray's Boathouse will assure you that Ray's doesn't lack fans. On weekends you'll probably have to wait for a seat, and harried service is the norm. The food (heavy on the seafood, natch) is fresh but not particularly inventive (though the happy-hour bar menu is a real steal), and the crowd is just having way too much fun. At Ray's, the postcard-perfect view's the thing, and that redeems the whole into something much better than the sum of its parts. Outstanding wine list, too. *Full bar; AE, DC, DIS, MC, V; local checks only; every day; map:EE9*

RED DOOR ALEHOUSE / 3401 Fremont Ave N; 206/547-7521 During the day, suits, salesmen, and salty dogs stop in to down a cold one with a burger and fries. At night it's so crowded with the fraternity/sorority crowd, you could mistake the place for a J Crew catalog shoot. There's a wide selection of beers, predominantly Northwest microbrews, to complement some terrific (inexpensive) pub grub. Order a bowl of mussels and eat 'em in the beer garden. *Beer and wine; AE, MC, V; local checks only; every day; map:FF7*

RED ONION TAVERN / 4210 E Madison St; 206/323-1611 Perfect in winter, when you can drink a beer beside the huge stone fireplace, this Madison Park institution is also known for its pool tables and its pizza. Mellow local crowd, except on Thursday nights in summer, when the Red Onion is invaded by the overflow of party-hearty students from the Attic down the street. *Beer and wine; MC, V; local checks only; every day; map:GG6*

ROANOKE INN / 1825 72nd Ave SE, Mercer Island; 206/232-0800 The Roanoke Inn isn't the kind of place most people will just happen upon. It resides on secluded Mercer Island, which is usually a destination only for its inhabitants. However, diehard pub-crawlers may want to seek this one out for its history alone. It's known for its somewhat checkered past—apparently the upstairs rooms once housed a brothel of sorts, and the main room was the site of many bloody barroom brawls. Today its biggest draw is the outdoor seating on a generous front porch reminiscent of a Southern estate. *Beer and wine; AE, MC, V; local checks only; every day; map:II4*

ROANOKE PARK PLACE TAVERN / 2409 10th Ave E; 206/324-5882 A gathering ground where the junior gentry of north Capitol Hill can feel like just folks. Good burgers and beers, but loud music often drowns out conversation. And the place is packed after Husky games. *Beer and wine; MC, V; local checks only; every day; map:GG6*

R PLACE / 619 E Pine St; 206/322-8828 This friendly, neon-lit pub caters mainly to youngish gay men, with three floors of pool, pinball, and microbrews. It's a great place to meet old and new friends, and the window tables on the Pine Street side offer additional entertainment as the parade of Capitol Hill street life rolls by. *Beer and wine; no credit cards; no checks; every day; map:J1*

THE ROOST / 120 NW Gilman Blvd, Issaquah; 425/392-5550 Smack-dab in the middle of Issaquah's eyesore strip-mall country, this Mick McHugh creation is equal parts pub and restaurant. Sporting life is the theme here: pictures of proud fishermen holding up their catch line the walls, and a larger-than-life moose trophy christens the fireplace. The backwoods-sports-bar motif is carried out to such an extreme that it's almost kitschy—making it worth a stop for those who'd usually not be caught dead in these kinds of places. The beer selection is on a par with the best pub fare this side of the United Kingdom. *Full bar; AE, DC, MC, V; checks OK; every day*

SALTY'S ON ALKI / 1936 Harbor Ave SW; 206/937-1600 The spacious West Seattle bar spills over onto the bay-level patio (warmed, thankfully, by high-rise heat lamps), where you can order from a lengthy menu of seafood appetizers and gaze at the twinkling lights of Seattle. *Full bar; AE, DC, DIS, MC, V; local checks only; every day; map:II9*

74TH STREET ALE HOUSE / 7401 Greenwood Ave N; 206/784-2955 An alehouse it is, with regulars lingering at the bar and taps pouring nearly two dozen brews. The food, however, is more than a cut above pub grub, including a delectable gumbo and several sandwiches and main dishes worthy of a "real" restaurant. It's a great place to meet after work, or to while away a rainy Sunday afternoon. *Beer and wine; MC, V; checks OK; every day; map:EE8*

SHEA'S LOUNGE / 94 Pike St, Pike Place Market; 206/467-9990 Don't let the near-hidden location (on the top floor of the Corner Market building) keep you from ferreting out this charming little offshoot of Chez Shea. Six small tables and a minuscule bar are set in a slender, elegant, dimly lit space with enormous casement windows looking out over Market rooftops to the bay beyond. A nice selection of Italian and Spanish wines is complemented by a short but tasteful, mainly Mediterranean menu. Utterly romantic. *Full bar; AE, MC, V; no checks; Tues–Sun; map:J8*

SHUCKERS (FOUR SEASONS OLYMPIC HOTEL) / 411 University St; 206/621-1984 Here you'll find Establishment and celebrity hotel guests enjoying Northwest oysters and shrimp or talking to bartender's bartender David Williams. Afternoons there's a light menu of seafood and good local beers. *Full bar; AE, DC, DIS, JCB, MC, V; no checks; every day; map:L6*

SIX ARMS BREWERY AND PUB / 300 E Pike St; 206/223-1698 Sister to McMenamins on Lower Queen Anne, this outpost offers a bit more funky character, albeit the same menu of tasty pub food and the fabulous brews for which the Portland brothers McM are known. Grab a window seat for primo people-watching. Service can be mellow to a fault. *Beer and wine; AE, MC, V; no checks; every day; map:K2*

SPACE NEEDLE / Seattle Center; 206/443-2100 If enjoying a truly sensational view means sipping one of the most expensive drinks you'll ever have in your life, cough up $8.50 for the hop to the top (only restaurant patrons ride free)—and then drink slowly. *Full bar; AE, DIS, MC, V; checks OK; every day; www.spaceneedle.com; map:C6*

TEMPLE BILLIARDS / 126 S Jackson St; 206/682-3242 It's not as glossy as Belltown Billiards, but that's just fine with the youngish crowd that shoots pool at the Temple. Word has it the regulars here include certain local band members, so keep your eyes peeled if celebrity-spotting thrills you. There's a decent selection of beer and wine, and some tasty sandwiches. *Beer and wine; AE, MC, V; no checks; every day; map:O9*

TINI BIG'S LOUNGE / 100 Denny Way; 206/284-0931 Located on the jumpin' corner of First and Denny, Tini's adds casual elegance to the KeyArena neighborhood. Perch at the bar, or grab a more intimate table and dish over a bracingly cold martini (Tini's offers 25 variations) or another favorite classic. Prices aren't cheap but the standard's a double; be forewarned, as these babies go down smooth. Tini's is also a purveyor of fine cigars and tasty little plates: specialty pizzas, quesadillas, and such. Weeknights are considerably less frantic than Fridays, Saturdays, and Sonics game nights, when the place packs out in elbow-to-elbow fashion. *Full bar; AE, MC, V; no checks; every day; map:C9*

TRIANGLE LOUNGE / 3507 Fremont Pl N; 206/632-0880 The congested crush up front has been eased considerably, thanks to a spacious bar remodel that also added cocktails to the fine selection of beers on tap.

Crowds come for the cheap, tasty food, and line up for their chance to grab a table on the patio (or one in the quirky-funky three-sided dining room). *Full bar; AE, MC, V; no checks; every day; map:FF8*

TROLLEYMAN PUB / 3400 Phinney Ave N; 206/548-8000 Couches and upholstered chairs abound in this renovated turn-of-the-century trolley barn that is attached to the Redhook Brewery and features its taps. A fireplace and piano add the touches that can make one forget it's pelting outside. The doors close earlier than legality dictates: around 11pm on weekdays. There's also a light snack menu. No smoking. *Beer only; AE, DIS, MC, V; no checks; every day; map:FF7*

TWO BELLS TAVERN / 2313 4th Ave; 206/441-3050 Even the most self-conscious hipster lets it all hang out at Two Bells. Good selection of local microbrews and imported gems, plus sporadic but always creative bookings of solo guitar acts, unusual art exhibits, and poetry readings. Great burgers and sausage plates, and a late-night happy hour. *Beer and wine; AE, DIS, MC, V; no checks; every day; map:F7*

211 BILLIARD CLUB / 2304 2nd Ave; 206/443-1211 Up one flight at Second and Bell you'll find the city's true pool sharks strutting their stuff all day and into the night. It's a big, smoky warehouse filled with tables of every kind: 2 snooker, 3 billiard, and 16 regular pool tables. *Beer and wine; no credit cards; no checks; every day; map:F7*

UNION SQUARE GRILL / 621 Union St; 206/224-4321 One of the best after-work downtown bars, where drinks go down easy with two or three of the grill's scrumptious miniature roast beef sandwiches. The barroom is long and narrow, with lots of dark wood. You may have to scramble for a table, but you'll be comfortable once you get settled. *Full bar; AE, DC, DIS, MC, V; local checks only; every day; map:K5*

VIRGINIA INN / 1937 1st Ave; 206/728-1937 What do you get when you mix arty Belltown dwellers, chic-seeking suburbanites, and babbling pensioners in a historic, brick-tile-and-avant-garde-art tavern? You get the VI, a very enlightened, very appealing, vaguely French-feeling tav with a fine list of libations (including pear cider) and character to burn. You'll have to burn your cigs elsewhere, though. *Full bar; AE, MC, V; local checks only; every day; map:I8*

VITO'S MADISON GRILL / 927 9th Ave; 206/682-2695 If you like a well-constructed cocktail (such as a gigantic martini) and enjoy watching a professional bartender in action, this old-timey joint is the place to go. All dark wood and maroon leather, it attracts police detectives, lawyers, the sports crowd, and judges on the road to intemperance, as well as a contingent of younger drinkers-in-training. *Full bar; MC, V; no checks; every day; map:M4*

WEDGWOOD ALEHOUSE / 8515 35th Ave NE; 206/527-2676 This congenial neighborhood pub draws a low-key local crowd that comes for the decent burgers and the good sampling of microbrews. The outdoor tables in front are the draw in summer. *Beer and wine; MC, V; local checks only; every day; map:EE6*

THE WILD ROSE / 1201 E Pike St; 206/324-9210 The center of the universe for the Seattle lesbian scene, the Wild Rose has served as community center, coffeehouse, music venue, pool hall, and just plain great tavern since 1984. Now that cocktails have been added, it's a great bar, too. Tables are just as likely to be filled with women reading alone as those dining with friends or drinking in uproarious groups. There's an extensive, serviceable menu of mostly comfort food. The other sex is gladly welcomed. *Full bar; MC, V; no checks; every day; map:HH6*

EARLY TO BED

Favorite coffee, tea, and dessert places that close before 8pm

Some places are filled with such a palpable sense of history and romance, they seem to have existed forever. One is the **Burke Museum Cafe** (17th Ave NE and NE 45th St; 206/543-9854; map:FF6), a civilized coffeehouse in the basement of the venerable Burke Museum, where classical music lilts in the background. Outdoor tables are lovely in spring. Open every day.

Espresso to Go (3512 Fremont Pl N; 206/633-3685; map:FF7) *is* Fremont, summarized in a stand-up-size espresso nook with two stools and a couple of newspapers. Open every day.

People come to Fremont from adjoining neighborhoods out of loyalty to **Lighthouse Roasters** (400 N 43rd St; 206/633-4444; map:FF8), where owner Ed Leebrick's excellent coffee is roasted on the premises. Open every day.

With a low-pressure location just beyond University Village, the **Queen Mary** (2912 NE 55th St; 206/527-2770; map:FF6) may never be a major stop on the coffee-tea-dessert circuit, but that doesn't diminish the teahouse's appeal as a refuge on gray Seattle days. Baked goods are the house specialty, along with a reassuringly proper pot of tea, correctly brewed and served in fussy china. Tea with a capital T is available from 2 to 5pm every day. Breakfast and lunch are served between 9am and 5pm every day.

A window sign declares "Fresh Sconage," and the scones at **Zu** (4850 Green Lake Way N; 206/632-6301; map:FF7) are some of the best in town. Try one, along with a beautifully presented latte, in the peaceful backyard rock garden. Or phone in your order for pickup at the drive-up window. Open every day.

Coffee, Tea, and Dessert

Coffee has become synonymous with Seattle for many people, thanks to the multiple branches of Starbucks, Seattle's Best Coffee (SBC), and Tully's, which it seems you can find on almost every corner in town. Though many of the chain espresso bars are open late, and some even feature occasional live music, we've concentrated here on independent tea- and coffeehouses. See also Bakeries and Candies and Chocolate in the Shopping chapter.

B&O ESPRESSO / 204 Belmont Ave E; 206/322-5028 ■ 401 Broadway E, Broadway Market; 206/328-3290 Legendary for espresso, extraordinary desserts, and serious conversation, this vigorous Capitol Hill coffeehouse buzzes from morning to 1am. It's a peaceful place for breakfast, for a steaming latte and a tart, or for a plate of fried new potatoes with peppers and onions. Lunches are thoughtful, out-of-the-ordinary creations like Chinese hot noodles and Egyptian lentil soup, and lighter fare is available for the later hours. Desserts and coffee are where the B&O really shines; these are some of the best (though they're not the cheapest) homemade desserts in town. The Broadway Market branch is a coffee bar with limited seating. *No alcohol; MC, V; no checks; every day; map:GG6*

BAUHAUS BOOKS AND COFFEE / 301 E Pine St; 206/625-1600 At Bauhaus, function follows form. It's a high-ceilinged place with a wall of bookshelves stocked with used art books (Bauhaus doubles as a used-book store—though we suspect the books actually look better than they sell). Big windows afford a view of the Pike/Pine corridor and the Space Needle, which appears oddly inspiring and appropriate in this context. The wrought-iron fixtures and greenish walls lend stylishness, as does the clientele. Sweets are typical—with the exception of single Ding-Dongs, served with reverence on a plate for a mere 56 cents. Kool-Aid is available; the vintage cold-cereal boxes displayed by the counter, unfortunately, are not. *No alcohol; no credit cards; checks OK; every day; map:J2*

CAFE ALLEGRO / 4214 University Way NE; 206/633-3030 People who got into the Allegro habit while they were at the UW still find themselves gravitating back. It's hard to pin down the cafe's appeal. Perhaps it's the moody dark-wood decor and often smoke-saturated air; or the cachet of the location (it's not easy to find, set in a U-District back alley); or the serious and interesting conversations among its wonderfully international crowd of students. You may feel as if you've been left out of a private joke on your first few visits, but it doesn't take long to become a regular. *No alcohol; no credit cards; local checks only; every day; map:FF6*

CAFÉ DILETTANTE / 416 Broadway E; 206/329-6463 ▪ 1603 1st Ave; 206/728-9144 The name of this Seattle institution is derived from the Italian word *dilettare,* "to delight." And that's exactly what its sinfully rich truffles and buttercream-filled chocolates do. No chocoholic is safe here—gift-boxed chocolates are available to go. In any case, be prepared to splurge. The Broadway location inevitably bustles (till 1am on weekends), and the First Avenue storefront acts as a retail shop only. Pssst . . . there's a small retail outlet at the candy factory (2300 E Cherry St; 206/328-1955; map:HH6), with seconds at reduced prices. *Full bar; AE, DIS, MC, V; checks OK; every day; map:GG6; map:I8*

CAFFE APPASSIONATO / 1417 Queen Anne Ave N (and branches); 206/270-8760 Perched on the top of Queen Anne, this sleek cafe offers outdoor seating and excellent people-watching opportunities. Visitors can sip espresso drinks made from beans roasted locally at the Caffe Appassionato Fisherman's Terminal location. The signature coffee beans are also available in bulk. If the weather takes a turn for the worse, slip inside and warm up in front of the fireplace. *No alcohol; MC, V; checks OK; every day; map:GG7*

CAFFE LADRO / 2205 Queen Anne Ave N; 206/282-5313 ▪ 600 Queen Anne Ave N; 206/282-1549 This hangout—with plum mottled walls adorned with the work of local artists and photographers—is usually packed, especially on weekend mornings, when locals vie for one of the few tables for a breakfast of homemade granola, French toast, or Italian-style scrambled eggs. The sweets and baked goods are way above average, made right in back. A second location is on Lower Queen Anne. *No alcohol; no credit cards; checks OK; every day; map:GG7; map:A7*

CAFFE VITA / 813 5th Ave N (and branches); 206/285-9662 Locals are rabid about this little cafe tucked in the unlikely neighborhood just north of Tower Records. All the beans are roasted to perfection, including the well-rounded Columbian Supremo, the Caffe Luna (French roast), and the smoky Guatemalan Antigua. Beware: all espresso drinks are made with double *ristretto* shots. Several of Seattle's better-known restaurants and cafes (among them Blowfish, Queen City Grill, and Caffe Ladro) sing the praises of Caffe Vita's signature coffee beans, distributed from their roasting company now at Fifth and Denny (2621 5th Ave; 206/441-4351; Mon–Fri; map:E7), under the Monorail tracks but soon to move to Vita's Capitol Hill branch (in Cafe Paradiso's old spot, 1005 E Pike St; 206/325-2647; map:L1). *No alcohol; no credit cards; checks OK; every day; caffevita@msn.com; www.caffevita.com; map:B5*

COFFEE MESSIAH / 1554 E Olive Way; 206/860-7377 If the gargoyles perched on each table could talk, they might have plenty to say about confessions they've heard at Coffee Messiah, where "Caffeine Saves." Religious sorts and atheists alike mingle over espresso drinks at this unique Capitol Hill coffee shop. Don't let the many artistic renditions of Jesus make you feel guilty; go ahead and order a dessert, they're made on the premises. *No alcohol; no credit cards; no checks; every day, and 24 hours on Sat; map:GG6*

ESPRESSO ROMA / 4201 University Way NE; 206/632-6001 The appeal of this minimalist place is that it doesn't have any: it's a big cinder-block space with a cement deck spilling out toward the Ave. Atmo or not, it's always packed with students, the drinks are good, the baked goods are standard, and service is always friendly. *No alcohol; no credit cards; no checks; every day; map:FF6*

THE FAMOUS PACIFIC DESSERT COMPANY / 127 Mercer St; 206/284-8100 Their motto says it all: "Eat dessert first; life is uncertain." This is the place that introduced us to the ultimate indulgence, Chocolate Decadence, and for that we'll be forever indebted. On any given night fewer desserts may be available than you might expect—considering the massive product line and reputation. But we have had some wonderful concoctions here: rich, incredibly silky cheesecakes; a custardy ice cream laden with chunks of chocolate; a hazelnut meringue cake with rum–whipped cream filling. *No alcohol; DC, MC, V; local checks only; every day; map:A7*

GARDEN COURT (FOUR SEASONS OLYMPIC HOTEL) / 411 University St; 206/621-1700 Spacious and grand, the formal Garden Court is the pièce de résistance of the Four Seasons Olympic. You come here to celebrate with expensive champagne, to dance on a parquet floor to the strains of a society combo (piano bar during the week), to hobnob with the pearls-and-basic-black set (although of late we've seen an influx of blue jeans too). Have lunch, high tea, a drink and hors d'oeuvres, or coffee and a slice of torte among the palm fronds. *Full bar; AE, DC, MC, V; no checks; every day; map:L6*

GRAND ILLUSION ESPRESSO AND PASTRY / 1405 NE 50th St; 206/525-2755 Attached to the last independent movie theater in town is the Illusion, where UW students (and their professors) rendezvous at the small tables, near the fireplace, or, on warm afternoons, in the tiny courtyard outside. Light lunch selections such as quiche and soup change daily, and the scones, cookies, and fruit pies are favorites; however, most customers come for postfilm conversation or late-afternoon quiet. *No alcohol; MC, V; no checks; every day; map:FF6*

GREEN CAT CAFE / 1514 E Olive Way; 206/726-8756 The Green Cat was a neighborhood favorite from the moment it opened. The tiny triangular kitchen turns out good vegetarian and vegan choices—salads, soups, and pizza by the slice—and the staff is chatty. There's a heavy sidewalk-society scene here, where people coming up from Fallout Records run into friends having lunch outside, but the crowd is not all mod; lots of joggers and casual types stop in for morning coffee. *Beer and wine; MC, V; checks OK; every day; map:GG6*

HONEY BEAR BAKERY / 2106 N 55th St; 206/545-7296 ■ 17171 Bothell Way NE, Lake Forest Park; 206/366-3330 Virtually all who walk into the warm, sweet arms of the Honey Bear adopt the place as if it were their own—from morning coffee and sugar-powdered whole-wheat sourdough cinnamon rolls to late-night steamed milk and German chocolate cake. Or stop by Saturday morning (the Bear opens at 6am) for a pumpkin or blueberry muffin to go; they'll still be warm from the oven. Earthy yuppies, ageless hippies, and just plain folk linger, converse, read, write, and listen to live acoustic music, regardless of the lines trailing out the door. True regulars bring their own mugs to avoid the paper cups. The nonsmoking Honey Bear also serves hearty homemade soups and salads. In late 1998, a second, larger branch opened in the Lake Forest Park Town Center. *No alcohol; no credit cards (MC, V in Lake Forest Park branch); checks OK; every day; map:EE7*

JOE BAR / 810 E Roy St; 206/324-0407 Partners Joanne Sugura and Mike Walker import baked goods from the Hi Spot Cafe to this comfortable bilevel space across the street from the Harvard Exit movie theater. The desserts and good espresso drinks add to the we're-all-friends-here atmosphere, fostered by the closely spaced tables and the eager après-film conversation. *No alcohol; no credit cards; no checks; every day; map:GG6*

LOUISA'S BAKERY & CAFÉ / 2379 Eastlake Ave E; 206/325-0081 Even the three bears would crawl out of winter hibernation to nuzzle up to Louisa's raspberry oatmeal, served in a Papa Bear–size bowl. The long lines along the display cases—especially during weekend breakfast hours—give you time to choose one of the mouthwatering baked goods. Whatever you choose, it'll be worth the wait. Make yourself comfortable; the friendly staff will bring your order to your table. *No alcohol; no credit cards; checks OK; every day; map:GG7*

PROCOPIO GELATERIA / 1901 Western Ave, Pike Place Market Hillclimb; 206/622-4280 Seattle's original gelateria still serves the most civilized Italian ice cream in town, in a stylish little nook right off the Hillclimb. At least 16 flavors (seasonally rotated) of freshly made ice cream are always displayed, and if you can get past these positively first-class ices, you can choose from an assortment of luscious desserts.

ESPRESS YOURSELF

Seattle is bean obsessed. The town spawned Starbucks, espresso bars and pushcarts (now in nearly every conceivable location, from gas stations to doctors' offices), and a nationwide caffeine habit. A specialized vocabulary has developed around ordering espresso—the high end of the coffee continuum. And, as at the Soup Nazi's place immortalized on *Seinfeld*, precise language is required. Woe to the person who gets to the front of the espresso line and asks for a "small" latte. An eye-roll from the *barista* is sure to follow. It's a "short," "tall," or "grande," if you please.

To help the espresso-ignorant fake their way through, here's a cheat sheet of espresso lingo. And, remember, half the trick is ordering with confidence.

THE BASICS

Americano: your basic cup of coffee (except for the price), prepared with the espresso method—a shot with hot water

Barista: espresso bartender

Breve: with steamed half-and-half instead of milk

Cappuccino: a third each of espresso, milk, and steamed milk, topped with foamed milk

Double or **doppio**: a drink with a double shot of espresso

Drip: regular brewed coffee, just like Folger's used to make

Latte (also caffe latte or café au lait): a shot of espresso with steamed milk, capped by foamed milk

Mocha: espresso, steamed milk, and chocolate

THE SLANG

Lid nerd: someone who can't attach an espresso lid

No form: no foam

No fun: a latte made with decaffeinated espresso

Rocket fuel or **red eye**: drip coffee with a drip of espresso

Schizophrenic: half decaf, half regular espresso

Tall skinny: a tall latte made with nonfat milk

Thunder thighs: double tall mocha made with whole milk, capped with extra whipped cream

Why bother?: nonfat decaf latte

With room: not filled to the brim

Now that you've got all the terms down, there's one last thing. The various components of an espresso drink must be strung together in a specific order: 1) amount of espresso; 2) size of cup; 3) type of milk; 4) foam; 5) whipping cream (if any); 6) beverage type. So a "double tall skinny formless no fun latte" is a latte with a double shot of decaf espresso made with lowfat milk and no foam.

Now, what could be simpler?

— Shannon O'Leary

Beverages include a great wintertime hot spiced cider, and espresso drinks. *No alcohol; no credit cards; checks OK; every day (closed Sun in winter); map:J9*

SIMPLY DESSERTS / 3421 Fremont Ave N; 206/633-2671 Simply Desserts cooks up a selection of classic pastries: chocolate espresso cake, berry and fruit pies, a white-chocolate strawberry cake that wins raves from everyone, and countless variations on the chocolate cake theme—the most popular being the chocolate cognac torte and the Bailey's Irish Cream cake. This small spot with an enormous reputation gets plenty busy evenings, when chocolate-cake fans from across the city sip espresso and enjoy what may be simply the best desserts around. *No alcohol; no credit cards; checks OK; Tues–Sun; map:FF7*

TEAHOUSE KUAN YIN / 1911 N 45th St; 206/632-2055 Depictions of Kuan Yin, the Buddhist goddess of mercy, preside over the serene atmosphere of "Seattle's first teahouse." It wasn't by chance that Miranda Pirzada located this peaceful getaway next to Wide World Books. A former travel agent with a longtime interest in Asia, Pirzada taste-tested many teas in Asia before selecting the Kuan Yin offerings: a full spectrum of teas, including plenty of blacks and greens, a few oolongs, and some herbals. Complementing these is a multiethnic and very reasonably priced assortment of quiches, humbao, and pot-stickers, as well as desserts such as green tea ice cream, pies, and scones. To-go cups are not available; instead, you're invited to sit in leisurely and lengthy contemplation (quilted tea cozies keep your tea warm for up to two hours). Be sure to chat with the staff: instruction in the ways of tea drinking is dispensed generously and with a philosophical air. *No alcohol; MC, V; checks OK; every day; map:FF7*

UPTOWN ESPRESSO AND BAKERY / 525½ Queen Anne Ave N; 206/285-3757 ▪ 3845 Delridge Way SW; 206/933-9497 This top-notch coffee hangout, with its own adjoining bakery, turns out a range of superb muffins, scones, and other sweet-and-semihealthy treats. The Uptown is always busy, whether with the quiet post-movie or post-theater crowd at night or with friendly tête-à-têtes throughout the day. Rightfully so, as these are some of the best espresso drinks you'll find in Seattle, and the morning treats are on their way to matching that claim. No smoking. The West Seattle branch (Mon–Sat; map:JJ7) opened in early 1999. *No alcohol; no credit cards; checks OK; every day; map:GG7*

THE URBAN BAKERY / 7850 E Green Lake Dr N; 206/524-7951 Morning, noon, and night you'll find Green Lake's urban yuppies hanging inside or out of this popular corner spot near the Green Lake shore. Enjoy excellent soups and vegetarian chili, the usual sandwiches and salads, and a world of freshly baked breads, pastries, pies, cakes, and cookies that taste as good as they look. All the requisite coffee drinks, too. *No alcohol; MC, V; checks OK; every day; map:EE7*

ZOKA COFFEE ROASTER AND TEA COMPANY / 2200 N 56th St; 206/545-4277 Owners Tim McCormack and Jeff Babcock bring more than 20 years of experience in the specialty coffee business to this spacious community coffee- and teahouse. Leather couches and tables with high-backed chairs invite neighborhood locals and visitors to settle in and read or challenge each other to a game of Scrabble. Zoka roasts its own signature coffees, with the roaster serving as an appropriate backdrop for live acoustic music on Friday and Saturday nights. Pick up a Roaster's Dozen card, which gets you a free pound of coffee after you purchase 12. A variety of loose teas are available by the cup, by the pot, or in bulk. Complement your drink of choice with a selection from the sandwiches, salads, and baked goods, all made here. *No alcohol; DIS, MC, V; checks OK; every day; map:EE7*

ITINERARIES

ITINERARIES

Whether you're a first-time visitor or a native, here are suggestions for spending one day—or an entire week—enjoying some of the best Seattle has to offer. More information on most of the places in boldface below may be found in other chapters (Restaurants, Lodgings, Exploring, Shopping, Day Trips, and so on) throughout this guide. Especially if you're staying in or near downtown, you won't need a car for Days One through Three; a car is recommended or necessary for Days Four through Seven, however.

DAY ONE

Note: Because the Seattle Art Museum and most galleries, as well as some of the following restaurants, are closed Monday, this itinerary is best followed on Tuesday through Sunday.

If you have just one day in Seattle, concentrate on the city's heart: Pike Place Market. Ideally you're staying in a view room at the **INN AT THE MARKET** (86 Pine St; 206/443-3600 or 800/446-4484)—if you've been savvy enough to secure a reservation months in advance, that is. The inn's close proximity to downtown and the waterfront, plus its reputation for excellent service, has made it legendary with those seeking an introduction to, or a return engagement with, the Emerald City. Some people think the views of Elliott Bay from the rooftop deck alone are worth the relatively steep price of a room.

MORNING: Watching the Market come to life is worth setting your alarm for, even if you're on vacation. Grab a fresh croissant from **LE PANIER VERY FRENCH BAKERY** (1902 Pike Pl; 206/441-3669) and a latte from the original **STARBUCKS** (1912 Pike Pl; 206/448-8762), and wander among the farmers and craftspeople as they set up their wares. Arrive before 9am, and you'll experience this most beloved of Seattle landmarks without the corresponding crowds that flock here on the weekends and every day in summer. You'll also get first pick of a wonderful array of produce—including berries, peaches, and apples, in season—to snack on as you wander or to take back to your room for later. Head into the depths of the Market to explore an unusual array of shops and oddities.

AFTERNOON: If weather permits, have lunch on the terrace at the **PINK DOOR** (1919 Post Alley; 206/443-3241), a favorite of local office workers and couples opting for a little Italian-style romance at midday. If it's raining, **CAFE CAMPAGNE** (1600 Post Alley; 206/728-2800), a French-inspired bistro, makes a cozy retreat. After lunch, shoppers take note: Western and First Avenues between the Market and Pioneer Square (and north on First into the Belltown district) are rich with more upscale treasure. Return visitors who haven't been back in a while will marvel at the Harbor Steps area, with its congregation of high-end, heretofore-unseen-in-Seattle shops and cafes. The SEATTLE ART MUSEUM (100 University St; 206/654-3100), with its intriguing permanent and visiting exhibitions, is directly across the street; just look for the giant *Hammering Man* sculpture, nearly impossible to miss.

Those wanting to explore more of the city—and get a glimpse of local history in the bargain—will hop a Metro bus (206/553-3000) or take the short walk down First Avenue to Pioneer Square (ride free on Metro until 7pm throughout the downtown core). This is the oldest part of the city, and you can learn about the early days by joining the UNDERGROUND TOUR (610 1st Ave; 206/682-4646), an informative and humorous, if somewhat campy, look at the city's early days. Literary devotees won't want to pass up a visit to the ELLIOTT BAY BOOK COMPANY (101 S Main St; 206/624-6600), considered by many to be the city's best bookstore, and art lovers will find plenty of galleries to peruse in the immediate neighborhood.

EVENING: After freshening up at your hotel, enjoy the Pacific Northwest's bounty with dinner at ETTA'S SEAFOOD (2020 Western Ave; 206/443-6000), then bring the evening to a rapturous close by watching the sun set over Elliott Bay from SHEA'S LOUNGE (Corner Market Building, top floor; 206/457-9990), a romantic aerie tucked above the Market.

DAY TWO

With two days to explore the city, you can range farther afield, taking in a few neighborhoods as well as more of downtown.

MORNING: Locals may scoff, but visitors are invariably drawn to the SPACE NEEDLE (Seattle Center; 206/443-2145). If you're staying downtown, catch the MONORAIL (206/441-6038) from Westlake Center (5th Ave and Pine St) for a quick but fascinating ride above the city streets to Seattle Center. If it's a clear day, take a ride to the top of the Needle and have breakfast in the revolving restaurant, where you can get the lay of the land along with your coffee and eggs. After breakfast, explore the rest of the Center, which is especially appealing to children. Visit the CHILDREN'S MUSEUM (Center House; 206/441-1768), stroll across the grounds to the PACIFIC SCIENCE CENTER (200 2nd Ave N; 206/443-2880) and its innovative, kid-friendly, hands-on exhibits, or catch a performance at the SEATTLE CHILDREN'S THEATRE (2nd Ave N and Thomas St; 206/441-3322), known for its excellent performances of old favorites and future classics. Or simply have a seat on a bench by the International Fountain, relax, and allow yourself to be mesmerized by the dancing water. Kids will love to see how close they can get to the water without getting wet, although most can't resist and come out soaked.

AFTERNOON: Some of Seattle's best Thai restaurants are in the Seattle Center neighborhood. Favorites come and go, but we still love **BAHN THAI** (409 Roy St; 206/283-0444). Later in the afternoon, spend time exploring one of the collection of neighborhoods that make up the soul of Seattle. We suggest funky **FREMONT**, a colorful, quirky commercial-and-residential district bordering Lake Union and the Ship Canal, with unusual shopping, great coffeehouses, and unique public art. Nearby is **GAS WORKS PARK**, an old industrial plant turned into a neighborhood gathering place. Climb the hill and try your hand at deciphering the sundial at the top, go fly a kite, or just enjoy the spectacular views of Lake Union and the city.

EVENING: See Seattle from the water. If you want to power your own boat, join a "Sunset Paddle" by kayak on Lake Union through the **NORTHWEST OUTDOOR CENTER** (2100 Westlake Ave N; 206/281-9694), or settle in for a boat tour through the Ballard Locks with **ARGOSY CRUISES** (206/623-4252), including a glimpse of the *Sleepless in Seattle* houseboat, among others. Enjoy a late dinner in burgeoning, boisterous Belltown at **MARCO'S SUPPERCLUB** (2510 1st Ave; 206/441-7801), a stylish and festive eatery.

DAY THREE

You won't need your passport or a car to travel out of the country on one of Seattle's most popular day trips: Victoria, British Columbia.

MORNING: Rise and shine for an early departure on the **VICTORIA CLIPPER** (Pier 69; 206/448-5000). The trip takes only a couple of hours—this is the fastest passenger ferry in North America, after all—and is full of splendid scenery and fabulous photo ops. Once you arrive, spend the next couple of hours learning about the history of the Pacific Northwest at the fascinating **ROYAL BRITISH COLUMBIA MUSEUM** (675 Belleville St; 250/387-3701) and visit **HELMCKEN HOUSE** (638 Elliott St Sq; 250/361-0021), the oldest home in British Columbia. Then head over to the Parliament buildings (on Belleville St) from where you can take a narrated horse-drawn-carriage tour (45–90 minutes at $80–$140 for up to six people; 250/383-2207) of **BEACON HILL PARK**, a vast expanse of forest and gardens with gorgeous water and mountain views.

AFTERNOON: Cruise in a tiny water taxi on Victoria's Inner Harbour to **BARB'S PLACE** (310 St. Lawrence St; 250/384-6515) for the city's best fish 'n' chips, then walk it off on your way back to town. There's no shortage of shopping available hereabouts, including Bastion Square, Government Street, and Market Square. Visit **CHINATOWN** to peruse the shops and get a bite, preferably of something exotic that you may never have tried before. Or hop on a bus to **BUTCHART GARDENS** (800 Benvenuto Ave; 250/652-5256) to marvel at 50 acres of elaborate horticul-

ALL ABOUT AIRPLANES

Boeing and Seattle both passed into aviation legend on August 7, 1954, when the company's famed test pilot Tex Johnston set out to demonstrate the airworthiness of Boeing's newest plane. It was the prototype of the 707, the first successful passenger jet. Boeing had had the plane in development for two years but had no buyers; doubts persisted about whether the plane could fly at all. So Johnston made an unauthorized flight that Saturday afternoon—1,000 feet above Lake Washington (and hundreds of thousands of Seafair spectators), flying the plane upside down and finishing with a barrel roll. Both the company and the city are still reaping the benefits of that stunt.

Eventually, buyers did order the 707; it was the dawn of the jet-travel age. Boeing prospered, becoming the preeminent aerospace company in the world when it merged with McDonnell Douglas in 1997. The 747, another plane that skeptics doubted could fly, rules the transcontinental airways; the 737, its smaller sibling, has sold more units than any other jet ever made. Boeing is now a $50-billion-a-year company employing 200,000 workers worldwide, one of the world's leading corporations, and remains the foundation of the Seattle economy: one in every six jobs in the Puget Sound region depends on Boeing directly or indirectly. All because Bill Boeing, the company's founder, happened to be in Seattle in 1916 when he decided to shift from boatbuilding to airplane manufacturing.

Corporate offices, defense work, and final airplane fitting occupy company facilities at and around Boeing Field, which is also the home of that first 707 prototype, called the Dash 80, and the first 747, both now the property of the Smithsonian Institution. Boeing's smaller jets are made in Renton, at the south end of Lake Washington. Defense and space work takes place at a huge complex in Kent, south of Renton. Access to all of these sites, especially the defense-related plants, is controlled. The bigger planes—the 747, 767, and 777—are assembled in Everett, and this is where Seattle visitors can get a taste of what it's all about by taking the hugely popular **assembly-plant tours**. The 747 assembly hangar is the world's largest enclosed building. There are seven daily tours weekdays in summer, six daily in winter. Prices are $5 for adults, $3 for kids and seniors (tour bus and charter groups pay $10 each); cash only is accepted. Tickets can be picked up on-site for that day; groups of 10 or more must make reservations; and no cameras are allowed. For information, call 800/464-1476 or 206/544-1264 in Seattle.

For more of Boeing's history, check out the Museum of Flight (9404 E Marginal Way S; 206/764-5720; map:NN6). It isn't a Boeing museum, but part of the facility is housed in the building where Boeing had its first home in 1910 (see the Exploring chapter).

— *Eric Lucas*

tural displays, a labor of love created by the wife of a local businessman. Once back in the city, fortify yourself with afternoon tea at the elegant **EMPRESS HOTEL** (721 Government St; 250/384-8111) or taste a hand-crafted ale at **SWAN'S PUB** (506 Pandora Ave; 250/361-3310) before taking an evening boat back to Seattle.

EVENING: If high tea leaves you hungry, and you're interested in seeing more of funky Belltown, grab a burger at the **TWO BELLS TAVERN** (2313 4th Ave; 206/441-3050), a casual but trendy diner, and throw off any lingering proper British atmosphere with a nightcap at the scruffy, grunge-classic **CROCODILE CAFE** (2200 2nd Ave; 206/441-5611).

DAY FOUR

Here's a chance to explore more Seattle neighborhoods and taste some of Washington's best exports. Because this itinerary covers a wider geographic range than the previous ones, a car is recommended.

MORNING: Breakfast at **MAE'S PHINNEY RIDGE CAFE**(6412 Phinney Ave N; 206/782-1222), a Seattle morning institution in the Greenwood neighborhood, featuring bigger-than-your-head cinnamon rolls and a whimsical atmosphere. Then head for the nearby **WOODLAND PARK ZOO** (5500 Phinney Ave N; 206/684-4800); the animals are most active in the morning (the zoo opens at 9:30am), and weekday morning crowds are sparse. If wildlife doesn't thrill you, opt for exploring Greenwood instead. Plenty of shops are ripe for browsing here, a good number specializing in antiques and home furnishings. Stop by **PELAYO ANTIQUES** (8421 Greenwood Ave N; 206/789-1333; or 7601 Greenwood Ave N; 206/789-1999) to look at nice selections of oak and pine pieces, as well as Latin American folk art and other one-of-a-kind finds.

AFTERNOON: Have a picnic at **GREEN LAKE**—you can pick up basic supplies at the nearby grocery store, **ALBERTSON'S** (6900 E Green Lake Way; 206/522-7273), or head to local favorites **SPUD FISH & CHIPS** (6860 E Green Lake Dr N; 206/524-0565) or **RASA MALAYSIA** (7208 E Green Lake Dr N; 206/523-8888), the latter for noodle dishes big enough to feed two. If you'd prefer to be served, sit by the windows at **SIX DEGREES** (7900 Green Lake Dr N; 206/523-1600), across the street from the lake, where you can watch all the walkers, runners, bladers, and bike riders jostle for space on the path around the lake.

Feeling inspired? Rent a bike or a pair of in-line skates at **GREGG'S GREENLAKE CYCLE** (7012 Woodlawn Ave NE; 206/729-5102) and head out around the lake. For a more ambitious ride, take the **BURKE-GILMAN TRAIL** to Woodinville, about 18 miles round trip. Once there (via bike or car), you can tour **CHATEAU STE. MICHELLE** winery (14111 NE 145th St; 425/488-1133), which also offers a very popular summer concert series, and the **COLUMBIA WINERY** (14030 NE 145th St; 425/488-2776), located almost directly across the street. Both are popular and award-winning Washington producers. Just a skip away is the **REDHOOK BREWERY** (14300 NE 145th St; 425/483-3232), which also offers tours, and has a pub that serves up the requisite grub and those by-now-famous Redhook brews. Take care on your return trip, especially if you've sampled liberally. And if you've ridden your bike here, the optimum scenario would be to arrange for a friend to pick you up and drive you and your bike back to Seattle.

EVENING: Yes, we know it's a touristy cliché, but **RAY'S BOATHOUSE** (6049 Seaview Ave NW; 206/789-3770) has one of the city's best waterside views of the Olympics and the endless boat traffic heading to and from the Ballard Locks and Lake Union. Head here for a sunset-inspired meal. After dinner, stop in at the **OLD TOWN ALEHOUSE** (5233 Ballard Ave NW; 206/782-8323) in historic Ballard for some acoustic jazz or blues, or the nearby **TRACTOR TAVERN** (5213 Ballard Ave NW; 206/782-3480), which features an eclectic schedule of touring rock groups, as well as country, Celtic, and zydeco acts.

DAY FIVE

Today you'll take your car on a ferry and explore the Kitsap and Olympic Peninsulas, to the west of Seattle. Getting there is half the fun, thanks to luscious views along the way; and your final destination, Port Townsend, makes for a good day trip.

MORNING: Take one of the Washington State Ferries (206/464-6400 or 800/843-3779) from downtown Seattle's Colman Dock at Pier 52 to Bainbridge Island, and in a mere half hour you'll be breakfasting at the delightful **CAFE NOLA** (101 Winslow Way; 206/842-3822). If you've planned in advance and made reservations, visit the **BLOEDEL RESERVE** (7571 Dolphin Dr; 206/842-7631), and stroll the breathtakingly lovely grounds and gardens of this former private estate. From Bainbridge, it's about an hour's drive to Port Townsend.

AFTERNOON: Once in Port Townsend, fortify yourself at the **SALAL CAFÉ** (634 Water St; 360/385-6532) for late-breakfast omelets and vegetarian specialties, or **KHU LARB THAI** (225 Adams St; 360/385-5023) for noodles and extra-fiery curry dishes. Explore **FORT WORDEN STATE PARK** (360/385-4730), home to more than 400 acres of idyllic woodlands, beaches, and grim bunkers left over from the Army base that was here at the turn of the century. Part of Fort Worden is a cultural center, where the **CENTRUM SUMMER ARTS FESTIVAL** (360/385-3102) takes place from June to September. This annual festival focuses on arts education, with classes and seminars in music and theater as well as performances open to the public. Browsing in the shops and galleries along Water Street back in town makes for a pleasant afternoon. On summer weekends, allow room in your schedule to attend a classical concert in a barn at Quilcene's **OLYMPIC MUSIC FESTIVAL** (7360 Center Rd, Quilcene; 206/527-8839) near Hood Canal. The Philadelphia String Quartet, a group of local musicians previously in residence at the University of Washington, has been entertaining young and old here since 1984, including folks who were convinced they didn't like classical music but who've been completely and charmingly won over by the farm's pastoral setting and the decidedly nonstuffy performances.

EVENING: Make your way back to Bainbridge, perhaps with a stop in Port Gamble for a look at a historic paper-mill town. Enjoy a burger with a waterfront view at the casual, convivial **HARBOUR PUBLIC HOUSE** (231 Parfitt Way SW; 206/842-0969) on Bainbridge's Eagle Harbor before catching the ferry back to Seattle.

DAY SIX

Today you'll head to the hills: the Cascade Range to the east of Seattle, and some of the prettiest mountain scenery in the state.

MORNING: Get an early start; head east on I-90 over the locally famous "floating" bridge (a portion of it sank somewhat dramatically into Lake Washington during construction work in 1990), and drive through Issaquah. Quaint **GILMAN VILLAGE** here makes a nice stop for shopaholics (with some fine restaurants, too), or continue east toward the town of North Bend, the place made famous by the TV series *Twin Peaks*. If you'd just like to spend the morning **HIKING**, try the hike to Talapus and Olallie Lakes (exit 45 off I-90), an easy jaunt as wilderness hikes go, and perfect for kids. For a longer, more strenuous hike, take the Denny Creek Trail to Melakwa Lake, with lots of spectacular scenery and waterfalls (exit 47 off I-90). The winter season offers cross-country and downhill skiing at several locations around the Snoqualmie Pass area; call 206/232-8182 for information.

AFTERNOON: Lunch on the trail, or head north off I-90 for some homemade soup and a hearty sandwich at Carnation's **RIVER RUN CAFÉ** (4366 Tolt Ave; 425/333-6100), where you can rub elbows with local farmers and anglers and maybe even pick up a few tidbits of local gossip. Pay a visit here to **REMLINGER FARMS** (32610 NE 32nd St; 425/333-4135 or 425/451-8740) for abundant locally grown produce, delectable baked goods, and plenty of amusements for the kids, including pony rides and a petting zoo. There's more in the way of lush, green, growing things in nearby Fall City at **THE HERBFARM** (32804 Issaquah–Fall City Rd; 425/784-2222 or 800/866-4372), including 17 herbal theme gardens, farm animals, and an intriguing gift shop. On the return trip to Seattle, stop at stunning **SNOQUALMIE FALLS**. Hike down to the bottom, or view the falls in all their thundering majesty from a platform at the top. If you're considering weekending in this neck of the woods, perhaps to celebrate a special romantic occasion, the **SALISH LODGE** (6501 Railroad Ave SE, Snoqualmie; 425/888-2556) makes a wonderful home base, with an acclaimed restaurant, a luxurious spa, and an unrivaled location overlooking the falls. The lounge is a cozy spot to sip something warm and gaze at the falls on days when the weather is less than cooperative.

SEATTLE SOFTWARE

Microsoft is not the largest company on earth. Unlike the older Seattle corporate heavyweight, Boeing, it's not even in the top 50 (based on annual sales, which are less than a third of Boeing's). So why is the Redmond-based software firm, founded in 1975, one of the world's most visible corporations?

Because its logo flashes on the opening screens of perhaps two-thirds of the world's computers, and because the many versions of Windows operating systems are ubiquitous. As a result of that hegemony, Microsoft's stock is among the most valuable in the world, with its market value at well over $300 billion. Many of those shares are held by Microsoft employees, more than 1,000 of whom (present and former) have become millionaires through stock options. That's also one of the reasons choice Seattle real estate has appreciated so much in the '90s.

Microsoft cofounder Bill Gates grew up in Seattle. Legend has it that when he and Paul Allen were looking for a location to build the company (once they'd secured the contract to supply DOS to IBM), Allen suggested Albuquerque, a much smaller and less expensive place than Seattle. But Gates said no way. Thus Redmond, east of Bellevue, eventually became the site of the Microsoft corporate campus, which at last count encompassed 260 acres, 38 buildings, and 3.2 million square feet. (The main corporate address is One Microsoft Way.) More than 13,000 people work there.

Want to visit? The Microsoft Museum is open to employees, their families, and their friends, as well as vendors and contract workers—but not to the general public. The latter are invited to tour the virtual museum, accessible through Microsoft's Web site (www.microsoft.com). And you're welcome to drive through the corporate campus, if you like, and look at the handsome but not very unusual office buildings.

Although Microsoft's fortunes still depend on its software, it has ventured into other enterprises related to electronic commerce, including widely publicized Internet magazines and services and a series of city-guide Web sites, the first of which covered Seattle (seattle.sidewalk.com). These sites evince a Gen-X, tech-savvy view of the world and our city—appropriately enough, since the Microsoft boom has been so much a part of creating the Seattle lifestyle.

— *Eric Lucas*

EVENING: Once back in town, visit another Seattle neighborhood, perhaps **MADISON PARK**, an oh-so-chichi enclave on the shores of Lake Washington. Sample satisfying Italian- and French-inspired cuisine at charming **SOSTANZA** (1927 43rd Ave E; 206/324-9701), and continue south on Lake Washington Boulevard to Leschi Marina for an after-dinner drink at the elegant bar at **DANIEL'S BROILER** (200 Lake Washington Blvd; 206/329-4191). The evening light reflecting off the lake is gorgeous, and if it's clear, you can gaze at the Cascades, where you began the day.

DAY SEVEN

Time to hit the road again. "The Mountain"—Mount Rainier—has been looming all week, and today you're finally going to get to see it up close and personal.

MORNING: Again, an early start is in order. It takes about 2½ hours to reach **MOUNT RAINIER NATIONAL PARK** (360/569-2211) by car from Seattle if you take the direct route. (See also the Day Trips chapter.) Those who are up for seeing a bit of the surrounding countryside and more wildlife than they can shake a stick at should take the roundabout way to the mountain via Eatonville, and visit **NORTHWEST TREK WILDLIFE PARK** (11610 Trek Dr E; 360/832-6117 or 800/433-8735). Or, for a longer and more scenic excursion, head to the village of Elbe and take a ride on a steam train via the **MOUNT RAINIER SCENIC RAILROAD** (360/569-2588). The train runs from May through October.

AFTERNOON: Past Elbe and farther along State Route 706 is the visitors center at **PARADISE**, with fabulous views of the more than six dozen glaciers that inhabit Mount Rainier. Here you can picnic and pick up a trail map. Several hikes starting from this point will get your circulation moving in anticipation of longer jaunts to come. Or you can turn off at the Grove of the Patriarchs for a great 1-mile walk through an impressive stand of thousand-year-old trees. If you choose, instead, to go to the visitors center at **SUNRISE**—with an elevation of 6,400 feet, the highest point accessible by car—you can see climbers scaling Emmons Glacier and mountain goats making their way up an adjacent peak. Take the 4-mile Sourdough Ridge trail, which winds through meadows of wildflowers to a breathtaking viewpoint.

EVENING: Back in the city, after a shower (and maybe a nap), end your stay in Seattle at **DAHLIA LOUNGE** (1904 4th Ave; 206/682-4142), one of three restaurants in town run by chef Tom Douglas, whom many credit with putting Seattle on the culinary map. Order his famous Dungeness crab cakes or other fresh seafood. You can reminisce about the time you've spent exploring the Emerald City, sigh about what you didn't get to see, and dream about making a return visit in the very near future.

DAY TRIPS

DAY TRIPS

Kitsap and Olympic Peninsulas

BREMERTON AND BEYOND

Take the Washington State Ferry from Colman Dock (Pier 52) in downtown Seattle to Bremerton (approximately 1 hour).

A naval city through and through, Bremerton makes the most of its waterfront and the nautical attractions of Sinclair Inlet. A broad promenade skirts the shore between First Street (where car- and foot-ferry terminals are) and Fourth Street. A stroll along this walkway provides impressive views, with picnic tables, benches, and sculpture along the way. The promenade leads to the Ship's Store Gift Shop, where tickets may be purchased for a tour of the **USS TURNER JOY**, a Forrest Sherman destroyer, moored nearby and famed for its role in the Gulf of Tonkin off Vietnam. A moving POW memorial has been installed on the ship, a replicated cell from the "Hanoi Hilton." The *Turner Joy* (360/792-2457) is open for self-guided tours, from fantail to fo'c'sle, daily in summer, Thursday through Sunday in winter.

The star of the harbor from 1955 to 1998, the battleship *Missouri*, has sailed off to Hawaii, but a harbor tour still provides thrills with close-up views of aircraft carriers, battleships, cruisers, nuclear subs, and the carrier *USS Carl Vinson*, the world's largest warship, when it's not at sea. Down at the west end of the harbor, the ghostly mothball fleet is moored. **KITSAP HARBOR TOURS** (360/377-8924) runs 45-minute narrated tours hourly, daily in summer and on weekends in winter (tickets are available at the Ship's Store Gift Shop). The same outfit runs a 45-minute cruise to **BLAKE ISLAND** for the salmon dinner in the longhouse and stage show by the Tillicum Village Dancers. (Also accessible from Seattle; see Boat Tours under Organized Tours in the Exploring chapter.)

On Washington Street, which parallels the boardwalk, the free **BREMERTON NAVAL MUSEUM** (130 Washington St; 360/479-7447) overflows with neatly displayed marvels: ships' models galore, including a 15-foot-long *Admiral Nimitz;* ships in bottles; ships' bells; and more nautical gear than you can shake a belaying pin at. Open daily in summer, daily except Monday in winter, 10am to 5pm. Two doors south on Washington Street the calm, comfortable **FRAICHE CUP** coffeehouse (360/377-1180) offers pastries, espresso drinks, and reading matter scattered on the tables. Tidy little City Hall Park, up the street at the corner of Fourth and Washington, with a great harbor view, is a handy spot to perch for a picnic lunch.

Several art galleries are found a block or so from Washington Street. The **AMY BURNETT FINE ART GALLERY** (412 Pacific Ave; 360/373-3187) displays works by Burnett and other contemporary and Northwest Coast artists in spacious, well-lit galleries. The adjoining frame-shop-cum-wine-shop is open for wine tasting every Saturday afternoon. The art of politics is also commemorated in Bremerton, with a plaque at Fourth and Pacific marking where the slogan "Give 'em hell, Harry!" was born, when a spectator shouted it to the campaigning Harry Truman.

A 5-minute drive on Washington Avenue north from downtown Bremerton and across the Manette Bridge, the **BOAT SHED** (101 Shore Dr; 360/377-2600) offers fine seafood, hearty sandwiches, and unusual salads (try the roasted vegetables and Brie). The clam chowder is as good as it gets. Have a pint of ale on the deck, watch scoters paddling in the bay and cormorants whizzing by, and enjoy the view straight down the water to the *Turner Joy*.

It's some 7 miles around the west end of Sinclair Inlet via State Route 3, State Route 16, and State Route 166 from Bremerton to **PORT ORCHARD**, but **HORLUCK TRANSPORTATION COMPANY** (Bremerton Ferry Dock or Sidney Dock in Port Orchard; 360/876-2300) runs foot ferries every half hour between Bremerton's ferry terminal and Port Orchard, year-round. Most of the boats are utilitarian (wooden benches, no amenities), but at peak commuter times you might luck out with the *Carlisle II*, a stalwart 75-year-old double-decker with historical photos from its Mosquito Fleet days. The trip costs $1.10 (free on weekends between October and May), takes 10 minutes, and lets passengers out just a block from Port Orchard's arcaded Bay Street with its antique shops, taverns, retro clothing emporiums, and espresso boutiques. Port Orchard, besides enjoying one of the best water-oriented locations on Puget Sound, claims to be the antique capital of the Kitsap Peninsula. You could spend hours in the **OLDE CENTRAL ANTIQUE MALL** (801 Bay St; 360/895-1902). Saturdays from April to October the **PORT ORCHARD FARMERS MARKET** takes over the three-block-long waterfront park. Wares, displayed under gaily colored canopies, range from pottery to scones to woodenware to fresh basil. The pavilion at the end of the park doubles as a bandstand and picnic shelter.

The cozy little **POT BELLY DELI** (724 Bay St; 360/895-1396) is a favorite hangout of Port Orchardites for breakfast, lunch, and gossip. Tasty sandwiches, soups, and salads are cheerfully dispensed from the counter at the back of the narrow, brick-walled restaurant. Place your order, then dash off a tune on the 1880s-era upright piano in the window while you wait for your meal.

A 5-minute drive east from Port Orchard, **SPRINGHOUSE DOLLS AND GIFTS** (1130 Bethel Ave; 360/876-0529) boasts the largest collection of modern dolls in the Northwest, as well as teddy bears and other cuddlies. Take breakfast, lunch, tea, or espresso in the flouncy Victorian Rose Tearoom or outside on the terrace. Reserve for the all-out Victorian High Tea (Wednesdays and Saturdays, 3pm) and your floral china teacup is yours to keep.

ELANDAN GARDENS (3050 W SR 16; 360/373-8260) is an enchanting 5-acre open-air gallery stretching along the shore of Sinclair Inlet. Priceless bonsai, collected over the decades by Dan Robinson, are the main attraction. Dozens of elegant little trees are artfully displayed, including tiny junipers and pines, and a ponderosa pine that was alive before King Alfred reigned. The gardens also feature native plants, Japanese maples, azaleas, and rhododendrons. Stone sculptures blend into the natural landscape, and spires of blackened cedar snags tower over all. A gallery/gift shop offers choice antiques, gifts, and wearables. Bonsai and other plants are on sale in the adjoining nursery. The gardens are in Gorst, between Port Orchard and Bremerton, just beyond milepost 28 on State Route 16, coming from Port Orchard. Closed Mondays and January.

A short drive up State Route 104 from Bremerton in Keyport, the free NAVAL UNDERSEA MUSEUM (610 Dowell St; 360/396-4148) is as shipshape as an admiral's flagship. Learn all about marine science, naval history, and evolving undersea technology. See dive suits seemingly designed for giants, fearsome torpedoes, and a submersible that helped explore the *Titanic*. The gift shop's wares are well chosen. For a post-museum snack, stop at the sandwich shop in KEYPORT MERCANTILE (Washington and Grandview; 360/779-7270) for fresh fare and a great view of the water.

HOOD CANAL

Take the Washington State Ferry from Colman Dock (Pier 52) in downtown Seattle to Bainbridge Island (approximately 35 minutes). From the Bainbridge ferry dock, take Highway 305 north to State Route 3, cross the Hood Canal Bridge to State Route 104, and take Highway 101 south.

The eastern arm of 65-mile-long, U-shaped Hood Canal runs from Belfair southwesterly along State Route 106 to Union. It's almost solid with mansions and modest homes built over the decades as summer retreats by urbanites, drawn by Olympic views and calm, swimmable waters. The less domesticated western arm, where Highway 101 hugs the littoral, still has long stretches of forested slopes and accessible beaches. Three rivers that plunge down from the Olympics to the canal offer trail access to the mountains: the DUCKABUSH, the HAMMA HAMMA, and the DOSEWALLIPS. The big peninsula bracketed by the canal's two arms is largely undeveloped.

On the northwest shore of this peninsula, tiny **SEABECK** is home to the Seabeck Conference Center (360/830-5010), which may be rented by nonprofit groups. Just to its west is **SCENIC BEACH STATE PARK**, with picnicking, campsites, and a view straight across to the Olympics. At the tip of the peninsula, overlooking the canal's Big Bend, sprawling **TAHUYA STATE PARK** is reached by the Belfair-Tahuya Road or by State Route 300, which follows the shore. The park embraces beach and forest and is sought out by mountain bikers, hikers, and horseback riders. Much more accessible **BELFAIR STATE PARK**, 3 miles south of Belfair on State Route 300, is one of the peninsula's busiest parks. Campers must reserve in summer: 360/478-4625. Some swim here, some fish, and some dig clams. For drama in the woods, check out the **MOUNTAINEERS' FOREST THEATER** (360/284-6310), on the road to Seabeck.

TWANOH STATE PARK, on State Route 106 on the eastern arm, is popular with families. It has a big, safe, shallow pool and a fast-food concession. More elevated cuisine is available near Union at **VICTORIA'S** (E 6791 SR 106; 360/898-4400): eat in the cheery, high-ceilinged dining room or al fresco by a tree-shaded brook.

At the **UNION COUNTRY STORE** (E 5130 SR 106; 360/898-2461), Bruce and Sheila Rosenstein offer exotic groceries, produce, wines, and wonderful fresh-daily dips (free tastings). Heavenly carry-out entrees such as prawn enchiladas, Parmesan scallops, or beef Stroganoff are created fresh daily by Bruce. They may be heated on the spot and eaten at a table by the window of this friendly, well-stocked store or at a picnic table outside. Or you may choose to have them packed in ice for the trip home.

HOOD CANAL–THELER WETLANDS (E 22871 SR 3; 360/ 275-4898), just south of Belfair, draws bird-watchers and nature observers to walk its 3.8 miles of wheelchair-accessible trails through saltwater marshes, bosky woods, and the Union River estuary. A wooden causeway over a tidal marsh leads to a grand view of the canal's south expanse. The interpretive center, with its native-plant garden, offers a quick course on the value of wetlands in general and this one in particular.

The west arm of Hood Canal, from Hoodsport to Quilcene, gives access to many recreational areas in the **OLYMPIC NATIONAL FOREST** and **OLYMPIC NATIONAL PARK**. Ranger stations along Highway 101 are generous with information on hikes, fees, and permits. Hoodsport Ranger Station (just off Hwy 101 on Lake Cushman Dr, 360/877-5254) has single-sheet maps for hikes along the southern sector of the canal, from a half mile to a serious backpack trip. At the Quilcene Ranger Station (360/765-2200), just south of Quilcene, ask about outdoor recreation at the north end of the canal.

Three miles south of Hoodsport, **POTLATCH STATE PARK** is a refreshing stop for a picnic or a dip. At low tide, oysters may be gathered on the beach. Other public beaches where oystering is permitted along the west reach of the canal include Cushman Beach, Lilliwaup Recreational Tidelands, Pleasant Harbor State Park, Dosewallips State Park (a choice stop, with 425 acres of meadows, woodlands, and beach), and Seal Rock Campground. Most of these have clam beds too. South of Quilcene, Bee Mill Road takes off eastward from 101 to the Point Whitney State Shellfish Laboratory and its interpretive display, and a good oyster and swimming beach. Check the state hotline (800/562-5632) for red-tide warnings. Shucked **OYSTERS** may be purchased at Hama Hama Oyster Company (360/877-5811), just south of the Hamma Hamma River; Triton Cove Oyster Farms (360/796-4360), near Brinnon; and Coast Oyster Company (360/765-3474), at the end of Linger Longer Road in Quilcene. Call ahead to make sure they're open.

HOODSPORT WINERY (360/877-9894), about a mile south of its namesake town, will match its wine to your oysters. The pretty tasting room looks out over the canal; the offerings include white varietals, four fruit wines, and, among the reds, the legendary Island Belle, made from grapes grown on Stretch Island, 30 miles away.

HOODSPORT, the largest town on the canal, is a gateway to the Lake Cushman area. Beyond the increasingly developed lakeshore, at the Olympic National Park boundary, there's a ranger station, campground, picnicking, and trailheads. A short walk along the **STAIRCASE RAPIDS TRAIL** beside the crystal-clear Skokomish River is a pleasure for both novice and veteran hikers.

From April to June the rhododendrons, azaleas, camellias, and kalmias at **WHITNEY GARDENS** (306264 Hwy 101; 360/796-4411), in Brinnon, burst out in a rainbow of colors. But any time of year it's a delight to stroll the leafy corridors of this 7-acre retreat, shaded by conifers, weeping spruces, colorful maples, and magnolias and bordered by exotic and native flora. The nursery has plants for sale, a picnic area is available, and catered lunches may be arranged. The gardens are open every day (small fee), but in December and January by appointment only.

HALFWAY HOUSE (360/796-4715), at Highway 101 and Brinnon Lane in Brinnon, serves three solid meals a day in a folksy, unassuming ambience where tourists and locals mingle.

Five miles south of Quilcene, invisible from Highway 101, is one of the canal's most sensational viewpoints: 2,750-foot **MOUNT WALKER**, accessed by a 5-mile dirt road (summer only) that snakes around the mountain to a topside view of Seattle, Mount Rainier, the Cascades, and the Olympics. Bring a picnic. You can hike the 2-mile trail to the top if you prefer. Near the Mount Walker turnoff from Highway 101, the

WALKER MOUNTAIN TRADING POST (360/796-3200) crams into a one-time pioneer home a variety of antiques, crafts, and locally made jewelry. Some wares are oddball, some are nice surprises. Also available: smoked salmon, fresh oysters, ice cream bars, and pop.

On the west side of Highway 101, north of the turnoff to Mount Walker, **FALLS VIEW CAMPGROUND** is a short hike from a lovely waterfall. For sustenance, stop at the substantial **TIMBER HOUSE** (360/765-3339), famed for its prime rib and local seafood (Quilcene oysters fresh from the bay), serving lunch and dinner Wednesday through Monday.

QUILCENE has the world's largest oyster hatchery and, in its bay, what's said to be the purest salt water in the West. The Quilcene Ranger Station (360/765-3368), just south of town, can help with advice on shellfishing. Quilcene's aged but mellow **WHISTLING OYSTER TAVERN** (360/765-9508) is where the knowing locals hang out for food, refreshment, darts, and shuffleboard. In the heart of town, the **TWANA ROADHOUSE** (360/765-6485) and its Trading House, with Northwest crafts and gifts, add up to a welcome excuse to break the journey. The menu won't dazzle, but service is quick and cheery, and everything is good and fresh: soups, salads, sandwiches, and pizza, plus homemade pies and hand-dipped ice cream.

North of Quilcene and just before the junction of Highway 101 with State Route 104, the **OLYMPIC MUSIC FESTIVAL** (360/527-8839) holds forth at 2pm Saturdays and Sundays, June through Labor Day, in a turn-of-the-century barn converted into a concert hall. Listeners sit inside on hay bales or church pews, or outside on the grass. Bring a picnic, or assemble one from the well-stocked deli on the premises. It's a real farm, and youngsters are encouraged to pet the animals. The music is sublime, performed by the Philadelphia String Quartet with guest artists from around the world. Reservations advised.

PORT TOWNSEND

50 miles northwest of Seattle (approximately 2 hours). Take the Bainbridge ferry from downtown Seattle, then head northwest across the island on State Route 305. Follow State Route 3 to the Hood Canal Bridge and continue on State Route 104 to State Route 20. Follow State Route 20 into town.

Known as the city with the finest display of Victorian architecture north of San Francisco, Port Townsend may also be the one that makes the most of its waterfront. A walk along Water Street reveals miniparks, benches, picnic tables, piers, and a profusion of modest and upscale eateries with sublime views of Admiralty Inlet. The town is a mix of 19th-century charm and the trendy, quirky 1990s. Hundred-year-old turreted and embellished buildings shelter a melange of colorful galleries and

FERRY RIDES

No activity better captures the spirit of Seattle than a ferry ride—both for commuters who rely on ferries as transportation and for sightseers who want to simply enjoy the sunset or the city skyline from an ideal vantage point.

Most of the ferries on Puget Sound are run by **Washington State Ferries** (206/464-6400 or 800/542-7052; www.wsdot.wa.gov/ferries). The largest ferry system in the country, it operates 10 routes serving 20 terminal locations and transporting 23 million passengers a year. On weekend and evening runs, ferries often don't have room for all the cars, so be prepared to wait unless you walk on or ride your bike (your fare will be much cheaper if you do). Food service is available on almost all routes, beer and wine on some. (However, in all cases you'll do better dining at your destination than on the way to it.) Rates range from $3.60 one way for foot passengers traveling from Seattle to Vashon, to $39.75 for a car and driver going from Anacortes to Sidney, British Columbia. The bike surcharge is 60 cents from Seattle to Bainbridge, Vashon, or Bremerton. Passengers pay only on westbound ferries (so if you're island-hopping, head to the westernmost destination first and work your way back).

Three ferries leave downtown from the main Seattle terminal at Colman Dock (Pier 52, Alaskan Way and Marion St; map:M9). A small, speedy walk-on ferry takes mostly commuters to **Vashon Island** (Monday through Saturday only; 25 minutes) or to the Navy town of **Bremerton** (35-40 minutes). The car-ferry trip to Bremerton takes an hour. The **Seattle-Bainbridge Island** run takes 35 minutes on a jumbo ferry. If sightseeing is your objective, take the Bremerton trip. It's a bit longer, but the scenic ride crosses the Sound, skirts the south end of Bainbridge Island, and passes through narrow Rich Passage into the Kitsap Peninsula's land-enclosed Sinclair Inlet.

In recent years, the population of Bainbridge and Vashon Islands has increased and more folks are commuting by ferry. As a result, drive-on ferry passengers should arrive early, especially when traveling during peak hours (mornings eastbound, evenings westbound; summer weekends: Fridays and Saturdays westbound, Sundays eastbound). Schedules vary from summer to winter (with longer lines in summer); credit cards are not accepted. Americans traveling to Canada should bring a passport or other proof of U.S. citizenship.

Other major Puget Sound routes are listed below:

Edmonds-Kingston (30 minutes)

Kingston, close to the northern tip of the Kitsap Peninsula, is reached from Edmonds (about 15 miles north of Seattle; take the Edmonds-Kingston Ferry exit—exit 177—from I-5 and head northwest on State Route 104).

Fauntleroy-Vashon Island-Southworth (15 minutes/10 minutes)

Vashon, an idyllic retreat west of Seattle, can be reached via passenger ferry from downtown Seattle Monday through Saturday, or via car ferry from the Fauntleroy ferry dock in West Seattle every day (15 minutes). Vashon is the first stop on a trip from the Fauntleroy terminal in West Seattle (exit 163 off I-5; map:LL9) to Southworth on the Kitsap Peninsula (10 minutes by ferry from Vashon; see Vashon Island in this chapter).

Vashon-Tacoma (15 minutes)

At the Puget Sound end of Vashon Island is the Tahlequah terminal, from which the ferry departs for Point Defiance Park, on the outskirts of Tacoma.

Mukilteo-Clinton (20 minutes)

From Mukilteo, 26 miles north of Seattle (take exit 189 from I-5), a ferry goes to Clinton, on pretty Whidbey Island (see Whidbey Island in this chapter).

Keystone-Port Townsend (30 minutes)

From Keystone, 25 miles up Whidbey Island from Clinton, another ferry reaches Port Townsend (on the Olympic Peninsula), one of the most enchanting towns in the state (see Port Townsend in this chapter).

Anacortes-San Juan Islands-Sidney, BC (crossing times vary)

The remote San Juan Islands are reached by ferry from Anacortes (82 miles northwest of Seattle, exit 230 off I-5). There are 743 islands at low tide, but only 172 have names, and only 4 have major ferry service: the boat stops on Lopez, Shaw, Orcas, and San Juan Islands. Once a day (twice a day in summer), the ferry continues on to Sidney on British Columbia's Vancouver Island, just 15 minutes by car from Victoria. It returns in the early afternoon. During the summer, you can reserve space for your car on this crowded run.

Seattle-Victoria, BC (2 hours)

The *Victoria Clipper* fleet (206/448-5000, 250/382-8100 or 800/888-2535; www.victoriaclipper.com) offers the only year-round ferry service to Victoria from Seattle. The waterjet-propelled catamarans carry foot passengers only between Seattle and Victoria four times a day from mid-May to mid-September, and once or twice a day the rest of the year. Reservations are necessary (see Victoria in this chapter). The BC ferry *Princess Marguerite III* offers the only car-ferry service between Seattle and Victoria, leaving Pier 48 in Seattle at 1pm daily from mid-May to mid-September for a 4½-hour trip, returning from Victoria at 7:30am daily.

Port Angeles-Victoria, BC (1½ hours)

The privately run Black Ball Transport's *MV Coho* (360/457-4491) makes two runs daily in winter and spring and four runs daily in summer from Port Angeles, on the Olympic Peninsula, to Victoria, on Vancouver Island.

shops. **CAPTAIN'S GALLERY** (1012 Water St; 360/385-3770) has an amazing selection of pricey kaleidoscopes, plus nautical prints, ships' models, and souvenirs. **EARTHENWORKS** (702 Water St; 360/385-0328) offers American crafts and fine art. The **ANTIQUE MALL** (802 Washington St; 360/385-2590) embraces some 40 purveyors of wares from toys to coins to jewelry to rare books. Below, there's a display of Chinese artifacts excavated from the burned homes of a Chinese colony from the 1890s. This area's Chinatown was destroyed by fire at the turn of the century, but when the Antique Mall basement was excavated, many items were discovered. **NORTHWEST NATIVE EXPRESSIONS,** in the lobby of the Waterstreet Hotel (637 Water St; 360/385-4770), features baskets, drums, masks, Salish blankets, and jewelry, most created by artists from the Olympic Peninsula. A superior bookshop, **IMPRINT BOOKSTORE** (820 Water St; 360/385-3643), is well stocked with classics and contemporary works and a fine selection of regional guidebooks.

Across the street, **WILLIAM JAMES BOOKSELLER** (360/385-7313) has a vast collection of used and rare books. At **APRIL FOOL & PENNY TWO** (725 Water St; 360/385-3438), the collectibles are high quality and the miniatures and dollhouses are appealing. The **WINE SELLER** (940 Water St; 360/385-7673) offers a large and well-chosen selection of wines as well as choice beers, teas, and coffees.

For the best ice-cream cone in town, head for the **ELEVATED ICE CREAM COMPANY** (627 Water St; 360/385-1156), with its elevated sundeck overlooking the bay. For the best sodas in the most nostalgic setting, visit **NIFTY FIFTYS** (817 Water St; 360/385-1156), where nobody is surprised if you order an egg cream or a Tin Roof sundae. For a nip with the natives, drop in on the legendary **TOWN TAVERN** (at the corner of Quincy and Water Sts; 360/379-8128), with its pool tables, huge bar, and startling mural. Below street level on Tyler Street, the brick-walled, cavernlike **CELLARS MARKET** (940 Water St; 360/385-7088) offers tasty lunchtime fare, espresso, homemade fudge, and idiosyncratic works by local artists. **CHEEKS BISTRO & CAFE,** upstairs at Flagship Landing (1019 Water St; 360/379-5244), has a super view, a balcony, and good seafood, salads, and wines. Longtime fixture **BREAD & ROSES BAKERY** (230 Quincy St; 360/385-1044) has great breads and pastries as well as espresso, soups, and sandwiches, plus open-air seating. **SALAL CAFE** (634 Water St; 360/385-6532)—voted "best breakfast" by locals—provides some of the freshest, most imaginative repasts in town. Eat in the streetside dining room or in the sunny atrium that overlooks Franklin Court, scene of Friday-noon concerts.

The exquisitely restored **ROSE THEATRE** (235 Taylor St; 360/385-1089) puts on daily 4:45pm matinees of current and classic films in its Rosebud Cinema. **FRONT STREET WATER TAXI** (360/379-3258 or

360/379-6266 Wed–Sun) offers summertime tours from the Boat Haven to Point Hudson, with stop-off privileges. Downtown parks include **JACKSON BEQUEST TIDAL PARK**, with its wave-viewing gallery and tidal clock (behind Elevated Ice Cream, on Water St). **POPE MARINE PARK**, at the end of Adams Street, is compact, with picnic tables plus logs and playground equipment for the young to climb on. The best views in town are from the pavilion at the end of the newly restored, 130-year-old Union Wharf: Mount Baker, Mount Rainier, and the back side of Water Street's historic buildings.

Reach "Uptown" by climbing the stairway at Taylor and Washington Streets, home of the voluptuous **HALLER FOUNTAIN**. Or drive up past the oldest Episcopal church in the Diocese of Olympia and the rusty-red **OLD BELL TOWER**, which once summoned firemen and now relaxes in the center of a minipark. Here atop the bluff, venerable mansions built by early moguls (many now elegant bed-and-breakfast inns) are just a few blocks from Lawrence Street's pizzerias, espresso bars, and galleries. **ALDRICH'S** (940 Lawrence St; 360/385-0500), a century-old general store, has quality wines, produce, fresh seafood, a deli, and a bakery. Stock up for a picnic here, then head for **CHETZEMOKA PARK** at Jackson and Blaine Streets, a beauty spot with emerald lawns, rose arbors, a playground, and access to the beach, where you can dig clams if the tide's right. Or go on to sprawling **FORT WORDEN STATE PARK**, once an Army base and now inexpensive lodgings (great for families) and the headquarters of the Centrum Foundation, which puts on an ambitious summertime program of concerts, plays, festivals, and workshops. **BLACKBERRIES** (in the heart of Fort Worden; 360/385-9950) serves appetizing meals in a pleasant, rustic dining room near the parade ground. Down on the beach, the **MARINE SCIENCE CENTER** (360/385-5582) shows off its touch tanks and aquaria; children may shake hands with a sea cucumber or tickle a starfish. Up on Artillery Hill, examine the slumbering bunkers and gun emplacements, recalling the days when this was one of the forts that protected Puget Sound.

Visitors have a hard time imagining the scandalous goings-on in this part of town during the town's heyday in the mid-1800s, when whiskey flowed free, brothels flourished, and the shanghaiing of sailors was a common occurrence. To get a handle on Port Townsend history, visit the buildings that are open for tours. The **HISTORICAL MUSEUM** in City Hall (210 Madison St; 360/385-1003) includes the city's original courtroom, its jail, and a replica of a furbelowed Victorian bedroom. The 130-year-old **ROTHSCHILD HOUSE** (360/379-8076 for group tour reservations) at Jefferson and Taylor Streets still displays many of its original furnishings; stroll through the herb and rose gardens. The **COMMANDING OFFICER'S HOUSE** at the end of Officers' Row at Fort Worden faithfully reproduces the life of an officer and his family at the turn of the century. Every September, Port Townsend holds a **HISTORIC HOMES TOUR** (Chamber of Commerce, 360/385-2722), including several noted bed and breakfasts.

This Victorian seaport boasts two marinas and an annual **WOODEN BOAT FESTIVAL** (360/385-3628) on the first weekend after Labor Day, centered at Point Hudson at the end of Water Street. Attractions include jazz concerts, strolling entertainers, and, of course, boats—ranging from dinghies to schooners.

Parking in downtown Port Townsend can be scarce. To avoid the hassle, leave your car at the Park & Ride at Haines Place near Safeway as you enter town and ride the free shuttle, which runs every half hour to uptown (Lawrence Street) and downtown (Water Street). Hidden away near the Park & Ride, **KAH TAI LAGOON PARK** is favored by birders, walkers, bikers, and waterfowl.

South Puget Sound

OLYMPIA

60 miles south of Seattle on Interstate 5 (approximately 1½ to 2 hours).

As the home of the state capitol and three colleges, Olympia plays host to a mix of bureaucrats, lawmakers, students, and professors, who constitute an eclectic and lively citizenry. You can plan an entire afternoon visit around the capitol campus alone, but because much of the town closes up shop over the summer, the best time to venture to this city is in springtime, when the legislature, the universities, and the businesses are all in full swing.

Most stages of the lawmaking process are open to the public, and a carefully scheduled trip to Olympia can reward visitors with glimpses of debates, demonstrations, speeches, and hearings. The **LEGISLATIVE BUILDING** (14th Ave and Water St; 360/586-8687), with the fourth-tallest dome in the world, is home to the Senate and House of Representatives chambers, as well as the governor's office. You can critique legislative debates from the fourth-floor visitors' galleries. Stop by the **STATE CAPITOL VISITOR CENTER** (14th Ave and Capitol Way; 360/586-3460) for information about exploring the campus. The grounds themselves are beautifully strollable, with their well-manicured lawns, centerpiece sunken garden, and conservatory. Free daily guided tours of the capitol buildings, including the **GOVERNOR'S MANSION** (Wednesday afternoons only), can be arranged by calling 360/586-8687. Drop by the **STATE CAPITOL MUSEUM** (211 W 21st Ave; 360/753-2580), a few blocks south of campus, which houses a permanent exhibit including an outstanding collection of Native American baskets and memorabilia from the state's founding and early days of government.

If you have little ones in tow, they're bound to get cranky with all of this boring government stuff. Treat them to a visit to the **HANDS ON CHILDREN'S MUSEUM** (108 Franklin St NE; 360/956-0818), where tons of interactive exhibits will keep them engaged and absorbed for hours. Nearby in the downtown area, you'll find a good variety of galleries, offbeat shops, cafes, and restaurants. Some of the best coffee you'll find anywhere brews at **BATDORF AND BRONSON COFFEE ROASTERS** (513 Capitol Way S; 360/786-6717), which has a sizable following of folks who don't care if there is a Starbucks across the street. A large blackboard lists all of the coffees, teas, and espresso drinks, and the smell of beans roasting just a few feet away is enough to make coffee lovers swoon.

Take your latte up the block to **SYLVESTER PARK**, a quiet spot nestled between the rushed paces of downtown and the capitol. Once the legislative and college sessions get rolling, this otherwise peaceful lawn with a gazebo becomes a choice venue for outdoor concerts, rallies, and demonstrations. At the corner of Capitol and Legion Ways, a boulder marks the end of the old Oregon Trail. Across the street is the classy and wholesome **URBAN ONION** in the old Olympian Hotel (116 E Legion Way; 360/943-9242). Its most famous creation, the Haystack—sprouts, tomatoes, guacamole, olives, and melted cheese piled high on wholegrain bread—draws crowds for lunch; it's open for dinner, too. Or indulge in a taste of the city's past at the **SPAR** (114 E 4th Ave; 360/357-6444), an old-timey joint decorated with historic photos and plenty of nostalgic character.

The **WASHINGTON CENTER FOR THE PERFORMING ARTS** (512 Washington St SE; 360/753-8586) has brought new life to Olympia's downtown, with a wide range of performances, including dance, symphony, and theater. **THE CAPITOL THEATRE** (206 E 5th Ave; 360/754-5378) is a showcase for locally produced plays, musicals, and Olympia Film Society–sponsored screenings, including a film festival in November. Toward the harbor, at the corner of N Capitol Way and W Thurston Street, the lively **OLYMPIA FARMERS MARKET** (360/352-9096) displays produce, flowers, and crafts from all over the South Sound; open Thursday through Sunday during the growing season.

At **PERCIVAL LANDING** (corner of State and Water Sts), the city's waterfront park, the highlight of 1½ miles of boardwalk is a viewing tower from which you can scan the horizon, from the harbor of Budd Inlet to the capitol dome to the snowy peaks of the Olympic Range.

THE EVERGREEN STATE COLLEGE (Evergreen Pkwy; 360/866-6000), one of the top liberal-arts schools in the country, has a beautiful, woodsy campus including an organic farm and 3,100 feet of beachfront property, and is host to a wide range of film, music, theater, and dance events throughout the year.

The area surrounding Olympia is rich in side-trip options. In neighboring Tumwater, the **OLYMPIA BREWING COMPANY** (Schmidt Place and Custer Way; 360/754-5000) offers free tours daily, April through September. The educational **WOLF HAVEN** (3111 Offut Lake Rd, Tenino; 360/264-HOWL) lies 8 miles south of Tumwater. This nationally renowned research facility, home to nearly 40 wolves, teaches wolf appreciation and invites the public to join the wolves in a summertime "howl-in" (Friday and Saturday nights, May through September, by reservation only). The facility operates hourly tours year-round (closed Tuesdays).

Outdoor enthusiasts will be drawn to the **NISQUALLY NATIONAL WILDLIFE REFUGE** (100 Brown Farm Rd; 360/753-9467), 10 miles north of Olympia. This wetlands sanctuary includes a spectacular 5.7-mile bird-watching hike and opportunities for canoeing and fishing (although you'll have to bring your own canoe). Brush up on bird identification at the small nature center at the boat launch.

TACOMA AND GIG HARBOR

30 miles south of Seattle (approximately 45 minutes). Take Interstate 5 south to exit 133. Gig Harbor is about 10 miles northwest of Tacoma via State Route 16 (exit 132 off I-5).

Flanked by Commencement Bay and the Tacoma Narrows and backed by Mount Rainier, **TACOMA** is no longer just a blue-collar mill town, but a growing urban center with a thriving cultural core.

The city has fervently embraced the idea of preservation. Historic buildings in the downtown warehouse district are being converted from industrial use to residential and commercial functions, and some of the old warehouses are being converted into a University of Washington branch campus. The stately homes and cobblestone streets in the north end are often used as sets for Hollywood's moviemakers, and students still fill the turreted chateau of Stadium High School. Old City Hall, with its Renaissance clock and bell tower; the Romanesque First Presbyterian Church; the rococo Pythian Lodge; and the one-of-a-kind coppered **UNION STATION** (now the much-praised **FEDERAL COURTHOUSE**, 1717 Pacific Ave)—all delight history and architecture buffs. The old Union Station rotunda is also graced by some spectacular work by glass artist and Tacoma native Dale Chihuly and is open to the public at no charge during business hours, so do drop in for a peek. The **RUSTON WAY WATERFRONT**, a 6-mile mix of parks and restaurants, is thronged with people in any weather.

The **BROADWAY CENTER FOR THE PERFORMING ARTS** (901 Broadway Plaza; 253/591-5894) often does shows at both the Pantages and Rialto theaters. The restored 1,100-seat **PANTAGES THEATER**, originally designed in 1918 by nationally known movie-theater architect B. Marcus Priteca, is the focal point of the reviving downtown cultural life,

FEELING SHELLFISH

A geoduck (pronounced "gooey-duck") is an ungainly creature, a huge, 2-pound clam with a foot-long siphon that it can't completely retract into its shell. Doesn't matter, though; geoducks inhabit deep sands in Puget Sound tideflats, from which only the tip of the siphon protrudes. They are rarely discerned, except by habitués of beaches at low tide—and by visitors to Pike Place Market, who stare in disbelief at the bizarre appearance of the limp harvested specimens displayed on ice. Geoducks are profoundly difficult to dig from their lairs, 3 feet deep in the sand.

Luckily for anyone interested in a genuine Puget Sound experience, many shellfish species are much easier to obtain than geoducks. Native butterclams and littlenecks, and introduced species such as Manila clams, are found in shallower habitats; and mussels and oysters live on subtidal rocks. If you're willing to make a day trip of it, hike a bit, and dig a little, you're sure to come back with a bucket full.

State regulations establish seasons and harvest limits for all shellfish, and you'll need a modestly priced license, available at sporting goods and hardware outlets where fishing licenses are sold. Make sure your destination is one that's open to public digging. Beginners need a tide table (you'll need at least a modest minus tide, and the lower the better) and a good guide (the Audubon Society Pacific Coast Nature Guide is excellent). Call the state's Red Tide Hotline (800/562-5632), which lists any areas in which mollusks are contaminated by paralytic shellfish poison (PSP) or other marine biotoxins; in some years, much of Puget Sound is off-limits by late August.

Unfortunately, when the legendary Seattle songwriter/entrepreneur Ivar Haglund rejoiced in his "happy condition / Surrounded by acres of clams," it was a more bucolic time. Today, because of urban pollution, no beaches in the immediate Seattle area are advisable for clam digging. The nearest spots are Dash Point and Saltwater State Parks in Federal Way, south of Seattle; the best places are a ferry ride away. The beach at Double Bluff Park, a 3-mile-long walk-in park on Whidbey Island, is an excellent spot (see Whidbey Island in this chapter). Hood Canal is the place to go for oysters: two of the best spots are Shine Tidelands and Hood Spit, both just on the west side of the Hood Canal Bridge, requiring a ride on the Bainbridge Island or Edmonds–Kingston ferry.

What to do with your loot? Steam clams or mussels in a pot, or use them to make clam chowder or mussel stew. Real enthusiasts like to take along an oyster knife and shuck a couple of their finds right on the beach. Add a dash of lemon juice and you can have lunch on the spot. And if you somehow manage to extract a geoduck from the sand, it's excellent diced up in a stir-fry—yes, siphon and all (dip the siphon briefly into boiling water and remove the skin first). With geoducks, you need only one for a meal.

— Eric Lucas

offering dance, music, and stage presentations. And the nearby **RIALTO THEATRE** has been restored for smaller performance groups. **TACOMA ACTORS GUILD** (253/272-2145), Tacoma's popular professional theater, offers an ambitious and successful blend of American classics and Northwest premieres that draw an audience from throughout the Puget Sound region.

The **TACOMA ART MUSEUM** (12th St and Pacific Ave; 253/272-4258), housed in a former downtown bank while its new digs north of Union Station are being built, has paintings by Renoir, Degas, and Pissarro, as well as a collection of contemporary American prints. The

WASHINGTON STATE HISTORICAL MUSEUM (1911 Pacific Ave; 888/238-4373), is housed in a handsome brick building just south of Union Station. The expansive facility offers a state-of-the-art museum experience, providing history and innovation under the same roof. From the outside, however, the museum has been carefully designed to blend into its surroundings and complement Union Station, built in 1911.

POINT DEFIANCE PARK (Pearl St off SR 16; 253/305-1000), on Tacoma's west side, has 500 acres of untouched forest jutting out into Puget Sound and is one of the most dramatically sited and creatively planned city parks in the country. The wooded 5-mile drive and parallel hiking trails open up now and then for sweeping views of the water,

Vashon Island, Gig Harbor, and the Olympic Mountains beyond. There are rose, rhododendron, Japanese, and Northwest native gardens, a railroad village with a working steam engine, a reconstruction of Fort Nisqually (originally built in 1833), a museum, a swimming beach, and the much-acclaimed **POINT DEFIANCE ZOO AND AQUARIUM** (253/591-5335). Watching the almost continuous play of seals, sea lions, and the white beluga whale from an underwater vantage point is a rare treat.

WRIGHT PARK (Division Ave and South I St) is a serene in-city park with many trees, a duck-filled pond, and a beautifully maintained, fragrant conservatory, built of glass and steel in 1890. One of the area's largest estates, and the former home of the late Corydon and Eulalie Wagner, is now **LAKEWOLD GARDENS** (12317 Gravelly Lake Dr SW; 253/584-3360), located on a beautiful 10-acre site overlooking Gravelly Lake in Lakewood, just 10 minutes south of Tacoma. It is recognized nationally as one of the outstanding gardens in America.

The **TACOMA DOME** (253/272-6817), the world's largest wooden dome, is the site of many entertainment and trade shows as well as a sports center. Its dazzling neon sculpture by Stephen Antonakos provides a dramatic background for events such as Tacoma Rockets hockey games, championship ice-skating competitions, and many other regional activities. Fans who like baseball played outdoors in a first-class ballpark arrive in enthusiastic droves at **CHENEY STADIUM** to watch the Tacoma Rainiers (253/752-7707), the Triple-A affiliate of the Seattle Mariners.

Nightlife options include **ENGINE HOUSE #9** (611 N Pine St; 253/272-3435) near the University of Puget Sound, a friendly beer-lover's dream of a neighborhood tavern (minus the smoke), and the **SPAR** in Old Town (2121 N 30th St; 253/627-8215).

ALTEZZO (1320 Broadway; 253/572-3200), at the top of the Sheraton with a great view of downtown and the surrounding area, serves some of Tacoma's best Italian cuisine, and the tiramisu is the real McCoy. Over the years, the **CLIFF HOUSE** (6300 Marine View Dr; 253/927-0400) has survived on its commanding view of Commencement Bay and Tacoma's north end and on its formal, airs. Masahiro Endo's stylish downtown Japanese restaurant, **FUJIYA** (1125 Court C, between Broadway and Market; 253/627-5319), attracts a loyal clientele from near and far with the best—and most consistent—sushi and sashimi around, plus feathery-crisp tempura and delicious yosenabe (seafood stew).

Other Tacoma eateries of note include **STANLEY AND SEAFORTS STEAK, CHOP, AND FISH HOUSE** (115 E 34th St; 253/473-7300), with a panoramic view of the city, its busy harbor, and, on clear days, the Olympic Mountains; **BIMBO'S** (1516 Pacific Ave; 253/383-5800), a family Italian restaurant serving hearty pasta dishes; **CEDARS III** (7104 6th Ave; 253/564-0255), for Mediterranean cuisine not far from the Narrows Bridge; **EAST & WEST CAFE** (5319 Tacoma Mall Blvd; 253/475-7755), a charming Asian restaurant; and for seafood, the **DASH POINT LOBSTER SHOP** (6912 Soundview Dr NE; 253/927-1513), and the **LOBSTER SHOP SOUTH** (4015 Ruston Way; 253/759-2165).

Accommodations in Tacoma include a number of fine B&Bs and hotels. Among the former is **CHINABERRY HILL** (302 Tacoma Ave; 253/272-1282; chinaberry@wa.net; www.chinaberryhill.com). This 1889 mansion (on the National Register of Historic Places) in Tacoma's historic Stadium District has been beautifully restored as a charming, romantic bed and breakfast. **THE VILLA BED & BREAKFAST** (705 N 5th St; 253/572-1157; villabb@aol.com; www.villabb.com), in the heart of Tacoma's historic residential North End, also stands out from the crowd. Built for a local businessman in 1925, it was designed with the Mediterranean in mind: open and airy, with high arched windows, a tiled roof, and a palm tree out front.

The best hotel in town is the **SHERATON TACOMA HOTEL** (1320 Broadway Plaza; 253/572-3200 or 800/845-9466), adjacent to the Tacoma Convention Center. Managed by the highly regarded Kimpton Group, the hotel has recently been renovated, and most rooms look out over Commencement Bay or have a view of Mount Rainier.

Not far from Tacoma is **GIG HARBOR** (253/851-6865: Chamber of Commerce), once an undisturbed fishing village and still home port for an active commercial fleet. The town is now part suburbia, part weekend destination. Boating is still important here, with good anchorage and various moorages attracting gunwale-to-gunwale pleasure craft. When the clouds break, Mount Rainier holds court for all. A variety of interesting shops and galleries line Harborview Drive, the single street that almost encircles the harbor. It's a picturesque spot for browsing and window-shopping.

Gig Harbor was planned for boat traffic, not automobiles (so traffic is congested and parking is limited), yet it's still a good place for celebrations. An arts festival in mid-July and a jazz festival in mid-August are two main events. May through October (on Saturdays), the **GIG HARBOR FARMERS MARKET** features locally grown produce, plants, and Northwest gifts.

Nearby **KOPACHUCK STATE PARK** is a popular destination (follow signs from State Route 16), as are **PENROSE POINT** and **ROBERT F. KENNEDY STATE PARKS** on the Key Peninsula, all with numerous beaches for clam digging. At **MINTER CREEK STATE FISH HATCHERY** (12710 124th Ave; 253/857-5077), you can watch the different developmental stages of millions of salmon of various species, every day.

PERFORMANCE CIRCLE (6615 38th Ave NW; 253/851-7529), Gig Harbor's resident theater group, mounts enjoyable productions year-round, with summer shows staged outside in the meadow (9916 Peacock Hill Ave NW). Theatergoers bring picnics and blankets and watch the shows beneath the stars—it's turned into a wonderful small-town custom.

Everyone in this area loves what Mark and Mimi Wambold have done for dining in Gig Harbor. The best option is the **GREEN TURTLE** (2905 Harborview Dr; 253/851-3167), one of two restaurants the couple owns in town. This one features Pacific Rim cuisine and outdoor dining on the deck overlooking the harbor in fine weather. Locals also love the busy, crowded bustle of the Wambolds' other spot, **MARCO'S RISTORANTE ITALIANO** (7707 Pioneer Way; 253/858-2899). The menu here ranges from the traditional (spaghetti and meatballs, handmade tortellini in fresh pesto) to more original specials (a dense, tender piece of tuna sautéed in red wine).

"Meet you at the Tides" has become such a universal invitation that the **TIDES TAVERN** (2925 Harborview Dr; 253/858-3982), perched over the harbor, often has standing room only, especially on sunny days when the deck is open. And people do come, by boat, seaplane, and car. Originally a general store next to the ferry landing, the Tides doesn't pretend to be anything other than what it is—a self-service tavern (no minors) with pool table, Gig Harbor memorabilia, and live music on weekend nights.

If you want to stay in town, check into **THE PILLARS** (6606 Sound-view Dr; 253/851-6644), just uphill from the harbor. From the windows of this landmark house, you can see Colvos Passage, Vashon Island, and Mount Rainier. Added bonuses are the covered, heated swimming pool, the Jacuzzi, and the morning's tasty home-baked breads and muffins. The inn is open only from May through October.

The **MARITIME INN** (3212 Harborview Dr; 253/858-1818) is right in downtown Gig Harbor, across the street from the waterfront. Most of the 15 rooms are comfortably appointed, but avoid the rooms on the front of the inn closest to the street.

VASHON ISLAND

Take the Washington State Ferry from the Fauntleroy dock in West Seattle to Vashon Island (approximately 15 minutes).

This bucolic, arts-and-crafty isle is a perfect example of an idyllic Puget Sound community: not enough civilization to detract from the main attractions (the serene countryside, the Rainier-to-Baker views) but just enough to make it a pleasing day trip or weekend jaunt. (Vashon, 12 miles long and 6 miles wide, includes Maury Island, which is joined by a mudflat to Vashon.) It's a short ferry ride from downtown Seattle, Fauntleroy, or Tacoma. The passenger-only ferry leaves from Seattle and the car ferry from Fauntleroy, at the edge of West Seattle (schedule info: 888/843-3779). With long country roads that wend through deep forests and peaceful pastures, Vashon is a wonderful island for exploring by bicycle, although the first long hill up from the ferry dock is a killer. Rent bikes on the island at **VASHON BICYCLES**, about 4 miles from the ferry dock, accessible by bus (17232 Island Hwy; 206/463-6225).

Few Vashon beaches are open to the public, but **DOCKTON COUNTY PARK** (Stuckey Rd and SW 260th St) on Maury Island makes one nice pausing spot. The lonely beach at **POINT ROBINSON** (SW 243rd Pl and Skalberg Rd) is presided over by a Coast Guard lighthouse that dates from 1915, and is looped by a beach trail. This is a fabulous spot to watch the setting sun's alpenglow on Mount Rainier. Hikers should hit the forest trail at **BURTON ACRES PARK** (on a peninsula east of the town of Burton that extends into Quartermaster Harbor). A small branch of the park offers a beach that, because the inner harbor waters are reasonably warm, is suitable for swimming. It's also a good place to rendezvous with **VASHON ISLAND KAYAKS** (206/463-9257). The company drops off kayaks or canoes here for visitors to use on an inner harbor paddle or at other island parks; staff also lead tours around the island.

You could spend an entire day just visiting all the island-based companies that market their goods both locally and nationally. Two that offer tours (call ahead to make arrangements) are **SEATTLE'S BEST COFFEE** (19529 Vashon Hwy SW; 206/463-3932), known locally as SBC, which offers fresh organic coffees and a 75-cent cup of fresh-brewed java; and **MAURY ISLAND FARMS** (20317 Vashon Hwy SW, by Sound Food; 206/463-9659), which sells berries, preserves, and other Northwest food products. **WAX ORCHARDS** (22744 Wax Orchards Rd SW; 206/463-9735) is no longer open for tours, but stop by to pick up preserves, fruit syrups, and apple cider.

Many island products are available at the **COUNTRY STORE AND FARM** (20211 Vashon Hwy SW, south of Vashon Center; 206/463-3655), a wonderful, old-fashioned general store that also stocks potted herbs, gardening supplies, and natural-fiber apparel. Across the street is **SOUND FOOD RESTAURANT** (20312 Vashon Hwy SW; 206/463-3565), a mellow, wood-floored place with healthy soups, salads, sandwiches, and aromatic home-baked goods. Next door, **MINGLEMENT MARKET** (206/463-9672) offers an extensive selection of holistic foods and dietary supplements, as well as an excellent collection of island-made pottery.

Stop by **BLUE HERON ARTS CENTER** (19704 Vashon Hwy SW; 206/463-5131), an art gallery displaying rotating exhibits that is also home to **VASHON ALLIED ARTS** (206/463-5131), offering live arts events—from literary readings to dance to folk music to plays on weekends from September through June (and occasionally later in the summer). Kids' programs, classes, and works in progress are also found here. The **HERON'S NEST GALLERY** (Vashon Landing, Vashon Hwy and Bank Rd; 206/463-5252), in the center of town, now houses the Blue Heron's former crafts gallery, featuring the pottery, woodwork, and textiles of Vashon's many crafters.

Vashon's biggest event is the **STRAWBERRY FESTIVAL** in mid-July, when a parade, music, and crafts celebrate the island's unique lifestyle. Parade highlights are performances by the Island Thriftway Marching Grocery Cart Drill Team and the Vashon Old Tractor Society. Some farms on Vashon have U-pick strawberries and raspberries, in case you miss the big day, and foragers will be pleased to note that blackberries abound, roadside and elsewhere, in late summer: bring a bucket. The best U-pick farm is **PETE'S FAMILY FRUIT FARM** (23724 Dockton Rd; 206/463-3256) on Maury Island, which offers berries, cherries, pears, figs, vegetables, flowers, walnuts, chestnuts, filberts, and 112 varieties of apples.

Dining options on Vashon are more varied than you'd imagine, a sign of creeping civilization that even isolationist islanders don't really mind. **EMILY'S CAFE AND JUICE BAR** (Vashon Hwy SW and Bank Rd SW; 206/463-6404), a streetside cafe, offers good espresso and interesting lunch fixings that lean toward the tofu/veggie side of the spectrum. Some locals just saunter by for a tall glass of juice, squeezed to order.

For dinner, Vashon Islanders favor **EXPRESS CUISINE** (in town on Vashon Hwy; 206/463-6626), a half-block south of Emily's. Here the menu features a superbly prepared variety of pastas, curries, salads, and stews, and in-store diners share tables. Vashon's most formal dining room is in the **BACK BAY INN** (24007 Vashon Hwy SW; 206/463-5355), a renovated turn-of-the-century landmark serving Northwest cuisine. Four rooms upstairs are available should you be charmed into spending the night. More than 40 other island B&Bs range from remote farm-houses to restored Edwardians; for information, call the Central Reservation Service (206/463-5491). One of the finest B&Bs, with a fabulous country locale and a view of Seattle's city lights, is **PEABODY'S** (23007 64th Ave SW; 206/463-3506) on Maury Island.

Round out your day with a return ferry trip from Vashon's southern terminal at Tahlequah (Tahlequah Rd, on the south end of the island) which drops you off at Tacoma's Point Defiance Park. (See Tacoma and Gig Harbor in this chapter.)

Mount Rainier and Mount St. Helens

MOUNT RAINIER

100 miles southeast of Seattle (approximately 2½ hours). Take Interstate 5 south to exit 142; then take State Route 161 south through Puyallup, Graham, and Eatonville; then head east on State Route 7 to Elbe. Take State Route 706 to the park entrance; 360/569-2211.

Mount Rainier, above all other natural wonders of this region, has garnered through the years the most grandiose adjectives imaginable. Suffice it to say that for Washingtonians, this abiding symbol of natural grandeur serves as landmark, symbol, moody god, and reminder of the geological glory that surrounds them. It seems fitting that Northwesterners feel a certain possessiveness about it.

This healthy reverence for the volcano reaches back into history. Native Americans who once inhabited its subalpine meadows told of the great goddess Tahoma, who took her child and fled her husband, Koma-Kulshan (personified by Mount Baker), in a jealous rage, but stretched her neck and looked back so many times along the way that she grew enormously tall. She finally stopped where she is today, 100 miles southeast of Seattle, and planted a garden around her. Today that "garden" is the 378-square-mile **MOUNT RAINIER NATIONAL PARK** (360/569-2211), a lushly forested reserve with the 14,410-foot-high active volcano as its centerpiece. Her "child" is Little Tahoma, a strikingly pointed peak on Rainier's east side. From Seattle the view of Mount Rainier's peak is often obscured by clouds or haze (the mountain is so large it creates its own weather), so when it appears, it overwhelms the landscape and imparts to locals a renewed sense of the dominance of nature in this region. If you hear Seattleites say "The mountain's out," you'll know what they mean.

You can choose among several ways to experience the mountain: tour it by car, see it by train, hike or snowshoe its flanks, ski nearby, or climb to the summit. By far the most popular option, however, is to drive a loop around the mountain in summer. It takes the 2½ hours to reach the national park from Seattle by car (entrance fee is $10 per car). Chinook and Cayuse Passes are closed in winter, and the road to Sunrise is open only when it's snow-free (roughly between late May and October). The road from Longmire to Paradise remains open during daylight hours in winter, but it's prudent to carry tire chains and a shovel, and check current road and weather conditions on the 24-hour information line (360/569-2211).

The most popular—and populated—visitors center is the one at **PARADISE**, which, at 5,400 feet, features the most complete tourist services in the park, including the circular Jackson Memorial Visitor Center, with a 360-degree view, and countrified accommodations (late May to early October) at the recently renovated **PARADISE INN** (360/569-2275 for reservations). Paradise also features a network of easy-to-moderate hiking trails that wind past waterfalls and massive glaciers and, in summer, through wildflower-laden meadows; in winter this is a good place to cross-country ski, snowshoe, or go inner-tubing.

The **SUNRISE** visitor area, at 6,400 feet, offers another take on the peak, from the northeast side. It's the highest point in the park open to automobiles—though it's open only during summer. Pack a picnic—the food at both visitors centers is mediocre at best. Diverse naturalist talks are available to enhance your trip: everything from a 6-mile alpine ecology hike (Paradise) to a 2-mile geologic walk (Sunrise) to a half-hour slide show (Paradise). On the half-mile evening walk, you can watch lights dim on the mountain while your senses of sound and smell become more acute. In winter, there's a guided snowshoe tromp from Paradise.

The **MOUNT RAINIER SCENIC RAILROAD** (360/569-2588; steam-powered trains run on a varying seasonal schedule) is a good way to view the mountain. Or you could opt to take the **CASCADIAN DINNER TRAIN** (888/773-4637 for reservations) from Elbe for a 4-hour round-trip tour, but it never gets as close to Mount Rainier as you'd like.

Those in search of more tranquil communion with the mountain can choose from 305 miles of trails within the park. The best known is the spectacular Wonderland Trail, which makes a 95-mile circle around the mountain, passing through meadows of wildflowers, across streams, and past glaciers and alpine lakes. Backcountry permits, available at the ranger stations and visitors centers, are required for overnight camping. The park also has several campgrounds: at Ohanapecosh, White River,

Cougar Rock, Ipsut Creek, and Sunshine Point (the only one open year-round). Call 800/365-2267 for campground reservations.

In winter, you can ski Rainier and stay at the Mount Tahoma Ski Huts, run by the **MOUNT TAHOMA TRAILS ASSOCIATION** (PO Box 206, Ashford, WA 98304; 360/569-2451; www.mashell.com/~mtta/), western Washington's first hut-to-hut ski trail system. There are more than 90 miles of trails, three huts, and one yurt in a spectacular area south and west of Mount Rainier National Park. Inquire at Rainier Overland (31811 SR 706; 360/569-0851), a restaurant/bar that serves as head-quarters for the MTTA. **WHITTAKER'S BUNKHOUSE** (30205 SR 706; 360/569-2439) is also a good place to meet the guides, climbers, hikers, and skiers of the mountain. Rooms are basic and cheap (bunks avail-able—bring your own bedding) but plush compared to a camping pad.

Also nearby is **CRYSTAL MOUNTAIN** (360/663-2265), believed by many to have the best skiing in the state. See Skiing in the Recreation chapter.

Finally, you can climb the mountain. There are two ways to do this: with the concessioned guide service, **RAINIER MOUNTAINEERING** (summer: Paradise 98397, 360/569-2227; winter: 201 St. Helens Ave, Tacoma 98402; 360/627-6242), or in your own party after registering at one of the Mount Rainier National Park ranger stations (360/569-2211); a fee of $15 per person or $25 for an annual pass is charged. Unless you're qualified to do it on your own—and this is a big, difficult, and dangerous mountain on which lives are lost every year—you certainly should climb with the guide service. In a one-day training session they will teach you everything you need to know to make the climb; all you have to supply is a sound heart. The climb itself takes two days and can be done year-round, but the period from late May to mid-September is the best climbing season.

One slightly less wild way to see the area is at **NORTHWEST TREK WILDLIFE PARK** (11610 Trek Dr E, Eatonville; 360/832-6116), 55 miles south of Seattle off State Route 161, a remarkable natural habitat 60 miles from the east entrance to the mountain. Bison, bighorn sheep, caribou, moose, elk, and deer roam "free" in pastures, peat bogs, ponds, and forests, while human visitors view (and photograph) them from trams. Naturalists narrate the hourlong 5½-mile trip, which is exciting for both kids and adults. General admission $8.25, reduced rates for chil-dren and seniors, kids under 3 free.

Inside Mount Rainier National Park, in the little village of Longmire, is the simple **NATIONAL PARK INN** (360/569-2275), as well as a small wildlife museum with plant and animal displays, a hiking information center, and a cross-country skiing rental outlet. The closest accommoda-tions to the mountain are near Ashford, just outside the southwestern entrance to the park. **WELLSPRING** (54922 Kernahan Rd, Ashford; 360/569-2514) offers two spas nestled in a sylvan glade surrounded by evergreens. If you don't want to leave after your massage or sauna (or one luxurious hour in a hot tub for $10 a head), ask about the log cabins or other rooms. **ALEXANDER'S COUNTRY INN** (37515 SR 706, Ashford; 360/569-2300 or 800/654-7615) is a quaint country inn (circa 1912) just east of Ashford. Rooms are bed-and-breakfast style, and the place has 1990s comforts combined with a turn-of-the-century feel. Make reservations in the dining room for a fine meal that includes pan-fried trout— caught out back in the holding pond. Six large guest rooms are available at **MOUNTAIN MEADOWS INN B&B AT MOUNT RAINIER** (28912 SR 706 E, Ashford; 360/569-2788). Reasonably priced and clean, the hotel-like 24-room **NISQUALLY LODGE** (31609 SR 706 E, Ashford; 360/569-8804) offers welcome respite to those willing to trade some charm for a phone, TV, and air conditioning.

MOUNT ST. HELENS

Approximately 150 miles south of Seattle (2 to 3 hours). Take Interstate 5 south to exit 49, then follow signs to the mountain via State Route 504.

Temperamental Mount St. Helens simmers about three hours south of Seattle off I-5. On a clear day it's well worth the trip to see the 8,365-foot remains as well as the mountain's regrowth since the incredible eruption of May 18, 1980 (it's 1,300 feet shorter than before the blast).

Before you begin the ascent to the ridge, you can stop in to see the Academy Award–nominated film *The Eruption of Mount St. Helens* projected onto the three-story-high, 55-foot-wide screen at the **CINEDOME** (360/274-8000). The rumble alone, which rattles your theater seat, is worth the price of admission (shows every 45 minutes). It's just off I-5 at the Castle Rock exit (exit 49, where State Route 504 begins).

There are now five places to stop along State Route 504 (also called the Spirit Lake Memorial Highway), and they all complement each other. The first is the U.S. Forest Service's **MOUNT ST. HELENS VISITORS CENTER** (360/274-2100), just 5 miles east of I-5 at Castle Rock. Built shortly after the eruption, it commemorates the blast with excellent exhibits, a walk-through volcano, hundreds of historical and modern photos, geological and anthropological surveys, and a film documenting the mountain's destruction and rebirth. It's a good place to get a broad perspective on volcanoes.

The second is the **HOFFSTADT BLUFF REST AREA AND VIEWPOINT** (milepost 27 on the Spirit Lake Memorial Hwy; 360/274-7750), run by Cowlitz County. Exhibits here explore the lives and deaths of those most directly affected by the blast. There's a restaurant and a gift store, and helicopter tours are available.

The third, operated by Weyerhauser at North Fork Ridge, is the **FOREST LEARNING CENTER** at Mount St. Helens (milepost 33.5; 360/414-3439), which focuses on how the tree farms were affected and the wood was salvaged in the wake of the eruption. The fourth, 43 miles east of I-5, is **COLDWATER RIDGE** (360/274-2131). It's a multimillion-dollar facility with a million-dollar view—of the black dome that rests in the 2-mile-wide steaming crater and of Coldwater and Castle Lakes, both formed by massive mudslides. This second U.S. Forest Service center focuses on the astounding biological recovery of the landscape.

The fifth stop up State Route 504, and the third facility run by the Forest Service, is the **JOHNSTON RIDGE OBSERVATORY** (milepost 52; 360/274-2140), which offers a bird's-eye view directly into the crater itself. The focus here (9 miles closer to the mountain than Coldwater) is on the eruption itself, how geologists monitor volcanoes, and what we have learned about volcanoes since the eruption.

The U.S. government requires an $8-per-person fee to visit any of the three Forest Service visitors centers in the region (the fee covers all three; children younger than 16 are free). Numerous other viewpoints line roads approaching the mountain (via Cougar from the south, or Randle from the north), but all the visitors centers are on State Route 504. Those who enter from Randle on Forest Road 99 will get a dramatic view of the blowdown destruction.

If you are interested in climbing the mountain, plan on about four hours up and two hours down. Be aware, however, that the registration procedure often adds an extra day. You need to get a permit ($15 per person) well ahead of time (call the monument headquarters at 360/247-3900 for the procedure), and you must then register at **JACK'S STORE AND RESTAURANT** (360/231-4276; 23 miles east of Woodland and just west of Cougar). Best times to climb are May and June (when there's still enough snow to tame the ash). Bring a good pair of hiking boots, drinking water, sunscreen, sunglasses, and an ice axe.

If you find yourself wanting to extend your mountain adventures, you can stay the night at the **SEASONS MOTEL** (200 Westlake Ave, Morton; 360/496-6835) located about halfway between Mount St. Helens and Mount Rainier. This moderately priced establishment has 50 rooms as well as a restaurant on the property. Heading east toward Mount Adams, you'll find an outdoor enthusiast's idea of heaven at the Flying L Ranch (25 Flying L Lane, Glenwood; 509/364-3488). This 160-acre guest ranch is popular for hiking, biking, fishing, and winter cross-country skiing and snowshoeing. A hearty breakfast is served in the cookhouse. The main lodge has a large common kitchen where guests can prepare their own lunches and dinners. If camping is the way you want to go, head east from Mount St. Helens National Monument and choose from more than 50 campgrounds in the **GIFFORD PINCHOT NATIONAL FOREST** (360/891-5000). The fishing is excellent in the lakes and rivers of this 1.3-million-acre wilderness. This is the most remote of the national forests and is traversed only by Highway 12. Call ahead for road and campground conditions.

Snoqualmie Valley

Approximately 30 miles east of Seattle (40 minutes). Take Interstate 90 east to exit 27 (Snoqualmie–Fall City).

The Snoqualmie Valley, a relatively bucolic stretch of cow country nestled just west of the Cascades, makes for a great Sunday drive or bike ride. No longer dotted with the sleepy farm hamlets of yesterday—thanks to the eastward ooze of Seattle suburbs—this rural valley holds a haystack full of charm nonetheless, complete with U-pick berry farms, roadside stands, and country cafes.

State Route 203 links Duvall, Carnation, and Fall City, then State Route 202 takes over through Snoqualmie and North Bend—both crisscrossed by a web of back roads leading the curious driver to dairy farms, quiet lakes, river beaches, and tree-lined drives. Cyclists should stick to the back roads to avoid weekend traffic. Better yet, mountain bikers, hikers, and horseback riders can hook up with the Snoqualmie Valley Trail, an old railroad right-of-way connecting Stillwater (between Duvall and Carnation) and Tokul (south of Fall City), then continuing north all the way to the Snohomish County border, and south to Snoqualmie.

Despite commercial growth, **DUVALL** has managed to preserve its small-town storefronts, including that of **DUVALL BOOKS** (15635 Main St NE), with a remarkable range of used books and a fascinating display of old photos and other collectibles. Be sure to visit the delightful **MAIN STREET GALLERY** (15611 Main St NE; 425/788-9844), an indoor sanctuary of plants, chimes, fountains, sundials, and other garden goodies. The **DUVALL CAFE** (15505 Main St NE; 425/788-9058) is an excellent spot to stop if hunger strikes as you explore, offering whopping-big breakfasts, fresh sandwiches for lunch, and surprisingly upscale dinners. Don't pass up dessert, especially if there's pie.

CARNATION is the home of a near-legendary eatery, the **RIVER RUN CAFE** (4366 Tolt Ave; 206/333-6100), where partaking of a giant cinnamon roll is practically mandatory and the small dining room is perpetually packed, rain or shine. **REMLINGER FARMS** (32610 NE 32nd St; 425/333-4135 or 425/451-8740) has one of the biggest and best produce markets around these parts. They sell their own farm-grown fruits and vegetables (U-pick or otherwise), plus baked goods, grains, gift items, and canned and frozen foods. The restaurant in back serves breakfast and lunch, as well as ice cream, pies, cookies, and candy. It's an especially fun place for kids in summer, with puppet shows, pony rides, and a petting zoo; autumn and winter bring the pumpkin patch and special holiday events. The farm takes a hiatus from January through March.

TOLT RIVER-JOHN MACDONALD PARK (31020 NE 40th St; 425/296-2964), at the confluence of the Tolt and Snoqualmie Rivers, is a fine place for a barbecue in one of the reservable picnic shelters. Throw a Frisbee on the rolling grass, ride an inner tube where the Tolt empties into the Snoqualmie, camp overnight, or watch brave teenagers take the plunge from the Tolt Hill Road Bridge.

Mountain bikers won't want to pass up a ride on the 7.4-mile trail that starts here and meanders over the Snoqualmie River into the Tolt River Campground and through a portion of the Snoqualmie Valley, with eye-popping views of the Cascades and Mount Si along the way. The perfect end to a day of biking—or inner-tubing, fishing, or canoeing—on the Snoqualmie is **SMALL FRYES** (4225 Preston–Fall City Rd; 425/222-7688), a great burger stand with specially seasoned french fries and a large range of milk shakes (try the banana or a mocha malt).

THE HERBFARM (32804 Issaquah–Fall City Rd; 425/222-7103 or 206/784-2222) in **FALL CITY** is a destination in its own right—an herbal oasis for gardeners (see Gardens in the Exploring chapter) and paradise to urban denizens seeking the kind of relaxation that only browsing among lush greenery can bring. The Herbfarm also offers year-round tours, classes, and workshops, and hosts a number of festivals and special events throughout the year, including beer and wine festivals in the spring and summer.

Then it's on to the town of **SNOQUALMIE**, where **SNOQUALMIE FALLS**, the region's 268-foot-high natural wonder, thunders past diners at the **SALISH LODGE** (6501 Railroad Ave SE; 425/888-2556 or 800/826-6124). Visitors can observe the falls from a cliffside gazebo, where the spray mists those standing close to the railing, or hike to the bottom for a closer look.

Railroad artifacts and old engines are on display at the Snoqualmie Depot, where, on weekends from April through October, you can board the **PUGET SOUND RAILWAY** (38625 SE King St; 425/746-4025 for fares and schedules) for a scenic round-trip train tour through the upper Snoqualmie Valley.

Across Snoqualmie's main drag, **ISADORA'S** (8062 Railroad Ave SE; 425/888-1345) is a funky country collectibles shop with a little bit of everything, merchandise-wise, and a cozy cafe. Nearby **NORTHWEST CELLARS** (8050 Railroad Ave SE; 425/888-6176) presents tastings of the Northwest's best wines and microbrews, and packages splendid gift baskets of the region's finest specialty foodstuffs, while **BIG FOOT DONUT**

SHOP AND BAKERY (8224 Railroad Ave SE; 425/831-2244) is where Sasquatch stops to assuage his beastly sweet tooth—and get a cuppa joe at 5am, if need be.

Factory-outlet malls are springing up all over the suburban Northwest, including in North Bend, where **FACTORY STORES OF AMERICA** (exit 31 off I-90; 425/888-4505) offer discounts on items from clothing and books to kitchenware and sporting goods.

North Puget Sound

SKAGIT VALLEY

60 miles north of Seattle (approximately 1 hour). Take Interstate 5 north, then take exits 221, 226 or 230 to La Conner.

For most of the year, to travelers on Interstate 5, the Skagit Valley is little more than a blur. During spring, however, the lush farmlands are brilliantly swathed in daffodils (mid-March to mid-April) and tulips (early to late April). Those who slow down and turn off the concrete artery discover that the pastoral Skagit Valley is a colorful excursion even after the tulips have been cut. The valley is a leading U.S. production center for peas, cabbage, and cauliflower, as well as seeds. For visitors, the fertile countryside is flat and ideal for bicyclists. Vehicle gridlock occurs during the **TULIP FESTIVAL** (360/42-TULIP) in April, diminishing the pastoral atmosphere but making bikes an even better way to get around; there's ample parking at several I-5 exit ramps. Another highly rational way to view the tulips is to take a boat/bus tour with the folks at Victoria Clipper (206/448-5000, 250/382-8100, or 800/888-2535; www.victoria.clipper. com). Tours leave the Seattle waterfront every morning during the festival, the boat docks in La Conner, and buses take visitors out through the countryside.

The rest of the summer and fall, U-pickers swarm the local farms, starting with strawberries in June, continuing through the summer with raspberries, blueberries, and sweet corn, and ending with pumpkins come October. Local produce stands offer a wealth of vegetables, fruits, and honey.

MOUNT VERNON, right off I-5 to the west, is a working town: it's really about fresh food and beautiful flowers, products of surrounding Skagit Valley farms. Here's a rural town in which good restaurants and bookstores outnumber taverns and video stores. The "Big City" to residents of Skagit and Island Counties, Mount Vernon is a college town for local folk, even though **SKAGIT VALLEY COLLEGE** is only a small community college on the eastern outskirts of town. The **BURLINGTON OUTLET MALLS** along I-5 between Mount Vernon and Burlington chewed up good farmland but boost the local retail economy with stores ranging from Liz Claiborne to Corning Revere to the Gap to Tommy Hilfiger.

LITTLE MOUNTAIN PARK (take Blackburn Road east out of Mount Vernon; it's on top of the hill) has a terrific picnic spot plus a knockout vista of the valley—look for migrating trumpeter swans in February. In winter, Skagit Bay is home to thousands of snow geese; when they fly, they look like a cloud taking wing. The entire Skagit Delta is an important stop on the Pacific Flyway, with dozens of migratory species dropping in at various times of the year. Best viewing is at the **PADILLA BAY NATIONAL ESTUARINE RESEARCH RESERVE** (360/428-1558), 10 miles west of Burlington.

Just off I-5, en route northwest to La Conner, you'll pass through tiny Conway, where locals congregate at the classic **CONWAY TAVERN** (360/445-4733) for charbroiled burgers and super onion rings. Head west about 5 miles to Fir Island and you'll come across **SNOW GOOSE PRODUCE**, an enormous roadside stand (open late February to mid-October) that is almost worth a day trip in itself. Stop for a fresh waffle cone filled with locally made ice cream, a pound or two of just-caught Hood Canal shrimp, an array of local produce, and specialty foods including cheeses, pastas, and fresh rustic breads.

LA CONNER was founded in 1867 by John Conner, a trading-post operator, who named the town after his wife, L(ouisa) A. Conner. Much of what you see today was originally built before the railroads arrived in the late 1880s, when the fishing and farming communities of Puget Sound traded almost entirely by water. During a later age of conformity and efficiency, the town became a literal backwater and something of a haven for nonconformists (Wobblies, World War II COs, McCarthy-era escapees, beatniks, hippies, and bikers), always with a fair smattering of artists, including Mark Tobey, Morris Graves, and Guy Anderson.

The town's long-standing "live-and-let-live" attitude has allowed the neighboring Swinomish tribe to contribute to the exceptional cultural richness of La Conner. Even the merchants here have created a unique atmosphere along First Street, an American bazaar with **SHOPS** such as Chez la Zoom, Cottons, Nasty Jack's Antiques, Ginger Grater, and Intimate Dwellings. Cafe Pojante is the place to go for coffee and a pastry, and O'Leary's Books is where locals stop for a read or a chat with owner Sally Cram. Hungry? Try Hungry Moon Deli for soup and a sandwich.

TILLINGHAST SEED COMPANY (623 Morris St; 360/466-3329), at the southern entrance to town, is the oldest operating retail and mail-order seed store in the Northwest (since 1885); in addition to seeds bred specifically for the Northwest growing season, it has a wonderful nursery, florist shop, and general store. **GO OUTSIDE** (111 Morris St; 360/466-4836) is a small but choice garden and garden-accessories store.

WINERY TOURS

Until fairly recently, Washington vintners traveling abroad or to the East Coast were used to being asked which side of the Potomac was better for growing their grapes. Now Washington State is regularly included in any survey of the world's best wine-producing regions. With 90-some wineries, Washington is second only to California in U.S. wine production.

Although the first European grapes were planted here in the late 1800s, fledgling winemaking efforts were hurt by icy winters and limited demand, and Washington vintners resigned themselves to producing safe, sweet dessert wines from winter-hardy vines instead. It wasn't until the late 1960s that the potential of Washington's soil and climate was fully appreciated and the first real premium wines were made. Washington's initial fame came from its full-flavored whites; only in recent years have reds equaled and surpassed the whites in reputation. Though most of the grapes are grown in the sun-soaked Yakima River and Columbia River Valleys east of the Cascades, the Seattle-area oenophile can find plenty of tastings close to home.

Most of the wineries in the greater Seattle area are located on the Eastside.

Chateau Ste. Michelle (14111 NE 145th St, off Hwy 202, 2 miles outside Woodinville; 425/488-3300; map:CC2) is the state's largest, occupying showplace headquarters on the 87-acre former estate of industrialist Henry Stimson. This is a popular destination for locals and visitors alike, since the winery offers the region's most comprehensive tour and, in summer, a lively outdoor concert series. The beautifully manicured grounds provide lovely picnicking opportunities (you can buy picnic food to go with your wine in the gourmet shop on the premises). The single-vineyard wines are the winery's most exciting, but winemaker Mike Januik also produces consistently well made whites and reds with the Columbia Valley appellation.

You'll get a different perspective across the street at **Columbia Winery** (14030 NE 145th St, Woodinville; 425/488-2776; map:BB2). Originally located in Bellevue, this is one of the region's pioneer wineries. Its varied picnic facilities, where you can sprawl out after a wine-tasting, are open daily and offer a pretty view of Ste. Michelle's grounds. To reach both wineries, take the NE 124th Street exit off I-405, proceed east across the valley, then turn left at Redmond-Woodinville Road and left again on NE 145th Street.

Now part of Columbia Winery, **Paul Thomas Winery** (17661 128th Pl NE, Woodinville; 425/489-9307; map:CC2) is widely recognized for both its classic vinifera wines (particularly chardonnay and merlot) and its good prices. Tastings are offered Friday through Sunday.

Smaller wineries provide an interesting counterpoint to the giants. To taste the wines made by Chateau Ste. Michelle alum Cheryl Barber Jones, stop by **Silver Lake**

GACHES MANSION (703 S 2nd St; 360/466-4288), overlooking the main drag, is a wonderful example of American Victorian architecture, with a widow's walk that looks out on the entire Skagit Valley. Open Wednesday through Sunday, it's filled with period furnishings and houses the only quilt museum in the Northwest.

WHIDBEY ISLAND

Take Interstate 5 north for about 25 miles, then take State Route 526 east for about 5 miles to Mukilteo. Take the Washington State Ferry from Mukilteo to Clinton (approximately 20 minutes).

Seekers of an island idyll needn't travel all the way to the San Juans when access to Whidbey Island is so close. The island boasts pretty villages, viewpoint parks, sandy beaches, and lovely rolling farmland. It makes for a nice family outing that combines browsing, sightseeing, and outdoor activities such as beachcombing and clam-digging. Whidbey's flat, relatively untrafficked roads make this long island great for biking.

The ferry docks at the town of CLINTON, at the south end of Whidbey Island. Ten minutes north is LANGLEY, where the main drag, First Street, is a browser's paradise of classy SHOPS AND GALLERIES and home to the CLYDE THEATER (360/221-5525), which hosts periodic local theater productions in addition to regularly scheduled films. Swap stories with John Hauser of Moonraker Books (360/221-6962). For singular shopping, try The Cottage (360/221-4747) for heirloom lace and

---

Sparkling Wine Cellars (17721 132nd Ave NE, Woodinville; 425/486-1900; map:CC2). There's not much to see here, but you can taste daily, noon–5pm. **Facelli Winery** (16120 Woodinville-Redmond Rd NE, Suite 1, Woodinville; 425/488-1020; map:BB2), inconspicuously tucked into an industrial office park, is worth a visit if only to meet one of the area's most exuberant (and entertaining) winemakers, Lou Facelli. Open Saturdays and Sundays, noon–4pm.

Other worthwhile winery stops in the region are **Snoqualmie Winery** (1000 Winery Rd, Snoqualmie; 425/888-4000), **Bainbridge Island Winery** (Hwy 305, Bainbridge Island; 206/842-WINE), **Hedges Cellars** (1105 12th Ave NW, Suite A4, Issaquah; 425/391-6056), and **Quilceda Creek Vintners** (5226 Machias Rd, Snohomish; 206/568-2389). This last winery produces one of the best reds in the state, a fine cabernet sauvignon (it's the only wine the winery has made since 1979). Quilceda Creek is a small operation and will show you around by appointment only. Tiny **Andrew Will** (12526 SW Bank Rd, Vashon Island; 206/463-3290), another notable winery, is open by appointment and has quickly gained a reputation among wine cognoscenti for its luscious merlot and cabernet sauvignon.

linens; Virginia's Antiques (360/221-7797), a repository of Asian and American wares; Whidbey Island Antiques (360/221-2393), a two-in-one shop with both restored and unrestored pieces; and Boomerang Books (360/221-5404), with selections in all genres. JB's Ice Creamery and Espresso (360/221-3888) is the place for java and ice cream. Annie Steffen's (360/221-6535) offers fine women's clothing and accessories. The Star Store (360/221-5222) is a genuine mercantile outpost where you'll find a grocery and deli, clothing, gifts, and kitchen gadgets galore. Upstairs, the **STAR BISTRO** (360/221-2627) is a Deco oasis with an outdoor deck, a snappy menu, and excellent margaritas.

A number of fine galleries line Langley's main street, including the **ARTIST'S COOPERATIVE OF WHIDBEY ISLAND** (360/221-7675), where 30 island artists and craftspeople sell their wares. **MUSEO PICCOLO GALLERY** (360/221-7737) offers work by local and regional glass artists as well as rotating exhibits from artists worldwide, while **HELLEBORE** (360/221-2067) features glass art in the making (stop to see glassblowers in action). Be sure to drive a mile south of town to **BLACKFISH STUDIO** (5075 Langley Rd; 360/221-1274)—just look for the huge mural of beluga whales—to see Kathleen Miller's hand-painted silk and wool clothing and enamel jewelry and husband Donald Miller's art photography.

If you're looking to spend the night in the heart of downtown Langley, where better than at Linda Lundgren's tucked-away retreat, the **GARDEN PATH INN** (360/221-5121), with two suites handsomely furnished with interior designs that are also on display at her adjoining First Street shop, Islandesign. **CAFE LANGLEY** (360/221-3090), with its Middle Eastern bent, is a busy, garlicky eatery. Join native islanders for a microbrew, along with a burger and fries, at the charmingly dumpy **DOG HOUSE BACKDOOR RESTAURANT AND TAVERN** (360/221-9996). Or take a picnic to **DOUBLE BLUFF BEACH** southwest of Langley—just the place to fly a kite, spot a bald eagle, watch a Puget Sound sunset, or stroll the length of an unspoiled sandy beach. When the tides are right, this is also one of the best clam-digging beaches on Puget Sound.

Numerous excellent B&Bs abound, such as **HOME BY THE SEA** (2388 E Sunlight Beach Rd; 360/321-2964). At **LONE LAKE COTTAGE** (5206 S Bayview Rd; 360/321-5325), you can spend the night on a (moored) stern-wheeler houseboat. Or you can try for a room at the idyllic **INN AT LANGLEY** (400 1st St; 360/221-3033), which marries a bit of Northwest ruggedness with Pacific Rim tranquility.

A mile south of town is **WHIDBEY ISLAND WINERY** (5237 S Langley Rd; 360/221-2040), which specializes in rhubarb wine and small bottlings from estate-grown grapes.

About halfway up the island, on the narrowest portion, stop by **WHIDBEYS GREENBANK FARM** (360/678-7700), known near and far for its loganberry products. After a short self-guided tour, sample the loganberry jams and jellies. Although Greenbank no longer makes the famous Whidbey's loganberry liqueur (manufacture was taken over by Chateau Ste. Michelle, and the farm is now operated by a local nonprofit organization), it has plenty on hand for you to sample or buy. Enterprising families can pick their own berries to take home—there's nothing better than a fresh loganberry pie. The farm offers lots of pretty picnicking spots. And don't miss the two-day Loganberry Festival in July, featuring food and craft booths, entertainment, and a pie-eating contest—of course.

COUPEVILLE, the second-oldest incorporated town in the state, dates back to 1852, when farming commenced on the fertile isle. A fort was built in 1855 after some Indian scares, and part of it, the **ALEXANDER BLOCKHOUSE** on Front Street, is open for touring. Amid the growing pressures of development, the town has set itself a strict agenda of historic preservation.

Coupeville's downtown consists of a half-dozen souvenir and antique shops and several restaurants. A must-see gallery is the **JAN MCGREGOR STUDIO** (360/678-5015), open on weekends throughout the year and every day in summer. McGregor has studied pottery around the world and specializes in rare porcelain techniques. **TOBY'S 1890 TAVERN** (360/678-4222) is a good spot for burgers, beer, and a game of pool. Homemade breads, pies, soups, and salads make a memorable meal at **KNEAD & FEED** (360/678-5431), and you can get a fine cup of coffee at **GREAT TIMES ESPRESSO** (360/678-5358). The **ISLAND COUNTY HISTORICAL MUSEUM** (360/678-3310) tells the story of Whidbey Island's early years. Annual community events include the Coupeville Arts & Crafts Festival the second weekend in August and the Penn Cove Water Festival (360/678-5434) in May. **ALL ISLAND BICYCLES** (302 N Main St; 360/678-3351) sells, rents, and repairs bikes and equipment. An extra bike lane follows Engle Road 3 miles south of Coupeville to **FORT** **CASEY**, a decommissioned fort with splendid gun mounts, beaches, and commanding bluffs. The magnificent bluff and beach at the 17,000-acre **EBEY'S LANDING** and **FORT EBEY STATE PARK** are good places to explore. The Washington State Ferry (206/464-6400 or 800/542-7052; www.wsdot.wa.gov/ferries), connecting Whidbey to Port Townsend, leaves from Admiralty Head in the town of Keystone, just south of Fort Ebey.

OAK HARBOR, Whidbey's largest city, is dominated by Whidbey Island Naval Air Station, a big air base for tactical electronic warfare squadrons. For the most part, Oak Harbor is engulfed in new military and retired military folk. An interesting stop is **LAVENDER HEART** (4233 N DeGraff Rd; 360/675-3987), which manufactures floral gifts on a 122-acre former holly farm. From the Hendersons' gift store, you can peek at the impressive 1,000-square-foot production facility. Kids at heart should visit **BLUE FOX DRI-VIN THEATRE AND BRATTLAND GO-KARTS** (1403 Monroe Landing Rd; 360/675-5667). Stop for good Mexican food at **LUCY'S MI CASITA** (1380 W Pioneer Way; 360/675-4800), then head upstairs to the lounge for a 27-ounce Turbo Godzilla margarita.

DECEPTION PASS marks the north end of the island, and is crossed by a bridge that links Whidbey to Fidalgo Island and the mainland. The beautiful, treacherous gorge has a lovely, if usually crowded, state park (Washington's most popular) with 2,300 acres of prime camping land, forests, and beach. But stay out of the water—the currents are highly hazardous.

British Columbia

VANCOUVER, BC

145 miles north of Seattle (approximately 3 hours). Take Interstate 5 to the U.S.–Canada border, then continue north on Highway 99.

It's a wonder Vancouver isn't overrun by visitors from Seattle and Portland. Not only is it beautiful and one of the world's great destination cities, but prevailing costs and the U.S.–Canadian exchange rate make almost everything in Vancouver essentially half-price. A full-scale deluxe dinner followed by a night at the symphony or the theater will run two people just $150 (U.S.) or so, and if you're inclined to stay overnight, a luxury hotel room can be had for not much more than $100 (U.S.) a night in the off season. (Summer travelers beware: everything is booked months in advance.) Furthermore, it's close. A commuter plane flight gets you there in 25 minutes. By bus or Amtrak, it's four hours; by car, three. (The much publicized lineups crossing the border almost invariably occur coming back into the States.)

As much as Seattle seems "European" in comparison to smaller inland American cities, Vancouver is even more so. The city proudly advertises that its West End, along Denman Street, is the most densely populated urban district in North America. What that means is a vibrant, always-bustling neighborhood of apartments and condominiums, and the myriad shops, cafes, and restaurants that serve them. It's a theme repeated throughout Vancouver. Here's a city truly made for walking (the various views are terrific) and the distinctive commerce that accompanies it.

Individually owned and operated retail and eating establishments still vastly outnumber chain stores, and the huge diversity of Vancouver's population colors the city's rainbow of offerings. On any block, you're liable to find a Northwest-style coffeehouse, an Asian lunch counter, an antique store, a European deli, a newsstand, a bakery, a small clothing store, and a restaurant serving "West Coast cuisine," Vancouver's unique amalgamation of Northwest, Asian, and continental cooking.

Denman Street is probably still the best place for visitors to experience this variety; it's also close to **STANLEY PARK,** one of the biggest and best urban parks anywhere. A walk, bicycle, or jog around the Stanley Park seawall is one of the quintessential Vancouver experiences. Follow that with a late lunch—try **BOJANGLES** (785 Denman St; 604/687-3622) for great soups, salads, and sandwiches—and an afternoon of strolling the shops along Denman and Robson. Long famed as Vancouver's **SHOPPING** street, Robson has recently suffered an attack of chain-store excess. Interesting spots survive, though, amid the brand-name uniformity; check out Lush (1118 Denman St; 604/730-0332), an aromatic soap, lotion, and cosmetics emporium; Duthie's (919 Robson St; 604/684-4496) is a large but nonetheless locally owned bookstore, one of the best for Northwest titles. Across the street, Murchie's (970 Robson St; 604/669-0783) is one of the world's best tea stores. Here you can buy tea that sells for $25C per ounce. Is it worth it? Only trial will tell. Next door, at La Casa del Habano (929 Robson St; 604/609-0511), fanciers of Cuban cigars can decide whether $35 to $50C is worth it for the tobaccos U.S. citizens are unable to obtain.

In Gastown, another famed shopping/dining district just five minutes' walk from Robson, **DOROTHY GRANT** (757 W Hastings St, Suite 250; 604/681-0201) turns First Nations patterns into exquisite (and pricey) clothing. A few blocks away, Vancouverites enjoy a marvel in **SIKORA** (432 W Hastings St; 604/685-0625), a store devoted entirely to classical music, with thousands of CDs and an expert staff. The **INUIT GALLERY** (345 Water St; 604/688-7323) offers the best First Nations artwork; it's pricey, too.

The **MUSEUM OF ANTHROPOLOGY** (at the University of British Columbia, 6393 NW Marine Dr; 604/822-3825) is a stunning glass-and-concrete building overlooking the Strait of Georgia and filled with totem poles, one of the most comprehensive collections of Northwest Coast Native artifacts in the world, and objects from other cultures for comparison.

Distinctive Vancouver dining can be found at dozens of downtown spots. Some of the best are **C SEAFOOD** (1600 Howe St; 604/253-4316), with a unique pan-Asian take on Northwest fish and shellfish; **DIVA** (in the Metropolitan Hotel, 645 Howe St; 604/602-7788), a famed, glitzy shrine of West Coast cuisine; and **BACCHUS** (845 Hornby St; 604/608-5319), a modern Italian restaurant, two blocks away at the Wedgewood Hotel. Budget-minded travelers will find all they can eat at **STEPHO'S GREEK TAVERNA** (1124 Davie St; 604/683-2555).

For more information on Vancouver, call **TOURISM VANCOUVER** (604/683-2000), or visit their huge information center in the Waterfront Centre (200 Burrard St), across from Canada Place. Also, check out our companion guide, *Vancouver Best Places*.

VICTORIA, BC

Take the Princess Marguerite car ferry from Pier 48 in downtown Seattle to Victoria (4½ hours), or the passenger-only Victoria Clipper *from Pier 69 (2 hours).*

Romantic as Victoria may be, with its delightful natural harbor and panoramic views of Washington State's Olympic Mountains, the provincial capital of British Columbia is less a museum piece now than it is a tourist mecca. Visitors pour in to gawk at huge sculptured gardens and London-style double-decker buses, to shop for Irish linens and Harris tweeds, to sip afternoon tea and soak up what they believe to be the last light of British imperialism to set on the Western Hemisphere. Raves in the travel press have brought a new crop of younger residents to upset Victoria's reputation as a peaceful but dull sanctuary for retiring civil servants from eastern Canada. As a result, restaurants are improving in quality and variety, and Victoria's streets are no longer silent after 10pm.

A ferry ride can be half the fun of a trip to Victoria. Fares run from as little as $8 to as much as $120 depending on the carrier, the season, your embarkation point, and whether you walk or drive aboard (you won't need a car if Victoria is your only destination). Call ahead for current rates. The **VICTORIA CLIPPER** (206/448-5000 in Seattle, 250/382-8100 in Victoria, or 800/888-2535 outside Seattle and BC; www.victoriaclipper.com), a waterjet-propelled catamaran, carries foot passengers between Seattle and Victoria, and leaves Seattle four times daily from mid-May to mid-September ($109 round-trip in summer), and once or twice a day the rest of the year. The best window seats for the 2½-hour voyage are on the upper deck and fill quickly, so board early. The **PRINCESS MARGUERITE III**—Clipper Navigation's cushy full-size ferry (206/448-5000 in Seattle, 250/382-8100 in Victoria, or 800/888-2535, outside Seattle and BC)—offers the only car-ferry service (mid-May to mid-September) between Seattle and Victoria, leaving Seattle at 1pm daily for the 4½-hour trip to Victoria, and departing from Victoria at 7:30am, arriving in Seattle at noon. Cost is about $150 round-trip for two people.

The fastest link from Seattle to Victoria is by air. Flights leave Lake Union and land in Victoria's Inner Harbour several times daily for about $142 round-trip on **KENMORE AIR** (206/486-1257 or 800/543-9595). You can also fly from Seattle's Boeing Field on **HELIJET AIRWAYS** (800/665-4354), or from SeaTac, through Port Angeles, on **HORIZON AIR** (800/547-9308).

In Victoria, your first stop should be **TOURISM VICTORIA** (812 Wharf St; 250/953-2033), a well-staffed office dispensing useful information on the sights. Then hop aboard one of Talley Ho's (250/383-5067) horse-drawn carriages for a lesson in city history. Two Belgian draft horses clop along to the cadence of the driver's hourlong narrated tour (complete with humorous historical anecdotes) starting at the Parliament Building, at Belleville and Menzies, and winding through Beacon Hill Park to the waterfront, then through the residential community of James Bay.

The **ROYAL BRITISH COLUMBIA MUSEUM** (Belleville and Government Sts; 604/387-3701) is one of the finest of its kind in Canada, offering dramatic dioramas of natural landscapes and full-scale reconstructions of Victorian storefronts. Of particular interest is the Northwest Coast Indian exhibit, rich with spiritual and cultural artifacts. The museum is open every day, as is the **ART GALLERY OF GREATER VICTORIA** (1040 Moss St; 604/384-4101), which houses one of the world's finest collections of Asian art (including the only Shinto shrine in North America), with special historical and contemporary exhibits on display throughout the year. **MACPHERSON PLAYHOUSE** (3 Centennial Square; 604/386-6121), a former Pantages vaudeville house done up with baroque trappings, offers evening entertainment throughout the summer. For a listing of local happenings, the free *Monday Magazine* offers the city's best weekly calendar of events.

An extraordinary city park spreading out over 177 acres, **BEACON HILL PARK**, just south of downtown, provides splendid views of the water, but the real interest here is in the landscaping (much of it left wild). Everyone will enjoy **BEACON HILL CHILDREN'S FARM**, where a modest donation is a small price to pay to visit this kid-friendly minizoo and its turtle house, aviary, duck pond, chicken yard, and petting corral (closed in winter). **CRYSTAL GARDEN** (713 Douglas St; 604/381-1213) is a turn-of-the-century swimming-pool building converted into a glass conservatory with a tropical theme (lush greenery, live flamingos and macaws) and a palm terrace tearoom. It's a fine place to spend a rainy day. Admission is charged; open every day. Just across the street is the **VICTORIA CONFERENCE CENTRE**, linked to the Empress Hotel by a beautifully restored conservatory and accommodating as many as 1,500 delegates.

The **EMPRESS HOTEL** (721 Government St; 250/384-8111; tea reservations 800/644-6611), grand and grandiloquent, is worth at least a walk-through. Built in 1908, it was one of the final flourishes of the Victorian era (even though it's technically Edwardian). Afternoon tea here at 12:30pm (in summer only), 2pm, and 3:30pm is a Victoria tradition—though it's not the city's best. Better, but lesser known, is the hotel's Bengal Lounge, where diners can sample surprisingly good curries—

another dim reflection of Empire days, when the city was a stop on the colonial circuit.

One of Victoria's most impressive sights is 21 kilometers north of the city. **BUTCHART GARDENS** (250/652-5256) is a miracle of modern horticulture, the creation of Jenny Butchart, wife of cement manufacturer Robert Butchart, who made it her life's work (with a small army of helpers) to relandscape her husband's limestone quarry. Decades later, the Butchart estate is an international mecca for gardening enthusiasts, with 50 acres of gardens and beautifully manicured displays (lighted after dark). In summer, it's best to go late in the afternoon, after the busloads of tourists have left. Concerts, fireworks (on Saturday nights in July and August), a surprisingly good afternoon tea, and light meals provide diversions. Admission is charged; open every day.

CRAIGDARROCH CASTLE (1050 Joan Crescent; 250/592-5323) takes you back to an era of unfettered wealth and ostentation. Vancouver Island coal tycoon Robert Dunsmuir built this 19th-century mansion to induce a Scottish wife to live in faraway Victoria. Open every day.

You can visit five of the better restored **VICTORIA HERITAGE HOMES** (with some seasonal closures; call 250/387-4697 for information): Helmcken House, behind Thunderbird Park, east of the Royal British Columbia Museum; Point Ellice House, at Bay and Pleasant Streets; Craigflower Manor, 110 Island Highway; Craigflower Schoolhouse, at Admirals Road and Gorge Road West; and Carr House, the childhood home of the painter Emily Carr, at Government and Simcoe Streets. Admission to each is $5.

The **ESQUIMALT AND NANAIMO (E & N) RAILWAY** (450 Pandora Ave; 800/561-3949 or 800/561-8630) leaves early in the morning from a mock-Victorian station near the Johnson Street bridge and heads up-island to towns with fine resorts. The trip is slow but scenic, and has no food service.

Victoria offers much for **SHOPPERS** (in addition to the favorable exchange rate for Americans, that is). British woolens, suits, and toiletries can be found in the area north of the Empress Hotel on Government Street. Piccadilly Shoppe (1017 Government St; 250/384-1288) specializes in good-quality women's clothes; Wilson W & J Clothiers (1221 Government St; 250/383-7177) sells English wool suits and women's clothes; Sasquatch Trading Company, Ltd. (1233 Government St; 250/386-9033) offers some of the best Cowichan sweaters; E A Morris Tobacconist, Ltd. (1116 Government St; 250/382-4811) carries a very proper Victorian mix of fine pipes and tobaccos; Munro's Books (1108 Government St; 250/382-2464), a monumental 19th-century bank-building-turned-bookstore, has a thoughtful selection; Murchie's Teas and Coffee (1110 Government St; 250/383-3112) offers the city's best selection of special blends; and don't forget Rogers' Chocolates (913 Government St; 250/384-7021) and the English Sweet Shop (738 Yates St; 250/382-3325) for chocolates, as well as almond brittle, black-currant pastilles, marzipan bars, Pontefract cakes, and more, or Bernard Callebaut Chocolaterie (623 Broughton St; 250/380-1515) for picture-perfect Belgian chocolates.

MARKET SQUARE (between Wharf and Store Sts on Johnson St) is a restored 19th-century courtyard surrounded by a jumble of shops, restaurants, and offices on three floors. A few blocks farther north of Market Square at Fisgard Street is **CHINATOWN**, marked by the Gate of Harmonious Interest; its original mix of Chinese restaurants and greengrocers is being encroached upon by a growing number of upscale boutiques and decidedly non-Chinese coffee bars and bistros. Walk through **FAN TAN ALLEY**, Canada's narrowest thoroughfare, and stop in at **LA PAZ RAKU STUDIO GALLERY** to see the ceramic work of owner Larry Sims and other local artists. On Fisgard Street, enjoy an espresso at the prettily appointed **GRACE BISTRO** or an unpretentious Chinese dinner at **WAH LAI YUEN**.

Antique hunters should head east of downtown, up Fort Street, to **ANTIQUE ROW** (on the 800 to 1000 blocks)—block after block of shops, including David Robinson, Ltd. (250/384-6423), with excellent 18th-century English pieces. Visit **BASTION SQUARE** (between View on Yates and Fort Sts) for sidewalk restaurants, galleries, the **MARITIME MUSEUM** (250/385-4222), the alleged location of Victoria's old gallows, and a great gardeners' shop called Dig This (250/385-3212).

RECREATION

RECREATION

Outdoor Activities

Seattleites are an active lot. We ski, sail, run, row, and rollerblade—and then we go on vacation and take up new sports. It's part of why people come here: you can drive to Snoqualmie Pass and ski the slopes in the morning, then be home in time for an afternoon sail on Puget Sound. If you're unfamiliar with the region, a good place to start planning your activity is at one of the four branches of REI (Recreational Equipment Inc.), the largest of which is located downtown at 222 Yale Avenue N (206/223-1944; www.rei.com; map:H2). REI has a generous stock of guidebooks for all outdoor sports as well as U.S. Geological Survey maps and equipment (see Outdoor Gear in the Shopping chapter). The U.S. Forest Service/National Park Service OUTDOOR RECREATION INFORMATION CENTER (located at the downtown REI, 206/470-4060; map:H2) offers trail reports, maps, guidebooks, and weather information. Its staff can also direct you to a ranger station near your destination. For some basic information on some of the city's best—or most accessible—outdoor activities, read on. And please remember, if you lack skills or experience, don't participate in any of these sports without getting training and guidance first.

BICYCLING

Despite the large amount of rainfall and fairly hilly terrain, cycling—from cruising to commuting to racing—is all the rage in and around Seattle. Many bicycle shops RENT BIKES for the day or week, from mountain to tandem to kids' bikes. Some even include helmets for free. Al Young Bike & Ski (3615 NE 45th St; 206/524-2642; map:FF6), Bicycle Center (4529 Sandpoint Way NE; 206/523-8300; map:FF6), and Gregg's Greenlake Cycle (7007 Woodlawn Ave NE; 206/523-1822; map:EE7) are all near major bicycle trails.

CASCADE BICYCLE CLUB organizes group rides nearly every day, ranging from a social pace to strenuous workouts. Call the hotline (206/522-BIKE; www.cascade.org) for current listings, information about cycling in the Northwest, and upcoming events. The legendary SEATTLE-TO-PORTLAND CLASSIC (STP) is a weekend odyssey in which approximately 10,000 cyclists pedal from the Kingdome to downtown Portland in late June or early July. Late February's CHILLY HILLY, a 33-mile trek on the rolling terrain of Bainbridge Island, marks the beginning of cycling season. Information for both rides can be found on Cascade's hotline.

The Seattle Parks and Recreation Department sponsors monthly BICYCLE SATURDAYS/SUNDAYS (generally the second Saturday and third Sunday of each month, May through September) along Lake Washington Boulevard, from Mount Baker Beach to Seward Park (map:II5–JJ5), which closes to auto traffic. Anyone with a bike is welcome to participate. This great activity offers a serene look at the boulevard and provides a haven for little cyclers who are not yet street-savvy (206/684-4075; www.ci.seattle.wa.us/parks/Bicycle).

Following are some of the area's favored rides. The city Bicycle and Pedestrian program (206/684-7583) provides a biker's map of Seattle, available at most bike stores. (See also the trails listed under Running in this chapter.)

ALKI TRAIL / This 8-mile West Seattle route from Seacrest Marina (on Harbor Avenue SW, by Alki Beach) to Lincoln Park is along a road wide enough for both bikes and cars. You'll get great views of downtown and Puget Sound. On sunny weekend days, be wary as you pass the Alki Beach area; it is often crowded and filled with skaters and slow-moving walkers. *Map:II9–KK9.*

BAINBRIDGE ISLAND LOOP / Start a bike expedition on the island by taking your bicycle on the ferry—porting a bike costs only 60 cents more than the walk-on fee and allows you to avoid waiting in long car-ferry lines. The signed, hilly 30-mile route follows low-traffic roads around the island. Start on Ferncliff (heading north) at the Winslow ferry terminal (avoid Highway 305) and work your way counterclockwise around the island, following the signs.

BLUE RIDGE / The view of Puget Sound and the Olympic Mountains is spectacular on this ride of less than 2 miles. From Aurora Avenue N, go west on N 105th Street, which turns into N Holman Road. Follow Holman southwest, turn right onto 15th Avenue NW, and follow it north to NW 100th Street, where the Blue Ridge neighborhood begins. *Map:DD8–DD9*

BURKE-GILMAN TRAIL / A popular off-the-streets route for Seattle cyclers commuting to downtown or the U-District, this 12½-mile path is also great for the bicyclist who wants great views of the city, waterways, and Lake Washington. The Burke-Gilman Trail, built on an old railway bed, has one trailhead on the Fremont-Ballard border (8th Ave NW and Leary Way). The trail then meanders past Gas Works Park on Lake Union, through the University of Washington, and along Lake Washington, ending at Kenmore's Logboom Park (Tracy Owen Station Park) at the northern tip of Lake Washington. From here cyclists can continue east to Woodinville on the Sammamish River Trail. *Fremont to Kenmore; map:FF7–BB5*

ELLIOTT BAY TRAIL / You get a grand view on this brief ride along Puget Sound. The trail, 1½ miles long, skirts the waterfront, passes between the grain terminal and its loading dock, winds its way through a parking lot of new cars right off the ship, and continues to the Elliott Bay Marina. It's full of runners and in-line skaters at noontime. *Pier 70 to Elliott Bay Marina; map:HH8–GG8*

LAKE WASHINGTON BOULEVARD / There are great views along this serene 5-mile stretch between Madrona and Seward Parks. The road is narrow in spots, but bicycles have a posted right-of-way. On Bicycle Saturdays and Sundays, the southern portion (from Mount Baker Beach south) is closed to cars; see above. On other days of the year, some riders may feel safer using the separate asphalt path that follows this portion of the road. Riders can continue south, via S Juneau Street, Seward Park Avenue S, and Rainier Avenue, to the Renton Municipal Airport and on around the south end of Lake Washington, then return via the protected bike lane of I-90. This makes for a 35-mile ride. Take a map with you. *Madrona Park to Seward Park; map:HH6–JJ5*

MERCER ISLAND LOOP / From Seattle, a bicycles-only tunnel leads to the I-90 bridge on the way to Mercer Island (the entrance is off Martin Luther King Jr. Way, through a park of concrete monoliths and artwork by Seattle's Dennis Evans). Using E and W Mercer Way, you'll ride over moderate rolling hills the length of this 14-mile loop. The roads are curving and narrow, so avoid rush hour. The most exhilarating portion of the ride is through the wooded S-curves on the eastern side of the island. This is a great route for perusing the varied residential architecture. *Along E Mercer Way and W Mercer Way; map:II4–KK4*

SAMMAMISH RIVER TRAIL / This very flat, peacefully rural route follows the flowing Sammamish River for 9½ miles. Stop for a picnic at parklike Chateau Ste. Michelle Winery, just off the trail at NE 145th Street (bring your own lunch or buy one there). Bike rentals are available at Sammamish Valley Cycle (8451 164th Ave NE, Redmond; 425/881-8442; map:EE2). *Near Bothell Landing, Bothell to Marymoor Park, Redmond; map:BB3–FF1*

SEWARD PARK / Take this paved and traffic-free 2½-mile road around wooded Seward Park, which juts out into Lake Washington. The peaceful ride offers a look at what may be the only old-growth forest left on the shores of the lake. Eagles sometimes soar overhead, as a few still nest in the park. *S Juneau St and Lake Washington Blvd S; map:JJ5*

MOUNTAIN BIKING

Though all of the aforementioned trails are great jaunts for those with mountain bikes, the advantage of bigger tires and more sophisticated suspension systems is that mountain bikes can be taken off-road.

Unfortunately, the booming popularity of mountain biking in the past few years presents something of a dilemma to environmentalists as

REDMOND CYCLING

In recent years, the Eastside town of Redmond has become known as the bicycling capital of the Northwest—thanks mainly to 522-acre Marymoor Park, which boasts both the Sammamish River Trail and the Marymoor Velodrome on its grounds. The Sammamish River Trail, a 10-mile trek through lush river greenery, hosts mainly casual, recreational cyclists, many of whom continue west to hook up with the Burke-Gilman Trail for a long and pleasant ride into Seattle.

The Velodrome, on the other hand, is the place to watch a more serious brand of cycling. Some of the region's best riders race here on the 400-meter oval track on Wednesday and Friday nights, May through August. Spectators are welcome—for an admission fee of about $3. Racers compete on brakeless, one-speed bikes in a number of different thrilling races that show off the competitors' speed and grace.

You can take a turn on the track yourself anytime during daylight hours if no events or races are scheduled. Better yet, spring for the $10 membership fee and join the Marymoor Velodrome Association (206/675-1424), a volunteer organization that offers discounts on racing, bike rentals, and spectator admission.

— Jo Brown

well as bikers. The very trails that provide an optimum off-road experience—the ones that were once quiet, remote, untouched—are those that often end up closed by the Forest Service because of the damage caused by increasing numbers of bikers. The Outdoor Recreation Information Center provides information on trail closures (see above; 206/470-4060). The **BACKCOUNTRY BICYCLE TRAILS CLUB** (206/283-2995; http://www.dirtnw.com/bbtc) organizes local rides for cyclists at all levels of experience and is adamant about teaching "soft-riding" techniques that protect trails from the roughing-up that can eventually cause closures. The best local guidebook is *Kissing the Trail: Greater Seattle Mountain Bike Adventures* by John Zilly, available at bookstores and biking and outdoor retail outlets.

If riding downhill is more your style, some ski areas, such as Crystal Mountain and The Summit at Snoqualmie, turn their snow trails into bike trails in the summer—complete with lift rides up the mountain (see Skiing in this chapter).

DECEPTION PASS STATE PARK / An hour and a half northwest by car from Seattle, Deception Pass is without a doubt one of the most beautiful wild spots in Washington. And it has more than 16 miles of bike trails that rise and fall over 1,000 feet of elevation. Trails climb to high rocky bluffs with views of the San Juan Islands, then descend to sandy beaches.

The trails are single-track, and not all of the park is open to mountain bikes. *South of Anacortes off Hwy 20 on Whidbey and Fidalgo Islands*

ST. EDWARDS STATE PARK / Up to 12 miles of varied terrain make this park great for all skill levels. Located in the Juanita neighborhood of Kirkland, it is the largest undeveloped area on Lake Washington and has 3,000 feet of shoreline. Be wary as you ride among the tall trees and up and down the 700 feet of elevation: the park's trails interweave, and it's easy to get lost if you don't pay attention. *Off Juanita Dr NE, Kirkland; map:CC4*

GOLFING

There are a number of fine public golf courses in Seattle and environs, many in wonderfully scenic surroundings.

BELLEVUE MUNICIPAL GOLF COURSE / **5500 140th Ave NE, Bellevue; 425/452-7250** This course (5,535 yards), the busiest in the state, is fairly level and easy. Eighteen holes, PNGA 66.6. *Map:FF2*

GREEN LAKE GOLF COURSE / **5701 W Green Lake Way N; 206/632-2280** Far from a full-fledged golf course (the nine holes run between about 60 and 100 yards), this conveniently located course adjacent to Green Lake might be just the ticket for beginners, families that putt together, or anyone looking for a fun weeknight activity. *Map:EE7*

JACKSON PARK MUNICIPAL GOLF COURSE / **1000 NE 135th St; 206/363-4747** An interesting—but crowded—course over lovely rolling hills, Jackson Park has a huge, well-maintained putting green, a nicely secluded chipping green, and a great short nine, which is sparsely played. Eighteen holes, 6,592 yards, PNGA 68.2. *Map:CC7*

JEFFERSON PARK GOLF COURSE / **4101 Beacon Ave S; 206/762-4513** You get great views of the city from the hilltop fairways of this enormously popular course, which has a driving range. Eighteen holes, 6,146 yards, PNGA 67.9. *Map:JJ6*

TYEE VALLEY GOLF COURSE / **2401 S 192nd St; 206/878-3540** At the foot of the Sea-Tac runway, this easy course is perfect for a fast game between planes, but it's noisy. Eighteen holes, 5,926 yards, PNGA men 66.0, women 70.6. *Map:PP6*

WEST SEATTLE MUNICIPAL GOLF COURSE / **4470 35th Ave SW; 206/935-5187** A good but forgiving course just west of the Duwamish River, tucked into an undulating valley, which makes for some surprising lies. Eighteen holes, 6,285 yards, PNGA 68.6. Tee times are the easiest to come by in the city, views of which are spectacular on the back nine. *Map:JJ8*

About an hour's drive out of the city are a number of fine, challenging courses, each with its own distinctive charms. Among these are the **SNO-**

HOMISH GOLF CLUB (7806 147th Ave SE, Snohomish; 360/568-2676 or 800/560-2676), a comfortable but solid rural course nestled among horse farms and towering red cedars northeast of Snohomish; **NORTH SHORE** (4101 North Shore Blvd NE, Tacoma; 800/447-1375), a bracing, salty-air 18 with first-rate practice facilities, including a covered, lighted driving range, restaurant, and pro shop; **KAYAK POINT** (15711 Marine Dr, Stanwood; 800/562-3094), an exciting, visually dramatic course carved out of dense forest and featuring head-scratching, imaginative holes; and **MCCORMICK WOODS** (5155 McCormick Woods Dr SW, Port Orchard; 800/323-0130), a fascinating shot-maker's course, impeccably groomed and laid out over beautiful, sylvan terrain.

HIKING

The hiking in Washington is superlative. Alpine lakes, rain forests, ocean cliffs, mountain meadows—all are within easy access of Seattle, and day hikers can count on reaching any of a score of trailheads within an hour or two. For this reason, the national parks, state parks, national forests, and wilderness areas nearby are heavily used, but conservation efforts have managed to stay a small step ahead of the abuse. Forest Service wilderness staff often practice triage—that is, letting a few popular spots take a pounding while quietly applying their energy and money to preserving more remote areas. Their efforts are supported by a statewide community of hikers, who maintain a strict creed of wilderness ethics.

Good hiking guides are published in association with **THE MOUNTAINEERS** (300 3rd Ave W; 206/284-6310; www.mountaineers.org; map:A9), a venerable and prominent outdoors club whose bookstore—open to the public—has the largest collection of climbing, hiking, mountain biking, and paddling books in the Pacific Northwest. A Mountaineers membership gives you access to skills courses, group hikes, and a variety of other privileges. Another reliable information tap to the outdoors is the Seattle branch of the **SIERRA CLUB** (8511 15th Ave NE; 206/523-2147; www.sierraclub.org; map:EE6). The **WASHINGTON TRAILS ASSOCIATION** (1305 4th Ave, Suite 512; 206/625-1367; www.wta.org/wta; map:K6), a nonprofit outreach group, welcomes telephone inquiries about hiking.

Like any other outdoor activity, hiking requires a marriage of caution and adventurous spirit. Always carry water and bring extra clothing (wool or synthetics such as polypropylene—not cotton) and rain gear, even if it's 80 degrees and sunny when you set out and you plan to hike for only two hours. Permits may be required for hiking or camping. Check with the local ranger station before setting out. Also beware having your vehicle ticketed and towed at the trailhead—be sure to buy a parking permit at a ranger station or outdoor equipment store. In general, national forests require daily (or seasonal) permits; national parks charge fees to enter the park but none to hike; and in some areas you can exchange two days of maintenance work for a free annual pass. Your best bet is to contact a ranger station or an outdoor store before you go to find out which kind of pass you need. Another good source is *Inside Out Washington* by Ron C. Judd.

Here are some popular nearby hiking areas, described broadly by region.

CENTRAL CASCADES / The best hiking near Seattle is in this section of the Cascade Range, one to two hours east of the city off Highway 2 or I-90. The Central Cascades are mainly national forest and include a stretch of the Alpine Lakes Wilderness, a scenic marvel. A gorgeous section of the Pacific Crest Trail cuts through the wilderness along the mountain ridges. *Between Snoqualmie Pass and Stevens Pass*

ISSAQUAH ALPS / The most easily accessible from Seattle, these comely Cascade foothills have dozens of day trails frequented by both hikers and horses. Every week the Issaquah Alps Trails Club (PO Box 351, Issaquah 98027; 425/328-0480) organizes day hikes through the hills, ranging from short and easy to strenuous—a good way to introduce children to hiking. *20 miles east of Seattle off I-90*

NORTH CASCADES / The high trails in this area are richly rewarding, reaching glaciers and old lookout shelters as well as offering majestic panoramas of this magnificent, brooding mountain range. Seekers of solitude will find it here. The alpine flowers are in their glory in early August; the fall colors blaze brightest in early October, with snow following soon after. *Between Stevens Pass and the Canadian border*

OLYMPIC MOUNTAINS / Journeying to the Olympics from Seattle takes a while longer (plan on more than two hours to get there via ferries and car), but is well worth the extra effort. Take your pick of glaciers, waterfalls, and mossy rain forests. Wildlife is abundant—you'll probably spot goats, deer, marmots, grouse, and, if you're lucky, a cougar or a bear. At Hurricane Ridge (visitors center: 3002 Mount Angeles Rd, Port Angeles 98362; 360/452-0330), a high point and hiking hub of the range, you'll also spot plenty of tourists. Rainfall is plentiful over the Olympic Range, so go prepared. *Olympic National Park, Olympic Peninsula*

SOUTH CASCADES / Mount Rainier, offering numerous trails, is one of the most popular hiking areas here (see Mount Rainier in the Day Trips chapter), and surprisingly close to the city. The rest of the South Cascades are a stunning contrast to the rugged northern peaks. The more arid landscapes here are in many places reminiscent of Montana or the Southwest. Sadly, clearcuts dominate the views, including those on the South Cascades segment of the Pacific Crest Trail. *Between Snoqualmie Pass and the Oregon border*

KAYAKING/CANOEING

In a city that is girdled by water, one of the best ways to explore is by boat. Several locations around Seattle will rent canoes and kayaks for day excursions. A good general resource is *Boatless in Seattle: Getting on the Water in Western Washington Without Owning a Boat!* by Sue Hacking. For those who want instruction on kayaking, perhaps in preparation for a whitewater trip, one of the oldest kayaking clubs in the nation is the **WASHINGTON KAYAK CLUB** (PO Box 24264, Seattle 98124; 206/433-1983), a safety- and conservation-oriented club that organizes swimming-pool practices, weekend trips, and sea- and whitewater-kayaking lessons in the spring.

DUWAMISH RIVER / From Tukwila (where the Green River becomes the Duwamish) to Boeing Field (map:QQ5–JJ7), this scenic waterway makes for a lovely paddle. North of Boeing, you pass industrial salvage ships, commercial shipping lanes, and industrial Harbor Island, where the river empties into Elliott Bay. Rent a canoe or a kayak at Pacific Water Sports (16055 Pacific Hwy S; 206/246-9385; map:OO6) near Sea-Tac Airport—the staff can direct you to one of several spots along the river where you can launch your craft. The current is strong at times, but not a serious hazard for moderately experienced paddlers.

GREEN LAKE / Green Lake's tame waters are a good place to learn the basics. Green Lake Boat Rentals (7351 E Green Lake Dr N; 206/527-0171; map:EE7), a Seattle Parks and Recreation Department concession on the northeast side of the lake, rents kayaks, rowboats, paddleboats, canoes, sailboards, and sailboats. Open daily, except in bad weather, March though October.

LAKE UNION / If you've always wanted to get an up-close look at houseboats, kayaking or canoeing on Lake Union is a great way to do it. You'll also find great views of the city and, if you are ambitious, you can paddle west from Lake Union down the Ship Canal, past the clanking of boatyards and the aroma of fish-laden boats, to the **HIRAM M. CHITTENDEN LOCKS**—which will lift you and your kayak up and down for free. A short distance past the locks, you'll find yourself in the salt water of Puget Sound. Rent sea kayaks at Northwest Outdoor Center (2100 Westlake Ave N; 206/281-9694; kayak@nwoc.com; www.nwoc.com; map:GG7). NWOC also offers classes and tours to the San Juan Islands and the Olympic Peninsula. Aqua Verde Paddle Club (1303 NE Boat St; 206/545-8570; map:FF6) also rents kayaks hourly and will give a quick demonstration on the dock before you paddle away. (Reservations are recommended on summer weekends for both of these Lake Union rental outlets.)

MONTLAKE AND ARBORETUM / On a typical hot August day, drivers sitting in bumper-to-bumper commuter traffic on the Evergreen Point Bridge gaze longingly at canoeists in the marshlands of the Arboretum (map:GG6). Rent a canoe or a rowboat at low rates at the University of Washington Waterfront Activities Center (206/543-9433; map:FF6) behind Husky Stadium. Here the mirrorlike waters are framed by a mosaic of green lily pads and white flowers. Closer to shore, vibrant yellow irises push through tall marsh grasses, while ducks cavort under weeping willows. Pack a picnic lunch and wander ashore to the marsh walk, a favorite bird-watching stroll that meanders from just below the Museum of History and Industry to the lawn of Foster Island. Those with their own canoes or kayaks can venture farther afield.

PUGET SOUND / Seattle's proximity to the open waters and scenic island coves of Puget Sound makes for ideal sea kayaking. Bainbridge Island's **EAGLE HARBOR** is a leisurely paddle in protected waters. Tiny Blake Island, a state park, is a short trip from Vashon Island, Alki Point, or Fort Ward Park on Bainbridge Island. Bird-watchers can head for the calm waters of the **NISQUALLY DELTA** and Nisqually National Wildlife Refuge south of Tacoma. And the **SAN JUAN ISLANDS** provide endless paddling opportunities, though the currents can be strong, and unguided kayaking here is generally not for novices.

SAMMAMISH RIVER / The trip up the gently flowing Sammamish Slough (map:BB5–FF1) is quiet and scenic. Ambitious canoeists can follow the slough all the way to Lake Sammamish, about 15 miles to the southeast, passing golf courses, the town of Woodinville, the Chateau Ste. Michelle Winery, and Marymoor Park along the way.

ROCK CLIMBING

Don't have time to travel several hours to learn how to climb a mountain face? You don't have to. In Seattle and its environs, several indoor climbing walls allow you to get vertical for after-work relaxation or for a good rush on the weekend.

MARYMOOR CLIMBING STRUCTURE / **Marymoor Park, Redmond; 206/296-2964** Otherwise known as Big Pointy, this 45-foot, concrete-brick-and-mortar "house of cards," just south of the Velodrome, was designed by the godfather of rock climbing, Don Robinson. It features climbing angles up to and over 90 degrees. East end of Marymoor Park, off Hwy 520. *Map:FF1*

REI PINNACLE / **222 Yale Ave N; 206/223-1944** Said to be the world's tallest free-standing indoor climbing structure at 65 feet, this looming structure, with more than 1,000 modular climbing holds, is very popular—waits can be as long as an hour, and you get only one ascent. You're given a beeper, however, so you can peruse the store while you wait your turn on the rock, and the climb is free. Or you can pay for a beginning climbing class and, while learning the basics and safety, have more time to clamber. *Map:H2*

SCHURMAN ROCK AND GLACIER / 5200 35th Ave SW; 206/684-7434 These West Seattle structures at Camp Long offer good climbing forays for the beginner. Both are unsupervised. Schurman Rock has separate areas so novices can take on one challenge at a time. The glacier is a child's dream structure with deep foot- and handholds. *Map:KK8*

STONE GARDENS / 2839 NW Market St; 206/781-9828 One section of the gym consists of low overhangs—allowing climbers to practice one of the most difficult maneuvers of climbing within a few feet of the ground. The rest of the gym offers faces that can be bouldered or top-roped, with climbs for beginners to advanced. Staff members wander around offering helpful advice, or you can take one of several classes ranging from one-on-one beginner instruction to several levels of technical erudition. *Map:FF8*

VERTICAL WORLD / The Redmond location of this rock gym (15036-B NE 95th St, Redmond; 425/881-8826; map:DD2) offers 7,000 square feet of textured climbing surface, while the newer, equally striking Seattle club (2123 W Elmore St; 206/283-4497; map:FF8) sports 35-foot-high walls and a whopping 14,000 square feet of climbing area. The walls are fully textured, making the more than 100 routes varied and interesting. Lessons are offered at both gyms.

Once you've attained the highest pinnacles indoors and in controlled outdoor settings, take your hardened hands and clenching toes to the *great* outdoors, where you'll find many challenging and breathtaking faces. **THE MOUNTAINEERS** (300 3rd Ave W; 206/284-6310; www.mountaineers. org; map:A9), the largest outdoor club in the region, is a superb resource, offering group climbs, climbing courses, and general information on climbs, both in the Northwest and elsewhere. For gear, both to rent and to purchase, and occasional free lectures about climbing, try the REI stores (flagship store at 222 Yale Ave N; 206/223-1944; map:H2).

ROLLER SKATING/ROLLERBLADING

Roller skaters—and their ubiquitous subset, the in-line skaters—compose an ever-widening wedge of the urban athletic pie. In fair weather, skaters are found anywhere the people-watching is good and the pavement smooth, including the tree-shaded Burke-Gilman Trail, the downtown waterfront, and along Lake Washington Boulevard. Farther afield, fine skating is found on the Interurban Trail south out of Renton, and north on the Sammamish River Valley Trail to Redmond's Marymoor Park. (See Bicycling and Running in this chapter.) Note: Skate-rental shops won't let you out the door if the pavement is damp.

GREEN LAKE (E Green Lake Way N and W Green Lake Way N; map:EE7) is the skate-and-be-seen-skating spot in town, where hotdoggers in bright spandex weave and bob through cyclists, joggers, walkers, and leashed dogs. The 2.8-mile path around the lake is crowded on weekends, but during the week it's a good place to try wheels for the first time. When the wading pool on the north shore of the lake isn't filled for kids or commandeered by roller-skating hockey enthusiasts, it makes a good spot to learn to skate backward or to refine your coolest moves. You can rent or buy skates, as well as elbow and knee pads, at Gregg's Greenlake Cycle (7007 Woodlawn Ave NE; 206/523-1822; map:EE7).

Another urban skating site excellent for practicing is the grounds of the **NATIONAL OCEANIC AND ATMOSPHERIC ADMINISTRATION** (7600 Sand Point Way NE, next to Magnuson Park; map:EE5). The facility can be reached via the Burke-Gilman Trail, and offers a quiet workout along a smooth 1-kilometer loop, with one low-grade hill and some exciting turns.

ROWING

In a city graced with two major lakes, many people opt to exercise on the water instead of jogging through exhaust fumes or skating through the crowds at Green Lake. They've discovered an affinity for the sleek, lightweight rowing shells, and relish slicing across the silver-black water of early morning. **LAKE UNION CREW** (11 E Allison St; 206/860-4199; map:GG7) offers an introductory weekend as a way to explore the sport. This eight-hour coached program (four hours on Saturday and four on Sunday) includes all the basics of safety, boat handling, and technique, plus a video review of your on-the-water rowing sessions. This floating boathouse also offers programs for both scullers (two oars) and sweep rowers (one oar each) from novice to competitive levels. After the row, enjoy a latte in front of the fireplace in the Great Room of the boathouse.

The Seattle Parks and Recreation Department runs two rowing facilities: one on **GREEN LAKE**, out of the Green Lake Small Craft Center (5900 W Green Lake Way N; 206/684-4074; map:EE7) and the other at **SAYRES PARK** on Lake Washington, through the Mount Baker Rowing and Sailing Center (3800 Lake Washington Blvd S; 206/386-1913; map:JJ6). Both operate year-round, offer all levels of instruction, host annual regattas, and send their top boats to the national championships. The Lake Washington Rowing Club (910 N Northlake Way; 206/547-1583; map:FF7) and the Pocock Rowing Center (3320 Fuhrman Ave E; 206/328-0778; map:FF7) are two boathouses where you can store your boat, find competitive rowing teams, or sign up for introductory rowing programs. Because Seattle has one of the largest populations of adult rowers in the country, you can find numerous other women-only, men-only, or age-specific clubs in the area. For a full list, contact US Rowing

(800/314-4ROW; www.usrowing.org). Most clubs allow guest rowers to ride in the launch with the coach; some will allow experienced oarspeople to row once or twice without paying fees. Contact individual boathouses to ask about guest policies.

RUNNING

Step out just about any door in the area and you're on a good running course, especially if you love hills. Flat routes can be found, of course, especially along bike paths (see Bicycling in this chapter). The mild climate and numerous parks make solo running appealing, yet the city also has a large, well-organized running community that provides company or competition. Club Northwest's *Northwest Runner* (pick it up in any running gear store) is a good source for information on organized runs and has a complete road-race schedule. Racers, both casual and serious, can choose from a number of annual races (at least one every weekend in spring and summer). Some of the biggest are the 4-mile **ST. PATRICK'S DAY DASH** in March, the **COLLEGE INN STAMPEDE** and the 6.7-mile Seward-to-Madison **SHORE RUN** in July, the 8-kilometer **SEAFAIR TORCHLIGHT RUN** through the city streets in August, and the **SEATTLE MARATHON** in November. One of the finest running outfitters in town, Super Jock 'N Jill (7210 E Green Lake Dr N; 206/522-7711; map:EE7), maintains a racing hotline (206/524-RUNS). Listed below are some popular routes for runners.

ARBORETUM / A favorite. You can stay on the winding main drive, Lake Washington Boulevard E, or run along any number of paths that wend through the trees and flowers. (The Arb's main unpaved thoroughfare, Azalea Way, is strictly off limits to joggers, however.) Lake Washington Boulevard connects with scenic E Interlaken Boulevard at the Japanese Garden. It then winds east and south out of the Arboretum and down to the lake itself. The northern lakeside leg, from Madrona Drive south to Leschi, is popular for its wide sidewalks; farther south, from Mount Baker Park to Seward Park, the sweeping views make it one of the most pleasing runs you will ever experience. *Arboretum Dr E and Lake Washington Blvd E; map:GG6*

GREEN LAKE / The 2.8-mile marked path around the lake has two lanes: one for wheeled traffic, the other for everybody else. On sunny weekends, Green Lake becomes a recreational Grand Central—great for people-watching, but slow going. Early mornings or early evenings, though, it's a lovely idyll, with ducks, geese, red-winged blackbirds, mountain views, and quick glimpses of rowers and windsurfers on the lake. The path connects with a bikeway along Ravenna Boulevard. A painted line establishes the cycling lane; runners can follow the boulevard's grassy median. *Latona Ave NE and E Green Lake Way N; map:EE7*

KELSEY CREEK PARK / This pretty Eastside park has a main jogging trail with paths that branch off into the wooded hills. *13204 SE 8th Pl, Bellevue; map:II2*

KIRKLAND WATERFRONT / The Eastside's high-visibility running path stretches along the water from Houghton Beach Park to Marina Park—a little over a mile each way. *Along Lake Washington Blvd, Kirkland; map:FF3–EE3*

LINCOLN PARK / Various paths and roads cut through this thickly wooded West Seattle park overlooking Vashon Island and Puget Sound. The shoreline is tucked below a bluff where auto traffic can no longer be heard. *Fauntleroy Way SW and SW Trenton St; map:KK9*

MAGNOLIA BLUFF AND DISCOVERY PARK / A striking run in clear weather, this route offers vistas of the Olympic Mountains across Puget Sound. From the Magnolia Bluff parking lot (at Magnolia Boulevard W and W Galer Street), run north along the boulevard on a paved pedestrian trail. Magnolia Park ends at W Barrett Street; continue north for four blocks to Discovery Park, which has numerous paved and unpaved trails. *Along Magnolia Blvd; map:GG9–EE9*

MAGNUSON PARK / Formerly part of the Naval Air Station at Sand Point, this park has many congenial running areas, including wide, paved roads and flat, grassy terrain, all overlooking Lake Washington. On clear days, the view of Mount Rainier is superb. *Sand Point Way NE and NE 65th St; map:EE5*

MEDINA AND EVERGREEN POINT / A scenic run along nicely maintained roads offers views of Lake Washington and of some of the area's most stunning homes. Two and a half miles each way. *Along Overlake Dr and Evergreen Point Rd, Bellevue; map:FF4–HH4*

RAVENNA BOULEVARD / Follow this course along the wide, grassy median strip beginning at Green Lake and dip into Ravenna Park's woodsy ravine at 25th Avenue NE, near the boulevard's end. *Green Lake Way N and NE 71st St; map:EE7–EE6*

SAILING

Seattle has a great deal of water but, in the summer at least, precious little wind. Thus many sailors hereabouts reckon that the real sailing season runs from around Labor Day to the beginning of May (although in summer, late afternoon winds will sometimes fill the sheets). And given a little wind, looking toward Seattle from its bodies of water will give you perspectives you can't get from your car (a glimpse of Bill Gates's house, for example). The wannabe sailor can find classes or chartered tours. **SAILING IN SEATTLE** offers three different staffed cruises on a 33-foot sailboat: past the houseboat communities on Lake Union, through the

Hiram M. Chittenden Locks on the Ship Canal, or past Gates's house on Lake Washington. Sit back and enjoy the sights or, even if you've never sailed before, try your hand at sailing with instruction from the on-board crew. Tours are regularly scheduled or can be chartered. Reservations are a must. Sailing in Seattle also offers a variety of courses for everyone from the beginner to the salty dog who wants American Sailing Association certification (2000 Westlake Ave N #46, Seattle 98109; 206/298-0094; skipper@sailing-in-seattle.com; www.sailing-in-seattle.com; map:GG7).

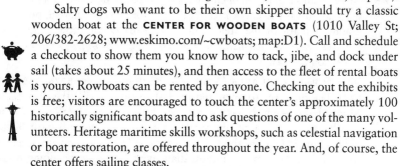

DISCOVERY CHARTERS AND SAILING SCHOOL offers cruises for one day or up to several days, as well as instruction, aboard the 40-foot yacht *Dream Catcher*, complete with teak interior (206/784-7679; saltydog@aa.net; www.members.aa.net/~saltydog/).

For beginning sailors who want to learn the art in a smaller boat and have a few days to pick up the essentials, the Seattle Sailing Association, headquartered at the **GREEN LAKE SMALL CRAFT CENTER** (5900 W Green Lake Way N; 206/684-4074; map:EE7), at the southwest corner of the lake, offers classes. Green Lake, no more than a mile across in any direction, is the perfect place to learn: it's free from motor cruisers, floatplanes, and barge traffic. Once you know how to sail, you can rent boats from the center with an annual membership. **MOUNT BAKER ROWING AND SAILING CENTER**, on Lake Washington, also offers sailing lessons in small boats (3800 Lake Washington Blvd S; 206/386-1913; map:II6).

Salty dogs who want to be their own skipper should try a classic wooden boat at the **CENTER FOR WOODEN BOATS** (1010 Valley St; 206/382-2628; www.eskimo.com/~cwboats; map:D1). Call and schedule a checkout to show them you know how to tack, jibe, and dock under sail (takes about 25 minutes), and then access to the fleet of rental boats is yours. Rowboats can be rented by anyone. Checking out the exhibits is free; visitors are encouraged to touch the center's approximately 100 historically significant boats and to ask questions of one of the many volunteers. Heritage maritime skills workshops, such as celestial navigation or boat restoration, are offered throughout the year. And, of course, the center offers sailing classes.

SKIING AND SNOWBOARDING

The rain that falls on Seattle turns to snow at higher elevations in the winter—making for wonderful skiing. And although some call the rain-thickened, heavy snow of the region's skiing areas "Cascade Concrete," most mornings a new layer of white has blanketed the slopes. Several ski areas have weekend shuttle buses leaving from Seattle. If you plan to drive, carry tire chains and a shovel, and inquire ahead about **ROAD CONDITIONS** (425/368-4499). All local downhill ski facilities rent skis, snowboards, and other gear. Many rental outlets are available in the city as well. REI (206/223-1944), for example, rents cross-country paraphernalia. And though commercial downhill ski areas have ski patrols, skiers in unpatrolled areas or in the mountainous backcountry should heed the constant danger of avalanche. Conditions change daily (sometimes hourly), so always call the Forest Service's **NORTHWEST AVALANCHE INFORMATION HOTLINE** (206/526-6677) before setting out. Finally, if you are heading off into the backwoods, most plowed parking areas near trailheads and along state highways require a Sno-Park permit, which costs $25 per vehicle for the winter season. One- and three-day Sno-Park permits are also available. These can be purchased at local retail outlets; check out www.parks.wa.gov/vendor1 for a full list.

Below are the ski areas most accessible to Seattleites, with information about both downhill and cross-country skiing. For daily updates on conditions in downhill areas, call the **CASCADE SKI REPORT** (206/634-0200, winter only).

CRYSTAL MOUNTAIN RESORT / 1 Crystal Mountain Blvd, Crystal Mountain 98022; 360/663-2265 Nine chairlifts lead to 55 groomed trails of more than 3,300 skiable acres of snow. On a clear day, the 7,002-foot vantage point at the top of Green Valley affords a tremendous view of Mount Rainier and Mount St. Helens. A new six-person chairlift makes getting up the mountain easier for the beginner or the expert, and there's weekend night skiing all winter long. Nordic skiers will be charmed by Silver Basin's big, broad open area. The ski patrol here will monitor your whereabouts if you check in and out, and for 50 cents they supply topographical maps of the area. Call 888/754-6199 for snow conditions. *www.csn.net/~mattcarl/state/wa/cm/cm.htm; 76 miles southeast of Seattle on SR 410.*

MOUNT BAKER SKI AREA / 1017 Iowa St, Bellingham 98226; 360/734-6771 The first area to open and the last to close during the ski season, Mount Baker—which has the highest average snowfall (595 inches) in North America—is a terrific weekend destination, though most of the lodgings are in Glacier, about 17 miles away. The view is remarkable; the runs are varied but mostly intermediate, with one bowl, meadows, trails, and wooded areas. Snowboarders can test their mettle at the legendary Banked Slalom Snowboard Race, held on the last weekend in January. Mount Baker accepts 250 entries on a first-come, first-served basis and awards $50,000 in prizes. No night skiing. On the northeastern flank of Mount Baker, Nordic skiers can find sporadically groomed trails. Rentals and lessons for all types of snow trekking are available in the main lodge. Snow conditions: 360/671-0211. *56 miles east of Bellingham off I-5 on SR 542.*

STEVENS PASS / PO Box 98, Skykomish 98288; 360/973-2441 Challenging and interesting terrain makes Stevens Pass a favorite for many skiers, with conditions that tend to be drier than Crystal's. Eleven chair-lifts lead to a variety of runs, not to mention breathtaking views of the Cascades. Snowboarders, welcome on all runs, tend to congregate near the Skyline Express and Brooks lifts, where nearby is a half-pipe. Other areas near these lifts are roped off for jumps. For Nordic skiing, head far-ther east on Highway 2 to the full-service Stevens Pass Nordic Center, complete with rentals, instruction, and hot food and drink. After you're suited up, you can choose from 25 kilometers of groomed trails over a variety of terrain. The Nordic Center is touted as having the best white stuff within 90 minutes of Seattle; the only problem is that it's open only Friday through Sunday. For winter conditions, call 206/634-1645. *78 miles northeast of Seattle on Hwy 2; the Nordic Center is 5 miles east of Stevens Pass.*

THE SUMMIT AT SNOQUALMIE / Information: 7900 SE 28th St, Suite 200, Mercer Island 98040; 206/232-8182 Now consisting of four neigh-boring sections along I-90—Alpental, Summit Central (formerly Ski Acres), Summit West (formerly Snoqualmie Summit), and Summit East (formerly Hyak)—this complex offers many options for skiers of all abilities. Linked by a free shuttle-bus service (three are also linked by ski trails), all four honor the same lift ticket, but each has its own dis-tinct appeal. Alpental, for example, boasts high-grade challenges, includ-ing the nationally recognized Internationale run. Summit Central offers intermediate-to-expert runs, and most of the mountain is open for night skiing. Summit West's gentler slopes are ideal for children and beginners as well as intermediate-level skiers. Dozens of ski and snowboard classes operate here. Summit East, the smallest and quietest, has a snowboarder's half-pipe. The Summit Nordic Center has a 5-kilometer lower trail system for beginners and racers doing warm-ups. Intermediate and advanced Nordic skiers can take the Silver Fir chairlift near the Nordic Center to the 45-kilometer upper trail system. On weekends, volunteer hosts will lead skiers along the 18 trails. Lessons and cross-country ski rentals can be found at the Nordic Center building. For up-to-date snow conditions, call 206/236-1600. *47 miles east of Seattle off I-90 at exit 52.*

I-90 CORRIDOR / The U.S. Forest Service offers a wide variety of marked cross-country trails here, which are free and close to Seattle, but you must have a Sno-Park pass to use the parking lots (see above). **CABIN CREEK** has 12 kilometers of trails; the ones on the south side are easy, and the ones on the north side are intermediate, with plenty of turns (10 miles east of Snoqualmie Summit, off exit 63). At **CRYSTAL SPRINGS/LAKE KEECHELUS,** Sno-Parks are at either end of a 11.2-kilometer trail that runs along the shores of Lake Keechelus. Crystal Springs has a conces-sion stand with hot drinks and snacks (top of Snoqualmie Pass off exit 54). At **IRON HORSE SNO-PARK,** about 10 miles of easy, flat trails around

Lake Easton and Iron Horse State Park are combined with a 12-mile trek from Easton to Cle Elum (not always accessible). (Iron Horse Sno-Park is off exit 71.) For more trails, or to learn which trails are at their best, contact local outdoor retailers.

METHOW VALLEY / One of the top Nordic ski areas in the country, the Methow Valley offers the charm of Vermont, the snow conditions of Utah, and the big sky of Montana. Too far from the city for a day trip, its 175 kilometers of groomed trails make for a great weekend getaway. The valley towns of Mazama, Winthrop, and Twisp offer an ample number of lodges, guides, lessons, and rental shops. Call Central Reservations, 800/422-3048, for hut-to-hut skiing or housing/rental reservations. For more information contact Methow Valley Sport Trails Association, PO Box 147, Winthrop 98862; 800/682-5787. *250 miles northeast of Seattle off SR 20.*

MOUNT RAINIER NATIONAL PARK / Several marked cross-country trails in the Paradise area (to Narada Falls, Nisqually Vista, and Reflection Lakes) have breathtaking views of the mountain, but they're hilly and tough for novices. Park rangers lead **SNOWSHOE WALKS** along the Nisqually Vista Trail from Paradise on winter weekends. They provide the snowshoes ($1 donation suggested) and guide those 10 years and older on two-hour treks. Snowshoe and cross-country ski rentals and instruction are available from Rainier Ski Touring, 360/569-2412. Mount Tahoma Trails Association (360/569-2451; www.mashell.com/Mt_tahoma.html) cuts almost 90 miles of trails through a spectacular area south and west of Mount Rainier National Park. The trail system includes two eight-person overnight huts (in the South District) and one 12-person hut (in the Central District). *86 miles southeast of Seattle off SR 706.*

SWIMMING

See Parks and Beaches in the Exploring chapter.

TENNIS

Tennis is popular here, but not so much so that it's impossible to get a public court. There's only one indoor public tennis facility in the city: **SEATTLE TENNIS CENTER** (2000 Martin Luther King Jr. Way S; 206/684-4764; map:II6), with ten indoor courts (there are also four unlighted outdoor courts). Bellevue has a similar facility, **ROBINSWOOD TENNIS CENTER** (2400 151st Pl SE; 425/455-7690; map:II2), which has four (lighted) outdoor and four indoor courts. Most public outdoor courts in the city are run by the Seattle Parks and Recreation Department and are available either on a first-come, first-served basis or by reservation for a small fee (usually under $5). Purchase of a one-year $15 reservation card enables players to make phone reservations up to two weeks in advance

(206/684-4082). Otherwise, reservations must be made in person at the scheduling office of Seattle Parks and Recreation (5201 Green Lake Way N; map:EE7). If it rains, your money is refunded. Eastside outdoor public courts cannot be reserved in advance. The best time to play is early in the day; in spring and summer, the lineups start at around 3pm.

Most private Seattle tennis courts do not allow non-member use and do not sell weekly or daily memberships. To use a private court, a tennis player would need a sponsor.

Following is a list of the best outdoor courts in the area.

Here are the best outdoor courts in the area:

BRYANT: two unlighted courts. 40th Ave NE and NE 65th St; map:EE5

GRASS LAWN PARK: six lighted courts. 7031 148th Ave NE, Redmond; map:EE2

HILLAIRE PARK: two unlighted courts. 15731 NE 6th St, Bellevue; map:HH1

HOMESTEAD FIELD: four unlighted courts. 82nd Ave SE and SE 40th St, Mercer Island; map:II4

KILLARNEY GLEN PARK: two unlighted courts. 1933 104th Ave SE, Bellevue; map:HH3

LINCOLN PARK: six lighted courts. Fauntleroy Ave SW and SW Webster St; map:KK9

LOWER WOODLAND PARK: ten lighted courts. W Green Lake Way N; map:FF7

LUTHER BURBANK PARK: three unlighted courts. 2040 84th Ave SE, Mercer Island; map:II4

MAGNOLIA PLAYFIELD: four courts (two lighted). 34th Ave W and W Smith St; map:GG9

MARYMOOR PARK: four lighted courts. 6046 W Lake Sammamish Pkwy NE, Redmond; map:FF1

MEADOWBROOK: six lighted courts. 30th Ave NE and NE 107th St; map:DD6

MONTLAKE PARK: two unlighted courts. 1618 E Calhoun St; map:GG6

NORWOOD VILLAGE: two unlighted courts. 12309 SE 23rd Pl, Bellevue; map:II2

RAINIER PLAYFIELD: four lighted courts. Rainier Ave S and S Alaska St; map:JJ5

RIVERVIEW: two unlighted courts. 12th Ave SW and SW Othello St; map:KK7

VOLUNTEER PARK: four courts (two lighted). 15th Ave E and E Prospect St; map:GG6

WINDSURFING

Definitely not for landlubbers, windsurfing takes athleticism, daring, and a lot of practice. The sport is big in this town, partly because the Northwest helped put it on the world map. The Columbia River Gorge (about 200 miles south of Seattle) is the top windsurfing area in the continental United States (and second only to Maui in the entire country), thanks to the strong winds that always blow in the direction opposite the river's current—ideal conditions for confident windsurfers. Closer to home, the windsurfing can be good on virtually any body of water. Here are some popular nearby locations.

GREEN LAKE / This is the best place for beginners; the water is warm, and the winds are usually gentle. Experts may find it too crowded, but novices will probably appreciate the company. You can take lessons and rent equipment at Green Lake Boat Rentals (7351 E Green Lake Drive

N; 206/527-0171) on the northeast side of the lake. *E Green Lake Dr N and W Green Lake Dr N; map:EE7*

LAKE UNION / Lake Union has fine winds in the summer, but you'll have to dodge sailboats, commercial boats, and seaplanes. You can rent equipment and catch a lesson from Urban Surf (2100 N Northlake Way; 206/545-9463; map:FF7). To launch, head to Gas Works Park (N Northlake Way and Meridian Ave N; map:FF7).

LAKE WASHINGTON / Most windsurfers prefer expansive Lake Washington. Head to any waterfront park—most have plenty of parking and rigging space. Magnuson Park (Sand Point Way NE and 65th Ave NE; map:EE5) is favored for its great winds. At Mount Baker Park (Lake Park Drive S and Lake Washington Blvd S; map:II6), you can take lessons at Mount Baker Rowing and Sailing Center (3800 Lake Washington Blvd S; 206/386-1913). Choice Eastside beaches include Gene Coulon Beach Park in Renton (1201 Lake Washington Blvd N; map:MM3), where you can also rent boards and get instruction, and Houghton Beach Park (NE 59th St and Lake Washington Blvd NE, Kirkland; map:FF4), with rentals nearby at O. O. Denny Park (NE 124th St and Holmes Point Dr NE, Juanita; map:DD5).

PUGET SOUND / On Puget Sound, which is warmer than Lake Washington in winter, windsurfers head for Golden Gardens Park (north end of Seaview Ave NW; map:DD9) or Duwamish Head at Alki Beach Park (Alki Ave SW; map:II9) in West Seattle. For rentals and lessons, try one of America's oldest windsurfing dealers: Alpine Hut (2215 15th Ave W; 206/284-3575; map:GG8).

Spectator Sports

Mere decades ago, Seattle was seen as a nonplayer when it came to big-time professional sports. The city nostalgically clung to the memory of the Seattle Supersonics' NBA championship in 1979, but, aside from a few brushes with winning seasons, it was a long time between celebrations.

Fortunately, as with any good sports story, it was only a matter of time before Seattle's losing streak was reversed. Things began looking up in the late '80s and early '90s with the arrival of such highlight-reel players as Ken Griffey Jr. and Alex Rodriguez of the Mariners and Gary Payton of the Sonics. These All-Star athletes quickly brought Seattle national media attention and a much-needed injection of hometown pride. A couple of division-winning seasons and a sports-facility spending spree (see "A Tale of Two Stadiums" box) has helped the city regain its sports swagger. Today, a tonsil-ringing enthusiasm makes itself heard in all three houses of the city's pro teams, as well as at the University of Washington and other local venues.

EMERALD DOWNS RACETRACK / 2300 Emerald Downs Dr, Auburn; 253/288-7000 or 888/931-8400 The sport of kings was dealt a royal blow in 1992 when the Northwest's historic thoroughbred racetrack, Longacres, was shut down to make way for a Boeing building. The ponies came back to Western Washington, however, when Emerald Downs, a sweet little track in Auburn, 25 minutes south of downtown Seattle, opened in 1996 (take I-5 south to the 272nd St exit; go east to West Valley Hwy and south to 37th St NW). There's plentiful indoor and outdoor seating (sixth-floor luxury suites can be reserved), cuisine that goes beyond the usual hot dogs and beer—with selections ranging from gourmet salads to Japanese yakisoba noodles—and about 700 color television monitors to ensure that race fans won't miss a thing from parade to post. A sports bar, a gift shop, and an attractive paddock area, where spectators can check out the horses as they're saddled, complete the track's attractions. Besides the on-site equine action, Downs visitors can wager on races at several tracks around the country (including simulcasts of big races, such as the Kentucky Derby). Racing season runs from late April to mid-September, Wednesday to Sunday. Post time is 6pm weekdays and 1pm weekends and holidays. General admission is $3 (free for children 10 and under), grandstand seating is $5, and clubhouse seating is $5.50. Free general parking is available (on busy days it can be quite a hike to the entrance, so grab one of the parking shuttles); preferred spaces (a shorter walk) are $3; and valet parking (no walk) is $5. *www.emdowns.com*

EVERETT AQUASOX / 39th and Broadway, Everett; 425/258-3673 or 800/GO-FROGS Real grass, real fans, real hot dogs—the AquaSox have it all, including a lime-green frog mascot, Webbly, that is a hot collector's item around the world. Watching this Class-A farm team of the Seattle Mariners is always worth the drive to Everett (30 miles north of Seattle on I-5; take exit 192 to Memorial Stadium), where the baby M's take their first steps toward major league careers. The AquaSox attract a loyal cadre of fans, who give equally enthusiastic support to the players and the endless between-innings promotional antics (ranging from a tuxedo- clad unicyclist to a giant walking hot dog named Frank to Harold, the pot-bellied pig who delivers the balls to the umpire throughout the game). The Sox season runs from mid-June through the first week of September. Games start at 7pm weekdays, 6pm Saturday and Sunday. Tickets for the 4,500 seats can usually be bought at the gate (the popular "Chicken Night" sells out fast, however) and are also available through Ticketmaster outlets or David Ishii, Bookseller (212 1st Ave S; 206/622-4719; map:O8). Tickets are $5 for adults, $4 for kids 12 and under; reserved seats are $7–$10. *aquasox@aquasox.com; www.aquasox.com*

HUSKY BASKETBALL / Hec Edmundson Pavilion, University of Washington; 206/543-2200 Around here, real women play hoops—and they play them very, very well. The members of the University of Washington's strong Husky women's basketball team have long put on a better show than their male counterparts, but the men are finally gaining ground, and both teams are fun and affordable to watch. The Dawg teams start play in early November and continue through March (games are usually Thursdays and Saturdays). General seating costs $6; reserved seats are $9 for women's games, $14 for men's. The Husky-Stanford women's games sell out early every year, so get 'em while they're hot. *www. gohuskies.com; map:FF6*

HUSKY FOOTBALL / Husky Stadium, University of Washington; 206/543-2200 Beginning in September, the UW's beloved "bad-to-the-bone Dawgs" play top-drawer football in the 73,000-seat Husky Stadium. Tickets are tough to get, so plan ahead, especially for big games (general seats are $15, reserved $30); when the Huskies are home, the games are on Saturdays. Be sure to pack rain gear, carpool (just follow the cars with the Husky flags), and wear purple. Also, plan to watch game highlights later on TV, as the lovely lake views from the stadium will likely distract even diehard fans from some of the gridiron action. *www.gohuskies.com; map:FF6*

A TALE OF TWO STADIUMS

Seattle is a town known for its good manners and laid-back nature. Oh, maybe locals get a little hot under the collar when it comes to dear-to-the-heart subjects such as depleted salmon runs or increasing traffic gridlock, but by and large such controversies are rare, and most civic issues are taken in stride.

So it was something of a shock to discover that what generated a full-bore rage in the city was a sports issue: the building of new stadiums for the Mariners and the Seahawks, the hometown baseball and football teams, to replace the clunky Kingdome. In perpetually polite Seattle, citizens loudly picked sides: it was anti-stadium citizens versus pro-stadium government; sports lovers versus sports haters; and tax-and-spenders versus spend-on-anything-elsers. Such a commotion.

The trouble all started with a winning season. The Mariners, aglow with their first division title in 1995, wanted a new outdoor park. While singing the virtues of outdoor play, the team ironically insisted its new park be topped by a costly retractable roof. When it seemed Seattle wasn't going to play ball, M's owners announced the team was for sale. Panic reigned. After much hand-wringing and finger-pointing, and despite a citizen vote against it, a deal was hammered out whereby Seattleites would pick up the bulk of the

SEATTLE INTERNATIONAL RACEWAY / 31001 144th Ave SE, Kent; 253/631-1550 SIR's season begins in February and continues with a busy schedule of races through the good-weather months. Though the dirt track for motorcycles is not much, the 10-turn, 2¼-mile European-style road-racing track (originally built in 1959 for sportscar racing) is a very good facility. The track's biggest draws are the NHRA Drag Race nationals, held the first weekend of August, and the vintage sportscar races, held on the Fourth of July weekend. Tickets for the big events cost $34–$134; regular races are $7–$10. Open February through October.

SEATTLE MARINERS / Safeco Field, between Royal Brougham Way and S Atlantic St; 206/346-4000 Until the team's thrilling foray into the play-offs in 1995, the Mariners' record for their first 18 years was uniformly horrible—as was fan interest. That stellar '95 season helped catapult attendance through the Kingdome roof and the M's right into a new $417 million, open-air ballpark. Though the bond issue that cleared the way for Safeco Field set locals at each other's throats, traditional baseball fans will be in heaven when they see their favorite players diving on *real* grass to rob opponents of runs. The park borrows from the classic design of other new ballparks, such as Baltimore's Camden Yards, but adds a state-of-the-art retractable roof. Not only are the Mariners faithful spared hauling rain gear to the park, but they can be entertained for the 20 minutes

$417 million park tab, mainly through bonds and lottery ticket sales.

Meanwhile, back at Seahawks headquarters, owner Ken Behring announced he was selling the city's NFL franchise. Microsoft co-founder Paul Allen saved the day with an offer to buy out Behring. Cheers quickly turned to groans, however, when residents learned the sale was contingent on a new home for the Hawks. Considering that Seat-tleites still owed $130 million on the aging Kingdome, this was an infuriating turn of events. Allen suggested the Hawks might share the Mariners' new home; the M's declined. Undaunted, in 1997 Allen rummaged in his pockets for $6 million to fund a campaign for a new Hawks home, including a statewide vote on the matter. The initia-tive passed, and a new bond-supported $386 million football/soccer stadium/exhibition center was born.

So the city that once wanted no new stadiums will soon be home to two new side-by-side sports facilities. Though most of the stadium fires are out, the citizenry bristled again when a local insurance company paid $40 million for the naming rights to the new Mariners park. After all, *taxpayers'* financial contribution was around $400 million. Instead of Safeco Field, how about calling it the People's Park?

—*Shannon O'Leary*

it takes to open and close the roof. Other amenities include an open bar-becue pit, several shops offering Mariners merchandise, and a baseball museum. Ticket prices range from $5 for center-field bleachers to $195 for "Diamond Club" membership seats directly behind home plate, with most seats costing $16. The $13 upper-deck seats may be the best in the park, with unobstructed vistas of Mount Rainier, Elliott Bay, and down-town Seattle. The season lasts from early April through the first week of October (game time is 7:05pm or 7:35pm weeknights; 1:05pm or 6:05pm Saturdays; 1:35pm on Sundays; and 12:35pm or 3:35pm on occasional weekdays). *www.mariners.org; map:R9*

SEATTLE SEAHAWKS / Kingdome (through 1999 season); 888/NFL-HAWK Time was—back when Steve Largent graced the gridiron before retiring to politics—Seahawks tickets were as hard to get your hands on as free parking spots. A series of bad seasons, though, along with charisma-free owners and a crime-ridden player roster, combined to drive fans away in droves. In recent years, you could walk up and get a good ticket on the day of the game. The turnaround began when Microsoft co-founder and Northwest sports mogul Paul Allen (who also owns bas-ketball's Portland TrailBlazers) purchased the Hawks in 1997. Following the pattern of modern-day sports deals, sealing this one was contingent upon building a new stadium to replace the much-maligned Kingdome. The new facility (which will also serve as a soccer stadium and an exhi-bition center) is set to open atop the rubble of the Dome in the summer of 2002. The Hawks finish the 1999 season at the Dome; at press time, a temporary home for the 2000 and 2001 seasons hadn't yet been deter-mined (though the UW Husky Stadium was one possibility). The Hawks' regular season starts in September (preseason games in August) and runs through December; games are Sundays at 1pm, except for the occasional Sunday or Monday night game at 5pm. Prices range from $10 to $52. The best bet is to take a free bus from downtown—parking near the Kingdome is an expensive nightmare. *www.seahawks.com or www.fir standgoal.com (for stadium news); map:Q9*

SEATTLE SOUNDERS / Memorial Stadium, Seattle Center; 800/796-KICK While some American cities are still discovering the world's most popular sport, professional soccer has been kicking around Seattle off and on since 1974, when the Sounders were founded. The profile of the soccer team will be raised even higher when the team moves into its new digs downtown (to be shared with the Seahawks football team) in 2002. In the meantime, the 1995–96 A-League champions play at the cozy 10,000-seat Memorial Stadium, north of the Space Needle, from April to October. Tickets range from $5 to $12. *www.seattlesounders.com; map:B6*

SEATTLE SUPERSONICS / KeyArena, Seattle Center; 206/628-0888 (Ticketmaster) Since winning it all in the '70s, the Sonics have been an uneven team, especially when it comes to the crunch time of the playoffs. On the other hand, unpredictability is part of the team's charm, and the Sonics are one of the consistent winners when it comes to drawing the home crowd—known as one of the loudest in the nation. The team tears up the courts from early November to late April, and tickets (ranging from a very cheap $7 to $63 for near-courtside) often sell out early. Most games are at 7pm. *www.sonics.nba.com/sonics/; map:B7.*

TACOMA RAINIERS / Cheney Stadium, 2502 S Tyler St; 800/281-3834 Many of the Mariners' current hotshots, such as shortstop sensation Alex Rodriguez, first honed their skills south of Seattle with the M's Triple-A farm club. On clear days at the team's Cheney Stadium facility, spectacular views of Mount Rainier play background for these boys of summer. The Rainiers play 72 home games, from early April to September. Games held Monday–Saturday are at 7:05pm; some midweek summer games start at 12:35pm; and Sunday and holiday games begin at 1:35pm. Tickets are very affordable, ranging from $5 to $10. *www.rainiers.fan link.com.*

THUNDERBIRDS HOCKEY / KeyArena, Seattle Center; 206/728-9121 Arguably the best ticket buy in local sports, the 1996–97 Western Hockey League champion Seattle Thunderbirds take to the ice in September and play through March—or May if they make the playoffs. No one could mistake these young icemen for the NHL, but what they lack in finesse (and years) they make up for with sheer energy and some of the most vocal, loyal fans in the region. The T-birds' 36 home games are mostly on weekends; tickets are $8–$20. *www.seattle-thunderbirds.com; map:B7*

CONFERENCES, MEETINGS, AND RECEPTIONS

CONFERENCES, MEETINGS, AND RECEPTIONS

Most hotels and inns and many restaurants recommended in this guide have meeting rooms for rent. The following is a list of other rental facilities appropriate for business meetings, private parties, and receptions. Private functions can also be held at branches of the Seattle Public Library, most museums, the University of Washington (which has numerous halls, auditoriums, and meeting rooms), and other educational facilities.

THE ATRIUM / 5701 6th Ave S; 206/763-0111 The Atrium holds up to 900 people for a reception (700 for a sit-down event) in a skylit, three-story, covered courtyard with plenty of tall greenery. A great place for corporate events, weddings, parties, and reunions. You must use their catering. Good PA system too. *Map:JJ7*

BASTYR UNIVERSITY CONFERENCE AND RETREAT CENTER / 14500 Juanita Dr NE, Bothell; 425/602-3061 This former seminary sits on 50 wooded acres next to a large state park on the northeastern end of Lake Washington. It is available to nonprofit groups only. Thirteen conference rooms hold up to 500, and overnight accommodations can sleep up to 50 people. Vegetarian buffet meals are served three times a day. *Map:CC5*

BATTELLE SEATTLE CONFERENCE CENTER / 4000 NE 41st St; 206/525-3130 Battelle Memorial Institute, a nonprofit research organization, operates this fully equipped conference facility on its attractive, 18-acre wooded grounds not far from the University of Washington. Battelle has 31 guest rooms, and the eight carpeted conference rooms can accommodate up to 115 people in the largest room. Catering is provided by Battelle. Rental policies are geared toward conferences of one day or longer. No weddings, but business-sponsored receptions are OK. *Map:FF6*

CAMP LONG / 5200 35th Ave SW; 206/684-7434 See Parks and Beaches in the Exploring chapter.

CHATEAU STE. MICHELLE / 14111 NE 145th St, Woodinville; 425/488-4633 In the quaint, original early-1900s Manor House on the grounds of this Eastside winery, you can hold a meeting or reception for up to 85 people. The house boasts hardwood floors, a cozy fireplace, and formal gardens. The Barrel Room, with a Mediterranean motif, accommodates gatherings of up to 250. Both rooms offer custom, in-house catering. *Map:CC2*

CHINESE ROOM, SMITH TOWER / 506 2nd Ave, 35th floor; 206/622-4004 Resembling a Chinese museum with its red and black carpets and hand-carved wooden furniture, this newly refurbished sky-level room in the classic 1914 Smith Tower is a stunningly elegant backdrop for a party. Other features include ceramic ceiling tiles, an outside wraparound balcony, and express elevator service (complete with tuxedo-clad elevator operator). The Chinese Room accommodates 99 for cocktail party–style receptions. Choose from a list of approved caterers. *Map:O7*

COURT IN THE SQUARE / 401 2nd Ave S; 206/467-5533 A glassed-in alley—now an atrium—between two brick buildings, the Court in the Square has a classy French Quarter ambience. A retractable glass roof allows for dancing under the stars. It's available evenings and weekends for parties of up to 300; all catering is done by the very high quality in-house restaurant. A favorite among wedding planners, who must book six months to a year in advance. A small adjacent conference center accommodates up to 50 for business meetings. *Map:P8*

DAUGHTERS OF THE AMERICAN REVOLUTION HOUSE / 800 E Roy St; 206/323-0600 Weddings and dance parties are the main events in this classic Capitol Hill mansion patterned after George Washington's Mount Vernon. The downstairs is Colonial and genteel; rent it by itself, or along with the barny upstairs ballroom for a total capacity of 250 people. Bring your own caterer and sound system; they have two pianos. Midnight curfew. *Map:GG6*

GOLD CREEK LODGE / 16020 148th Ave NE, Woodinville; 206/296-2966 (King County Recreation) The wooded trails of Gold Creek Park surround this rustic, pine-paneled room. The place holds 100 people for a meeting or reception, and sleeps 40—who are accommodated on cots and bunks (bring your own sleeping bags). *Map:BB2*

KIANA LODGE / 14976 Sandy Hook Rd NE, Poulsbo; 360/598-4311 The waterfront lodge and garden atrium at Kiana on the Kitsap Peninsula have a genuine Northwest flavor—good for both weddings and corporate get-togethers. You can even dock your boat right in front. The specialty is alder-grilled salmon dinners for large groups (up to 1,000). Kiana is usually booked several months in advance for weekend weddings. No overnight accommodations.

LANGSTON HUGHES CULTURAL ARTS CENTER / 104 17th Ave S; 206/684-4757 A large multipurpose room, a 287-seat theater, and a restaurant-capacity kitchen are available for rent at this Seattle Parks Department facility. Fees are reasonable and based on event use (public or private; when and for how long). *Map:HH6*

LUTHERAN BIBLE INSTITUTE / Providence Heights, 4221 228th Ave SE, Issaquah; 425/392-0400 Religious groups and nonprofit organizations can rent this comfortable Issaquah conference facility with rooms seating 12 to 400 people. The institute has dorm rooms and motel-style lodgings, dining rooms, a gym, an indoor swimming pool, and a 400-seat chapel. No smoking or alcohol consumption anywhere on the grounds, but they provide catering.

THE MEETING PLACE AT PIKE PLACE MARKET / 93 Pike St, Suite 307; 206/447-9994 Located in the Economy Market Building in Pike Place Market, the Meeting Place has two unprepossessing rooms (one with a bay view) for rent on an hourly or daily basis. They can be used separately or together, with a maximum capacity of 200. No in-house catering service, but the staff will assist you with planning. The facility has a small kitchen with a microwave oven, a deli cooler, and a freezer. *Map:J8*

MUSEUM OF FLIGHT / 9404 E Marginal Way S; 206/764-5706 This museum houses an impressive cross-section of aviation history and has seven different event spaces for between 4 and 2,500 people. You can hold a reception for up to 2,500 people in the Great Gallery, where great flying machines are hung. A stroll around the balcony above the gallery takes you to the view lounge (a view, that is, of Boeing Field to the east and Mount Rainier to the south), with its handsome chrome wet bar. The Skyline Room, on the second floor, overlooks downtown and accommodates about 180. Best atmosphere: the Red Barn, the original home of Boeing, where a stripped-down Curtiss Jenny occupies center stage. Catering is provided by McCormick & Schmick's. Parking is free. *Map:LL6*

MUSEUM OF HISTORY AND INDUSTRY / 2700 24th Ave E; 206/324-1126 Located on Union Bay just west of Foster Island and the Arboretum, the museum rents out a 392-seat theater/auditorium and a carpeted room that accommodates 200 people for a sit-down gathering, or up to 300 for a stand-up reception. The room has an adjoining kitchen. Two smaller rooms accommodate a reception for 100 and a meeting for 25. Meetings, parties, and receptions only; no wedding ceremonies. Plenty of parking in the museum lot. *Map:FF6*

OLD WINERY / 37444 Winery Rd, Snoqualmie; 425/831-7700 This newly renovated wine cellar, formerly the home of the Snoqualmie Winery, retains its winery ambience. The Barrel Room accommodates up to 350 people auditorium style. The tasting room has a fireplace and a bar, and accommodates up to 160 for a reception or 110 for a banquet. The terraced lawn has a wonderful view and picnic tables; the amphitheater can accommodate several thousand people for corporate picnics and wedding parties.

ROBINSWOOD HOUSE / 2432 148th Ave SE, Bellevue; 425/452-7850 A comfortable, nicely furnished two-story house that holds up to 120 people for parties is part of a well-tended 60-acre park. Parts of the house can be rented for smaller gatherings on weekdays, but on weekends the entire facility is rented as a unit. An additional 75 guests can be accommodated outdoors (there's an English garden on the premises). Robinswood is a popular place for weddings, and is suited to DJ music or a small ensemble. The facility provides a list of preferred caterers. *Map:II2*

SEATTLE AQUARIUM / Pier 59, Waterfront Park; 206/386-4300 Several hundred people can party right in the exhibit area, amid the fish and octopi. The underwater dome is an especially atmospheric spot for wedding ceremonies. The Aquarium also has a 200-seat auditorium and a conference room that holds 20 people. Available evenings only; the aquarium provides catering service. *Map:J9*

SEATTLE ART MUSEUM / 100 University St; 206/654-3100 or 206/625-8900 A lecture room and a 300-seat, acoustically perfect auditorium lend themselves to lectures, films, music, and dramatic performances. Evening parties staged in the main entrance lobby can flow up the Grand Stairway, which is graciously interrupted midway by a comfortable cafe run by the Seattle Sheraton, which provides catering services. *Map:K8*

SEATTLE CENTER / 305 Harrison St; 206/684-7202 The largest and most varied meeting and conference center in the city, Seattle Center can handle just about any need, from roundtables for 8,000 to small monthly workshops. The center also can provide catering services, planning assistance, and support staff. *Map:B6*

SKANSONIA / 2505 N Northlake Way; 206/545-9109 Permanently docked on Lake Union not far from Gas Works Park, this retired Washington State ferry is available for groups of up to 400. Besides the romance of it all, there's a large dance area, dining room, parlor, two garden decks, grand piano, full stereo system, working fireplace, and a postcard view of the city. Weddings and corporate parties are its main business. Catering is available. *Map:B6*

SPACE NEEDLE / Seattle Center, 219 4th Ave N; 206/443-9800 The rooms themselves aren't much, but they face outward for a spectacular 360-degree view from 100 feet up. There are three rooms, with a total capacity of about 300 people with seating or 350 for a reception-style gathering; the Space Needle provides all catering. *Map:C6*

STIMSON-GREEN MANSION / 1204 Minor Ave; 206/624-0474 Two of Seattle's prominent industrialist families—the Stimsons and the Greens—have called this stately turn-of-the-century brick Tudor mansion home. It is now a designated historic site. Since the early 1980s, the house has been available for meetings, parties, and weddings, with room for 48 for a sit-down meal or up to 200 for a reception. We like it best on wintry evenings, when the opulent place is infused with a rich, cozy glow. *Map:L2*

UNION STATION / 401 S Jackson St; 206/623-2434 Entertain up to 1,500 of your closest friends in the enormous Great Hall of Union Station, once the Grand Central of the Northwest. The booking agent provides a list of approved caterers. With its high ceilings, mosaic tile floor, and stately ambience, Union Station is a top-choice venue for political fund raisers, wedding receptions, and corporate parties. *Map:Q7*

WASHINGTON STATE CONVENTION & TRADE CENTER / 800 Convention Place; 206/447-5000 Draped artfully across I-5, this gargantuan facility has reception rooms that accommodate from 50 to 4,000 people, exhibit halls, press facilities, conference rooms, ballrooms, indoor parking for 900 cars, and wheelchair accessibility. Catering is available. The center is within walking distance of all major downtown hotels. *Map:K4*

Index

We Stand By Our Reviews

Sasquatch Books is proud of *Seattle Best Places*. Our editors and contributors go to great lengths and expense to see that all of the restaurant and lodging reviews are as accurate, up-to-date, and honest as possible. If we have disappointed you, please accept our apologies; however, if a recommendation in this 8th edition of *Seattle Best Places* has seriously misled you, Sasquatch Books would like to refund your purchase price. To receive your refund:

1. Tell us where and when you purchased your book and return the book and the book-purchase receipt to the address below.
2. Enclose the original restaurant or lodging receipt from the establishment in question, including date of visit.
3. Write a full explanation of your stay or meal and how *Seattle Best Places* misled you.
4. Include your name, address, and phone number.

Refund is valid only while this 8th edition of *Seattle Best Places* is in print. If the ownership, management, or chef has changed since publication, Sasquatch Books cannot be held responsible. Tax and postage on the returned book is your responsibility. Please allow six to eight weeks for processing.

Please address to Satisfaction Guaranteed, *Seattle Best Places*, and send to:
Sasquatch Books
615 Second Avenue, Suite 260
Seattle, WA 98104

Seattle Best Places Report Form

Based on my personal experience, I wish to nominate the following restaurant, place of lodging, shop, nightclub, sight, or other as a "Best Place"; or confirm/correct/disagree with the current review.

_____

_____

_____

_____

(Please include address and telephone number of establishment, if convenient.)

REPORT

Please describe food, service, style, comfort, value, date of visit, and other aspects of your experience; continue on another piece of paper if necessary.

_____

_____

_____

_____

_____

_____

_____

_____

I am not concerned, directly or indirectly, with the management or ownership of this establishment.

_____

SIGNED

_____

ADDRESS

_____

_____

_____

PHONE   **DATE**

Please address to Seattle Best Places and send to:
SASQUATCH BOOKS
615 SECOND AVENUE, SUITE 260
SEATTLE, WA 98104
Feel free to email feedback as well: **BOOKS@SASQUATCHBOOKS.COM**